LEO

LEO

July 23–August 22

ASTROSCOPE PROFILE

ARTHUR BARKER LIMITED   LONDON
A subsidiary of Weidenfeld (Publishers) Limited

Contents

Introduction to the *Astroscope Profile* System

Astroscope Profile—
Your Personal Horoscope

How will this book help you, a distinct individual, know yourself better? Whether you are a Gemini or a Virgo or any other "sign," your experience tells you that you are different from other Virgos or Geminis. This *Astroscope Profile* series of books confirms your experience. *Astroscope Profile* presents the elements of a personal horoscope—an astroscope, as we call it—that are often missing in traditional descriptions of the basic types Aries through Pisces.

To be a Gemini or a Virgo or any other sign simply means that the Sun was in a particular part of the Zodiac on the day of birth. If the position of the Sun was all that mattered, there would be only those twelve types of people. Although the descriptions of the twelve Sun types are astonishingly accurate, they are nevertheless limited.

Our individuality arises from the fact that there are *ten other factors* to consider: the Ascendant (Rising), the Moon, and the planets Mercury, Venus, Mars, Jupiter, Saturn, Uranus, Neptune, and Pluto! All these have distinct and inescapable influences on individual character and personality. Their combined effect on us as individuals is equal to that of the mighty Sun's!

Every genuine astrologer knows that the traditional Sun sign descriptions, as valuable as they are, tell only half the story about the individual. The other half of the story, contributed by the Rising, the Moon, and the planets, seldom ever gets told short of a visit to a professional astrologer.

The problem has always been in devising a system for publication whereby the positions and interpretations of all the planets are worked out in advance for everyone. This problem has been solved in the *Astroscope Profile* series. Each book in the series provides, in addition to a full description of your Sun sign, complete positions and interpretations of the Rising, the Moon, and the other planets for all signs! Now you have the opportunity to read both sides of your own astrological story.

HOW TO USE THIS BOOK

With the book for your Sun sign, you can construct your own astroscope. Tables of planetary placements are conveniently located on colored/banded pages at the end of the book, so you won't have to skip around to list the various placements for your astroscope. Interpretations of each placement are presented in separate chapters, so you can easily find the ones that apply to you. You won't have to make any guesses, calculations, or interpretations. All the tables and interpretations have been done for you, based on the data of professional astrologers.

You might be interested to know how these astrological data are obtained in the first place. What an astrologer does when erecting a personal horoscope is to plot on paper a minimap of the heavens at your moment of birth. But the minimap cannot be made until the astrologer pinpoints the positions of all the planets at the time of birth. To do this, prepared tables of planetary positions, called ephemerides (from the Greek *ephemeris,* meaning "calendar"), are used. Years ago the positions of the planets had to be laboriously worked out each time a horoscope was cast, which introduced a wide margin for error. Today ephemerides are prepared years ahead, mainly by computer, ensuring accuracy within seconds of a degree.

If you glance at your birthday tables—the Planetary Tables that end on page 477—you will see that they are given up to the year 1990. Because the planets move in mathematically predictable orbits, astrologers can predict their positions for the future.

Here is what you need to chart your astroscope, and how this book organizes your search.

Your Sun sign. You know your birthday, but it may be on the cusp, or edge, of a sign for that particular year. Check the Cusp Tables for all Signs, pages 379–83, to find out for sure which Sun sign is yours.

Your Rising sign—the Ascendant. If you know the time of your birth, consult the Ascendant Tables, pages 387–92, to discover your Rising sign. If you don't know the time, a suggestion is given to help you identify your Rising sign.

Your planetary positions: Moon, Mercury, Venus, Mars, Jupiter, Saturn, Uranus, Neptune, and Pluto. Use the Planetary Tables, pages 397–477, to discover what signs each planet is in.

Once you've listed the various placements for your astroscope, you will want to interpret them. This book provides the following material for that purpose.

Sun sign description. Separate chapters on character analysis, work and business, love and romance, and parents and children for your Sun sign.

Cusp sign description. A chapter describing each cusp combination from Aries and Taurus through Pisces and Aries.

Rising sign description. Separate chapters for each of the twelve signs Aries through Pisces.

Moon and planets in the signs. Separate chapters for each planet covering the twelve signs Aries through Pisces.

Look through the Contents for the chapters that apply to you specifically. Then you may want to read up on your friends. Or peruse other chapters of interest as you go along. You can also construct your astroscope on a wheel, just as professional astrologers do. The next chapter, "Planets of the Solar System and the Signs of the Zodiac," shows you how. Read through the chapter first, so you have a visual picture of the heavens that corresponds to your wheel.

ADVANTAGES OF THE *ASTROSCOPE PROFILE* SERIES

The first advantage of the *Astroscope Profile* series is simplicity. Simply by turning to the birthday tables—the Planetary Tables—for any day in the eighty-one years covered, it is possible to see at a glance the astrological makeup of the person concerned. Reading across the page from the birth date, you can see instantly that each planet is in a certain sign.

The second advantage is the in-depth profile. You match the placement with its interpretation. Take a random example. Moon in Taurus, which makes a person artistically practical. Then Mercury in Leo, giving a dominant turn of mind. Venus in Cancer, making someone deeply protective of loved ones. Mars in Aries, which gives great energy and determination. Jupiter in Aquarius, endowing a detached, scientific capability. Saturn in Scorpio, an intense urge to discover the truths of life and sex. Uranus in Pisces, love of the unusual and a psychic sensitivity. Neptune in Virgo, fondness for detail, artistic precision, and wit. Pluto in Leo, the desire to operate creatively on a grand scale.

Fun and enlightenment are two other advantages. Astroscope can be a game for friends and at parties. Or it can be a means of developing a hobby, more serious study, finally even a career. Astrology's growing popularity creates the demand for new astrologers.

A fourth and very important advantage is understanding other people. The *Astroscope Profile* series helps you estimate the types of people you deal with: relatives, friends, mates, lovers; teammates and bosses; prospective employees and employers; rivals in love or work; professional contacts; children and their companions.

A final advantage concerns children. The birthday tables are supplied up to the year 1990. Parents and expectant parents can assess their children's qualities and needs. People who are planning families can look up the influences that will be present when they become parents. Teachers and other guardians can understand more about their youthful charges.

Most of us have had some experience of youngsters being forced to take up interests, studies, or jobs incompatible with their natural inclinations and abilities. Even a bit of astrological knowledge can help parents and teachers prevent this. The *Astroscope Profile* series provides insights that enable the caretakers of the young to build nurturing, encouraging environments for each child's development.

We create much of our own fate, as well as influence the fate of those we are responsible for. The *Astroscope Profile* series helps us to see what can be done, what probably cannot be done, and what may be possible. Applying these understandings is a safe and sure way of taking destiny out of the hands of chance and putting it firmly in our own.

Planets of the Solar System and the Signs of the Zodiac

Planet Earth is part of the Solar System. This huge solar family has nine planets that revolve around the Sun, our star, and any moons that belong to a planet. Earth has one moon. Jupiter has twelve moons! Figure 1, on page 14, shows the Solar System in space.

Planet Earth is also part of the larger environment defined by the space around the Solar System. That environment stretches billions of miles and contains billions of stars. One fascinating series of stars, which could be seen to early cultures observing the nighttime sky, is the Zodiac.

The Zodiac—a far, far distant series of stars—seems to extend around the Solar System. The Zodiac seems to occupy, at least to the Earth observer, a band of space around the Solar System. The Zodiac contains twelve characteristic star groups, or constellations, that have been variously studied by astronomers and astrologers both ancient and modern. The twelve constellations are known as the twelve star signs or, simply, as the twelve signs of the Zodiac.

A model of the Solar System and the signs of the Zodiac is pictured in Figure 1. This model, though fancifully artistic, is similar to the model astronomers and space scientists use. When they depict the constellations of the Zodiac, they use dot patterns instead of animal or human forms. It doesn't take much imagination to see that their dot patterns resemble the sign symbols used in astrology.

Astrologers have always believed that the Solar System and the Zodiac interact to produce cosmic influences. Astronomers and space scientists confirm that the Solar System and the Zodiac constitute an interacting field of matter and energy. Astrologers talk about the qualities and forces of matter and energy. Astrophysicists and astronomers talk about gravitational forces, electromagnetic fields, and the transformations of matter and energy.

Although the terms are different, the concept is the same. The planets and signs constantly interact, affecting all life on Earth. Their interaction, measured on a day-to-day basis, is the fact on which the system discussed

13

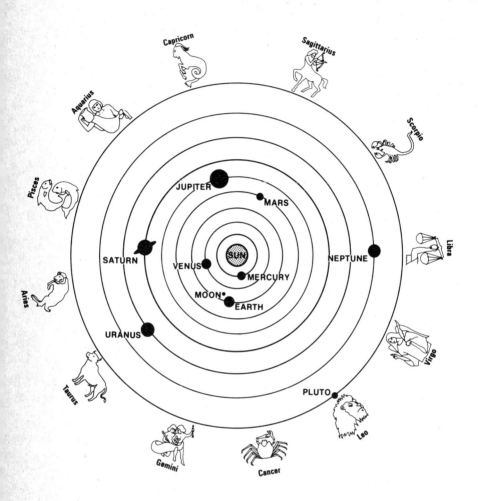

Figure 1   Model of the Solar System and Constellations of the Zodiac

in the *Astroscope Profile* series was built. That is why Ascendant Tables and Planetary Tables are provided for you to find your own placements. And the chapters on the meanings of each planet in each sign help you zero in on your personal characteristics.

THE RELATIONSHIP OF PLANETS TO SIGNS

In Figure 1, look at the outer band depicting the signs of the Zodiac. Notice that the band is drawn so that the sign of Aries is on the left center. Then all the other signs follow Aries counterclockwise until the band is completed with Pisces.

Why start with Aries? Why not start with Gemini or Capricorn or any other sign, for that matter? In fact, Aries doesn't even correspond with our January 1, the beginning of a calendar year. Starting the Zodiac with Aries is a correct convention, respecting the wisdom of our first astronomers. These early peoples were the first to classify the planets and the signs as well as to develop other fundamentals of astronomy that exist today in every textbook.

Aries is the sign that begins on March 21. That date is called the spring (vernal) equinox. It is the date when the length of day and night is *the same everywhere on earth*. (The Sun's rays at the time shine vertically on the equator.) So it is an appropriate time. It is springtime in the Northern Hemisphere, where our early astronomers observed the nighttime sky. It is the beginning of a new growing season, the herald of summer, the expectation of harvest.

Aries is the Rising sign of the natural Zodiac.

Look back again at Figure 1, noting the rest of the signs in the Zodiac. The Zodiac is so far distant from the Solar System that it is considered to be a relatively stationary system in space. It is not moving *relative* to the motions of the Earth and the other planets around the sun.

The Earth, for example, moves around the Sun completely in one year. Other planets take shorter or longer times to revolve around the Sun, as you can tell from the lines that represent their orbits. But relative to the Earth's motion and the motions of the other planets, the Zodiac seems to stay put. So we always draw the natural Zodiac starting with Aries on the left and going around as shown in Figure 1.

As the Earth or any other planet revolves around the Sun, it passes through the space defined by each of the twelve signs of the Zodiac.

THE SUN SIGN

As the Earth revolves around the Sun, the Sun and Earth together appear to be in line with one sign of the Zodiac approximately once a month. The Sun is said to be "seen" in that sign; then it is "seen" in the next sign, and so on. By the time the Earth has made one complete revolution—a year—the Sun has been in every sign of the Zodiac.

You can check this for yourself by referring again to Figure 1. Put your finger or a pencil point on the planet Earth. Trace an imaginary straight line connecting the Sun, the Earth, and the closest zodiacal sign. Be sure to start from the Sun, then draw the line through the Earth, and go out to the Zodiac band. Try it. What sign do you hit? Your line should hit Gemini. So for the day shown by Figure 1, the Sun is in Gemini. Or, more accurately stated, the Sun is in direct line with the Earth, which is in line with Gemini. This is how the Sun sign is determined throughout the year. From astrological calculations, generalized dates for the Sun signs are used. Sometimes the dates vary slightly from year to year. The *Astroscope Profile* series takes this fact into account by providing for you the cusp dates (see Cusp Tables for All Signs, pages 379-83) if you need them. Sun sign dates are given below, but every astrologer calculates from slightly differing dates (the ones we use are listed on the back cover).

Sun Sign	Date
Aries	March 21–April 20
Taurus	April 21–May 20
Gemini	May 21–June 20
Cancer	June 21–July 20
Leo	July 21–August 21
Virgo	August 22–September 21
Libra	September 22–October 22
Scorpio	October 23–November 22
Sagittarius	November 23–December 20
Capricorn	December 21–January 19
Aquarius	January 20–February 18
Pisces	February 19–March 20

Cusp

For your particular birth year, you may need to check the Cusp Tables, pages 379-83, to be sure which is your Sun sign. If you are born near the cusp—say, within six days from the end of one sign to the beginning of another—you may want to read the cusp description that applies to you in the chapter "The Cusps of All Signs," pages 139-47.

THE MOON AND PLANETS IN THE SIGNS

Sun and Earth were considered together for the Sun sign. What about the signs for the Moon and for the eight other planets in the Solar System? The planets, too, fall into different zodiacal signs as they revolve around the sun.

Astrologers use the same method as was used for the Sun sign to figure out the signs for the Moon and planets. These are the data in the Planetary Tables, which the *Astroscope Profile* series has provided for you on pages 397–477. For your Sun sign, the Planetary Tables give the signs for the Moon and each planet on each day of the eighty-one years from 1910 to 1990 inclusive.

You could play with Figure 1, taking a planet, imagining it revolving around the Sun, stopping every now and then at a point on its orbit, then drawing a line from Sun to planet, and seeing in what sign the planet is at that moment of its year. But can you imagine doing that challenge for *every planet* on *every day* of the *eighty-one years!* This is the compiled work given to you by the Planetary Tables of the *Astroscope Profile* series.

CHARACTERISTICS OF THE PLANETS AND SIGNS

Our Solar System forms one huge interacting force (gravitational) and energy (electromagnetic) field, as you can imagine even from the simple model shown in Figure 1. Each of the planets is a cosmic force. And each has a special brand of energy. That the planets continuously radiate energy is documented by evidence from space probes. We moderns have been lucky enough to see infrared photographs taken at night from space showing the Earth's otherwise invisible energy glow.

Every planet receives the Earth's energy. (If Martians are constructing their astroscopes, they will certainly note what sign the Earth was in when they were "born.") And the Earth receives the planets' energies. The Sun's energy is so powerful it is easy to see why so much emphasis is placed on the Sun sign. But the Moon and the other eight planets, each with their characteristic energies, significantly modify the Sun sign character. (You may know or have noted in reading that the Sun is a star and that the Moon is a satellite of Earth. From the astrological framework of force and energy, the Sun and Moon are considered planets.)

The Solar system also interacts with the Zodiac, as we saw in the last section and in Figure 1. Now that we have introduced the idea of the Solar System as an energy field, the fanciful depiction of the Zodiac as a band of stars takes on a new meaning. There is nothing abstract about the Zodiac. Though pictured as an animal or human form, each sign is in reality one or more groups of stars. Like our Sun, these stars generate tremendous energy. Our Sun is only one star. Each sign consists of many stars, and so generates energy fields many times more powerful than the Sun's. These fields stretch across space, intersecting and interacting with the energy fields of the Sun and planets.

Even though the signs are very far away, their energy fields affect us here on Earth. Their energy fields also affect the Sun and planets. Each sign, consisting as it does of different kinds of stars—white, blue, red, yellow—has its own brand of energy. So each sign is associated with specific modes of energy expression and specific elements of matter.

Energy Keys

Energy principles or modes of expression for the planets and signs are as follows:

Planet	Energy Principle
Sun	Being, Life
Earth*	Embodiment, Physicality
Moon	Response, Instinct
Mercury	Mind, Intellect
Venus	Attraction, Union
Mars	Action, Force
Jupiter	Expansion, Wisdom
Saturn	Restriction, Responsibility
Uranus	Change, Independence
Neptune	Dissolution, Spirituality
Pluto	Upheaval, Renewal

*This may be the first time you have ever seen the Earth included as a planet in an astrology book. Because the *Astroscope Profile* series is based not only on your Sun, Moon, and planets, but also on your Rising sign, the Earth is included. Our Rising sign is most important because it transmits the Earth's own energies to the individual as an indestructible part of self from the moment of birth on. The Earth's energy principle, in positive form, is the human body; its negative form is pure materialism.

Sign	Energy Expression
Aries	Assertive
Taurus	Possessive
Gemini	Communicative
Cancer	Protective
Leo	Creative
Virgo	Critical
Libra	Related
Scorpio	Intense
Sagittarius	Enthusiastic
Capricorn	Conservative
Aquarius	Detached
Pisces	Impressionable

Element

Fire, earth, air, and water and the four natural divisions of matter associated with the twelve signs of the Zodiac. Each element is associated with three signs, as you can see in Figure 2. Fire represents an energetic and assertive person. Earth denotes a practical and cautious person. Air represents an intellectual and communicative person. Water signifies an emotionally sensitive person.

Quality

Cardinal, fixed, and mutable are three other designations associated with the twelve signs. Each quality represents four signs. Cardinal signs tend to produce outgoing people, oriented to action, movement, and change. Fixed signs tend to produce stubborn people, resistant to change but determined to build and create. Mutable signs tend to produce adaptable people, intuitive, creative, and responsive to change.

Polarity

Signs have been represented by dualities of nature or convention. Positive and negative, aggressive and passive, expressive and repressive, introverted and extroverted, male and female have been used. The duality shown in Figure 2, active and receptive, is suggestive but no sign is completely one or the other. Some of the signs themselves show opposites or doubles. Pisces, the Fishes swimming in opposite direction; Gemini, the Twins; Sagittarius, the Archer, half man, half beast. Note that these signs are also mutable ones.

THE ASCENDANT: YOUR RISING SIGN

The Rising Sign, or Ascendant, is the second most important placement in your astroscope, almost equal in importance to the Sun sign. The Sun sign was determined by considering the Earth's revolution, its yearly trip around the Sun. The Rising sign is determined by considering the Earth's rotation. The Earth turns, rotates, completely around once every twenty-four hours on the circuit of night and day.

The Rising sign is your Earth placement. At the moment of your birth, it is the sign "rising" with the Sun somewhere on Earth at that moment of time. That's why astrologers say it is the sign rising on the eastern horizon at the moment of birth. The eastern horizon marks sunrise, where daylight is breaking. Even though you may have been born at night on a certain day in a certain place, somewhere on Earth at that very moment sunrise is also occurring. And that place designates the eastern horizon for that moment of time.

SIGNS OF THE ZODIAC

Signs and Symbols			Element
Aries	Ram	♈	Fire
Taurus	Bull	♉	Earth
Gemini	Twins	♊	Air
Cancer	Crab	♋	Water
Leo	Lion	♌	Fire
Virgo	Virgin	♍	Earth
Libra	Scales	♎	Air
Scorpio	Scorpion	♏	Water
Sagittarius	Archer	♐	Fire
Capricorn	Goat	♑	Earth
Aquarius	Water Bearer	♒	Air
Pisces	Fishes	♓	Water

Quality	Polarity	Planetary Ruler	
Cardinal	Active	Mars	♂
Fixed	Receptive	Venus	♀
Mutable	Active	Mercury	☿
Cardinal	Receptive	Moon	☽
Fixed	Active	Sun	☉
Mutable	Receptive	Mercury	☿
Cardinal	Active	Venus	♀
Fixed	Receptive	Mars,	♂
		Pluto	♇
Mutable	Active	Jupiter	♃
Cardinal	Receptive	Saturn	♄
Fixed	Active	Uranus,	♅
		Saturn	♄
Mutable	Receptive	Neptune,	♆
		Jupiter	♃

Figure 2   Signs of the Zodiac. Each sign is ruled by one or more planets. Where there are co-rulers, each planet is considered equally important.

The Earth is constantly turning. Every place on it is turning also, as you know when you experience the full range of day and night in and out of sunlight. As the Earth turns, the eastern horizon is in line with a specific sign of the Zodiac at any given moment. And, as the Earth turns, about every two hours another zodiacal sign comes into line with the eastern horizon. This means that within the twenty-four-hour period of rotation, all the twelve zodiacal signs appear to rise. (No observer on Earth can actually see the sign that is rising. The light of the Sun blocks a view of the signs at sunrise. We see signs only at night.)

If you know the time of your birth, you can use the Ascendant Tables on pages 387–92 to find your Rising sign quickly. These Ascendant Tables give the Rising sign for each hour of the day for every day in your Sun sign. If you do not know the time of your birth, consult the chapters for each Rising sign. Read a few paragraphs of each, or skim through. See which Rising sign description best fits you.

RISING SIGN AND THE HOUSES OF THE ZODIAC

The Rising sign is a major indicator in your personal astroscope. The Rising sign influences how other people see you. It influences your body type, appearance, temperament. It helps to fashion your "face" to the world. It is a very real part of your identity.

The Rising sign always "starts" the astroscope. Look at Figure 3. It shows a flat model of the Zodiac without sign names or symbols. The Earth is in the center of the model. Lines like spokes of a wheel radiate from the Zodiac band to the center, and mark twelve equal divisions. Each division is called a house.

The Rising sign is always placed on the first house—that is, on the line dividing the twelfth house and the first house. The bubbles in the drawing are merely artistic devices so that a sign can be placed on the house and not in it.

Your Rising sign determines the sequence of signs around the wheel from the second house through the twelfth house. Figure 4 shows a sample wheel for someone whose Rising sign is Leo. See how each sign follows in natural zodiacal sequence once Leo is placed on the first house. In Figure 4 there are no planets listed, so the astroscope wheel is not complete.

Let's take another example based on obtaining from the appropriate Planetary Tables all the positions for this person with Leo Rising. See Figure 5. First we list the planetary positions. Then we transfer the planets to the wheel and put them in the houses where their signs fall. The signs are on the lines. The planets are in the houses. The astroscope wheel is complete. There remains only the job of interpretation.

You see from Figure 5 that planets are in certain houses. The term "house" is an apt one, and the Zodiac wheel is aptly termed "the wheel of life." The twelve houses are regarded as spheres of life experience. Together these twelve houses represent most of what makes up everyday living. Brief meanings of the twelve houses of the Zodiac are sketched on the wheel of life in Figure 6.

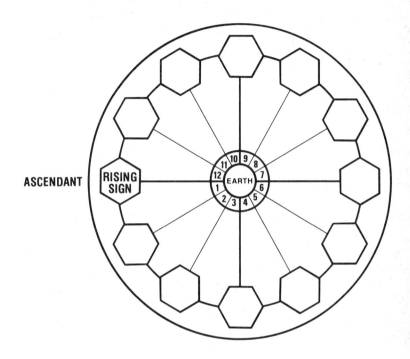

Figure 3 **The division of the Zodiac into 12 houses. The Rising, or Ascendant, sign is always placed on the 1st house (left center of the wheel). The houses go around counterclockwise from 1 to 12 as shown in the inner circle surrounding Earth.**

The twelve chapters "Your Rising Sign" for each specific sign detail the meanings of these houses for the individual. When you read the chapter that applies to you, you will see how you react and relate to these life experiences defined by the houses of the Zodiac. As the *Astroscope Profile* system has emphasized all along, your Rising sign modifies the characteristics of your Sun sign.

For example, a Capricorn Sun sign tends to make an individual conservative, especially with money. But a Capricorn Rising sign tends to make an individual unpredictable about money. These distinctions and modifying influences are thoroughly covered in each of the twelve chapters describing a different Rising sign (pages 151–245).

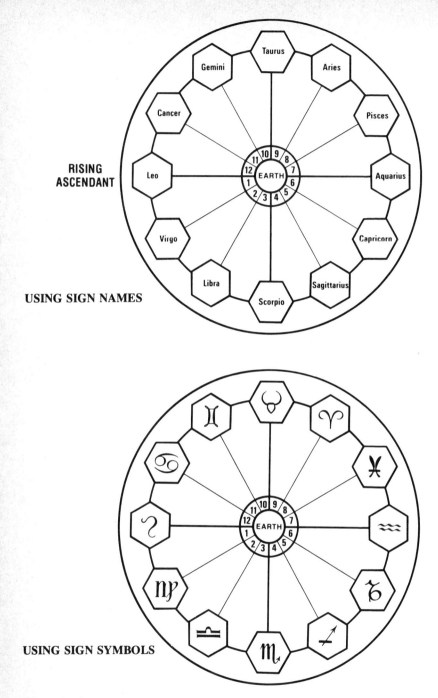

Figure 4 Astroscope wheels showing how to sequence the signs on the houses for someone with Leo Rising. The Rising sign is placed always on the 1st house. On each successive house, the natural sequence of the Zodiac follows.

Positions

Rising in Leo
Sun in Gemini
Moon in Sagittarius
Mercury in Cancer
Venus in Leo
Mars in Libra
Jupiter in Virgo
Saturn in Pisces
Uranus in Taurus
Neptune in Virgo
Pluto in Cancer

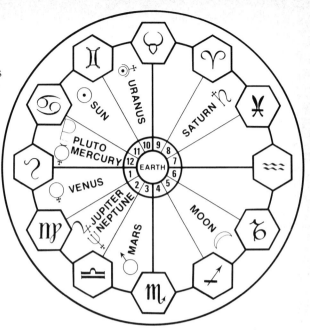

Figure 5 Completed astroscope wheel. The names of the planets, followed by their symbols, are written in the appropriate houses.

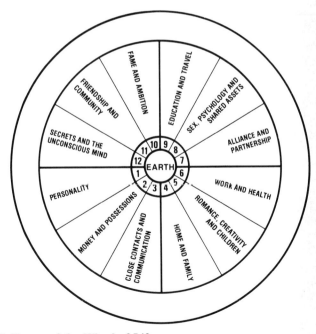

Figure 6 The 12 Houses of the Wheel of Life.
Each house defines specific life experiences.

CONSTRUCTING YOUR ASTROSCOPE WHEEL

This page is reserved for you. Fill-in blanks are provided to list your planetary positions. The astroscope wheel is reproduced. Go ahead! Write in this book. It's yours, and you will have a permanent record for study and fun.

YOUR ASTROSCOPE WHEEL

Planet	Sign	Birth Date

Rising   _____   Time _____

Sun   _____   Day _____

Moon   _____   Year _____

Mercury   _____

Venus   _____

Mars   _____

Jupiter   _____

Saturn   _____

Uranus   _____

Neptune   _____

Pluto   _____

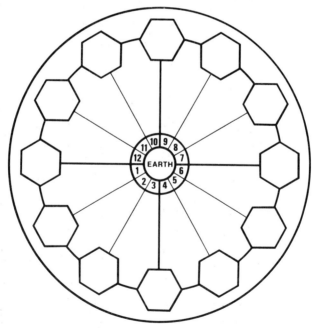

Astrology:
Tradition and Frontier

SCIENCE AND THE STARS

Tuesday, July 20, 1976, was a triumphant day for science—and astrology. America's *Viking* spacecraft had just bumped gently down to a perfect landing on Mars.

For twenty-five hundred years, astrology had associated the red planet Mars with the metal iron. To science, such an assumption was laughable. It was impossible for an ancient tradition to know such detail about a cosmic object thirty-six million miles from the Earth.

Yet one of the first signals received from the spacecraft confirmed that the planet's red surface was formed of oxidized iron. The Martian rocks were covered with rust. In fact, the probe indicated that the planet's pink sky and its reddish appearance from the earth were probably caused by the iron dust particles in the atmosphere scattering the Sun's rays.

The Mars probe indicating its iron composition confirmed something astrologers have always known. As a planetary influence, Mars in the individual astroscope adds its ironlike qualities of courage and strength to the character. Mars is associated with many aspects of life on Earth, as was emphasized in the preceding chapter.

Each of the planets has its own particular qualities, as were described in that chapter. No doubt existing and future space probes traveling even farther than Mars will reveal similar astrological parallels.

The recent probe of Saturn in 1980 is evidence of this thinking. Saturn was shown to be shrouded in ice crystals and frozen gas particles. Its chilly atmosphere surrounding the planet is only slightly colder than the freezing temperatures on its surface—equivalent to about $-270°$ Fahrenheit. Again, modern science has confirmed certain astrological qualities assigned to the planet Saturn.

Where did the ancient astrologers get their information? How did they know?

No one can answer this question. Astrology is so old that it predates history. We cannot even say *why* astrology works. But we can satisfy ourselves that it *does* work by observing the amazing accuracy of its insights into our characters, together with the discoveries of science that are constantly confirming its principles and beliefs.

THE WORLD'S OLDEST TRADITION

Astrology is one of the oldest ideas in the world. It also was the world's first science. It goes back so far into antiquity that it is the basis for much myth and legend. Mercury, Venus, Mars, Jupiter, Saturn—all the planets were said originally to have been gods. How this could be possible defies any rational speculation, much the same as applies to ancient religious traditions. But it does help to make the point that in that imponderable beginning of history, astrology was there.

Astrology is the science of circles or cycles. It is founded on the principle that people and the world evolve to the rhythm of circular motion, wheels within wheels, symbolized by the planets orbiting the Sun, and the Solar System as a whole appearing to move against the background of the Zodiac, an even larger "circle" in space. (See Figure 1 in the preceding chapter.)

The end of every zodiacal round or cycle heralds a fresh new start in which a person, or on a larger scale a society or the world, is wiser and more capable of handling life's challenges. Out of this idea emerges the strong astrological suggestion that reincarnation or recurrence is a fact. According to that tradition, every individual gets another crack at life, having been all the better equipped for it by their previous experience.

FROM THE AGE OF LEO
TO THE AGE OF AQUARIUS

Astrological cycles have a curious connection with one of the most pressing problems facing the world today—the search for an alternative power source to our fast-diminishing oil supplies. It looks as though history might be about to repeat itself with the recurrence of a very ancient cycle.

The connection goes way back to around 12,000 B.C., into fables and astrological traditions. That was the time when the world was passing through the Age of Leo. According to traditions, it was a very different world indeed from that of today.

Most people have heard about the Age of Aquarius, which the world is said to have entered recently. Each astrological age lasts approximately twenty-one hundred years. The age just ended was the Age of Pisces, which started a bit before the birth of Christ. The ages succeed each other around the zodiacal circle in a direction *opposite* to the Aries to Pisces sequence we are familiar with. In other words, after the Age of Aries comes Pisces, and now Aquarius.

Way back in the Age of Leo, we are told, there was a civilization called Atlantis, an island just west of the Strait of Gibraltar. Atlantis was developed socially, economically, and politically beyond our wildest dreams. The Atlanteans had mastered the problem of obtaining power from the Sun. They powered their space vehicles with solar energy and had even succeeded in using it to regenerate human bodies. The whole Atlantean world was run on Sun power!

Atlantis, according to the tradition, was literally ripped apart as a result of Leonine power struggles among its rulers. It finally vanished beneath the Atlantic ocean. Does history repeat itself?

Astrologically, there is no justification for suggesting that our civilization over the next two thousand years is going to reach Atlantean heights of harnessing solar power. But the law of astrological cycles does indicate that this Aquarius Age could at least be a beginning toward that end.

Aquarius is the sign of scientific discovery, originality, progress, radical change, and invention. It is exactly opposite Leo across the Zodiac. So we are now halfway around the circle from the days of Atlantis. The "dark" ages that followed the loss of Atlantean technology are at last behind us.

The cycle is on the way up and heading toward Leo again. This point will be reached in 12,600 years. It is to be hoped people will have evolved and matured enough not to repeat the same disastrous mistakes.

HOW ASTROLOGY BEGAN

There are two main schools of thought about how astrology began. The first is that it was the product of divine inspiration handed down by the sages of Atlantis. These sages included the spiritually evolved guides of the human race, the legendary figures who during this epoch gradually withdrew from the world and became known as Hermes, Minerva, Apollo, Isis, Osiris, Dionysus, Diana, and Vesta—in other words, the gods and goddesses.

The other and more popular idea is that the science of astrology must have evolved purely out of man's observations of celestial phenomena. These supporters picture early peoples observing phases of the moon, eclipses, meteors, and comets, then correlating them to such earthly events as floods, famines, wars, disease, earthquakes, and, later on, the characters of people.

But when the principles, functions, and formulas of astrology are studied as a whole, it becomes clear that the idea of astrology having been invented and put together piecemeal, like assembling a model of some new animal, is even more preposterous than giving it a "divine" or inspirational origin.

The answer probably lies somewhere in between.

There can be no doubt that astrology existed in prehistoric times. Out of early man's fears and dreads in coping with a hostile and cruel environment emerged a natural yearning for order. For this, his closest example was nature itself. Even its extremes of floods, droughts, and gales offered a predictable cyclic pattern. And there was the regularity of the seasons and the rhythm of the tides and the repetition of the climates year in and year out.

Early peoples linked these periodic phenomena with the apparent path of the Sun and the motions of the Moon which followed periodic and predictable routes. It must not have taken early peoples long to rationalize that almost every aspect of human existence was dependent on these two mysterious heavenly bodies.

Alexander Marshack, writing in the journal *Science,* has suggested that nicks found cut into mammoth ivory and reindeer bones dating back to the Upper Paleolithic period (up to around 20,000 B.C. were "records" of such observations of the lunar cycles.

Early man's inability to explain celestial phenomena probably led him to identify them with the work of superhuman intelligences and spirits. He even invested the Sun and Moon with "characters" of their own, giving rise to religion, rites, and unlimited superstitions. But magic was the beginning of science!

THE EGYPTIANS

For written evidence we leave early peoples' possible inferences and move forward to around 4200 B.C., to the Egyptians. It is a giant leap in time from the first human beings to these sophisticated people of the Nile who by this date had been able to erect finely accurate charts of the fixed stars. Some of these charts survive today; they evidently are copies of even earlier charts.

There is no concrete evidence from this time that the Egyptians practiced astrology. They were, though, extremely skilled astronomers. Their calendar was so accurate that only in relatively recent times was it possible to improve on it.

But it is inferred by many modern scholars that astrology was practiced by the Egyptians before any other Mediterranean race. The Egyptians practiced it in the strictest secrecy, something like an exclusive cult. This hypothesis is supported by folk traditions that maintain that the original astrological knowledge, presumably issuing from Atlantis, first passed to the Egyptians, who later disseminated it to the Babylonians. The main wave of the knowledge, it is said, was from Egypt to India to China, and then across the Bering Strait between Russia and Alaska down to the vanished civilizations of South America, where innumerable astrological relics have been discovered.

The supporters of the Egyptian theory point to the findings of a French scholar, R. A. Schwaller de Lubiscz. During the last thirty years, de Lubiscz produced extraordinary evidence to show that astrological principles were built into Egyptian art and architecture in such as way as to be obvious only to those who were in sympathy with the idea of a harmonious, unified universe—the actual basis from which astrology begins.

It is said that the whole Egyptian astrological tradition was handed down orally from master to pupil and only allowed to be expressed publicly in art and architecture. Some examples exist among the acknowledged masterpieces surviving today.

THE BABYLONIANS AND THE EGYPTIANS

On purely historical evidence, the Babylonians, or Chaldeans, were the first people to develop astrology systematically. These were the ancestors of the people of old Mesopotamia and today's Iraq. Their civilization grew up between and around those two most famous rivers of the ancient world—the Tigris and Euphrates, which empty into the Persian Gulf.

On the evidence, it was the Babylonians also who were the first to put 2 and 2 together and so to invent mathematics. It was a fairly simple system, but it did allow them to translate their observations of the heavens into meaningful records and especially calendars.

The Babylonians were originally desert people. For thousands of years their acenstors had been shepherds. They had every opportunity to observe the ceaseless comings and goings of the heavenly bodies in the clear and cloudless desert sky and to make mental notes. In fact, skywatching probably was their equivalent of TV!

By 3,000 B.C. the Babylonians had developed a relatively advanced system of organized observation and interpretation of celestial phenomena. They were a people who had always depended on divination, including the examination of animals' entrails for "signs." It was a natural step for them to see a correlation between the movements of the stars and certain earthly events.

The Babylonians erected a series of watchtower observatories, which for those times were impressive structures. These watchtowers, set around the kingdom and manned full time by the priests, were up to two hundred feet high and hundreds of feet long. Some consisted of seven terraces, one on top of the other, representing the seven known planets. They were lined with glazed brick, and the topmost chambers were sometimes finished elaborately in gold and precious stones.

The Tower of Babel mentioned in the Bible is a likely reference to one of these towers, which were said to "reach unto heaven."

The Babylonians had no telescopes. Yet they were able to discover and name at least two constellations—Orion and the Pleiades. The Babylonian priests were deeply steeped in the occult. To them, there was no doubt that the brightly shining planets were gods, and they had no difficulty identifying them with mysterious forces and powers that affected terrestrial affairs.

For two thousand years they charted and studied the heavens, discovering the ecliptic—the apparent annual path of the Sun around the Earth. They eventually divided this path into twelve divisions, the signs of the Zodiac, although they did not identify them as such.

Astrology in those early days was practiced differently, though the principles were the same. No individual horoscopes were cast, at least not for ordinary people. It was the custom of the early priest-astrologers to link the fortunes of the nation with the fate of the King. If the King prospered, so did everyone. If ill luck befell him, it was bad times for all. So only the King's horoscope was erected and interpreted. This one horoscope was the basis for a continuous reading that helped to guide the running of the country from day to day.

Across more than four thousand years of history have come down to us some of the written maxims of these ancient astrological pioneers. In fact, more than thirty thousand of their cuneiform clay tablets have been recovered near the site of ancient Babylon.

The most famous Babylonian predictions in existence are those of Sargon the Old (2470–2430 B.C.). These are mainly concerned with the Sun and the Moon.

He wrote: "If the moon can be seen the first night of the month, the country will be peaceful; the heart of the country will rejoice. If the moon is surrounded with a halo, the king will reign supreme.

"If the setting sun seems twice as large as usual, and three of its rays are bluish, the king of the land is lost.

"If the moon is visible on the 30th, good tiding for the land of Akkad, bad for Syria."

It is not reported whether the astrologers were able to predict the end for Babylon, which came around 1000 B.C. Then the country was overrun by the Assyrians from the north.

Meanwhile, however, to the south, Egyptian astrology was becoming more mundane and Babylonian in flavor. It was losing any purely esoteric connections with art and architecture. It had begun the long journey toward the marketplace.

The argument that the Egyptians learned astrology from Babylonian sources receives support from the evidence of the Old Testament. It could well be that the old esoteric system became "lost" through excessive secrecy and that the later system developed along conventional lines.

The Bible shows that the Israelites were well versed in the subject. Abraham, the prophet, actually lived in Ur, part of the Babylonian Empire. According to another old work, Abraham "wore an astrological clay tablet on his chest." The enslavement of the Hebrews by the Egyptians around 1300 B.C. also would have resulted in a wide exchange of ideas, no doubt including astrological ones.

On the other hand, the oldest horoscope relic in the world is one that was cast in 2767 B.C. by Imhotep, the architect responsible for the first of the Great Pyramids of Zoser. The earliest Egyptian horoscope known to have been drawn up was for Nectanebo II in 358 B.C., more than two thousand years later. But this, of course, proves nothing. as earlier relics may yet be found.

Using their tremendously advanced astronomical knowledge, the Egyptians were able to align the pyramids to the cardinal points of the compass within a few seconds of a degree of error. The Great Pyramid of Gizeh, finished around 2800 B.C., was originally 481 feet high and covered 13 acres. It incorporated measurements said to correspond to astrological relationships and cycles.

Also at Giseh, in front of the Great Pyramid, was built the Sphinx, claimed to be another example of astrological symbolism.

Pliny, the Roman scholar writing about A.D. 50 observed: "In front of the pyramid is the Sphinx, a still more wondrous object of art, but upon which rests a spell of silence, as it is looked upon as a great deity." The Sphinx even then was more than twenty-five hundred years old. Wrote Plutarch, the Greek biographer about the same time: "The Sphinx symbolizes the secret of all occult wisdom."

Nevertheless, with Ptolemy's works astrology no longer needed to defend itself. Ptolemy's works were the bible of astrology for more than twelve hundred years—until Copernicus.

But trouble was coming. Although the early Christian fathers seemed to have no trouble living with astrology, the later leaders of the Church came out hard against it as a pagan practice. By A.D. 323 the first Christian Emperor, Constantine, sat on the throne of Rome. And under the fierce attacks of St. Augustine, who had once been an adherent, the science virtually disappeared from Europe.

Meanwhile, however, astrology was thriving in the Middle East, where it had begun. The Mohammedan conquests of the seventh century interfered for a time, while millions of people turned to embracing the new faith. Then Islam became the center of astronomical and astrological effort.

In Baghdad, the successors of Mohammed surrounded themselves with the greatest mathematicians and scholars from the Arab world. They were employed in making observations of the heavenly bodies, measuring distances along the meridian, redetermining the size of the Earth, and inventing a new calendar for civil affairs based on the Moon.

At the same time, a "House of Wisdom" was established where translations were made of Ptolemy's *Almagest* and *Tetrabiblos* as well as many Greek texts. Over the next six hundred years the Arab contribution to the world's knowledge of astronomy, mathematics, medical chemistry, biology, and geology was enormous. From the point of view of astrology, it was these gifted people who kept the science alive while Europe lay prostrate under priestly rule and the ignorance of the Dark Ages.

THE COPERNICAN MODEL OF THE UNIVERSE

With the Renaissance, the period of renewed cultural and intellectual endeavor around the start of the fifteenth century, astrology once again attracted the leading minds of the day. One was Roger Bacon, the English philosopher and scientist whose writings contain prophecies of the telescope, microscope, steam engine, and airplane.

Bacon believed that the nature or character of an individual was determined by the sky at conception and birth. Bacon also thought that health and disease of the body were under the influence of the stars, so "the wise physician should be aware of the fact that hour by hour the bodily states vary with changing positions of the planets."

Thomas Aquinas (1225–74), one of the guiding lights of the Church, also averred that "no wise man doubted that all natural motions of the inferior bodies are caused by movements of the celestial bodies." Dante, the devotional poet of the same period, believed that the power, wisdom, and love of the Almighty were transmitted to man through the stars and planets.

Shakespeare wrote: "The fault . . . is not in our stars but in ourselves that we are underlings."

Then came Nicolaus Copernicus (1473–1543). He spent several years studying in Italy, where he became familiar with the Ptolemaic model of the

Aristarchus made the incredible deduction from mathematical calculations that the Sun and Moon must be of very different sizes, even though they appear in the sky to be approximately the same. He also concluded from the shadow of the Earth cast over the Moon at an eclipse that the Earth was twice as large as the Moon. (It is actually about four times larger.) Eratosthenes was the first to estimate accurately the circumference of the Earth. And under Empedocles and especially Hippocrates, often called the father of modern medicine, a system of medical astrology was started.

It was Empedocles also who formulated the doctrine of the four elements in astrology: earth, air, fire, and water. These elements were said to distinguish the temperaments of people.

THE PTOLEMAIC MODEL OF THE UNIVERSE

From the Greeks, astrology passed to the Romans. Greek slaves are reported to have first brought this art and science to Rome. But it was coldly received by the traditional Roman diviners, who, feeling their power and livelihood would be threatened, had the star readers banned from the city.

However, the appeal of the old science lingered. With the support of the Stoics and other schools of philosophers and intellectuals, it gradually gained ground. By the first century A.D. it was firmly entrenched. Every leading citizen, including Emperors Caesar and Octavius, had their horoscopes cast in great detail.

Nevertheless, astrology did have its ups and downs, usually due to the fluctuating temperature of the Roman political scene. Emperor Augustus, although a firm believer, outlawed the astrologers in 33 B.C. because he feared Marc Antony, his archrival, would cause unfavorable predictions to be made about him by his enemies. As soon as Antony had been removed, Augustus restored astrology to its former respectable place in Roman society. And, as though to reaffirm his own allegiance, he had a special coin struck showing Capricorn, his Moon sign, dominating the world!

In A.D. 137 astrology received probably the greatest boost in its history by Ptolemy's publication of his two books the *Almagest* and *Tetrabiblos*. Ptolemy (Claudius Ptolemaeus of Alexandria) was the greatest astrologer and astronomer of that time. His two books brought together all the known astrological and astronomical knowledge to that date.

Ptolemy's model of the solar system had the Sun and all the planets moving around the Earth. The planets moved in tiny circles, called epicycles, as they revolved in larger circles around the Earth. It seems quite natural to think that the Earth is at the center of the universe. It is also natural to assume that the Sun and stars move around the Earth, since every day and night we see these objects appear to rise, move across the sky, and set.

But predictions of the positions of the planets did not always work out based on the Ptolemaic model. It kept being revised, and it was still clumsy. Not until Nicolaus Copernicus revolutionized the model in the sixteenth century could celestial motions be accurately explained.

And understandably so. The riddle of the Sphinx and its hidden astrological significance are intriguing.

THE GREEKS

According to Greek mythology, the Sphinx originally was a living monster, part man and part beast. It used to ask passersby to answer a riddle, and when they failed ate them alive.

The riddle was: What creature walks in the morning upon four feet, at noon upon two, at evening upon three?

Oedipus, the future King of Thebes, guessed the riddle. In amazement the Sphinx turned to stone.

The answer was: man. The allusion is to his walking on hands and knees as a baby, on two feet later, and with a staff in old age.

Astrologically, the Sphinx is said to represent the fixed signs in a cross: the Bull (Taurus); the Lion (Leo); the Eagle, which was the ancient symbol used for the Scorpion (Scorpio); and Man. It also is said to embody the four elements: Bull, earth; Lion, fire; Eagle, water; Man, air.

After the Babylonians, the Greeks became the main custodians of astrological lore in the Western world. Babylonian astrologers, fleeing from the Assyrian conquest of their country, filtered through the Hellenic islands and gradually passed on their knowledge.

Under the keen minds of the Greeks, astrology developed even more swiftly. But for a while, around 600 B.C., it was somewhat neglected. The Greeks had other things on their mind. This was the unique period of Greek enlightenment during which philosophy and the arts received an impetus that was to influence succeeding civilizations for thousands of years.

The period also marked the foundation of the scientific method as it is understood today. The result was that when the Greeks once again turned their attention to astrology, they were better equipped than ever to pursue it.

The Greeks welcomed astrology as the natural partner to the divine science of mathematics. Their philosopher scientists pursued the subjects with extraodinary insights. Over the next three hundred years they added tremendously to the concepts of astrology. This plus their astronomical achievements resulted in a completely new intellectual view of the world and the universe. It was the era of such memorable names as Thales, Anaximenes, Pythagoras, Empedocles, Anaxagoras, Aristotle, Plato, and Hippocrates.

Although Copernicus of the fifteenth century A.D. is credited with being the first to propose that the Earth orbited the Sun, this fact had already been discovered and recorded by Aristarchus of Samos in 300 B.C. Democritus correctly surmised that the Milky Way consisted of myriads of stars. Leucippus declared that the Moon's markings were caused by hills and valleys casting shadows on its surface. Empedocles taught that the solar eclipses were due to the Moon passing between the Earth and the Sun.

These are all well-known facts today. But it has to be remembered that the invention of the telescope was still a long way off. With no instruments, all the Greeks had to assist them were their extraordinary minds.

Solar System. Copernicus returned to his native Poland and took about thirty years to develop a new model of the Solar System.

The Copernican model, with slight improvements, is the model of the Solar System used today. In it, the Sun is at the center. The planets and their satellites, including our Earth and Moon, revolve around the Sun. Now the planets' positions could be accurately predicted.

The Copernican model also explained the apparent daily motion of the Sun, Moon, and stars. He suggested that the Earth is rotating on its axis from west to east, and that the celestial objects appear to us Earth observers as passing scenery. But it is we, not they, who are moving. Because we are not aware of our rotation, the objects we see appear to be moving.

The Copernican model has been one of the most useful tools of discovery in science. It, together with Newton's theory of gravitation, made it possible, for example, to predict the position of the unknown planet Neptune in 1843 and the even more distant planet Pluto in 1930.

After Copernicus came the scientific discoveries of Galileo (inventor of the telescope), Tycho Brahe, Johannes Kepler, and Isaac Newton. All of these scientists took an interest in astrology.

Brahe, by his meticulous observations of planetary orbits, paved the way for the genius of Newton to define the laws of gravitation in 1693. A practicing astrologer, Brahe predicted the years of birth and death of Gustavus Adolphus of Sweden, a hero of the Thirty Years' War.

Johannes Kepler, a student of Brahe, used Brahe's observations of planetary orbits to refine the Copernican model. Kepler discovered that the orbits of the planets were ellipses, not circles as Copernicus and the others had assumed. Kepler, also an astrologer who published astrological calendars, put the finishing touches on the model of the Solar System that is used today by astronomers, space scientists, and astrologers.

THE SPACE ERA

The Copernican model of the universe, Kepler's laws of motion, and Newton's laws of gravitation, inertia, mass, and acceleration were the scientific "launching pads" for the space era. Now astrology was put to the real test. Could the world's oldest tradition and first science possibly survive in such a climate of supertechnology?

Astrology has certainly survived, and it is booming. Never in the history of the world have so many people taken such an intelligent interest in astrology. Each week, hundreds of thousands of copies of specialist books, magazines, and other publications on astrology are bought and studied.

Astrology today has demonstrated the validity of its principles in modern scientific terms.

Despite official obstinacy, more and more individual scientists, especially those of the last couple of generations in this new Age of Aquarius, are acknowledging the validity of astrology as a tool for helping them unravel the mysteries of the universe. It makes absorbing reading to bring together some of the major scientific discoveries of recent years, which help to confirm astrological practice and theory. It is, in fact, quite an astounding record.

THE MOON AND BEHAVIOR

The Moon's effect on aspects of life around us is so much a part of normal experience that it often passes without being noticed. However, its vital influence on terrestrial existence has been a key factor in astrology since time immemorial.

As everyone knows, the Moon controls the tides. Scientists also have established its connection with the menstrual cycle, births, and blood flow. Medical astrologers of old were respectfully aware of the latter connection. They would refuse to perform operations during certain phases of the Moon because of the danger of patients bleeding to death.

In modern times, it was the observation of an alert nurse in Florida that prompted research into this old belief. The nurse reported to Dr. Edson Andrews of Tallahassee that his patients seemed to be hemorrhaging more frequently at certain times than at others.

Ignoring his first impulse to dismiss the idea, Dr. Andrews made a quick check, which convinced him that here indeed was something that needed closer investigation. In subsequent tests covering a thousand cases of tonsillectomy, he found that 82 percent of the bleeding crises occurred between the Moon's first and third quarters. "These data have been so conclusive and convincing," he is reported to have said, "that I threaten to become a witch doctor and operate on dark nights only!"

Japanese and American researchers, in studying the frequency of more than 530,000 births over a period of years, found a significant peaking one or two days before the Moon's first and last quarters. Similarly, studies of thousands of menstruation cases over a period of fourteen years showed a maximum at Full and New Moons.

Leonard J. Ravitz of Duke University, by comparing the electrical potential of normal and disturbed people, found that patients were markedly more affected at times coinciding with Moon phases and seasonal changes. Astrology has always linked the Moon with mental disorders, a tradition perpetuated by the word "lunatic."

One of the first medical men to publicize the apparent connection between lunar cycles and physical illness was William Peterson of Chicago. He reported that deaths from tuberculosis were most frequent seven days before the Full Moon. In 1961, a significant correlation among lunar phases, pneumonia cases, and uric acid in the blood was discovered by a German scientist, Hans Heckert.

Perhaps the most interesting and revealing experiment is what has been called "The Strange Case of the Evanston Oysters." Frank A. Brown, professor of biology at Northwestern University, had done a tremendous amount of research work into "biological clocks." It was known that every living organism, from man to the tiniest living cell, operates according to predetermined rhythms. But the disputed question was: What controls those rhythms?

From rhythm tests with beans, flies, and rats and from color changes in fiddler crabs, Brown and his colleagues found that solar factors, probably the Sun and Moon, must be responsible, not climatic changes, as had been generally supposed. His next experiment with oysters gave the breakthrough and forced a major, though somewhat reluctant, change in scientific thinking.

It had been long assumed that the trigger for the oysters' biological clock, telling them when to open their shells to feed, was the movement of the tides. No one ever bothered to check this assumption. Brown did. He took a batch of oysters fresh out of the sea from New Haven, Connecticut, to Evanston, Illinois, a thousand miles from the nearest tidal waters. There he placed them in specially prepared pans of salt water in a dark room. For two weeks, the oysters opened and closed to the tidal rhythms back in New Haven. But then they began to alter their timing, soon settling into a routine of opening their shells when it would have been high tide in Evanston—had there been tides there!

Brown's experiment proved conclusively that gravitational forces coming from the Moon, and not immediate external conditions, were responsible.

THE SUN AND BEHAVIOR

From the Moon we now switch to the Sun. The Sun is the most powerful of all the cosmic influences in astrology, for the simple reason that it is the source of life for us and the brightest object in the sky.

In the 1920s, a Russian historian, Tchijevsky, was struck by the cyclical pattern in which wars, epidemics, and major social changes occurred. Science by then had discovered sun spot activity. Huge electromagnetic storms on the Sun every 11.1 years spew into space huge flares of solar gases. Tchijevsky figured that there might be a connection between sunspot activity and world-shaking events. Over the next fifteen years, he assembled historical data from seventy-two countries dating back twenty-five hundred years. His findings revealed that peaks in sunspot activity coincided with the world's major epidemics and plagues, including the Black Death.

Since then, a great new world of scientific research into cyclical rhythms has opened up, especially in America and Russia. These cyclical patterns have been found to exist in a range of phenomena—flu epidemics, heart disease, world rainfall, icebergs, and even droughts in India. Russian scientists were able to link the solar activity, especially a particularly violent eruption in 1959, with a blood deficiency due to destruction of lymphocytes, a form of white blood cell.

But it was a persistent and brilliant Japanese professor, Maki Takata, who put his finger on the Sun's power to affect the human bloodstream. Takata found that the composition of human blood changes in relation to the sunspot cycle, solar flares, and eclipses. He also found that just before sunrise the blood becomes enormously active. For some astrologers this immediately suggested a correlation with the Sun sign and the Ascendant, or Rising, sign (the sign that was rising on the eastern horizon at the time of an individual's birth).

Solar activity has been found to affect the incidence of road accidents. Russian scientists and engineers reported that research carried out over a number of years at the Tomsk Medical College had found a relation between roads accidents and solar activity. Their statistics show that the day after the eruption of a solar flare, road accidents increased, sometimes as much as four times above the average. Similar findings had also been obtained by investigators in Hamburg and Munich.

THE IGY EXPLORATION AND
PLANETARY INFLUENCES

The existence of an electromagnetic link between the Sun and the planets, which would help to prove the functional validity of astrology, was actually established as a result of discoveries made during the International Geophysical Year (IGY), 1957–58.

During the IGY exploration, rocket probes and brilliant deskwork led scientists to the discovery that the Earth was "cocooned" in vast "local" radiation layers. These were named the Van Allen Belts, after American scientist James A. Van Allen, who first explained the phenomenon. The Earth's own magnetic field interacted with the Van Allen Belts. In the vast space around Earth was created a tremendous electromagnetic field. This field is called the magnetosphere.

For a further fifteen years, the space scientists labored. Finally, through the U.S. *Pioneer* space probes, they established that the other planets also had magnetospheres of their own. This meant that one secret of the Solar System was at last solved. It consisted of a single gigantic electromagnetic field of force and "information," in which the orbiting planets act as magnets and "cut" and change the field continuously.

Electromagnetic radiation is "sensed" by all organisms in different ways. What "information" is conveyed has become a rich area for speculation and organized research. For example, scientists investigating earthquake areas found that shortly before an earthquake occurred, the local magnetic field collapsed. This was immediately sensed by the wildlife in the area, which promptly fled. The magnetic field had acted as a warning system.

Medical science for years has been utilizing the electromagnetic fields in the human body to evolve more effective and precise diagnostic techniques. Much research still remains to be done. But it has been established that during magnetic storms in cosmic space, the incidence of heart attacks and mental and nervous disorders increases.

To astrologers, all this is yet another demonstration of their much-maligned craft being made scientifically respectable.

The work of a famous German geophysicist, Rudolph Tomascheck, has helped to give scientific credence to one of the most ridiculed aspects of traditional astrology. This concerns the astrological tradition of assigning to each planet a symbolic character, which is either intensified or diminished by the planet's position relative to other planets. Even that most benign planet Jupiter, which is supposed to symbolize luck and good fortune, can create very disturbing conditions when in an adverse aspect.

Tomascheck, an ex-chairman of the International Geophysical Society, is one of those rare Western scientists who also takes an active interest in astrology. In making a statistical analysis of 134 major earthquakes and comparing them with the positions of the planets at those times, he found that Jupiter, Uranus, and Pluto were in bad or stressful aspect "to a statistically significant degree."

This becomes even more interesting when it is remembered that modern astrology attributes qualities of revolution and drastic change to Uranus, and upheaval and chaos to Pluto. Pluto also was "god" of the underworld. According to the Greeks, the benevolent god Jupiter was not beyond turning nasty and throwing thunderbolts when his cronies and mere mortals upset him.

Another physicist who believes in applying traditional astrological principles to modern scientific research is Konstantin Kobysev of Moscow University. His researches have produced such positive results he is confident that one day it may be possible to predict natural disasters such as earthquakes, floods, and epidemics from the study of relationships between and among celestial bodies. He thinks the laws behind these phenomena could eventually be clearly defined, thus ushering in a new era of hope for thousands who die annually in natural disasters.

Two Western scientists who were not afraid to suggest that astrology might deserve more respect from official scientific circles are John R. Gribbin, a British astrophysicist, and Stephen H. Plagemann, an American astronomer who worked with eminent astronomer Fred Hoyle, as well as for NASA. "To the surprise of many scientists," they said, "there has come evidence . . . that the astrologers were not so wrong after all: it seems that the alignments of the planets can, for sound reasons, affect the behavior of the earth. The trail [of evidence they had assembled] links astrology—for that is really what the study of planetary alignments is even though we can explain their effects in sound scientific terms—astronomy, meteorology, geology, geophysics and other sciences."

SUN SIGNS AND PERSONALITY STUDIES

Hans Eysenck, professor of psychology at London University, has come up with some extraordinary results. His research has shown that astrology can and does make accurate assessments of personalities. Eysenck says that the position of the planets when a person is born is an accurate guide to how introverted or extroverted the person will become and also to how emotional the person will be.

His research was based on the traditional astrological premise that extroverts are born when the Sun is in Aries, Gemini, Leo, Libra, Sagittarius, and Aquarius, and that introverts are born when the sun is in Taurus, Cancer, Virgo, Scorpio, Capricorn, and Pisces. According to astrologers, people born under the three water signs—Cancer, Scorpio, and Pisces—are the most emotional types.

Professor Eysenck asked more than two thousand people to complete a personality questionnaire, which included their dates of birth. The answers were computer-analyzed and gave "an overwhelming verdict supporting the predictions of astrology."

Publishing his findings, the professor said: "I must admit this was a great surprise to me. My instinctive skepticism had led me to expect failure from an investigation of astrology."

Sybil Eysenck, also a psychologist and the professor's wife, has found that the position of the planets Mars, Jupiter, and Saturn at the moment of birth is significant in the forming of an individual's personality. In France, she studied the research of another famous husband-and-wife team, Dr. Françoise Gauquelin and Dr. Michel Gauquelin.

PLANETARY PLACEMENTS AND CAREER STUDIES

Michel Gauquelin, who originally set out to disprove astrology, has done more perhaps than any other scientist in modern times to prove the validity of its assumptions.

With his wife, he traveled through Europe collecting data from birth registers to combine with similar statistics obtained from his native France. His object was to discover any correlation between the positions of the planets at the time of birth and the professions people follow.

The two researchers compiled data for large groups of eminent professors of medicine, soldiers, politicians, artists, sportsmen, clerics, writers, and musicians. In all cases, their comparisons showed an inexplicable correlation between the planets and the chosen professions.

In the horoscopes of scientists and academicians, as astrology would maintain, Mars and Saturn figured prominently. Sportsmen were strongly influenced by Jupiter and Mars, as tradition would predict. In the charts of musicians and painters, the influence of the not-so-artistic planets Mars and Saturn was noticeably diminished.

At the odds of half a million to one against, Mars occupied dominant positions in the charts of scientists. At astronomically greater odds against chance, the hard-driving, energetic planet Mars was prominent among the 1,485 athletes surveyed. And among 3,142 military leaders whose charts were examined, Mars, the planet that symbolizes war and self-assertion, was strong in 634 cases—at odds of a million to one against.

An interesting point about the leading Nazis of the Third Reich came out of Michel Gauquelin's research. It concerns the position in their horoscopes of the planet Jupiter. Jupiter symbolizes expansion and power. Strongly positioned in a chart, it also induces a fondness for exaggerated ceremony and theatrical display. In the horoscopes of Hitler and his henchmen Himmler, Heydrich, Goebbels, and Bormann, all of whom hungered for power and possessed a love of the dramatic, Jupiter was the dominant factor in the power-sensitive angles.

SUN SIGNS AND CAREER STUDIES

Other scientists have also done studies to ascertain whether the twelve zodiacal Sun sign types are inclined to be drawn to particular jobs, careers and professions. In both America and England, two independent research teams have culled through hundreds of thousands of birth dates and come up with much the same answer. Astrological notions are correct to a statistically significant degree.

The English team comprised Alan Smithers of Manchester University, and his colleague, Bradford sociologist Joe Cooper. In the United States, Edmund Van Deusen, a scientific consultant, and his team of researchers checked through the birth dates of 163,953 individuals to ascertain which of the Sun signs had been successful in 37 specific professions.

In an interview with Ann Leslie in the *London Daily Mail*, April 25, 1977, Van Deusen explained: "Let's suppose, for example that it takes a certain type of personality to become a good doctor. By the law of averages the birth pattern of doctors should match the birth pattern of general population. If (in the final analysis of such a research project) to a statistically significant degree the doctors' birth pattern is very different—then something extraordinary is happening."

And so it was.

Van Deusen and the British team, although working independently on the evidence of more than 750,000 birth dates between them, found that the birth dates of 6,413 British and American doctors clustered well beyond chance in the summer and autumn months, with the British Army medical officers peaking in Scorpio. Scorpio, according to astrologers, is the sign of natural-born soldiers and surgeons.

Samples of 6,677 British and American lawyers revealed that they tend to be born in early summer and midautumn, with the American birth dates peaking particularly in Gemini. The sign of the Twins, astrologers say, is noted for the ability to argue any issue or case from either side.

Geminis also came out on top as the people most likely to become diplomats and advertising executives. Traditionally, Gemini is the sign of communication, salesmanship, quick thinking, and a facility for learning languages.

Of the 2,696 bankers studied by Van Deusen, a statistically disproportionate number were Virgos. "Astrologically speaking," Van Deusen is quoted as saying, "this would be predictable. Virgos are supposedly accountants by nature—life is a ledger in which every event must be neatly entered."

American and Birtish composers, the researchers found, tend to be born between late autumn and late winter—that is, in Sagittarius, Capricorn, Aquarius, and Pisces.

Of the 5,111 American and Canadian librarians surveyed by Van Deusen, the dominant sign was Libra. And Librans "according to astrologers need to work in a quiet, congenial, harmonious environment."

British politicians, according to the researchers, tend to be born under Aries, the sign of go-getting, self-asserting, and often crusading people.

Both surveys bore out the astrological tradition that Scorpios (and Leos because of their leadership qualities) are drawn to the army. The birth dates of 16,000 British Army officers and 12,000 American Army officers showed that 34 percent more than would be expected were born in late summer and early autumn, with the peaks occurring in Leo and Scorpio.

Of 5,056 schoolteachers, the dominant signs were Leos and Virgos. Said Van Deusen: "A schoolroom can quickly degenerate into chaos unless the teacher exercises a degree of authority. This, an astrologer would maintain, makes it the right setting for Leos, who can command a situation by their very presence. And it is also appropriate for the everyone-in-his-place Virgos.''

Virgo also was the sign under which a disproportionate number of the 3,927 leading British and American authors were born. Virgos are methodically analytical, as the distinguished classical Virgo writers Tolstoy, Goethe, and H. G. Wells showed.

Top signs in the laughter stakes are Aquarius, Pisces, Aries, Taurus, and Gemini. The British survey found that the most comedians were born between January 21 and June 20.

ASTROSCOPE PROFILES

Astrology, as it is practiced today, is far easier to follow and understand than at any other time in its long history. Still, you can recapture that old-time magic and mystery even as you read here the commonsense, factual connections between the planets and the signs that make you a unique individual. Astrology is a personal art and science. The *Astroscope Profile* series, which enables you to construct your own profile, opens up that exciting new world of discovery. The subsequent chapters of this book take you on a journey through your Sun sign, your Rising sign, and the signs in which the Moon and other planets appear for you. *Bon voyage!*

Sun Sign Leo

Leo:
Character Analysis

The Sun in Leo at birth produces a character that can be aptly summed up as lordly Leo. Like the Lion, which is their symbol, these men and women often create an impression of power and authority. In a crowd they tend to draw the eye, even the plainest of them. Their manner, movements, and gestures usually have a certain flair, an assurance that suggests the person might be more than they appear.

No wonder. Leo represents the kings and queens of the jungle—those men and women born between July 21 and August 21.

No other sign is so bountifully endowed with positive, creative, and attractive potential. These people are capable of bringing a great deal of happiness, sunshine, and achievement into the world. They have drive, organizing ability, staying power, and an inborn instinct for command. They radiate energy and vitality.

The font of all Leo's attributes is the Sun, ruler of the sign of Leo. Being the center of the solar system and the source of life, the Sun is the most powerful influence in the Zodiac. Astrologically, it is as children of the Sun that Leo men and women acquire their tremendous sense of self-importance and indomitable faith in themselves.

A HEART OF GOLD

The Sun, as the center of life, represents the heart. And Leos have a lot of heart, as well as a brave heart. Generosity is one of their best characteristics, although it is not always in the form of money or what it can buy.

Warmth of heart is a typical Leo characteristic. They are spontaneously generous in their affections. Their genial and encouraging manner often acts as a tonic to their associates.

Leos frequently take it upon themselves to make the lives of others happier and more fulfilling. They will invite lonely acquaintances to their homes, where they can meet and find common interests. They also try to act as romantic matchmakers.

No type in the Zodiac is more generous with their time, their possessions, or their sunny personalities. A Leo smile of encouragement or thanks is so open, warm, and sincere that it is very difficult to continue to be peeved or angry with them. They are easy people to forgive. For all their strutting, self-glorification, and bossiness, they are at heart simple but highly principled characters. There is much that is noble and good in these children of the Sun.

After receiving due homage, the Leo man or woman will go to extraordinary lengths to pay a person back in kind. In the royal tradition, once loyalty or love is shown, Leo's habit is to distribute largesse and favors far beyond the value of any tokens received.

But it does not pay anyone to expect anything from a Leo. They can't stand other people presuming on them. Even if they are millionaires, they will be stonyhearted and aloof to anyone who expects a handout, no matter how deserving their position may appear. Leos often have trouble with their relatives in this way, and prefer to avoid or ignore most of them.

Although generous in the entertainment of their friends, Leos do not take kindly to being asked for something beyond what is offered. They expect a high level of good manners. Anyone who does not measure up will not be invited again.

Leos love buying gifts for people. They get a big kick out of making others happy, especially their nearest and dearest. Their presents at times can be very expensive, but on other occasions may be more of a token, depending on their mood and whether the person is currently in good favor.

A Leo will be more generous with the people whom he or she feels deserves it, rather than hand out the same valuable gifts to everyone. To qualify for a Leo's material generosity usually means the recipient is appreciative of the Lion's other qualities and is one of his or her admirers.

Leos do not have much to do with people on a halfhearted basis. To them, a friend is a supporter whom they feel admires them and speaks well of them. They are not interested in wishy-washy friendships. They like to feel a heart bond between them and their true friends.

PRIDE GOETH BEFORE A FALL

The monster that stalks Leos in everything they do is pride. Even with so much that is natural working for them to ensure the limelight and admiration they crave, they can't help going to extremes. They often are guilty of arrogance, smugness, conceit, and boastfulness.

True Leos never are daunted by fears of failure. Failure is something they refuse to consider—not because they can't fail, but because they are too proud to contemplate the prospect of it. These individuals often back themselves into difficult corners. Their pride in their ability to perform will seldom allow them to turn down a challenge. They are bold and impulsive, often too confident.

When they give their word, their pride again prevents them from admitting that they can't deliver. As a result, Leos frequently work themselves to a frazzle to complete what they promised in a rash moment.

Leos throw themselves completely into every project they start. They are inclined to concentrate on one activity at a time because this enables them to give it all they've got. But one pursuit invariably leads to another in the same field, and they often are in danger of being swamped by sheer lack of time.

Their stubborn determination not to ask others for help frequently adds to their difficulties. In a Leo who has other planets in Cancer or Pisces, this can produce a desire to play the martyr in a bid for sympathy. Such people will attempt to draw attention to their hard-pressed plight while continuing to wave aside offers of help.

In spite of their massive self-assurance—or perhaps because of it—there is a naiveté in the Leo character that makes these people appear sometimes childishly inept as judges of character. They can be conned. Their defenses are infiltrated by devious and complicated types who wheedle favors or advantages out of them or through them.

Leos detest pettiness. They are contemptuous of critics, cynics, faultfinders, backsliders, and renegers. Their arrogant disdain can be so pompous that they may refuse to take action against people they have been warned are plotting their downfall.

Their faith in their ability to meet any challenge or danger head-on is supreme. Many Leos have had to climb sheepishly out of the ruins and dust themselves off after being undermined by those they trusted against better advice.

THE POWER OF AUTHORITY

Typical Leo men and women are disdainful of danger when it stands in their way. Their physical courage can reach the point of foolhardiness. It must be remembered that Leo has always been associated astrologically with royalty, with the old-time kings, queens, and emperors who personally led their armies into battle. Leos are excitable under stress, but do not lose sight of their objective. They work relentlessly toward it

Pressure is something they will not give in to. They will proudly, stubbornly refuse to bend to another's will, sometimes quite unreasonably. Leo believes in the divine right of Queen or King Leo to refuse to compromise with anyone. They stick to their guns regardless of the cost. It helps to know that Leo also is one of the four most obstinate signs in the Zodiac. The others are Taurus, Scorpio, and Aquarius.

Leos thrive on responsibility. It heightens their sense of power. They love to be in positions of authority where they can throw their weight around. Yet the typical Leo does not lose sight of his or her obligation to those who work for them. They have a strong sense of justice and fair play. They will not exploit their subordinates knowingly, but they do expect unquestioning loyalty and obedience. This does not go down too well with independent individuals of other signs. There often is friction 'when a Leo takes over until those who are rebellious quit or submit.

Leos in authority have an annoying way of hogging the work and refusing to delegate it. They are quite prepared to handle everything—except the dull detail. If they can get away with it, they make all the decisions without deigning to consult or confer with anyone. They do not realize how frustrating and annoying this is to others. If told so, their reaction is likely to be one of deep hurt that anyone could think they were not acting in the best interests of the job and all concerned.

One Leo public-relations executive, faced with an imminent deadline, decided on his own to correct proofs of a client's color brochure printed in Norwegian. He had a smattering of the language, but that was all. With a Norwegian-English dictionary on the desk beside him, he attacked the task with great concentration. All his underlings saw the danger, but not Leo. With the job done, he gave the go-ahead for twenty thousand copies to be printed. Of course, he had missed a couple of serious misspellings and through changes in the idiom had altered the sense of the text. The whole lot had to be dumped and reprinted at great cost.

Leo men and women's power over others stems from a compulsive determination to enforce their own will. Most other types can't take themselves so seriously as to be continuously projecting their personality. But Leos can and do. Rather than bother to argue with a Leo, who will never admit they are wrong anyway, many people just end up agreeing with them to get some peace and quiet.

Leos often reflect the old-fashioned autocratic royal traditions of this sign by being bossy and high-handed with those they consider are inferior. Any privileges Leos believe they are entitled to they insist on being made available, even if they don't use them. Service or any product a Leo pays for is expected in full measure. They love pomp and ceremony, and occupying official positions where they are waited on.

Leos are ambitious. All of them from an early age imagine themselves to be famous and successful. They are driven by dreams of glory. They never lose hope. Even in old age when fortunes or positions may have been won and lost several times, they still expect to be called upon to perform a last spectacular service.

THE POWER OF PUBLICITY

Leos can't resist taking and holding the floor. They are showmen and showwomen. They will do practically anything to attract attention. They will start an argument, do a belly-dance, make an outrageous comment—all for an audience. As they mature and get wiser, they become more dignified, aloof, and less impulsive. Although the need for admirers remains just as compelling, they aim at a higher class of audience.

Leos are forever looking for exaltation. Their appetite for praise and admiration is insatiable. It is here that they can come closest to corruption. Although for the most part a proud and noble sign, Leos can be tempted to sell their soul for public recognition. They are the easiest people in the world to flatter. This is because they believe every nice thing that is said about them. Even the most exaggerated compliments will be good-humoredly tolerated by a Leo, whereas another type may regard such blarney as an insult to the intelligence.

Leo men and women invariably get themselves into the news media at some time in their lives. Their whole existence is calculated to draw attention to themselves. It is never a huge step from their regular performance to be in the public eye.

Although the publicity Leos attract is often due to their undoubted accomplishments, they are not the types as a rule to work quietly behind the scenes. They revel in the spotlight, even if it burns. They adore the opportunity to be out front. Even if the publicity is gained, as it sometimes is, through notorious behavior, Leo men and women are not averse to seeing their picture in the newspapers or on the television screen.

Leos are among the great pretenders of the Zodiac. Even when appearing to be aloof and disinterested—a favorite guise of famous Leos—they are keenly aware of other people's reactions, of the impression they are making. Their love of performing and make-believe often draws them to the acting and entertainment professions.

Leos can be exceedingly charming and persuasive when they want to. They speak well. Although forthright to the point of being hurtful at times, they also know how to be tactful when necessary.

It is important to them to make a strong first impression: Their entry into a room usually manages to be dramatic even if they are not really trying. Their main device in impressing others is to overwhelm them with words, with stories of their success, prowess, and cleverness. They enjoy discussions, debates, and arguments—friendly or otherwise. Any opportunity to air their knowledge gives them pleasure. They always convey the impression they know what they are talking about.

The air of superiority that Leos so frequently adopt can be most irritating, even to those who love them most. Leos sometimes are inclined to dismiss other people's views as rubbish before hearing them out. Or they may show conspicuous disinterest by gazing elsewhere, or getting up and walking around while others are speaking. They really are happy only when they have the floor.

THE POWER OF POSITIVE THINKING

Leos are born positive thinkers. Although they have their down days, they are remarkably resilient and soon able to shake off the blues. They have tremendous faith in human relationships as a power for good in the world.

Although not necessarily religious in the formal sense, they have an awareness of divine power. Almost everyone born under this sign believes they have a personal mission to perform in life. They often feel they are directed and guided by a higher force. It is easy for Leos, especially when they are successful, to suffer from delusions of grandeur.

These individuals are big thinkers. Nothing is planned on a small scale. And they have the natural organizing ability to assemble resources and helpers to get their grandiose schemes moving. One of their problems is that they may not know when to stop. In their enthusiasm, and disregard for failure, they can overstretch themselves disastrously.

It is not surprising that Napoleon was a Leo. His unbounded ambition, king-making games, flamboyance, and conscious awareness of his place in history were all typical of the true Leo. Although he met his Waterloo and died ignominiously, the reputation he left behind would make any Leo lady or gentleman's mouth water.

To a typical Leo, going under on a grand scale is preferable to surviving in comfortable obscurity. When they dream their dreams, Leos put more emphasis on glory than on money.

THE POWER OF LEARNING

The wellspring of Leo activity is the desire to expand the mind, to learn, and to understand. They have a great thirst for higher knowledge. The more evolved types are not interested simply in gathering information and retailing it for their own self-glorification. They want to know why and how things happen. Consequently, Leo men and women usually are engaged in some sort of formal study.

In adolescent years, because of their fondness for pleasure and especially romance, they may neglect school lessons and fail to qualify as they should. But sooner or later the urge to acquire knowledge as a serious pursuit asserts itself.

Leos are often avid readers, well versed in literature, history, politics, economics, or the arts. They have a strong practical side, which insists that what is learned should be of some value to society. Leos are not intellectuals in the abstract sense. Their minds are too straightforward for mental convolutions. They are not good plotters or conspirators, either.

Neither are Leos time wasters or dalliers. Every study is pursued wholeheartedly and at considerable depth. They genuinely see themselves as fountains of knowledge from which others can draw a greater understanding—if only these people will listen! There is something of the headmaster or headmistress in all true Leos.

It is part of the gigantic Leo ego image of themselves to imagine that their opinions are more thoroughly thought out and superior to most other people's. They can't resist an opportunity to air their knowledge. Sincerely believing they are being helpful, they will gratuitously criticize and offer advice. They can usually spout forth with the authority of an expert on practically any subject.

But it has to be said that the true Leos do have an original streak. They can summarize the essence of a problem or a subject in a few simple words. They have a remarkable facility for filling in the spaces left by the experts they have read or listened to. They do, however, tend to present all their knowledge as a personal discovery. They are not inclined to give their teachers much credit until their own recognition as some sort of oracle seems assured.

AND A LITTLE CHILD SHALL LEAD . . .

Leo, being the fifth sign of the Zodiac, is traditionally associated with children. Leos take a great interest in the young. Although very attached to their own children, they enjoy being involved with other children from all walks of life.

However, the Leo interest focuses on transmitting knowledge and training the younger generation to cope with the problems of life rather than establishing any particular emotional ties. The Leo man and woman believes in freeing people from their ignorance. Leos can lecture, and this is why they frequently have a reputation for being know-it-alls.

Of course, the unevolved type is a collector of any spurious information or half-digested knowledge that he or she can use to draw attention to themselves. These poorly developed Leos bore the pants off everyone in earshot with their incessant outpourings of fixed opinions, advice, and boasting. They are loudmouths. With pompous superiority they force their ideas down people's throats. These are generally overbearing and obnoxious characters.

It is not a well-known fact, even among astrologers, that the roots of the Leo character reach down into the masterful sign of Scorpio—another fixed sign like Leo. It is from Scorpio that the Leo man and woman receive their love of power. Leos are powerful enough characters in their own right, being children of the Sun. But this Scorpio influence makes them want to see the reflection of that power in the adulation of the crowd.

Older Leos are usually found in some kind of honorary, part-time, or occupational teaching position. They are the types found in university chairs, or as principals and deans in schools and colleges. Youth movements, workers' education programs, management courses, and rehabilitation and retraining schemes are all likely to attract the conscientious exertions of Leo men and women.

. . .OR THE PARENT WILL!

Being the sign of children, Leo produces intelligent parents. Far from being indulgent, they are determined to see that their kids are well educated and follow a fairly strict routine toward that end.

The pleasure-seeking Leo man or woman takes the responsibilities of parenthood very seriously. They are likely to embark on a serious program of training and instruction for Junior that entails a good deal of personal hard work. If necessary, they are prepared to get in and coach the youngsters in lessons.

The Leo pride makes these parents intent on raising a child who will be a credit to them. Natural talents will be encouraged, and professional instruction will be provided if possible.

As always with Leos, there is a danger they will overtax a youngster. Being capable of handling a great deal of work and responsibility themselves, they are inclined to expect similar performance from others. An overburdened child trying to please his or her parents may be unable to take the pressure.

Perhaps this character analysis will help Leo men and women to understand how easy it is for them to expect too much of their youngsters. The parent should ease up and make sure that Junior gets plenty of time to play with friends. A more relaxed atmosphere may help to avert future problems.

Leos, being intense and powerful personalities, are often held in awe by their children. Although Leos would be the last to bully a boy or girl consciously, they can be dominating and overbearing in their drive to make a success of the child. Often, too much is expected too soon.

Any child of a Leo parent will be loved and pampered. In fact, a child who measures up to expectations is likely to be rewarded with frequent gifts and ample pocket money. Leos like to use a carrot to encourage people close to them to help themselves.

ROMANTIC LOVE AND IDEALISM

Leo also is the sign ruling romantic love. Again, the distant influence of Scorpio, the sex sign, shows itself. But the idealistic, sunny, and warm-hearted Leo temperament spins around the raw mating urge, a cocoon of romance, of mystery, of delicious expectation, and of promise between the sexes.

Although Leo is a hot-blooded, passionate sign, love is regarded first as a romantic game. The woman must be won, the man enticed. The proud peacock with its brilliant, colorful feathers must strut, Leo style, and do his or her stuff.

Romance and love mean more to Leo men and women than anything else. It is their romantic notion of themselves that allows them to hog the floor with such incredible self-confidence. They believe they have a mission to brighten and entertain an otherwise bored and humdrum world.

Leo men and women imagine themselves in every kind of romantic situation, but always as the hero or heroine. Who else could possibly be the handsome prince, the beautiful princess, the courageous rescuer, the noble conqueror, the magnanimous ruler? Anyone other than Leo would obviously be miscast.

These men and women have high ideals. Being true romantics, they are prepared to believe the best of people, to accept them at face value. They are not a suspicious sign, although this will be modified by the position of other planets besides the Sun.

Leo men and women, like the other fire signs, Aries and Sagittarius, are frank and open. They say what they mean. Their directness and outspokenness are often regarded as bluntness and lack of tact. More sensitive types frequently find them noisy and overpowering.

No one enjoys material comforts and the good life more than Leo men and women. In fact, Leo is the sign governing pleasure, games, amusement, and recreation. There is always the desire for spectacular display, whether it is in the choice of a restaurant, a sport to play, or a place to go for a vacation. Leos will spend money like water as long as it enables them to attract an admiring and appreciative circle around them.

But friendship is another matter. They will not consciously pay for friendship. They are too proud, too aloof, and too selective of who enters their inner circle. They have to be convinced and continuously shown that their closest friends love them for themselves.

Leo the Lion is genuinely prepared to believe that anyone who seeks his or her company does so without an ulterior motive. When unsuspecting Leo accepts affection only to be tricked, the bottom drops out of his or her world—for a while. The destruction of an ideal is painful in the extreme, for the Lion's greatest strength lies in faith. And when that faith goes, he or she is finished.

Fortunately, a Leo's ideals are infinite in number. After one is shattered, he or she quietly withdraws until faith is restored. Leos are not revengeful. Shabby thoughts and actions are usually beneath them. Being magnanimous, they will always be treated with a cold aloofness and never trusted again.

ME TARZAN—YOU JANE!

All is not pure romanticism and idealism in the Leo person's love attachment. Man or woman, there is role playing with Leo as the heavy. Leo, for whom life surely is love, and love is true life, has to guarantee that maxim. So Leo believes there is no better way to control both ends—life and love—than to beat the chest, roar, stalk, paw, and pamper. In these poses, the kings and queens of the jungle more resemble the apes than the lions.

The Leo partner in love or marriage, whether man or woman, invariably wears the pants, or tries to. Where another strong sign is involved, there has to be compromise all the way. Otherwise arguments culminate in breakups. Power struggles and confrontations have to be avoided at all costs, or Leo will retain only a meaningless throne and an empty realm.

From their families, Leos expect a good deal of adulation and praise. Their efforts to provide a good home, as well as their sacrifices and kindness, have to be recognized or there will be trouble.

Leos, especially the man, can be a headache around the house. They will insist on interfering. With the best of intentions to be helpful, their habit is to try to show their partners "better" ways of doing things. Many a wife and husband has gone nearly bananas trying to maintain their individuality and faith in their own competence under such a constant barrage of leonine knowledge.

"Let me do it, honey," may be very appealing to a woman or a man in the heady days of romance or early marriage. But when "Do it this way, dear," becomes the daily order of things, partnership tempers start to snap.

Leo people married or in love have to come to terms with a basic contradiction in their character. On the one hand, they want to be loved with the sort of reverence that binds people to them. On the other hand, they are confirmed believers that people, especially their partners, should be able to stand on their own two feet and determine things for themselves. Browbeating close associates into submission one minute, then preaching freedom and autonomy the next, is a sure recipe for confusion or revolt.

To make the most of love and marriage, Leos have to expand by letting go. It can be a sure road to maturity for them. A partner provides Leo with the audience he or she needs, a mirror to reflect Leo's nature. But Leo's self-glorifying performance is not so important as the effect it has on the partner. If the lessons of tolerance, patience, and restraint are not learned, Leo is likely to find himself or herself suddenly all alone—and very lonely.

RELATIONSHIPS

How Leos get along with and react in love and marriage with other signs of the Zodiac is given in detail in the next chapter, entitled "Leo: Love and Romance." Here we will deal generally with the Leo love nature, and take a brief glimpse at what makes the Leo male and then the female tick.

The Leo man and woman both have to be adored or adulated by their partner for there to be any chance of making an affair permanent. And as it is difficult to worship anyone after living with them for a while, Leos figure prominently in the divorce rate.

They start off being among the most love-struck types in the Zodiac. They love being in love. But really, it is the romance of it that they love most. Every affair is dramatized, played to the romantic hilt. Nothing is too good for the one who is loved, no gift adequate to express the ecstasy of feeling. Except one: Leo himself or herself! This is the consummate offering. Who could ask for more?

Well, from the other side the view can be different. There is no doubt that Leo lovers put their heart and soul into every romance. They are as passionate and exciting as anyone who ever swept a man or a woman off their feet.

But it can be irksome having to keep up the compliments, the oohs and aahs of exaltation that Leos demand from all who would love them. Leos' self-love makes it impossible for them to give themselves to anyone who has not surrendered or is not completely devoted to them.

It is a vicious cycle that drives the Lion round and round until he or she finds someone they truly love. This person is often a quieter type who is prepared to accept a dependent position without being servile. This person the Leo man or woman will love and serve. And they can truly live happily ever after.

Love fills the Leo man with ardent enthusiasm. His boyishness, his naiveté bubble straight to the surface. He knows the woman he wants. He knows what he's got to offer and how to present it. He lays it all before her with a dramatic flourish, and a good deal of boasting and exaggeration to make sure she gets the point.

When in love, he wants the whole world to love with him. He is ennobled, generous, determined to bring sunshine into the life of his beloved—and anyone else who passes by as he treads on air. He is as easy to read as a book. Nothing is hidden in his sincere and open countenance. He has no subtle games to play, no time for coquetry or teasing. He is in love.

He also is extremely vulnerable. He is a romantic, an idealist. He often allows love to blind him to reality. Although courageous enough to face any danger, he cannot bring himself to face the flaws that would destroy his love dream. He is disillusioned as often as the times he falls in love. Each disappointment shreds his heart. For a while he is able to sublimate his pain in numerous worldly activities until once again his romantic nature hears the love call. Where their emotions are concerned, Leo men often make the same mistakes over and over well into maturity.

As a boyfriend, the Leo male can be ruthless if he feels he is not receiving the undivided attention of his woman. He will walk off and leave her, firmly believing that she asked for it. Leo believes he is the only one who knows how to love. So why would any woman want anyone else?

He also knows the torment of jealousy. Because of his pride, it is difficult for him to bring himself to complain. His usual resource is to sulk or to make ridiculously transparent efforts to appear unconcerned. But in the end his fiery and impulsive nature gets the better of him, and he prepares for a showdown. At that moment the affair is either on or over.

The Leo female is a cooler customer than the male. She is as passionate, impulsive, and headstrong, but not so fixed. Her emotions are more ambivalent.

In her case, every affair is not a demand that she must be loved and worshiped forever. That ideal she keeps tucked away for the day when Mr. Right comes along.

This woman is a flirt. Like the male, she loves to be in love, too. But the sensation of power that her sexual magnetism implies hooks her every time. The Leo power complex is never more evident than in the way a beautiful Leo woman conducts her love life.

Lady Leo gets what she wants. She is a self-sufficient female. There is hardly another type, even among the men, who can look after themselves as well as she can. Leo is considered a masculine sign as well as a royal one, and the women often come out in the mold of imperious queens.

This woman likes money. She tends to fall in love with men who can keep her in the royal manner she expects. She likes good clothes, jewels, and plenty of idolizing attention. She is restrained when she wants to be, promiscuous if it suits her. Her personality gradually takes her men over. Then she loses interest. If she can't boss a man, she certainly won't let him boss her. She is a very together creature.

But, like Napoleon, her Waterloo comes when she falls truly in love. This is what she has been searching for. Her attempts to gain public prominence, her drives into the commercial or artistic worlds, and all those superficial affairs were merely ways of filling in time—or at least this is what she thinks. When this woman gives as much love as she receives to her devoted man, she is emotionally fulfilled.

Then a new cycle of her life can begin either as wife, mother, or career woman.

Like all Leos, what she must eventually discover is that the struggle for power has only one successful end—service to something larger than self.

Once the Leo person marries and passionate love has cooled, there are the inevitable adjustments to be made. The Leo woman wants to be busy and creative, either with her family or her work. Her husband, however, she will always put first, as long as he is wise enough to give her the freedom she requires.

A HEALTHY BODY

Healthwise, Leos do not as a rule suffer from much serious illness. Their positive way of looking at the world and handling their problems keeps them psychologically fit and eliminates the ailments more negative types are prone to.

Because of their full and busy lives, Leos feel they can't afford to get sick. They haven't got the time even to consider it, which is another protection. One problem, however, is their enormous vitality. They have so much of it they can push themselves too hard. Their bodies and nervous systems are unable to cope, and they end up exhausted and susceptible to sicknesses they should not have.

When a Leo man or woman does get ill, they usually have the good sense to lie there, perhaps for a day anyway. But then they start to panic. Their responsibilities loom like accusing visions, reminding them that everything will indeed fall apart without them. Leos never learn that graveyards are filled with indispensable people.

Astrologically, the weakest point of the Leo physical system is the heart. These people in middle age are prone to heart attacks and other cardiac troubles. Stress, which they continuously impose upon themselves, is one of the main contributing factors. They have to learn to relax during the day in between their many comings and goings. Simple yoga exercises, and particularly deep breathing, can help to keep tension down.

It also is important for Leos to get all the exercise they need. Many of them are writers and executives who grind away all day at the typewriter or desk and don't get out and about enough.

Leos sometimes suffer from throat infections and back trouble. They should avoid trying to be their own doctor, diagnosing what is wrong with them from medical books and dictionaries.

As Leos get older, they tend to react sharply to anything or anyone that crosses their path. Irritability can become an unfortunate habit.

A WEALTHY HOME

Both the Leo man and woman want a nice home and are prepared to work hard for it. It should be something of a showplace to which they are proud to invite their friends and many acquaintances.

Leos like to entertain a lot, and as lavishly as possible. Both male and female are excellent hosts. Their dinner parties are often occasions that none of their friends would miss. Besides, there is sure to be good entertainment, probably provided by the Leo host or hostess themselves.

Leo men and women like bright colors, especially yellow and gold.

They like to dress their bodies and their homes in the latest fashion, and to display distinctive styles. Although inclined to be ostentatious by normal standards, they usually go for the best quality they can afford in clothes and furnishings.

The Leo home usually reflects the colorful personality of these people, as well as their creativity. They surround themselves with as many luxuries as they want, yet may still try to save on the bathroom soap. Leos believe in comfort as well as hard work.

Periodically, they need to be silent and alone. The Lion withdraws into his or her pad, disconnects the phone or doorbell, and flakes out—perhaps for a whole weekend. Leos do know how to be lazy when the mood is on them. On these brief and necessary occasions, nothing at all, not even housework, is likely to get done. Revitalization, it is called.

A Leo's home is always a challenge to their artistic talents. They are great ones for moving or for redecorating and refurnishing the whole place. There is no shortage of mirrors. Both male and female Leos enjoy frequent glimpses of themselves from all angles. Appointments in a Leo home seldom leave any doubt about the kind of person who lives there—a larger-than-life character with strong tastes for the dramatic and spectacular.

If there is not a huge, sunken, gold bath in the bathroom, there will be an emperor-sized bed in the main bedroom, a bronze chandelier in the room, or a startling Picasso in the lounge. The Lion's den is always impressive, if not in everybody's taste.

Leos like to own their own home after passing through the rental and apartment stage. They move a number of times on the way up. They usually manage to make a tidy profit on each house if they get into the habit of buying and selling.

SPENDING, SPECULATION, AND THE SPECTACULAR

Money is something that Leos are very good at managing. They can put it away; they also can spend it. But it is unusual for anyone to run into a broke Leo. Temporarily out of funds, perhaps. But this probably means that he or she does not intend to disturb that nice little nest egg gathering high interest every day on fixed deposit. Leos always have a buck or two between them and the skids.

These men and women have expensive tastes. And they indulge them when it suits them. They also spend a good deal on their loved ones. But no one squanders Leo's hard-earned cash except Leo, or someone he loves to whom he's extending a treat.

Leos are impulsive spenders. In company with other high-spending, fun-loving characters, especially Libra, they can be a positive danger to their own solvency. Once on a wave of pleasure and high living, Leo shoots it all the way. When the bills come in, the Lion just shrugs and works a little harder.

Leo men and women like to invest in property and solid securities. They have a good head for business, and often make money out of creative enterprises. There is always an area where Leos get a regular income, even when they are temporarily unemployed.

In understanding these people, it helps to remember that Leo is the sign of speculation and gambling. Leos do take chances with money. If they get hooked on the horses or the tables, they can be in big trouble. But usually they are more cautious than the sign suggests. Most of them reserve their big gambles for business and real-estate ventures, the risks of which they have considered and worked out in advance.

Leos have their gambling moments, but they are seldom any match for Sagittarius, the gamblers of the Zodiac. The position of Jupiter in a Leo profile will indicate the possibilities of losing money through speculation. Jupiter is the ruling planet of Sagittarius. For Leo it rules, among other things, the extent of the love of pleasure and the tendency to take risks, financial and romantic. The position of Jupiter, as well as all the other planets, can be seen in the Planetary Tables at the end of the book.

Leos figure prominently among the big promoters of the world. Being essentially showmen and showwomen, they often are the organizing brains behind top entertainers' tours, world boxing championships, international sports events, and the like.

Romantic affairs are usually fairly costly for Leos. They are extravagant in their attempts to make a good impression on the people they are attracted to. They can be too generous with gifts, entertainment, weekends, and vacations. Because they are a fun-loving sign and really enjoy a good time, they can easily be led on, even while the more prudent side of their nature is aware of the danger.

As Leo's first marriage frequently ends in divorce, these people often find themselves paying or arguing over alimony. Joint savings and mutual assets and resources are regular sources of trouble or confusion. It is not unusual for Leos to be taken or deceived in joint financial affairs. They need to keep firm control, or to be constantly vigilant.

In astrology, the Sun usually stands for people of influence. And it is remarkable how often Sun-ruled Leos are helped in their projects by the support of such individuals. Leos often are on friendly terms with the most important people in their communities, as well as the wealthiest and most famous in the land.

CREATIVITY AND CAREER

Leos are productive but restless people. Fired with solar energy, their enthusiasm is as boundless as their need to be continuously immersed in projects. If a day ever dawns when there is nothing to absorb or occupy them, they are bored, fidgety, and cantankerous. Leos usually plan their schedule so that there is always something stimulating to fall back on.

The basic conflict in the Leo nature is the pull between activity and fixity. Activity is represented by fire, which is their element. The quality of the sign is fixed, shown by their stubbornness. It is difficult to be creative while at the same time fixed. As fire also stands for energy and self-assertion, the irresistible urge for these people is to lay down the law and become overbearing and dominating.

Leos groan under this discrepancy in their nature. The best of them do something about it by using their fixity of purpose to control the self-assertive element, which can force on others their great sense of pride and authority, and make them unpopular.

People are often envious of them. They can't figure out how they accumulated so much so soon, not realizing that nine times out of ten it is due to Leos' sheer hard work and perseverance.

However, Leos do not like handling tedious detail. Anything that is petty or unimportant is inclined to be waved aside. They enjoy intelligent conversation, but the higher type is not much interested in hearing gossip. They certainly will not spread it; talking behind people's backs they regard as personally debasing.

When it comes to a career, the fields that a Leo can succeed in are almost unlimited. Their ability to lead and get along with others, to organize resources and work, to take responsibility and direct personnel fits them for any kind of executive or administrative role.

But their natural urges usually drive them into work where they can dramatize their talents and gain some measure of public prominence. They gravitate toward politics, the stage, moviemaking, directing, column writing for newspapers—anything that can lead to their name going up in lights, their photo in the press, or their views being discussed in public.

To be in front of a television camera talking about his or her pet subject is a Leo's dream.

Because of their vivid imagination and interest in reading and acquiring knowledge, they often make successful writers and authors. Being able to sit for hours at a typewriter in front of a blank wall day after day, week in, month out, with the single idea of fame planted firmly in their brain, they can turn out an immense amount of work and powerful ideas.

Leos long for public recognition but underneath crave power. Wealth is indeed a worthy by-product that these men and women can make good use of. But all their ambitions add up finally to the drive for power, to be the last authority, the benevolent dictator, the king.

Leo men and women seldom fail to reach a top job by the time they are in their thirties or forties. Sometimes they even make it in their twenties but change because the job is not big enough. Seeming to sense a destiny that awaits them, the most successful Leos in the early years despair of the time they appear to be wasting.

Even though often making more progress than others around them, they refuse to be satisfied with the pace. They are always endeavoring to grab the rung of the ladder a little higher than they can reach.

In professions such as law, medicine, and science, Leos usually become an authority in their field. Their love of publicity and flamboyant manner often make them public favorites, sometimes much to the chagrin and disapproval of their more staid and conservative colleagues.

Leos are good for high government, legal, and judicial positions. They are able to keep the public informed of what is going on behind the scenes without betraying confidential interests.

Smug and superior, they may be in powerful positions. But the true

Leos do not forget the hopes and aspirations of the common man or woman. In the highest positions they can be fighters for justice, even though the incumbent attitude is to preserve power and privilege.

Many a Leo sits on the boards of the world's most powerful companies, having come up through the ranks of the industry. A desk job is not enough for Leo. Glamour, globe trotting, and excitement such as provided by top jobs in publishing, public relations, advertising, oil, aerospace, fashion, cosmetics, and newspapers are typical Lion territory.

Successful Leos are sometimes considered a bit eccentric. Encouragement from their public or the media can turn their love of playing to the gallery into buffoonery.

ALTERNATIVELY . . .

Every sign of the Zodiac has a negative side. No one is perfect. Most people have their faults and flaws. But there are individuals in this world, as everybody knows, who are villainous to their associates. Leo produces its share of mean, destructive, and antisocial types.

One of the values of astrology is to provide the opportunity for people to see themselves as they really are, and then to make any personality corrections they themselves decide are necessary. The following is a description of the negative side of the Leo character.

The negative Leo has many facets, but each reflects the determination of these people to force their will on others. They will go to any lengths to attract praise and adoration in some form or other.

Weaker Leos use their attractiveness to gather even weaker and parasitical flatterers around them. They don't care that their admirers don't mean what they say. Leos are so vain and filled with their own importance that the truth is never realized. These people live miserable lives, for the friends they choose keep failing them and betraying them.

These Leos can be empty-headed and lazy, especially if they are good-looking. They take lovers who praise their non-existent virtues and worship their spurious charms. They frequently have the power to make others feel they are beholden to them, and in this way bully them into providing for their needs.

Leos seldom turn totally bad. But when the strength and vitality of the sign are directed into sensual and dissolute channels, the depths of depravity can be plumbed.

Strong desires are characteristic of this sign. Many Leos have to go through the fires of uncontrolled desire to begin to master themselves and start to realize their full potential. The downfall of people born under this sign is often a prelude to their discovering new powers of restraint and control within themselves.

Leos can turn to crime. They are more the type to be the boss man or boss woman, even though their operation might be small. They extract a high price from those who are associated with them. They can be ruthless and cruel toward anyone who does not treat them with the admiration and respect they feel they deserve. Punishment of some kind is the just dessert for all offenders.

Leos are dangerous when they become antisocial. Because it is their nature to immerse themselves completely in what they undertake, their lawbreaking efforts are often spectacular and bring misfortune down on numerous people. Even in a crime situation, the crooked Lion seeks to establish a public reputation. That it might be for infamy does not matter. All unevolved Leos tend to be loudmouthed show-offs. Their conceited opinion of themselves can make them very unpopular. They grab the limelight from others and try to force their opinions or self-glorifying brand of humor on anyone who will listen.

These Leos also think about nothing else but making money. They can be extremely materialistic. Everything of value is measured in terms of what is in it for them. And they use their wealth or influence to make them seem important in the public eye.

The uncultivated Leo man or woman cares little about how others feel or think. They are so full of themselves that they will crush other people's dreams unnecessarily, perhaps just for the feeling of power that it gives them.

These Leos love lording it over others. In positions of authority, they can make life miserable for everyone under them. Any indication of independent thought from other people is regarded as a personal slight to Leo. Original ideas are disdainfully rejected because Leo did not think of them first.

Such Leo bosses force their associates to shoulder most of the responsibility and burdens. They themselves seek the praise for such work, and bask in the glow of their superior's unknowing satisfaction.

One of the most annoying negative traits of Leos is a tendency to be snobbish. In their pursuit of veneration, the worst of them are quite prepared to enjoy reflected glory by being associated with people in high places. These Leos are the worst kind of social climbers. Their attitude toward others less well placed can be pompous and patronizing in the extreme.

Undeveloped Leos are often able to give an appearance of strength that is only skin deep. Bravado and bombast replace courage and achievement.

Leo:
Love and Romance

How successful will you be in sex and romance, love and marriage? And doesn't that depend on with whom? In the preceding chapter you read a description of how you react in relationships in general. Here the following sections describe your attitudes and behavior and the likely attitudes and behaviors of individuals born under each of the twelve different Sun signs.

First there are the sections for the Leo woman in combination with each of the twelve zodiacal signs Aries through Pisces. Then there are the sections for the Leo man in combination with each of the twelve signs Aries through Pisces.

You can build on this in-depth view of yourself if you read the sections of chapters that apply to your Moon, Venus, and Mars placements. The Planetary Tables at the end of the book give you your placements. The chapters "The Moon in the Signs," "Venus in the Signs," and "Mars in the Signs" describe each placement in your profile.

The Moon, Venus, and Mars figure prominently in love, sex, affection, passion, response, instinct, unconscious motivation—the whole ball of wax. Venus essentially influences affections. The Moon influences emotions. And Mars influences sexuality. But how these broad capacities are expressed specifically varies with the individual, as described in the chapters mentioned.

You can also learn more about an individual born under a certain Sun sign this way. You may want to buy the relevant book in the Astroscope Profile series to read his or her Moon, Venus, and Mars placements. For this individual, you might also want to read his or her Rising sign, for as has been emphasized, the Rising sign indicates how a person appears to others on the basis of what he or she is showing the world. Perhaps a person's come-on is so much a part of the nature that it can't be changed. And you, Leo, don't want to be fooled!

WHEN LEO WOMAN
MEETS ARIES MAN

The Aries man is a positive, hardworking guy. He will have many innate qualities that attract a Leo woman. The Ram is the no-nonsense kind. A female will soon know if he has taken a liking to her. The subtle approach is not for him.

Some people may say this pairing would not work out satisfactorily. They would point out that both are fire signs and both like to dominate, so a harmonious relationship would be impossible. This is not true. When two people are in love, they find a way to make decisions through mutual agreement. And besides, fire respects fire!

It would be wise, however, for these two to have a fairly long courtship. Aries men do jump in feet first. To make sure this attraction is the real thing, they should get to know their lover really well before thinking of an engagement or marriage.

A Leo woman usually is straightforward in her love relationships. If she decides she has met Mr. Right, it is unlikely she will be coy, flirtatious, or hard to get. She won't cheat, either.

The Leo woman knows her own mind. But she will resent Aries if he tries to organize her life in any way. She tends to be an organizer too, and expects her independence to be respected. The Ram will want to make demands on this woman, but she won't let him take over her life.

Trust and sharing are important between these two partners. Fiery displays of jealousy on either side can flare up, making understanding difficult if not impossible. The Leo woman does not want to be questioned on her motives, and will grant the same freedom to her Aries mate.

The Ram is more fickle. It is not easy for him to settle down in a one-to-one relationship. He is perhaps the most passionate of all the signs. With the Lion, their sexual and physical contact should be enriching and deeply satisfying. They will find themselves in agreement about many things.

This couple is likely to show a lively interest in what is going on in the rest of the world. It also is probable they will be attracted to the arts. They should find they have pretty much the same tastes in music, theater, and movies. He is likely to have many hobbies. The Ram gets interested in subjects very quickly but, unfortunately, tires of them nearly as swiftly. His enthusiasms are boundless but short-lived.

They will have arguments, of course. It would be wise for the Leo woman to make sure she doesn't dent this man's ego. Aries cannot stand to be nagged or criticized too sharply. The way to get him to do things is to adopt the subtle approach and by gentle persuasion get him to follow the path she wishes him to take.

This woman will be a tower of strength for an Aries man. Leo is the sort of woman to bring out the best qualities in him. He likes a woman with drive and energy. So he will admire the way Leo fights for her rights, and he will be in there rooting for her all the way.

WHEN LEO WOMAN
MEETS TAURUS MAN

The Leo woman will not be bossed around, nor will she give up her pride or independence to cater to the whims of any man. If the Bull has to prove his masculinity in terms of dominance, he won't get too far with the Leo female. She tends to be fairly dominating herself.

Trust and sharing are crucial if this relationship is to build beyond the dating stage. Taurus must let a Leo woman go on her own, respecting her choices and not throwing fits of jealousy if he is left out of some of her activities. Taurus has to cool his temper. He can be as stubborn as a mule. It is impossible to get him to do anything against his will. He can be difficult to pin down and cannot stand to feel trapped or hemmed in in any way. However, Leo is just the strong kind of female to capture him. This man likes to play the dominant role in a relationship, but Leo won't let him. He usually runs a mile if he feels he is being chased by a member of the fairer sex, but Leo won't chase. He takes time making important decisions, and Leo will wait for the outcome without becoming impatient.

Taurus usually has a shrewd business head on his shoulders. He is quick on the uptake, as well. It is unlikely that anyone will get away with sharp practices when he is involved. Leo will feel secure with him.

He likes his home comforts. Although he is something of a social butterfly, he does like to have a permanent and comfortable place in which to live. Taurus has quite a roving eye. Lady Leo is likely to be surprised when she discovers how many females have fallen under his spell before she came upon the scene.

A love of beauty and art is highly marked with this couple. Possessions are important to the Bull, perhaps far more to him than to his Leo mate. He will take great care furnishing and decorating the home and will never stint on purchases for it.

He usually is an expert handyman. He can make himself useful by dealing with all the odd repair jobs without having to go to the expense of calling in a professional builder. He also is a whiz in the kitchen and makes an imaginative and distinctive cook.

Taurus is a hardworking type and will do all he can to ensure that his woman never goes without. He is careful with money without being stingy. This couple are likely to be great friends as well as lovers. This is terribly important when thinking in terms of a lifelong relationship.

He also is lots of fun and will keep his Leo woman twinkling and young at heart. He is a fine storyteller, embellishing a tale with his vivid imagination. When recounting his escapades, he likes to embroider the truth to make sure he gets the attention and reaction from his audience that he wants.

As long as both agree about what their priorities in life are going to be, and how they are going to go about getting what they want, there is no reason why they should not be very happy together. Both of them have inquiring minds. It is unlikely they will ever get into a rut or feel bored with each other.

WHEN LEO WOMAN MEETS GEMINI MAN

A Gemini is not an easy man to get along with. This is something that has to be understood right away. When a Leo woman first meets him, she is likely to be swept off her feet by his charm, his sense of humor, and his naughty schoolboy air. That glint in his eyes will make her think he is about to stage a mischievous scene at any moment. The Leo woman takes instantly to the charming, on-the-go Gemini man. At least on the surface, their relationship sparkles with bright feelings, high spirits, and a meeting of the minds. But on a deeper level of commitment, Leo may find the Gemini male too unpredictable. The Lion likes to make plans and see that they are pushed to fruition. Gemini can be too scattered or too interested in social activities to knuckle down and make a go of the relationship. But even if Leo regards Gemini as a poor marriage prospect, she will enjoy dating him and having a whirlwind affair.

Any woman who is going to form a permanent relationship with the Twins will need to have a strong maternal instinct. A man born under this sign usually has a very youthful quality. Most people find his company stimulating. With a man born where Mercury rules, there is never likely to be a dull moment.

He will admire many of the fine qualities that his Leo woman possesses and displays. And if she is prepared to make the effort, she could bring out the best in him. He will like her for her strong personality. But it is very important that Leo makes him stand up for himself and does not allow him to hide behind her petticoats.

If she is not vigilant, she will find he has manipulated things in such a way that she gets stuck with making all the difficult decisions. Leo will certainly need to give him a kick in the pants at these times. He needs incentive. He can easily become bored and dispirited if he does not succeed immediately in getting what he wants.

Gemini needs to be in a job that gives him a certain amount of freedom. He cannot stand too much of routine in his life. Travel is exciting for this man. He likes to keep on the go. Very often he is to be found in jobs that give him the opportunity to visit distant places.

Friends are especially important to him. He has no difficulty mixing with people from varied walks of life. Although he likes to be involved with a woman who has strength and character, he must never get the feeling he is tied down. He'll run a mile if he feels he's being ordered around.

He is a bit of a flirt, but it is unlikely he would get too deeply involved with another woman once he had committed himself to a permanent relationship. As long as Leo can keep up with the all-action life he is bound to lead, all will be well.

When they start a family, she must make sure his nose is not put out of joint. He won't like it if he feels that Junior has taken his place and comes first in the affections of his woman.

WHEN LEO WOMAN
MEETS CANCER MAN

Cancer is not an easy man to get to know. On the surface he is likely to strike a Leo woman as a happy-go-lucky sort of guy who does not really have a care in the world. After two or three dates, however, she may discover he is a more complex character than she thought.

The Crab is basically an introvert. Very often he feels he has to put on a big front in order to hide his basic shyness. At a party or gathering of strangers, he is likely to take the place by storm and people will soon be crowding around him. It takes a long time for any woman to discover exactly what makes this man tick and what he wants out of life.

A Leo-born woman has such an inquiring mind that she easily becomes fascinated by this guy and willingly takes on the challenge of getting to know him really well. He hides his true feelings because of his insecurity. He tends to withdraw because he is terrified of being hurt. His tough outer shell hides a sensitive and gentle soul.

The Leo woman is not the maternal type and not particularly the home-body type. She doesn't like sitting around the house fulfilling domestic duties. And she gets impatient trying to comfort a mate or lover who may be as sensitive as the Cancer man usually is.

A Leo woman's love expression is flamboyant. She likes showing off her man. Cancer may feel he's got a tiger by the tail. If he does, he may not have the emotional stamina to deal with this openly passionate female.

But the Leo woman should not run away with the idea that he is a weak man. Far from it! He is a hardworking type. Security and success are important to him. However, certain sacrifices are going to have to be made on both sides if this couple is to form a permanent relationship.

Neither of them likes to be bossed around. Cancer will tolerate it, but not for long. These two have to build a power-sharing partnership if it is to succeed. He is not stingy with money, but he does like to have enough cash behind him to feel that at least the immediate future is secure.

This man needs a bit of a push. His Leo woman will have to make sure he is making the most of his talents. He needs to have his confidence boosted from time to time. It is important for him to be continually reminded of his talents and capabilities.

Cancer will love the way his Leo woman runs a home, for run it she will. He is good at making himself handy, and always is willing to share the household chores as well as the cooking.

There should be no problems with lovemaking. He is an understanding person who will instinctively know how to make his woman feel secure and turned on by him physically. Family life is very important to him. It is likely he will want to have more than one child. He is very good with youngsters.

WHEN LEO WOMAN
MEETS LEO MAN

This may at first glance appear to be the perfect match. The pairing of the King and Queen of the jungle sounds ideal. However, there are two very powerful and proud personalities here. The question must be asked: Could they survive long under the same roof? It may be they will find they have gotten themselves into a situation that is too hot to handle.

Leo is a born leader. It is here that the problems are likely to start.

Lady Leo certainly will have to tap all of her undoubted qualities of generosity and loyalty to make Lord Leo feel secure and wanted. He is not going to play second fiddle to anybody. It must be remembered that we are dealing with a big male ego here. A friendship is likely to blossom quickly between this couple. They intuit each other's personality. They have many mutual interests. It is important, though, that the Lioness does not mistake friendship for love. She may find that if she really gets deeply involved with him, he will want to dominate and perhaps organize her life more than she could bear. This is mistake No. 1. As the Leo male should know, his female counterpart is born to rule. No one dominates her, not even the male of the species. In fact, she may be the really tough one in the union, slapping him around and boxing his ears when his childish nature threatens to assert itself and put everyone in jeopardy.

The Leo woman is also a born organizer and fiercely protects her territorial and emotional rights. Being the female, she also has a more mature sense of nurturing. She knows how to take care of the things in her ken, and will not gamble away her security on foolish ventures.

Her pride and courage are tempered with caution, whereas his pride is straightforward, coming right from that great big ego that doesn't acknowledge limits or danger. He will never shirk a challenge, no matter how foolhardy.

He does not mess around when it comes to making big decisions. He makes them with a flourish. He has fixed ideas about most things. Once his mind is made up on a certain course of action, it is almost impossible to get him to budge.

The Leo male also craves a great deal of attention. When he gets home from work, he will expect his woman to drop everything and make a big fuss over him. For a woman who treasures her independence, his demands may be excessive. He cannot take other people finding fault with him and he cannot stand to be criticized.

Leo-born people are jealous types. This is another area where there could be problems. He will not take kindly to any flirting, even if it is only in fun. Their lovemaking will be exciting. Both are passionate individuals.

Because of the strength and honor of the Leo personality, it is possible that many of the problems in this relationship could be overcome. It must be stated that when the Lion seriously takes on a challenge, he or she rarely fails. As long as she can put up with his demands, they have a great chance of finding lasting happiness together.

WHEN LEO WOMAN
MEETS VIRGO MAN

The Virgo man is a cool customer. He is underestimated by many people. When he wants to score, he is prepared to bide his time. Whereas some other signs are in a great rush to get to the top, this guy will show unbelievable patience. His staying power is his allure.

Virgo plans for the future carefully. Although he may not get spectacular results, he is still likely to climb high in his career steadily. He is vigilant. His pristine ways may be a little too good to be true for a realistic woman like the Leo female. His approach with women is subtle. Usually it is his mind that women are drawn to rather than his fun-loving personality. Of course, Virgo men do love fun, but of a subtle sort. They tend to be droll in their humor, and they seek mystery rather than crude adventure. These men have an uncanny knowledge of human nature. Amusement for them may consist of dissecting the motivations of people around them rather than joining hectic sports, games, and social activities.

The Leo woman, who loves raucous entertainment and socializing, may discover an entirely new dimension to her own character with the Virgo man's choice of fun and games. When she participates in the quiet but fascinating sport of analyzing people with Virgo, she reaches down and plumbs her own depths and strengths of thought and feeling.

For the slightly reckless Leo female, the Virgo man has a great deal to offer. As a marriage partner, no woman could ask for a more loyal or devoted mate. He will do everything he can to make this woman happy. He is likely to be an adoring and faithful husband. He is the perfect counterpart for this vital and fiery woman, who needs a cautious, down-to-earth influence in her life.

He is a creature of habit, though, and his fussy ways could drive Leo crazy. He is a man who is ruled by logic. If he cannot work something out systematically, he will not have any time for it. It is essential that this couple have many mutual interests if they are going to share a life together. It would be a good idea also to have a fairly long courtship.

Virgo is the sort of guy that a Leo woman should get to know really well before considering throwing her lot in with his. It is important that they share similar tastes in art, movies, theater, and music, as these subjects are likely to mean a lot to him. His woman should try to get him to take a more active interest in sports. A stay-at-home Virgo can get very set in his ways and go to seed early through shirking physical regimens and exercise.

When it comes to making love, it might be up to the Leo woman to get him going. He is a shy man and sometimes has problems throwing himself into the physical side of a relationship with a carefree abandon. She will be able to bring him out of himself and show him that sex can be more fun than he would ever have imagined.

It is unlikely that this couple will wish for a particularly large family. But as parents they can make an exceptionally fine combination. He will have quite a lot to teach this woman. He is careful with money and quick at summing up the strengths and weaknesses of people.

WHEN LEO WOMAN
MEETS LIBRA MAN

A relationship between a Leo woman and a Libra man should have a very good chance of going places. There will be many qualities in this man that will impress the Lion. He has a quick mind and is a great believer in fair play. He is super company and makes a charming and amusing companion. His taste is impeccable, and he usually knows the best places to go. Libra does not make a big song and dance about how he conducts his life. But it will not take a Leo woman very long to discover what a caring and compassionate person he is. He is very sensitive about not hurting other people's feelings. He does everything in his power to make the shy and retiring feel easy and relaxed in his company.

But there will be certain differences that have to be faced. When it comes to setting up home together they may find their ideas about lifestyle different. A Leo woman looks for consistency in a man, and this guy could be something of a puzzle. When it comes to romance, he is known to blow hot and cold. He has problems settling down into a one-to-one relationship.

A Libra male often likes the courtship stages of a relationship best. He prefers to sing or hear romantic songs, go on exotic cruises, take madcap trips, celebrate in a party atmosphere. It is not that he is wildly promiscuous. It is just that he feels uncomfortable functioning in the daily routine of a love affair.

He is such a romantic, though, that he finds himself getting deeply involved before he is ready. This can make his private life rather complicated. However, he usually feels lost alone. So he thinks it's better to be married or at least settled down. But it's hard for him to make that decision.

He will do anything he can to avoid head-on confrontations. He cannot stand scenes. He feels no dispute is so great that it cannot be settled by reasoned discussion. He cannot stand to get into a rut. Any woman who decides to settle down with him must find a way of coping with his moods and sudden changes of mind.

The Libra man usually is a great talker. His Leo woman will never be bored hearing him spouting his pet subjects. He has a magnetic quality about him and has little difficulty in holding an audience. He will love taking Leo out and showing her all the things that are important to him. He usually has a strong creative streak and an avid interest in the arts and music as well.

This man does have a cutting and cynical side to his nature. Homelife is important to him, although it may not always appear to be so from the amount of time he spends away from it burning up his energy. He is a tolerant father, but not too good at meting out discipline.

WHEN LEO WOMAN MEETS SCORPIO MAN

A level-headed woman like Leo may wonder what has hit her if she ever gets involved with a Scorpio man. It can be honestly said that she won't be the same again if she flips her lid over Scorpio. He certainly is a heavy number and not one to take on lightly.

He is a very passionate type. There are no half measures with him. When he takes a shine to a woman, he makes a big play for her. No woman should attempt to dominate this man. He will not tolerate the law being laid down to him. When this couple have a disagreement, it will be like an irresistible force meeting an immovable object. Neither of them is prepared to give ground.

If she is one of those leonine types that relishes a challenge, she need look no farther. He is likely to find this female devastatingly attractive. There will be a challenge about her he may not be able to resist. Having an affair with this guy will make Leo realize what being a woman is all about. When it comes to lovemaking, they should have a ball. Their physical relationship is likely to be uninhibited. He may not be the most romantic person in the world, but he is passionate and exciting.

Sex, however, could become a source of trouble and set the scene for conflict. Scorpio males enjoy the feeling of power evoked through sex. He may try to make his dominion over the Leo woman felt through their sexual relationship. Certainly, no Lion will tolerate this. Her resentment is likely to be expressed openly and fiercely, leaving Scorpio no other option than to smolder in silent anger.

Another word of warning is in order. Any woman who gets involved with this man mustn't flirt. He is an intensely jealous lover and will not wait to listen to excuses if he feels he is being two-timed. A Scorpio man is quite capable of resorting to physical violence when aroused. But the Lion can slap, too, and may slap him down.

His tastes in music and art are not the most refined. This couple may have different preferences in this area of their life. He needs to be given quite a bit of freedom, and he enjoys having his nights out with the boys. Leo may find he has a definitely chauvinistic attitude to the fairer sex. He often has the old-fashioned philosophy that when a woman gets married her place is in the home. This idea is going to have to be brought up to date if he is to make it to first base with a Leo woman.

Scorpio is an exceptionally hard worker. Success in his chosen profession is likely to be very important to him. A Scorpio man likes to keep his home life and business affairs in distinctly different compartments. He usually broods alone on his problems and requires solitude to work out difficult situations. He is a strict father and a bit old-fashioned with kids.

WHEN LEO WOMAN
MEETS SAGITTARIUS MAN

The Sagittarius male enjoys the game of love. Seduction is a sport for him, the more conquests the better. Being the Archer, he has a keen eye and a splendid aim. When he shoots his arrow, it truly finds its mark. The Leo woman, though, is not likely to be felled easily. She will go along on the hunt and the chase. She might be caught if he changes his childish tactics to reveal the romantic and dreamy side of his nature.

The Archer can be quite a handful for any woman to cope with. He is a bit of a rogue in many ways, although a lovable one. A Leo woman could find that the challenge of taking him is one she cannot easily resist.

He is a fun-loving character, and some may even go as far as to say that he is downright irresponsible. Very often he remains something of an adolescent till very late in life. It is often more fortunate for a woman to get seriously involved with him when he has had the opportunity to gain experience. He has great difficulty settling down to any routine and often can be easily led astray.

Sagittarius is a difficult man to trap. He has a fear of getting into a rut. Leo may be going out with him for some time before he gets around to discussing the question of her becoming his wife. It could be said he is marriage-shy.

He often is to be found at the very center of a crowd. He has a way of gathering people around him. He is the sort of guy that everyone wants to have at their party. Time spent in his company will not be forgotten in a hurry.

Sagittarius usually does not end up in a nine-to-five job. His freedom is important to him. He likes to keep on the move as much as possible. He loves excitement and is often caught in situations that border on the dangerous. However, there is the other side to the Archer's nature. He is not exactly what he appears on the surface.

Sagittarius happens to be an extremely shy and sensitive person underneath that façade of style. He always is going out of his way to help people who are having a rough time of it. Underneath that flashy exterior is a man who basically suffers from an inferiority complex. Leo could be the woman to help him take an adult and responsible view of life.

In marriage, he is likely to be extremely faithful. He may fool around at an office party, but he would never dream of getting involved in a heavy scene that could put his marriage in jeopardy. Taking everything into consideration, Leo and Sagittarius might have a better chance of working out a long-term relationship than most people would have imagined.

He is extremely generous with money. He is likely to spoil his woman with expensive and decorative presents. There is something of the gypsy about him, though, and it is important she gives him plenty of freedom.

WHEN LEO WOMAN
MEETS CAPRICORN MAN

The Capricorn man will be spontaneously drawn to the Leo woman, partly through admiration and partly through attraction. Leo is glamor, representing success and status to him. Leo is open and flamboyant, awakening in him those sexual urges he constantly represses. He will also admire her for her ability to display warmth and sexuality.

The Capricorn man may worry too much about his reputation, on the one hand, and his sensitive inner nature, on the other, to get beyond the dating stage. The Leo female must take the lead, developing his attraction to the point where he trusts enough, allowing himself to let go sexually and emotionally—to take the plunge.

Capricorn is not an easy man to get close to. He is shy, almost to the point of being standoffish. It would take a go-getting, no-nonsense woman like Leo to bring him out of himself. He is afraid of being hurt. Often he appears to be rude and abrupt because he is terrified of anyone getting through to him and discovering what a gentle soul he is.

This man does require a lot of attention. He is likely to get the sulks if he feels he is being ignored. He may like to give the impression of not having a care in the world and being able to stand on his own two feet. But an intuitive female like fiery Leo is not going to take very long to see through the façade that he attempts to put up.

He needs discipline, mainly self-imposed, and he is a great conformer, always veering toward conservatism. He does not make friends easily. But when he does allow people to be included in his intimate circle, he will prove himself to be most loyal and trustworthy. He has a wry sense of humor. It is also true to say he can be a bit of a gossip at times. That petty streak in his nature is something his Leo woman will have to watch out for. She must make sure it does not become too dominant, as it can easily warp his outlook on life.

One may wonder if this man has enough push and drive to keep the lioness interested and content for the rest of her life. He is not all that good as a social animal, preferring the company of small groups of intimates rather than flitting about at big functions and gatherings. He has a private world that he does not readily allow people to enter.

It would be simpler for Leo to make him content than the other way round. Perhaps the best chance of this couple hitting it off will come when Capricorn has matured and come to terms with his own deficiencies. It may be that he will then see clearly just how much he needs a strong woman. Perhaps he will then be able to accept her advice and, what is more important, act upon it.

As a lover he does not beat around the bush. Leo will have to show him there is more to a relationship than plain and simple physical attraction. He is the faithful type, and is unlikely to get involved in an affair that would upset the balance of his orderly life in any way.

WHEN LEO WOMAN
MEETS AQUARIUS MAN

The Leo woman may be attracted to an Aquarius man simply because she has never met anyone like him. He, too, will be struck by the differences she presents. Their teaming up may be a case of opposites attracting. Leo and Aquarius are on opposite sides of the Zodiac, six signs apart. And they are totally unlike each other. But whether opposites can make a go of a long-term relationship is another matter.

Leo will be taking on more than she had bargained for if she decides to make a go of it with the Water Bearer. It must be said from the outset that Aquarius probably is one of the most difficult signs with which to form a permanent relationship. He will be particularly exasperating for a passionate, straightforward female like Leo.

This man has so many interests it will be difficult for any woman to keep up with him. He is very enthusiastic and gets deeply and quickly involved in causes. One of the problems for him, however, is sustaining interest. He is very good at throwing himself body and soul into reforming activities, as long as there is something glamorous and exciting about them.

Once he has to face dealing with the routine side of issues, he often becomes vague and disinterested.

He does not have a great deal of interest in domestic life. It will be up to the Leo woman to make the home an attractive and comfortable place to live in. He can be disorganized, too. It will be most upsetting for her to realize that her Aquarius man is never aware of all the hard work she has put into the place.

Aquarius can count himself a lucky man indeed if he successfully courts a Leo female. She is just the sort of woman to bring out the very best qualities in his nature. He needs a woman who has vision and can see the light he often hides under a bushel. She should not forget that his is the sign of impersonal friendship. He is very adept at communicating his ideas in a forceful and persuasive manner.

It is important that Leo keeps him in touch with reality and stops him thinking too abstractly. There will have to be a lot of give-and-take in the relationship. Tolerance may be easier for him to achieve than for Leo, although both of them have fixed ideas about so many things.

He is not the sort of fellow who always is on hand to offer a shoulder to cry on when things get rough. He will realize what a strong-willed woman she is and will expect her to fend for herself when he is not around. The interesting thing about this pairing is that they are such opposite types in many ways. She should be able to teach him a thing or two about close personal relationships, of which he has very little understanding.

WHEN LEO WOMAN
MEETS PISCES MAN

The union of Leo and Pisces can be as strong as the blazing sun, as deep as the vast ocean. Their elements, fire and water, do indeed represent the extremes—the sun on the one hand, the ocean on the other. Love and sacrifice characterize their relationship. It is not always a heavy, emotional affair. It can be light and bright and fun.

But there is never likely to be a dull moment when this couple gets together. In this relationship, no middle ground is possible. Their life together is going to be full of surprises, mostly happy ones.

Strangely enough, Leo is not likely to be instantly attracted to Pisces on first meeting. He may seem far too dreamy and vague for a go-ahead female like her. He may appear to wander around with his head in the clouds. But appearances can be deceptive. This guy is no slouch when important action is called for.

He usually has a very astute business brain on his shoulders. He does not mess around when it comes to clinching deals. Once he has decided on a certain course of action, he moves. It must be remembered, though, that his symbol is two Fishes swimming in opposite directions. He is certainly a puzzle. He can be everything a woman wants one moment, and everything she would prefer to live without the next.

Still, part of the fun of this liaison is never knowing what is coming next. Variety being the spice of life, this couple will not become bored in each other's company. It is true to say that this guy does need to be given a sense of direction and general purpose in life. It also is true to say that if he has not found that direction by the time he has reached early middle age, then it is unlikely he will ever get it together.

Being an ambitious woman, Leo can give him the extra push and the inspiration he often is unable to motivate within himself. He is a bit of a loner. It is possible for him to be extremely self-reliant. He would prefer to be on his own rather than link up with someone for the sake of companionship.

Pisces is tolerant and fair. He is not the type to judge people by the size of their bank account, their religion or the color of their skin. He also will make special efforts to get on with his mate's family—a fact that will please Leo.

Pisces can be very romantic. This couple is likely to spend quite a few evenings at home together snuggling in front of the fire. He is great with kids, but perhaps not too good on the discipline. His youngsters are likely to regard him more as a friend than as a father figure.

WHEN LEO MAN
MEETS ARIES WOMAN

The concept of the battle of the sexes could have been modeled on a relationship between these two zodiacal types. Nevertheless, this couple could hit it off right from the word go. They both are fire signs. Apart from that, they have a lot of other things in common.

The Aries woman is every bit as bossy as the Leo man, just as proud, just as demanding, and just as fiery. Their passions will blaze with a fierce yet abiding light, although they can fight over any and every petty thing they share. Power struggles characterize their union. But Aries and Leo are so equally matched that the competition between them becomes a strong feature holding the relationship together and binding them in true love and friendship.

She is sexy, an upfront woman, a real charmer. There are certain difficulties to face when Leo teams up with his Ram counterpart. For instance, it is definitely going to be a power-sharing relationship if it has any hope of succeeding. Both are born leaders, and this, of course, could cause the sparks to fly. Leo could find that his Aries woman is like no other female he has ever come across. A woman born under the sign of the Ram is feminine enough, but she also is likely to be a women's liberationist. She will not be happy settling for a pink-frilled apron and a life at the kitchen sink.

The Lion may be King of the Jungle, but if he tries to lay down the law he will not get very far with this freedom-loving powerhouse. She doesn't play around with emotions. Like the Lion, she is a straightforward and open-minded person. And it does not take very long for a man to know whether he has any chance of getting to first base or not.

There are many things about the Lion she will admire. His practicality, for one thing. Nothing irritates the Ram more than a person who does not speak his mind fairly and squarely. For many a man the very thought of having a heavy affair with this female is a daunting proposition. She is a real flattener of ego because she has high standards.

This duo will know exactly what they want from life together. Their individual aims are similar, so mutual goals could work out very well. But she has an independent streak that is very pronounced. It might be too much for Leo to take.

As business partners they would be unbeatable. In fact, if this couple were to meet under working conditions they might form a company together as well as having a close emotional relationship. They both are very good at divorcing business from pleasure when it is expedient to do so.

It often is the case that an Aries woman will be an aggressive pursuer if she meets a man she likes. It is not uncommon for her to take the lead in romantic and sexual relationships. This attitude to sex could rock the Lion on his heels, especially if he is a Leo who has an image of himself as an all-conquering hero. Aries can be an extremely jealous woman. He had better watch out if he is ever caught having fun on the side. She won't think twice about creating a scene and dumping the relationship.

WHEN LEO MAN
MEETS TAURUS WOMAN

The Taurus woman is a little toughie as well as being a gentle, romantic female. People get mixed ideas about her. She gives the impression of being able to take care of herself, with her proud and strong bearing. But underneath the cool and placid exterior burns a passionate and sensitive heart, which she is averse to showing.

The Taurus woman hides behind an introverted personality. She does not believe in wearing her heart on her sleeve. Many men may think she is a cool cucumber, aloof and unemotional. But if they scratch the surface, they will find one of the sexiest and most romantic females in the Zodiac.

How will the Leo male hit it off with the Venus-born female? He will have many qualities she will admire. She likes a man who knows his mind. Contrary to popular belief, she is perfectly prepared to be led—provided she feels the person who's doing the leading is taking her in the direction she wants to go. She is a woman who has a great deal of self-control. This is not the type of woman to chase after a man and humiliate herself.

In many ways, she is rather an old-fashioned woman. A stable, affluent relationship is a cornerstone in her life. Once she has given her heart, she is unlikely to waver. When it comes to the loyalty stakes, she is not very far behind the Lion. A Taurus woman would never let a friend or lover down. It is important to her to show that she is a person who keeps her word. Woe betide the guy who double-crosses her. She can be extremely jealous. And if she has been played for a fool, the fat's in the fire.

The Taurus woman is conservative and adept at saving. This economizing trait in her character will go down swell with Leo. He should not try to change her ways. She can be very obstinate. Once she has a fixed opinion on something, it would be best to accept the situation.

She will not mind a bit of harmless flirting. A Taurus woman is no prude, and flirts herself. She will understand it if her man winks and talks with an engaging female. She would never make a scene unless she felt that her relationship with her man was really being challenged.

Some problems in the relationship can come from the similarities between these two. Both Leo and Taurus are after power. Both of them are incredibly stubborn. The Taurus woman likes to revel in the comforts and luxuries of the home. The Leo man likes to receive the praise and flattery that a beautiful home inspires. They could get in each other's hair here.

Both Taurus and Leo are conscious of good looks and money. She will be proud of this guy, who likes to dress and entertain royally. She may think he's a bit flashy, but because his character is as firm as hers, she will feel secure with him.

Leo is not likely to have any regrets if he does decide to get hitched to a Taurus woman. She is a home lover and would be willing to sacrifice many of her outside interests to be by the side of her man. She is very good with children, but perhaps can be too anxious about their manners and appearance.

WHEN LEO MAN
MEETS GEMINI WOMAN

If he is the Leo type who cannot resist a challenge, a Gemini woman is the one for him. To be honest, this relationship would appear to be a bit of a nonstarter. But then love can conquer all, and stranger things have happened than a pairing like this.

A Gemini woman has plenty of glamor and sophistication, qualities that will dazzle the Leo man. He, too, is a charmer, outgoing and popular. These two are likely to have a swell affair, enchanting each other and their public. They are a wonderful couple in the social whirl.

In private, though, the emotional mix between them could get a little sticky. The Leo man can be heavy, demanding a lot of affection and attention, and complaining about the Gemini woman's flighty ways. If Leo can be a bit more casual and if Gemini can be a bit more serious, the relationship will survive and grow.

The Lion is a methodical type of person in many ways. He likes to have order in his life. In personal relationships he certainly likes to know where he stands. He is going to run into all sorts of difficulties if he gets deeply involved with the Gemini woman.

She is always changing her mind. That may be a woman's prerogative, but Gemini does take it to extremes. People born under the sign of the Twins do have great difficulty in making decisions and finding a direction in life. No sooner do they decide which way they should turn than they see a perfectly good reason for going ahead and doing the exact opposite. These antics can be infuriating even for a patient man.

Age can be an important factor. If Leo comes across a Gemini female after she has had the opportunity to gain a lot of experience, they might have a good chance of making a go of things.

It does take this woman a long time to come to terms with herself and to slow down. Leo must not get angry or lose his temper with her. It would also be a mistake to try to lay down the law. Gemini simply cannot stand to feel she is being hemmed in or trapped.

The way to help a Gemini woman is by example. She is quick on the uptake and will catch on when she sees it would benefit her to follow a particular course. Gemini loves to keep on the move. Travel means a lot, and she cannot stand to stay in one spot for very long. This woman needs a lot of loving. It also is very important that the romance never goes out of a relationship.

She does not like routine. Leo will have to get used to her flirting, too, although it is not likely to be harmful. She makes a great hostess. When he brings important people home, she will entertain them magnificently. When a party is arranged, he should leave it to his Gemini woman to do the organizing. Social occasions are never likely to be dull affairs when she is in charge.

WHEN LEO MAN
MEETS CANCER WOMAN

The Cancer woman is a constant puzzle for any man, and particularly for a straightforward guy like Leo. She is a Moon child. So it will be difficult to fathom whether she is totally ruled by the lunar vibrations or if she is the sweetest and most intelligent lass he has ever come across.

Her element is water, which has a big influence on her personality. She turns like the tide itself and is as fathomless as the deepest regions of the sea. It would be best not to try to delve too deeply; this woman cannot bear analysis. Leo is going to have to accept her as she is or not at all.

In many ways, Cancer is rather unsure of herself. It often appears to an observer that she does not know in which direction she is heading or, for that matter, what she truly wants out of life. It is vital that she has a strong and steady man at the helm. She does not like to be bossed, but it is important that she has a partner who can be a guiding force and a positive influence when the going gets tough.

Her moods can change with the blink of an eye. It is no good trying to tie her down to promises she made yesterday. What she feels at the moment is all that is likely to have any significance to her. When this woman gets the blues, she gets them bad. It is no good trying to shake her out of her mood. But perhaps a powerful and positive guy like Leo can help her face reality more readily.

When the Lion first meets this woman, he will find she has a way of involving others in her personal and emotional problems. The Crab likes to be the center of attention. She is not a woman who thrives on competition, though. When she withdraws into her shell, it will be because she does not wish to face problems and responsibilities. When the blinds come down, it is impossible to get through to her. She cannot stand criticism, and refuses to face the truth about herself unless it suits her purpose.

She can be extravagant on herself, and loves pretty clothes and decorative jewelry. However, she worries a great deal about the future. She can be stingy if she feels a cutback in her spending habits is called for. When she falls in love, Leo will know all about it. She is all woman and will give herself totally to the man who has won her heart.

There is a lot of affection shared between these two. The Cancer woman is strongly maternal, and the Leo man is openly loving. Their emotional availability to each other engenders trust. Even though their affections fluctuate from hot to cold and back again, there is always the flow of emotions between them.

Domestic life keeps the two of them together through hard times. There will always be spats, especially around relatives and children, but the mutually strong feelings for home and family keep disagreements from becoming irreconcilable conflicts.

WHEN LEO MAN
MEETS LEO WOMAN

On the surface this may appear to be a perfect match. However, a liaison between two people born under the sign of the Lion might not be so compatible as would first appear. There could be a clash of personalities. These two are very forceful types. The coming together of two people who are born leaders demands that some power-sharing formula has to be worked out.

When a couple is similar in so many ways, they are bound to see reflected certain aspects of their own personality they find very difficult to accept. The Leo woman is proud and determined. She is not the type to bow down and give up her career and outside interests willingly. This woman has far too much going for her to be prepared to settle for a mundane life, living in the shadow of her mate's success. Freedom is very important to her.

A Leo guy, on the other hand, does like to be the provider for his woman. He wants to be head of his household. It might be very difficult for him to accept his choice of a woman who is perfectly able to take care of herself and to stand on her own two feet.

It might be even more difficult for him to admit that the Leo woman could be better adapted to the game of life than he is. She has all the courage and fierceness that characterize the Lion; she wasn't shortchanged being a female. Moreover, she may be a lot more subtle and cunning than he, so she has a chance of gaining advantages by strategies he never thought of.

The Leo woman also has a more pronounced nurturant streak. This enables her to protect her position and her possessions, and to develop them without running foolish risks. Her decisions tend to be carefully considered and therefore are more likely to succeed than are her male counterpart's.

But Lady Leo is no fool. If she falls for a man, she will be prepared for him to make many of the important decisions. As long as he does not try to take her freedom away from her or to stifle the individual streak in her nature, she will play along.

Their sex life should be most compatible. Lady Leo is all woman. She is very physical and has a great imagination in bed. The Leo man will have to get used to her flirting ways. She will love playing up to his best friend.

But it is all likely to be harmless fun. Leo will have to learn to keep his possessive tendencies under control.

Other women are likely to be jealous of her. Most women would like to have her strength of character and singleness of purpose. Having a woman like this around will be a great help in business. He will never have to worry about bringing important people home for cocktails or dinner. Pretty clothes are important to her. Her mate may find there is not much room in the closets to squeeze in his own wardrobe.

It is unlikely that this couple will be planning to have more than one or two kids. Both will make sure the children know all about the world.

WHEN LEO MAN
MEETS VIRGO WOMAN

The roar of the Lion could easily frighten off a shy and reserved woman like Virgo. The King of the Jungle is going to have to adopt a far more subtle approach if he is to stand any chance of making her his steady date or lover.

Leo does have a tendency to rush in feet first. But this up-and-at-'em tactic is not likely to be the right one in this particular union. It would be unwise for a Leo man to try to push this liaison too far too quickly. Virgo the Virgin is a mighty cautious female. She requires respect, and will not be won over by brashness or wildly amorous advances.

The best way to appeal to her is through her intellect. Of course, this does not mean to say there will not be an obvious physical attraction in the first place. But Leo will have to be interested in more than a casual affair and to woo her as only a Leo can when he cares enough. Any man will have to prove his loyalty and devotion before a woman born under this sixth sign of the Zodiac is willing to team up with him.

She is a shy female. But here still waters run deep. She can often surprise people by acting completely out of character. She is capable of sudden changes of direction that can catch her nearest and dearest completely off guard.

The changeable nature of Virgo's intellectual and emotional apparatus will fascinate and hold the Leo man, especially because he sometimes can be so fixed in his ideas and feelings. She can lead him quietly in many new and challenging directions that he would never think to explore on his own.

She can spot truth from falsehood, sense hidden motivations, separate the wheat from the chaff. These qualities of mind and spirit are an enormous asset to Leo. Her subtlety more than once will get him out of a tight spot or threatening situation. The Virgo woman can be an abiding guide and helpmate for her Leo man.

Virgo women never like to admit they are in the wrong. She cannot stand criticism. A Leo man would do well not to try to change her basic personality. She is very good at summing up people. When he brings prospective business partners home to meet his Virgo woman, he is likely to find that her analysis of their characters is right on. She can pinpoint the strengths and weaknesses of people at first meeting.

A Virgo woman will try very hard to make a success of marriage. She cannot stand to fail, especially in something as important as a lifelong partnership. She hates sloppiness, and the home they share is likely to be kept as neat as a pin. She makes a very good mother.

In lovemaking, the Lion should always be gentle and never forget to treat her with respect. She is a passionate woman who also needs to be wooed romantically. Evenings at home will mean a lot to her, but she also likes to get out and around. She loves the company of stimulating people and can usually hold her own in conversations on the important issues of the day.

WHEN LEO MAN
MEETS LIBRA WOMAN

A Libra woman is the essence of charm, grace, and refinement. That smooth yet glamorous exterior tantalizes Leo, who wants the woman in his life to be admired and praised in her own right. She fills the bill beautifully there. The Libra woman also casts a subtle love spell that the Leo man finds irresistible. Leo is looking for love, Libra is looking for partnership, and the two of them can trade splendidly on such a romantic bargain.

A Libra woman would make a fine partner for the Lion. He is likely to find in her everything he has been looking for. She is an independent woman, yet has a way of making a man feel like a man. She will never lose her individuality for all her feminine ways.

This lady will never make her man feel he is tied down in any way. Her interests are many and varied, and she feels at home with people from different walks of life. She has an inquiring mind, an active intelligence. She carries on with her career after the wedding bells have stopped ringing.

However, her outside interests will never interfere with her responsibility to her home and family. She would never dream of continuing with her job if her man or her kids were to be neglected or feel deprived in the slightest. But she remains the sole judge of that state of affairs. No man could con her into dependence.

Harmony and balance are essential to her life. Like Leo, she likes to conduct her affairs in an orderly and adult way. What will appeal to Leo is her little-girl-lost persona hidden behind the sophisticated female. She will bring out the protective instincts in his nature. She will be quite happy for the Lion to be head of the house. So it should be a relatively simple matter for this couple to decide who will be in charge of what.

A Libra woman has a logical mind and holds her own in company and in discussion. It must be remembered that Libra is the sign of human relationships. So it is obvious how important it is for a woman born under the Scales to make her marriage work out successfully in the broad context of people. She doesn't want a private or isolated relationship.

There is one area where there could be problems. This woman cannot help flirting. Leo will have to accept that this is all harmless fun and it would be silly for him to get jealous. The fact is she knows she is attractive to men and cannot help playing games.

A Libra woman is a great ego booster. She will know how to make her leonine mate purr with contentment. She will make sure her guy fulfills his potential, though. She is a great driving force for any man whose ambition is to get to the top. She never allows her emotions to get the upper hand when the time comes to make important decisions. If she feels a relationship is going wrong, she will break it off no matter how much it upsets her. She is great with children and has a genuine and deep love for them.

WHEN LEO MAN
MEETS SCORPIO WOMAN

With Scorpio, it is true that the female of the species is more deadly than the male. Leo, who prances around pretending he's King of the Jungle, will find all such poses regarded as playful gestures by the Scorpio woman. She will let him know immediately that his chest-beating ways are preposterous. With her, the Leo man becomes a pussycat, manageable, lovable, and loving—if he sticks around.

A Scorpio woman is a real challenge for any man. Leo may not wish to take on such a challenge. This is not an easy female to live with, especially for a guy like Leo, who likes to live in an orderly sort of way. She is a very passionate person. Being a water sign, she is also a deep and mystical one.

If this lady loves a man, she will go to almost any lengths to make him hers. There is also the reverse side. If she feels she has been let down in any way, woe betide the man who she feels is the guilty party. The saying, "Hell hath no fury like a woman scorned" would seem suitable for a Scorpio female on the warpath. She has the devil's own temper. Once her feelings are aroused, there is no telling what will happen.

This woman is quite capable of resorting to physical violence if this is the only way she can work out her feelings of frustration. It is not easy to have a smooth and harmonious long-term relationship with Scorpio. She does not like to be dominated—she will not be. She is suspicious of men who try to take away her individuality.

She does not go for the heavy-handed approach in romance, either. She is not easy to persuade. She likes to make decisions for herself. She can't stand to feel she is being manipulated or coaxed. Life with Scorpio will not be a smooth passage. Although she will cry out that she craves the simple life, the truth is this woman cannot get by without a certain amount of internal conflict.

Her feelings are intense. An affair with this woman is a once-in-a-lifetime experience no man is likely to forget in a hurry. Scorpio is an individual, and she has no time to be the simpering little girl who plays Miss Innocent with men. Scorpio women are leaders and not followers.

Work is vitally important to her. Not because she is ambitious for fame or greedy for money, but because holding down a job gives her a certain amount of independence. She enjoys earning her own money, as she feels it is a measure of the control she retains over her own destiny.

Sex is one of the dominating factors in this woman's life. The physical side of the relationship will have to be particularly good if she is going to stay loyal to one man for any length of time. She is not promiscuous, though strict monogamy may be too limiting. She would not like to have more than one serious relationship going at a time. But if the one she has is failing, she'll strike up another with no qualms.

WHEN LEO MAN
MEETS SAGITTARIUS WOMAN

A Sagittarius female is likely to take Leo's breath away. As fiery as he, as independent as he, and as fun-loving as he, she appears to be the perfect match for the Lion. As companions, they will have a swell time on the swing circuit, bopping here and there, delighting the crowd. They both enjoy noisy, raucous entertainment. As lovers, though, with thoughts of permanence, their clashes could mount into one long, loud explosion.

Sagittarius women are great to be with as long as they are not bossed around. One thing this woman cannot stand is to be told what to do. Leo will have to go easy on the Archer. In his leonine way, he often feels he knows what is best for people and with the best will in the world tries to put them straight.

This is not the right approach with Sagittarius. She may make a lot of mistakes in her life, but she would turn around and say, "Well, it's my life, isn't it?" A lady born under the third fire sign—he is the second—is ablaze with energy. She will be happy for her man to make big decisions, as long as he never tries to interfere with her energy and the areas she feels are hers.

Sagittarius people do have a habit of trapping others—and themselves—by putting their foot in the worst situation at the wrong time. Sometimes her statements will make Leo cringe. She means well, but she does say things truthfully, and that hurts. She can make announcements that put people's backs up and start arguments. He will get it straight from the shoulder from her. She believes in saying what she thinks. This blunt approach does not go down too well with a guy like Leo, who needs truth sugar-coated and his ego boosted regularly.

A Sagittarius woman is super company. They will enjoy meeting each other's friends and partying. She certainly knows how to have a good time and live life to the full. Sagittarius is an ambitious woman, not only for herself but also for her man. She also is loyal and will stand up for her man no matter what the odds.

People born under the sign of the Archer excel at sports. She is likely to be a willing and winning partner in outdoor games like tennis. Sagittarius is a trusting female. She will want to believe her man. She would be terribly hurt to think she had been let down or taken for a fool, especially if he tries to bluff his way on the sports field.

Sagittarius women are sometimes shy when it comes to settling down. She will need lots of understanding to bring her out of herself and into another's family. She also is not one of the greatest cooks in the world. Leo may often feel like going home to Ma for his Sunday lunch, leaving his Sagittarius mate and the kids to their TV dinners.

As a mother she cannot be faulted. She will do all she can to make sure her youngsters get the best possible start in life. As the kids get older, though, it is important that she maintains other interests and does not try to live her life through them. As a lifelong partner and companion, this woman could turn out to be tops for a Leo.

WHEN LEO MAN
MEETS CAPRICORN WOMAN

The Capricorn female has an air of refinement and style that will turn Leo's head. Always on the lookout for glamor, Leo will sense a subdued excitement about this woman that will make his blood run hot. He loves a challenge. He also is intuitive enough to know that his flamboyant advances will melt that icy reserve by which the Capricorn female protects herself. And she is game enough to let him get by the first few defenses, then cautious enough to wait and see what develops.

Any woman born under the sign of Capricorn could be an ideal partner for go-ahead, forceful Leo. She is the perfect female to be the power behind the throne. The King of the Jungle needs a queen—someone who is ambitious behind him to give him that extra impetus to get to the top.

Most Leo men are bent on being leaders. A Capricorn woman is an able administrator, the choice of a man who is out to make his mark in the world. People born under Capricorn, the third earth sign, can get hung up on material possessions. So the Capricorn female is likely to make sure that her man keeps his pile when the profits come rolling in.

She regards wealth and security with esteem. It is very important to her to have a secure and stable home life. She must know where the next meal is coming from and how much she can afford to spend on it. This is not to say she worships money, only that she is unlikely to fritter away the hard-earned spoils of her man's or her own toil.

Capricorn is not easy to get to know. On first meeting she may appear to be the shy and retiring type. The female Goat is not prepared to let people get too close to her until she is sure she can trust them. Any man can count himself fortunate if he is able to win the hand of this choosy lady.

She is an astute and high-principled female. If she does accept a date with the Lion, it is because she has spotted his qualities of leadership and honor. He better live up to her standards. She is prepared to take the rough with the smooth in the early days of a relationship. Capricorn always will make sacrifices for the sake of the future.

Emotions are deeply felt by her. If she gets hurt, it will take her a long time to recover. She will not feel like getting involved with anyone else quite so deeply for a long time to come. A Leo-born man is not likely to have any complaints when it comes to lovemaking. Few people would believe from her demeanor that her sexual appetite is insatiable.

As parents they are likely to make a fine combination. Both will feel that a good education is most important for their youngsters. Leo will have to accept that his Capricorn lady is a bit of a flirt. But he should take this in the right spirit when he knows finally that she is his. She will not be unfaithful while he remains true.

WHEN LEO MAN
MEETS AQUARIUS WOMAN

A female born under the sign of Aquarius is a difficult nut for a Leo man to crack. She is a nut, idiomatically speaking. This woman defies being put into any one category. Just when a fellow feels he has gotten through to her, she will act completely out of character and throw him into a state of utter confusion.

Yet the Aquarius woman has many sides to her character, so the unpredictability is not unusual—it is just maddening. Leo will come to realize that he and she are virtually opposite in personality, in lifestyle, and perhaps in ultimate priorities. Aquarius and Leo occupy opposite sides of the Zodiac, being six signs apart from each other. The differences in their natures are real and not easily resolved.

It would be advisable for this couple to have a long courtship if they are contemplating any kind of permanent relationship. It would be most unwise to have a whirlwind affair and decide that they were meant for each other. After a month, Leo may suddenly realize that he has, in fact, become involved with a stranger.

It must be stated that there is quite a lot to be said against this liaison working out. Still, love can find a way, and it is true that opposites do attract.

There is a marked independent streak in this woman's nature that could be infuriating for the Lion. She does not act within the framework of any set rules or regulations. It is important for Leo to know where he stands with a woman. His life could become so confused by her that in the end he finds he really is at a loss as to how to handle her.

The Leo male is a possessive character. He does not like to be diddled. Home life means a lot to him. Coming back from a hard day's work, he could find the house empty with a note saying his Aquarius lady is out somewhere pursuing her own interests. If the King of the Jungle can accept his life being full of surprises, then all will be well and good.

It might be that a whirlwind affair would suit this couple best. Perhaps a stormy few months together would be that once-in-a-lifetime experience neither of them would be likely to forget in a hurry. Of course, marriage could not be ruled out completely. It is possible that a permanent relationship could grow and blossom over the years—with lots of separations in between.

Certainly, an Aquarius woman will do all she can to make sure her Leo man makes the best possible use of his potential. It might surprise many people to discover that she also makes a fine and responsible mother. It is important to her that the next generation are properly equipped to sort out the problems that will face them in adulthood. This woman's ideas are ahead of the times.

WHEN LEO MAN
MEETS PISCES WOMAN

There are not many men who would not fall under the spell of the mysterious and enchanting female born under the sign of Pisces. Leo, in particular, will find himself inextricably drawn to her. A Pisces female can entice him emotionally, sexually, and creatively. She brings out the romantic in him, taps his mysticism, turns him on to the creative joys of sex and love. Leo often is in love with love, and the Pisces woman, he senses, can fulfill this seemingly impossible dream.

On a down-to-earth level, too, the Pisces woman has many qualities the Leo man will find attractive and appealing. For a start, she makes a guy feel all man. Any fellow who is lucky enough to have her fall head over heels in love with him will feel like a million dollars. When she gives herself totally to a man, he will experience a relationship that money could never buy. Leo sees her as an inspiration. She may be the missing piece of the jigsaw puzzle of life he has been trying to put together for so long.

She is the dreamy type, but her dreams have a strange and uncanny way of coming true. When Pisces puts her mind to it, she can make the impossible become a reality. Never can she be underestimated. Yes, she gets confused and can change her mind about things to an alarming degree. But with the stability that she is likely to find in a relationship with the Lion, she will have a great chance of fulfilling herself.

It is important that the man in her life takes the lead. She will be prepared to give him the responsibility for making the big decisions. But whenever he is in doubt, Pisces will be there and able to give him invaluable advice. She is an intuitive woman. What is more, her instincts are never far off the mark.

This couple makes an excellent combination. The differing strengths and weaknesses create the perfect balance. She may take many people in with that dreamy expression. But when it comes to summing up people's characters, she is rarely wrong.

Leo can be niggling where small amounts of money are concerned. Although Pisces can go on a spending spree—especially if the sales are on and she wants some fine clothes to add to her wardrobe—she also is astute. She staggers her purchases, never running up bills in one fell swoop that would put the account in debt.

After a hard day's work at the shop or office, the Lion will be pleased to get home to his Pisces woman. She often will have prepared a delightful surprise to show him just how much she cares. In lovemaking, they are likely to be on the same wavelength. As a lover, she is inventive and giving, which will appeal to this lovestruck, romantic guy. A Pisces woman easily combines the dual roles of wife and mother.

Leo:
Work and Business

No matter how important ambitions and desires may be, happiness is usually decided by human relations—the ability to get along with others. The preceding chapter, "Leo: Love and Romance," gave you insights into the deeply personal relationships of love, sex, and marriage.

How do you relate to other people as a friend? An employer? A partner? What is the best career field for you? And if you strike out on your own and seek a partner, what can you expect from him or her in a work and business relationship?

The chapter describes your personality as a friend and employer. It highlights your career motivations and capacities. It details your work and business relationships with individuals born under each of the twelve Sun signs.

You can extend the in-depth view of yourself as a friend and partner if you read the sections that apply to you from the chapters "Your Rising Sign," "Mercury in the Signs," "Jupiter in the Signs," and "Saturn in the Signs." The pertinent descriptions there will add to your understanding of yourself as developed in this chapter and in the chapter "Leo: Character Analysis."

The Rising sign, as the *Astroscope Profile* series has emphasized, indicates how others see us and how they may relate to us on the basis of what we are showing the world. Mercury, Jupiter, and Saturn are significant in work and business partnerships, too. Mercury influences the individual's capacity for mental work and communication. Jupiter indicates how an individual might develop and expand a venture and the capacity for taking chances and risks. Saturn indicates how an individual might deal with money, obstacles, and the plain hard work involved in a venture.

You can also add to the descriptions of specific business partners given in this chapter. If you are interested in finding out more about a particular individual, you may want to read the relevant book of the *Astroscope Profile* series for that person. The tables in that book will give you the Rising, Mercury, Jupiter, and Saturn placements for him or her. These descriptions should be read together with the person's Sun sign description.

LEO AS A FRIEND

Leo people are warm and loving to their friends. No occasion is too small for a Leo man or woman to demonstrate a token of their love. They give gifts in abundance.

Sometimes the gifts are neither insignificant nor sentimental. They can be expensive purchases, which Leo went out of his or her way to buy. But Leo will explain that the gift is an investment, not merely a present. And the friend better hold onto it—or else! Leo's friends alternate between gratitude and resentment toward such behavior.

Leos have a lot of friends, so they can't buy "trifles" for all of them. Entertaining is a substitute. The Lion's household, whether he or she is single or married, is the center of social life for a particular set of friends and acquaintances at any given time. Food, drink, music, dancing, games, and sports flourish there on these occasions.

Because Leos always enlarge their social circle, either they must get larger living quarters or contrive somehow to lose some friends, acquaintances, or associates. They do manage to lose some in all innocence of their own motives. Leo's domineering ways can drive certain people to abandon Leo temporarily. If Leo feels slighted, that person is not a welcome guest in Leo's home or heart anymore.

Leos give, but they also like to receive. There are two sure ways to a Leo's heart and hand in friendship. These are flattery and praise, which may be sincere or insincere. Leo doesn't distinguish false adulation from true admiration. As long as a person shows recognition of Leo's self-image, Leo counts him or her as a friend.

Leos don't particularly appreciate generosity from their friends if it is expressed through material gifts or products. Leos are finicky; they frown on things that do not exemplify their tastes. Leo men and women are perfectly capable of returning an unwanted item and being annoyed for a while at the friend who presented it.

Leos can become unreasonably irritated with friends whose tastes and manners clash with their own. They are always lecturing people on the right ways to do things and say things. But despite such differences, Leos are never petty, mean, or vengeful. They remain loyal and loving to these people. If Leo does break with a friend, it is intended to be a permanent separation.

LEO AS AN EMPLOYER

Leo employers are sunny, sincere, and enthusiastic, at least when a staff member first joins up. The Lion has great faith in the operation he or she is running, and this confidence is contagious. Soon, however, the domineering parts of the Leo personality infect the staff, possibly causing resentment.

As bosses, Leos are tough. They expect everyone to work as hard as they do. To them, good employees are respectful and obedient workers. These exemplary staff members are treated with paternal kindness, encouragement, and continual reminders of good advice.

Less devoted workers either reform under the Leo look of stony disapproval, or tear their hair out, quit, or get fired. The quiet and placid types merely collapse under the pressure of the Lion's relentless intensity and noisy performing. These workers are allowed to resign or retire, but only with passing grades—no honors.

Leo employers were once workers, so they know the motives of their staff. As workers, Leos are conscientious and filled with bright ideas for improvements. They become unhappy and disgruntled if unimaginative people are over them. Leos are prepared to work hard and to support a boss whom they respect as someone who knows their job.

But most Leos believe they can do the immediate boss's job better. As Leos are always waiting for the opportunity to prove it, they are dangerous people for an incompetent superior to have around. Once Leos finally oust the boss and sits in the royal roost, not forget what it took to get there. So they rule with a powerful scrutiny. But they also promote creativity. And this makes up for their bossy ways.

LEO IN A CAREER

Leos work conscientiously and consistently once they have found a career area that suits them. Despite their tendency to speculate and move around in other areas of their life, they do not like job hopping—unless it is up in their chosen field.

Leo people are consummate actors. They believe totally in whatever they are doing. That does not mean Leo men and women all seek a career on the stage. Indeed, any job is a stage upon which the Leo personality can dramatically display belief in an idea, product, or service.

With Leo, a job is not just a job; it is an investment in the future. It is also a tool for teaching other people. Leos believe they have a personal mission to teach all with whom they come in contact.

Leos have a talent for making any person they deal with feel important. Leos demonstrate their love for the common man or woman by putting their heart into fulfilling his or her needs.

This talent makes Leo shine in a range of careers and fields from real estate to education, and in a variety of jobs from salesperson to president. These men and women can create catchy slogans and powerful phrases that persuade people of the sincerity and genuineness of any idea, product, service, or institution Leos represent.

LEO AND ARIES
IN BUSINESS TOGETHER

The two fiery leaders of the Zodiac in partnership? Both trying to be boss at the same time? On paper, few would give this business relationship much chance. Yet it can produce an extremely well-proportioned team, able to excel in any creative field or where the going is competitive and rough.

Aries and Leo both are inclined to play for high stakes. These two are gamblers at heart, naturally optimistic types. Both have supreme faith and confidence in their own abilities. Aries is more the action man or woman, ready to slog it out with anyone or anything who might get in the way.

Leo is more conscientious and takes what comes down more regally than does the Ram. Lions and Lionesses are happy sitting on their thrones in the office, handing out lectures and advice, writing persuasive promotion copy, and handling finances and administration. As a rule, the Lion will leave most of the outdoor work and organizing to the Ram.

The Lion may, though, feel there's an occasion where he or she can leave the royal roost and take the floor elsewhere to receive much-desired compliments or flattery. These two partners have to reach a sensible agreement about whose territory is whose, or they will get in each other's way and there may be a bustup.

The Ram and the Lion basically are compatible. But neither will surrender any ground under threat or confrontation from the other. If they can work out how to handle each other, they are an unbeatable team. The Ram and the Lion can lie down together, though Aries is more a wolf in sheep's clothing than a lamb. If they do, there may be some peace at last.

Aries will soon spot the Lion's weakness for flattery. He or she will use this with great seriousness to get their own way, and probably will succeed more often than not. Even for the independent Aries character, such a tactic will be fairly painless due to its entertainment value. Leo falling for compliments in exchange for favors is something the Ram can easily laugh or yawn off.

Aries and Leo genuinely respect strength and the power to command. Both these partners have an abundance of courage and leadership. But Leo will have to get used to or at least understand the Aries fondness for handing out orders. Aries wants something to be done immediately. Leo is less urgent.

These two will fight. But they have sufficient sentiment and good sense to forget the whole thing as soon as it is over. Then they can get down to practicalities, and to making money.

LEO AND TAURUS
IN BUSINESS TOGETHER

Taurus and Leo will respect each other, an important factor in any partnership. They will have much in common that may not appear on the surface. They will work together on the positive side of the relationship. But there will be some tensions. Fiery Leo will always be a little anxious about the ability of earthy Taurus to put the Leo light out or to overshadow him or her in any way.

Taurus and Leo are practical people. They should be able to put aside their emotional hangups for the good of the partnership. Once they agree on their aim, they will have no trouble sticking to it.

They are both fixed signs. That means there won't be any fooling around or switching and changing their goals. If they can give and take a little regarding their personality differences and the strategies to succeed, they will be able to make a very successful business team.

The main problem is that the Lion and the Bull will have to come to some power-sharing arrangement. Both like to dominate their relationships. Taurus will have to face the fact that the King of the Jungle needs a lot of praise and flattery. But being a hardheaded sort of person who knows that the purpose of business is to make money, the Bull will not be too worried about pampering the Lion in order to obtain his or her full cooperation and support. And very valuable the Lion's contribution will be!

Leos are great organizers. They also are one of the most imaginatively creative signs in the Zodiac. But the Leo partner could find the Bull staid and unimaginative when it comes to putting up original ideas. The Lion may have to be the inventive part of the outfit.

The Bull is top-notch at turning artistic and creative ideas into practical ventures. These people have a feel for color and harmony that is seldom equaled. They are especially good at interior decorating and design. But they do tend to use the tried and trusted ideas. Nevertheless, they polish them up with their special kind of Taurus shine.

The Bull will help to keep the Leo partner's feet on the ground when he or she gets carried away with some of their foolishly imaginative schemes. Taurus will also check the Lion's extravagance in entertainment expense.

Both these partners like to put on a show. Here there could be sharp rivalry. Taurus, with his or her quiet charm, may often attract more admiring attention than the Lion will be able to stand. These two are very hard workers, and a great deal will be accomplished each day if they put their competitive instincts toward each other aside.

LEO AND GEMINI
IN BUSINESS TOGETHER

Gemini and Leo are naturally compatible in most things. In business, this combination could really go places. Once they have sorted out a few minor details and sized each other up, there should be no personality problems. Both are realistic when it comes to making money. They will do everything they can to make the most of the other's positive qualities.

Leo and Gemini make an imaginative duo. Both are creative and inventive. They probably would do better in a business that caters to one of the artistic fields. But they are both go-getters in harness. Between them, they could make an impression in just about any business line that was not a monotonous drag. They do like their excitement and public acclaim.

Leo is a born leader. The Lion is called the King of the Jungle for good reason. This partner is unable to control his or her dominating ways. Leo must run the show. As long as the Lion is wise enough not to put pressure on the Gemini Twins, they will be pleased to work under the Lion's mature direction.

Geminis, in spite of their many positive qualities, are always a bit lost in themselves. They are happy for someone they trust to tell them which way to go, as long as they have had a hand, or two hands, in creating the idea, product, or service. With Gemini's brilliance, this team will never lack innovation.

Being a realist and a hard worker, the Lion will be unhappy if his or her Gemini partner starts flitting around, making more with the chat than the sweat. It is to be hoped that these particular Twins have learned to face the facts of life. They mustn't get bored and distracted when it comes down to the nitty-gritty of making the business pay. Not with Leo around!

At times, the Lion will be mystified by the Twins. Leo is one of those fixed and obstinate signs that do not like changing direction once the targets have been set. Gemini finds it very difficult to stick to any decision or course of action for long.

Of course, the common business aim of making money does offer much scope for variety. But it will be vital to the success of this partnership that the Twins' activities offer a change of surroundings and people to keep them mentally stimulated. Otherwise, the Gemini partner will start getting moody and difficult, and the whole thing will be a washout.

These two like a swell party. The office entertainment expenses could roll sky high. Leo, however, has a cautious financial mind, and probably will be better at balancing the books than Gemini. Gemini, though, will be better at gaining the advantage in tricky financial negotiations.

LEO AND CANCER
IN BUSINESS TOGETHER

This is not going to be an easy combination. The Lion and the Crab are so very different. Cancer people get terribly wrapped up in their own emotional problems. They find it difficult to be objective about other matters when they are down. Also, when they have a touch of the blues, they have trouble relating to the outside world. In fact, they retreat within themselves to try and get away from it.

The Lion, not happy having to play mother every now and again in a business arrangement, will growl and carry on. Although kindhearted and sympathetic, a Leo business partner will expect his or her opposite number to leave their emotional hangups at home, where they probably originated.

But despite the emotionalism, the Crab has much to offer in any business venture. It is likely, and probably most advisable, that this partnership will choose a commercial line that allows both partners to employ their creative talents. Cancer people have deep romantic natures and fertile imaginations, which need only a positive direction to be translated into lucrative talents.

The Crab often does not make the most of his or her undoubted abilities. The Leo partner, with characteristic energy and drive, will be a great help. The Cancer person cannot help but be impressed with the way the Lion genuinely tries to help those who help themselves.

The Leo partner must try to be more tactful and diplomatic in dealing with the Crab. The Lion tends to call a spade a spade. Cancer people cannot stand personal criticism. Even when none is intended, they are inclined to see imagined slights. This will be very difficult for the Leo person to come to terms with. If the Cancer partner becomes too emotionally demanding, the Lion may call the whole thing off.

But the Lion has much to learn from this gentle and intuitive person. Cancer often puts on a far tougher front than he or she feels. This works splendidly in pressured financial negotiations.

These two partners should have no problems with the financial side. Both are economical when it comes to ensuring future security. Yet both enjoy their comforts and stylish entertaining. On the lighter and less serious side, they will forge strong personal ties. If they can last as a business combination, they should go from strength to strength.

LEO AND LEO
IN BUSINESS TOGETHER

Two Leos could get very competitive with each other over people, territory, profits, ideas—you name it! A lot of concessions are going to have to be made on both sides here. Although these two enthusiastic and warm-hearted people, with their imagination and flair for organizing, appear to be a perfect business duo, it is very doubtful whether they could operate for long in harness together.

These are two very strong personalities. They cannot help but impose their will and presence on everyone with whom they have close contact. As genuinely and sincerely as they may agree to work together toward the common aim, eventually the dominant sides of their characters will clash—and claw.

A partnership might possibly work better if they could each have a section of the business that they feel is their own. Leos love responsibility. As long as they are the one making the immediate decisions, they will work day and night to achieve a mutual objective.

It is often wrongly thought that Leo people have to be the big boss at the top. If that were true, there would be no Leos on the way up. Or else everywhere they operated would be chaos, as they scrambled over the next person's desk. Leos are very good at following an overall plan, as long as it has been drawn up by someone whom they respect at the top.

Leos have a sincere way of accepting the authority of anyone who has already made it, as long as they are still well down the ladder and climbing. In fact, it is this ability to follow top policy and instructions that is very much the key to their ultimate rise to success.

If two Leos can agree on a plan, the first hurdle is jumped. Then if they work in separate but equal bailiwicks toward its fruition, they might just manage to stay together.

Leos are straightforward. There will be no grudges harbored here. If either has something to say, it will be said. Leos manage to keep the air clear around them. The trouble is that others sometimes are inhibited by their manner and are not as honest to the Lion as the Lion likes to imagine. One partner will have to see that this does not happen with the staff; and also that certain members of the staff do not make use of Leo pride to play one partner against the other.

It is not a good idea for these two Leos ever to start competing. The strength of their personalities should be directed to achievement. It will allow them to overcome many of the problems in the business, rather than in their personalities. The question is, for how long can two Leos maintain a nonpersonal set of objectives?

LEO AND VIRGO
IN BUSINESS TOGETHER

Leos are born leaders. They have to be boss. They are creative and broad-minded. They cannot be bothered much with details. Virgos work best acting under instruction or following a blueprint. They are excellent at handling detail, but they are not particularly concerned with personal power and authority. Could there be a better business match? It is doubtful!

The areas where these two partners would possibly clash are fairly minor. But the clashes will not become grudges.

The Virgo person loves to analyze people. They are the kind who manage to stay in the background while observing everyone and everything going on around them. They want to know why things happen and especially what makes others tick. The Virgo partner will have plenty of material to explore in his or her Leo partner. The Lion's way of parading out front and his or her magnificent self-confidence will be eternal mysteries to the modest and cautious Virgo partner.

But Virgo will admire the energy and drive that the Lion brings to the partnership. Virgo also will appreciate the imaginative ideas of his or her partner that will help to keep the business up to date, and probably ahead of their rivals. Virgo people, on the other hand, are very good at solving production and personnel problems. They can devise systems out of apparent chaos. And they are not afraid of hard work.

The Leo partner cannot help but notice and learn from his or her Virgo partner the refreshing quality of modesty. Virgo people are seldom ego trippers. They are prepared to do their best. They leave it to others to extoll their virtues. They do like to be appreciated, though. They never boast and draw attention to their achievements like Leos are inclined to do, but wait for a perfect moment of recognition.

Being shrewder than they may appear on the surface, the Virgo partner in this combination will be aware of the Leo contribution to the partnership. Rather than dwell on Leos' conceited and patronizing ways, Virgos graciously allow Leo the floor.

But there will be times when each gets on the others' nerves. Virgos are inclined to be fussy and critical. They want everything to be in its right place. A creative person like Leo the Lion may fail to see overseeing as anything more than getting into a rut. Also, the Lion does not take kindly to any personal criticism. There will be loud roaring around the place if Virgo tries to tidy Leo up.

LEO AND LIBRA
IN BUSINESS TOGETHER

A business partnership combining Leo and Libra talents will go a long way fast. They would do very well together in any field requiring creative work and imagination or in any area dealing with the public. From party caterers to public relations, Leo and Libra could make a swell team.

Libras have quick minds. They admire a good intellect. They are great believers in fair play. This partner would never do anything underhanded if it could be avoided. He or she will admire the way Leo also insists on giving everyone as fair a deal as possible. Together they could easily make some worthy cause a sideline to their partnership activities. Both are likely to have strong views about the rights of the underdog.

What these two have to guard against is becoming a mutual admiration society. Leo people can listen to flattery all day without ever doubting the sincerity of the offering. Libras like to maintain harmony at any cost. When the Lion starts roaring for attention or action, the Libra partner could easily be guilty of buttering him or her up.

Libras are not fond of hard work, especially of the physical or boring kind. They are better at public relations, probably the best of all the signs in the Zodiac. They have a natural and easygoing charm that will be very helpful to the partnership, especially if there are influential people or clients to entertain. No one makes a better host or hostess than the person born under the sign of Libra.

Where this partnership could shine would be in the entertainment industry. Leo is the showperson of the Zodiac. And Libras like nothing more than to be associated with glamorous people and situations, which are synonymous with showbiz. Libras also make wonderful restaurateurs and chefs. With Leo out front and Libra preparing the goodies and decorations inside, any of the pleasure industries could provide the partnership with a comfortable living.

One problem is that Leo looks for consistency in his or her partners, and Libra does tend to blow hot and cold. What is supported today with boundless enthusiasm may tomorrow leave Libra detached and disinterested. The Lion and Lioness have short tempers, and they will be showing their partner just what it's like to be surrounded by disharmony if Libra starts any of this nonsense. The Libra partner with the Lion around better come to a quick decision and then stick to it.

LEO AND SCORPIO
IN BUSINESS TOGETHER

At the roots of the Leo personality is the sign of Scorpio. Both Leo and Scorpio are fixed signs. So these two partners are going to have something in common. It needs to be something more than the desire for power, which both possess so strongly. Otherwise, this relationship is doomed from the start.

Fortunately, Leo people really want only one thing out of power—their own personal aggrandizement. They are the types who like to strut around at the center of things, feeling the admiring gaze of an audience focused on them. They are harmless in their lust for applause. They do not like using petty or shoddy methods to get ahead. They have a strong sense of justice and fair play.

Scorpio is a different kettle of fish. This person loves power for power's sake. To the Scorpio partner, Leo's conceited parading around probably would be regarded as immaturity or weakness. Scorpio would note the fact and file it away for use on some future occasion.

Partnership with Scorpio can be a risky business. They are secretive and uncommunicative. Heaven help the partner who tries to fool or cheat him or her. Scorpio does not forgive or forget easily.

Yet there will be many qualities about the Scorpio partner that the Lion or Lioness will admire. Their capacity for hard work, for one thing. No other sign in the Zodiac has quite the same staying power. Leos are no slackers themselves, but to keep up with Scorpio's drive and stamina could mean endangering the Lion's health.

Scorpio people also have good business heads on their shoulders. They are realists. Their vision is not limited, just cautious. They do have a long view, and can spot opportunities for making money in the future—years ahead. They will work toward these aims with unwavering determination.

Leo will be a great help in this partnership by providing imaginative ideas and sparks of creativity. The Scorpio partner will also appreciate the Lion's organizing abilities.

Scorpio and Leo will, of course, have to come to some power-sharing agreement. Without this, the partnership will not fall apart but burst apart. Both are fixed signs, which makes them obstinate and unwilling to change their opinions or admit they are in the wrong. Both are realistic enough to appreciate the other's qualities and overlook flaws for the sake of making money.

LEO AND SAGITTARIUS
IN BUSINESS TOGETHER

Sagittarius and Leo can be a very profitable and rewarding business relationship. Besides, the two partners are likely to become the very best of friends. They will have much in common, including a similar sense of humor. After a busy day working together, they have the heart and spirit to team up for a night on the town.

The Leo partner probably will assume the role of leader. But this will only be with the tacit consent of the Archer, who will not take orders from anyone unless he or she feels like it. Sagittarius are not vitally interested in taking on responsibility or power, mainly because these roles interfere with their freedom to get around.

With Leo running things back at the office, the Archer will be able to get out and around and meet people, which she or he loves doing. Sagittarius individuals are especially good on the marketing and sales side of an operation. They have the gift of gab and a natural way of making most people they meet feel as though they are long-lost buddies. The Sagittarius way of doing business is frequently to turn a conference into a party.

Although Leo will not always approve of his or her Sagittarius partner's unconventional methods, the Lion will be the first to acknowledge their undoubted success. Sagittarius fixes their own patterns for living and business, and will not be browbeaten into changing their habits by anyone.

Some people might think that these two extroverts in partnership together may clash when it comes to grabbing the limelight. Both love to be at the center of attention, as well as the life and soul of the party. But Leo does have a regal approach, which limits the lengths he or she will go to. Not so for Sagittarius. These free spirits feel bound by no conventions except their own moods of the moment. Even Leo will be in the front row applauding.

In spite of a fun-loving nature, Sagittarius has a natural feel for business. These men and women have uncanny insights that enable them to make decisions with little preparation and reference to detail. They seem to be lucky. Even when they make mistakes, they usually land on their feet.

The Archer is very good at earning money but not at holding onto it. It would be a good idea if Leo took charge of the finances. Sagittarius is a sincere and outspoken character. There will be no secrets or behind-the-scenes shenanigans with this partner.

LEO AND CAPRICORN
IN BUSINESS TOGETHER

The Capricorn man or woman sometimes lacks the drive and initiative to get to the top of the peak. Perhaps they are content on level ground. They have lots of ambition and desire to be successful, but often fail to make the most of opportunities. A Leo partner could be just the person to get the Goat highly motivated.

Once Capricorn people start climbing in the right direction, they seldom fail to realize their objectives. It could be that Leo, the born leader, eventually finds himself or herself happily hanging onto the shirttail of the Goat as they clamber up to the summit.

Leos do not like having emotional hangups introduced into their business world. They let others know where they stand and expect the same treatment. The trouble with the Goat is that he or she is so wrapped up in his emotions that often he cannot see the forest for the trees. He needs bringing out of himself. He also needs lots of attention if his full potential is to be realized. This will not go down too well with the Lion, who needs a lot of attention himself.

Capricorn individuals are often their own worst enemy. They are so afraid of being laughed at or made a fool of that they often venture nothing and end up in a deep rut. They make their decisions in terms of security. A Leo partner will be a great help in showing them that there is not so much to fear in the big wide world, after all.

For a long time, Capricorn people do not really know what they want out of life. They have tremendous potential locked up in them, but cannot seem to get it out. If Leo can manage to get close to this person, not only as a partner but also as friend, he or she will discover a very capable and efficient person underneath.

The Capricorn person is disciplined, and has a ruthless streak that few people would ever believe he or she possesses; they keep it well hidden. But anyone who crosses them in business will soon find out they have taken on more than they had bargained for.

The Leo partner will certainly be impressed by the way his or her opposite number can shift the work. When it comes to taking responsibility, the Capricorn partner will accept it without showing any flap or strain, even under the most sustained pressures.

Leo may be put out by the offhand and brusque manner his or her partner displays at times. But for Capricorn, this rude reserve is merely a means of covering up the sensitive feelings that lie inside.

LEO AND AQUARIUS
IN BUSINESS TOGETHER

Leo and Aquarius gaze uncertainly at each other across the Zodiac. They are opposite each other in the sequence of signs. It is not so much that they are incompatible, because opposites often manage to fit in quite well together in a business linkup. The trouble is that these two never seem to be able to understand each other. If they can just get down to business and forget about trying to work each other out, all will be well.

Both are outgoing, outward-looking people, and this is good. There will be no emotional hangups to get in the way. In fact, the Water Bearer is probably the most unemotional type in the Zodiac. He or she likes to approach life from a logical point of view. The Lion will appreciate this.

However, the Aquarius person can be too detached and offhanded. They are not really the business types, mainly because they are interested in people and humanity as a whole. They really want to put the world to rights. Business, with its purely material aims, is likely to be felt as a compromise. It will be easy for the Aquarius partner to lose interest. This tendency has to be judged accurately by any Lion contemplating a commercial arrangement with Aquarius.

Still, the Water Bearer has much to contribute to any undertaking that maximizes his or her talents. For instance, Aquarius are extremely intelligent people. They are among the most progressive thinkers in the Zodiac.

If this business is connected with inventions, scientific research, social welfare, writing, broadcasting, publishing, and even space technology, the mental skills of this partner will soon be apparent. However, if he or she is an unconventional type, it may disturb the Leo partner suddenly to find his or her opposite number acting completely out of character.

One danger will be that Aquarius has too many varied interests. He or she will often be missing or absent attending to matters outside the business relationship. These people need plenty of mental stimulation to keep them absorbed in any project. They are not particularly good at hard physical work, either.

If they are discontented, they become more and more cranky and irritated, until finally they may just walk out without any explanation whatsoever. The hardworking, conscientious Lion is never going to figure this guy or gal out. As a result, the whole thing could be quite a gamble.

LEO AND PISCES
IN BUSINESS TOGETHER

No one, especially the Lion, should be fooled by the Pisces air of idealism or mystery. Even though this man or woman appears to have his or her head high in the clouds, shrewdness is never lacking. People born under the sign of the Fishes often have very astute business minds. It suits their purpose to appear vague and dreamy. Very often they are able to lull their competitors into a false sense of security.

This man or woman is capable of achieving marvelous results when they put their mind to it. But concentration could be one of the main problems. The absent-minded professor could have been born under the sign of Pisces. The Fishes are evasive and difficult to pin down. These people change their minds with alarming regularity.

How is all this going to go down with a Leo business partner? Well, the Lion is not the King of the Concrete Jungle that represents the business world. So he or she will benefit splendidly from a close commercial association with the Fishes, who do know how to swim in that tough world.

For a start, Leo, whose ideas are generally fixed, will learn the value of being more flexible and relaxed as a means of getting the best of a deal. The Fishes never lay down the law or start pounding a table. He or she just swims away, or round and round, perfectly content to let matters take their course, while relying on their fabulous intuition to tell them what to do next.

A Pisces business partner will at times drive the Lion up the wall with exasperation. Pisces people are very unpredictable. Their moods change like lightning. One minute they will be saying one thing, the next minute doing the exact opposite. For the Lion, who likes to know where he or she stands every moment, this could be very annoying.

Also, the Pisces business partner is likely to get down in the dumps suddenly for no apparent reason. One day they may be shooting ideas across the table twenty to the dozen. At the follow-up session they may sit in a moody silence that can last for hours or days.

What the Pisces business partner lacks in practicality he or she will make up for in imagination. These people are wonderful at thinking up business ideas that have never occurred to anyone before. Naturally, some of their schemes are so fanciful that no one in their right mind would go along with them. But Leo will find that it is mostly the Fishes' ideas that turn out to be the money-makers.

Leo:
Parents and Children

How will a child born under a different Sun sign respond to a Leo parent? And how will the youngster be as a toddler, an adolescent, a teenaged boy or girl? Will there be changes? What kind?

These questions and suggested answers make up one of the most overlooked aspects of astrological psychology. The *Astroscope Profile* series provides in-depth discussions of these questions and answers in this chapter.

Parents who take the trouble to read and understand the Sun sign descriptions of their children may certainly save the kids from future psychological problems, and at the same time make life easier for themselves. The child's natural urges can be anticipated, and opportunities provided for the youngsters to express these in positive ways. The negative side of the nature also can be watched for and handled with intelligent understanding as soon as it appears.

But parenthood is a kind of partnership. Success usually means turning out a balanced and integrated young personality capable of coping with the adult pressures and creating a reasonably fulfilling life. This depends a great deal on the temperament and character of *both* child and parent. How will each take to the other despite the natural bond of parental and filial love?

This chapter describes the likely interaction and compatibility between the Leo parent and children born under each of the twelve signs. Each section first describes family togetherness and likely modes of behavior and response. Then there follow points about the child's developing character as an infant, a youngster, and a teenager.

LEO PARENTS
AND ARIES CHILDREN

There will seldom be a quiet moment in this household. Aries and Leo are both fire signs. This means that parent and child will have something very subtle and precious in common. It also means that they both will want to rule the roost together and will be quite noisy about it as they attempt to divide up territory.

The Aries child will love to be with a Leo mom or dad. The other parent could sometimes feel left out. As these two fire signs will argue, play, and generally clown around together, other people get wearied. Leo is the sign of children. A Leo parent often dotes on his or her youngsters to such an extent that the parent fails to see any faults in them. Yet when they do discover the inevitable failings in their little idols, they can be extremely strict. This is not going to go down too well with the Aries boy or girl, who does not like to toe the line. But Leo is in a way just as determined as Aries. The youngster will soon learn that Dad or Mom Lion, when they say they are going to do something, stick to it.

Aries children are often precocious, mentally far more advanced than their years. They love activities that exploit their vivid imaginations. Leo is the sign of creativity. The Aries youngster can count on many stimulating hours of lively conversation as well as plenty of suggestions for exciting things to do. Aries children usually have one or two projects going at the same time. The Leo dad or mom will take just as much interest, if not more, in any that requires the injection of bright new ideas.

There will be some tears from young Aries as the Leo parent insists on taking the lead in whatever they are doing together. This will be more of a problem as the teenaged years are reached, unless the Lion parent learns to take more of a back seat. The Aries child also has a fundamental urge to take the lead and should be allowed as much freedom as is reasonable without always having to account to a higher parental authority.

Leo parents have to learn to listen to the good advice of others. In their desire to turn a child into a person who can cope with the demands of adult life, they can be too strict and at times overbearing. Although they are usually not nearly as fierce as their leonine roar, they may on occasion go to extremes and create unnecessary tension around the house.

The Aries child even as a teenager will tend to respect the Leo parent. Leos have a commanding presence and are not the types to bow down to anyone. These are qualities very much a part of the Aries nature as well. In this regard, the relationship could become something of a mutual admiration society.

The impulsiveness of the Aries youngster is likely to get on Leo's nerves. Leos are fairly fixed in their opinions. They want life to keep going in the direction they have become used to. The Aries son or daughter is much more flexible and inclined to dart and weave from one activity to another, often without bothering to finish those they know they can complete. The Leo parent will be inclined to frown on this, but should eventually get around to realizing that once an Aries person sees they have mastered a project they tend to lose interest. The Aries boy or girl never turns down a challenge, though he or she is disdainful of routine.

Aries teenagers will soon get the idea that flattery will often allow them to curl Mom or Dad Leo around their little finger. But the Leo and Aries combination should produce a young adult who becomes a worthwhile member of society.

Infant Aries

The Aries infant will soon demonstrate to doting Mom and Dad that he or she was born under the restless first sign of the Zodiac. "Me first" will be the message right from the start. Words will not be necessary: just a boisterous, full-blooded cry for instant attention. Aries types, young and old, never can wait. If a thing is in reach, they grab it. If it catches the eye outside the crib, they are up and over—and possibly down, with a fall. Aries is the sign of pioneers and adventurers. Falls, bumps, bruises, cuts, and scratches, especially from the cat, are all in a day's experience to these young daredevils. It is especially important not to leave boiling saucepans on the stove or other dangerous things within tumbling distance of an Aries infant. Somehow they can usually manage the impossible when it comes to action.

These are very active and energetic little people. They are early talkers and walkers. They are as bright as buttons and full of life. They are angry in a flash and forget it the next moment. They can be destructive, especially of toys they cannot work. If they can't master a game, they are likely to throw it down and break it just to have the last word.

Young Aries

At school, Aries youngsters will not learn too well if they are forced to delve into detail. They excel in work and activities that allow them to show off their lively imagination. Once their interest is aroused, they learn very quickly. But the danger is that they will race ahead, depending on their quick minds and good memories for answers, instead of understanding what they are doing. They are very impatient young people. They become easily bored by repetition.

Aries boys and girls are extremely curious. They are always asking questions. They are eager to experience life to the full and to learn all about it in three seconds flat. Parents have to make sure these children understand the basics of what they are supposed to be learning. Often they skip over fundamentals. When exam time comes around, they flunk—to everyone's surprise, especially their own.

These youngsters are likely to roam. Parents of Aries children have to be prepared for them getting lost. They can't resist the urge to explore the unknown even if it is only hopping on a passing bus or streetcar. They usually are good at sports. But unless they can take a leading or impressive role, they are inclined to lose interest.

Teenage Aries

The Aries teenager is a very independent young person. Both he and she are inclined to think they know more than everyone else. At least they are very sure of what is best for them.

They are often brash and inconsiderate, a law unto themselves. Unless they have received a good deal of understanding and love in the early years, they can start to take it out on the rest of the world.

Aries teenagers exude an air of self-sufficiency that can make adults believe they are not in need of much affection and love. They are inwardly sensitive and need more loving guidance and attention than their independent airs indicate.

These young people are naturally honest and trusting. It is only through others that they learn to be otherwise. They should be put into positions of trust. They should be given the opportunity to meet challenges that will win them admiration and praise, instead of pursuing dares that get them in trouble.

Sex is one of the dares that Aries teenagers will meet when challenged by their peers. Sex is an area in which the young Aries has not had much independence and precious little experience. So early experimentation serves a dual purpose: showing off to friends and proving something to themselves.

Here is where the parent must come in. Their teenage Aries youngsters are too likely to plunge into sexual freedom without knowledge or protection. Pregnancy is one danger, worse for their daughter than their son. But the Leo parent is not likely to preach the double standard. Escapades in fast cars are another danger, often attracting the unfavorable attention of the law.

Suitable parental guidance, and it can't be too subtle, can forewarn their teenage Rams. The parents can discuss the dangers of freedom without responsibility, as well as the intricacies of social acceptance and pressure with all the price tags. The parents' message to their teenage youngsters should help to modify any behavior the kids exhibit with companions outside of the home.

LEO PARENTS
AND TAURUS CHILDREN

At no time from infanthood to adolescence should this relationship between a Leo parent and a Taurus son or daughter become a battle for supremacy. The Leo mom or dad will understand right from the start that the young Bull is unbelievably obstinate. This will reveal itself well before the child starts talking. In fact, Taurus children are often late talkers, but they make up for it by being quite active movers.

Leo people, with their great sense of pride and authority, tend to think that everyone should do as they say. They know very well themselves that all they want is the greatest good for the other person and that all this talk of their being on a perpetual ego trip is sheer nonsense.

Taurus at any age is not going to be browbeaten. Taurus at any age does not acknowledge that anyone knows what is good for them better than they do. Added to this, Taurus is the most stubborn sign in the Zodiac.

The Taurus child, especially the boy, may take longer than most to get out of diapers. These young Bulls are inclined to be lazy. Any activity that demands that they exert themselves more than necessary except toward something that they want is ignored or refused. The reason is that Taurus is the sign of physical comfort. These people are well into their senses. They learn only by experience, not by being told.

It is not easy to reason with a Taurus youngster once he or she has made up their mind. This will upset the Leo mom or dad, who pride themselves on their ability to explain things. The Leo fur is likely to fly when the young Bull, being given a good talking to, looks right through Mom or Dad. That "gone elsewhere" expression that Taurus people get when they are determined not to hear can be maddening.

On the positive side, a Leo parent and a Taurus son or daughter will not only love each other, but also will have mutual respect. Once they find a way around their natural inflexibility, they will admire the way each gets down to brass tacks. The Taurus nature is very much down-to-earth. These young people can see a situation as it is without getting carried away by imagination.

The Leo parent should watch for any early signs of creativity in this child. Venus, the planet of beauty and beautiful things, rules Taurus. With their practical turn of mind, they are often able to use their hands to make things. Giving the youngster a little bit of training and encouragement, the Leo parent could have a budding young sculptor, woodworker, weaver, or maker of handicrafts in the family.

However, Taurus youngsters will need gentle leading until they discover what they like to do. On no account should the Taurus boy or girl be allowed to get their own way more than is reasonable. They will usually choose the self-indulgent way if left to their own devices. They can become quite selfish. It is unlikely that a Leo mom or dad would stand for this, but the other parent might if they like a quiet life.

The Leo parent at some time or other will be struck by this young person's sense of loyalty. The Taurus youngster will stick by their parents or their friends through thick and thin, even though on many occasions it may be found that their faith in others has been misplaced.

A Taurus boy or girl usually is born with a sound sense of material values. They often do well in their adult lives because they are prepared to work hard to earn money and provide themselves with the luxuries they enjoy so much. They have strong likes and dislikes, but seldom are guilty of impulsiveness that may endanger their sense of security.

Infant Taurus

This is a child who is very easy to spoil. The young boy or girl Bull is usually very soft, round, and cuddly. They are not demanding types. That comes later. They are not silly, either. But when Mom or Dad can't resist picking them up often enough, they soon get the idea and start squealing for attention.

It has to be remembered that Taurus is a luxury-loving sign. So anything that comes near to making life more comfortable and congenial will quickly be seized on even by the Taurus infant. If handled intelligently, this little boy or girl will probably be a model of quiet and contented babyhood.

As long as they feel comfortable, Taurus infants will be easy to keep amused. They receive most of their assurances through their highly developed senses. They love to be cuddled and made a fuss of, to feel warm and loved. Even having soft and fine materials next to their skins can mean more to these children than it does to other infants. Furry toy animals and squeezable objects are good company in the crib.

Very early it will become apparent that Taurus infants have a mind of their own. If challenged, they can become very difficult. It is easier for a parent to go along with them or change the subject or distract the attention than to persist in trying to make them do what they do not want to do.

Young Taurus

Taurus children learn slowly. They are more physical than mental. They have to absorb the feel and situation of things by handling and touching. Parents and schoolteachers have to remember that it is no good rattling off facts and numbers and expecting these young people to remember them. They won't! And if this is the attitude of their teachers, these children can seem to be dull or backward.

Taurus children above all need educational toys. Handling them and moving them around and playing with them help the youngsters learn their arithmetic and spelling. Given the time to take things in their own way, they learn mathematics and language arts thoroughly.

It is seldom that the young Bull cannot be made to take an interest in music. Music is something that people born under this sign seem to have a natural aptitude for and appreciation of. Any musical talent should be encouraged as soon as it is revealed. Taurus youngsters often make good singers as well as instrumentalists.

It is easy to teach a Taurus youngster to be methodical. They fall quickly into habits. They should be given little chores to do around the house, which they will take pride in if given a good example. Anything they can touch, move, and put into place reinforces a careful and systematic approach to problem-solving.

Teenage Taurus

Taurus youngsters are usually attractive physically at an early age. They grow into fine-looking teenaged boys and girls who are very much in demand among their friends and acquaintances. Their ear for music and ability to dance make them popular in the disco scene.

Taurus teenagers always make a point of understanding in depth what interests them. They can build a reputation among their friends for being a whiz or expert in one hobby or another. They are fairly serious, although cars do turn them on. It's possible that the Taurus teenager likes cars more for the comfort and status they confer than for any love of mechanics or driving.

However, there is a great love of entertainment and being entertained. These teenaged Taurus boys and girls can quickly become bored, especially if they have been spoiled by their parents. They can get into selfish habits. Indulgence can be a problem in sharing situations.

Taurus teenagers are much more cautious than their confident manner may suggest. They are not inclined to take physical risks. They would much rather stay safely in the group than take the lead. Sports that require strength catch their interest more than show-off sports of skill, speed, and daring.

Sex on the experimental level may not become a pursuit of the Taurus teenager. Slightly shy and lacking the natural curiosity that characterizes other youngsters, they express sexual urges and sexual interests more through clothes, the company they keep, and the extracurricular activities they pursue. The parent should watch for these strategies in order to help their teenager learn the social graces so important to dating.

Some Taurus teenagers secretly wish to go steady, but may be too emotionally immature to handle such a situation. So they make a big splash with one set of costumes, companions, and cliques. Then they abandon these for new fashions, fads, and friends. Such behavior is uncharacteristic of the adult Taurus or one who has matured beyond the family scene. Again, the parent can point out how extravagant behavior creates problems and dangers, especially in relating sincerely to people.

LEO PARENTS
AND GEMINI CHILDREN

Leo and Gemini are basically compatible signs. The fire of Leo responds cozily to the airy, communicative nature of Gemini. But a Gemini child will often try the patience of a Leo mom or dad. This parent will laugh at and enjoy the spontaneous antics of their son or daughter born under the sign of the heavenly Twins. Normally, enough is enough, but never for Gemini. The love of activity, variety, and change goes on and on. Something will have to give pretty often, and it probably will be Leo cracking down on this extraordinarily mercurial character.

Mischief is the one thing that young Gemini cannot help getting into. The problem is that these kids are so active mentally and physically they soon run out of things to keep them entertained. It will be a ceaseless task for the parent thinking up activities to keep this boy or girl busy.

The Leo mom or dad will appreciate the lively intelligence of their Gemini youngster. No doubt, with their own self-expressive nature, they will help this youngster find some creative outlet for the high-strung energy. Geminis learn quickly and easily. It is a good idea to watch for any special aptitudes they may show and to encourage them as much as possible in this direction.

It should be remembered that, unlike Leo, Gemini is extremely adaptable and is quite capable of carrying out two or three activities proficiently at the same time. Leo, the sign of creativity, is more inclined to find one thing to do well and to concentrate on that to the exclusion of anything else. In fact, this can become a fault with the Lion. Leos may not appreciate that other people, especially Geminis, need variety and change in their pastimes.

However, it is true that the Gemini youngster does tend to start numerous projects without finishing them. But with a Lion giving half of the parental guidance, this young person probably will be taught early the value of consistency.

The Leo parent could easily despair at times as his or her Gemini charge enters adolescence. Leo will worry what the future holds for this changeable and restless young character. It is a good thing if the studious urge of the youngster in the early years has been applied to learning a trade or skill. But it has to be said that Geminis frequently end up jacks-of-all-trades and masters of none.

They are usually well suited for any vocation requiring quick thinking and a constant change of scene or things to do. They are clever and skillful at light manual work, but seldom are to be seen when jobs involving hard labor are handed out. This youngster may succeed as a secretary, short-hand-typist, computer programer, salesperson, lecturer, teacher, or writer.

It also has to be said that Geminis can be con artists! This is due to their very plausible attitude. They are great talkers and able to sense what the other party wants to hear. Sometimes they may be accused quite rightly of answering questions purely to please so as not to create any ill feeling.

The Leo mom or dad with their strong ideas about straight talking are likely to put an early end to any Gemini tendency to be two-faced and cunning. These young people are so mentally dexterous that if not checked, they can grow into the habit of starting arguments to practice their quick wit.

Like their leonine parent, Gemini youngsters have a great sense of drama and like to be the center of attention. These kids instinctively know how to praise the Leo parent in order to get their own way.

Infant Gemini

A Gemini infant is very quick to learn and to mimic. It will not be long before this child is amazing its parents with the things it can do and say. It is especially quick at picking up words and actions.

The parent of a Gemini toddler will soon learn that this little boy or girl cannot be left alone for more than a few seconds without getting into some sort of mischief. They are extremely quick at moving, whether on their knees or feet. They can be out the door in no time, or into the cupboard where the best china is stored.

Gemini children at a very early age show an intelligent interest in what is happening around them. They should be given crayons and pencils and paper as soon as their deft little hands can hold them. Then they can express themselves and work off their abundance of mental energy.

The curiosity of these children makes it very difficult for them to concentrate on any one thing for very long. They need great variety in their toys and games. It is not unusual for parents of these kiddies to become wearied, either chasing after them or answering their incessant questions, which they frequently cannot wait to be answered before asking the next.

Young Gemini

The immediate environment is of vital interest to young Geminis. They will draw what they see and think. Soon they are stringing letters into words, and words into phrases on paper. It is important to get the Gemini child down to silent reading and written expression as soon as possible. Otherwise, they will interrupt classmates and teachers and parents with endless though spirited recitations.

At school, young Gemini is likely to have some problems. He or she will be among the brightest in the class, probably first up with their hands when questions are being asked about current events or controversial topics. But when it comes to anything old or routine, the Gemini youngster is likely to be disinterested or just plain bored.

Young Gemini may disturb his or her parents by the number of activities that are started but never finished. Parents may despair at their child's inability to concentrate. But this is typical of the Gemini nature. Parents are advised to encourage them in each new project, helping them to see the broad overview, even though they won't see the project through to a conclusion.

The Gemini urge is to learn by experimentation. Anything novel is immediately absorbed. Their minds are always active. It is not a good idea to allow them to become too excited before going to bed. Chances are, they will not sleep. Sometimes Gemini children develop a stutter because their minds work faster than their tongues. Nevertheless, this impediment doesn't stop them from verbalizing.

Teenage Gemini

The Gemini teenager as a rule does not spend as much time at home as most other types do. Geminis are often among the first teenagers to leave home. It is not that they can't stand the family or their homes. They just need constant variety and change. These youths are not runaways or truants, just absentees for short periods of time.

The Gemini teenager probably will roam often but not far, especially if he or she is handled with understanding. Although their curiosity often leads them into dubious company and situations, they have a knack for avoiding trouble. They are survivors once they have learned something of the ways of the world. And a little knowledge does not take them long to absorb and use.

But it seems to take a long time for the Gemini teenager to grow up. Not only do they look younger than their years, which is often annoying to them, but also they refuse to satisfy their parents' expectations by eventually settling down. Geminis can be in their thirties before they start to show a desire to quit their restless, chattering, gallivanting ways.

It is essential for parents to see that their teenage Geminis get sufficient sleep and rest, or their health may suffer. But the youngsters themselves usually have a hand in whatever regime is plotted for them. They will show up at mealtime, maybe; they will endure piano lessons, sometimes; they will abide by curfew, seldom.

Romance and sex usually interfere with Gemini teenagers' regime of exercise, rest, and nutrition. Studies and sports certainly do not get these youngsters off stride. But the excitement of the unknown can upset all their daily routine.

Sex and romance, their final youthful plunge into knowledge, can take them far afield, making them abandon piano lessons or basketball practice or early snacks at the hangout. They even can stay away from the house for a few days, or sneak out when they have been punished. But this little knowledge does not lead them into danger.

Somehow Gemini teenagers manage to avoid violence, pregnancy, venereal disease, and the long hand of the law or their companions' family when they break into this new frontier of experience and feeling and insight. Their own parents are usually amazed at the scrapes they get into and out of.

But then, of course, Geminis, teenagers notwithstanding, have lots of knowledge they picked up somewhere or other, here and there. They are always using this knowledge to protect themselves and their companions.

A mature head for responsibility on youthful shoulders seems like a contradiction. But Geminis, contradictory to the core, perform splendidly in emergency situations. Romantic and sexual adventures to the teenage Gemini are seen as emergency situations. Novelty and knowledge, which are secondary considerations, are the ones they will brag about, though.

LEO PARENTS
AND CANCER CHILDREN

It is terribly important for a Leo mom or dad to take it easy in dealing with this young Moon child. Cancer children can be a bit clinging in the early years. Their extreme sensitivity makes it difficult for them to let go of the apron strings. Leo, one of the most self-assured and authoritative signs of the Zodiac, can easily come on too strong in trying to make these youngsters stand on their own two feet.

The Leo mom or dad will find that as young Cancer grows into adolescence, he or she becomes far more independent and resourceful. In fact, as the years roll by, the Leo parent may feel at times that here is someone as tough and self-assured as themselves.

But there is a catch. Sure, Cancer is a far stronger sign than the evidence often suggests. But inside, behind the swagger and bravado, is a very soft and emotional person. In the early years, these Moon children depend on their almost mystical ability to absorb and interpret the feelings of the people and places around them.

The Leo parent is affectionate and loving. But they seldom carry their demonstrations of affection to the lengths that are likely to be demanded by the emotional needs of their Cancer kids. These children born under the sign of the Crab hunger to be loved with tenderness and sentimental devotion.

However, when this youngster grows up, and the Leo parents are looking forward to the ease of retirement, they need never worry about seeing their Cancer son or daughter and their grandchildren. Cancer always gives back the affection they received in their growing-up years. Also, these very loyal people have an innate urge to mother and protect. As the Lion and his or her mate grow old together, they will always be grateful that they had a Cancer youngster.

There will be times when the emotionalism of the Cancer young person becomes infuriating for the Leo parent. Leos have more than their share of emotion. But it is all outgoing; they rant, rave, and roar but seldom brood. Cancer people, on the other hand, often retreat emotionally within themselves, leaving others around them completely bamboozled by their inexplicably sudden change of mood. The sunny nature of the Leo parent will help to counteract these Cancer depressions.

However, it must be remembered that a Cancer child is ruled by the Moon. Their emotional natures ebb and flow something like the tides, controlled by the Moon. Half the time, a Cancer person is outgoing and surprisingly enterprising. They can be particularly ambitious and very tough business customers to deal with. The other half of their life is spent withdrawing from the world. This is how they repair their self-confidence, which, unlike Leo's, is not a fixture.

Leo is the sign of creative endeavor, and this is very good for Cancer. The parent will help to inspire their Cancer youngsters to make the most of any artistic inclinations they may have. Cancer people have a way with words. They are able to express themselves in pleasing and gentle ways, which under the right influence may be cultivated to become a writing ability. They are often natural poets.

However, there is a lazy side to the Cancer nature unless it is corrected in the early years. They can be inclined to moon around, to socialize idly, and to talk about their plans instead of getting on with the job of implementing them.

These youngsters love their home and the security it gives them. To have a strong and warmhearted Leo parent around, who does not overlook their deep sensitivity, can provide them with everything they need.

Infant Cancer

This child needs love more than anything else. Whereas the Taurus infant needs the reassurance of cuddling and touch, the Cancer infant needs even more. These little ones born under the sign of the Crab are deeply emotional beings. They need, above all, to feel they are wanted.

The Cancer child needs to be brought up in harmonious surroundings. Parental and family arguments create emotional strain in the child, even in the tenderest years or months. Any excessive crying and fretfulness that cannot be explained are often attributable to anxiety about a hostile environment.

During the infant stage, Cancer children are not very demanding as long as they feel affection around them. They will sit for hours playing quietly by themselves. They are usually very good with younger brothers or sisters, being quick to accept them as members of the family, for which they want to feel responsible in some little way or other.

The Cancer infant is often a slow developer. These littles ones learn more through their emotional feelings about things than through any concentrated mental activity. To encourage the growing Cancer infant, music and art should be introduced into the environment as early as possible. Musical toys and objects representing people, animals, and buildings should be available for the little one to play with and relate to.

Young Cancer

Growing up is often a painful process for the Cancer youngster. In spite of all the love and care lavished on these little people by their parents, their sensitivity causes them to feel hurt more often than most other types of children.

School days are sometimes an agony for them. They do not mix easily in the beginning. They tend to wait on their own for someone to approach them, rather than making any attempts at contact themselves. They are often teased, sometimes because they are inclined to be a bit fat or dumpy. Every hurtful jibe and comment, even though it may not really be meant, goes straight to the soul of the young Cancer person.

Parents should try to remember that appearances with a Cancer child do not always tell the full story. They may suffer in silence. Sympathy and understanding will help to bring them out of themselves, and perhaps help the parent to remedy a situation.

Cancer boys and girls, once they feel accepted by a group, are very active and vivacious. The more familiar they become with their surroundings and companions, the more likely they are to start showing their considerable initiative.

Teenage Cancer

By the time Junior Cancer reaches teenage, he or she is likely to be showing a good deal of swagger and self-assurance, at least on the outside. There can be something of the rebel in the late teenagers. They are not nearly as quick to obey as they were in their earlier years.

Also, in teenage, Cancer youngsters are likely to start showing the moody side of their nature. For a while they can be sunny and bright and outgoing. Then without warning they retreat deep inside themselves. They transmit inexplicable waves of gloom that are likely to affect everyone else in the household.

The slightest criticism is likely to send the Cancer teenager into a black mood. Even imagined hurts and slights will have the same result. There is something of the martyr in the Cancer nature, which makes these young people inclined to keep their problems to themselves. An intelligent parent has to endeavor to get them to open up, or the mood may go on for days. Love and sympathy displays can be the solutions.

The Cancer teenager has to be encouraged as much as possible to see his or her own emotional weaknesses. Otherwise, they can become intolerably demanding in later life.

Dating and sex could be the areas where the Cancer teenager first discovers how painful his or her emotions are. They want a steady boyfriend or girlfriend, but they may have a reputation for being difficult. It is not that the Cancer teenager is picky. Just moody!

Also, peer pressures around cars and clothes and spending money and sexual experimentation might be hard for the Cancer teenager to handle. This youngster may not be daring enough either to rebel against parental restrictions or to tell their friends off. And he or she is not likely to confide these worries to the parent.

Parents should try to draw their Cancer teenager out on such subjects as dating, sex, and peer pressures. Appearance and good looks, so important to these youngsters, must be considered. Also, it is never too early to explain the consequences of sexual freedom, for their Cancer teenager, deeply attached to home and family, may be thinking of starting their own family prematurely!

LEO PARENTS
AND LEO CHILDREN

Two Leos can be a rollicking combination. But there could be a problem for the other parent if he or she has to withstand the combined self-confidence and arrogance of these two cats. A Leo parent needs a loving though firm counterbalance from his or her partner in bringing up a Leo, or the child could grow into an unbearably bossy character.

It is to be hoped that the Leo parent has over the years learned some measure of humility and tolerance. Leos mean well. But the fact is they insist on thinking they know what is best for everyone. They try to turn their children into versions of themselves. The dangers here obviously do not have to be spelled out.

Given the right upbringing, the Leo child of a Leo parent is almost sure to make a success in life. They love to do things in a big way, with themselves at the center. If the creative side of this child's nature can be developed, they can make a name and fortune for themselves in several possible fields.

The Leo parent should watch for signs of writing ability. If the youngster in the teens spends hours a week writing love letters, it does not matter about the quality; the urge to literary expression is there. Leos also make good speakers. They have powerful presence. They also make fine teachers, although usually at the middle of their careers. Then they are successful and able to pass on their secrets, which they will do willingly, to others coming up the ladder.

The organizational ability of this boy or girl will be evident at an early age. Also, it will be nothing new to the Leo parent to realize that young Leo has a distinct flair for the dramatic, which may indicate future success as an actor, entertainer, or promoter.

The Leo mom or dad should endeavor to see that their youngster gives sufficient attention to detail in school studies. Leos can be inclined to cut corners. However, when they eventually discover what they want to do with their lives, they are among the most painstaking and conscientious workers in the Zodiac.

It is not a good idea to encourage a young Lion to spend his or her life competing. They are born with enough of the competitive instinct. What they need to be taught is that it is not always necessary to win or to be on top.

Leos need to feel needed. They also need lots of parental love. It would be a pity if the Leo parent was so caught up in their own world that they could not give sufficient time to this child in their leisure hours.

One of the most admirable qualities in a Leo that the parent will help to bring out is their sincerity and straightforwardness. These youngsters should never be exposed to praise for outsmarting the other fellow through devious means. This sort of thing from any authority conflicting with their own simple idea of honesty can create confusion and possibly lead to sharp practices in later life.

It has to be remembered that no matter what a child's natural propensities may be, the conditioning he or she is exposed to in the early years will have a great influence. Leo is the sign of born leaders, often associated with the kings and queens of old. This is because of their natural dignity, generosity, and sense of justice. Under the wrong conditioning, a Leo can just as easily end up leader of the local gangsters.

In teenage, a Leo boy or girl will be extremely popular. Mom or Dad will enjoy having many young friends in the home. Leo is the sign of pleasure and entertainment, as well as romance. Young Leos fall heavily in love when they do fall, as the adult Lion indulgently remembers.

Infant Leo

It will soon become evident to the parent of a Leo infant that this little person has to be the center of attention. The Leo child, even at the tender age of a couple of years, starts showing off. This behavior will not be quite the same as when other children go through a stage of juvenile exhibitionism. Other children grow out of it. The Leo child never does, but rather grows into it with a vengeance.

Any parent who shows a Leo infant true love will seldom have to worry about being lonely and neglected in old age. The Lion, like the elephant, never forgets. A loving mother or father always will have a secure place in the Leo heart.

This child knows unconsciously whether a parent really needs him or her. Leo is the sign of children. Although a natural show-off, right from the start the Leo child is extremely sympathetic. He or she should never be loaded even in jest with any sort of responsibility that is not intended. There is a tremendous seriousness in these toddlers under all the lightheartedness that compels them to do what is expected of them.

Although they will be as naughty and as mischievous as the rest, Leo children will fret about letting their parents, or those who love them, down. Their anxiety may express itself in unexpected bursts of tears or tantrums, especially when they are not able to converse more than with baby talk.

Young Leo

Young Leo's mind is quick. But his or her instinct to grab the limelight is quicker. At school, Leo children will work in the direction that gives them the most recognition. They are likely to be good scholars or tops at sports or the best fighters or the leaders of the gang.

Leo youngsters may take up numerous activities and abandon them while they endeavor to find one that suits them. When they do, they work imaginatively and conscientiously and seldom fail to reach their objectives.

Leo is a born leader. But it takes some time for these youngsters to get to understand themselves. Until they do, they cannot assume the powers of rulership that lie dormant within them. They can be little devils and bullies, boasting more than they can deliver. They need intelligent direction—and plenty of loving understanding.

Teenage Leo

Parents should endeavor to set their Leo youngsters on a positive course early in their teens. These boys and girls want to make a success of their lives. And if a certain direction seems to offer this, they will be inclined to cooperate and work toward it.

The teenaged Leo can be extremely proud and arrogant. They are not easy young people to control, especially if there is any attempt to boss them around. In their eyes they know all the answers, and any that they don't they will not admit to. Leo teenagers are not the types ever to admit they are wrong. Even when standing in the ruins of their own disastrous decisions, they are likely to justify their actions.

But these Lion-hearted boys and girls will be inclined to follow the advice of their parents, as long as they respect them and their opinions. Once they are disillusioned, however, as often happens in teenage, they are not likely to take advice from that place again.

Seldom are Leo adolescents successful both academically and physically. These young people put their heart and soul into whatever they attempt. They do not divide their energies.

Underneath the bravado of Leo is a loving and warmhearted individual who is only trying to find a mission in life.

Youthful sexual and romantic experiences can temporarily sidetrack the Leo teenager from discovering his or her true mission in life. Teenage Leos get hung up in love, possibly more so than other youngsters of the same age.

The Leo in love radiates immense happiness and enthusiasm, but often the enthusiasm is focused strictly on the girlfriend or boyfriend. Homework and sports practice can go by the boards. Unrequited love will send the Leo teenager into a spell of gloom and inactivity. Moping around the house and refusing invitations from friends, this lovesick cat will abandon all the things that gave him or her such pleasure before.

It is not unusual for Leo teenagers to put off college or job training to hang around with the object of their affection. They may take a "leave" from school or a year off before pursuing future goals just to travel with their romantic partner.

Such situations may result in an early marriage and a premature family. Leo is the sign of children, so when Leo teenagers outgrow their childhood, they think it's perfectly natural to start the next generation.

Parents are wise to help their Leo teenager see the options open to them, as well as the consequences. Love, romance, and children, pursued too early, might interfere with the youngster's mission in life. On the other hand, these pursuits might very well be Leo's true mission.

LEO PARENTS
AND VIRGO CHILDREN

A Leo parent will find a Virgo son or daughter a pleasure to bring up. These youngsters seldom give any trouble. They are diligent at their school-work, obedient and self-contained, neither aggressively independent nor fretfully dependent. They seem to do everything in moderation.

The only area in which the Lion is likely to have any problems with this child is in relation to the Virgo tendency to be prissy and fussy. Leo is a sign of people who are big thinkers. They like to do things in a big way and don't have much tolerance for handling detail.

Virgo is the sign of detail and discrimination. People born under this sign have analytical minds. So mom or dad Leo is not going to take it too well when Junior Virgo starts complaining about the cap being left off the toothpaste and little things being overlooked.

The Leo parent will do well to teach this youngster to use his or her imagination as much as possible. Usually, Virgos tend to use their imagination to break topics down, a sort of reverse process to what most others do. As a result, when a Virgo youngster looks at a thing or a situation, they see what has to be done to correct it, to restore it to normal. They may not see the infinite possibilities that could expand it and make it more interesting.

Leo, being the sign of creative imagination, will have much to give this child. However, the Lion, especially the parent who looks after the house, will be very grateful for the way their youngster keeps his or her room neat and tidy and is prepared to help around the house. It will be up to the parent to see that the methodical Virgo nature never is allowed to go to extremes. Otherwise, they could find this boy or girl following them around cleaning out ashtrays as soon as they have used them or putting away the Sunday paper before it has been read.

There could also be territorial squabbles for rights to the bathroom, which will have busy Leos tearing their hair out. As they grow into adolescence, Virgos can become extremely hung up on hygiene and cleanliness. Most people who take two or three baths or showers a day have the Sun or other important planets in Virgo.

Virgo youngsters are very cautious people. They never intrude. They are not the types to propose outlandish pranks or escapades to their young friends. In fact, to an up-and-at-'em self-assertive Leo parent, it may seem at times that Junior Virgo is just too staid and mature in the head for his or her own good. The Leo parent must be patient with this sensitive young person and understand that he or she has a totally different temperament from fiery Leo.

Virgo is an earth sign, which means they are restrained and like to look before they leap. But these people also can give Leo a good lesson in practicality. Everyone knows that Leo's ideas are sometimes just too grandiose to work. In any important plans it will not hurt to listen to Junior's observations. They can be incredibly discerning.

This brings us to the problem of faultfinding. A Leo parent frequently is going to be upset by young Virgo's well-intended criticism. Leo people can put up with just about anything except being told what is wrong with them. From a youngster—even worse, their own teenager—this may be unbearable for the proud Lion.

The Leo parent should remember that when it comes to a career, the Virgo nature responds to specialized training. They can easily make a name for themselves in the fields of science, mathematics, teaching, and the graphic arts. They are usually more contented working for someone than having to cope with top-management responsibilities.

Infant Virgo

This child is quite an early developer. Mercury, the planet that rules mental ability, governs the sign of Virgo. In a very short time, the parent of a Virgo toddler will be struck by the little one's quick comprehension. Even before he or she begins to talk, the child will be noticed to listen intently to what is being said.

These children are good mimics. It is important always to set a good example for them, or their antics in company may cause some embarrassment. Not that they are pushy or show-off types. Far from it! Virgo children are more inclined to sit in the background observing everything that is going on. As they develop and learn to converse, which is astonishingly early, they make very adult and wise comments or answers to questions.

Good common sense will start to be evident in this child at a very early age. A tendency to be shy may have to be corrected. Virgo toddlers learn very quickly and can be taught to put away toys and to keep their rooms tidy. To these little ones, helping around the house comes naturally and is often played as a game.

Young Virgo

At school, Virgo youngsters are likely to be regarded as ideal students. Their minds are very orderly, and they do things methodically. They have a love of sorting out detail, which many other children despise. Virgo children are quick to learn mathematics. They soon become proficient at writing and speaking.

Young Virgo is very sensitive. It takes these youngsters a longer time than usual to mix freely in company. They are inclined to sit apart, reading books or concentrating on writing or drawing. They would dearly love to join in, but find it extremely difficult to make the first move.

Parents have to be careful not to try to push this child into company. The entrance should be slow and natural, possibly through the device of a party where children can informally get to know each other. It is important for Virgo children to have at least one little friend early in life who can help them across the relationship barrier.

Once sure of their ground, Virgo children are active and happy in play as well as in formal company. They are popular among their playmates for their ability to think up interesting games for wet afternoons. Their minds naturally go to activities requiring pencils, paper, counting, and problem-solving. They are usually good at puzzles and games.

Without materials for writing or drawing and without puzzles or games to work out, the Virgo child nevertheless is a master at entertainment. Virgo youngsters can spin tales of mystery and adventure that keep their companions delighted for hours.

Teenage Virgo

The Virgo teenager is not usually rebellious. For this there will need to be some unsettling influences from other planetary placements. The Virgo teenager is likely to be fairly serious, aware of what is going on in the world and what needs to be done to make it a better place to live in.

Virgo teenagers are inclined to be studious, often avid readers. They enjoy discussions and debates. They have excellent memories for details. They can be interested in religion and any other formalized system of morality or philosophy.

But by this time, the Virgo teenager's main fault is likely to be evident. Virgos cannot help being critical. The Virgo teenager is likely to turn his or her critical eye on parents, friends, relatives—anyone at all—and make the most bone-chilling and disturbingly accurate observations.

What motivates Virgo people to do this is that they strive to make the world a perfect place, an obvious impossibility. They try to correct any fault or disorder that they spot. And with their discerning attention, they can find a lot to criticize. Virgo teenagers can be precocious in their knowledge of worldly affairs.

Precociousness, however, is not apparent in the Virgo teenager's attitude and approach to sex. These young people may already have an obsession with neatness and cleanliness. Fears about personal well-being may be aroused at the thought of actual sexual experiences.

Virgo teenagers are fairly knowledgeable about sex, even if they are completely innocent, because they read and listen so much. They probably know more about abortion, birth control, and pregnancy than some adults do. But young Virgos, whose concerns around health and hygiene may become phobic, are afraid to experiment.

The parents of a Virgo teenager probably sigh with relief, thinking they don't have to worry about the youngster getting in trouble. But if not intelligently guided, the Virgo teenager can get into another kind of trouble—unpopularity.

The teenager may avoid all physical demonstrations of affection and even mild sexual fun. Parents must help him or her develop prudence, rather than prudishness, and so go forward to enjoy dating and romantic attachments.

LEO PARENTS
AND LIBRA CHILDREN

Leo and Libra get along together like a house on fire, as a rule. The Leo parent, although more forceful and self-confident than a youngster born under the sign of the Scales, lives the kind of active life that will keep young Libra mentally stimulated.

Libra is an air sign, which means these people are communicative and need lots of company around them and a changing scene. In fact, as the youngster grows up, this parent-child combination could be too much of a good thing. Both Leo and Libra take to the social scene like ducks to water. It could be that the other parent may feel left out at times when these two swingers get going.

Leo parents often fail to see the faults in their children. They are so busy trying to bring them up as little versions of themselves that they fail to keep an eye on other aspects. It is not enough to make a youngster straightforward and outgoing.

·For instance, the Leo parent should know that a Libra youngster has to be taken very gently along the path to teenage. Although young Libras are enterprising, they are basically shy and find it hard to respond in a natural way. They are very aware of and disturbed by any kind of disharmony. Any shouting, particularly leonine roaring, is likely to make them nervous and uncertain of themselves.

A parent of a Libra child has to remember that Libras are continuously at work in their unconscious minds trying to redress any imbalance they see in their environment. They have the kind of nature that wants everyone to be happy and everything to be perfect. Anything less makes them tense. As this is mostly an imperfect world, it is not hard to understand the stresses and strains that pull at a Libra under the surface.

These young people have to be taught to relax, to release their emotions as naturally as possible, and not try to cover them up. Libras are so desirous of peace and quiet around them that they often say only what they know-will please the other person. They are not beyond telling fibs if they feel it will make them more acceptable to the company they are in.

On the positive side, this young person has a natural charm and easiness of manner, qualities that make them extremely popular. They are intelligent and diplomatic, and possess a strong sense of social duty. They grow into much stronger personalities than their youth may suggest. As much as they abhor violence and discord, they can't bear to see another human being unjustly treated. All their pacifist ways are likely to be discarded instantly if they decide to take up a case for an underdog.

Although Libra is a sign of peace, it also is a sign of war. This probably explains why these gentle people have a way of gliding through situations and leaving a trail of unrest or mayhem behind them.

The Leo parent has to be very careful not to overindulge a Libra son or daughter. These youngsters do not have to be taught what is good quality and what is expensive; they naturally select both. It is possible to make good use of their appreciation of beauty and beautiful things by encouraging them to make a career for themselves in one of the beauty-aid or beautifying industries or professions. Libras often are food and wine connoisseurs, beauty specialists, hairdressers, restaurateurs, and hotel managers. Their social conscience often draws them to occupations such as social worker and welfare officer.

The teenage Libra of both sexes should be encouraged to discuss their romantic lives with their parents. They are not always the best at handling this area of experience.

Infant Libra

A Libra infant usually has something attractive about him or her that goes beyond good looks or a sturdy body. A parent who feels that their newborn Libra baby is the most beautiful in the world may not be all that far-out.

Libra is ruled by Venus, the planet of beauty and love. And this universally attractive though subtle quality of Venus tends to pervade all her little children born at this time of the year. The placements of the other planets, and especially the child's Venus, will have an important moderating effect. But generally, Libras tend to be beautiful people.

As a toddler, the Libra child will be popular with aunts, uncles, and all the family friends. "Cute" and "adorable" will be words frequently heard. There will be a constant succession of young friends coming in to play. And young Libra will hardly miss a birthday party in the whole neighborhood.

But there will be a fair number of squabbles in the neighborhood as this youngster grows a bit older. Then he or she learns to play off one playmate against another. Surprisingly, Libras don't get too much dust on hands or costume. They prefer wheedling or crying to a parent or nearby authority figure. They have a real fear of pushing, shoving, tumbling, or fist fighting.

Young Libra

At school, the Libra child will be regarded as bright, intelligent, and cooperative. These boys and girls often become teachers' pets and are able to think like adults at an early age. They assume certain social responsibilities that threaten other youngsters their age.

The young Libra person is more likely to be interested in mental and creative activities than in sports. Although they may join school teams to keep up identification with their group, they will prefer to remain on the sidelines organizing the off-field and after-game activities.

This youngster has a natural love of harmony, which may be expressed in color, music, or human relations. Parents should be alert for any particular artistic aptitude they may show. Libra adolescents are often drawn to painting and sculpturing.

The Libra child should not be exposed to harsh or uncongenial surroundings. These young people have a temperament that is particularly sensitive to any kind of discord or conflict. They will never be able to do their best under such conditions.

The Libra youngster thrives in an atmosphere of refinement and good taste. The kids themselves have learned the difference between charm and force. They always prefer a charming technique to get what they want, though they will resort to street violence when they are pushed beyond endurance.

The parents of a Libra youngster may be undecided whether to send the youngster to private school or to public school. Private school has all the benefits of selectivity and tact that encourage the Libra child in learning. But public school teaches him or her how to get along with other kids, sometimes the hard way, and to mistrust the easy and extravagant ways of charm and refinement.

Teenage Libra

Libra teenagers, especially the girls, are usually very conscious of appearance. They are likely to spend a great amount of time in front of the mirror. They can tie up the bathroom for hours, luxuriating in hot baths or attending to their well-cared-for hair.

The Libra teenager is sometimes a bit lazy. They can drive their parents mad by not being able to make up their minds about what they want to do. They may go in one direction one moment and in another direction the next. But when they eventually find what they want to do most, they can be very determined.

With Venus being the ruler of Libra, an interest in the opposite sex usually occurs very early in the teens. Libras are aware of their innate ability to attract others and make the most of it, often leaving behind them a trail of wounded young hearts.

Libra teenagers are not rebels. They usually depend on their charm and tact to get their own way. They are cheerful, easygoing, seemingly cooperative. They know the value of compromise, which is often the key to their success.

Sex is of vital interest to the Libra teenager, but not so much for adventure or learning purposes. Libras do not get kicks out of cheap thrills or foolish experimentation. And they are not burning to discover the great mysteries of life.

Libra teenagers' curiosity about sex has to do with their popularity. And the niceties of partnership, even the most innocent attachment. How far can Libra go? How far should they go? What is the appropriate line to draw before they turn off their date, on the one hand, or get a fast reputation, on the other?

Libra teenagers discover a middle ground very quickly. They show an almost adult ability to be coy, play the field, and promise but never dare. They always keep their date or steady dangling but interested, while they toy with the next eligible partner hankering for a chance. Libra boys and girls are terrible flirts, and charming heartbreakers.

LEO PARENTS
AND SCORPIO CHILDREN

The Leo mom or dad is going to find it difficult to understand just what makes their Scorpio son or daughter tick. Leos are fairly simple and straightforward characters. Black and white sum up the subtlety of their outlook. They are not complicated people.

Scorpio is exactly the opposite. Whereas Leo is fire, Scorpio is water. When they come together in a family, there is usually a lot of steam let off.

The Leo mom or dad must try to understand that emotional people like this boy or girl are very secretive. Whereas the King of the Jungle proudly marches through his or her domain, the Scorpio male or female prefers to remain hidden. It's just a matter of two different styles. But to the Lion, it could be very hard indeed to get used to.

There will be many clashes of will between these two. Both are two of the most intense signs of the Zodiac. They give out vibrations that are either repellent or attractive to others just by standing where they are. Scorpio is known as a masterful sign, and Leo, of course, is the sign of rulership. Both also are fixed signs, meaning they can be impossibly stubborn when they want to. Let us hope it never comes to a real battle between these two powerful personalities.

As long as the parent does not allow power struggles to develop, Senior and Junior will get along well together. They will admire each other's strength. The Leo mom or dad will soon become aware of their youngster's strong reasoning powers. The imagination of Scorpio is impressive, not because of its flights of fancy but for its sheer ability to create future opportunities.

The Leo parent cannot help but admire the penetrating way in which their youngster is able to go to the heart of any problem. Scorpios often make wonderful investigators, spies, and psychologists. This innate talent is something to be kept in mind when the time comes around for talking about a career.

It is the emotional side of the Scorpio boy or girl's nature that will most perplex the Leo parent. These young people can become extremely depressed and moody at times; they may lock themselves away in their room and not talk to anyone. It is necessary for them to have time alone without anyone banging on the door asking them to explain their own nature. They also need to be able to keep what they consider their secrets to themselves. They should not be expected to confide all their problems, for the simple reason that one of their main problems is a compulsive need to be secretive.

It will, of course, be up to the parents to make sure that this secretiveness does not develop into deception or duplicity. It has to be said that the Scorpio nature is one of the most perverse if allowed to develop negatively or along antisocial lines.

There is also often a vindictive streak in people born under the sign of the Scorpion. It induces them to think and to take revenge. Leo, whose nature impels them to confront or disdainfully ignore their antagonists, but never to stoop to vengeance, may find this tendency distressing.

The Scorpio teenager is seldom short of admirers among the opposite sex. It is a good idea to encourage them to bring their romantic partners home and to talk about their ups and downs without any attempt to pry.

The courage and ability to persevere under hardship are admirable Scorpio qualities. The Leo parent will find these very close to their own heart, and certainly will respect this steadfast though complicated young person.

Infant Scorpio

The Scorpio infant needs plenty of love and attention. Even though these little people may seem strong and tough and able to look after themselves, the parent who demonstrates how much they are loved will be doing much to prevent problems for the child when he or she grows up.

Inside every Scorpio-born human being is an affectionate and jealous person. If they are not shown the love they need in childhood, they can become disillusioned and bitter people who are likely to take it out on the rest of the world.

Parents of Scorpio toddlers should remember that their nature is fixed. Once they get an idea in their head, it is very difficult to change it. They need to be shown the value of being flexible in dealing with their little friends. They should be discouraged from taking rigid attitudes and putting people into compartments of their own making.

Young Scorpio children are sensitive and sweet to animals and to babies younger than themselves. Here they can show an incredible kindness, almost an instinctive understanding of the other creature. Scorpio infants are not likely to get scratched by the cat or bitten by the dog.

But as Scorpio children grow a bit older, they may get into rough-and-tumble fights with playmates. Here they may develop cruel and insensitive speech and actions, a capacity to hurt and hurt hard.

The Leo parent, always proud when their youngsters defend themselves, may not fully appreciate how defense for the Scorpio child can take on antisocial attributes. This is an area where the parent can help the child learn to fight fair, get over failures, and not hold grudges.

Young Scorpio

Scorpio youngsters have good intellects. They are not the frivolous kind. They like to delve into things with their minds, to get to the bottom of what they think are mysteries.

It is a good thing if at an early age they are encouraged to take up some hobby or study that will utilize their analytical capacities. Chemistry sets, a telescope, or a microscope are the kind of educational toys that may have an important bearing on the child's future development.

A Scorpio child can be a bit of a loner. He or she is not the type to engage in silly and superficial games for long. It is also a good idea for parents to try to encourage them to join groups such as the Scouts, where they can get used to working in cooperation with others.

A Scorpio child needs constant though unobtrusive supervision. Both boys and girls can get into bad company. They have deep emotional needs, and often they think they can get their kicks through taking unnecessary risks.

There is a strong secretive streak in these youngsters. Wise parents will acknowledge it by respecting their privacy. A good strategy is to allow the youngsters to have a "secret" drawer of their own with a key where they can keep writings and relics free from probing eyes.

Teenage Scorpio

The good sense and understanding parents have shown to the Scorpio child in earlier years will start to pay off in the teenage years. If the child has been neglected or unloved, there is likely to be trouble.

Scorpio teenagers are direct, often blunt. They say exactly what they mean, even though they often resort to sarcasm. Any scars of disillusionment with parents are likely to show in independent and aggressive behavior.

The Scorpio person is a great survivor. If these teenagers leave home early, they are very capable of looking after themselves. However, their tendency to look for heightened sensations can lead them to experiment with drugs and alcohol.

Sex is an area that Scorpio teenagers are almost sure to investigate. These youths have plenty of knowledge under their belts by the time they are ready to leave home. And they're not the shy or inhibited type. These youthful experimenters may already have won, or lost, a reputation with their friends.

There is little in the way of practical knowledge that the parent can offer a Scorpio teenager when he or she is set on discovering their sexuality. But the parent can advise the teenager on the tricky ins and outs of each tender relationship, and help him or her decide the emotional and ethical conduct appropriate to each relationship.

By impressing on the Scorpio youngster from an early age the qualities of honesty and consideration for others, the parents will help to ensure that this teenager realizes his or her considerable potential. Consistency is especially important in raising a Scorpio successfully. They are practical, down-to-earth people who are not impressed by anyone who does not practice what they preach.

LEO PARENTS
AND SAGITTARIUS CHILDREN

A Leo parent can expect to get along just fine with a Sagittarius son or daughter. Leo and Sagittarius are basically the same temperaments—energetic, assertive, and happy. As the youngster grows up, these two will be more like buddies than parent and child. They are both positive thinkers and enjoy the lighter side of life.

However, a time will come when the Leo mom or dad may wonder whether Junior is shaping up well enough to accept the inevitable obligations of life. When there are chores to be done, this young person is likely to be missing, probably down by the river with a fishing rod or up at the park horsing around with the gang. The Sagittarius youngster loves the wide-open spaces. Even a Sagittarius girl is tomboy enough and daring enough to be the leader of the local juvenile pack.

The Leo parent, although an outgoing fire sign like Sagittarius, is inclined to be more serious and aware of conventional responsibilities. Young Sagittarius people have all the makings of success in whatever occupation they follow in the future. But the problem is to get them to settle down and apply themselves long enough to get started.

It is the Sagittarius nature always to look to tomorrow. Then the pot of gold will be found at the end of the rainbow. The thing is to try to prevent them from going off enthusiastically on hopeless explorations. When they get older, they must be cautioned against putting all their money into one risky venture.

Sagittarius optimism is a dangerous infection unless it is matched by good common sense. These young people are highly intelligent and have sound judgment. But when they allow their enthusiasm to overrule their intuition, they often make terrible blunders.

The inordinate love of freedom and independence in this young person is sure to clash with Leo's idea of what is meant by individual freedom. Leo is the sign of children. Although they can love them to the point of not seeing their most glaring faults, it is unlikely that they will tolerate the freewheeling instincts of young Sagittarius.

However, there is much to be admired in the Sagittarius nature. This boy or girl has a heart of gold. They will always be helping someone who is in trouble. They are particularly fond of animals. Mom or Dad will have to be prepared to take in all sorts of strays, and to help administer to their assorted injuries.

One thing the Leo parent will have to watch for is that in their teenage years the Sagittarius boy or girl does not get too tied up in the search for pleasure. Of all the signs of the Zodiac, no one is more of a natural partygoer than the person born under the sign of the Archer. Sometimes, if these people have been allowed to indulge their natural instincts excessively in their youth, they become playboy and playgirl types who cannot settle down to an ordinary existence.

However, there is a serious type of Sagittarius who is just the opposite of the life-of-the-party type. This young person may display an early interest in religion or philosophy. They may spend a lot of time reading and studying. They may eventually travel widely in their search for higher knowledge.

All Sagittarius individuals love to travel, and the young ones are no exception.

When it comes to selecting a career, they usually succeed in anything to which they will apply themselves. They are strongly ambitious, far-sighted, and versatile.

One thing that may strike the Leo parent before their old age is how often a bit of good luck saved their youngsters from what might have been disaster. Sagittarius often amass fortunes or lose a couple of fortunes in their lifetimes, by sheer luck.

Infant Sagittarius

The Sagittarius toddler needs plenty of fresh air and space outdoors to play in. Frequent visits to the park to see the bigger kids playing football and other games will help to keep this active and curious little person entertained.

Sagittarius children usually are fairly healthy and robust types. They are likely to crawl early in their attempts to find out just what is happening around the corner or up the stairs. They may also disappear smartly out the front door, if it is left open.

These infants do seem to get more bruises and bumps than other children, due to their clumsiness. It takes them some time to get their bodies properly coordinated in spite of their incessant physical activity. Sports should be encouraged.

They do not like to be hemmed in. They are inclined to put up a raucous fight when stopped from doing what they want. It is easier to coax and humor a Sagittarius toddler into submission than to use force.

Young Sagittarius

Sagittarius youngsters are bright and intelligent. But they are more likely to distinguish themselves on the sports field than in the classroom. Sagittarius kids have the brains to make good students, even scholars, but seldom have the time to devote to their homework.

This young person should be handled with a fairly firm hand so that homework and chores around the house get done. The Sagittarius boy or girl longs to be outdoors. They relish any kind of games and sports requiring physical movement and prowess. They are inclined to treat the whole of life as a game.

These youngsters usually love pets. A cat, a dog, and especially a horse can mean more to these young people than imaginable. The Sagittarius boy or girl often finds it easier to express love by caring for animals than by trying to communicate it to human beings. They are spontaneous little people with a strong desire to share without a great need to possess emotionally, as many people are inclined to do.

Teenage Sagittarius

Sagittarius teenagers usually are extremely popular among their young friends. They do not spend a great deal of time at home in one sitting. If they do, usually it is spent in the company of friends who come and go, day in and day out at a bewildering rate.

These teenagers seldom go through the moody-blues period that so often afflicts the adolescent. They manage to remain cheery and optimistic most of the time. Their sense of humor is well developed and matches their love of fun.

__ There is often a strong religious interest in Sagittarius individuals that develops in their teens. They respect the need for the golden rule and tend to remember it all their lives, even though they may abandon regular church attendance. In spite of their rash and rascally ways, they have a due regard for moral and social responsibilities.

These teenagers have to be trusted. And they are usually worthy of it. Otherwise, with any kind of narrow supervision, the parent will face an adolescent rebellion.

Sex is a lot of fun and games to the typical Sagittarius teenager. These youths are not too fond of passionate attachments. They think that the mysteries of love and sex are a bit too heady for them. "Nothing heavy" is their motto. Easy come, easy go characterizes their dating patterns.

The girls are just as independent as the boys and can chase and hunt with the best of the Archers. Sagittarius teenagers may get a love-'em-and-leave-'em reputation. As far as actual sex is concerned, Sagittarius teen-agers often retain their innocence while they are promoting their reputation. Crushes, even the most romantic attachment, will not lure these kids too far from their sports and hobbies. Of course, they will use their boy-friend or girlfriend as an excuse to get out of homework. And they may make a big thing about each new steady. Their enthusiasms burn brightly for a while, then disappear as these teenagers discover a new horizon.

LEO PARENTS
AND CAPRICORN CHILDREN

A Leo mom or dad is just the parent to help bring out the best in a Capricorn son or daughter. However, these two zodiacal types are very different in temperament. It will be a good thing if the parent understands this right from the start and does not try to push the Capricorn child too far too early.

Capricorn is an earth sign, restrained and cautious. These youngsters, once they get into the school years, like to put one foot very carefully after another. This boy or girl born under the sign of the Goat is one day going to be a very together person. He or she will end up close to the top or become an authority in whatever field they choose.

But it takes them a long time to get started. Although they are often studious and take their schoolwork seriously, it is usually not until they are well into adulthood that they really take the long strides in a positive direc-tion.

The Capricorn youngster usually is not a ray of warmth and sunshine. The Leo parent, with a cheery, outgoing personality, may wonder at times how he or she came to have a youngster so different in nature. Although the young Goat will get up to the usual juvenile pranks and have boister-ously happy moments, there will be an unmistakable element of seriousness in their makeup.

The Leo parent's warm and enthusiastic influence will have a great positive effect on this young person. It would be hard to find a more ben-eficial kind of conditioning. Leo the Lion will recognize the strength that underpins the young Capricorn personality. And it is to be hoped that Leo will also appreciate that the young Goat does have a problem expressing feelings. He or she is not the type to respond to any hearty and insensitive urgings to "get it out" and "snap out of it." Leos can be awfully bombastic in their own self-assurance.

The Lion will have to get used to his or her Capricorn son or daughter getting a touch of the blues. The child should be gently encouraged to forget themselves, perhaps by helping others less fortunate. They may join move-ments or organizations, not because they are by nature great joiners but because there is a worthy self-sacrificing quality in Capricorn that needs drawing out.

Through being taught the value of compassion in the formative years, a Capricorn person often can be saved from feelings in middle age of loneliness and failure. They are a rather melancholy and even morose sign by nature. Anything a parent can do to expand contact and interaction with the rest of humanity, from whom Capricorns are inclined to cut off, will be worthwhile.

Another thing that the Leo mom or dad should work at eradicating in this youngster is the fear of failure. These are practical, methodical, and resourceful youngsters. There is very little that, given the time, they cannot achieve. Yet the fear of failure makes them afraid to venture. Too often the world is denied their contribution because they didn't think it would be appreciated or worthwhile.

Capricorn youngsters have to be taught that everything necessary for their success is already within them. Their main problem is in overcoming their own anxiety. This can be done by a Leo parent who with warmhearted sincerity can instill a faith in Capricorn kids that otherwise the child may never discover.

Capricorn is a down-to-earth sign. The young Goat can become interested in any activity that draws upon his or her ability to be constructive and responsible. They are careful and cool people who are very good to have around when an emergency arises. Whereas Leo probably will overreact and start shouting and giving orders, Capricorn is likely to go straight to the heart of the problem and deal with it.

Infant Capricorn

The Capricorn infant may seem to be developing a bit slower than other toddlers of his or her age. But the proud parents—and proud they will be—should not be disturbed by this. The Capricorn influence tends to be slow to express itself at all stages of early development.

Although these children take their time, they are absorbing their surroundings. They should not be hurried. They are much more sensitive than they may appear. They need plenty of love and affection, especially the physical kind.

Capricorn children need to feel that they are really needed. They need to be cooed over and told how good they are. This is more important than one would think, for as they grow up, these little ones can very easily obtain a poor opinion of themselves and become too self-conscious.

Brother, sister, or children of other signs may show more promise than little Capricorn. But parents should know that in this lovable bundle is a character that will develop into a conscientious, patient, and courageous individual. In maturity, this person is likely to have a prominent and responsible place in society.

Young Capricorn

At school, these children are likely to be good students. Study comes naturally to them. They are not easily distracted by the regular pastimes of children. They are likely to be avid readers and eager listeners to adult conversations.

It is important for the parent of a Capricorn boy or girl to see that they get out and play with the other children. If these youngsters born under the sign of the Goat get interested in collecting stamps or a similar hobby, they are likely to pursue it to the exclusion of other interests.

It is a good thing if they can be persuaded to take up a sport. They should be given some coaching lessons, so they can prove their ability in front of their schoolmates early. If left to their own devices, they may become more conscious of their failings than their successes. That pushes them more than ever to retreat into themselves where they feel secure.

Young Capricorn is not usually the type to have many close friends. They are very selective and take their time to make sure the other child does not criticize or ridicule them. They find it hard to take a joke against themselves. They are extremely sensitive about what others may be thinking about them.

This young person should not be allowed to mope around the house. They will respond to any parental request for help in running the house. They should be given small chores to their liking, which they can regard as their own personal contribution to the efficient operation of the household.

Teenage Capricorn

The Capricorn adolescent usually has a fair idea of what he or she wants to do in life. Although this may be in the distant future, they are inclined to work assiduously toward that objective. Their interests and pastimes probably in some way will be connected with it. These are serious young people who like to prepare themselves.

The Capricorn teenager in normal circumstances is not likely to be a rebel. They enjoy the warmth and closeness of family life. They respect their parents and are not a problem in teaching the merits of law and order. They are not particularly adventurous and would rather keep things as they are. However, they do have an acute regard for social injustice, especially if they have seen their parents or families deprived by the system.

Contact with the opposite sex is not easy for Capricorn youngsters. They are shy and painfully determined to avoid rebuffs. Yet more often than not, Capricorns in their teenage years go steady. They seem to attract outgoing types who want someone to nurture.

Such a warm and private attachment is perfect for the Capricorn teenager. Their steady won't be fooled by Capricorn's reserve or seeming detachment. Capricorn thaws with a loyal steady who can show him or her the ropes. And Capricorn thrives if their girlfriend or boyfriend is popular in the gang and insists on dragging Capricorn along.

Through this attachment and vicarious popularity, the Capricorn teenager is introduced to social and cultural events that this introverted type might be too frightened to attend alone. Parents of Capricorn teenagers are wise to encourage such love affairs, especially when they include plenty of socials, sports, and fun activities that their son or daughter might otherwise skip.

LEO PARENTS
AND AQUARIUS CHILDREN

A Leo parent and an Aquarius youngster are not likely to be separated by a generation gap. The Leo parent will understand the intellectual needs of this boy or girl. Leo will help to give them the mental stimulation and encouragement they require.

As this youngster grows up, there will be more and more interesting discussions, not to mention good-humored arguments, about the news of the day, politics, religion, and the economic state of the nation. Aquarius kids take a mature interest in what is happening in the world, when many other children are just starting to make eyes at the boy or girl next door.

Fortunately, Leo the Lion has fairly strong intellectual leanings. A Leo usually is able to give an opinion, whether it is wanted or not, about any subject under the sun. They have very strong and definite views. They invariably think that they are right.

In an Aquarius son or daughter, the bighearted, big-talking, and big-thinking Lion might at times feel they have met their intellectual match. Although mom or dad probably will manage to bluster through an argument to their own satisfaction, the odds are an observer would think that young Aquarius had won the day.

Aquarius kids are smart. They love to debate, often taking the opposite side of a question just for fun. It will soon be evident to the Lion that their youngster has the sort of mind that would be suitable for a career in science, radio, television, publishing, writing, or any field where their fertile mental qualities can be exercised and developed.

Leo is the sign of children and creative thinking. This will help to awaken the artistic inclinations that Aquarius tends to have. It is not a good idea for Aquarius youngsters to be left too much to their own devices when it comes around to thinking about a profession. They need guidance. They are inclined to go for change and variety, and so may not settle down to anything in the end.

Sometimes, especially when young Aquarius is in their teens, both parent and youngster are going to have serious clashes of will. These are two of the fixed signs in the Zodiac. When these characters get an idea in their head, no one will shift it. With Leo the Lion being one of the most autocratic and dominating people in the Zodiac, all the ingredients are there for a battle royal.

However, the Leo parent should try to remember that Aquarius people are extraordinarily reasonable. Although they have strong ideals, they are prepared to listen to any intelligent statement. If the Leo parent can keep emotion out of the situation and avoid issuing ultimatums, they may be surprised at the cooperation they receive.

Sooner or later this Aquarius youngster will start to exhibit the strong humanitarian leanings of the sign. No one cares more about the welfare of mankind than an Aquarius, once they have started to develop their potential. They are filled with reformist ideas to make the world a better place to live in. These are the young people who are often found in the front line of a demonstration.

They are not particularly emotional people. The strong romanticism of the Leo mom or dad will be absent. This will be especially noticeable when it comes to romance. Aquarius people certainly have their passionate moments, but often they make their loved ones feel they are not the main thing in their lives.

Infant Aquarius

When this little one starts toddling around and taking an interest in things, it will not be mere childish curiosity. Aquarius endows a child with an unusual type of intelligence that can best be described as the ability to synthesize, to put ideas together, and to draw the essential meaning out of that combination. It will not be long before the parents of this kiddie will start remarking, with justifiable pride, that he or she is a bit unusual and bright.

These boys and girls of Uranus, the unconventional planet that rules Aquarius, are not concerned about being kissed and cuddled. They do, of course, need to be surrounded by love and affection. But the demonstration of these in emotional ways is not so important to them.

Intellectual rapport—even for baby Aquarius—is the vital thing. Somehow parents communicate their interest in the unformalized ideas of baby Aquarius just by listening intently to their coos and squeals and watching carefully the thrusts and grasps of hands and legs.

Aquarius is a high-octave mental sign. It is advised that parents gradually establish common ground in the way of interests and mental pursuits. This child will enjoy playing. But he or she wants to know how and why things are done in a particular way. They are likely to be very good at inventing games and things to do.

Young Aquarius

At school, the young Aquarius boy or girl will have a lot of friends, but perhaps not many close ones. He or she will be regarded as intelligent and full of strange ideas and imaginings. These children are too alert and observant to be called daydreamers. But they do make fanciful and inventive use of their imagination.

The Aquarius youngster's chief interest is experimentation. This can range from dressing up in bizarre combinations of clothes to becoming absorbed in the wonders of the glassware and chemicals in the school laboratory or the intricacies of system and design in architectural and electronic models.

Aquarius kids often begin an early fascination with adult topics, such as questions of law and ethics, justice and politics. Philosophical issues turn them on. They can spend more time reading and researching the whys and wherefores than in recreational pursuits.

They don't take to sports and games, especially the strenuous variety. But all study and no play cannot become too much the rule, or these youngsters get an unbalanced picture of life—the very thing they're trying to understand. Parents can guide them here.

Aquarius are truthful youngsters. They look to their parents and teachers to guide them with honesty. They should not be fobbed off with superficial answers to questions, and should certainly not be misled by "white lies."

Aquarius children will quickly lose respect for anyone who lies to them. This could largely account for the fact that in adult life, all Aquarius people tend to question, and deride as necessary, established authority in the person of mere mortals.

Teenage Aquarius

The parent of an Aquarius teenager will have learned by now that this young person can be very fixed in his or her opinions. It's true they have some amazingly advanced ideas at times for their age. And they show a great capacity to move even ahead of the times.

But these teenagers can be as stubborn as mules when it comes to such familiar things as household chores, attendance at family gatherings, curfews, clothes, and appearance. Once these teenagers get an idea into their head—their own idea of these things, of course—they will not abandon it until experience has proved it to be misguided, or until their defiance has been met by restriction of their personal liberties.

Normally, the Aquarius teenager is not a rebellious type. He or she is extremely independent, but not unreasonable. They will listen to the good advice of their parents. They genuinely do not want to make trouble for those they love. Their motivation is to be helpful. Although inclined to go to extremes when their feelings are strong about certain issues, they tend to lead a fairly moderate kind of existence.

They have many casual friends, some of whom may have ideas as strange as their own. When it comes to romance, the Aquarius teenager is more likely to act like a friend most of the time than a youthful lover. There usually must be a mental compatibility and a sharing of intellectual interests before any more serious attachment starts.

Sexual experimentation, though, is likely to start for the Aquarius teenager with a good friend or even a casual pal. These youngsters do not have to wait for the love of their life, or even a serious crush, before getting down to what makes the world go round.

Pursuing kicks, they manage to experience sex but not necessarily the emotions of the attachment. Somehow, in their love for kicks, they do not even give the impression that they are capricious.

Their seriousness, though, should be a comfort to their parents. Methodical and cautious, typical Aquarius teenagers are not likely to be caught in embarrassing situations, risk pregnancy, or set the law on their trail. The latter they reserve for their more purposeful forays into political agitation.

LEO PARENTS
AND PISCES CHILDREN

A Leo parent will be able to give this lovable child all the love and affection they crave. A Pisces youngster is probably the most sensitive and difficult to understand of all the twelve types. There is a bit of every other sign in these people. But they do lack, probably for this very reason, a sense of identity. They need to be reassured constantly and praised to keep up their self-confidence.

The Leo mom or dad must try to avoid being too bossy and assertive with this youngster. Pisces are extremely sensitive. It is not an exaggeration to say that they can become physically ill if harshly criticized or rebuked. The Leo parent will have to be more careful with his or her quick temper. Although these parents are seldom the type to hurt a child deliberately out of anger, they must realize that just the noise and look of anger can disturb these youngsters profoundly.

This is not to say, however, that young Pisces should be coddled. This is the worst thing that can happen to them. Because of their extreme sensitivity, they tend to depend on an air of helplessness as a means of defense. If allowed to become a habit, this dependence can produce an adult who sits around waiting for others to do the dirty work for them.

At their best, Pisces youngsters are charmers and a delight to have around the home. They are unobtrusive children, who are usually content to play for hours enacting the fairy tales that they love so much. They do this with paper drawings, by dressing up in costumes, and through daydreams.

The Leo mom or dad is usually a straightforward, no-nonsense type, so this youngster's dreamy and idealistic approach may be hard for Leo to take. It is no good, however, for the Lion to bring the Pisces child harshly down to earth. These kids need their dreams, which are really their exceptionally creative imagination out of control. By gently coaxing them to face up to reality more and more as they grow up, Leo can help them to turn this imaginative faculty into a particularly creative instrument.

Most Pisces have artistic leanings. Leo should encourage their youngster to draw and write. It is the most natural thing in the world for a Pisces to write poetry and to have a natural fondness for good literature. When this child grows up, he or she could make their Leo parent very proud of them in fields such as art, music, dancing, writing, and acting. The Leo parent will soon realize that their youngster spends most of his or her life acting out some role or other.

Pisces are especially kind, compassionate, and understanding people. They are particularly suited for work as caretakers, nurses, and welfare officers. They are often found working in institutions for the aged, the orphaned, and the underprivileged. They have a way with children that brings out the best even in the most aggressive and unruly children.

The Leo mom or dad is not going to find it easy to come to terms with the extreme emotionalism of a Pisces youngster. They are very easily hurt. If overindulged and coddled, they can become impossibly thin-skinned, unable to bear the slightest personal criticism. The tendency of all parents is

to spoil their Pisces child. But for the child's own good, this behavior has to be resisted.
It will be up to the Leo parent to make sure that their youngster goes to school and keeps up with studies. Pisces easily get bored. They have a way of finding excuses and of being missing when any work requiring concentration and effort has to be done. Once they get behind, they are not likely to catch up.

Infant Pisces

There is something about the Pisces child that most people take to. Although all infants are lovable and cuddly, this tiny baby seems more vulnerable than others. Its skin is so soft and translucent, its miniature fists and feet curl so close to its body. Parents, even brothers and sisters, are moved to hold the little creature just a little more tightly in order that nothing may befall it.

There is nothing delicate about baby Pisces, soft and sweet and silent though it may be. Baby Pisces, boy or girl, is just expressing the basic Pisces nature. It is made for love and loving. A little older, and this infant will be showing salty tears, rough tantrums, and tough rebellions that its babyhood never betrayed.

The Pisces kiddie is extremely affectionate. Both boy and girl relish the demonstrations of love. They feel comfortable in loving arms. They respond immediately to any show of warmth aimed in their direction. They love to be loved and liked.

This toddler is usually spoiled. Parents, relatives, and friends seldom resist indulging the child's desires. The child's delight in receiving attention of any kind is most charmingly expressed.

Parents should be warned, however, that this child of the deceptive planet Neptune, which rules Pisces, can be very demanding emotionally. They may cry at being left alone or in unfamiliar surroundings. They can have inexplicably odd likes and dislikes.

Young Pisces

Pisces children are extremely sensitive and cannot stand harsh treatment or surroundings. Although quite able to take care of themselves when left to their own devices, they are inclined always to be on the lookout for others who will help them. This can lead to dependence and lack of initiative.

Pisces youngsters start out full of life and enthusiasm. They love plenty of change and excitement. They are often happiest only when they are looking forward to something. Because of their heightened expectations, they frequently are disappointed and disillusioned.

Pisces children are more emotional beings than mental ones. They may be regarded at school as being slow learners. They need to be taught with patience and understanding. They have to be emotionally involved in what they are learning to absorb and retain it. Otherwise, it is like water off a duck's back.

These children, born under the water sign of the Fishes, are day-dreamers. They tend to go off into a world of their own at the first sign of pressure or hostility. They do not like to be criticized. They are very easily hurt and put out.

Sometimes these young people worry their parents by not eating much. Or they can be finicky and inclined to pick. They do not need a great deal of food as children.

Teenage Pisces

The secretive side of the Pisces nature usually surfaces in the teenage years. This side must be respected by their parents if these young people are ever to develop their full potential.

Pisces teenagers need privacy. They must be allowed enough spare time from homework, household chores, sports, games, and lessons to cul-tivate their own hobbies. In fact, these youngsters need more extensive periods alone than most other kids do. It may be difficult for parents to understand this, especially if they are outgoing types themselves. Pisces is essentially a self-repressive and passive sign.

These teenagers can be the life of the party one moment, down in the dumps or in tears the next. Their emotions change with bewildering swift-ness. They often appear to be two people who never seem to meet each other.

Pisces teenagers need discipline, not the harsh but the understanding kind. Without being taught restraint, they can become self-indulgent and demanding. They may grow into very discontented and uncertain people. The Pisces charm, their favorite device, should not be allowed to win them their own way all the time.

As teenagers they are inclined to overeat, believing they are indulging sophisticated tastes. Sex, drugs, alcohol, and daredevil sports may become lures and possible dangers for the Pisces teenager. Their tendency to go to excess, on the one hand, and their idealistic belief in romantic purity, on the other, make them careless of chances and risks.

Here is where the parents must take a firm hand. They should dem-onstrate by subtle and not so subtle means the need for knowledge, protec-tion, and responsibility. The real world can be more hurtful and sordid than the Pisces teenager ever imagined it would be.

Cusp Signs:
Aries Through Pisces

The Cusps of All Signs

Being born on the cusp means that you were born between the nine-teenth and twenty-fourth of any month. This is the period when the signs change. The actual day a sign changes is different from month to month and from year to year because the time used to measure planetary motion differs from calendar time. The actual day the signs changed from 1910 through 1990 is given in the Cusp Tables for All Signs, pp. 379–383.

Being born on the cusp means that you exhibit characteristics of two signs. If you were born on any of the days nineteenth through twenty-fourth of a month, you will want to read the cusp description that applies to you in the following sections. Through it, you will learn another set of influences that make you uniquely you.

Cusp Days for the Signs

Aries and Taurus Cusp	April 19 through April 24
Taurus and Gemini Cusp	May 19 through May 24
Gemini and Cancer Cusp	June 19 through June 24
Cancer and Leo Cusp	July 19 through July 24
Leo and Virgo Cusp	August 19 through August 24
Virgo and Libra Cusp	September 19 through September 24
Libra and Scorpio Cusp	October 19 through October 24
Scorpio and Sagittarius Cusp	November 19 through November 24
Sagittarius and Capricorn Cusp	December 19 through December 24
Capricorn and Aquarius Cusp	January 19 through January 24
Aquarius and Pisces Cusp	February 19 through February 24
Pisces and Aries Cusp	March 19 through March 21

CUSP OF ARIES AND TAURUS

People born between April 19 and April 24 are on the cusp of Aries and Taurus. These people have some of the drive of Aries and some of the slowness of Taurus. They have wonderful ideas and great energy to implement them as well as tremendous enthusiasm, all of which they get from the Aries side of their personality. The Taurus side gives them a practical, thorough approach and an ability to finish what they have started. Together, these energies can be a formidable combination.

Individuals born on this cusp will take risks, but not unnecessary ones. They will try new things but with a practical approach. They have the ability to initiate *and* to follow through. They will start new businesses on a thoroughly practical foundation. The chances of success with this combination are very high.

On the negative side, people born on the Aries and Taurus cusp can be at war with themselves. They want to take risks, but may be too afraid. They may feel that their innovative ideas are not practical enough. The Taurus resistance to change is at odds with the Aries need to create something new. Taurus wants to be slow and sure, and Aries is too impatient to wait. Taurus wants to be secure and will not take risks, while Aries wants new challenges and hates the too familiar. People born on this cusp may feel that they are going through life with one foot on the accelerator and one foot on the brake.

CUSP OF TAURUS AND GEMINI

People born between May 19 and May 24 are born on the Taurus and Gemini cusp. They combine strong practicality and a lightning-quick mind. The Taurus brawn and the Gemini brains make them particularly well suited for athletics. The Taurus placidity can make the person not want to move at all, so the Gemini restlessness is a perfect balance.

These people are much more open-minded than a Taurus is likely to be, and much more practical and patient than a Gemini. They can give practical application to their ideas. They will see a project through, and not take the rest of their lives to do it. They are excellent students and probably have more than one degree. They are often found improving their homes. They have a whole library of do-it-yourself books. They like all kinds of handywork. Some of them write books. These people are generally successful in life because they have good mental discipline.

On the negative side, people born on the Taurus and Gemini cusp can be so intent on getting all the information they need that they never get started. Some of them are professional students, being attracted to learning but afraid of the real world. They spend a lot of time talking about what they are going to do and very little time actually doing it.

The Taurus resistance to change can be well supported by the Gemini inability to make a decision. These are people who are mentally agile but never move beyond square one. They spend a lot of time doing crossword puzzles and other brain teasers. They like nothing more than a wonderful dinner and stimulating conversation. They give away many good ideas because they do not have the drive to use the ideas themselves. They also find it easy to think up excuses for not changing. Some of these individuals can be accident-prone; their mind moves faster than their body, and so they have a tendency to trip over their feet.

CUSP OF GEMINI AND CANCER

People born between June 19 and June 24 are on the Gemini and Cancer cusp. This combination of energies provides the intellect of Gemini and the intuition of Cancer. These people have tremendous communication skills. Not only do they instinctively know the right words to say, but they also put feeling into those words, so they can move any audience. They are well suited to political speechwriting, public relations, and advertising. They know what the public wants to hear. They can also write best-selling novels. Their understanding of people's feelings plus their facility with words make them particularly well equipped to create characters and situations.

Cancer and Gemini cusp individuals are social animals, providing excellent food and scintillating conversation. Some love to entertain and do it so well they make a career of it. Other Cancer and Gemini people are psychologists and teachers, and still others do very well writing cookbooks.

On the negative side, people born on the Cancer and Gemini cusp spend too much time talking about their feelings. They want sympathy so much they think that if they tell you how bad they feel, you will provide the appropriate amount of sympathy. When they don't get the emotional support they think they deserve, they assume it is because they haven't explained their needs well enough. They will explain and explain, feeling that they have not found the right words, rather than the right person. They go back and forth between their intuitive side and their thinking side rather than integrating these two sides. As a result, they will mistrust their intuition if their logic does not agree, or try to reason out matters when their intuition already knows the answer. Their reasoning tends to be circular because the clarity of their intellect is clouded by their feelings.

CUSP OF CANCER AND LEO

People born between July 19 and July 24 are on the Cancer and Leo cusp. These people have excellent dramatic skills. The flamboyance of Leo together with the sensitivity of Cancer make them award-winning actors and actresses. Even those not involved in the entertainment field create drama in their everyday lives. Their lives *are* soap operas.

These people also have a great sensitivity to the feelings of others. They are very generous with time and affection. These are natural nurturers. They will make such a dramatic event out of your being sick that you almost hate to get well.

They are particularly sensitive to the needs of children, having the mothering quality of Cancer and the childlike quality of Leo. Cancer and Leo cusp people give memorable parties; they are particularly fond of costume parties. These people provide entertainment for everyone around them. On the negative side, Cancer and Leo cusp people are extremely demanding emotionally. They must be the center of attention at all times. They throw temper tantrums if someone else has the limelight for even one minute. The Cancer insecurity together with the Leo need for ego gratification can make them very difficult to live with. When they do not receive all of the other person's attention, they feel unloved and they sulk. They can be very possessive and manipulating, and no matter what is done for them, it is never enough.

They blame everyone else for whatever goes wrong in their lives. They feel indignant and outraged at what they consider the lacks in their lives, and refuse to take any responsibility for them. They see themselves as tragic figures on the stage of life, and no amount of evidence to the contrary will change their mind. They prefer dramatic suffering to undramatic happiness.

CUSP OF LEO AND VIRGO

People born between August 19 and August 24 are on the Leo and Virgo cusp. These people combine the drama of Leo and the service of Virgo, and so are often teachers of dramatic arts. They produce children's plays, teach in acting schools, and use dramatic expression as a tool in psychotherapy.

The precision of organizational ability of Virgo, together with the executive ability of Leo, makes these people particularly well suited to run any business. The Leo and Virgo person appears at home in any situation because the poise and competence of Virgo, together with the Leo confidence and flair, command attention and respect. Because of Virgo's communication skills and Leo's dramatic skills, these people are naturally suited to writing plays, television scripts, and best-selling novels. They are generally wealthy in later life.

On the negative side, the Leo and Virgo cusp person never feels adequately rewarded for his work. The Virgo side of him feels no one could ever do it as well, and the Leo side demands to be in charge. As a result, he has to do everything and feels that no one appreciates his contribution. He is intensely sensitive to criticism, as he cannot admit his mistakes. In an effort to get a job done, he bosses others around, points out their imperfections, and then wonders why others do not like him; he is therefore often quite lonely. He cannot understand their attitude, because he feels he was only trying to be helpful.

Leo and Virgo individuals tend to overdo everything. They are flamboyant with details and showy about the amount of work they do. They sometimes have trouble distinguishing between the essential and the trivial. They tend to make an opera out of blowing their nose, yet will handle a car with perfect ease.

CUSP OF VIRGO AND LIBRA

People born between September 19 and September 24 are on the Virgo and Libra cusp. The precision of Virgo together with the artistic quality of Libra make them particularly well suited for fine arts. They have an eye for line and color, and like to design their own pictures or needlework. Their creations are often meticulous and lovely. They make very charming hosts and hostesses because of the Virgo need to serve and the Libra need to bring peace to the environment.

These people are very popular because they listen well and provide adequate solutions to people's problems without becoming emotionally involved. They are found most often helping other people dealing with their lives. They are fair and unbiased in their dealings with others. They work hard at their relationships. They try to help other people work as hard. They are usually very attractive, and take great care with their appearance and their surroundings.

On the negative side, they can be too cold and calculating in their relationships. They can find it difficult to be emotionally involved and are often considered very distant. This is hard to deal with because they always want to keep everything pleasant. Others find it hard to believe that such an attractive person would have so little feeling. The Virgo inability to accept criticism together with the Libra refusal to confront situations make it very difficult for these people to deal with the emotional problems of their own lives. It can also be frustrating for those people who have to deal with them.

Virgo and Libra cusp individuals can be very indecisive because of the Virgo insecurity and need for perfection and the Libra need to consider both sides of a question before taking action. Their inability to make decisions leads many of them into escapist activities such as living in a fantasy world of perfection and harmony.

CUSP OF LIBRA AND SCORPIO

People born between October 19 and October 24 are on the Libra and Scorpio cusp. The charm of Libra and the intuitive qualities of Scorpio make these people extremely attractive. The Libra side knows how to please and the Scorpio side knows what others want. They can often achieve prominence in the field of their choice. The Scorpio stamina and persistence together with the Libra ability to create harmonious working conditions enable them to rise at a meteoric rate. There is no one more skilled at drawing people out and finding out what makes the other person tick, often without that other person's realizing what is happening.

Such individuals have an ability to manipulate others so gracefully that people seldom feel used and actually give them what they want joyously. They can move mountains because they can charm other people into helping them.

On the negative side, the Libra and Scorpio cusp person can be cold and calculating to the point of being insensitive to the feelings of others. He can manipulate those around him to serve his needs with little regard for what they need. Such a person charms others into service, and it isn't until after he is gone that they realize they have been had. A master at illusion, he will create whatever environment is necessary to achieve his ends.

He is secretive in the extreme, hardly letting his right hand know what his left hand is doing. He is conceited, as he truly believes he is more attractive and brighter than almost everyone. He is possessive of his family and expects them to adhere to his rules. He can be extremely vindictive when his feelings are hurt. He can ruin a career without the victim's ever realizing what has happened. This is one to be wary of. He would never forgive you if you disappointed him.

CUSP OF SCORPIO AND SAGITTARIUS

People born between November 19 and November 24 are on the Scorpio and Sagittarius cusp. These people have the Sagittarius optimism and the Scorpio realism. Such a combination enables them to fulfill their dreams. They are spontaneous and enthusiastic as well as passionate and deep. They accomplish what they set out to do and have unbelievable energy and drive.

The Sagittarius curiosity and the Scorpio need to get to the bottom of things lead them to learn everything possible about the subject of their choice. Their powers of concentration are formidable, as is their physical stamina. They are able to accomplish goals that others aspire to but rarely achieve. The Sagittarius side gives them high ideals, and the Scorpio side gives them the fixity of purpose to achieve those ideals. The Sagittarius desire for travel and the Scorpio need for constancy lead them often into careers in which travel is an integral part.

On the negative side, the Sagittarius and Scorpio cusp person has trouble trusting others. The Sagittarius need to believe the world is wonderful, and the Scorpio realization that it is not, make it difficult for them to be open and honest about their feelings. These people can be very immediate in their relationships, and they are the ones who invented the phrase "out of sight, out of mind."

Although they are most charming, they can disappear without a trace, leaving people wondering what happened. Their humor can be sarcastic or black, and they are not above destroying somebody for the sake of being funny, a combination of the Sagittarius humor and the Scorpio sting. Their rapier wit is their greatest tool, and they thrust it where it will do the most damage. These people are extremely secretive and sometimes have two separate lives, complete with aliases. They are not trustworthy.

CUSP OF SAGITTARIUS AND CAPRICORN

People born between December 19 and December 24 are on the Sagittarius and Capricorn cusp. The Sagittarius optimism that everything will work out well is combined with the Capricorn willingness to make things work. The Sagittarius immediacy is tempered by the Capricorn foresight and planning. The natural curiosity of Sagittarius to cover as many bases as possible, together with the innate ambitiousness of Capricorn to get to the top, enable these people to achieve professional success early in life. The Capricorn side enjoys working hard, being responsible, and keeping his finger on the pulse of things. The Sagittarius side is able to deal with multiple factors simultaneously with efficiency and good humor. These people are successful because they can set more far-reaching goals and see possibilities that others would miss, and then design and implement the methods by which the goals can be attained. There is often therefore a fruitful combination of idealism and practicality.

On the negative side, the Sagittarius and Capricorn cusp person has trouble integrating his idealism with his innate practicality. The natural conservatism of the Capricorn side is at odds with the flamboyance of the Sagittarius side. Here is a person with idealism, but his Capricorn pessimism makes him think he can never realize it. He wants the best of all possible worlds, but doesn't think he will ever achieve it.

These people resent all authority, whether parental or organizational, because the Sagittarius need for freedom is in conflict with the Capricorn need to be in control. They are difficult to work with because they are either too bossy or too cavalier, and sometimes alternate between the two. The Sagittarius belief that he knows the truth and wants to share it, together with the Capricorn need to be an authority figure, can make these people tyrannical in their dealings with others. They can be extremely self-righteous, even when they are wrong.

CUSP OF CAPRICORN AND AQUARIUS

People born between January 19 and January 24 are on the Capricorn and Aquarius cusp. The Aquarius ability for abstract thinking, together with the Capricorn practicality, make this combination formidable for problem solving of all kinds. Since Aquarius individuals are usually the most scientifically minded people of the Zodiac, and Capricorns are the people who deal with the practical details of daily living, people born on this cusp are often very good troubleshooters.

They often have mechanical ability and are amateur as well as professional inventors. The Aquarius desire to improve the quality of life plus the Capricorn ability to see practical solutions to problems leads these people into social reform and political organizations. They are clear-thinking and unbiased by the emotional environment in which they are operating. They tend to see life's problems as solvable like a mathematical equation. These people will establish social structures that will guarantee the freedom of each individual.

On the negative side, the Capricorn and Aquarius cusp person can be too detached from the people around him. He can be so busy organizing the community that he neglects his family. He has trouble establishing close emotional relationships. He's more comfortable being a friend to all. His natural intellectual gifts may make him arrogant and condescending to those around him. He can run into difficulty because he keeps his eye on the goal and forgets the needs of the people doing the work.

Such a person can have a pessimistic view of life and deal with every situation with too much seriousness. Although he can get things done, it is not necessarily enjoyable to work with him. He can push the people around him unmercifully because he has no tolerance for emotional weakness. His lack of success in relationships often leads him into dealing with abstract ideas and mechanical devices.

CUSP OF AQUARIUS AND PISCES

People born between February 19 and February 24 are on the Aquarius and Pisces cusp. These people combine the Aquarius ability for logical reasoning and the Pisces ability to fantasize and imagine. Many of these people are talented in the arts, particularly in areas in which they can create an illusion out of time, such as science fiction, fairy tales, or allegories. They have an abiding awe of the universe and a great desire to understand how it works. Many are led into the study of higher physics. They can often envision future events. They are sensitive to the harshness of life and will often turn to music for solace.

Basically the Pisces side has faith that things will work, and the Aquarius wants to know how. The Pisces creativity is given expression by the logic and fixity of Aquarius. Many Aquarius and Pisces cusp individuals are exceptionally fine painters and musicians. Many others are excellent psychiatrists because of the Pisces sympathy and the Aquarius analytical ability.

On the negative side, the Aquarius and Pisces cusp person is caught on the horns of the dilemma of wanting to know, which is an Aquarius quality, and having faith, which is a Pisces quality. Such a person may have trouble integrating the creative and logical sides of his nature. He is likely to have very structured thinking and deny his creative impulses. As a result, he stalls in his progress and accomplishes very little. He can be facile in his talk but lazy in his accomplishments. Such a person will escape into fantasy and abstract thinking. He will construct crossword puzzles and Double-Crostics. He would tend to be a dabbler, rather than pursue anything thoroughly.

Because of the Aquarius need for freedom and the Pisces confusion about this world, such a person can have a great deal of trouble surviving in the real world. The problem is that he can be too easily distracted, so that he has difficulty finishing things and therefore has no sense of accomplishment.

CUSP OF PISCES AND ARIES

People born between March 19 and March 21 are on the Pisces and Aries cusp. It should be noted that because the Sun moves into Aries on

March 21 of each year, this cusp is very small. These people combine the creativity of Pisces with the drive of Aries, so they often achieve renown in some artistic field. The Aries need to be first, coupled with the Pisces ability to generate fresh ideas from the imagination, often puts these people in the forefront of their field.

The enthusiasm and energy to initiate is tempered by a sensitivity to the needs of others, so that such a person often has an enthusiastic team working with him. He can encourage others to take risks, and is sympathetic to their fears. He appreciates creativity in all forms. He encourages his associates to express their own creative urges. He has great compassion, and will think of new ways to take care of people's needs. His optimism inspires others to have faith in themselves.

On the negative side, the Pisces laziness together with the Aries impatience can cause this person to give up any creative endeavor before he has completed it. He tries everything once, perfecting nothing. This person wants to be a leader and be respected for his executive abilities, but will get very hurt and upset if this does not happen. He can get arrogant about his own ideas.

Such individuals have an ability to create a fantasy world for themselves, and they do not let the facts interfere with that fantasy. They are past masters at not dealing with issues whenever they so choose. They put the Aries energy into the Pisces fantasy. They are willing to take risks, but are terribly upset when those risks fail. In an effort to overcome the insecurity of Pisces, the Aries side can make such individuals domineering. They can become angry if others do not share their fantasy. They find it difficult to live with themselves, so naturally it is difficult for others to live with them.

Rising Signs:
Aries Through Pisces

Consult the Ascendant Tables at the end of the book,
pages 387–92, to find your Rising sign for the hour and day
of your birth. When you have determined your Rising sign,
read the chapter relevant to you.

Your Rising Sign: Aries on the Ascendant

Aries Rising people are self-starters. Like the Ram, the symbol of Aries, these people are headstrong. And like Mars, the planet that rules Aries, these people give the impression of fiery energy, courage, speed, and skill. With the iron and steel of Mars in their sinews, they are tough and commanding. But whatever they do, Aries Rising individuals relate everything back to the self, which gives their personality a sharp focus and colors how they experience the twelve life houses as described below.

FIRST HOUSE: PERSONALITY

People born with Aries Rising make their presence felt. Even their gait and manner suggest an attitude of "Here I come!" Their bodies and minds are finely attuned to their immediate environment. This gives them a sense of urgency and the confidence that they can handle whatever happens.

These people are prepared to take on anything or anyone around them. They are so lacking in fear that often they will take great physical or professional risks to carry out the most ordinary tasks. Their friends may ask, "Is it worth it?" Aries people will reply, "It is, if I do it." They are fiercely self-reliant.

Never are these people prepared to sit back and let life come to them. They are the self-starters of the Zodiac, men and women who create their own destiny and are often followed by the multitude. They have great faith in their stamina, their survival power. They love nothing more than action, especially if it involves challenges and dares.

People with Aries Rising are often more idealistic than practical. They can quickly be talked into supporting hopeless causes, particularly if they

151

see themselves as the rallying point. Their imaginations are extremely active. New ideas and schemes crowd their minds, often forcing them to abandon pending projects for new ones. Once a project catches their imagination, though, their enthusiasm is unlimited. But a desire for instant results makes them ignore proper planning and detail. Impatience is a major flaw.

Aries Ascendant people tend to have quick tempers. Feelings of frustration or indignation can trigger immediate action, sometimes anger or even violence. But such rages are usually short-lived. When temper subsides, Aries Rising people are not too skilled at coping with subtler situations. Masters of action and direct thought, they are bewildered by the less direct and more emotional sides of life.

Their hearts and feelings are vulnerable. Sensitive to the self but insensitive to others is more the rule than the exception. Thoughtless actions and blunt words often hurt the people they care for most. Such behavior can occasion loss or regret. Yet Aries can take the bitterest of blows and start all over again.

SECOND HOUSE: MONEY AND POSSESSIONS

Money and possessions are more important to Aries Rising people than one would think by casually knowing them. A lifestyle geared to being constantly on the go and involved in endless activities may suggest slight interest in things material. But Aries Rising people are keenly aware of the advantage of a stable base. And then they like to build on it.

They also like to acquire their own property—bought independently, owned independently, and managed independently. They have more faith in land and buildings than in cash or credit. Money in the bank is idling, and it should be active. So they pick one of two general alternatives: spending cash impulsively or tying it up safely in property investments.

Aries Ascendant people can be surprisingly conservative as far as their assets are concerned. Sometime they can be almost rigid. In spite of their spontaneous and open ways in other areas of daily life, they can miss valuable opportunities by sitting on investments and not moving with the trends or varying their assets to get a broad mix. Many people with Aries Rising have complained that inflation has left them behind the eight ball; their holdings have dwindled or the interest on their holdings is lower than for other available investments.

Such people can be obstinate about taking good financial advice, believing they already have all the answers. Mistrust of experts and professionals is a trait developed in order to survive independently. But once it backfires, Aries will reluctantly admit that good advice is also an asset to acquire. Although slow to make changes, Aries Rising people show a sound practicality in financial matters, sometimes even flashes of brilliance. Once they start building and acquire a feel for wealth, they can amass fortunes.

The most important asset of all to Aries Ascendant people is the physical body. Although they will not hesitate to risk it to achieve their objectives, they like to keep it in fine shape. A fit and agile body is their best security.

THIRD HOUSE: CLOSE CONTACTS AND COMMUNICATION

Close contacts and communication keep Aries Rising people continuously active. They are forever on the move, visiting people, writing letters, making phone calls, and generally spreading their ideas and themselves about. Getting in touch rather than being in touch is the hallmark, and it is for the sake of moving pet projects along rather than an interest in other people.

Aries Ascendant folks have brilliant notions about most of the problems facing their friends and society. There is no subject that stumps such people. But too often their brainstorms lack the maturity of experience. Solutions are plucked out of thin air with admirable dexterity, but not out of the solid ground of consideration and analysis.

These individuals make first-rate speakers. Indeed, Aries Rising people are known to be fast and voluble talkers. Sometimes, though, they may develop a verbal block because too many swift ideas crowd the mind and cancel each other. Words come so easily that they can be careless about the way they put things; often they are guilty of putting their foot in their mouth, creating long silences of embarrassment or resentment.

Aries Rising finds it fairly easy to keep emotion out of debate. Being able to see and adapt to many points of view, such people can take a stand fully aware of the legitimate arguments of the other side. This sometimes make them appear to be opportunists, a reputation that can destroy their credibility and persuasive power. They may come on as individuals who do not believe in what they say. But come what may, Aries does not stop expounding.

FOURTH HOUSE: HOME AND FAMILY

Home and family attachments can be unexpectedly strong for Aries Ascendant people. Their action-packed, on-the-go existence can create a false impression, as though outside activities are far more important. But the basic Aries impulsiveness leads to idealistic attitudes about close ties, so that home and family are never ignored or abandoned for other alliances.

Home and family affairs are areas where the emotions of Aries Rising people can be surely touched—and touched in ways that may render the Aries brand of relating inadequate. Even single Aries like to keep in touch with home base. But verbal contact of a simple and direct variety is easier than sentiment. Although they may spend a lot of time away from house and kin, the home is a place they long to return to, even if it is only to leave quickly.

Aries Ascendant people are often softies at home. These individuals believe in the old-fashioned family traditions. They are inclined to feel that the modern approach to family life is not as desirable as the good old days when "families were families," staying together and playing together.

Aries people with their own family are likely to move many times in their adult life. Rather than leave their families behind, they like to take them along—at whatever expense. The isolated Aries for whom such an endeavor is not possible makes frequent return trips over long distances or sends regular caring communications so that the feeling of separation is not allowed to become excessive.

FIFTH HOUSE: ROMANCE, CREATIVITY, AND CHILDREN

Love and romance, creations of the mind or body are resources of immense pride for Aries Rising people. In romance, they are romantics. They love to give fine and expensive gifts, to dine and wine in the best places, to put on a show. A casual date or an intimate dinner party at home can have all the excitement of Aries on a dare. He or she love to dramatize their part as host or hostess, doing all the right things, and especially creating spectacular little surprises to add to the occasion's entertainment.

Aries Rising people can be arrogant about their talents, but they have every right to be because they guard them so jealously. They often will take all sorts of risks, financial or otherwise, for the opportunity to display their particular abilities. Sometimes they appear to be gambling all. But this is unlikely to be the case; they are very clever at creating the effects of suspense.

The Aries Ascendant person has a great need to show off. When he or she becomes a parent, children become the focus of their zeal. Aries parents strive to give children every advantage in order to be proud of them, as well as to develop young ones in the Aries model who can do and think and say everything. Aries parents try hard to spend a lot of time with children, but inevitably other activities interfere. The justification for absences is that the child will learn to be a loner, just like their parent.

Aries craves applause for personal efforts. The appeal of being accepted by glamorous people or being in glamorous situations is often a compulsive drive for Aries Rising individuals.

SIXTH HOUSE: WORK AND HEALTH

In work and health matters Aries Ascendant people are not afraid to be analytical, as long as emotion is kept out of the problem-solving. At work they are likely to display an impressive talent for getting to the heart of the matter instantly and for offering sharp ways to proceed.

They are not great ones for getting immersed in detail, but they quickly size up a problem. If given control, they will do their energetic best to remove the difficulty in record time. These are no clock-watchers or slouches once they accept an assignment—and stick to it.

They are inclined, though, to get distracted from their labors unless they are physically involved or in a position where they can set the pace. Aries Rising folks can be perfectionists, always on the lookout for ways of introducing greater efficiency. This aggressive manner can appear self-serving and get on the nerves of associates. When Aries perceives resentment, criticism of coworkers' effort is quick to be expressed, though never in a vicious way. Given the chance to do better, they take swimmingly to a leadership role, but are not always as effective as they imagined they would be.

People with an Aries Ascendant take an intense interest in diet, analyzing for themselves and by themselves its possible effects on their total health. They are then inclined to adopt delicately contrived measures—which others may call fads—to improve their resistance to illness. The Aries person really believes in purity of mind and body, but never quite manages to achieve this high ideal.

SEVENTH HOUSE: ALLIANCE AND PARTNERSHIP

Partnerships are not so easy for people born with Aries on the Ascendant. They resent a yoke. But if there is a basic compatibility and understanding, they can work loosely in tandem with a mate.

The trouble is that Aries cannot help trying to be boss. They are often accused of trying to control people and to dominate situations. On the one hand, if they link up with a similar forceful and independent type, there is little chance of a harmonious relationship, let alone a permanent one. On the other, more reserved and placid folk become ruffled and uncomfortable under the aggressive, get-up-and-go Aries influence.

But Aries Rising people do need others, even if only to be admired and encouraged. Sharing can become fairly one-sided. To be completely happy in partnership, Aries must feel they are in charge of the people and the events around them.

In business and social alliances and often in marriages, Aries can be very choosy, carefully selecting a suitable type who will put up with their need to give orders, their frankness, and their lack of diplomacy. However, if they impulsively fall in love, they often manage to choose exactly the wrong partner, with disastrous results.

In partnership, it is extremely important for Aries to be associated with someone who does them credit or whom they can look up to. It is then easier for them occasionally to surrender those independent and self-assertive ways.

EIGHTH HOUSE: SEX, PSYCHOLOGY, AND SHARED ASSETS

The Aries approach to sex is straightforward. There is very little sentiment involved. When a suitable mate has been found and the romantic preamble, if any, is over, they are concerned with getting to the point as quickly as possible, expressing themselves through the action rather than unnecessary words or game-playing.

The Aries psychology is expressed in a similar rugged realism. These people do not like pretense or pose. They can be rude to a fault in the company of others or on social occasions where great delicacy and tact are required. Their no-nonsense directness often arouses hostility and hurt feelings.

Aries Rising people seldom confide their inner secrets to others. They may be aware of a compelling urge to achieve a higher freedom, a sense of being beyond the limits of the physical body. Sex often is felt to be a way of achieving this freedom, as well as the means of self-renewal.

A person with an Aries Ascendant often can make money through alliances and marriages. The presence of a partner, perhaps even a silent one, helps them to maintain a sense of financial responsibility. A lover or mate, a teammate or colleagues help them to conserve and improve shared money and resources.

Aries people like to impress. Increasing joint funds often is a painless way to win admiration and respect.

NINTH HOUSE: EDUCATION AND TRAVEL

In their more relaxed moments people with Aries Rising believe in looking beyond the limited horizon of immediate circumstances in which they are so often deeply involved. They feel that only by looking to the future can they receive the insights that help them cope with today.

Aries Ascendant people's strong faith in themselves helps them to be philosophical about the ups and downs of life. They are highly intuitive, sometimes prophetic. They often are inspired in their ability to cope with fast-moving situations. They are optimistic. They like to believe in something. In religious matters they are broad-minded but cannot help adhering to convention.

These people love to travel—the farther the better—and to observe the cultures of other nations. They learn more easily from people and experience than from books and lectures. Time-consuming and complex studies can be a bore for most Aries Rising folks. Trying their hand at a situation is far more appealing.

Aries people often visit strange and exotic places in an effort to find something new to believe in. But usually they return to the accepted religious and philosophical views. It is difficult for them to change their opinions once they have been formed. It may take an emotional upheaval in their personal lives for them to develop a workable philosophy of their own.

TENTH HOUSE: FAME AND AMBITION

Success and image figure prominently in the thinking of Aries Rising people. Because they must always be out in front, they have strong urges to get way ahead of the pack. Fame for its own sake doesn't interest them so much as the public recognition of being a leader.

Their basic motivation is to get to the top where they will be respected and free from the demands that interfere with their need to be in charge and give orders. It is not so much the prospect of material reward that impels these people, as the prize of power. Such power will allow them to implement their schemes and enterprises without having to refer them to higher-ups.

Aries people are particularly fitted to control large organizations. Their tremendous capacity for physical work often enables them to outflank rivals who may have more smarts and persistence. The Aries stamina, gift of initiative, and pioneering spirit are tremendous assets for reaching a chief executive position. Aries have little taste for monotonous desk jobs, no matter how important the job may be regarded. Their ambition is to rise to such a position of authority or prestige that they can select the adventurous assignments and leave the mundane operations to others.

ELEVENTH HOUSE: FRIENDSHIP AND COMMUNITY

Aries Rising people cannot stand dull companions. They are very selective about the company they keep. As a result, they have many acquaintances but few close friends.

An emphasis on physical fitness makes Aries sports-minded and exercise-oriented. So they continually join recreational or health clubs, searching for the perfect formula. Here they pick up pals and casual acquaintances. Aries also knows a lot of people at work or from business on a first-name basis, and enjoys the endless socializing such contacts provide. Some of these people may regard themselves as friends, but few ever reach this degree of intimacy with Aries.

Basically Aries people are attracted to others for their ideas. Aries Ascendant types like to be associated with free thinkers whose beliefs are so advanced that they have not yet been accepted by society. Only in their religious and philosophic views do they tend to be conventional, and their friends often help them gradually to change such beliefs. Aries people surround themselves with odd types whose eccentric ways are tolerated as long as their minds are sharp and stimulating.

Aries people often have radical ideas, which can attract an extreme type of person. Although fairly socially conformist when it comes to action, they can be drawn unsuspectingly into political intrigues in which their fearlessness may be exploited. They are not very good at playing people off against each other; their frankness gets in the way.

TWELFTH HOUSE: SECRETS AND THE UNCONSCIOUS MIND

Aries Ascendant people seldom come to terms with their own emotions. They are so used to being brave and self-assertive, they fail to notice that the tender side of their nature is constantly repressed. This tenderness pops up unexpectedly, most embarrassing for steely Aries, and is immediately pushed down again.

Emotions and sentiment are things Aries Rising people associate with their homes and families. Here their feelings are nicely compartmentalized, so there are no unforeseen problems.

The area in which Aries individuals are least equipped to handle their emotions is in their love lives. This is a secret they frequently manage to keep even from themselves. They confuse boldness with openness.

Emotions are involved in every facet of life, even for clear-thinking Aries. If they are constantly repressed, they have to surface somewhere. For Aries, they break out as compulsive urges and sudden impulses—so often the cause of problems, loss, and regret.

A bit of self-analysis and introspection, especially by Aries men, would help them to understand their emotional complexes. But pioneering Aries folk, forging ahead in the world of action, seldom have the time and patience.

Your Rising Sign:
Taurus on the Ascendant

People born with Taurus Rising tend to be security-conscious in everything they undertake. An inhospitable environment makes them anxious. But money, things, and love (a possession to them) make them feel comfortable. Taurus Rising folk sometimes amass possessions more for the sake of security than for the pleasure or prestige they offer. This need affects how Taurus Rising people experience each of the twelve life houses as described below.

FIRST HOUSE: PERSONALITY

Taurus Ascendant people are slow to start, but long and strong on the finish. They are particularly tenacious. Once they decide to take on a project, they can be counted on to complete it. The quality of follow-through makes them desirable workers and partners.

You always know where you stand with Taurus Ascendant people. They are renowned for their straightforward and honest approach. But it isn't always easy to get them to change their mind once it is made up. Taurus can be very stubborn. Strongly opinionated, too, they do not sheepishly follow what other people say.

The symbol of Taurus is the Bull. Like the Bull, Taurus Rising people usually have powerful constitutions, which enable them to work long stretches at a time without tiring. And, like the Bull, they resent being pushed or pressured. Methodical and deliberate, they plod along at their own pace. In one day Taurus can often achieve more than flashy and dynamic types.

Loyalty is an outstanding characteristic of Taurus Rising people. Once they give their word, their heart, or their hand, they would rather suffer than let a person down. And suffer sometimes they do. Their loyalty can

159

land them in tricky situations. But even when betrayed, they refuse to acknowledge it until the fact is driven home in a painful way.

Taurus Ascendant people are uncomfortable with doubts and insecurities, so much so that they prefer to shut their eyes to difficult realities. They are reluctant to doubt the sincerity of loved ones and friends until they themselves have examined all the possibilities. When Taurus people finally accept the fact of betrayal, their hearts turn to stone as far as the betrayer is involved. He or she is written off without another thought.

Taurus Rising people sometimes find it hard to make decisions. They try to avoid radical changes. They try to leave nothing to chance. They prefer to fix a goal well into the future and then work slowly but constructively toward it. Change puts them off balance. Their thought processes are geared to follow accepted and reliable patterns.

Taurus is not the gambling type. Security in all its forms means more than virtually anything else. Such people like to surround themselves with solid possessions. Their ruling planet is Venus, planet of attraction, harmony, and beauty. But being an earth sign, they express their fondness for beautiful things in practical ways. They are good with their hands, and they have an eye for design and texture. Taurus craftspeople enjoy fashioning jewelry, clothes, furniture, and objects of art out of the sturdy materials of the earth.

Taurus people love their homes. They take great pride in their families. Their sense of possessiveness dominates the people in their life. Taurus can treat loved ones like "things." And because Taurus folk like the things around them to be desirable to others, they unwittingly foster situations where flirtation and competition go on right under their noses. When the Bull finally gets a whiff, the jealous rage is something to behold!

SECOND HOUSE: MONEY AND POSSESSIONS

Money and possessions mean security to Taurus Ascendant people. Their peace of mind depends on it. They have no illusions about the world and its worship of material things. Taurus people are not grabbers, but they know the value of money. For them, there may never be enough tokens of ownership to give them an adequate sense of security. When they do have the funds, they put them into tangible assets—especially those they can touch and gaze upon.

Jewelry and precious metals, paintings and ceramics, stamp and coin collections give Taurus the feel of wealth. If they cannot afford these things, they dream about having them. When Taurus people invest in land or buildings, you can be sure they are not absentee owners. They enjoy the experience of seeing and feeling part of the earth they own.

Taurus Rising folk often reach their goal of stability and comfort because they do not divide their time. They tend to fix on one aim early in life—to acquire enough material wealth to feel good—and never get distracted from it. Even though they marry, raise families, and enjoy the good life, all these activities are geared to the driving ambition to be as well off as possible.

Taurus people are naturally conservative. If they buy something, it must be the best quality. Their possessions are durable and eye-appealing; some of them last long enough to become valuable antiques. The home is the place where Taurus Rising people like to show off their artistic sense. They strive to make everything attractive and comfortable.

Extravagance is the middle name for some of those with Taurus on the Ascendant. They like rich food, heady drink, flashy clothes, and fast cars. These flamboyant desires are in direct contrast to the steadfast and sober nature of most Taurus Ascendant folk. And even though they watch their pennies grow into nickels, dimes, and quarters, they cannot help spending on luxuries for themselves and loved ones.

Taurus Rising people seldom have all their eggs in one basket. They manage to spread their savings in various ways so that a disaster in one sphere will not wipe them out. When Taurus people complain they have no money, they don't mean cash in hand; they mean a large and comfortable margin in savings or investments. They try to allow nothing to threaten their very precious feelings of security.

THIRD HOUSE: CLOSE CONTACTS AND COMMUNICATION

Taurus Ascendant people are neither garrulous nor gregarious. Casual contacts can frighten them. But close ties are very important. Taurus people make a point of keeping in touch with their nearest relatives and all associates with whom they feel a close bond of affection.

Quick visits and brief phone calls can rattle the Taurus Rising person. He or she needs time to react to a new situation, then settle into it. So letter writing and overnight or weekend trips are the preferred means of keeping in touch. Taurus people like to talk and think about things gone by, and to return to places to which they were attached in the past.

Taurus people operate at a far deeper emotional level than would seem to be the case for these practical, down-to-earth types. They are not quick thinkers. They deliberate; they weigh all the pros and cons before reaching a decision. Some of these people seem to be slow learners because teachers fail to give the subject matter an emotional content to which Taurus Rising can relate.

People with their Ascendant in the sign of the Bull are sensitive to their immediate environment. They are more dependent on what they feel than on what they think. If they rely on their minds too much, they often make mistakes. Having learned this lesson once, they tend to mistrust snap judgments in themselves as well as in other people.

Taurus Rising folk feel most comfortable in an environment that appeals to all the senses. They rely on touch and sight and sound more than many other people do. Taurus people love nature in all its splendid variations. It is important that these people settle in a neighborhood where beauty, balance, and harmony can be achieved and maintained.

FOURTH HOUSE: HOME AND FAMILY

Home life is a matter of personal security for Taurus Ascendant people. It also reflects their own value and status in the world. So do their loved ones, whom they often regard as objects to be admired and shown off. Family members for whom they are responsible must be clothed and presented in the best possible light. They are adamant about schooling youngsters in good manners and socially acceptable ways.

Their pride in their home and family borders on fierce possessiveness. It is not unusual for Taurus people to treat loved ones as if they were precious china dolls. Nor is it unusual for loved ones to feel objectified and stifled.

Taurus Rising folk are happiest entertaining at home. Here they can bestow the kind of hospitality they enjoy receiving, but seldom get, when they go out. Their surroundings must be plush. But no matter how modest their incomes and circumstances, they always try to be lavish in one way or another. What they cannot do because of lack of money, they will say in other ways—eye-catching flower arrangements or pleasing combinations of color and fabric.

Taurus Ascendant people often deprive themselves of certain pleasures to make their home more luxurious and comfortable. Food and drink must be of the best quality, and quantity is no object. If Taurus folk have a lot of money, they can become gourmets or gluttons. At the very least they are self-indulgent to an extreme.

Everything to do with the home and hearth is performed with a flourish. Here is the unconscious urge to impress. People whose Rising Sign is under the Bull would love to own a mansion and stock it with every lovely object imaginable. But their practical nature balances this expansive urge. That ever-present need for security prevents them from stretching fantasy to the reality of bankruptcy.

FIFTH HOUSE: ROMANCE, CREATIVITY, AND CHILDREN

People with Taurus on the Ascendant are not gambling types. They would never dream of approaching love life or artistic ventures with a speculative eye. Such matters are earnest ones for Taurus, who typically see them in terms of security. Will security be threatened or can it be relaxed? With that as the abiding question, Taurus folk go forward with a good deal of common sense and discrimination.

In romance, Taurus Rising people have a bent toward the sensuous and sensual. But this tendency is offset by a cautious, even prim, approach. They do not make bold advances, and they abhor this trait in people whom they are dating. A flamboyant come-on from a prospective partner can turn Taurus right off. They like their romantic companions to be modest and conventional, at least in public.

Taurus people experience strong emotions, but have a hard time expressing them verbally. Statements of ardor and passion embarrass them. They frown on displays of affection and emotion, which they believe are unnecessary and tend only to make them look frivolous to the onlooker. Reserved and shy out of bed, in bed the story is different. With a responsive lover, Taurus people abandon inhibitions for the full gratification of their senses.

Taurus Rising people can be extremely critical in romantic matters. Their usualy live-and-let-live attitude fails them in this area. They set high standards of morality, and then find it hard to live up to them. They try to choose lovers and mates who share the same moral code. Fidelity is paramount. Taurus people are severely threatened when promises are broken and commitments betrayed.

A common-sense attitude characterizes the Taurus approach to creativity and artistic endeavor. They don't daydream about talents they don't have or those that cannot be made practical and lucrative. Such people usually know their limitations. They try to make the most of their abilities. Applied arts and handicrafts are areas where Taurus Rising folk excel. Rather than being original and pioneering, their imagination is more suited to rearranging ideas that have already been absorbed by experience.

Children are a source of pride for Taurus Ascendant folk. It is not unusual for Taurus to plan well in advance when to have a family. The job of overseeing the family never quite ends. Taurus people want their youngsters to be a splendid advertisement of their fine parenting tradition. So they can be strict with the kids, not putting up with any nonsense. Taurus Rising people spend a great deal of time with children, seeing they get a good education and that they practice all the social graces.

SIXTH HOUSE: WORK AND HEALTH

Taurus Ascendant people are often drawn into trades or professions connected with music and art. The application of beauty is their special skill. But it is terribly important to them that the work surroundings be harmonious. They become uptight and irritable if conditions grate on their senses. Thrust among noisy and unruly people, Taurus will quit the job before adjusting to it.

It is the noise that really bothers Taurus Rising folk. They like sweet and melodious sounds, a gift from the planet Venus. Otherwise they probably would get along swell with teammates, no matter how distracting job relationships and job politics become.

Taurus folk work well with others. They bring tact and diplomacy to disputes. They are reasonable and cooperative workmates. They have a knack for bringing together people with clashing opinions. They are good peacemakers. And they have a strong sense of justice. They will not stand around indifferently while their coworkers are exploited or badly treated.

But Taurus Rising people do have a stubborn streak. It can infuriate bosses and colleagues. On the other hand, this trait enables them to follow through with painstaking detail all the requirements of a task and to complete it to near perfection. Only their bosses and colleagues would complain that the Taurus method is too exacting, too trivial, and too time-consuming. But for Taurus it is the only method!

The health of people influenced by the sign of the Bull depends on their working and living conditions. Their feeling of well-being is attuned to peace and quiet. Sensitive to jarring impressions, they can easily be upset. If conditions are harmonious, fine. If not, all manner of imagined ailments plague them. They are inclined to worry unduly about minor health problems, despite the fact that they have a naturally robust constitution. Strong as an ox, nevertheless they often feel weak as a kitten. But when the question of professional diagnosis and treatment comes up, Taurus Rising people characteristically ask, "How much will it cost me?"

SEVENTH HOUSE: ALLIANCE AND PARTNERSHIP

Personal relationships for people with Taurus Rising cover the vast terrain where angels fear to tread. Close relationships, especially of love and marriage, make these people uptight and skittish. Taurus Ascendant people are not afraid of commitment. They are afraid of betrayal. They guard their security by adopting whatever pose seems to work with a partner or mate who could threaten them.

The truth is that their emotions are intensely concentrated, not casual, and always ready to blow the calm, cool, and collected pose. Taurus Rising people try to handle partnerships with a matter-of-fact grace, but a great deal of ferment is going on under the surface.

Taurus Rising is possessive and jealous. These people suffer agonies when a lover or mate keeps them pawing at the air, seeking solid ground. Uncertainty is the brink of a pit of terror. They cannot endure to be dangled on a string or kept at bay. Their emotional tranquillity and happiness demand their knowing exactly where they stand.

Marriage is a matter of great moment. Taurus Ascendant people do not enter it lightly. Serious planning must go on before the commitment is made. As long as Taurus feels that his or her love and affection are returned, faithfulness will override all. Except frustration! Once intimacy is established, Taurus folk demand a fulfilling physical relationship.

In business and social alliances, Taurus Rising people expect open and aboveboard behavior. They want full disclosure; no detail, no secret, no nuance of feeling is too trivial for their partners to omit. But Taurus people themselves may not be as emotionally honest or straightforward as they expect others to be.

Nevertheless, Taurus people work well in business partnerships, and business partnerships usually work out well for them. Their dislike of financial risks combined with their capacity for dogged effort usually ensures that the partnership reaches a solid financial footing.

EIGHTH HOUSE: SEX, PSYCHOLOGY, AND SHARED ASSETS

Modern attitudes about sex are not likely to meet with the full approval of people who have Taurus on the Ascendant. They believe in maintaining a strict code of behavior. Their tendency toward prudishness makes them regard sexual freedom as a threat to the traditions of family, loyalty, and security.

Taurus people might be surprised to hear themselves criticizing the effects of "loose morals" on society as a whole. Until the subject comes up, they probably never realized they worried about the subject. If questioned closely, and if they give in to their basic honesty, Taurus folk will admit that there really is nothing wrong with sexual freedom except the uncertainty it generates—and that is a Taurus bugaboo.

A live-and-let-live attitude is the Taurus psychology. They are prepared to take people and conditions as they find them. If the conditions are too grating, Taurus will leave. And if people are too upsetting, Taurus will flee. But they won't seek to change the environment. The exception is when people and conditions interfere with their money and possessions. Then they react in a narrowly focused way. It is not unusual for them to stand pat and fight to the finish.

People with Taurus Rising often inherit money or a position of prestige. Through a desirable marriage some of them achieve wealth and fame that would not be theirs otherwise. Although they do not take marriage lightly, they have an eye for improving their financial position. If marriage involves more than material security and prestige, all the better. It can be said that the number of Taurus folk who marry poorly is fewer than those who marry into money.

Taurus Ascendant people bring fine personal assets to business partnerships, and help to increase shared assets. Their tireless energy and patience carry an endeavor far beyond the initial stages. They work hard to develop a project and bring it to completion. Preferring to work in the background and avoid upfront risks, nevertheless they are able to teach other people how to achieve a good image and material success.

NINTH HOUSE: EDUCATION AND TRAVEL

People born with Taurus as the Ascendant are not the types to fall for highfalutin doctrines or creeds. If any aspect of learning is not true in their experience, it is suspect. Although many of them adhere to traditional philosophic or religious codes, it is not with zeal; it is the expected thing to do to get ahead.

These people are the pragmatists of the zodiac. They feel their way as they go. They test every idea and suggestion by their own practical leanings. They would never mislead anyone. The only trouble is that they can often miss the spirit of an idea.

Taurus Rising folk are sticklers for the letter of the law, whether it is religious, philosophical, or legal. They must guard against being too cautious and conservative. On the one hand, they accept only what can be proved by concrete evidence. On the other, they easily experience the subtleties of art and beauty through pure sensation.

These people are inclined to support established authority whenever they are in doubt. In spiritual matters they are often orthodox, until their own experience teaches them otherwise. Then they can rise to great heights of enlightenment.

Knowledge for its own sake is seldom a priority for people with Taurus Rising. Many of them, as youngsters, were chided for being slow learners. Of course, that was probably because the subject matter was so abstract. Taurus people need to feel that whatever they study has a definite and tangible purpose, a purpose that immediately or ultimately improves their basic security.

Taurus Ascendant people are not the type to travel long distances without a good reason. Long journeys to other nations purely for pleasure do not motivate them. And the expense of the tickets can turn them off! But if they can combine travel with commercial goals, they are happy to slip the anchor that holds them so securely to home ground.

TENTH HOUSE: FAME AND AMBITION

The Taurus desire for fame and attainment is not so self-centered as it is in many other zodiacal signs. The Taurus Ascendant person genuinely wants his or her job and career to benefit as many people as possible. The fact that his or her prestige is enhanced is swell, but it is not vital to involvement or performance.

Taurus Rising needs to feel needed. Such people want to be of service in their vocation. Although not highly original in other areas, in business and public affairs these men and women display ingenuity and invention. They have a way of turning unexpected changes to advantage, as long as they themselves are not too unsettled by the changes.

Determined to build something out of their lives, they do their very best even without approval. If they feel secure, they will work with a persistence unmatched by other zodiacal signs. Although they like to measure their personal success in wealth and status, they are capable of working day in and day out on pursuits aimed solely at benefiting society as a whole.

It is not unusual for Taurus people to become involved in scientific projects. Their inventive minds, pragmatic goals, and tolerance for detailed technical work enable them to sustain long periods of frustrating work. In music or art, technology or trade, they endeavor to contribute something tangible to the sum total of human knowledge in that area.

ELEVENTH HOUSE: FRIENDSHIP AND COMMUNITY

No one is more loyal to their friends than a person with Taurus on the Ascendant, except perhaps someone whose Sun sign is Taurus. When Taurus makes a friend, it is not a casual occurrence. And it is not an event that takes place at an intellectual level.

Taurus Rising people are particular about whom they call friend. They are not fussy, but there has to be the right chemistry. The link is emotional, and the bond can be deep. That bond won't be broken as far as the Bull is concerned. When a friend lets Taurus down, there can be a definite cooling-off period. But if the friend sincerely apologizes, Taurus is prepared to forgive and forget.

They are no fools, of course. They are too practical to be used by so-called friends. You can't force a Taurus person against his or her wishes. Opportunists don't get far with these folk. And high-pressure types might just as well not try to develop that special bond called friendship.

The way to lead a Taurus is not by the ring through the Bull's nose, but by love. Taurus people give love and affection freely, and they expect their close friends to reciprocate in kind and quantity. These sons and daughters of Venus feel hurt at the slightest evidence of neglect.

Taurus Ascendant people are not types to join clubs and groups that highlight intellect over sentiment, or that feature large-scale impersonal goals over the nitty-gritty everyday ones. A group must have a useful purpose for them.

Yet Taurus people easily become involved in humanitarian efforts if they feel secure with the group members. They often are dedicated for purely altruistic motives. They can immerse themselves in projects that seem to have no extrinsic or material rewards for them. Taurus Rising people do not resent volunteer work or the helping and caring services.

Taurus people need to exchange ideas with others, but superficial contacts are difficult for them. Acquaintances are few. Taurus folk are a bit too insecure to approach strangers or newcomers merely on the basis of group interest. Friendship, preferably of an intimate and long-standing nature, is preferable to casual companionship.

Taurus are wonderful listeners. They are staunch and understanding; theirs is the shoulder to cry on. Their practical turn of mind offers solutions to problems that baffle their friends. They have a deep, seemingly endless, well of sympathy. They often sacrifice for their friends, providing a sense of total support and caring.

When a person is in need, a Taurus friend is a friend indeed.

TWELFTH HOUSE: SECRETS AND THE UNCONSCIOUS MIND

People born with Taurus on the Ascendant have strong and sympathetic imaginations. Their fears and compulsions have a terrifying reality. They worry, especially as youngsters, that their imaginations will take them over.

The slightest fear can be exaggerated into enormous proportions. Once their vigorous fantasizing gets going, it often gives rise to compulsive behavior that they cannot understand. Such uncontrollable impulses shock the cautious and reserved side of their nature.

This is their big secret. They would not care to admit that there was a time in their life when they were unable to control a longing for pleasure, pure and simple. A large part of their adult psychology centers around pleasure and its forbidden aspects. They try to control their constant need for sensual gratification. Or they learn to live with the consequences of overindulgence in food, drink, and erotic experience.

Strong-willed and patient, these people try to control their actions by repressing their emotions. They also try to put down feelings of rage or sadness even when such feelings are justified. They do succeed in avoiding a lot of trouble this way. But repression is repression. Taurus Rising folk repress their passions to such an extent that they can explode at the slightest thing.

Your Rising Sign:
Gemini on the Ascendant

People with Gemini on the Ascendant inherit the mercurial character-istics of the Sun's closest neighbor. These daughters and sons of Mer-cury are indeed "neighborly." They need to be constantly in touch with all facets of their environment, especially the people in it. They are forever rushing around, checking on this one and that one, asking questions, noting replies, and trying to complete what they started. Communication for Gemini Rising people is a two-way street, coloring how they approach the twelve life houses described below.

FIRST HOUSE: PERSONALITY

Gemini Rising people are adaptable and communicative. They are rest-less individuals in mind and body. They are, or try to be, continuously active and on the go. Their favorite pastime is getting out and about, meeting as many new people as they can, touching base with the regular crowd.

Being the first air sign, Gemini bestows a keen and active intellect in these people. They love to exchange ideas. Geminis are often accused of chattering rather than speaking. Their ideas come so fast that they hurry their speech to keep up with their minds. Talking, performing, and traveling come naturally to them.

Gemini is a dual sign. Its symbol is the Twins, for Castor and Pollux, the two bright stars in Gemini. Gemini Rising people are very changeable, often contradictory. They set out to do something with great zeal, get dis-tracted after a short time, and end up doing several other things without returning to their original intention.

Change and variety are their spices in life. Unexpected events and interruptions often disturb other zodiacal signs. But Gemini Rising people thrive on such developments. They can adapt with lightning quickness to virtually any situation that arises.

Excitement and stimulation are basic requirements if Gemini people are to pursue an activity to its end. They become bored and irritable if they are forced to stick to a routine. It is not easy for them to perform in a routine occupation if it does not offer changing surroundings and contacts.

Gemini Rising people are quick-witted, always eager to learn new things. The speed with which they absorb facts makes them appear merely to skim the surface. They seem to be incapable of deep and profound study. This is probably not the case. Gemini people have a serious bent. You would be surprised at the deliberation going on in their heads while they appear to skip from one concern to another.

People with a Gemini Ascendant appear to suffer from a lack of concentration. What is really going on is a powerful mind beaming on all angles of a question. Just one more bit of data is needed to weigh all that has been absorbed. But Gemini people then have a hard time resolving the issue. It is their own fault. They have gathered so much information, it may be impossible to cut through the nonessentials to the heart of the matter.

Gemini Rising folk have a fine knack of doing several things at once. They are usually deft with their hands. They are fine inventors, able to fix any gadget or tool. Some of them can write with both hands; many play musical instruments. Artistic and witty, they have a keen aptitude for languages, writing, lecturing, and teaching.

Geminis are great to have around in emergency situations. Logical and quick, their bright ideas more often than not provide an instant solution. They will help to carry it out, too, because they do not worry about danger or consequences. Their ability to adapt makes them accept the unexpected as a challenge to their considerable mental abilities.

Gemini people are nearly obsessive about their personal freedom. They will not be tied down long. They can walk out without explanation if they find themselves trapped in a relationship. They cannot stand pressure. Hard manual work is something they seek to avoid. They are mental creatures whose silvery qualities tarnish under prolonged physical effort.

SECOND HOUSE: MONEY AND POSSESSIONS

Gemini Rising people are romantic about money. It should be used for having a good time, according to them. They seem to throw it around as they go on their merry way from one person or event to another. They give the impression that money is not very important to them.

But they know exactly what they are doing with their cash. Their agile minds are as efficient as computers, noting everything they and other people are doing. They are always aware of whose turn it is to pick up the tab, and who has missed out. Their nonchalance masks a real concern about every penny, nickel, and dime. Perhaps Gemini folk are too embarrassed to expose this petty concern to view. So they are not above posing as a spendthrift or wastrel.

They can be extravagant. But seldom do Gemini Ascendant people waste all their money. They like to have a solid core of funds invested for a rainy day. They tend to put funds into their home or into a family enterprise. What is not invested can be spent lavishly at times.

They like to have variety in things, especially for the home and their families. They think nothing of abandoning old things and buying new ones to fit the trends. The intrinsic value of things is of little importance to them. Possessions for them must be exciting and appeal to the senses. But their senses get easily wearied. Gemini can have a million gadgets around the house, all performing the same task.

Although not emotional themselves, Gemini Rising people are sensitive to others in their environment. They often depend on their ability to excite people's emotions as a means of earning money. This talent enables them to range successfully from actor to con artist. They can be financially successful in the role of agent, broker, merchant, or banker.

A Gemini Ascendant person uses his or her ability to communicate with the public as a means of increasing income. They may take part-time jobs as actors, writers, agents, and teachers. They are modern people who keep up with the times. Their ideas have a fashionable appeal. And they know how to excite the minds of their audience.

THIRD HOUSE: CLOSE CONTACTS AND COMMUNICATION

Close contacts, and plenty of them, are lifelines for Gemini Rising. People are most important assets in the lives of these mercurial types. They sincerely want to know what makes you tick. If anything is askew, there is Gemini trying to figure it out for you.

They take great pride in their ability to persuade and influence people. They realized, probably early in life, that they have the gift of gab. And they make the most of it in their social and occupational affairs.

Gemini Ascendant folk are clever talkers and apt writers. They are chatty and witty. They easily entertain a crowd of people with fascinating stories. They can spellbind the individual with amusing conversation. They never tire of injecting everyday life scenes with the unusual. They have a childlike interest in everything, and it helps them to see with a fresh perspective.

Geminis appear to be intense talkers. They think so fast that words tumble out in a great urgency. Sometimes their tongues cannot keep up with their thoughts. In youth some of these people develop a stutter or other speech impediment.

Gemini Rising folk are habitual telephone users. They like to keep in touch with relatives and pals, although they try to avoid a deep involvement with relatives. They love hearing other people's troubles and discussing them. The logical Gemini mind can always find something of interest in the most trivial detail.

Gemini Ascendant people make many short trips and visits. They prefer traveling by public transportation. It gives them an opportunity to chat briefly with people from all walks of life. Besides, if they drive alone, they probably wind up talking to themselves.

They love listening to news from other people and about other people. Sometimes they get a reputation for being gossips. Gossip, though, is an important tool for Gemini Rising. It enables them to learn about the world and communities and people with whom they are not directly involved.

FOURTH HOUSE: HOME AND FAMILY

A Gemini Ascendant person is fussy about where she or he lives. Although such people like to be on the move, they need to have a place to unwind and retool. A quiet and small niche is all they really need in order to relax and renew their spent energies.

But Gemini Rising people get bored fast. They are unlikely to spend a lot of time at home, especially if they live alone. They are not prone to loneliness. But visiting other people's homes has an instant appeal. Nevertheless they do need the psychological assurance that something solid is waiting for them at the end of their restless day.

If their own private niche has outlived its usefulness, Geminis are quick to make a family of their own. Geminis like the emotional freedom of being single, but they like the physical security of having a family or at least a mate to come home to. Another dilemma for the dual Gemini!

Geminis can be chaotic in the house, either maddeningly sloppy or maddeningly neat. They may throw their belongings around with abandon, leaving them strewn about without any regard. But sooner or later they confront the mess as if they just discovered it. Then they vehemently attack the job of tidying up and putting everything back in its place. Until the next whirlwind change descends!

They can be quick-tempered with their families. Little things that others do or do not do in the house annoy them. Although their lives are usually lived as a constant revolt against routine, they like their home to be run on methodical lines.

They find it easier to organize their home and the people in it than adjusting to the demands of an outside workplace. It is not unusual for people influenced by the sign of Gemini to work at home. Here they can do the writing or make the handicrafts and artistic objects that suit their temperaments at their own sequence and pace.

Gemini Rising people sometimes feel that they want to live in the country, away from the hectic pace. Especially away from the telephone! But isolation rarely works. Living in a rural commune or near a big city is a choice that fulfills the dual needs for privacy and stimulation.

FIFTH HOUSE: ROMANCE, CREATIVITY, AND CHILDREN

Romantically, Gemini Ascendant people are not too reliable. When they are in love, they are charming, attentive, and eager to please. They mean what they say at the moment. But unfortunately it is often difficult for them to maintain a close personal relationship for a long time. After the initial passion has receded, they tend to lose interest and to go their own way.

Gemini Rising folk are often flirts. They can have too or three affairs going at the same time. They are mentally curious rather than physically passionate or emotional. But their love of variety enables them to be skilled and inventive lovers. They can be cold and aloof when it suits them or when the party is over.

Gemini Ascendant people have strong artistic and mechanical abilities. Sometimes they do not spare the time to develop them. Writing and speaking come naturally. They also like to fool around with any and all conceivable machines, tools, and appliances. Their hands and minds are nimble and quick. Gemini is a bit of a culinary whiz, too. They make first-rate actors, entertainers, and caterers.

Children are second nature for Gemini Rising people. Being something of an eternal Peter Pan themselves, they get along splendidly with youngsters of most ages. They do prefer children who have passed the nursing and baby stage, for such tiny creatures baffle Geminis and also tie them down. They truly believe in a live-and-let-live attitude, so they are not too concerned with discipline. Their own forever-young approach to life helps them to understand and to teach youngsters at most stages of development.

SIXTH HOUSE: WORK AND HEALTH

Gemini Ascendant people take their work more seriously than they are given credit for. An observer only sees them flitting from task to task without seeming to finish any of them. But Gemini people do not rigidly adhere to an expected sequence of beginning, middle, and end. In fact, they abhor routine. So they usually vary the way in which they will perform—and ultimately complete—a job.

The Twins have a heaven-sent gift for doing several things simultaneously, without sacrificing efficiency or neglecting any detail. They have an extraordinary memory. Many an employer thankfully remembers the day a Gemini worker joined the staff—and probably regrets the day Gemini, as is his or her tendency to do, left it.

Geminis are exceptional at getting to the bottom of things and finding facts. They make topnotch reporters, researchers, and investigators. Often they are born psychologists and sociologists, with a shrewd and discerning logic. Even if they do not pursue such professions, they nevertheless develop a keen insight into people because they have a tireless interest in what makes people tick.

Gemini Rising folk must find a job that utilizes most of their skills and interests. Otherwise boredom sets in fast. Repetitive tasks unvaried as to time and space chafe at them. If they don't quit, they will rebel by giving far less to the job than it deserves. They will spread themselves thin by becoming involved in outside activities that assume more importance than the job. To be truly happy, they need work that thoroughly challenges the application of their talents and the absorption of their mental energies.

The Twins never seem to run out of energy. In fact, they revitalize by pushing themselves to the limit. They work frantically, sometimes till the wee hours. They seem to get a second, third, and even fourth wind through this incessant activity. With just a tiny bit of peace and quiet, even a refreshment break, they quickly recover.

The health of Gemini Ascendant people is fairly stable, despite their nervousness and intensity. They work off a lot of repressed energy by having their mouths and their hands constantly engaged. So they are not too likely to succumb to psychosomatic ailments. With a great fondness for food and a love of variety, it is predictable that many Gemini Rising folk are diet faddists and exercise bugs.

SEVENTH HOUSE: ALLIANCE AND PARTNERSHIP

Partnerships òf an intimate variety are something of a one-way street where Gemini Ascendant people are concerned. Impersonal or group alliances, on the other hand, are eminently suitable for these dual folk. In business partnerships and other mutual endeavors, the Twins often find the variety of experience necessary for them to work as a team.

Marriage is regarded as a meeting of the minds. But Gemini changes his or her mind so often, it is hard for them to find a partner whose personality is exciting enough to sustain their interest. Gemini people also have the capacity to think about their partners while not being with them. After the honeymoon Geminis think nothing of roaming here and there by themselves.

Gemini Rising people cannot stand to be fenced in. The responsibilities and obligations that go with married life may be experienced as intolerable bonds. It is important for people born under the influence of the restless Twins to find a partner who is capable and who knows his or her mind. Then Geminis won't have to do all the work in the marriage.

Gemini people are inclined to need looking after. They want to be looked after, babied even. Although they present a fiercely independent front, they secretly yearn to be taken care of and given direction. They feel guilty about their aimless ways, and imagine that a strong and helping hand can lead them from childishness to sober adulthood.

With a partner who takes charge, but still allows Gemini plenty of latitude, the marriage can be a happy one. But these people need a long leash, and they will revert to those aimless and childish ways if their sense of freedom is threatened. Geminis do not like to be bothered with the details of domestic life that have nothing to do with other people. They prefer to organize the social side.

EIGHTH HOUSE: SEX, PSYCHOLOGY, AND SHARED ASSETS

Gemini Rising people are unsentimental about sex. Although they have a sweet line of patter and a charming approach, they are down to earth, almost businesslike, when it comes to lovemaking. Nevertheless, they are inventive lovers. They like experimentation. They approach sex naturally, and they usually have few, if any, inhibitions or hangups.

But a love of variety and experimentation does not lead them into promiscuous ways. Geminis are fussy about whom they want to play games with. Either they are interested or they are not. It's hard to seduce them. They, of course, can be the seducers. But their flirtatious ways are often a game that never comes to anything. In fact, flirtation may be their strategy for fending off real sexual contact. It is their way of saying "Nothing doing!"

Gemini-influenced people do not dwell on abstract issues, nor do they worry about the abstract sides of such everyday issues as death and survival. They will not probe too deeply into the problems of life unless those problems happen to be affecting them at the moment. It is enough for them to keep moving with the moment, and not to presume that the moment is ever going to end.

But when Gemini people do put their minds to deep investigation, they can become seriously involved. Invariably they discover a truth that is meaningful to them. And they assume that the truth will be meaningful to others. Their need to communicate with other people leads them to share their insights generously.

Sharing resources as well as insights can be a bond of interest that keeps a partnership going long after Gemini Rising people become bored with other aspects of the partnership. When money and possessions are involved, Geminis can display an admirable degree of responsibility.

It is often best if Geminis are allowed to manage shared assets. The responsibility brings out the best in them. Flighty Geminis often settle more comfortably into double harness when they have the obligation to oversee joint funds. If a partner insists on taking control of the financial side, Geminis as a rule will forget about economizing. Sooner or later they will spend whatever they can get, even if it means dipping into the cookie jar.

NINTH HOUSE: EDUCATION AND TRAVEL

Gemini Ascendant people learn quickly and easily. They are interested in everything. They appreciate knowledge for its own sake and also in order to communicate tidbits of information to their cronies. If they get deeply involved in studies, they will not keep the project to themselves. It is important for these people to share their knowledge with others.

But Gemini is a rebel. He or she will not accept orthodox doctrines merely on faith or as a fashion. Some of these people do belong to established religions, but probably because belonging offers social contacts or because the rigorous logic of the belief challenges the Gemini intellect.

Gemini Rising folk can be fanatical about their love of freedom. Their dislike of established authority often makes it difficult for them to pursue college or university studies to the end. They become distracted or rebellious. They spend a lot of time supporting worthy causes on campus. They like to spread their own ideas on philosophy, religion, and the law. Nonconformists to the end, they enjoy exhorting others to rebel.

Gemini-influenced people like to roam among people of all persuasions and beliefs. They travel at any and every opportunity. Trips to new and different lands intrigue them. Culture contrasts fascinate them; they enjoy discovering how people of other cultures think. It is not unusual for Gemini visitors to shun the tourist role and live with the people. Going "native" is easy because Geminis quickly pick up a new language.

TENTH HOUSE: FAME AND AMBITION

Gemini Rising people have lofty dreams about what they would like to be. But when it comes down to the reality of making decisions, they often are uncertain. Too many careers have appeal for them to decide, once and for all, that this is it. And they have too many talents to focus on one and cordon off the others.

Their ambitious urges tend to take the form of enthusiastic spurts. They get a romantic notion of a field of endeavor, then pursue it only to discover that it really isn't as glamorous as they thought. When the drab reality starts to show through, they lose interest.

It isn't easy for typical Gemini-influenced people to know exactly what they want out of life. Undefined dreams of fame and glory make it almost impossible for them to put up with routine. They want to fly before they can walk. But their mercurial wings are not made to soar like those of eagles, and sometimes they do not get off the ground.

Gemini people are extremely versatile. They can do and adapt to just about anything that requires swiftness of mind and movement. They often achieve maximum fulfillment when they are handling several jobs at once. One job must be mightily challenging to hold their interest for long. The danger is that their versatility may lead them to go from one job to another.

Public image is not a priority concern for Gemini Rising people. Of course, they want to be recognized for their alert minds and their easygoing ways. But they are too nonconformist to assume the conservative pose that befits high standing in the community. In fact, they rather enjoy the reputation for being mischief makers and scandal lovers.

ELEVENTH HOUSE: FRIENDSHIP AND COMMUNITY

No one in the Zodiac makes more contact with people than does the typical Gemini Ascendant person, except possibly someone whose Sun sign is Gemini. The act of communicating is fun. It is also a reason for existence. Geminis do not care whether the ideas exchanged are inconsequential tidbits of information or serious insights about life problems. The important thing is the communicating.

Geminis are vigorously enterprising at establishing relationships. Among their many acquaintances are usually just the right people to help them at any particular time and for any particular situation. If they are isolated from people for even a few days, they start to show strain. They become irritable and stale and frustrated. Their health can be affected.

Typical Gemini Rising people have many friends, associates, and acquaintances. They love to debate. Arguing the issues of the day keeps them vital and young. Their agile minds are usually more than a match for their companions, but they do not always try to win. They will start a verbal dispute for the pure pleasure of exercising their intellectual muscles.

Gemini Rising folk are often in the forefront of radical movements. They are good at starting clubs, associations, and collectives. They like to get involved in community work or burning social issues. They get along well in groups. They have an extraordinary ability to inspire others to support causes they believe are important. But once the initial enthusiasm fades, they move on.

TWELFTH HOUSE: SECRETS AND THE UNCONSCIOUS MIND

Gemini Ascendant people are determined that no one will ever get close enough to them to discover their motives. What makes them tick is a private affair, although they certainly can be nosy about the lives of other people.

Geminis sometimes feel that their true emotions are buried so deep that they can never express them. They often are aware of their own coldness and lack of sympathy. They worry that their interests and intensity might be shallow.

Gemini Rising folk assume many poses and play many games: mischief maker, storyteller, gossip, scandalmonger, petty tyrant, jack or jill of all trades. They appear to be flighty and superficial. But underneath, and not as deep as Gemini fears, is another facet of the Gemini nature.

They possess a solid core of seriousness. This can surface easily in their approach to material matters. Their possessions are more important to them than their breezy manner suggests. They also yearn for security. But it is hard for them to admit that fact and to stay put long enough to attain it.

The underlying need for security is reflected in the way Gemini people refuse to put all their financial eggs in one basket. They depend on their versatility to see to it that the baskets are tended, and that there is more than one source of income.

Gemini-influenced people are often secretly anxious about what others think about them. They want to be accepted. As a result, they are generous and hospitable. They give expensive gifts to mark special occasions. Their memory always serves them in this regard, much to the amazement of their friends. They have a sixth sense about what will give others pleasure, so generally they are able to select just the right gift.

Your Rising Sign:
Cancer on the Ascendant

C ancer Rising signifies instinct and response. People with Cancer on the Ascendant are deep ones, but changeable. Like the Moon, ruler of Cancer, their enthusiasms wax and wane. Like the waters of the Earth, their element, their spirits rise and fall, trickle and stream, then take a sudden turning. Cancer Rising people seek to stabilize themselves through links with tradition and the past. Ties to home and family become a central theme, affecting their experiences in the twelve life houses as described below.

FIRST HOUSE: PERSONALITY

People born with Cancer on the Ascendant are extremely sensitive. They live in and on their emotions. They display a brave front to the world, which manages most admirably to hide the uncertainty within. Like the Crab, their symbol, they scuttle away when they sense danger.

Cancer Rising people know what it is like to be hurt. They feel miserably offended at the slightest criticism. They are often thin-skinned, imagining slights and insults where none are intended. They yearn to be respected and appreciated. No one can ever seem to love them enough.

Deep, black moods are one of the prices Cancer Rising people have to pay for their hypersensitivity. They can get so far down in the dumps that it is sometimes impossible to coax them out until the emotional buildup has been worked out. In these moods they can be demanding of the people around them.

But their sensitivity has a positive aspect. Cancer Ascendant people are very understanding. They will listen for hours to other people's problems. Their sympathy is unbounded. A person in trouble pouring out his or her heart to a Cancer feels truly understood. And the Crab's ability to relate emotionally to others is so great that these people can at times actually feel what the other person is going through.

Cancer Rising people are spasmodically active. When the pressure is on, they can wade into the work and get a lot done. But they are not the staying type. Dogged, unremitting effort leaves them exhausted and lethargic. They need frequent breaks from any prolonged physical or mental effort.

Excessive pressure, which many other signs regard as the normal strains of living, is something Cancer people cannot stand. They put on the toughest and bravest front possible. But at the first opportunity they scurry off to a quiet place where the pace is easy and undemanding, and the surroundings comfortingly familiar.

Cancer Rising people love their homes. They try to make them as attractive and comfortable as possible, in keeping with their strong artistic leanings. They make excellent cooks and considerate hosts. Cancer people are very protective of their loved ones, so much so that they often make their nearest and dearest feel stifled.

SECOND HOUSE: MONEY AND POSSESSIONS

Cancer Rising people like to use their money to put on a show. One of their fondest possessions is their home. They love to entertain. They spoil their guests with the best of everything. They enjoy having a reputation for being attentive and generous hosts. They are prepared to work hard at maintaining that image.

Cancer people are generally conservative with their cash. They like to save up for a home and for all the nice things that go into it. They make it a most desirable place, because they like to spend much of their time there. They frequently collect old books, antiques, and relics of the past. They have a flair for displaying their nostalgic treasures in most attractive ways.

The typical person with a Cancer Ascendant has a great need for security. If they cannot feel materially secure because of lack of money, they will attempt to surround themselves with people or family who love them or are dependent on them.

They try to put something away for a rainy day. They are quite happy to spend as much as necessary to give their children a good education and start in life. They often regard their youngsters as possessions and may be reluctant to let them grow up and go their way.

THIRD HOUSE: CLOSE CONTACTS AND COMMUNICATION

Cancer Ascendant people like to keep in touch with their kin, no matter how distant they are from relatives and family friends. They also like to have more than a nodding acquaintance with their neighbors. Close relationships, near or far, are the stuff of life for Cancer-influenced folk.

Although they are particular about choosing close friends, they have many informal contacts. Cancer people love to invite people to their home. Chatting and exchanging ideas are fine in familiar or domestic situations. Cancer people worry a good deal about the future. Details and little things seem to stick in their minds. Mistakes get blown up beyond all proportion by their vivid imaginations. They also tend to brood about the past, remembering this and that minor thing that most others have long ago forgotten.

Cancer Rising people usually express themselves very precisely when they want to. They can be quite sharp-tongued and critical. They are seldom entirely happy with any current state of affairs. They tend to feel that life was far more desirable in the good old days.

As a rule, people strongly influenced by Cancer are great storytellers, with an eye for quaint and romantic detail.

FOURTH HOUSE: HOME AND FAMILY

Home and family affairs are usually the most important part of a Cancer Ascendant person's life. At the hearth of the home and the heart of the family—here is where they imagine themselves to be.

They want their home to be as attractive as possible and to fill it with the nicest of people. They are often disappointed with the way their families turn out, possibly because their expectations are so high. But their love of their nearest and dearest, as well as their dependence on them as a guarantee of future security, allow these rather critical people to live with human frailty.

Cancer Rising people will forgive anything if they feel appreciated and loved. But if neglected by their families, they are likely to be gloomy and disgruntled. They complain how little they have received in return for all the sacrifices they have made.

Cancer people are charming and diplomatic in their close relationships with friends and neighbors. But they can be picky and mean with lovers or mates. They allow the spiteful side of their nature to surface in the bosom of family.

People born under the influence of Cancer do not like to live alone. If they cannot find a lover or mate who meets romantic or idealistic standards, they are likely to spend much time in intimate clubs or community activities.

FIFTH HOUSE: ROMANCE, CREATIVITY, AND CHILDREN

Cancer Rising people can suffer terribly from jealousy. They desire a love that is complete and perfect. They see anything less, even a harmless word or action, as betrayal of their faith. When badly hurt, these people scuttle back to a safe place. It is almost impossible to reach them then.

They can be passionate lovers but rely on their vivid imaginations to maintain their erotic interest. They are in love with the idea of romantic love. The want to get to the bottom of the mystery of love, and they use their emotions, true or false, to do so. They often put their loved ones on pedestals, failing or refusing to see the faults or shortcomings.

Secret love affairs have a fascination for Cancer Ascendant people. The element of risk provides an extra stimulation that excites their emotions.

The natural talents of people influenced by the sign of the Crab lean toward the artistic. They have an inborn appreciation of beauty and an extremely reliable intuition. They make splendid painters and designers; fine arts and applied arts utilize their moody talents. Their sensitivity and sympathy make them ideally suited for the caring and helping services.

Cancer parents can be rather strict one moment with their children, lovingly indulgent the next. They find it difficult to maintain a middle-of-the-road emotional course.

SIXTH HOUSE: WORK AND HEALTH

Cancer Rising people are excellent workers as long as they believe in the importance of what they are doing. It also is essential for them to feel they are among congenial people and surroundings. They are good organizers who can bring together masses of details.

They are always looking beyond the immediate task to the future. If they are not happy with their present position, they are inclined to dream and speculate without taking much action. Or they leave and drift with their moods, longing for a perfect and safe niche.

The work of Cancer Ascendant people often requires them to travel. Or they are in frequent contact with other countries. They may be obliged to take on extra study and to develop their minds.

Cancer-influenced people shine in any job that makes use of their quality for protecting and caring for others. They are often attracted to the medical and nursing professions, as well as social and child-welfare occupations.

They cannot work efficiently or happily if they have to submit to a rigid or harassing authority. They are easily hurt and start worrying and brooding. Their moods affect everyone around them.

The health of people born with the influence of the Crab demands that they have plenty of change, either in people or surroundings. They are drawn to people who share their fondness for occasional isolation, especially for communing with nature. If they become ill, they recover much more quickly with tender loving care. Their loved ones must not allow these sensitive folk to worry.

SEVENTH HOUSE: ALLIANCE AND PARTNERSHIP

Partnerships are never entered into lightly by typical Cancer Rising people. They like to weigh every angle, especially in love and marriage unions, before taking the plunge. But often they load themselves with partners who have difficulty coping with the pressures of life.

Cancer Ascendant people have an inborn desire to protect and look after others. Often the prospect of having to shoulder a partner's particular problems or responsibilities provides them with a sense of purpose and fulfillment. They may complain from time to time if they feel they are not being appreciated, but otherwise are quite prepared to play a nurturing role. The Cancer woman can be the makings of her man as he is trying to get to the top. She will be prepared to accept more than her share of any sacrifice that may be necessary. Cancer men and women are ambitious for their partners; they want them to make the very best use of their skills and talents.

Nevertheless, people born with the Crab as their Rising sign often feel restricted by the partnership role. They can become especially demanding and even nagging if they feel their partner is not making the full effort.

With an aggressive and fairly competent business partner, Cancer Rising people happily submit to the alliance. They are dependable and encouraging; they would never think of abandoning ship for the kinds of picky reasons that so often mar their love relationships.

EIGHTH HOUSE: SEX, PSYCHOLOGY, AND SHARED ASSETS

Cancer Rising people are fairly strict about marriage vows. They do their very best to stick to the straight and narrow. But if they are not committed in marriage or partnership, they are inclined to believe in sexual freedom. They are more outspoken about these matters than their reticent natures would normally suggest.

They are often in the forefront among advocates of a more liberal approach to abortion, homosexuality, and birth control. They may not personally support any particular issue, but they do champion the right of the individual to make his or her own decisions.

People born with a Cancer Ascendant have a natural interest in occult subjects, unless they have been frightened off by their own experiences. These individuals are strongly intuitive and very impressionable to psychic influences. They frequently are mediumistic.

People with Cancer on the Ascendant have a strong desire to share what they have with those who are closest to them. Where shared resources and finances are concerned, such folk are very dependable. They would never as a rule do anything to endanger joint security. They are the sort of people who are very good at managing community funds.

NINTH HOUSE: EDUCATION AND TRAVEL

Cancer Ascendant people fall into two types. There are the wishful thinkers who only dream about what they would like to do or be. And there are those who relentlessly pursue their objectives.

The more evolved Cancer type is not a follower where education and learning are concerned. These people as a rule do not conform to orthodox religious beliefs unless they have some sort of personal reality for them. They are not prepared to accept other people's explanations of what life is about, or why they are here. Cancer folk have a strong urge to serve others, or at least to protect and help them. Therefore a Cancer person's personal ethics embody the highest religious principles of service and surrender.

At the wordly level, people born under the influence of the Crab frequently have a strong desire to improve their minds. They delve into history and traditions. From these studies they extract the most desirable aspects and try to apply them to improving present conditions.

They love to travel physically, as well as mentally and emotionally. Journeys of the mind are enlightening. Through their vivid imaginations they discover new worlds of creative thought, which inspire them to artistic expression. They also may journey through their emotions into psychic experiences.

TENTH HOUSE: FAME AND AMBITION

The urge of ambition is often extremely strong in Cancer Rising people. This is something of a contradiction in their nature, for much of the time these people are retiring types. They like to be in a comfortable position where demands upon them are not too great.

But the desire to get ahead in the world and possibly make a name for themselves periodically overtakes them. And they become filled with new enthusiasm and a strong determination that often catches their competitors napping.

Cancer Rising folk have a way of putting on an air of self-assurance. Such a pose may not be matched by any feelings of certainty within. They can carry off the big bluff. They have a way of appearing detached, which often forces others to act along the lines they wanted. Cancer can be a manipulator.

People born under the influence of the Crab are often difficult to get close to in business and career affairs; they are more suited for occupations where they can operate on their own.

Cancer people are often more interested in honor and prestige than in the material gains from their ambitious efforts. They have a strong desire for power. They enjoy being in a position of authority, which leaves them free to pursue their lives without reference to superiors.

ELEVENTH HOUSE: FRIENDSHIP AND COMMUNITY

Cancer Ascendant people enjoy doing things for their friends. They like to be of some practical value. A Cancer person is the type who will help a friend to decorate or build a house, giving up a great amount of his or her spare time and thinking nothing at all of it.

Although Cancer Rising people can be difficult and demanding in close relationships, they are far more easygoing and tolerant with their friends. Their affectionate and caring ways usually guarantee them a staunch circle of good friends. They will never let a friend down if it is up to them. And they will forgive their friends any human frailties except disloyalty. Cancer folk regard their friends as essential to their enjoyment of life. Although loners in many ways, they cannot stand to be prevented from circulating regularly among their many acquaintances.

Ties within the community are most important for Cancer Rising people. They like to number among their friends or acquaintances a few important people. The Cancer generosity is geared for public events, which they enjoy hosting. They enjoy sharing the customs and traditions that keep the community together.

It is the desire of Cancer Rising people to leave something lasting where they have been. They make very good members of clubs and societies. They endeavor to make a solid contribution that will be remembered by posterity.

TWELFTH HOUSE: SECRETS AND THE UNCONSCIOUS MIND

Cancer Ascendant people are frequently not very sure of themselves. They have far more faith in their feelings than in their intellectual ability. They are highly intuitive and not a little mistrustful of so-called facts.

In childhood there may have been the possibility that parents or teachers put a mistaken emphasis on learning, putting too much store in memorization or other mental tricks. This could make the Cancer Rising youngster seem a bit slow on the uptake. Both youngsters and adults are more suited to learn through feeling and experience. They also are best at expressing themselves in these ways.

Cancer Rising people are often moody. Whereas other types spend much of their time in their thoughts, Cancer people spend much of their time in their emotions. They are introspective and need time alone to try to work out some of the ideas that enter their heads.

Cancer folk have such vivid imaginations that they can create, at times, an inner world that competes with the real world for their attention.

Like all water signs, Cancer people are inclined to be secretive. This is because they are emotional creatures. They regard their feelings as something very private. They prefer to chat about their problems rather than analyze the causes of them. They often feel that deep down inside there are other parts of their personality they are never quite in touch with.

Some of the pressures from the unconscious mind of Sagittarius people relate to sex. As long as they do not dwell on the subject they have no difficulties, being fairly direct and straightforward in their lovemaking. Any tendency to brood about sex or become preoccupied with sex can trigger conflicts leading to excess or unnatural attempts at repression.

Your Rising Sign:
Leo on the Ascendant

L eo Rising beams the radiance and creativity of the Sun, as well as its
power, centrality, and domination. Leo Rising people want love and
pleasure, but they also need to rule. They want a mate and family, but
they also must be alone with their hobbies. Will the Lion play or will the
Lion stalk? What is the Lion's domain? Self-expression can be a dilemma
for Leo Rising people, coloring how they experience the twelve life houses
as described in the following sections.

FIRST HOUSE: PERSONALITY

People born with Leo on the Ascendant have a strong taste for leadership. There are powerful and intense personalities, with all the qualities
that fit them for positions of authority.

The sign of Leo has always been associated with monarchs and rulers.
In this liberated Aquarius Age, it is possible for Leo to overdo the power
act and to alienate the admirers he or she is so intent on attracting.

Leos are theatrical. Showpeople at heart, they have a keen sense of the
dramatic. They cannot help but imagine themselves always at the center of
attention. In any kind of gathering, they endeavor to dominate the conversation, often becoming quite dogmatic and overbearing in the way they put
their opinions across. Leo Ascendant people find it very difficult to concede
that others may know as much as they do about one of their pet subjects.

People influenced by the sign of the Lion are extremely good organizers. They have a talent for directing others and for getting the very best out
of them. They are often able to inspire their associates with their creative
imaginations and their boundless enthusiasm. Leos are great optimists.

But they do have faults. If they are not receiving sufficient attention
and admiration, they are inclined to demand it. They become noisy, sulky,

or boisterous. Too much applause and acknowledgment often make them conceited and patronizing. The less evolved type of Lion is often snobbish, boastful, and pompous. They love to throw their weight around and to lord it over others.

Typical Leo Rising people have a strong sense of justice and great pride. They find it difficult to do anything underhanded. They are truly sincere people, but mainly they don't want their actions to reflect on their image. They like to think they are above the need to be shady or petty.

At their best, Leo-influenced individuals are generous, warm, and outgoing. They have a great capacity for attracting friendship, loyalty, and respect. Although they expect others continuously to praise their good points, they are always the first to admire and encourage the talents of others.

Leo Ascendant people are ambitious and usually seek a career in a field in which there is a chance for them to become a leader or public figure. They like to do things with a flourish.

SECOND HOUSE: MONEY AND POSSESSIONS

Money and possessions are things that Leo Ascendant people like to keep careful track of. In spite of their rather fancy and often extravagant lifestyle, they usually know where every penny is and exactly how liberal or generous they can be.

The typical Leo Rising person can often be a bit of a contradiction where money is concerned. They can argue and perform endlessly with dependents over the spending of a few pennies. Then they go and buy them a gift that costs the earth! Even then, Leos tend to spend their money only on those who have proved themselves to be loyal and appreciative of what they do.

However, money can be wasted or misspent on the hangers-on. Anyone who satisfies the strong Leo need for compliments and flattery has a good chance of cashing in.

Leo-influenced people are shrewd and discerning when it comes to buying property, or large resources. Although they are not great ones for attending to detail where their possessions are involved, they are seldom neglectful. They take good care of their investments. They see that insurance premiums are paid up and that property is kept in good repair.

Financial problems can affect the health of Leos. They are a fixed sign. As long as there is a chance of holding onto what they own, they will fight to the end without respite. They worry about money more than their confident natures will allow them to admit.

THIRD HOUSE: CLOSE CONTACTS AND COMMUNICATION

Leo Ascendant people are very persuasive. They exude a magnetism that at the physical level is difficult to ignore. When a Leo person walks into a room, everyone seems to know about it. Their vibes are intense and often provocative.

Leos are always trying to get others to agree with their ideas. They are the "professors" of the Zodiac, always trying to teach someone something. They often have deep insights. It pains them not to share this knowledge with their companions. To their companions, they can seem to be "know-it-alls." Leos have to learn that not everyone wants to know what is good for them.

The typical Leo Rising person can often become argumentative if his or her ideas are challenged. Although they will endeavor to be tactful and diplomatic, these devices are often cast aside at the first sign of opposition.

Leos usually have little difficulty in winning the sympathy of an audience, even if there is not unanimous agreement with the points that are being made. They seldom try to speak on any subject they do not believe in wholeheartedly. So their sincerity comes across.

Leos love to bring sunshine into other people's lives. They often are instruments for matchmaking. Love is so important to Leo people, they figure it must be equally important to others.

FOURTH HOUSE: HOME AND FAMILY

Home is the "King of the Jungle's" castle. Leo-influenced people are inclined to rule both home and family with a fairly strong hand. Although they are kind and considerate, they do not stand for any rebellious talk or action on the home front.

But the very dominating manner of Leo brews trouble on the home front, rather than quelling it. Leo people often have to contend with domestic difficulties. Their partners and dependents are seldom as submissive and obedient as the Leo nature expects.

People born under the influence of Leo are often not aware of their own faults. They think in a compartmentalized way, failing to recognize the contradictions in their own actions. Leos will insist on certain procedures in the home or in family affairs, and then fail to follow the guidelines. They offer a transparent excuse that they really believe to be true but that fools no one else.

Leos do not like family laundry washed in public. Their pride requires that skeletons be kept in the closet. They can be very secretive and hedgy about such matters.

Leo Rising people also tend to be quite proud of their roots and traditions. The family tree is immensely valuable if it contains important ancestors, scoundrels notwithstanding.

FIFTH HOUSE: ROMANCE, CREATIVITY, AND CHILDREN

Romance is Leo's sphere. Leo Ascendant people can be romantic about anything, given half a chance. They approach many of life's activities with the unspoiled pleasure of a child on a romp. Recreation, sports, theater, art, and of course love—these are the pleasure-filled niches for these romantic people.

Leos are inclined to gamble. If they don't gamble with their cash, they certainly gamble with their hearts. Leo Rising folk seldom do anything by halves. When they love, they go all the way.

When they fall in love, they fall hard. They put their sweethearts on pedestals, usually far above the limits to which human frailty can aspire. As a result, they are frequently disappointed and sometimes brokenhearted.

Leos have considerable creative talent. They are often good with words and can be writers and lecturers. Their enthusiasm for high ideals often inspires others to make creative efforts and to discover unsuspected or undeveloped talents in themselves. Being dramatic types, Leo men and women often make fine actors.

With children, Leo-influenced people endeavor to bring them up with a good knowledge of the ways of the world. Leos make very conscientious teachers. They can be fairly strict, but this is usually to instill some particular lesson in the child. They often can spoil their children, being far too generous when the times for giving come around.

SIXTH HOUSE: WORK AND HEALTH

Leo Rising people are very conscientious employees as long as they are doing the type of work that makes full use of their capacities. They have a strong sense of duty once they have taken on a task. Their natural pride will not allow them to do any less than their very best. To them, failure to deliver the goods is a self-inflicted insult.

They can often push themselves to the point where their health is affected. Although they usually have strong constitutions, they make heavy demands on themselves. However, Leos are quite health-conscious. They like to look after themselves and to keep fit.

Leo Ascendant people have a natural ability for leadership. They seldom stay on the same rung of the ladder for long. Although they are prepared to follow orders in which they believe, they are always moving toward the top. Higher-ups soon learn to trust them and to admire their way of organizing people and work.

Leos prefer to stay in one job or profession in which they can make a name for themselves. But they will make changes in direction if they find their way blocked. Their driving urge is to be able to express their sense of power and authority.

Their enterprising qualities and reliability seldom go unrecognized by people in charge.

SEVENTH HOUSE: ALLIANCE AND PARTNERSHIP

Leo Rising people do not find partnerships particularly easy, especially those of the love and marriage kind. Although they love to be with their partners, they cannot stand any interference with their independence. Partnership being a two-way affair, there are often domestic fireworks in the Lion's household.

One of the problems for Leo-influenced people in their close relationships is that they frequently choose partners who are as independent-minded as themselves. Even if they picked a more docile type, the Leo nature is to try to awaken the sense of independence in others. The more they succeed in doing this with their partner, the more they add to their own troubles.

Leos want their associates to be free but cannot stand rebellion against their edicts. This is a basic contradiction in the Leo nature. It affects their close relationships more adversely than business and social ones.

In business partnerships, Leo-Ascendant people are more down-to-earth. They are prepared to give and take more for the sake of the business. They can maintain a more detached attitude when their personal emotions are not involved.

Social and intellectual alliances can be a boon for Leos working on a project. An atmosphere of teamwork triggers original and progressive ideas for making money. They also prefer a mutual endeavor to have some sort of benefit for the community. In harness, they like the idea of serving a cause.

EIGHTH HOUSE: SEX, PSYCHOLOGY, AND SHARED ASSETS

Leo Rising people are inclined to be sensual. But their sexual relationships usually have a sense of the romantic about them. This romantic idealism can prevent Leo from surrendering to passionate lust.

They are prepared to make sacrifices as a rule for people with whom they have an intimate association. Their sense of responsibility and justice does not allow them to exploit others for long. There are, of course, the romantic scoundrels. But even they find their Don Juan ways unsatisfying after a while.

Leo-influenced individuals are inclined to use their many attributes to indulge their personal desires. They often live a very active social life. But to mature and reach the highest state of development the sign is capable of, they have to learn eventually to serve others in some selfless way.

Where partnership funds are concerned, Leo Ascendant people are inclined to run into difficulty. Other people may be to blame, through woolly-headed thinking or actions. Some confusion for Leos is never very far away when they have to combine their money or resources with others.

Legacies and inheritances may not come up to expectations. Or there may be misunderstandings due to the imprecise instructions of the person who made the bequest.

NINTH HOUSE: EDUCATION AND TRAVEL

The starting point of the Leo pattern of destiny is the desire for knowledge. Leo Rising people at every level of development are continuously endeavoring to broaden their minds. The less evolved Leo type cannot help showing off his or her knowledge and can be quite a bore. They are often boastful and conceited.

The more mature Lion or Lioness is a born teacher. They pursue the highest knowledge they are capable of absorbing. They spend their lives trying to impart it to others. People influenced by the Sun's own sign often feel they have a mission in life. This, of course, can lead to delusions of grandeur.

Leos are often natural philosophers. They are more interested in the inspiration behind the world's religions than in particular dogmas. They like to make up their own minds—and then to spread their own dogmas!

They have great faith in the future. They like to envision a worthwhile goal and then to stick to it. They know the importance of ideas as the fount of effective action.

The more serious-minded Leos regard travel as the best learning tool. Of course, the pursuit of pleasure is never entirely absent from the numerous trips and visits Leo people undertake. But long journeys to faraway places satisfy their craving for knowledge. And they prefer such travels to formal studies.

TENTH HOUSE: FAME AND AMBITION

Fame and ambition are very important to a person with a Leo Ascendant. It probably would be safe to say that in most cases such people would rather be famous than rich. They love the idea of being surrounded by applauding and admiring crowds.

Leo Rising people are prepared to work very hard to get to the top. Although they enjoy their leisure, they are ready to postpone recreation, even vacations, to satisfy their driving ambition. They will not give up once an objective is firmly fixed in their mind.

Leos take to power like ducks take to water. When recognition and fame do come to them, they are never in doubt that they deserved it. They have a natural ability for handling the public. They use their keen sense of the dramatic to obtain as much publicity as possible.

They enjoy the trappings and ceremonials of power and status. They are secretly offended if anyone fails to observe the formalities they think are due. They entertain in a regal manner. Queenly or kingly to all in their realm, their generosity is truly a magnificent thing.

The trouble with Leos is that they often continue to perform and to demand applause, even after the act is over. In retirement, forced or otherwise, they can be very disillusioned people. They find it very difficult to cope with the fickleness of the public when the tide has turned.

ELEVENTH HOUSE: FRIENDSHIP AND COMMUNITY

Leo Rising people are seldom short of friends. They have an easy way with people, which guarantees that wherever they go they make numerous new acquaintances. The Leo person likes engaging in conversation and trying to win others over to his or her ideas.

Leos are good listeners—as long as the talker is being informative. Otherwise they would prefer to do most of the talking. They believe that what they have to say is more important or entertaining. They cannot stomach bores and know-it-alls, often other Leos.

Leo Ascendant people often associate with the younger, intelligent crowd. They frequently make links with youth clubs. They like to have around them people who represent the thinking of the day. They are stimulated by discussions and debates, which give them the opportunity to display their knowledge and understanding of difficult subjects.

These people born under the influence of the Lion usually hold down prominent positions in clubs and groups. Here they are capable of a relatively impersonal attitude toward problems, projects, and progress. Their personal pride does not get in the way of promoting endeavors that have benefit for the community or society at large.

Leos are inclined to select their closest friends from among the people who support their humanitarian ideals. When and if they change these ideals, they usually change their friends.

TWELFTH HOUSE: SECRETS AND THE UNCONSCIOUS MIND

The greatest fear that a Leo Ascendant person can imagine is not to be loved or appreciated. It is the compelling desire for love and appreciation that makes Leos capable of giving up just about everything else. Their loved ones and admirers hardly expect this sacrifice.

Until he or she realizes some worthwhile purpose to their existence, the Leo person will tend to substitute daydreams. Their vivid imaginations can place them in positions of authority where, in exchange for loyalty and obedience, they take on the problems of the world.

Leo Rising people are more easily slighted than their self-assurance would suggest. Although they are forward-looking characters, they can be inclined to brood about incidents in which people have not shown them sufficient appreciation or respect.

Leos often give out vibrations that make them unapproachable. Their expectations of special treatment often come across to others as pomposity and pretentiousness.

Leo Ascendant people can become sulky and disagreeable if they feel they are being neglected—which is fairly often. Their demands for equal time and treatment in the spheres of love and appreciation are impossible for most people to fulfill.

Your Rising Sign:
Virgo on the Ascendant

Virgo Rising signifies "worldliness." The symbol of Virgo is the Virgin, or Maiden. This ancient designation is not synonymous with chastity. The Virgin is the woman, fertile and productive, the only zodiacal sign that is a human female. Virgo is an earth sign; Mercury, her ruling planet, is the planet of mind and communication. Worldliness means instruction in such vital matters as inheritance and progress. The process is personal. Virgo Rising people, rooted in their own minds and bodies, are the guardians and teachers of other people. The identification of Virgo Rising people with productivity and well-being—work and health—affect their experiences in the twelve life houses as described below.

FIRST HOUSE: PERSONALITY

Virgo Rising people are active, practical, and sharp. Work is their context, service their aim. They appear to be unemotional, impersonal, and detached, as though their efforts were obligatory. But these people are totally absorbed in their projects. Their sense of self comes from the involvement, the more complex and the more intellectual the better.

Nevertheless, Virgo Ascendant people appear to be unassuming. They are not ones to put on airs and graces, or to go on ego trips. They just like to do the job to the very best of their considerable ability, and without drawing much attention to themselves. For them, work is natural and work is cyclical. It goes on without rules being imposed or rewards offered.

But it must go on, especially when there is stress. So Virgo Rising people are the great teachers, mediating what is natural and what is imposed. And they are critical teachers, sparing neither feeling nor defense. They often upset their associates by pointing out their faults and failings. The fact that their criticisms are usually right on the mark does not help, either.

Virgo Rising people have a fine analytical talent. In fact, they enjoy analyzing things. Confronted with a great mass of complicated detail, they coolly and methodically translate it into a straightforward and intelligible pattern.

They also enjoy analyzing people. Their sharp logic enables them to define other people's weaknesses. And their sharp tongues express such weaknesses succinctly.

Virgo people have strong intellects. They are fond of art, literature, science, and mathematics. They have very good memories but are not particularly original, despite their strong reasoning powers. They are better at getting things in order, especially the messes left behind by muddled and confused minds.

These people influenced by the sign of the Virgin can be prudish. They tend to follow the letter of the law rather than the spirit of it. They have a good respect for authority. They would rather trust to precedent than break new ground reaching decisions.

Virgo-influenced people are often health faddists. They are particularly careful about following a healthful and balanced diet. Of course, their quirks in this regard can make them go to unbalanced extremes. The results often surface in unusual ailments.

Virgos are the hypochondriacs of the Zodiac. They are also worrywarts and fussbudgets. They focus intensely on their health and personal well-being. No ailment, real or imagined, is too slight to arouse their anxiety and care.

Down-to-earth Virgo types like to maintain a low profile. They often immerse themselves in their work, not worrying unduly about promotion or pay raises. They often hide their light under a bushel. They can become too subservient. They would rather persevere in a dead-end job on many occasions than face the disturbance of moving on.

Virgo Ascendant people do not like changes. They tend to be old-fashioned. They have a passion for orderliness and neatness. These qualities help to make them careful and conservative administrators.

SECOND HOUSE: MONEY AND POSSESSIONS

Virgo Ascendant people seldom live beyond their means. They like to budget their monthly income and stick to it. They are good savers, mainly because they follow the method of putting a fixed sum away out of each paycheck.

But Virgo-influenced people do have their extravagant and expansive moments. They like to spend their money on finely made objects. They are often collectors of works of art, musical instruments, manuscripts, and old books. They do not like cheap and shoddy articles.

Virgos are not spendthrifts as a rule. They are shrewd shoppers, cautious consumers. They believe in getting their money's worth as well as getting an attractive item. They also have an idea about resale if that should ever be necessary. They are no fools.

People born with a Virgo Ascendant are security-conscious. They like to be prepared for the proverbial rainy day. Fussy and conservative, they manage their money well.

They are extremely good at handling other people's money or possessions. They make fine brokers, accountants, managers, and auctioneers. With their methodical and meticulous minds, they know where every penny is.

But Virgo Rising people often have their well-laid financial plans upset and even ruined by their partners or associates. Virgo Rising people are often the victims of extravagance by others.

THIRD HOUSE: CLOSE CONTACTS AND COMMUNICATION

Because of their mercurial nature, Virgo Ascendant people enjoy a variety of contacts. They like the changing scene—as long as it is not personally unsettling. They are the type of individuals who like to stand unobtrusively on the sidewalk and observe the rest of the world go by.

Virgo Rising people tend to be shy in groups and with new acquaintances. They do not like to intrude until they are very sure of their ground. Then they come out with shrewd but extremely critical remarks about what they have seen in situations and in people.

Virgos maintain fixed opinions. They believe in order. They are looking for perfection in the world around them. Anything they see out of place irritates them. They can be blunt in their attempts to weed out the faults in other people. But they often fail to see their own imperfections.

People with a Virgo Ascendant have a natural flair for writing, especially the analytical variety. However, they are not especially communicative when it comes to their personal affairs. They would rather deal with others than have the spotlight put on thmselves.

Virgos are among the most logical characters in the Zodiac. They can be relied on to stick to the facts and to adhere to traditional systems. They are easy people to educate.

FOURTH HOUSE: HOME AND FAMILY

The home is one place where the Virgo Ascendant person feels confident to insist on establishing rules and order. With family members, the usually modest and unassuming Virgo can become something of an authoritarian. The object is not to impose a rule of power on the household, but one in which neatness or tidiness dictates the state of things.

Their homes are frequently larger or more spacious than their needs require. They do not like to feel hemmed in, especially if there are more than two people in the household. Virgo, the hypochondriac, tends to be claustrophobic.

There are some Virgo Rising types who can be surprisingly untidy, even sloppy, around the house. Much will depend on the positions of the planets other than the Sun. In these cases, domestic disorder is ignored.

The emphasis is placed on mental order. There can be a wearying insistence on logic and rational method. Virgos have a strong belief in the power of the home and family to keep society morally intact. They are inclined to be very critical of any doctrine, or person, who opposes this belief. These people like the idea of traveling to broaden their minds. Short trips and visits have a magical appeal. But Virgos often feel restless and at loose ends when far away from home.

FIFTH HOUSE: ROMANCE, CREATIVITY, AND CHILDREN

Virgo Ascendant people are rarely able to let themselves go in pleasurable or romantic situations. They often have the reputation for being a bit staid and straight-laced. They are people who enjoy themselves most by being part of the scene, rather than at the immediate center of it. They are self-conscious.

The Virgo-influenced woman finds it difficult to be unrestrained in romance, especially lovemaking. She needs a very understanding and patient lover to make her gradually abandon her preconceptions about sex. Once this is done, she can be free. The Virgo male is more sex-oriented because he is driven to prove his masculinity.

Virgo Rising people have a great talent for devising methods. They are often able to introduce new methods into areas of art that artists themselves are incapable of. Virgo Rising people have computerlike minds. They often have a talent for music. And their sharp minds and sharp tongue make them splendid critical writers or satirists.

Virgos as a rule prefer not to have large families. They are cautious types who do not like to take on more than they can afford. They are factual and straight with children. But they do have to be careful not to neglect children's emotional needs. It is hard for Virgos to give love and affection. They are not usually the types who go in much for physical displays.

SIXTH HOUSE: WORK AND HEALTH

Virgo Ascendant people arc happiest when working as part of a team. They are extremely cooperative and very considerate toward the people they work with. They like to be appreciated. But they are rarely guilty of putting on temperamental scenes. They like to do a good job and to keep personality problems out of it.

These people influenced by the sign of the Virgin are conscientious and dependable employees. They would prefer to work under someone and with instructions. Being a boss frightens them. But they do make capable administrators; they have an extraordinary ability to cope with details and to create systems. They are not the types to lose their heads in an emergency.

Virgo-influenced people are often employed in scientific and industrial laboratories. Their ideas about food and hygiene can be innovative. They are especially good at setting up production lines and devising methods for dealing with delays and logjams.

Virgo is the sign of health. People with Virgo Rising are health-conscious to an extreme. They may not be the best at getting regular exercise, but they do try to keep fit and trim through a sensible diet. They have to avoid excessive worry, which can upset their nervous system as well as lead them into spurious health fads.

SEVENTH HOUSE: ALLIANCE AND PARTNERSHIP

Virgo Ascendant people often turn out to be the long-suffering partner in love and marriage relationships. Once they commit themselves to a partnership, they will do all in their power to make it work. They are the types who will constantly forgive and forget in their efforts to discover a perfect harmony.

These people seldom walk out until all else has been tried and has failed. Their kind and considerate natures can be exploited if they are unlucky in picking a partner. They need a sympathetic mate who can appreciate their finer points.

Virgo-influenced people are easily upset by conflict in love. They do not like wrangling and arguing. They would rather give in to the partner than try to live in a depressing or unharmonious atmosphere. They will make considerable sacrifices to keep a marriage together.

It is not difficult for Virgo people to remain single. Unsatisfactory experiences early in life can put them off forever. Or they will wait for the right person to come along, without making any aggressive effort to find that person. Sometimes they appear to be unpopular or left on the shelf. But Virgo people are not short of admirers. Any decision not to marry is a considered one.

In social and business alliances, people with Virgo Rising take conflict situations more in their stride. Their caustic wit and acid tongue often provoke clashes with their partners. Virgos enjoy the ensuing debate or argument, for in the long run it improves the relationship.

EIGHTH HOUSE: SEX, PSYCHOLOGY, AND SHARED ASSETS

The Virgo reputation for chastity is farfetched. Virgo Ascendant people enjoy sex as much as any other sign. But because of their self-consciousness, they are slow to get started. And their desire for inner purity often clashes with their ideas of sex. However, Virgo-influenced people think a great deal more about sex than would seem. Often their sexual complexes are expressed in indirect ways.

The Virgo nature personifies the desire to be rid of everything less than perfect. As this is impossible, these are usually highly strung, nervous people. They tend to know what they don't like very definitely and to be outspoken about it.

But what they want out of life, they are not so sure of.

Virgo Rising people are considerate and conservative when it comes to assets or resources shared with a partner. They can be depended on to treat as carefully as their own anything left in their care. They are impelled by an urge to achieve maximum efficiency. They will never allow their own personal interests to interfere with a shared asset. Virgo-influenced people like to take control of joint finances and possessions. They endeavor to turn them into something better. They have a way of getting rid of unnecessary expenditures and poor investments. They make very good accountants and financial advisers.

NINTH HOUSE: EDUCATION AND TRAVEL

In their search for knowledge, Virgo Ascendant people prefer to stick to tried and trusted ways. They do not have much faith in speculation and experimentation. As a rule, they are more likely to support an established religion or philosophic method. Virgo-influenced people are often the staunchest members of the local church.

The Virgo nature does not like any idea that does not have a practical value. These people will translate lofty teaching, into down-to-earth ethics. They truly believe that brotherhood and sisterhood will bring peace and harmony into the world. They probably could not accept a philosophic code that has no concrete application.

Virgo Rising people can be dedicated teachers. They know the value of a higher education. They have a great deal of patience and understanding with slower-thinking people. They like people to have an appreciation of the artistic side of life. They often spend their time writing and simplifying for popular consumption lesser-known aspects of music, painting, poetry, and classical literary works.

Virgo-influenced people usually travel for a purpose rather than for pure sightseeing or pleasure. Curious about other customs and systems of belief, Virgos will take long journeys to observe, compare, and classify people of other cultures.

TENTH HOUSE: FAME AND AMBITION

Virgo Ascendant people often appear to have very little ambition. They may seem content to accept what comes. They appear to make the best of their lot without going out of their way to push their interests.

Virgo Rising people often become famous, just as often as people of other signs. Their modest and unassuming ways have a great appeal, especially to the dynamic folk who try to run this world. But Virgos seldom allow fame and position to go to their head.

Virgo Rising people are intelligent and shrewd. They do not complain about hard work. They are practical and love solving problems. They are great with detail, which usually drives others up the wall. To employ a Virgo is often the answer to the harassed boss's prayer.

Virgo-influenced people have no difficulty doing two jobs or handling several things at once. In fact, they enjoy a variety of small challenges in whatever work they do. They become completely absorbed. If they are happy, money becomes a secondary consideration.

Virgos do not have many enemies. They are likable people who never give the impression that they are after another person's job. Sometimes when rivals are angling for senior positions, the unassuming Virgo is promoted over them as the reasonable compromise choice.

ELEVENTH HOUSE: FRIENDSHIP AND COMMUNITY

Friends are very important to Virgo Ascendant people. They like to gather around them a select circle of companions who appreciate them for themselves and who do not resent their tendency to be critical. Virgo-influenced people and their friends both know that no offense is meant.

Virgo people's friends usually are the quiet and sensitive types. But Virgo does enjoy occasional outings with boisterous acquaintances, observing their antics from the sidelines. Virgos are always interested in how other people behave.

Virgo-influenced people like to entertain their friends at home. They enjoy the intimacy of a small dinner party, and will go to a great deal of trouble cooking and presenting the meal in an artistic way. They love to talk about the past with their closest friends. In familiar company they are often good storytellers.

Virgo Rising people take close friends to their bosom. They enjoy fussing around any pal who is in trouble, endeavoring to make things as easy as they can. They try to provide a nurturing environment for anyone hurt or ailing.

They also are inclined to join or support groups whose aim is improving the lot of less fortunate people. Virgos can be active animal lovers and frequently possess pets of their own.

TWELFTH HOUSE: SECRETS AND THE UNCONSCIOUS MIND

Virgo Rising people love secrets. They keep their own secrets well hidden. But they like to unearth other people's motives and compulsions. They make a mystery out of it. Prodding and prying, detecting and solving give Virgos an enormous sense of glee.

Virgo Ascendant people have a tendency for self-sacrifice. It may appear quite normal to them. It lies behind their ability to perform work that other people might consider boring or beneath them.

Virgo-influenced people have a most admirable modesty. It often expresses itself in doing the dirty work of society, such as cleaning up after others. They make first-class nurses and institution workers. They care for the sick and weak uncomplainingly.

These people influenced by the sign of the Virgin draw their strength from within. They are not dependent, like many others are, on outside recognition of their accomplishments. They do what they do because to them it is worth doing. Sometimes Virgos feel more inwardly fulfilled and satisfied if they exert themselves on behalf of others. These are people who often rule behind the scenes. They possess a quiet sense of dignity. It soon communicates itself to anyone who tries to impose on them or take them too much for granted.

Your Rising Sign: Libra on the Ascendant

Individuals born with Libra Rising are people-oriented. Sharing activities with date or mate, lover or spouse, partner or ally makes life more interesting. Venus, the planet that rules Libra, is the planet of love. Libra, being an air sign, does not foster possessive love. Libra's affections are breezy, and Libra Ascendant individuals like to circulate. But they always seek some kind of personal relationship. Their need for relatedness colors how they experience the twelve life houses, as described below.

FIRST HOUSE: PERSONALITY

People born with Libra on the Ascendant are constantly striving for harmony and balance. Like the Scales, their symbol, they seek equilibrium, poise. These people try to avoid any kind of conflict or disagreement. But when they are pushed to an extreme, they will take a stand.

If their basic beliefs are at stake, they can hit out as hard and effectively as anyone. Usually, however, they do all they can to bring about compromise. If they cannot mediate an argument, they tend to disappear from the scene. They flee to peaceful surroundings.

Libras are basically mental creatures. They have to be surrounded by people who interest them. Once a person has been understood by a Libra, there may be little mystery or originality remaining. If they are not constantly amused, Libras tend to lose interest. They usually have many friends, but not of the intimate type. They are inclined to go from one friend to another, sometimes neglecting old friends for a newly discovered one.

It is not that Libra Rising people are disloyal or would abandon any of their friends who are in trouble. On the contrary, they are very sympathetic and understanding people. But it has to be remembered that Libra is the sign of partnership. Relating to others is their basic impulse. They need to spread themselves around as much as possible.

Libra Ascendant people usually are physically attractive. If they are not beautiful or handsome, their skin, hair, and bodies usually have an indefinable attractive quality. They tend to be vain about their appearance. Their friendliness, charm, and dislike of conflict make them popular. In social situations the Libra personality reaches its glittering best. These people are natural hosts and hostesses. They do not consider expense when they are entertaining, either at home or in restaurants. They select the best places and food, often being prepared to run themselves into temporary debt to make an occasion just right.

Libra-influenced people sometimes are unable to face up to their difficulties. Their love of harmony makes them put off disagreeable tasks. Their dislike of conflict tends to make them postpone decisions. They would prefer to wait for something to happen to provide an alternative.

Libras have the reputation for being lazy. It is more that they refuse to do what their hearts are not in. Because they are people who are attracted mainly to beautiful things and pleasant activities, there is much in this world that they tend to shy away from and to neglect.

SECOND HOUSE: MONEY AND POSSESSIONS

Libra Ascendant people tend to have a basic contradiction in their personality where money is concerned. Their strongest impulse is to spend their money on beautiful things. They tend to select the most expensive of objects, being shrewdly aware that as a rule you get the quality you pay for. But deep down, they tend to worry about financial insecurity. Though aware of their extravagances, these trouble-hating people seem unable to compromise their taste for luxury.

Libra-influenced people seldom manage to avoid financial problems for long. They are extremely generous with gifts, often going beyond the bounds of good sense. In addition to the lavishness of the gifts, they often hand them out to people who are mere acquaintances and who have no particular connection to justify such generosity.

The Libra influence also makes a person enjoy the good life. They like fine food, flashy cars, rich clothing, and posh accommodations. They often cannot earn enough to support their taste for exotic things. Characteristically, they depend on a partner or lover to help pay their way.

Libra Rising people are successful with property investments. Their shrewd business minds are capable of seeing the resale value in land and other products of the earth, especially finely crafted pieces of furniture, jewelry, fabric, and metal. Libras tend to buy art objects and other valuable things for trade purposes rather than for lifelong possessions.

THIRD HOUSE: CLOSE CONTACTS AND COMMUNICATION

Close contacts and communications keep the Libra Ascendant person very active mentally. They love to be in touch with one segment of their considerable circle of friends and acquaintances, then to move on to a new segment. In this way they obtain the variety and change that are so necessary to their feeling of well-being.

Libra Rising people also like to communicate with their relatives and to visit them from time to time. They usually leave a longish interval between calls to particular relatives, so that the contact is stimulating and informative. They do not stay long in any one place. Daily routine easily bores Libra.

Libra-influenced people love to travel long distances, especially to other countries. They often write books or keep diaries about their travels. They are not the type to journey without due attention to maps, food and hotel guides, and information on local beauty spots and interesting things to see.

Libras are talkative but also good listeners. They make many casual contacts wherever they go, some of whom become firm friends. They often have numerous pen pals. Libras prefer letter writing to phone calls as a means of communication, because it is more formal and doesn't put them on the spot to make quick decisions.

These people have good judgment. Sometimes, though, they weigh things in the balance so long that they become indecisive. Easily distracted by petty details, they have to work hard at keeping their mind focused on the task at hand.

FOURTH HOUSE: HOME AND FAMILY

Home and family affairs are extremely important to Libra Ascendant people. Although they appear to be easygoing and even a bit flighty in other matters, they have a no-nonsense attitude about family life. Here they are very much down-to-earth. Their sense of luxury is tempered by an uncharacteristic thriftiness.

Libras organize their households to operate efficiently. They take responsibility to see that the home is well equipped with the latest gadgets and labor-saving appliances. Although they probably work harder in their homes than anywhere else, they always have an eye for anything that will save them time and effort.

Libra-influenced people are neat and tidy. They regard their homes as a reflection of themselves. They would hate to be criticized for the way they run or furnish their homes. In keeping with the Libra fondness for being surrounded by beautiful things, they do all they can to make their homes attractive and comfortable.

Libras like to be proud of their families and will work conscientiously to win their respect. Their keen sense of fair play enables Libra folk to see all sides of a family dispute. Playing the role of referee or peacemaker, they manage to keep family squabbles to a minimum.

Libra Rising people regard the home and family as the cornerstone of a successful society. They believe that justice and fairness on the home front help family members see the wisdom in the law and order of the larger society, as well as help them to enjoy a better life.

FIFTH HOUSE: ROMANCE, CREATIVITY, AND CHILDREN

In romantic affairs, Libra Ascendant people do not easily fall in love. They love the game of love but do their best to keep their emotional distance. Even so, they frequently underestimate the degree of involvement that others are capable of. So they tend to get embroiled in complicated situations. They are quite capable of walking away from a situation once it becomes too demanding.

Libra-influenced people often fall in love with an idea, and then attach that idealism to a person. However, they usually choose attractive or socially desirable people as their romantic companions.

Libra Rising people have a talent for combining mind with beauty. They are especially gifted for bringing social improvements into community life. Libras have been responsible for making many towns and cities more harmonious and attractive through their efforts in local government.

Libras are very good with children. They have a natural way of winning their confidence and respect. They are neither too strict nor too easygoing. Children regard them more like friends and learn quickly under their instruction. Libras have a happy knack of being able to treat all children the same; their own do not receive special treatment. They make very good elementary school teachers.

SIXTH HOUSE: WORK AND HEALTH

Libra Ascendant people are not enthusiastic about hard physical work. They lack the necessary stamina and will. They need an occupation that stimulates their mind and interest. They do not like to remain in one place for too long. They get bored in mind and body very easily.

Libras have a way of getting others to do the more strenuous and monotonous work for them. They are quite prepared to do nothing or make no move in a situation that cries for volunteers. They rely on tactful and cooperative noises as a smoke screen. They do not like making commitments that might tie them down for long.

Libra Rising people are very good at maneuvering behind the scenes. They are first-rate diplomats, able to convey disagreeable information in the nicest of forms. Often they are accused of being connivers. But it is just the situation Libras want to manipulate, not the people; for in a harmonious environment, Libras believe that all sides can come to a compromise.

They work best in occupations that allow them to express their strong sense of social duty. Any job that taps their arbitrating and peacemaking skills suits them very well. They also gravitate toward artistic fields that enable them to blend color, line, and texture in harmonious patterns.

Libras worry a great deal about failure. That fear affects their performance. They are not the type of people to take chances; they tend to swing back and forth in a debate. They stay alert for the first sign of a winner, to whom they can give their support.

Libras often suffer from health problems that are difficult to diagnose. They can worry about their health and yet do nothing about it. The twin fears of conflict and of failure make them prone to psychosomatic ailments affecting the nervous system. Their obsession with appearance lures them into diet, exercise, and beauty fads.

SEVENTH HOUSE: ALLIANCE AND PARTNERSHIP

Partnerships are the most important thing in the life of the typical Libra Ascendant person. These people are happiest and most efficient when living and working in a close relationship. They have a gift for getting along with others, more so than probably any other sign in the Zodiac.

Libras are prepared to accept other people as they find them. This takes a lot of the tension out of a partnership. Although they may recognize the slightest failing in their partner, they are not the kind to argue about it. They look for peace and quiet in their close relationships. Anyone looking for heightened emotional responses or kicks would have to look elsewhere than at Libra.

However, Libras also have a way of provoking aggressiveness in others. When they do, they are not the type to sit back and take it. They have an unexpected fiery streak. They will allow no one to impose on their rights without their permission. Nor will they allow others to undermine the rights of people with whom they feel identified.

Libra-influenced people receive pleasure out of bringing together potential romantic partners. They often arrange to have unattached men and women at their social functions in order to couple them off.

Social, intellectual, and professional alliances are lifelines for the typical Libra Rising person. He or she works splendidly in tandem on a job. Projects are always more interesting if they are mutual endeavors. The chitchat and back-and-forth relieve the boredom of routine that Libra people so abhor.

EIGHTH HOUSE: SEX, PSYCHOLOGY, AND SHARED ASSETS

Libra Ascendant people are romantics at heart. But where sex is involved, they can be detached enough to be mercenary. Sex, for many of these people, is a function of their security. And security is always measured in material terms. Libras can flirt, often meaninglessly. But they won't commit themselves unless the affair heightens their social or professional prestige.

Libras are not shy once past the flirting or courting stages. Even though they are matter-of-fact in bed, there is always the Libra vanity to contend with. Suitors get much father with a Libra Rising person if they remember to flatter him or her, and bring plenty of expensive presents to arouse Libra's desire for lovemaking.

Libras are often lucky. They tend to attract good things and good people consistently. What they gain through their relationships is often more than they earn through solitary efforts and endeavors.

Although their lives are seldom without financial strains and crises, they have a way—especially when the chips are down—of turning troubles to profit. They frequently manage this through partnership. They sometimes marry into money. And their financial problems are more than occasionally solved through legacies, insurance policies, the stock market, and business transactions.

Libras are usually financially successful in partnership. They have good business heads when they apply themselves. They have a knack for spotting lucrative investments. They often make successful husband and wife teams in business.

Libra Ascendant people have to feel they are responsible for joint funds or resources. If not, they can easily become extravagant and cause their partner considerable worry and anxiety. They are usually quite prepared to take the easy way out if the other person is foolish enough not to involve them.

NINTH HOUSE: EDUCATION AND TRAVEL

Libra Ascendant people are constantly endeavoring to broaden their minds. They love to meet people from all walks of life, to listen to their problems, and to exchange ideas. It is essential that they try to find a consistent philosophy for life. Until they do, they are always in danger of flitting from one belief to another.

They can easily become dabblers in religious and philosophic subjects. They have an ability for expressing the most abstract ideas in down-to-earth terms. But much of their outlook is based on pure reason and logic; the emotional and experiential sides may be neglected.

Libra Rising people enjoy any kind of travel, from short trips to world journeys. They often regard the world as their university, and the people in it as their teachers. Even when tied to the home by a family, they always manage to get out and about and to meet interesting people.

People influenced by the sign of the Scales are usually avid readers, especially if they cannot travel. Being mental types, they easily enter the world of adventure through the written word. And not being particularly energetic individuals, unless an exciting journey lures them, they often are happy to settle down with a good book and travel in their minds.

TENTH HOUSE: FAME AND AMBITION

Any success in the world that Libra Rising people have is reflected in their home. The home is a status symbol to them. They aim with all their heart and soul to make it as attractive, comfortable, and luxurious as possible.

Libras feel deeply about their careers. They are ambitious but choosy about the kind of work they are prepared to do. They like to feel respected and appreciated; they would rather do nothing than a job that others might regard as inferior.

Many people born with the sign of the Scales as their Ascendant make a name for themselves by catering to the public taste. They often own or manage good restaurants, beauty establishments, interior decorating concerns, and motels or hotels. They have a superb way of making people feel at home and at ease.

Their professional lives frequently have ups and downs. Depending on their moods, they make hasty changes, which may not always be well advised. Sometimes Libras will quit a career for solitary pursuits. This may be a mistake, because these people need to work with others in a harmonious environment.

Libra Ascendant people often work from home. If not, they rearrange their work space to suit their own concepts of harmony and design. They are not trendy, relying more on traditional schemes of color and line balance. A Libra's cubicle, shop, or office is a pleasant and inviting niche.

ELEVENTH HOUSE: FRIENDSHIP AND COMMUNITY

Libra Rising people love to mix with famous and socially prominent people. They are at ease in any company and have no trouble taking their place among celebrities. They are flattered to number such people among their friends.

Venus-ruled Libra has a weakness for beautiful people and beautiful things. But Libras do not always look deep enough below the surface when selecting their companions. They often go by appearances—and are then let down. But they have a natural ability to attract others, which means that they seldom are lonely.

People born under the influence of Libra know how to give their friends the royal treatment. They are generous and charming hosts and hostesses. They know just the right thing to say. They have a gift for avoiding controversial subjects if people of opposing beliefs are present.

Although they are not disloyal to their friends, they do tend to blow hot and cold. All over their friends one day and seemingly disinterested the next, Libras expose this unbalanced and contradictory side of their nature. It is maddening to their friends.

Libras like to be members of clubs and societies where their particular enthusiasms can be expressed. They are interested as a rule in humanitarian and cultural projects that propose justice for all. Libras can be equally active in establishing the rules of fair play and in organizing the social functions of such groups.

TWELFTH HOUSE: SECRETS AND THE UNCONSCIOUS MIND

A secret about themselves that few Libra Ascendant people are aware of is that they are constantly trying to suppress an unconscious urge to criticize others. For a sign that is said to epitomize the desire for peace and harmony, this is a very disturbing state of affairs. This urge drains some of

Libra's vital forces. It also explains why Libras sometimes feel inexplicably lethargic, and why to others they may even appear to be lazy.

Libras spend a lot more time in front of the mirror than many other signs do. Although they seldom are guilty of displaying vanity in egotistical ways, they are inclined to work hard at keeping up an elegant appearance. Their sense of style in costuming is highly developed.

Although Libra people usually are among the most naturally attractive types in the Zodiac, they find it difficult not to find fault with their own looks. They often resort to cosmetics and artificial devices to cover up what is more likely to be a form of neurosis than a noticeable defect.

In spite of their easygoing appearance, Libra-influenced people are worriers underneath. They feel obliged to make every effort to keep the peace, even when there is no need. Carried to extremes, this compulsion can make them appear gushing and insincere.

Your Rising Sign:
Scorpio on the Ascendant

Scorpio Rising is a powerhouse placement. The planetary rulers of Scorpio, Mars for force and action, Pluto for control and spirituality, pack plenty of punch. Scorpio Rising individuals can go to extremes. The stinging venom of the Scorpion, symbol of Scorpio, can be destructive as well as protective. Scorpio Rising individuals are deeply involved with the great psychosexual mysteries of life. They are always seeking to understand their own sexual natures and their own psyches, and to transform their everyday reality through such understanding. This search affects how individuals with Scorpio on the Ascendant experience the twelve life houses as described below.

FIRST HOUSE: PERSONALITY

People born with Scorpio on the Ascendant are proud and temperamental. They do not like others to know what they are doing. They are secretive. They feel quite capable of handling their own affairs without help from others. They certainly expect their associates to respect their privacy. They can be cutting and hurtful to anyone they suspect of being personally curious or too friendly.

Scorpio Rising people are often a riddle, not only to others but also to themselves. They are constantly endeavoring to discover the secrets of their own nature. But no one else should pry. They maintain privacy by repressing any emotional displays that would betray them to others.

There is always a danger of Scorpio Ascendant people exploding into an emotional rage. Their self-repression can get too much for them. They need to be handled tactfully and carefully. They are the types to remember insults and slights for a long time—as long as it takes to get revenge.

These people possess great powers of leadership if they are sure of themselves. They are extremely good in situations posing danger. They have steady nerves and steel-trap minds. They can keep their cool and operate efficiently while others around them are in a panic. They are great people to have around in an emergency.

Scorpio-influenced people are often aloof. They do not make close friends easily. And they keep gregarious types at bay. People have to prove their worth in one way or another before Scorpio will allow them into their private world. These people can be blunt to the point of cruelty. They are especially intolerant of anyone who starts fishing for compliments. Scorpios like to tell the truth. They are not always so talented at seeing their own faults, but they certainly have a way of summing others' up. They are especially good at spotting other people's weaknesses. And if they are in any way competing with them, they play on these weaknesses.

Scorpios have tremendous endurance. Once they fix their mind on an objective, they will work toward it until it is achieved. Time means nothing to them. They also are able to withstand any physical discomfort inherent in the pursuit of their aims. They are intensely ambitious, determined to make a name for themselves in whatever they do.

SECOND HOUSE: MONEY AND POSSESSIONS

Money and possessions are vital to Scorpio Ascendant people. They have been called greedy. But the intrinsic value of things is not as important as the feeling of abundance. Scorpios need to have a sense of plenty around them. And they are prepared to work extremely hard for it.

Scorpio-influenced people are enterprising and shrewd. Their judgment in business and money matters is first-rate. Although their natural astuteness usually ensures that they have an adequate cash flow, they tend to work toward long-term profits. They have an ability to look ahead and imagine conditions in the distant future, then make their day-to-day moves accordingly.

Scorpio Rising people, however, can sometimes be so engrossed in looking to the future that they fail to note current changes and trends. Once they get an idea fixed in their head, it is difficult for them to see any other point of view.

If Scorpios ever do become wealthy, they like to surround themselves with items of value. They can buy enormously expensive works of art, even though their aesthetic appreciation may not be strong.

Scorpio Rising people have a compulsive desire for power. Often they command obedience from others through intimidation. They are not above trying to instill fear in people, especially if they possess the financial muscle to back up their threats.

THIRD HOUSE: CLOSE CONTACTS AND COMMUNICATION

Scorpio Ascendant people play their cards close to the chest. They are not among the most spontaneous or communicative of people. They are at their best, down-to-earth. They express ideas in a purposeful, practical, and economical way. They are most reticent, though, when they have serious business matters on their mind.

However, there is another side to them that their closest companions will recognize. At times, Scorpio-influenced people are extremely talkative. It is often necessary for them to talk out their emotional hangups. Doing so prevents a buildup that would otherwise end in an outburst of rage. Scorpios honor close contacts within the traditional family unit. They tend to be more respectful of relatives, especially older ones, than of their acquaintances or daily associates. In fact, Scorpios frequently complain to their nearest and dearest about the attitudes and shortcomings of the people who stand in the way of their ambitions.

Scorpio Rising people think nothing of taking weekends off to visit relatives and family friends out of town. They also like solitary trips for the purpose of communing with nature, or possibly communing with a lover whose whereabouts, even existence, is kept secret. Scorpios love to make a mystery out of their contacts, viewing them as much as conquests as routine interactions between people who know each other.

FOURTH HOUSE: HOME AND FAMILY

Scorpio Ascendant people often have odd ideas about how to run their homes and bring up their families. In this area they often display an originality that may not be appreciated by those around them. They can even be ahead of their times. Their innovations, which initially cause raised eyebrows or even domestic rebellions, may one day be adopted by society as the latest thing.

Scorpio Rising people can often appear to run their households with a severe hand. But mature Scorpios know the meaning and importance of discipline in helping to forge character. They try to teach family members a sense of freedom by insisting that each one accept responsibilities for his or her own lives and actions.

People born under the influence of the Scorpion often have to contend with radical changes in their home and family affairs. Unforeseen events can change their place or mode of living overnight. Often these changes are associated with their deeper emotional needs.

Although Scorpios maintain stubbornly fixed ideas as a rule, they do have an extraordinary way of suddenly throwing off their old beliefs for a new truth. Change and renewal are basic to the Scorpio nature. So these people find no contradiction in adopting a new doctrine, especially because they embrace it with characteristic zeal and fanaticism.

FIFTH HOUSE: ROMANCE, CREATIVITY, AND CHILDREN

Romance is something that a Scorpio Ascendant person can enjoy as much as anyone. Romance, though, is usually secondary to the need for intimacy. These people are seriously concerned with what is at the bottom of the attraction between male and female, not the surface effects.

Scorpios need to experience intimacy in its deepest emotional contexts. And as often as they can! Their search for intimacy leads them from experimentation to commitment. The search has also given Scorpio a reputation for sexual excesses.

These people often get involved in secret love affairs. They have a love of danger that is almost suicidal as far as their emotions are concerned. They tend to push events beyond limits, seeming to court disaster in an effort to experience heightened sensations. They are fearless people. They will court disaster to plumb emotion.

Scorpio Rising people are talented in the arts. They bring artistic expression down to earth. They are frequently connected with the entertainment industry because of their love of dramatic effects, as well as their ability to create such effects.

They are often surprisingly compassionate, and may spontaneously give away large sums of money or make other sacrifices when faced with the suffering of others. Scorpios' creative drive is linked with their compassion. They make powerful painters and skilled surgeons when they are dedicated.

Scorpios can be quite sentimental about their children, although they may succeed in hiding the fact. Children represent to them the mysterious life forces of change and renewal. So Scorpio people are either intimidated by their youngsters, or are deeply concerned with understanding their motives and following their development.

SIXTH HOUSE: WORK AND HEALTH

Work is often the Scorpio Ascendant person's reason for being. They throw themselves into work with conviction and purpose that usually leave their competitors straggling behind. The only problem is that they first must find something they want to do. If they do not, they may waste their talents and become discontent and bitter.

They are self-sufficient people. They have no trouble making their home wherever they happen to be. Scorpios make extremely good explorers. They are able to put up with all kinds of discomfort in order to reach their goal.

Scorpio-influenced people have immense physical stamina and enduring powers of leadership. Their aggressive instincts are well developed. They make good soldiers, especially commanders. They also are suited for the stage and public arena, where their qualities of intensity have a magnetic effect.

Scorpio Rising people are usually successful as doctors, engineers, politicians, lawyers, detectives, psychologists, and energy and conservation specialists. They are often in the forefront of attempts to deal with industrial pollution, waste, and recycling of matter and energy.

Scorpio people's main health problems are those that arise from an emotional source, especially through indulging their senses. The pursuit of erotic pleasure can lead them to burn the candle at both ends, neglecting their rest and nutrition. Or they can become obsessed with a part of their body and imagine ailments they do not have.

SEVENTH HOUSE: ALLIANCE AND PARTNERSHIP

Typical Scorpio Ascendant people never enter into a partnership without a great deal of soul searching. Being realists, they weigh all the pros and cons. They are not adverse to marrying into money as a substitute for more idealistic expectations of a partner.

Scorpios are prepared to have their casual affairs before settling down. Often such relationships do not last once brief physical or emotional expression is over. But their more serious love and marriage associations mean a great deal to them.

Scorpio Rising people know exactly the sort of person they want for a permanent partner. It takes time for them to be sure that the person they have selected measures up. They do not intend to make any mistakes. But they often do. Their ideas are too fixed. They frequently fail to see possible areas of incompatibility, especially when they put a lover on a pedestal.

Scorpios are loyal. But they are very possessive. Jealousy often is the cause of much domestic disharmony. However, they do their best to persevere even with an unhappy marriage. They have fairly conservative ideas about marriage. They find it difficult to forgive a partner who cheats. However, their own emotional needs often require them to look elsewhere for physical gratification.

Business and social alliances pose a dilemma for Scorpio Rising people. On the one hand, mutual endeavors challenge their creative and leadership drives. On the other, they can abuse trust and misuse power. If they feel threatened in any way, they can subvert the partnership to serve their own ego needs. The mature Scorpio nurtures alliances by sharing knowledge and offering compassion in need.

EIGHTH HOUSE: SEX, PSYCHOLOGY, AND SHARED ASSETS

The Scorpio reputation for being preoccupied with sex is exaggerated. Scorpio Ascendant people are early experimenters, for they have little shame about their bodies and the sensations of pleasure. They enjoy variety, either in partners or experiences, in their love life. They need a sense of mystery and novelty to maintain their sexual interest.

Scorpio Rising people have a deep intellectual need to get to the bottom of mysteries. They are also keenly curious about death and the afterlife. They often are students of the occult.

Scorpios will write and lecture about their findings in sexuality and spirituality. They enjoy sharing their discoveries with other people. But they prefer to keep private thoughts and emotions a secret. Verbally sharing intimacies on a one-to-one basis is hard for them to do.

Sharing material assets is also something of a problem for them. Scorpio-influenced people are usually shrewd with money, and believe they are better managers of it than their mates or partners. It is sometimes their capable management of joint funds and resources that helps the partnerships to endure. Many a husband or wife who has been prepared to let their Scorpio mate look after the finances has lived comfortably and watched their money grow.

Scorpio people seldom put their investments in one basket. They believe in spreading the risk. Their business interests often cover a variety of fields. In their financial dealings, they are more adaptable and flexible than in most other areas of their life.

NINTH HOUSE: EDUCATION AND TRAVEL

Scorpio Rising people are natural philosophers and psychologists. It is not enough for them to learn what other people have reported; they have to experience the truth of it for themselves. In religious matters, they hold wide-ranging views. They are inclined to look beyond the limited scope of orthodox dogmas.

They are inclined to take up studies later in life that may have been neglected in earlier years. As they get older, they discover the value of education as a means of realizing their ambitions. They have great powers of concentration once they put their minds to a subject.

In their search for the truth, Scorpio Ascendant people depend a lot on their own emotional states. They can sometimes become completely self-absorbed, so much so that they may go into temporary isolation or refuse to converse with anyone. They often become depressed and moody. They can feel deeply identified with the futility of existence.

Scorpio Rising people enjoy the sea and voyages across water. They do not usually travel for sightseeing reasons. When they visit other countries, it is usually in quest of personal enlightenment. Or they undertake journeys on behalf of other people. A long and distant search challenges the Scorpio love for danger and imperiled survival.

TENTH HOUSE: FAME AND AMBITION

Scorpio Ascendant people are intensely ambitious. They are determined to make good in whatever field they choose. They are not as interested in the egotistical side of fame as in the power that it conveys.

Their aim is to be the person in charge of whatever they do. If they enter politics, they would have their eye continuously on the most powerful position in the land. When they do make it to the top, they expect others to show them respect and obedience.

However, Scorpio Rising people have a deep sense of justice. It often prevents them from going to extremes with power in public life. They are more inclined to become protectors of the people than their oppressors. But if they lead minority groups, they can clash with established law and order and be ruthlessly efficient in their tactics.

Scorpio Ascendant people will work day and night to achieve positions of prestige and authority. They are prepared to work under others but usually only while they feel they are on the way up. They do not work well as a member of a team unless they are leading it.

ELEVENTH HOUSE: FRIENDSHIP AND COMMUNITY

People influenced by the sign of the Scorpion are very choosy when it comes to making friends. Although they are affable enough in formal situations, and at first meetings, they are inclined to give an impression of aloofness. They cannot help summing up immediately everyone they meet. And their judgments are usually uncannily accurate.

These self-sufficient people do not make many friends. Few of the people they meet come up to their exacting standards. They can at times be critical of their associates and acquaintances. But to their real friends they are loyal and true. They will work quite selflessly to help a friend.

They do not like much close contact. Too many people in close proximity make them feel uncomfortable. They feel there are not many people they can trust. They sometimes settle for pets instead of friends.

Scorpio Ascendant people will work hard for any clubs or societies of which they are members. These groups usually promote cultural or artistic aims in which Scorpios have a personal interest. Community welfare projects also interest them, especially if the project taps their sense of social and political justice. These people can be tireless fighters against oppression of any kind. Brilliant strategists, they understand that it takes power to challenge authority.

TWELFTH HOUSE: SECRETS AND THE UNCONSCIOUS MIND

Scorpio Ascendant people are suspicious types. They are subconsciously on their guard. They are not at all susceptible to flattery. Displays of charm and tact team to make them suspect another person's motives.

Typical Scorpio Rising people learn fairly early in life that any form of partnership contains deception for them. They are invariably misled at one time or another. Disillusioned by close relationships, they seek privacy and solitude.

Often they are the victims of gossip. They are not usually lucky with lawsuits. They easily become mistrusting and secretive as a result.

There is always a battle between war and peace going on inside a typical Scorpio person. They are often contradictions to themselves. In times of peace, they will be inclined to provoke situations that soon land them in a sea of trouble. In the midst of their emotional storms and self-inflicted problems, they will yearn for peace.

Scorpios live on an emotional edge that is very demanding of the people who share their lives. Their marriages and other close relationships often turn out to be tests of fortitude for both Scorpio people and their mates.

Your Rising Sign: Sagittarius on the Ascendant

Sagittarius Rising signifies a love of freedom that is seldom ever satisfied. Such people won't allow themselves to get stuck for long in dead-end situations. Jupiter, the ruling planet of Sagittarius, propels these people on a search for excitement, wisdom, and truth. Bitten by the wanderlust, they are always seeking. A need to know and to learn colors how people with Sagittarius Rising approach the twelve life houses, as described in the following sections.

FIRST HOUSE: PERSONALITY

Sagittarius Rising people are enthusiastic. Being influenced by a fire sign, they exude seemingly boundless energy, and appear always to have something cooking. Sagittarius Rising people are also restless, both physically and mentally. They are always on the move; new people, new places, new things beckon. They are on the lookout for interesting new ventures, some of which take them far from their starting places.

Sagittarius on the Ascendant inspires a great fondness for travel. Such people will seize any opportunity to visit other countries. Frequently they combine travel with their jobs. They are often professional sportsmen and sportswomen who compete in other countries. They are active and friendly hostesses and stewards who even after exhausting trips, bounce right back to see the sights and sample the local entertainment until the wee hours.

People influenced by the sign of the Archer have a great love of pleasure. They are often born entertainers. They are cheerful, optimistic, and friendly. People feel good in their company and seldom resist laughing with them. They are often the life of the party.

In spite of their easygoing and often lighthearted manner, Sagittarius-influenced people are serious. They enjoy discussing profound subjects, and their views are usually well worth listening to. They have a way of seeing

215

the basic truth in a maze of detail. They make very good teachers and managers. Sagittarius Rising folk are renowned for their love of the great outdoors. They are animal lovers, having a special attachment to horses and dogs. Sometimes this interest leads them to the racetrack; here they can lose—and sometimes win—a lot of money. Sagittarius people are gamblers at heart. Even if they do not gamble with money, they love to stake themselves against the challenge of life. These people can easily become involved in the most hair-raising business schemes. And they are great promoters. An untried challenge turns them on. They seldom worry about failing; they have too much faith in the chances of succeeding. They tend to depend a lot on luck. Strangely enough, they often are lucky. Sagittarius Ascendant people have to guard against making promises they cannot keep. They are so used to expecting the best they can become dangerously optimistic.

SECOND HOUSE: MONEY AND POSSESSIONS

Sagittarius Ascendant people have a deeper regard for money than their open-handed ways suggest. They may be tempted to take more chances than most. They will invest in dubious moneymaking schemes. Or they will gamble a large piece of their financial future on a fast horse or a throw of the dice. But underneath, they like to know that there is something in the kitty. They often fail to look at their actual financial situation because they cannot bear the thought of having no security to fall back on.

With money, Sagittarius people are often contradictions. When they spend, they spend big. They often run into debt, then refuse to consider where the next penny is coming from. They would rather count on something turning up than face facts. More often than not, their philosophy works for them. Their faith in the future can pay off at the very last moment.

Sagittarius people have a great talent for planning for the future. In this way they can amass wealth. Influenced by Jupiter, the sign of abundance and good fortune, Sagittarius Ascendant people see golden opportunities knocking at every door. But they have to be careful not to become impatient and through speculation try to win tomorrow's gains today.

Sagittarius Rising folk like to have valuable possessions around them; it helps to satisfy an unconscious craving for security. But these people are never so attached to their belongings that they would not pick up and go, leaving everything behind. The need to roam, to gather experience, is deeper than any need to acquire and keep material things.

THIRD HOUSE: CLOSE CONTACTS AND COMMUNICATION

Sagittarius Ascendant people never tire of making contacts—here, there, and elsewhere. Like their Gemini cousins, they probably have more acquaintances than most other zodiacal types. And, like Geminis, they often get a reputation for being gadflies of the Zodiac. They do not as a rule form very close relationships; they are terrified of any involvement that might tie them down. These are very progressive-minded people. Their intellects are sharp and inventive. They are often original. Their writings and commentaries display keen wit and irony without sarcasm. Their understanding of humanity, especially its comic side, is great. They are usually good storytellers with a wonderful sense of humor.

Sagittarius folk believe in free education for all people. They feel that everyone should receive the best education available, not just to earn a living but also to share insights with each other. Communication, they believe, is vital to human progress.

People influenced by the Archer are independent and have a hearty belief in freedom of speech. In spite of their originality, they often become fixed in their ideas and inclined to support orthodox traditions. When they do speak out, it is often from the podium or recording room of an established group. They make good preachers, whether in person, in print, or on radio and TV.

FOURTH HOUSE: HOME AND FAMILY

Sagittarius Ascendant people are roamers. They spend a lot of time away from home base. But they are intensely sentimental about their families. No matter how far they wander, they keep in touch—not on a regular basis, but when an intense longing for loved ones overtakes them. And by phone, which is quicker and more personal than writing.

Sagittarius people are kind to their families. They will listen to their troubles, and do all in their power to fulfill their desires. They go out of their way to make things easier in times of worry. They are a soft touch. They are generous with gifts and seldom fail to remember birthdays and anniversaries.

At the core of the Sagittarius personality is timidity. These individuals are not as sure of themselves as their extroverted ways suggest. They look to their families to provide a sense of belonging. Once assured of this, they can happily pursue their carefree rushes into the world.

Sagittarius Rising folk usually furnish and decorate their homes in quiet harmony, with only a few mementos and trophies proclaiming their worldly enthusiasms. They like to regard where they live as a sanctuary, a place to which they can escape when the world becomes too much.

FIFTH HOUSE: ROMANCE, CREATIVITY, AND CHILDREN

Sagittarius Rising people are fun lovers. They seldom tire of pleasure and entertainment. And they seldom tire of the chase. Hunters of the heart, they pursue variety and challenge. Any conquest is fair game, which often gets them into trouble.

Though ardent lovers, Sagittarius-influenced people do not allow romance to dictate their lives. They seem to put heart and soul into a love affair, but they are really enthusiastic about the lovemaking. They infuse sex with idealism. Then they get on with the next exciting activity. Their loved ones can at times feel neglected. It is impossible to tie Sagittarius down. Any interference with their freedom makes them unhappy and rebellious. They are inclined to walk out on anyone who consistently tries to put an emotional rope round their neck.

Sagittarius Rising people have a talent for all occupations or hobbies involving plenty of human contact and movement. They are very good at sports. They have a way with animals, especially horses and dogs, and like careers breeding, training, racing, and showing animals. On the intellectual side, they make first-rate teachers and scholars. Politics, promotion, coaching, and exploring also attract them.

Sagittarius Ascendant folks are good with children as long as they do not have to stay indoors with the kids too long. The men, being somewhat boys themselves, never seem to be able to take on the role of father comfortably. They are either too heavy or too indulgent. The Sagittarius woman makes a better all-round parent, blending freedom with discipline in judicious amounts.

SIXTH HOUSE: WORK AND HEALTH

In spite of their fondness for amusements and the good life, Sagittarius Ascendant people are hard workers. They are prepared to put in a full day's work without shirking, as long as this will provide them with the financial means and freedom to do as they please in their spare time.

This often means that Sagittarius folk burn the candle at both ends, working and playing with equal zest and vigor. However, most Sagittarius-influenced people like to keep fit. They are interested in sports and games, which help them to keep the weight down and to stay in balance.

These pleasure-loving people are susceptible to rich food and drink. When they eat or drink too much, an expanding waistline often is a problem. However, people influenced by the fleet-footed Archer are usually diet-conscious. In between their excesses they try to keep to good natural foods.

In both work and health, they aim to establish a good foundation to support their many activities. They usually choose work that will allow them to fulfill their visions of future security. They tend to live for the future, having great faith that they will find the pot of gold at the end of the rainbow.

Their work usually has an element of speculation in it; they often choose to work on commission, or on a time or production basis, so that there is always the possibility of exceeding fixed expectations of one salary.

Sagittarius Rising people, though, do have a strong conservative streak. It often projects them into professions such as teaching, which offer plenty of time for them to follow their other interests.

SEVENTH HOUSE: ALLIANCE AND PARTNERSHIP

Partnerships of the love and marriage kind are not an easy thing, especially for the male Archer. He is terribly conscious of his independence and freedom, and is most reluctant to do anything that may endanger these precious assets. He is one of the most marriage-shy types in the Zodiac. In this age of liberation, female Archers are settling the score. They, too, demand an independent life, free of the usual constraints.

Both male and female Sagittarius require a special kind of partner. They need a mate who is a friend and who will not make undue emotional demands. They look for a partner who is able to share their many interests. It is imperative for a happy marriage that the husband or wife be intelligent, versatile, and easygoing.

Sagittarius people love to share their lives with their friends and acquaintances. They are often away from the home. Or they will invite all manner of companions back to the house for dinner and drinks. Their instant sociability can be tough on mate and the kids at home, giving Sagittarius people a reputation for being somewhat irresponsible. But their social and business allies flock around them.

Sagittarius Rising people make good business partners, provided the field offers scope for them to move around and experience plenty of human contact. Some never wed, preferring to settle down with their intellectual pursuits and studies. As they get older, their preoccupation with physical activity, tripping around, and meeting people matures into a philosophy of life that younger generations can find both illuminating and practical.

EIGHTH HOUSE: SEX, PSYCHOLOGY, AND SHARED ASSETS

Sex means a lot to Sagittarius Rising people. They are passionate and ardent but suffer sudden changes of mind. This can be difficult for their lovers and those seeking a fulfilling union. The Sagittarius male and female are ill equipped for devotion to one partner and long-term or permanent relationships.

There are two distinct types of Sagittarius: one is the playboy type, and one is deeply reflective. The easygoing Sagittarius nature belies a deep emotional connection with such questions as death and survival. These people have the ability to look deep within themselves, but rarely are they able to come to terms with what they sense is there. They are inclined to skate over such subjects or to express their feelings in traditional ways.

Sagittarius-influenced people can be protective of joint funds and resources. In spite of their generous, spendthrift, ways, they manage to respect shared finances and property. Sagittarius folk like a stable foundation. They are wise enough to know that a partnership arrangement can offer this. So they try to brake their irresponsible impulses before they reach such momentum that both the money and the partnership are endangered. With the Sagittarius luck, they squeak through just in time.

NINTH HOUSE: EDUCATION AND TRAVEL

Sagittarius Rising people are justifiably proud of their ideas. They present them with the confidence that comes from knowing they are an expression of themselves. Whatever they learn, from formal sources or from the school of hard knocks, they adapt to suit current needs and purposes. These people are natural teachers. They are capable of becoming professors and philosophers. Their minds can delve deep into complex subjects and understand them. But they do have to control their urge to move around too much. A diversity of interests can distract their concentration.

When Sagittarius embraces a religious or philosophic point of view, he or she is never in doubt that it is the correct one. They have supreme faith in their ability to see the truth. The only thing that prevents them from being truly original is a tendency to conformity. They often express their truths through established positions. In this they can be stubbornly conventional.

Sagittarius people are the travelers of the Zodiac. Fresh horizons broaden their mind. They regard long journeys and extended stays in other countries as a learning experience. They see them also as a teaching experience. They love to present their own ideas to people of different cultures, even to the extent of trying to convert them. Sagittarius Rising makes an ideal missionary.

TENTH HOUSE: FAME AND AMBITION

Typical Sagittarius people are vigorously ambitious. They aim for the highest in whatever they do, even though their final goal is probably not definitely clear to them at any time. They work toward an indescribably broad future where freedom, space, and opportunity are unlimited. It is not that they are dreamers. They are optimists, with tremendous faith in the unknown.

When famous, Sagittarius Ascendant people have an element of modesty about them. They often enjoy participating in the ceremonies and trappings of their office, but they are able to retain a basic simplicity that comes across. Arrayed in colorful robes or surrounded by worldly splendor, they can still be simple at heart. They also can be swashbuckling and boastful.

Sagittarius people have a gift for critical analysis. They are able to see the merits of a complex proposition. Intuition is keen. They do not like handling details, but they can cope with a variety of claims on their time and talents at one time. They are often writers and lecturers.

In spite of their independent natures, Sagittarius Rising people are good at following orders, as long as they respect the aims of the authority issuing them. They are not too independent to seek conventional careers in the fields of law, politics, and religion.

ELEVENTH HOUSE: FRIENDSHIP AND COMMUNITY

Sagittarius Ascendant people are most expansive among friends. They love nothing more than to be at the center of a group of congenial people exchanging ideas, telling amusing stories, and relating their experiences. They are enthustiastic raconteurs, seldom short of a joke or a parable.

People like their easygoing and jovial manner. They do not have as much interest in making close friends as in collecting acquaintances. Their dearest friends are those who usually share their many interests and accompany them on their ceaseless trips and adventures.

These sons and daughters of Jupiter, which is the ruling planet of Sagittarius, are very good at bringing together people of opposing points of view so that compromises can be reached. They make efficient chairpeople and mediators. Although in their personal lives they are often outspoken to the point of bluntness, in group and community work they can be exceedingly tactful and diplomatic.

Still, they are great believers in justice. They will not shy away from an unpopular decision if they deem it to be necessary. Firebrand Sagittarius speakers can rouse their audience to take action toward some societal or political goal.

TWELFTH HOUSE: SECRETS AND THE UNCONSCIOUS MIND

Deep within the subconscious of the frank and outgoing Sagittarius is a secretive side. This often makes these people feel uncomfortable whenever they are forced to consider the truly mystical elements of their own experience. There is something there they do not want to face. Although they are capable of great insights, they would prefer to stick to the safety of familiar conventional religious and philosophic views.

However, if they can overcome this reluctance, Sagittarius people can delve deeply into the subconscious. They can become perceptive investigators of the occult, and reveal to the world new explanations for psychic phenomena.

Your Rising Sign:
Capricorn on the Ascendant

Capricorn Rising people tend to be concerned with their public image. What they do, even what they think, may be measured against conventional standards of acceptability. These people are strongly motivated by a need for success, as it is defined through such wordly ambitions as recognition and prestige. In a broader sense, achievement is what Capricorn Rising people are striving for. It colors their approach to the twelve houses of life experience, as described in the following sections.

FIRST HOUSE: PERSONALITY

People born with Capricorn on their Ascendant are determined and patient. These people have a tremendous capacity for hard work. They are not the types to expect favors. They are down-to-earth realists. Their early life often teaches them that living is no bed of roses. They are prepared to accept conditions as they are and to get on with the job of whatever has to be done.

Capricorn Ascendant people are proud and aloof. They know what they want out of life when they reach maturity. Whereas many other signs are never quite sure what they should, or should not, have done, the developed Capricorn does not look back. He or she is no dreamer. Things are as they are because they had to be that way, as far as they are concerned. With long-suffering patience, these people move inexorably toward their goals.

That doesn't mean such people have never experienced loss or sadness or failure. Capricorn Rising people know there are limits to everything, including their ambitions. But their quality of patience allows them to look at the record, to size up the alternatives, and to work and wait. With restraint and through responsibility, characteristics inherited from Saturn,

Capricorn's ruling planet, they work their way steadily upward. Indeed, the Goat, symbol of Capricorn, makes their climb sure-footed and steady.

Capricorn Ascendant people usually succeed in the end because of their sheer persistence. They are not deterred by setbacks or obstacles. They grind away like the "mills of the Gods," wearing down any resistance. What they lack in imagination they make up for in dogged determination to succeed.

People born under this cardinal sign of action are more interested in gaining prestige and respect than in amassing large sums of money. They like to be looked upon as authorities in their particular line. They can become so preoccupied with work that they live for little else. Their loved ones must sometimes see to it that they get enough recreation and leisure.

Capricorn Rising people are more sensitive than their manner often suggests. An inferiority complex often lurks behind their tough, skeptical exterior. They love their homes and families, although they are shy about expressing their feelings. They worry whether their undemonstrative ways will cool off loved ones. Their pride often won't allow them to ask for the affection they need.

These people influenced by the sign of the Goat are also contradictions within themselves, to themselves, and to the world at large. One type of Goat may in youth exhibit a rather irresponsible attitude. Their parents may think such youngsters are never going to settle down. But when their wild oats are sown, they become the most serious and law-abiding of citizens. The other type of Goat can start life being serious and studious, and in maturity become more yielding and young at heart.

There are seldom any half measures about Capricorn. Life demands discipline and restraint, as well as joy and fulfillment. Which sequence comes first and which last seems to vary with the individual. With Capricorn Rising, the sequence tends to be conservative in early life, expansive and enthusiastic later in life.

SECOND HOUSE: MONEY AND POSSESSIONS

Capricorn Ascendant people can be unpredictable where money is concerned. This tendency wars with their basic nature, which is cautious and methodical. They want to take responsibilities seriously, so they try to be conservative. When it comes to saving, they certainly can put the pennies away—but sometimes not long enough to grow.

They will often spend their money on an impulse, frequently without getting much value for it. And they are not the type of people who take unsolicited financial advice easily. They are independent thinkers in this respect. They can even spend their money in unconventional ways, which may seem out of character but is typical for Capricorn Rising.

Capricorn Ascendant people do not allow money to rule their life. They can be quite detached from it, although keenly aware of its practical value. In their business lives, they can amass wealth through bold and original investments. They have a canny way of thoroughly investigating a proposition. And after getting the best of advice from competent authorities, they are able to act swiftly.

Capricorn Rising people usually like to surround themselves with the latest gadgets and scientific equipment. They are the types of people who after acquiring wealth may support worthy causes, especially scientific research into humanitarian problems. They are likely to do this anonymously.

THIRD HOUSE: CLOSE CONTACTS AND COMMUNICATION

The typical Capricorn Ascendant person plays his or her cards close to the chest. They are not ones to confide in all and sundry. They are very careful to whom they tell their inner thoughts and private problems.

Capricorn people, however, do like to listen to others. They enjoy working out the reasons why other people make certain statements. They are especially quick at noting any unguarded statement; they are interested both in the information it may contain and what it reveals about the person making it. Logic and sentiment, according to Capricorn Rising people, should combine to make sense.

People influenced by the sign of the Goat live in a deeply emotional world that seldom gets expressed. They are far more sensitive to what other people say and think about them than they ever let on. They are often deeply hurt and pained, but would consider it weakness on their part to show it. They hide their vulnerability behind a cynical shell, sometimes coming out to express disapproval in verbally cutting ways. Or they bury their vulnerability so deeply, they remain inhibited and silent even with close associates.

These strong and proud individuals have to work harder than most other types to express themselves through language. When they do develop this facility, they can become speakers and writers of rare depth and sensitivity.

Capricorn Rising people often are music lovers who find it easier to enjoy emotions that are communicated without the complication of words.

FOURTH HOUSE: HOME AND FAMILY

Home is where Capricorn Rising people feel most comfortable. Family gives them a basic sense of selfhood and reinforces that image of self that they want to show the world.

No one takes more interest in their domestic affairs than these people. They need a stable base to make them feel psychologically secure while they pursue their ambitious enterprises. Gradually, as they become older and more fulfilled, the Capricorn Ascendant type tends to spend more time in the bosom of his or her home and family.

It is surprising how often Capricorn people are influenced in their formative years by an ambitious mother or father or other parent figure. If adult pressure to succeed has been excessive, there can be a revolt in later years.

If mate or family members have great expectations, Capricorn may perversely fail them or demonstrate a tough, rebellious streak. The Capricorn Goat can be led to water but cannot be made to drink. These are people who usually know what they want around the home. They can become quite dictatorial. Their know-it-all and bossy ways can provoke arguments with other members of the household.

Capricorn Ascendant people are extremely loyal. They want the very best for their families. They endeavor to provide a comfortable home. In return, they expect to be respected, and their efforts appreciated. They are capable of handling a large family if they blend discipline with tenderness.

FIFTH HOUSE: ROMANCE, CREATIVITY, AND CHILDREN

Capricorn Rising people do not rush into love affairs. But physical affection is terribly important to them. They find lovemaking the easiest way in the world to express their feelings, which often are so difficult for them to put into words.

No one at the beginning of a romance should expect a Capricorn person to bare his or her soul. These people are intensely afraid of being hurt. They will not confide in anyone until they feel they can trust them completely. Where their emotions are concerned, Capricorn types would rather proceed at a snail's pace than risk the possibility of rejection.

Capricorn Ascendant people are resourceful and practical. They are very good at making the most of whatever is available. They have a talent for organization and administration. The women are usually more artistically inclined than the men. Both sexes, however, enjoy their creature comforts. Art and music attract them. Some of these people become the strong, silent artists of their generation, speaking to others through the languages of soul and senses.

Capricorn people are at their creative and enterprising best when they are juggling money problems and investments. They have a way of grasping intricate details of higher finance that would leave others confused and despairing. These are people who can become leaders in handling merger operations and the complications of big business.

With children, Capricorn Rising people are fairly firm. They like to turn out their offspring as socially acceptable individuals having due respect for law and order. They like their children to be a favorable reflection on themselves.

SIXTH HOUSE: WORK AND HEALTH

Capricorn Ascendant people produce their best work when they have plenty of variety. But this does not mean they have to be darting hither and thither. These people have intense powers of concentration. Nothing delights them more than coping with a stream of detail that they can arrange into orderly patterns.

They make very good researchers in scientific fields. They can put their finger on the salient facts among a welter of detail and trivia. They can make boring statistics interesting and more meaningful with their ability to write clearly and concisely. They make competent accountants and engineers.

They also manage to bring versatility into their work. They are good examples to the younger generation of how work can be handled efficiently and without fluster. Capricorn-influenced people are not the types to lose their heads or panic when the pressure is on. They have faith in method and order. They endeavor to bring structure to all their activities, so they do not have to depend solely on imagination.

Capricorn Rising people are usually physically strong. They will stay on a balanced diet trying to keep fit, because they worry so that ill health will interfere with their work. But they tend to ignore leisure activities; they often do not get enough exercise and rest. They sometimes suffer from nerves through keeping their emotions repressed.

SEVENTH HOUSE: ALLIANCE AND PARTNERSHIP

Partnerships represent an emotional area for the usually cool and serious Capricorn-influenced person. They are never sure of their ability to cope with this area of life experience. They don't want to give up control, so they can be suspicious and aloof with a new lover or potential mate.

These people are very protective toward their marriage partners. They try to avoid arguments, even to the point of giving in. Or if their behavior is the cause of complaint, they may refuse to discuss it and walk off. They cannot bear any situation in which their emotions are brought to the surface.

A Capricorn person is not the type to cheat after marriage, unless there is a compelling reason. Once they have given their word, they do their very best to stick to it. The problem is that they have a great need for physical affection. If it is not forthcoming from their mate, they may feel compelled to go elsewhere.

But these people will not break up a close relationship for any trivial reason. They take their responsibilities very much to heart. As long as a marriage is still intact, they will be inclined to let their partner have his or her way.

Capricorn Rising people are usually successful in work and business partnerships. In these relatively nonemotional alliances, they don't worry too much about being tricked or used. They have the patience and endurance to take bad times with good; they would never wittingly let their performance fail the goals of the alliance or their partner's expectations.

EIGHTH HOUSE: SEX, PSYCHOLOGY, AND SHARED ASSETS

Capricorn Rising people usually are good lovers. They enjoy the physical side of romance. This is an area where these naturally cautious and modest people can really let their hair down with the right kind of partner.

Until they find the right partner, though, they tend to feel inadequate about sex and love. They worry about intimacy, how it might expose their sensitive emotions or how it might threaten their need for control. But it is through the intimacy of love and sex that Capricorn Rising people find the true meaning of success and achievement—the joy and fulfillment of sharing with another human being.

These people influenced by the sign of the Goat find hope in their own accomplishments. The more they succeed, the more they tend to relax their stern outlook on life. They become younger at heart. No types in the Zodiac respond more positively to success than Capricorn; to them it can be a reason for living.

A person with a Capricorn Ascendant is often proud of his or her ability to manage money. They enjoy demonstrating this talent to others, especially to their partners. This makes them ideal people to be in charge of shared funds and resources. Besides, Capricorns truly get a sense of pleasure from providing partners and loved ones with a solid base, often exceeding everyone's expectations and building a large nest egg.

NINTH HOUSE: EDUCATION AND TRAVEL

A person with a Capricorn Ascendant is naturally skeptical. They are not the types to accept any radical ideas about religion or philosophy. They find their truths in their own experience or in practical, down-to-earth rules of living.

They are most suspicious of beliefs that engender an emotional response. They feel that whatever is true can be described in rational terms. Their inner feelings may tell them that there are other purposes to life, but these have not been revealed. Until they discover these truths for themselves, they will continue to adhere to their own ethics.

Capricorn Rising people believe in higher education. Often their own education is interrupted in youth. They resume it in later life to help them attain their ambitions.

These people tend to be supporters of law and order. Their general outlook is that in an ordered society, people have the opportunity to reach their own conclusions, political and moral, free from emotional demands.

Capricorn people are seldom interested in extensive travel unless there is a good reason. They will visit other countries for business and educational purposes but seldom for pure pleasure or sightseeing. They believe in having a responsible attitude to life; sometimes they become narrow-minded, with shrunken vistas. The more they learn through formal courses of study, the more they are attracted to travel, mainly to compare book learning with actual, everyday experience.

TENTH HOUSE: FAME AND AMBITION

Many Capricorn Ascendant people become leaders in their field. Their way to the top is usually along a steady gradient. They become so much a regular part of their field that often they are far more renowned than they know. They are the "authorities" to whom others come for advice. Capricorn people usually know their job in and out.

Capricorn Rising people frequently are successful in partnership. They have a flair for being able to control diverse and scattered activities. They make excellent managers, administrators, and public officials. They frequently are attracted to law and accounting. They can handle heavy responsibilities without any sign of stress.

Capricorn rarely appears to get flustered. They often make topnotch arbitrators with a pronounced ability for weighing alternatives.

Capricorns are among the most ambitious people in the Zodiac. But they seldom make any noise about it. They are prepared to work and wait. They do not like to take shortcuts, which they feel may be a sign of shirking.

On many occasions the quiet, hard-working Capricorn person gets to the top ahead of the favorites as well as the whiz kids. People can make the mistake of underestimating the Goat, then end up working for him or her.

ELEVENTH HOUSE: FRIENDSHIP AND COMMUNITY

Capricorn Rising people are steadfast in friendship. But they choose their companions carefully. No one can expect to become a close friend of the Goat just because they have enjoyed a few days or nights out together. Capricorn people regard friendship as a private, intimate relationship in which both parties are likely to know each other's secrets. They want to be sure first that whoever they call a friend is absolutely trustworthy. They do not have many close friends.

Capricorn Ascendant people cannot stand disloyalty. Anyone who lets them down is banished but not forgotten. If the rascals ever ask for favors in the future, their request probably will be turned down. Both the male and female Goat enjoy the kind of friend who does not make excessive demands on their time. They like to spend a good deal of time alone.

Capricorn-influenced people are not indiscriminate joiners. They frown on clubs where company and conversation are the main activities. Their affiliations with groups and societies require more meaningful objectives, work-oriented ones as a rule. Their public image often demands that they join conservative groups whose emphasis is law and order and where radical ideas are suspect.

Capricorn Rising people do have a liking for secret societies. Mystery intrigues them. They often cultivate people who have an interest in the occult, then amuse themselves by being skeptical and demanding demonstrations of proof.

TWELFTH HOUSE: SECRETS AND THE UNCONSCIOUS MIND

A Capricorn person can keep a secret. They have many of their own, which will never be revealed to anyone.

Their deepest religious convictions are seldom discussed. Even if they have mastered the art of communication and can verbalize their feelings, it is unlikely that they will disclose any really private opinion. These people can enjoy an argument or debate, using them as means of discovering the hidden connections that make their opponents tick.

As a result, Capricorn Rising people are very good at making plans in the background. Their minds are alert to what is going on behind the scenes. In their business and work affairs, they usually have figured out all the possible angles well in advance of any decisions that have to be made. They are seldom taken by surprise.

Despite appearances, Capricorn Ascendant people may be secret optimists. They don't believe in chance nor will they rely on other people to solve a problem. But they do put their faith in themselves; they attend to the practical matters of the present, then trust that this preparation will insure a favorable result in the future.

Capricorn Rising people privately nurture their secret hopes and wishes, which are more expansive than their conservative behavior suggests. They also have a hidden rebellious streak. A sudden shift from conformity to radicalism, for example, comes as a shock to friends and loved ones, but it is really the maturing of a long emotional and intellectual process.

Your Rising Sign:
Aquarius on the Ascendant

A quarius Rising creates a free spirit, interested more in human considerations than personal ones. Such people look to friendship and community networks for stimulation and satisfaction. Group ties may supplant intimate alliances. But in all involvements, even in day-to-day relationships, people with Aquarius on the Ascendant tend to be detached. An impersonal approach characterizes their experiences in the twelve life houses, as described in the following sections.

FIRST HOUSE: PERSONALITY

Aquarius Rising people are fiercely independent. They are not prepared to follow for long in the footsteps of others. They yearn for change, but not for the sake of variety. Change breaks up old patterns and allows the new to come. Change is progress to these often misunderstood people.

Being born under the influence of Aquarius makes a person impatient to discover new truths. They are sometimes regarded as the truth seekers of the Zodiac. They often are attracted to scientific and humanitarian occupations. Where they can apply their intelligent, intuitive minds to discovering keys to the universe or solutions to society's ills.

Aquarius is an air sign; it bestows intellect and the ability to communicate ideas. Once an idea is planted, it must germinate and grow. The symbol of Aquarius is the Water Bearer, signifying fertility, creativity, and nurturance. The sons and daughters of Aquarius are destined to spread their ideas, then take part in the growth and development. Saturn, one planetary ruler of Aquarius, charges them with this responsibility.

Aquarius Rising people are among the most original thinkers of the Zodiac. Uranus, the other planetary ruler of Aquarius, gives them a quality of genius. Frequently their ideas are so advanced that society turns them down only to adopt them at some later date.

230

Aquarius Rising people are as a rule friendly and cooperative. They make many acquaintances but few close friends. They resist alliances and friendships that are emotionally demanding. Aquarius like to keep their relationships as impersonal as possible.

These are people who show in some way a love for humanity. Sooner or later, they endeavor to take responsibility for making the world a better place to live in. They are supporters of worthy causes and often at the head of protest groups. The intense believers can become revolutionaries, taking their place in the forefront of movements aimed at radicalizing society and government.

Aquarius Ascendant people are often intent on reforming the people or organizations they associate with. They are quick to notice when others try to become leaders or authorities. Then they do their best to pull them down, often by the very despotic means they have deplored. Their abuse of people in the name of freedom is destructive of their goal of changing society's thinking.

Aquarius can be very stubborn, in spite of a freewheeling personality. Once they get an idea fixed in their heads, they will not amend it until they have proved to themselves that it is unworkable. With their tendency toward intense beliefs, they can go to extremes of fanaticism.

As artists, Aquarius Rising people can make their best statements. Here their attraction to the unusual and their stubborn need for self-expression enable them to produce truly individualistic works.

SECOND HOUSE: MONEY AND POSSESSIONS

Aquarius Rising people are idealistic about money. How they make it and how they spend it are concerns that plague their social conscience. Usually they wind up compromising their idealism with pragmatism.

Money and possessions actually mean more to Aquarius Ascendant people than they are prepared to admit. They need a sense of material security behind them. Then they feel free to pursue their consciously expressed concerns for the betterment of society.

Unless Aquarius folk find some ideal to work toward, they can get too attached to the power of money and the pursuit of money. Attractive possessions and a comfortable life undermine their social values.

Aquarius can be uncharacteristically impractical where money and possessions are concerned. They frequently have a blind spot that can mystify those closest to them. They can be good managers of household budgets, but may easily endanger their assets by investing in fanciful schemes.

They are not stingy with money. They will help people who are down on their luck. They are more inclined to believe a hard-luck story than to reject it. They genuinely want to help people. If they are able to do it with money, as well as progressive ideas, they feel fulfilled.

The basic Aquarius unpredictability is likely to reveal itself at any time in regard to money and possessions. However, home and family responsibilities make these people more stable.

THIRD HOUSE: CLOSE CONTACTS AND COMMUNICATION

Airy and friendly, typical Aquarius Ascendant people stay socially alive and active. They love to circulate among their many friends and acquaintances. They make frequent short trips and use of the telephone. They like to know all that is going on in their immediate environment.

People influenced by the sign of the Water Bearer have alert, logical minds. They are not generally the type to engage in superficial gossip. Their conversations usually have an instructive purpose; they are always endeavoring to communicate the truths they have discovered. Aquarius Ascendant people have a knack of expressing the truth in a few words.

Aquarius Rising people can make quick decisions. They have active imaginations. They can envisage several courses of action at the same time, then draw an acceptable compromise line to follow.

Sometimes these Uranus-influenced characters are a bit eccentric. Their independent attitudes and progressive ideas put them outside conventional opinion. If they believe enough in a cause, these are the types who are not deterred by libel or other man-made laws from declaring their convictions.

It is not unusual for them to get into temporary disfavor with their current circle of friends and associates. Their companions do not like to be lectured on social and political priorities. However, Aquarius Rising people can be so affable and sociable, their idiosyncracies are soon forgiven—but not forgotten.

FOURTH HOUSE: HOME AND FAMILY

When Aquarius Ascendant people fail to make use of their fine minds and natural inventiveness, it usually means they are tied up with their homes and families.

Although these people are fiercely independent and reluctant to fall into a rut, they do settle down quite well. Family life is a minisociety; here they can preach and practice the ideals of brotherhood and sisterhood. Aquarius singles, who before marriage were probably the envy of their friends, may overnight change into responsible and dutiful parents.

Aquarius people have an underlying need for power, which is often satisfied by involvement in family life. In spite of their ideals of brotherhood and sisterhood (these are usually reserved for the kids in the family), they tend to take and hold onto the reins of power at home. They believe wholeheartedly in their own ideas. In a family scene they insist on demonstrating the practical value of their ideas by running a capable household in which they are undisputed boss.

The Aquarius home is usually modern in decor and furnishings, as light and airy and spacious as economy permits. They enjoy entertaining on a large scale where space, or even the lack of it, encourages impersonal contact rather than intimate exchanges. They will, though, invite friends or associates to drop by any time to examine an ingenious household appliance or a bizarre artistic creation.

Aquarius Rising people can settle into a home fast and are not easily threatened when uprooted. Unexpected events may force them to move, a not uncommon occurrence in their lives.

FIFTH HOUSE: ROMANCE, CREATIVITY, AND CHILDREN

Aquarius Ascendant people are not hot-blooded lovers. Their approach to romance is cool and controlled. Their friendly, broad-minded ways make them popular. So they are seldom short of romantic companions or opportunities. They are able to maintain a fairly detached attitude, which often makes them appear more desirable to the pursuer.

The Water Bearer prefers to keep his or her love affairs as free as possible from emotional demands. Articulate and civilized, these people believe that disagreements should be settled by logical discussion. If they do get involved with possessive or jealous mates, they are likely to split. They also seek a lot of experimentation in love and romance before they are willing and ready to settle down.

Aquarius Rising people are innovators, talented in the arts as well as in politics and the sciences. They try to bring progressive and original ideas to whatever work they do. They have vivid imaginations and a natural aptitude for using words. They are fine public speakers and writers.

Aquarius people are good with children. They usually suggest interesting games and things to do, a form of structured play for the child. They are likely to take more interest when a child is older and able to converse. Aquarius parents are not possessive of their children. They try to pass on to them their own love of independence and truth.

SIXTH HOUSE: WORK AND HEALTH

Aquarius Rising makes a person take work very seriously, provided it interests them. They can become so immersed in their work that time means nothing to them. As these people are often attracted to science, logic, mathematics, philosophy, and similar studies, it is not difficult to imagine the absent-minded professor being one of their type.

However, Aquarius Ascendant people are not daydreamers. They are indeed idealist, but they try to give their notions concrete expression. They are usually found in some field or career that is of benefit to society. As owners or bosses, they make a point of providing good working conditions.

Aquarius Rising people make first-rate politicians, social and charity workers, broadcasters, writers, and psychologists. They often are attracted to the study and practice of astrology. Regardless of field or occupation, they like to be involved in both the theory and practice of it.

People with Aquarius on the Ascendant hold strong views about health and nutrition. They can become identified with efforts to feed the world's starving millions. They sometimes become so absorbed in their mental activities that they fail to take sufficient exercise. They are not enthusiastic about sports, especially the strenuous variety. They prefer introspection and meditation as ways of relaxing and putting their thoughts into perspective.

SEVENTH HOUSE: ALLIANCE AND PARTNERSHIP

Aquarius Ascendant people marry for love, but seldom without other considerations. For one, they have to feel proud of their mate. They like to imagine that their friends and acquaintances also share this esteem.

Second, it is vital for a person influenced by the Water Bearer to marry a partner who has similar intellectual interests. Aquarius are mental creatures, foremost, and they need someone equally intelligent with whom to share their creative ideas.

Typical Aquarius people are often attracted to partners who are as stubborn as themselves. Their homelife can be fraught with periodic tension, battles of minds, and struggles for power.

Aquarius Rising people work very well in a team, but usually gravitate toward a leading role. They are often found as prominent members of laboratory teams, orchestras, and other groups concerned with reform and social welfare.

Aquarius are modest people. They would prefer the group with which they are associated to receive the praise rather than themselves. Even when their originality and inventiveness may have been the main reason for success, they generously share the stage with colleagues.

EIGHTH HOUSE: SEX, PSYCHOLOGY, AND SHARED ASSETS

In sex, Aquarius Rising individuals are never lacking in imagination. But they do have a detached approach which can give a wrong impression—that they lack passion. This is not so. People influenced by the Water Bearer must be mentally attracted to their lovers, as well as physically. Often physical love develops out of shared intellectual interests or pursuits.

Aquarius people have fairly strong critical tendencies. But their friendly nature and genuine interest in the welfare of people as a whole check them from expressing these tendencies. They are more inclined to put their analytical faculty to work in practical ways. They become researchers, technicians, scientists, and psychologists.

Aquarius Ascendant people are quite good at managing joint funds and resources, probably better than they can manage their personal financial affairs. They are suited for controlling large investments for business corporations and pension funds, where practical attention to minute detail is required.

However, it must be remembered that Aquarius types need a sense of purpose and plenty of novelty in whatever they do; they will not allow themselves to be bogged down by mere statistics. They make very good investigators of financial frauds; they can keep secrets discovered in the course of their inquiries. It is not easy for a partner to pull the financial wool over their eyes.

NINTH HOUSE: EDUCATION AND TRAVEL

Nothing is higher in the mind of the typical Aquarius Ascendant person than his or her idea of justice. Whereas others have a limited idea of justice, these people believe in justice for all—that all men and women should have equal opportunities. And they are prepared to do something practical about it.

The Aquarius Rising person is not one who just preaches idealism. They are always active in their conversations or writings. They point to what needs to be done. They often assume the role of reformers in politics and social life.

The Water Bearer is diplomatic and tactful as a teacher. He or she will defend individualism, and will encourage students to develop their own philosophies of law and justice. Aquarius teachers like to present their own strong beliefs, then challenge students to debate.

Aquarius Ascendant people are unemotional. They are able to make balanced assessments. They enjoy listening to other people's viewpoints, and do not have preconceived ideas about how others should run their private lives. They are prepared to accept people as they are. Yet at the same time they work toward helping people understand society better.

Aquarius Rising people love to travel as often and as extensively as possible. They are interested in the unusual, and can be snobbish about their exotic journeys. Travel can be a way of life for some of these individuals. They prefer traveling with a like-minded partner. But lone journeys never remain solitary for long; Aquarius people easily join up with strangers at public events and on sightseeing tours.

TENTH HOUSE: FAME AND AMBITION

Once Aquarius Rising people decide on a definite career, they will work vigorously and with great dedication. Although they enjoy fame and renown, these factors are not usually their main motivation. They take on a profession or job because they feel it should be done. Through it, they hope to contribute something to the world's store of knowledge.

But it is not always easy for these people to decide what field to enter. Without a definite commitment, they can waste their talents. They can become absorbed in projects that have no practical use. Sometimes, they get a reputation for being eccentric.

It is in the fields of science, medicine, space research, electronics, engineering, aviation, television, writing, broadcasting, and music that Aquarius individuals usually make their name. They love nothing more than a challenge, the more complex the better. If they can get to the bottom of some problem that is impeding progress or affecting the welfare of society as a whole, they feel they are fulfilling their destiny.

Although they are more mentally inclined than physical, Aquarius Ascendant people have no trouble finding the necessary stamina and vitality to see their enterprises through. No matter how long a project might take, they can be relentless about completing it. Their work and their causes can inspire deep passions not often aroused by other life experiences.

ELEVENTH HOUSE: FRIENDSHIP AND COMMUNITY

People born with Aquarius on the Ascendant have a natural way of getting along with others. They are affable and sociable, enjoy themselves in all company, like to meet new people, and have many acquaintances.

They select as their friends the more liberally minded types like themselves who believe in freedom, justice, and equality. But they are interested in all types and enjoy exchanging views, even with the most conservative people.

On these occasions, Aquarius does his or her best to present the more broad-minded principles in which they so firmly believe. But their friendly and diplomatic natures seldom give the impression that they are imposing their views on others.

Aquarius Rising people are usually active members of associations and societies. They prefer to mix in circles where their original and progressive ideas are likely to have the most effect in bringing about reforms in society. They know that change takes time. But they also know that it is the conditioning of public opinion that provides the ground for improvement.

TWELFTH HOUSE: SECRETS AND THE UNCONSCIOUS MIND

Aquarius Rising people are often unable to express their feelings in personal ways. They rely on expressing their sympathies for other people, usually in practical ways, and hope that other people will not try to probe into their souls. It's hard for Aquarius people to be emotional about themselves, to look at the deep conflicts that surround their self-image.

Sooner or later Aquarius Ascendant people have to face up to some sort of self-discipline. These freewheeling, intelligent people have much to give to the world, especially to their fellow man. But they often want to give too much too soon. As they can be ahead of the times with their inventive and reforming ideas, they can be ahead of themselves, too. They need to keep a firm hand on their enthusiasm for causes—as well as on their preoccupation with their own independence—until they reach a state of maturity.

Aquarius can become frustrated. The slowness of society to accept their brilliant ideas can make them bitter, rebellious, erratic, and perverse. They have to practice patience to reach their full potential.

These people, however, do have a conservative side to their nature, although it usually remains in their unconscious. This allows them to temper their more revolutionary and radical views with good sense. Then they are able to argue their ideas in rational and socially acceptable terms.

Your Rising Sign:
Pisces on the Ascendant

Pisces Rising personifies the human dilemma of impression, repression, expression. The two planetary rulers of Pisces present contradictions. Jupiter develops wisdom, but also promotes indulgence. Neptune creates vision, but can offer illusion. Like the Fishes, symbol of Pisces, Pisces Rising individuals caught in turbulent eddies may plunge into the dangers of the deep or swim to the safety of shore. Pisces Rising individuals are always trying to integrate their contradictory natures. They dive into the unconscious, then surface to adapt poses for everyday situations. This approach colors how individuals with Pisces on the Ascendant experience the twelve life houses as described in the following sections.

FIRST HOUSE: PERSONALITY

Pisces Ascendant people are exceptionally intuitive. They know instinctively the right thing to do. They don't have to weigh the pros and cons of a situation with rational thought. When, under pressure, they do try to reach decisions intellectually, they often make mistakes.

Pisces Rising are among the kindest and most compassionate people in the Zodiac. They would never harm anyone if it were up to them. They are conscious of the suffering and sorrows of others, and will do all in their power to alleviate them. They can be generous to a fault. These people are soft touches for the hard-luck story. They are true humanitarians.

Pisces-influenced people are often artistic. They have a fine appreciation of music and poetry, and a love of natural beauty. Their creative talents are multifaceted, leading them into fields where they combine physical and emotional expression, especially theater. They make accomplished dancers, singers, and actors. They have a natural aptitude for psychic communication.

These people influenced by the sign of the Fishes, each swimming in opposite directions, vacillate. They can be vague in their personality and approach to life. They are inclined to live in a dreamland, where everything seems to drift. They have difficulty facing the harsh realities of life. Submerged in their fantasies, it is hard for them to surface and make for shore.

Pisces Rising people as a rule do not stand up well under pressure. Of course, much will depend on the position of the other planets in the astroscope. But these people do tend to shy away from action and decision. Unlike the rosy dreams of their fantasies, the real roses of life have thorns, and they prick.

Their extremely sympathetic natures make them attracted to caring for the sick and underprivileged. Pisces Ascendant people often become nurses and social workers, especially in hospitals and institutions. They love children, who respond to their gentle and understanding ways. Their compassion also extends to animals; they frequently have a peculiar empathy with flowers.

Pisces Rising people have a love of the sea. They are deeply emotional. Sometimes they suffer long depressions. They are inclined to spend a good deal of time alone and in introspection. But they also are happy people in between their emotional lows and highs.

They love the good life. They are frequently extravagant with money and may indulge to excess. Isolation doesn't suit them for long. They are incessant talkers when the sociable side of their nature is foremost. They are not very good at keeping secrets, except their own.

Pisces Rising people are lovable individuals who often have a deep understanding of mystical experience.

SECOND HOUSE: MONEY AND POSSESSIONS

It is typical of the nature of a Pisces Ascendant person to scheme like mad to acquire wealth and security—and then yearn to give them away. Frequently they do, for they are generous and unselfish people. But their innate desire to keep some hold on material reality checks them. They retain a sense of proportion in their charitable and philanthropic urges.

Pisces Rising people are contradictions. They blow hot and cold. When the mood is on them to make money, they are intensely active and capable. They tend to resist outside financial advice. Their intuition serves them extremely well in business, especially in connection with land and other real-estate transactions.

But Pisces are impulsive. They are just as likely to blow their entire savings on one wonderful vacation and refuse to think about tomorrow. When tomorrow comes, they are likely to be depressed at the thought of owning anything. Or they may decide with great enthusiasm to start afresh. Pisces people are usually up or down, wild with joy or confused with self-reproach for having more than the needy person next to them.

Pisces Ascendant people are promoters. They look for a quick profit—

probably so they will not have time to change their mind. They are big spenders when they have it, and quick-to-recover-their-spirits losers.

THIRD HOUSE: CLOSE CONTACTS AND COMMUNICATION

From their first day in elementary school, Pisces Ascendant people tend to find the learning process a bit of a drag. Education taught with an emphasis on detail, facts, and memorization is at the opposite pole from them. Their sensitive, feeling natures intuit. They are capable of absorbing the big ideas, as opposed to the nitty-gritty, and they can make broad generalizations based on seeing things as a whole.

To learn, Pisces Rising people have to be involved emotionally. The best way of doing this is to appeal to their sense of beauty or creativity. Having them observe the natural world around them leads to deep understandings of the interconnections in all of life.

Naturally, in adulthood, Pisces Ascendant people tend to mix in circles where feelings are easily communicated. They are often found in the arty domains of the community, among the poets, writers, dancers, and dramatic performers.

Pisces get most of their kicks out of their feelings. So they look for a constantly changing scene. They love to be in the city one day, yearn for the country the next. They would prefer to have a home in both so that they could pack up and move the instant the mood overtook them.

In spite of their easygoing ways, Pisces Rising people can be extraordinarily obstinate. Once they get an idea in their head, they are extremely reluctant to budge from it. It usually requires a deep emotional experience or shock to dislodge an attitude once it is formed.

FOURTH HOUSE: HOME AND FAMILY

Pisces Ascendant people love their homes. But this does not mean they are prepared to settle down in the vine-covered cottage for the rest of their lives. They like to move fairly regularly, if it is possible. And it seems that they always move toward a more expensive residence. Their thoughts about material security are often more solid than their love of change suggests.

Like the Fishes tied together, Pisces Rising people often are not sure in which direction they want to go. Sometimes they want to get away from it all and live in the country. At other times, they yearn for the bright lights. It is a typical Pisces wish to have both a town and a country residence.

For the less mature Fish, this inclination toward the gypsy life can make them wanderers. It is difficult for them ever to settle down. These are the individuals who cart their young families around in circles while they try to find the impossible ideal they are looking for.

All Pisces people love their families. Being one of the most sympathetic and kindly folk in the Zodiac, they frequently overindulge their loved ones.

Yet at times they can become quite irritated with family members. If they feel they are being unduly tied down or if their ideals are criticized, they may just pick up and go. Certainly, open conflict will be unavoidable.

FIFTH HOUSE: ROMANCE, CREATIVITY, AND CHILDREN

Romantic dreams and ideas are almost more important than reality to Pisces Rising people. They spend a great deal of their time drifting on the currents of their emotions, feeding all sorts of romantic imaginings.

In romantic love, they are idealists and dreamers. Quite frequently, they do not see the man or woman they fall for as a real individual. They see only the romantic vision of a lover. Naturally, Pisces Rising folk can be disillusioned and heartbroken in love.

Pisces Ascendant people have a keen sense of the dramatic. Their emotional sensitivity provides them with a talent for artistic pursuits, including writing, poetry, dancing, entertaining, and acting.

Pisces is the last sign of the Zodiac, and so instills in its children a capacity to see all of life's variety as an interrelated whole. Such a collective view enables Pisces Ascendant people to become the theoreticians of art, science, philosophy, and sociology, always within the framework of the humanities.

Pisces people are very sensitive where their children are concerned. They react strongly to criticism of their youngsters. Yet they do all they can to try to correct any shortcomings in their children. The kids should always appear as attractive in looks and behavior as possible. The Fishes want to be proud of their youngsters, for these creations are reflections of themselves.

Pisces-influenced individuals are not consistent enough to be good disciplinarians. They can be quite strict at times, then forget the rules. They tend to give in fairly easily. They are more likely to spoil their youngsters than to be bothered trying to deny them for long.

SIXTH HOUSE: WORK AND HEALTH

Pisces Ascendant people will seldom do a job they consider beneath their dignity. In their way, they probably have a greater sense of pride about work than any other type in the Zodiac.

Pisces Rising people are a bit of a paradox. They are often prepared to do the most menial and self-sacrificing work for the sick, handicapped, or underprivileged. They make wonderful nurses, caretakers, orderlies, and houseworkers. But on no account will the mature Pisces work as a second-rate citizen in his or her own eyes. These people have a way of "disappearing" or not turning up when the work is likely to fall short of their expectations.

Pisces at heart are show-offs. They love to display their talents in their own way. They prefer work where they feel they are at the center of activity yet not under any pressure to perform in established ways. They like to set their own pace, which usually does not involve much physical exertion. Mature Pisces Rising individuals do not complain about ill health. They are too proud to let others think they are not up to coping, even though this often is the case emotionally.

The emotional highs and lows that Pisces can experience as a matter of course can affect their constitutions, which are never too robust at any time, making them feel ill when they really are not. Their self-absorption and vivid imagination also lend a tendency to hypochondria.

SEVENTH HOUSE: ALLIANCE AND PARTNERSHIP

Pisces Ascendant people are not particularly efficient in an organizational sense. They are wonderfully kind and understanding human beings. Their artistic and moneymaking ideas are often uniquely brilliant. But generally, they need a mate or partner who can get down to brass tacks and compensate for their rather impractical ways.

Pisces people usually make a point of choosing a solid, down-to-earth partner. Other things being equal, the relationship can work out very successfully. But if Pisces individuals are immature, they may expect everything to be done for them. Or they just refuse to think about their responsibilities to mate or lover. If so, the partnership almost invariably ends up a stormy and emotional affair.

Pisces Rising people can be extremely critical of their mate or lover. They often blame their partner for their own failings and shortcomings. Their emotional sensitivity makes them prey to deep depressions in which they can appear to be cold and unloving.

Pisces individuals are fairly adaptable and easygoing. They can swing with the ups and downs, and so manage to make their partnerships work when they put their minds to it. They are the sort of people, however, who often are happier remaining single.

Pisces Rising people tend to go to extremes in business and work alliances. They throw themselves in and get swallowed up. Then they resent their backstage role and worry about losing their independence. At this point they may either act uncharacteristically bossy or simply walk out on the scene.

EIGHTH HOUSE: SEX, PSYCHOLOGY, AND SHARED ASSETS

Sexually, Pisces Rising people are inclined to be more curious than deeply sensual. They are avidly interested in understanding the emotional subtleties behind the attraction of the sexes. They can blow hot and cold in physical relationships, leaving their partners confused at their sudden changes of mood.

There are Pisces individuals who through their curiosity get so involved at a sensual level that they find it easier to continue their indulgent way of life than to stop. They can be lazily permissive, being able to "forget" their bodies by going into dreamland.

Pisces Rising people are often mystically inclined and psychically sensitive. They often understand people intuitively, without need for verbal explanations. They can so identify with another person that they are in danger of losing their individuality. This tendency may be behind their abrupt changes of partner and the constant search for satisfaction.

Pisces Ascendant people often breeze into money through their partners. But they can just as often make mistakes in their financial partnerships, and end up being let down and losing their cash.

They have to be very careful with whom they decide to share their funds or resources. Agreements that are made today may fall apart tomorrow through no fault of their own. Partnerships can involve them in taxation and insurance worries.

But probably more often than many other signs, Pisces-influenced people do tend to share at some time in their life in inheritances or legacies through mates and partners.

NINTH HOUSE: EDUCATION AND TRAVEL

Pisces Ascendant people are usually keenly interested in subjects connected with the mysteries of existence. They are natural philosophers who tend to disdain formal metaphysical and religious doctrines. They rely on their own deeply introspective natures to reveal to them the truth about life, death, and purpose.

Pisces Rising people are among the most mystically inclined types of the Zodiac. They tend to meditate naturally, even if they have never had a lesson. They love to examine relationships minutely and to work out what makes other people tick.

People influenced by the sign of the Fishes find it easier and more interesting to understand abstract ideas. They follow a true intellectual process. The boring jobs of concentrated study and memorizing are not for them. These are individuals who depend on their sensitive emotions and intuition more than their reasoning abilities when making important decisions.

Pisces Rising people love to travel. They enjoy the variety of emotions that contact with people in other countries rouses in them. They also are compulsive daydreamers, who often are just as happy performing in their own fantasies as in the real world. They often escape into their dream world when the pressures outside become too much for them.

Pisces Ascendant individuals are impressionable. They are wise to avoid excessive use of drugs or alcohol, which can induce in them rougher trips than other people might experience.

TENTH HOUSE: FAME AND AMBITION

Pisces Ascendant people are great optimists where their careers are concerned. Once they have found what they want to do, their enthusiasm is boundless. Their strong sense of fantasy allows them to visualize with great conviction a rosy end to their dreams. And very frequently these highly adaptive and intuitive people manage to make them come true.

Pisces-influenced people will express their full potential only when they are doing what interests them. If they settle for a humdrum job where their vivid imaginations are not utilized in practical ways, they tend to become incorrigible dreamers.

These individuals are anxious to leave their mark on the world. But they are not the egotistical types who strive for power for power's sake. Once they have achieved their ambitions, they are inclined to do all they can to help other people achieve theirs.

It is important for a Pisces Rising person to aim high. They are rather easily discouraged. They need more than one objective, so if one door shuts they do not feel depressed. These people are inclined to judge themselves too harshly. They are often their own strongest critics. They need the support of their loved ones, who should never allow them to lose heart.

Pisces Ascendant individuals usually have many ups and downs in their professional and working lives. But after the knocks, they have a way of getting up again, often due to a lucky break.

ELEVENTH HOUSE: FRIENDSHIP AND COMMUNITY

Pisces Rising people love their friends and need them. Their friends provide them with a feeling of social security, which is so essential. They often suffer from an inferiority complex, hiding guilts and inadequacies that are mostly figments of their imagination. When meeting people for the first time, they may experience agonies of embarrassment that nevertheless are carefully disguised under a cheery exterior.

Their companions love them despite all, and seldom catch on to their poses. Pisces-influenced individuals are capable of playing a part convincingly because they believe in it. They totally immerse themselves in the persona of the moment.

They are not the types to have many close friends. They require a certain sort of person for an intimate companion, one who will be prepared to ignore or put up with their frequent depressions, changes of mood, and desire to be alone. And one who will not rip the mask off their hidden faces.

Pisces Rising people are often helped in their careers by their friends. They tend to cultivate companions who are ambitious, solid, and reliable.

Although not practical and efficient themselves, they generally look for these qualities in their friends.

When their emotions are outgoing, Pisces Ascendant people like to have many casual contacts. They have a fondness for excitement and novelty provided by new faces and new places. They are talkative in familiar company.

But they do not usually become members of groups, clubs, or societies. They are inclined to feel that such affiliations tie them down. They will, however, actively support movements and causes aimed at helping sick and deprived people. They are idealistic, and identify with the suffering and exploitation of other people.

TWELFTH HOUSE: SECRETS AND THE UNCONSCIOUS MIND

Mystery, rather than secrecy, comes naturally to the Pisces Ascendant individual. Neptune, the planet of mystery and illusion, enhances the effects that sleight of hand and sleight of mind can produce. Pisces Ascendant individuals are always playing with these possibilities, perfecting them in the unconscious—or conscious—mind, and practicing them on real-life people. So they get a reputation for being mysterious and secretive.

Nothing could be farther from the truth. Such individuals will tell all, even about themselves once their hidden persona is penetrated. They can be secretive about their private affairs, but only until they have found the right person, or source, in whom to confide.

Then they can be unguarded. They are perfectly willing to divulge other people's confidences, especially if such a disclosure supports a general principle or belief. Idealistic to the core, Pisces Rising individuals think nothing of betraying personal secrets—in order to make an impersonal judgment or point.

Also, Pisces Ascendant individuals need to share their thoughts with other people. So their private affairs can be a vehicle for sharing. So can the private affairs of other people! But when they do tell secrets, it is with the best of intentions.

The hidden personas of Pisces Ascendant people serve definite purposes. Although the conscious mind may not make the connections at the time, the process can be fulfilling as it goes along and when it is completed. The process is one of immersion and analysis and synthesis and creation—all proceeding without noticeable starts and stops.

As a result, Pisces Rising people often appear confused and vague in wordly affairs. Yet they are never short of original and inventive ideas. Their pioneering thoughts often emerge after a period of apparent daydreaming. Pisces-influenced people are the most imaginatively creative types in the Zodiac.

However, they are frequently disillusioned. They yearn to be loved. But often they are linked with people who do not feel the same attachment as they do. The attachment can be personal, as in love and friendship, or it can be impersonal, as in work and study. Yet somehow Pisces Rising individuals have more commitment than their partners do.

The relationship gap and the difficulty in coping with worldly affairs and expectations can lead Pisces Ascendant people into solitary pursuits, such as exploring the frontiers of knowledge.

Through their emotional sensitivity, they often possess an awareness of occult and spiritualistic states that are not normally in the experience of others. Pisces-influenced people are frequently mediumistic and able to receive messages from the psychic world. They have remarkable intuition and sometimes can tell the future.

The Planets in the Signs: The Moon Through Pluto

Consult the Planetary Tables at the end of the book, pages 397–477, to find the position of the Moon and the other planets for your individual astroscope profile. When you have determined your placements, you can read the descriptions relevant to you in the next chapters.

The Moon in the Signs

The Moon stands for response. Its quality is sensitivity. A positive influence from the Moon enables a person to express sympathy. A negative influence breeds moodiness and suspicion.

The Moon is the planetary representative of the forces of the past, preserved in memory. Instinctive and habitual modes of mind and body are inherited from the Moon.

The Moon is associated with the ebb and flow of the tides, as well as the rise and fall of sensation and emotion. All that is cyclical in nature, and nearly everything is, draws upon the Moon's ever-changing faces, shapes, and movements.

Whereas the Sun vitalizes our senses and makes us conscious of what we have and want to do *now,* the Moon makes us look back. It reflects our tradition and heritage. It makes us cling nostalgically to what used to be, and endeavor to create the past through the present. In so doing, we learn from our mistakes. This is evolution.

The Moon draws us into sleep, into the unconscious. It ensures our safety for a while. Dreams and introspection give us pause. We do not proceed so swiftly into action that we endanger our physical and emotional mechanisms.

But the Moon is constantly changing—moving, turning a new face to Sun and Earth. And sometimes it is hidden, invisible to view. It appears and disappears. Change, changeability, birth, death, and disappearance are phenomena we accept as naturally as we accept the Moon's familiar phases, though not without sentiment.

The Moon also helps us to express such sentiment. Its phases proceed gradually, such as emotions build. First there is awareness of a feeling; then its gradual development; conscious desire, climax, and descent follow in similar rhythms, although they may appear to be stepped up or slowed down.

We think broadly in terms of crests and waves, beginnings and ends.

We forget the gradualness and the connections. The Moon, representing a complete cycle with all the nuances, reminds us, forces memory into impulse.

The Moon is the nature principle, the nurturer, the protector, the mother, the antecedent. The Moon activates our everyday experiences with the expectation of newness and the guarantee of familiarity.

The Moon is associated with the sign of Cancer, which it rules.

THE MOON IN ARIES

This is a good placement if other planetary positions enable a person to handle it. Moon in Aries gives a tendency to stop and start, to swing between action and inaction. One day the person may be fiercely ambitious and ready to mow down any opposition. The next, he or she may feel sorry for their rivals and go out of their way to be helpful, considerate, and understanding.

The marriage of the Moon and Aries can create inner conflict and nervous tension. The Moon tends to make individuals sentimental, while Aries urges them to shake off hindrances or attachments that might hamper freedom of action.

But much can be accomplished in practical ways. Moon in Aries combines intelligence with feeling. These people sense situations because they are attuned to the emotions of others and to their environment. They know instinctively the best thing to do. They are extremely handy to have around in emergencies.

The combination does present problems for emotional relationships. Seldom do attachments of any kind go smoothly. The watery emotions of the Moon often reach boiling point in fiery, impulsive Aries. Arguments and walkouts frequently occur. Despite some moodiness, hard feelings are seldom nursed. These people are quick to forgive. And if they do remember slights or insults, they will not try to get even or be petty.

Moon in Aries people often have a strong desire to work in the public eye. Or their work allows them to influence public opinion. They are confident, enthusiastic, idealistic, and enterprising. Frequently they will be attracted to creative and artistic occupations. In their spare time they may write poetry.

There is likely to be a strong interest in travel, especially to other countries. These people can be surprisingly patriotic. They may be among the first to defend established order and past traditions.

Moon in Aries individuals take an active and somewhat demanding pride in the family. Loved ones are expected to live up to certain standards and to show their affectionate appreciation of what is done for them.

Irritableness can be a problem. Temper has to be controlled. Difficulties can arise in parent-children relationships, especially affecting the mother. Moon in Aries people often can become a bit fussy.

These are people with powerful instincts. Their feelings are easily aroused. Their intuitions often are more reliable than their deliberative decisions. They are especially capable when responding to the challenges of moving situations; a sixth sense seems to guide their reflexes.

The imagination of Moon in Aries individuals is extremely active. They are quick to be drawn into any projects that take their fancy. They can be impetutous and inclined to forget about the consequences of their actions in their eagerness for immediate results.

People with Moon in Aries are independent. They tend to go their own way even when they are working as a team. If they do not occupy a position of authority or leadership in the group, they are inclined to lose interest and look elsewhere.

The danger with Moon in Aries people is that they may start projects and not finish them. They can be restless, forever looking for stimulating changes. They may lack stability. There also is a danger of enthusiasm developing into fanaticism.

Their enthusiasm, though, is often an inspiration to others, especially in the artistic field. Even if they are not particularly creative themselves, they have an eye for art and an urge to encourage self-expression in their associates.

THE MOON IN TAURUS

Here the Moon is especially strong and helpful. Moon in Taurus people are practical, reliable, and earthy. They have a strong feeling for nature and beautiful things. But there is nothing dreamy about their sensitivity. They usually succeed in bringing their ideas into the world, where they can be enjoyed in books, handicrafts, design, and the like.

Success for these individuals often comes through dealing directly with the public. There is a keen sense for business and making money, which often brings material success and enviable reputations.

Moon in Taurus people are among the builders of the Zodiac. Even though they are creative and inventive in artistic ways, they like putting down solid foundations, and especially deep roots. They may travel a bit, or wish to, in order to find just the right place to settle. Surroundings must be harmonious. Ideally, there has to be a link with nature, a lifeline to them, especially if they are crowded in cities. Once they find a suitable place, they settle.

These people are conscientious, imaginative, and keenly productive. They can be relied on to do what they say. They do not undertake things lightly. Nor do they ever give up just because the going gets rough. If they have faith in a person or a project, they will doggedly pursue it to the end.

Moon in Taurus confers an emotional temperament, which enables these individuals to make friends very easily. Such persons are quietly confident, courteous, sympathetic, and unobtrusive. They can be secretive about some of their activities. But they do not try to probe into the private affairs of others, either. They are intensely loyal to their friends.

They are especially fond of the home and their family. Being slow to make changes, they are content to build step by step as the years go by. Their aims are a comfortable home and an affectionate, tight-knit family group.

Moon in Taurus people are not revolutionary in their thinking. They even can be suspicious of new ideas. They like to see first that ideas are workable. They specialize in adapting established ideas—upgrading them with a new or attractive or profitable twist.

Moon in Taurus gives a natural skill in handling money, especially on behalf of others and in connection with public enterprises. These individuals are the perfect guardians of partnership funds and shared assets of a group. Sex for Moon in Taurus individuals is sensuous. They have a deep need to be loved and cherished and to feel the physical warmth of affection. If they are promiscuous, it is usually because they are looking for the ideal partner. They are great romantics but manage to retain a keen eye for practical advantages and disadvantages of a relationship. They would love to love a partner who could also provide them with the economic security they deeply crave.

Moon in Taurus people have considerable capacity to enjoy life. They love comfort and good things. Although they insist on having their pleasures, they are usually prepared to work hard for them. Once they set their minds on a material objective, they are not inclined to give up.

The Moon signifies instinct; Taurus signifies persistence. So these people can be supremely focused. Their powers of endurance are impressive. But they need an aim outside of merely satisfying their desire for creature comforts. They can become too contented and get into a rut.

Moon in Taurus people often have musical appreciation. Artistic pursuits can help them toward a greater sense of self-fulfillment. On the negative side, they can be fiercely possessive. Their jealousy can make the lives of their loved ones a misery. There is always a danger that early marriages may be based on physical attractions and so fail.

THE MOON IN GEMINI

This person can be a born writer, talker, or speaker, popular to everyone. But Moon in Gemini individuals need to understand themselves if they are to make the most of their talents. They can too easily become superficial and spend their time gossiping, absorbing useless information, and visiting others as a need to share their own restlessness. Not facing up to problems can be a fault. So can the tendency to tell untruths to gain popularity or attention.

But with a little self-understanding, Moon in Gemini people can combine the wonderful feeling world of emotions with the interesting and stimulating world of the mind. They can present to the public all kinds of new ideas and perceptions. Their intellects are extremely sharp. They can reach deep into themselves and express the most complex feelings in clear and entertaining ways.

Moon in Gemini individuals can pick up atmospheres instantly. They are very adaptive but inclined to change their minds or moods without warning. They should try to write down what they think when they are feeling creative. Later, their record of insights and inventions may be put to profitable use.

Moon in Gemini can make a person secretive about home and family affairs. Although they may not want the household to know everything they are doing, they expect to be kept informed of what the others are doing. They enjoy reminiscing about the past. They are very good storytellers if they put their mind to it.

It is sometimes one of their bad habits to insist on getting their own way in close relationships. They can even take pleasure out of rubbing others the wrong way just to trigger a response. Then they try to use their superior mental qualities to win the argument.

Moon in Gemini people find learning very easy. What they can't quite understand with their minds, they pick up with their feelings. This placement of the Moon often gives an aptitude for music, either as a composer or a player. Languages are easily mastered. The imagination is particularly vivid and colorful and can be used to make money and to get ahead in practically any profession or line of work.

Moon in Gemini people are versatile. They can turn their hand and mind to practically anything. In business, they are alert and shrewd, sometimes even described as crafty. They have good ideas for obtaining publicity and influencing public opinion.

These people can make good actors, speakers, and entertainers. They can switch their emotions very swiftly, almost to order. Sometimes they are guilty of using this ability to play on the feelings of their loved ones, especially family members. They can be opportunists who just cannot resist taking advantage of a situation.

The Moon in Gemini often produces individuals who have difficulty finding what they want to do with their lives. Even when they achieve enviable heights of success, they are still likely to be dissatisfied. They always seem to be looking for something else or something more. Because of this, they are often accused of being restless and superficial.

Moon in Gemini individuals need to cultivate a purposeful attitude. They can be too easily distracted from whatever they are doing to have much success in finishing anything worthwhile. They tend to love novelty and change. They seldom stay in the one place for long. They are likely to move house and change their jobs frequently. They can be talkative and may enjoy gossiping.

THE MOON IN CANCER

Cancer is the Moon's own sign. So a person with this combination enjoys the best that the emotional world, represented by the Moon, can give. They are deep-feeling people, who enjoy a rich inner life. But this must not be allowed to take over too much from the external world, or they will become disjointed and lapse into moodiness.

Moon in Cancer individuals are inclined to become mentally lazy; they depend unduly on the sensitivity of their feelings. A Moon in Cancer person needs to mix and talk and give verbal or written expression to feelings and instincts.

These people are nature lovers. Like the Moon and the tides, they easily fall into rhythms and can reach great heights of enjoyment and beauty. They are artistic and very impressionable. They like to think things over rather than make quick decisions. When they get a creative idea or thought, they should try to do something with it. It is easy for them to let their best impressions fade. So they often miss opportunities for having their talents and skill recognized.

With effort, Moon in Cancer people can easily become famous. They have a way with the public. They also possess a remarkably good business sense, which they should apply if they are not already aware of it. They often are much more ambitious than their retiring nature suggests. These people can show uncharacteristic aggression and determination when they are moved to.

Moon in Cancer folk make loving parents and successful marriage partners. The family and the home are extremely important to them. They are great homemakers. They have a knack for creating a haven. They are nurturers, inclined to cluck over their loved ones with the protective care of a mother hen.

Moon in Cancer people are sentimentalists. They look at people through their own deep emotional experiences, and so understand immediately what the other person is feeling. Their sympathy is especially comforting to those in distress, especially those who are experiencing loss of loved ones.

It is easy for Moon in Cancer people to be imposed on. They also must be careful of excessive intake of drugs or alcohol. And they must choose more selectively prospective lovers, partners, and mates—even casual contacts whom they let into their lives.

These are people who love to relive their experiences. They frequently go into daydreams about the past. They love to wander down memory lane, not only in their minds but also by visiting the places in their past, especially of their childhood.

Moon in Cancer individuals are among the most romantic types in the Zodiac. The women are cherishing, loving, emotionally responsive. The men are protective, sensitive, understanding. All of them radiate an Old World style and charm. These are people who love to entertain at home, to prepare succulent and fine dishes. They are the most hospitable folks. They love to make visitors feel at home.

People born with the Moon in Cancer are generally fine raconteurs. Although initially reserved in their talk, they become more and more voluble and communicative as they settle into pleasant company. Their stories usually show an ability to observe the nuances of life and living. They possess a subtle sense of humor.

Moon in Cancer people can be lazy. They may be inclined to discuss their grandiose plans with all and sundry, but never get around to making a start. They can be selfish, demanding, and cranky to live with.

THE MOON IN LEO

Moon in Leo individuals often become very successful in life. They make good entertainers, professional or amateur. They are often among the leaders in creative and artistic fields. Moon in Leo confers an extremely fine ability to gauge the mood of the public.

But Moon in Leo people often get carried away by their importance. They often try too hard to get their own image across, and so fail to give their audiences what they want. Through conceit, and an inordinate desire to be at the center of everything, they can make mistakes that ruin their chances.

Moon in Leo individuals have to be loved. They don't care whether it is family love, romantic love, or hero worship, as long as they feel an emotionally appreciative response from others. They have a flair for dramatizing situations, and are not beyond using these to get the attention they want. They are born actors and actresses, as their loved ones will be the first to attest.

Moon in Leo people take a great pride in their homes. They like them to be comfortable, attractive, and a little out of the ordinary. They are particularly fond of giving dinner parties to which their special friends are invited. To them, the home is the place where they enjoy showing off their social graces, their collections, their good taste in food and wines—and their lovers, mates, or children.

Moon in Leo people are romantic individuals who have no trouble attracting admirers. They fall in love easily and usually very deeply. Their affection can be so intense that the beloved feels smothered. With all the best intentions in the world, the Moon in Leo person can become just too emotionally attached.

But they are loyal and will not go back on any undertakings. They have a high sense of honor that cannot condone pettiness or backbiting. Yet if not appreciated sufficiently, or if they feel left out of situations, they can become moody and sulky.

Moon in Leo individuals have a great deal of initiative. But they can balk getting started. They need to feel a project is going to bring them some form of personal acknowledgment. They would usually rather be famous than rich.

Moon in Leo folk are generous. But their sharing can be a bit heavy-handed. They have a sense of dignity that can make them appear affected and patronizing. They have considerable self-confidence and like to hear themselves talk. They want to be at the center of attention. They can be show-offs and conceited. They are frequently luxury-loving and in danger of self-indulgence.

These people have a capacity for leadership. Their perceptions are geared to other people; they instantly pick up how people receive them and respond to them. They have a persuasive way with groups and a sixth sense for measuring the mood of the public. They make good public-relations consultants.

People born with the Moon in Leo have passionate feelings. They seldom become involved in anything, or with anyone, in a halfhearted manner. They are outgoing and optimistic. They often refuse to recognize personal limitations. They have fertile imaginations and are inclined to get along well with children.

Moon in Leo individuals make loyal friends. They usually have numerous acquaintances from whom they enjoy receiving admiration and praise. Anyone who does not appreciate them to their satisfaction is likely to be ignored and banished from their inner circle. Although radiating fun and warmth, these people can be self-opinionated and so run the risk of alienating friends and realizing their worst fear—isolation.

THE MOON IN VIRGO

People with Moon in Virgo are competent and conscientious. They have a unique ability to analyze problems and to come up with solutions. Once involved in a project or task, they become totally absorbed until their work is completed.

Given even a small share of appreciation, Moon in Virgo individuals will work as though they really enjoy it—and they do—without fuss about pay or privileges. Employed in a job, they are usually there as long as it suits them. Employers find them willing, uncomplaining, trustworthy, and undemanding.

Moon in Virgo individuals may appear much more self-confident than is the case. They are likely to have some problem understanding their own emotions. They may feel in a way that they can't trust their emotions and therefore get inwardly uptight trying not to show them.

There are chances that childhood misunderstandings, involving a parent or parent figure, have never been resolved and become the basis for adult attitudes. The tendency to criticize and find fault is strong. Old prejudices picked up from elders in childhood may be unconsciously applied.

Moon in Virgo people have very practical minds as long as they do not allow their emotional uncertainties to get the better of them. They can become woolly thinkers if they start to worry about what others are thinking about them, instead of dealing with the facts in hand and getting on with what has to be done.

Moon in Virgo people are modest and unassuming. They make extremely good teachers who are able to appreciate the feelings of their students without allowing personalities to get in the way. They genuinely wish to help people. And even their critical tendency has this object behind it.

In business and work, Moon in Virgo people believe in giving service. They are industrious and unassuming, sometimes inclined to be a bit timid. They are very good at dealing with detail. Although their personalities can at times be cold, they have a knack for being able to analyze other people's feelings. They can remain detached from a problem and are capable of giving first-rate advice.

They have to be careful that their practical way of looking at things does not make them calculating. They may need to cultivate a more imaginative outlook. There is a tendency for these people to concentrate on mental activities to the exclusion of emotionally stimulating ones.

Moon in Virgo individuals can wait for romance to come to them, then end up let down. They need to make more effort to communicate their deeper feelings. They can be too sensitive about maintaining appearances. Displays of affection in public are likely to embarrass them.

These people are inclined to make good doctors, nurses, administrators, and teachers. Even so, they have to work harder at accepting progressive ideas. They can be too conforming and conventional. They may need to relax and enjoy life more.

With the Moon in Virgo, a person can be particularly interested in health and diet. These people have to avoid becoming unduly imaginative about ailments or feelings; their imaginings can be exaggerated to the point where phobias can develop.

Fault-finding is one of the most annoying traits of Moon in Virgo people. They are usually looking for some kind of perfection. This tendency can make them tidy and efficient around the home. Or they may concentrate all their attention on their family, putting its comfort and welfare before neatness and tidiness.

A love of the past, combined with analytical ability, can lead to hobbies such as souvenir collecting, and tracing family trees.

THE MOON IN LIBRA

This person can make the ideal partner. Libra is the sign of partnership, and the Moon the energy of emotional response. Between them they make the sweetest music.

But the combination of Moon in Libra can confer a changeableness, sometimes a flirtatiousness. It is not conducive to lasting relationships. While everything is going smoothly, an association with this person can be idyllic. They are undemanding, understanding, charming, courteous, agreeable, and diplomatic. They accept their partners as they find them, and are not out to reform or correct them.

Then the mood is likely to change. The attention is likely to shift. If distracted by something out of the past, these people can withdraw deeply and uncommunicatively inside themselves. Or if a new and interesting person or event happens on the scene, they respond.

The need to be accepted by others is extremely strong, so Moon in Libra individuals are never alone for long.

Moon in Libra people have a habit for a while of giving everyone the response he or she wants. They tend to agree with whatever is said without noticing any contradiction in themselves. They feel the need to adapt to the emotions of the other person. It is this that makes them so popular. And after a while so exasperating to the person who takes them seriously!

Moon in Libra people often have a lot of ups and downs in their love life. Not so much because they are sensual, but because they are always out to please. And it's very difficult to please several people at the same time, especially if one of them is the marriage partner or primary lover. Libra, energized by the Moon, responds and relates to every contact, mostly innocently, but this does have its obvious complications.

Moon in Libra individuals seek harmony. Even though they may be the cause of much falling out, they hardly ever see it—they have moved on to a new relationship. And besides, they would not want to be involved in any nasty scene or argument if they could possibly avoid it.

Moon in Libra also produces persons who finds it hard to make up their mind. In their indecisiveness, they often wait for events to pick them up and carry them along. They have a powerful appreciation of beautiful things.

Their tastes in clothes, food, and amusements are expensive, frequently exotic.

Moon in Libra people can be passive. Their desire for peace may be so strong that they avoid making any effort for fear of the disturbance it might create. This is not to say that these people are lazy. Far from it! But they may exert themselves only along channels of their own choosing. Unfortunately, such channels may lead to a dependence on others to do the dirty work.

These are friendly people with sensitive instincts. They know how to make a partnership or a relationship really work. They rely on an emotional sixth sense that makes them aware of what will please others the most.

Moon in Libra individuals are most charming, pleasing hosts and hostesses to all. They love to entertain in style and beautiful surroundings. They are particularly tolerant, accepting others as they are. But they are snobs. They would like to find their closest associates among a privileged group, people who have more money than most. Even if Libras cannot afford this kind of life, they gravitate toward it.

Moon in Libra individuals can be undependable. Their emotions blow hot and cold. They can be all over someone one day, then aloof and uninterested the next. They can be too easily influenced, unable to pursue a definite line of action for a sustained period of time.

THE MOON IN SCORPIO

Scorpio can be an emotionally hazardous placement for the Moon. The sexual appetite is likely to be stimulated. There are dangers of problems and difficulties through indiscretion. A way has to be found of directing the emotions into productive channels. There is too much tendency to use the imagination along self-indulgent lines.

With the necessary restraint and positive direction—to be found in the other planetary placements—Moon in Scorpio can produce a determined and successful person. Through the energy of the Moon, their passions can be translated into creative, artistic, and inventive work. They can have access to heights and depths of emotions unknown to others.

Moon in Scorpio people can be scientists, psychoanalysts, researchers, investigators, occultists, and deeply moving painters and writers. They are likely to excel in any occupation that requires deeper than average insight.

Such individuals are strong-willed, secretive, intense, and seldom spontaneous. Staunchly helpful and brave, nevertheless these people can be jealous and spiteful. They tend to repress their feelings so that they get tremendous buildups that can explode into anger, corruption, or near genius.

Moon in Scorpio does not produce a person with great tenderness. The urge may be there, but seldom can it be expressed. There is too much self-suppression. The sentimentality and softness of the Moon get burned up in the volcanic intensity of Mars and Pluto, planetary rulers of Scorpio. But it has to be remembered that all this will be modified by the positions of the other planets. In this way, the Moon in Scorpio placement can reflect positive and helpful values for the integral personality.

For instance, Moon in Scorpio confers great strength of will whether it is used for good or ill. The person is less dependent on others, enabling him or her to work for long hours in isolation and difficult conditions or circumstances. These people can get to the top through sheer endurance and personal discipline. They have a way of grasping difficult subjects instantly. They don't like change and are fixed in their views, often to the point of absurdity.

Moon in Scorpio individuals have a special magnetism about them. They are not the type of people who blend into a crowd. It is difficult not to be aware of their presence even though they do nothing to draw attention to themselves.

Their emotional sensitivity enables them to have deep insights into other people's characters. They are not fooled by pretense. They dislike affectation. They want people to be themselves. Yet in spite of their directness and sometimes bluntness, they are very secretive people. They never reveal their deeper feelings except in the intensity with which they approach projects they are interested in.

Sometimes Moon in Scorpio people are subject to deep depressions. They feel compelled to penetrate their souls in order to identify with their own core, the source of their feelings. At times like these, life can be difficult for their loved ones. People they live with may feel rejected or excluded. Moon in Scorpio individuals can be weird and self-tormenting.

But they do have a great capacity for getting to the bottom of things. They never give up once their emotional interest has been aroused. They like to relive their experiences. Because of this, they often make the same passionate mistakes more than once.

Moon in Scorpio people are not ones who forget or forgive quickly. Perceiving an insult, they vow to get even. It is within their nature to retaliate and get revenge no matter how long it takes.

THE MOON IN SAGITTARIUS

People with the Moon in Sagittarius often find it hard to remain in one place for long. They yearn to travel to distant and exotic places, preferably across the sea. If they can't journey physically to foreign lands, they make frequent visits through their imaginations.

These individuals are idealists. They are always looking for new horizons, new goals. They make plans in their heads, which they may have no intention of implementing at the moment. But one day they probably will.

The Moon in Sagittarius often makes a person move house a lot. Even if such people have large families, including children or elders, they are likely to pack them all up and move on to new pastures without a backward glance or any thought of inconvenience.

These people have to feel free. They will not tolerate any kind of partnership if it makes them feel tied down. They can be very good providers and family men and women, which may seem to restrict them as much as anyone. But it all depends on how *they* feel about it whether they stick at it or not.

With the Moon in Sagittarius, a person can easily become something of a wanderer. But they will never let their family down, if they have one. They will be interested in having the nicest home they can afford, a place where they can entertain friends and acquaintances. But once the family unit is established, they will be inclined to use it as a base, a place for joyous homecomings with gifts and parties—and frequent departures.

People with Moon in Sagittarius are invariably popular. They have an optimistic outlook on life that others often envy. And they seem to have more than their fair share of good luck. They can be disastrously overconfident, and lose their money gambling or backing untried business ventures. But they are not ones to worry or to blame others.

They are generous, sometimes foolishly so. But their losses have a way of being made up. Moon in Sagittarius people have spontaneous feelings. They are intuitive and quick to do others a good turn. So their generosity often is paid back, getting them out of trouble in the nick of time. Such is their good luck.

Moon in Sagittarius individuals love nature and the outdoor life. They are most active in sports and games. They are fond of animals, especially racehorses. Gambling often attracts them, and is one cause of their irresponsibility.

These people can be devils for making promises that are not kept. They can be very irresponsible. They may be a constant headache to their dependents, who have to make excuses for their easygoing casualness.

Moon in Sagittarius people are outspoken. They say exactly what they feel and very often put their foot in it. They are not the types to indulge in deception and lies. These are people with a high sense of honor and a regard for tradition. Although they sometimes want to break authoritarian rules and positions, they have a respect for established law and order.

These are freedom lovers, but they do not believe in anarchy. They can, however, be rather superficial and tend to ignore the bigger social issues for the trivial. They can be too indulgent of their need for emotional stimulation through companionship and change. They can be the tireless party types, always in search of a good time.

These people are great raconteurs. They may be successful writers about history and cultures without necessarily ever having visited other lands.

There is something of the explorer about Moon in Sagittarius people. They love to be free to roam, both mentally and physically. They do not take easily to conventional nine-to-five occupations. They need excitement in their lives, the prospect of new discoveries around every corner. They can make good professional people if their profession allows them to extend their knowledge and vision.

THE MOON IN CAPRICORN

The Moon in Capricorn is not a good position for expressing love or emotions. These feelings may be felt quite intensely, but getting them out is the problem. With this combination, people feel self-conscious about any displays of sentimentality. They can be afraid of seeming foolish. The female side is very important to this combination. The men are likely to link up with women much older or younger. Their first attempts at marriage may not be as successful as their second, which they may studiously avoid through fears of making the same mistake. The women in their lives may lack warmth.

The women with Moon in Capricorn will not be happy unless they find a man who loves them; they should not settle for less. And it is important to have sexual rapport. It is through the act of lovemaking that all people with this combination can communicate their deeper feelings to the person they love.

But the Moon in Capricorn is a very favorable position for achieving worldly success. It may mean, though, a lot of hard work and the sacrifice of many of the normal distractions and pleasures that people enjoy. It is as if people with the Moon in Capricorn decide to put their unreleased emotions into mobilizing their ambitions. They feel more secure and confident in company when they communicate from a position of reputation or influence. So prestige becomes their aim early in life, once they discover something they are good at.

The Moon in Capricorn gives a remarkable capacity for working under pressure and in conditions that most other people would find impossible. In this way, much ground can be covered, and the favorable attention of helpful people in authority gained.

These people have an aptitude for wielding power. Instead of depending on personality and charisma, their strength lies in an extraordinary ability to know everything that is going on in the operation under their command. These are the potential captains of industry, as well as the all-seeing eyes of the bureaucratic "big brother."

Wherever the public is concerned, Moon in Capricorn individuals will eventually receive the recognition and authority so dear to their hearts.

Moon in Capricorn people have to be careful not to take too serious a view of life. They can become gloomy and brooding. They need to get out and around as often as possible, and not settle into any ruts. They can be inclined to put too much emphasis on work and achieving their ambitions. They often neglect relaxation and entertainment in which other people are involved.

These individuals are careful, sometimes too cautious. They can miss out on opportunities through a fear of taking any chances at all. They can be reluctant to venture beyond the familiar.

However, these people can be very self-demanding. They are inclined to put a great deal of pressure on themselves. They may be acutely conscious of their emotional restraint, which in turn will cause them to become even more uptight. They must find a happy way of releasing their feelings.

The sign of Capricorn energized by the Moon can make these individuals a bit self-centered in their feelings. They are inclined to relate everything to themselves. Sometimes, they appear unsympathetic. They are, however, deeply attached to their homes and families. They make a point of seeing that the people and things they love most are protected.

THE MOON IN AQUARIUS

A person with the Moon in Aquarius is usually a person with high ideals. These people are not sentimentalists, however. They believe that any good that is done should be for the benefit of all people in the community, not just for individuals. Moon in Aquarius people are the humanitarians, the reformers of the Zodiac. A person with this combination has very strong feelings about what should and should not be done. They see things very clearly. They translate everything they feel into a mental image. In this way they are able to identify with their fellow man. They can initiate ideas that will help to solve problems rather than just relieve them.

Moon in Aquarius individuals are often scientists. The power of invention is strong. They also can make farsighted politicians, and dedicated leaders of good causes and crusades.

These people are friendly. They like to get around, to circulate, to enlarge their circle of contacts and interesting acquaintances. They are not too enthusiastic about close friendships; they prefer looser relationships.

But Moon in Aquarius folk are loyal. They love the idea of freedom and independence, for themselves and for everyone else. It is this urge that makes them so effective in their endeavors to help others. They don't want anyone to be unnecessarily dependent.

This, of course, creates its problems. Their own loved ones can feel a bit neglected. It is very hard, almost impossible, for these people to settle into a one-to-one relationship, especially if it demands a lot of their time and attention. They are not the type to cuddle up by the fire for long. They don't forget what is happening in the cold, cruel world outside.

Moon in Aquarius people live a regulated life. They seldom go to extremes, emotionally or physically. They are not self-indulgent. They may, though, be fanatical in their views of society. But they are conservative in their own affairs, which they handle with efficient detachment.

These people are interested in unusual subjects and usually have a strong intuitive flair for understanding them. They are often original thinkers, tending to use the past to demonstrate what is possible in the future.

Moon in Aquarius individuals are quietly obstinate people. For all their friendliness and understanding, they will not budge from a position or an idea once they have made up their mind. Sometimes their views are very difficult for their associates to identify with. They sometimes feel isolated. They often go out on a limb; few people really understand what they are trying to do.

These individuals have to beware of becoming eccentric. Their deeper unconventional attitudes can impel them to mix with groups that are on the fringe of established society, acquaintances who may have odd and even revolutionary inclinations.

People born with the Moon in Aquarius are good judges of character. Their instincts are well developed. They often are able to provide their associates with logical solutions to their problems that no one else may have suggested or seen.

These are individuals who can understand people undergoing stress and strain and crises of adjustment. In a helping way, they are very straightforward; they will not pull any punches in what they say if they feel it is necessary. They often use shock as a device for trying to wake people up. Moon in Aquarius people can come on as rebels. If they want to win the support of the public, it is important for them not to display excessive independence. The public can be quick to turn against them if it is sensed that their efforts are for self and not for service.

THE MOON IN PISCES

A Moon in Pisces person is very difficult to understand. Their emotions change with the drama and frequency of a flashing light. The true person is seldom ever seen. They are a parade of different moods and personalities.

These people are dreamers. There is a great need for a strengthening influence through other planetary positions. These people find facing up to reality an excruciating experience. They can't stand pressure, disharmony, ugliness, conflict, argument, or competition. They are very happy when they are winning, but fretful and difficult when losing.

It is not so much that Moon in Pisces individuals cling to their material possessions. Just the opposite! They can be commendably philosophic about that kind of loss. But they are terribly concerned with what others think about them. They want to be liked and, even better, loved.

Moon in Pisces people usually manage to have someone strong and reliable in close contact. They need someone to depend on; they can become clinging vines. They have a happy knack of making confessions that confuse their partner but free themselves from their own feelings of guilt or doubt.

The feeling of continuous failure seems to afflict Moon in Pisces people whenever they become introspective, which is fairly often. Things that other people shrug off as the price of being human can psychologically torture these supersensitive souls.

People with the Moon in Pisces need to get out of any regular environment. Without constantly changing faces and scenes, they become highly emotional, depressed, even morbid. They need more than just the person they love—and they do love very, very deeply. They need lighter, even superficial, relationships to compensate for the depth that is in them.

These people are generous, self-sacrificing, and cooperative. They can easily be taken advantage of. They have to avoid excessive intake of alcohol or unnecessary use of drugs. They are inclined to use these aids under pressure to escape from reality.

The Moon in Pisces is an extremely creative and poetic combination. It gives people a great capacity for love and service to those less fortunate. Dedicating themselves to the hurt and needy can be an artistic and awe-inspiring mission.

Moon in Pisces individuals have a deceptive side to their nature. They have a horror of revealing their true feelings. They often adopt poses that help them release their emotions. Other people mistake the pose for the real person, only to be disappointed when this Moon child changes again. Such emotional games give the Moon in Pisces person a reputation for being unreliable and unstable.

People born with the Moon in Pisces have powerful imaginations. However, they need to channel their feelings and thoughts into constructive activities. They need to work toward definite objectives. Otherwise, they will drift off into dreamland, which is their refuge when the pressures of life become too much for them to cope with. There is a risk of self-indulgence in food, alcohol, sex, and comfort. These people can be very sociable. They enjoy the stimulation of entertaining and visiting, at home or out. Attached to their families, they are capable of making considerable sacrifices for the ones they love—as long as they are allowed their private world.

Although gentle and kindly, Moon in Pisces individuals are often restless and seem to be inconstant in their affections. They may turn their back on an established relationship for a while, so they can enjoy the distraction of a newer or more novel one. They are usually true to lovers, mates, or friends in the long run, and certainly when a situation is serious and demands a clear show of allegiance.

Mercury in the Signs

Mercury stands for communication. Its quality is intelligence. When positive, it is discerning; when negative, cunning. This quicksilver planet can create lightning-swift intuition and heightened awareness, or mental restlessness and lack of concentration.

Mercury's influence on an individual also depends on the other planetary placements. If some planetary placements are stabilizing ones, Mercury's contribution can be positive.

Mercury gives adaptability. It intensifies the power to communicate information or knowledge. There is always a risk that without mature restraint, the influence of Mercury can make a person frivolous, superficial, and inclined to scatter mental energies. Pursuing numerous activities may interfere with an individual's ability to accomplish anything of value in one activity.

When balanced, Mercury makes a person alert, active, and quick to spot opportunities.

Mercury is strongest in association with Gemini and Virgo, the two signs it rules.

MERCURY IN ARIES

This combination makes a person mentally active and able. Their mind is seldom still. They can produce an abundance of ideas about practically any subject brought to their attention. If they do not understand something, they are inclined to head straight for the encyclopedia or the library. Ideas are as necessary to them as food.

These people often enjoy debating. They are likely to provoke arguments just for the sake of exercising their mental dexterity. They can be

265

very clever, sometimes brilliant. But there is a tendency to become pat and stale. They may collect information for the sake of displaying knowledge instead of using it productively.

People with Mercury in Aries have a gift for summing up situations at a glance. They make good executives and administrators. They are at their best when the action is coming thick and fast, and ideas are needed for solutions. Pressure triggers their sharp wits.

But these people are not so good at making long and detailed studies. They are inclined to become bored with repetitious situations. They can bring their minds brilliantly to bear on specific problems with figures or details. But to have to concentrate on long columns of numbers day in and day out would drive them mad.

Mercury in Aries people love to read and learn subjects in which they are interested. But here, too, they are inclined to skim the surface. They will take what they think is needed off the top, then depend on their own undoubted ingenuity to fill in the rest.

This zippy approach can produce a person who may seem to know a tremendous amount. But he or she is likely to be exposed as a dabbler in any particular subject when confronted by an expert. Cornered, these individuals shift into high gear—pioneering topics, their best conversational gambit.

These people like to put forward new ideas. They are good conversationalists. But they do find it difficult to listen for long to others. Then they are compelled to put their oar in, knowledgeable or not.

Mercury in Aries can make a person blunt and outspoken. There is an impulse to say anything that is felt, even though it may offend or hurt. The excuse for this lack of diplomacy is the feeling that the truth should not hurt. But, of course, it often does, and it can hurt these people themselves.

Mercury in Aries individuals are fast movers, physically and mentally. They like to get around, making frequent short trips and visits to their friends and relatives. Friendship means a great deal to them. They are spontaneous and generous in their responses to friends. They do, however, tend to collect numerous friends, not a great many to which they are deeply attached. This tendency, of course, has to be considered against the placements of the other planets.

They have a direct and forceful manner of expression. Sometimes they are in such a hurry to communicate that their utterances become disconnected. They do not think much before they speak; what comes into the mind usually passes right out of the mouth.

These people are often impressive in engaging in repartee. Their first thoughts usually are best. Their lack of deliberation, unless their Sun is in Taurus, allows them to deliver volley after volley of clever retorts and remarks.

There may be a tendency in people with Mercury in Aries to exaggerate. They may not allow the facts to destroy a good story. It is important for them to try to cultivate greater concentration, as well as more careful regard for the truth.

These individuals are often inspired in their perceptions. But they may lack continuity. They often lack patience and restraint. When others do not agree with their ideas, they may become hostile and argumentative.

MERCURY IN TAURUS

Once Mercury in Taurus people get an idea fixed in their head, it is very difficult to change their minds. They can be as obstinate as a mule. They may take an interest in an opposite view or play the devil's advocate. If so, they appear to be won over, at least convinced of their misconception. But this is like water off a duck's back. Mercury in Taurus will only change an opinion in his or her good time.

Of course, this mental determination can be a great asset. Certainly it is helpful to a partner or a boss who relies on Mercury in Taurus individuals. When they have the right idea, they pursue it with a stubborn resolution that can produce wonderful results.

Mercury in Taurus people are methodical thinkers. They proceed cautiously from one fact to another. They are not subject to flights of fancy, unless other combinations in the chart introduce this element. They are practical. They don't jump to conclusions. They are conservative and inclined to put their faith more on what has been proven that in speculative ideas.

A person with Mercury in Taurus makes a good politician who will be known for his or her solid policies. There is a strong tendency to want to build for the future, to make provisions against possible future needs or shortages. The impulse is to resist changing the status quo. Much that has been good, and bad, in the past has been retained by the intransigence of the Mercury in Taurus individual.

These people are diplomatic and conventional in speech and writing. They may appear to be slow-thinking. But they have swift comprehension, which requires time for thought before making their responses. They are not mentally adaptable. They have to live with an idea for a long time to come around to accepting it. Even then, the attitude may be only a tentative tolerance of "newfangled" notions.

What goes into the Mercury in Taurus mind is indelibly registered. These people have a natural feeling for making money. Their ideas are usually directed toward this endeavor. They may sit on an idea for years before implementing it. When they do, the time is usually ripe. They put a lot of store in experience. They will never undertake a project unless it has been thoroughly examined. And, wherever possible, they will avoid giving snap decisions.

Mercury in Taurus folk can be a bit opinionated. They may think they have worked out the only worthwhile philosophy or approach to life. So they are inclined to ignore any other. They usually adopt a fairly dogmatic method of expression, which goes with their self-assured manner.

They are diplomatic people, however. They do not go looking for arguments even though their stubborn refusal to see the other person's point of view often puts up the backs of their associates. It is easy for Mercury in Taurus individuals to get into mental ruts.

These people lack adaptability. They tend to settle into a situation very gradually, judging it all the time on its practical advantages. They seldom embrace a new scheme or idea without a great deal of consideration. They hate to be put under pressure to make up their minds if any change is involved.

Mercury in Taurus people are intuitive. But they often lack inspiration because they will not give up their already formed hardheaded notions. They are not trustful of imagination. Everything needs to be pinned down and explainable in concrete terms.

MERCURY IN GEMINI

Now here's a person who can have a flashing wit. If the other planetary positions are favorable, Mercury in Gemini minds can be as incisive as a razor's edge. They are logical, quick-thinking, able to outdistance most of their rivals and competitors in any mental gymnastics.

But Mercury in Gemini people can be very shallow. Unless they have a solid planetary support, like the Sun in Taurus, they may be as light as feathers. They may use their mental gifts for nothing more edifying than gossip, criticism, or light reading—for example, newspaper headlines.

They want the news, near and far, but not a detailed account. They are seldom able to settle down to any serious mental activity, such as reading a good book, without having to put it down and start something else.

Without support, this combination can produce a person who is restless and lacks any powers of concentration. They may be great mimics, but cannot sustain the effort long enough to put it to any good or profitable use. They may jump from one activity to another, so nothing worthwhile is ever really accomplished.

For some Mercury in Gemini individuals, nervous problems can develop, including near breakdowns. Speech can be affected by impediments, such as stuttering or incoherence. The mind may race far ahead of the body's capability to give it voice.

Mercury in Gemini people can become con artists. The necessity to earn a living when there is no chance of sticking to one occupation turns mental dexterity into cunning. The plausibility of these people can be amazing.

But with good support from the other planets, the Mercury in Gemini person can be extremely successful. They can adapt to other people's moods in an instant without any negative reaction. As a result, other people feel they are understanding and intelligent individuals. They are often helped to get ahead by those more influential than themselves. Such allies appreciate their swift-minded versatility.

People with Mercury in Gemini are ideally suited for careers in journalism. They make first-rate linguists, interpreters, shorthand writers, typists, agents, and lecturers. They are friendly, entertaining, and fun. They have a knack for making people laugh and feel at ease.

They need travel as often as possible to change the scene and to make interesting new contacts. They have a great love of independence and freedom. Nerves get on edge when they feel hemmed in. Routine drives them up the wall. Their tolerance for repetitive tasks is almost nil.

Mercury in Gemini individuals have to guard against being slapdash. Persistence and determination to reach fixed goals are seldom among their virtues. They receive most of their life satisfaction from mental stimulation, which often is gained by going from one relationship to another.

They are not particularly easy people to live with, although the position of the other planets, especially the Sun, will have a strong bearing on this. They change their minds so often they can be very difficult to follow. They are inclined to be selfish because they take the line of least resistance. It invariably leads to new experiences, which they love so much. To resist their impulses, however, can mean a continuation of the status quo, which they hate.

There is never a dull moment when Mercury in Gemini people are around. They are inventive and curious. They sometimes act like children even in adulthood, playing tricks, joking around, and making mischief. Gemini, it has to be remembered, is the sign of the Twins. When they are stimulated by their eternal playmate Mercury, there is little time for seriousness.

These people have to guard against a tendency to become too excited. They may suffer from nerves and nervous ailments. They have a strong tendency to worry about all sorts of things, jumping from one problem to another when they are upset without any intention of pausing long enough to find practical solutions.

MERCURY IN CANCER

People with Mercury in Cancer are extremely sensitive. They want desperately to be liked and respected. This does not always show, but it is there behind their façade. They try hard to seem easygoing and nonchalant about what others think. They are tactful, discreet, and diplomatic.

The conversation of these people will usually get around to the past. They often have a repertoire of reminiscences, which can be entertaining and delightful to the ear. They have a simple way with words that communicates just the right feelings and atmosphere.

Mercury in Cancer does not confer a great amount of originality. But it does make a person a natural psychologist. Such individuals can look into people and deliver amazingly accurate descriptions of their mental states and feelings.

They love nature and can't abide cruelty to animals or people. They have strong feelings about what they like and don't like. Sometimes they can be irritable and moody. Their memory is usually first-rate. But these people can be indecisive and live in a world of fantasy if Mercury is not supported by other solid positions.

With Mercury in Cancer, a person can be an excellent scholar. They can become professors, curators, historians, lecturers, and writers of unusually perceptive autobiographies. There is a depth to these people, which shows in their manner, speech and turn of phrase.

Their mind is not busy but it is introspective. They like to go inside themselves, to explore and to interpret their own feelings. This exercise gives them a great capacity for understanding how others feel, and for describing these things.

They usually possess a strong hankering for the past. In whatever work or profession they may follow, they rely on precedent and tradition for their values and standards. They are inclined to think that things were better in the old days.

Mercury in Cancer people do not like stress and strain. They are not the competitive type. They certainly can have a surprisingly good head for business when they want to put their minds to it. But usually they are more content to stay out of the rat race. They will pursue their ambitions in areas less likely to create the feeling of competitiveness.

Although timid, Mercury in Cancer individuals are enterprising. If they can summon up the interest and the energy, they are frequently successful in influencing the public to support their schemes and business ventures. They have an appealing way of expressing themselves. Their emotional sensitivity combines with clarity of thought, as long as moodiness does not intervene.

These are people who usually have strong family ties. They also are inclined to worry and fuss about their loved ones. Their active imaginations allow them to fear the worst if loved ones are late getting home or keeping an appointment.

As parents, people with Mercury in Cancer have to learn to let go when their youngsters reach the age for venturing out into the world. They can be too protective, and may deny a teenager the freedom that is necessary for mature development.

Mercury in Cancer individuals can become very polished writers if their Sun is in Gemini. The Sun in Cancer will confer more tenacity and ambition. With the Sun in Leo, this person will be more outgoing and optimistic, alert for opportunities to organize and lead on a grand scale.

MERCURY IN LEO

Mercury in Leo instills pride of mind. And these people, proud of their ideas, do spend a lot of time putting them across to the public. They can be writers, lecturers, teachers, public-relations agents, or promoters. They favor the entertainment and amusement industries, in which they can exploit their sense of the dramatic.

Mercury in Leo people tend to be self-confident and outgoing. They have a strong regard for the worth of their own ideas, which often are quite good. But the tendency is to try to foist their opinions on others, mainly out of an impulse to give others what is good for them. This, of course, is not always appreciated. If there is not restraint indicated by other planetary positions, such a person can get a name for bossiness, boasting, and showing off.

There also is a strong tendency toward conceit. Mercury in Leo individuals think their ideas are what the world has been waiting for. They are especially haughty if the Sun also is in Leo. Although these people can be great leaders, they can make such a din about it that respect turns to laughter and derision.

Mercury in Leo people are very sensitive about how others regard them. They like plenty of praise. Anyone who doesn't react warmly and enthusiastically to their ideas is likely to be regarded as a nincompoop. There is very little leeway for intelligent criticism of their proposals. They hold their beliefs so passionately, to question them is to insult them. Although they do not hold grudges, they are inclined to ignore anyone who disagrees with them. People can suddenly feel very much out in the cold if they have dared to question the Mercury in Leo's judgment or opinions. The fact is that Mercury in Leo often makes a person too fixed and narrow-minded. She or he may fail to move with the times. Disdainful of detail, these individuals often make careless mistakes. They tend to take the broad and grandiose view—which has won a lot of empires, but lost a lot of friends.

The urge to be imperious has to be avoided if these people want to get their ideas accepted. Then they are more likely to reach a position of authority, in which they have the scope to express their skills and talents.

Mercury in Leo individuals are not very adaptable. Anyone who is trying to influence them has to avoid confrontations, which immediately get their backs up. Like the Lion, the symbol of Leo, they have a strong fighting spirit. At the first sign of opposition they are ready for a fight. These people need time to think through new ideas. Even though they may oppose a viewpoint, it can be counted on that they will go away and consider it. One of their maddening habits is to come back and propose the very same action to the person who originally suggested it to them.

Mercury in Leo people have breadth of vision. But they are not the types to fill in the details, unless their Sun is in Virgo. Mercurial Leos need the backing of a good team of associates to handle the less interesting side of their plans.

There is an intolerably inflated sense of pride associated with Mercury in Leo, especially if the Sun is in Leo. These people can become very wearing on the people they live with. They are likely to be know-it-alls, and literally try to take over the other person's life. They are often badly shocked and for a while contrite when a loved one fights back, as often happens. But they soon resume their high-handed manner.

There is, throughout all, a distinct air of dignity about Mercury in Leo people. Their bearing can be impressive, and their demeanor attractive. They are magnetic personalities.

MERCURY IN VIRGO

Here Mercury is in a very strong position. It gives the person a bright and balanced intellect. There is no tendency to go to extremes, as is often the case with Mercury. And the ideas that the person holds are likely to be practical and to appeal to a wide segment of the public.

Mercury in Virgo individuals have great powers of discrimination. If they are dealing with details, they can select all that is relevant with a smooth and flowing precision. They will never allow emotional considerations to interfere with their judgment. They are capable of making decisions on the facts alone, regardless of their own personal feelings.

In their personal behavior, Mercury in Virgo people also exhibit the same discriminating faculty. They are seldom likely to be indiscreet. They are very aware of the value of a good reputation. Reliability is extremely important to them. They are not late for appointments. They enjoy doing the right thing.

People with this combination can be a bit cold and intolerant. They may be more concerned with the details of a situation than with the human element. If some compassion is called for, they will be inclined to insist on the letter of the law being followed. This can be good for business but tough for people.

A Mercury in Virgo person is strictly a no-nonsense individual. They are conscientious and serious in whatever they undertake. They respect method and order. They make very good employees. They can solve production problems at a glance, seeing all the practical alternatives and focusing on the best one.

These people have to guard against being too critical. They may strive for perfection to such a degree that they see faults everywhere, especially in people. Although they mean to be helpful, their critical observations can get others' backs up and create ill feeling against them.

People with this combination are modest and unassuming. They work extremely well under direction or without it. They can be relied upon to work, not slacking even when left alone.

Mercury in Virgo people can become unduly obsessed with their health and diet. This is the only area in which they are likely to show extreme behavior. They have a fear of ill health, mainly because it interrupts their enjoyment of their work and mental pursuits.

Mercury in Virgo individuals are often found in scientific occupations. They have a well-drilled mentality, which allows them to pursue long trails of detail toward worthwhile ends. They like to be involved in work that has humanitarian value. They make excellent laboratory workers and researchers.

However, these people can become too narrowly focused in their objectives if left to their own devices. They can put too much store on being correct in every little thing. They can become exacting and fussy. The desire for cleanliness or neatness can be accentuated to the point of getting on other people's nerves.

Mercury in Virgo confers a facility for mathematics and verbal expression. Problems are approached in a practical way, which does not allow much room for imagination. But what these people say is well worth listening to. They have a knack for putting the most complex issues into simple language.

They are quick thinkers, analytical, and systematic. Their minds work like well-arranged filing systems. They have good memories. They are best able to utilize their talents and skills when working to design or prearranged plan.

Mercury in Virgo people are easy to educate. They seldom go off into daydreams. With the Sun also in Virgo, they have to avoid suppressing their emotions and feelings. Otherwise, they become too logical.

MERCURY IN LIBRA

This is a person with a finely balanced intellect. Mercury in Libra people make extremely good judges and executives whose job is to sum up alternatives and give a balanced opinion. They are better at working with data presented to them than trying to make decisions regarding their own life.

Personally, where tne emotional element comes in, such individuals can be so torn between thought and feeling that they do nothing. Opportunities are often missed through indecision. This is especially so if these people also have the Sun in Libra.

With the Sun in Virgo, on the other hand, the mind is more practical, highly legalistic, and coldly logical. Emotional considerations are less likely to affect the judgment. But without a softening influence from other planets, there can be too much head and not enough heart.

With the Sun in Scorpio, another alternative, the logic of the mind can be used for more selfish reasons. In any judgments, points will be added up, with the weight given to personal advantage. And such individuals will definitely look for those advantages.

Mercury in Libra people usually are extremely broad-minded. They are prepared to accept people exactly as they are. They seldom try to improve or reform others, even though they may have noticed all their faults.

When confronted with a dilemma, they have a strong intuition about the right course to follow. But their nature is to weigh all the pros and cons. They do this with such precision, noting all nuances, that eventually they are back where they began. They have thus evened out the possibilities into an impeccable balance of equilibrium, or poise.

This poise is basic to Mercury in Libra people. They are often charming and serene, exceedingly friendly and diplomatic. They possess a love of refinement and artistic things. And they avoid as much as possible becoming involved in arguments.

Their intuition is sometimes brilliant. When balanced, they make very good constructive critics. They are able to provide perceptive suggestions for improving literature and works of art.

Mercury in Libra individuals are extremely social creatures. They need numerous relationships, both friendly and romantic. Their agreeable natures make them easy to talk to and get along with. They like to be liked, and so will say the kind of things that make the other person warm to them. These people have to be careful of dropping old friends for new ones.

Mercury in Libra individuals can be shallow and flighty. Libra is an air sign, mental and intellectual; it creates a need for stimulation of the mind through diverse and entertaining relationships. The presence of Mercury, the planet of swift communication, exaggerates this need. So these people may not be able to concentrate too long on one thing.

Mercury in Libra creates a personality that is enterprising and spontaneous. But unless other planetary placements give more stability, there can be a lack of direction. These people can be plagued by indecision. They are likely to compare one alternative with another so long that nothing concrete gets done. They are inclined to shove problems under the table, then hope that circumstances will eventually sort them out. ·

These people can be polished and persuasive speakers. They are diplomatic and able to appreciate the many sides of an argument. They are often in demand as after-dinner speakers and masters of ceremonies at weddings and celebrations. They can be extremely flattering without appearing to be insincere. Mercury in Libra individuals are well suited for partnership ventures. They are smooth-working members of a team. They are more inclined to contribute mentally than to be much help physically; they do not generally enjoy physical exertion.

MERCURY IN SCORPIO

A person with Mercury in Scorpio can go either one of two ways—up or down. At their best they can use the extraordinary clarity and strength of their mind for the benefit of mankind. They make topnotch psychiatrists, researchers, scientists, investigators, and medical men and women. At their worst they can use their mental faculties in self-seeking and cruelly deceptive ways, so that other people are more likely to be enslaved or degraded than helped and uplifted. Such is the power of Mercury in Scorpio.

As has been mentioned frequently in these planetary descriptions, all depends on the positions of the other planets; they usually modify the undesirable propensities of any one placement. Scorpio is a sign of extremes. When considered in isolation, it can produce a totally unwarranted impression. The effects of all the planets must be synthesized into a whole, which makes up the real individual.

Mercury in Scorpio denotes a person who is active both mentally and emotionally. The emotions are usually the strongest, especially if the Sun is in Scorpio also. These people are extremely shrewd. They have a talent for spotting opportunities that will occur in the future, and for working toward them with unalterable determination. They are fixed and stubborn in their views. They often repeat the same mistakes.

Mercury in Scorpio tends to produce a person who is secretive and sly. They are able to put their finger on other people's weaknesses, which they frequently exploit. They are gifted players of the cat-and-mouse game, encouraging the foolhardy toward doom. Such a fate may be inflicted by circumstances that the Mercury in Scorpio person has perceived, even manipulated, long before.

These people often take a great interest in investigating the occult and other mysteries of life. Although they are down-to-earth and realistic, they have a fascination for trying to work out both the future and the past.

They often exhibit a steely mind, which is especially encouraging to people in emergencies. With other favorable planetary placements, they can be brilliant surgeons, fearless soldiers and commanders, and inspired mystics.

People with Mercury in Scorpio sometimes have irresistible urges to fantasize about sex. They often start their search for sexual excitement at a young age. They may get a reputation for being cool experimenters, unable to commit themselves or to achieve real intimacy.

Mercury in Scorpio people seldom give up once they have fixed their mind on an objective. They are forever probing the ground around them to make sure they have not missed anything to their advantage. They are outspoken in their relationships, not hesitating to tell another person exactly what they think. Yet their private feelings about their own life are seldom revealed.

These people do not find it easy to adapt to new ideas. They are inclined to be studious and to stick to their own opinions through thick and thin. They can be so closed to new ways of thinking that in the commercial world they may get left behind, or be forced to make costly innovations in midstream.

Mercury in Scorpio individuals can be intolerant and bitter. Intent on revenge, they can be implacable and unforgiving enemies. Without helpful contributions from other planets, they can poison their own minds brooding and plotting. They need to cultivate a positive outlook, which sees more good in the world than may be immediately apparent.

These people often have very few interests in their lives. They tend to pour themselves into a single channel of activity. Their narrow focus makes people in other areas of their lives feel secondary and neglected. They can spend too much time working and not enough on relaxing.

Mercury in Scorpio people are resourceful, especially in a crisis. But they must be confronted on a deep personal level. It often takes a whacking surprise or shock for them to see the error of their close-minded ways.

MERCURY IN SAGITTARIUS

This is a rather happy-go-lucky placement. It often marks a person who is always on the move, both mentally and physically. The urge to roam over the land or through the mind is irresistible. Mercury in Sagittarius individuals need an occupation like writing or lecturing, which can be followed without interfering with their travels and adventures.

The mind of these people is clear and sharp. They have a gift for delivering one-line observations of shattering accuracy. But their insights seem to rise from deep down in their subconscious, a place where these people seldom consciously go.

Mercury in Sagittarius can confer a great interest in gathering information, but little in expending much effort through study and mental discipline. There is a need to feel free and unfettered, which can make the person a bit of a lightweight when it comes to serious thinking.

Mercury in Sagittarius people like to do several things at once. As a result, there is a tendency to do nothing really well. Variety becomes the spice of life. And unless they can get around to putting their experiences or thoughts on paper or on the airwaves, there is not much opportunity for them to excel in anything.

If there is a stabilizing influence from other placements, Mercury in Sagittarius can be used in positive ways. It can develop in a person philosophic interests that may contribute remarkably good ideas to the store of human knowledge. Such individuals can become great defenders of the underprivileged and downtrodden.

A person with Mercury in Sagittarius believes in freedom of expression. They do not take kindly to any kind of authority, especially if there is any attempt to muzzle the truth. In spite of their freedom-loving ideas, they can be too conventional where religious beliefs are concerned. They may don the cardinal's hat or the archbishop's robe, then preach freedom of thought and not be aware of the contradiction.

This combination can make a person inclined to forget his or her promises. They can get carried away with camaraderie and so make friends of people who are not good for them. Although their business judgment can be first-rate, they may lack discretion where pleasure and amusements are concerned.

Mercury in Sagittarius people are versatile and adaptive. They can usually turn their minds to just about anything—for a while. It is not that they lack the intelligence needed for concentration, merely that they fail to find it productive in their particular case. They depend more on inspiration. Their faith in this is often vindicated by the quality of their suggestions and ideas.

These people often have the gift of gab. They are not beyond doing a bit of moralizing and preaching, which can get on the nerves of their associates. Yet they can be very casual in their approach to life, ignoring responsibilities that other people regard as essential to an ordered existence.

Mercury in Sagittarius people are always looking for pots of gold at the end of the rainbow. They may not be as interested in the spoils as in the search. They are not the types to worship money; such a love of it would tie them down to having to make it. They would rather move on and trust to luck. Luck, surprisingly, often comes their way.

These people often say the wrong thing at the wrong time. Although their insights can be inspired, their sense of timing is inappropriate, usually because they are so enthused they cannot restrain themselves. When it comes to personal observations, they can provoke embarrassment all around.

MERCURY IN CAPRICORN

Here is a person with all the mental attributes of the proverbial strong, silent type. In a man or a woman engaged heavily in worldly affairs, this combination can be impressive. But it does not allow enough free play for the expression of femininity, which is such an important part of our enjoyment of life. A woman with Mercury in Capricorn needs to work harder to bring the female lightness of touch to the surface of her personality.

But for those with serious things to do, Mercury in Capricorn is an admirable placement. These people are clear and methodical thinkers. Unless they are careful and pay tolerant attention to the views of others, they can become unimaginative and rigid.

They are cautious individuals. They will not do or say anything that might make them look foolish. But if they become too tight-lipped and guarded, they can appear to be a caricature of the strong, silent type, and so bring on themselves the derision they are endeavoring to avoid. This combination needs some lighthearted balancing, such as the Sun in Sagittarius or even the Sun in Aquarius.

Mercury in Capricorn gives the sort of mentality that enables a person to persevere to the top of any profession or trade. These people are mentally tough. They are able to withstand long hours working on detail and other tedious tasks without losing interest. They are ambitious in a quiet and unobtrusive way. They like to get control of situations and people. They are curious about anything that might affect their future, but are not distracted by superficialities. They have a good memory, into which they pack useful information and facts, ignoring anything that is trivial or likely to sidetrack them from their objectives.

Mercury in Capricorn people have to avoid becoming bigoted. Their tendency to be diplomatic to protect themselves from being criticized can turn into bitterness and cynicism. They have a good sense of timing and are able to cultivate, through mental determination, some of the virtues that usually come through more emotional temperaments.

Mercury in Capricorn individuals have a dry and appealing sense of humor. Their tongues also can be sharp and cruel, all the more so because of their knack for encapsulating their feelings into a few words. They can be sardonic. However, because these people have a compulsive need to be respected, their method of expression usually is diplomatic.

They often have to cultivate greater faith in the human race. Sad or unhappy experiences in their younger days are never quite forgotten or outgrown. They are often the victims of neglect or other people's unhappy circumstances. It is not difficult for them to adopt a skeptical and suspicious outlook.

Mercury in Capricorn induces a high regard for tradition and law and order. These people can become staunch and brave defenders of the conventions of society. Sometimes they can be misunderstood and branded reactionaries when all they are doing is trying to preserve what is best in society.

These are not the most optimistic of people. It is easy for them to get down in the dumps. They are inclined to feel the world pressing down on them, when probably it is their own lack of flexibility and gloomy view of life.

But if Mercury in Capricorn individuals have their Sun in a more joyous sign, such as Sagittarius, they will be more optimistic. They will be less self-concerned and more enthusiastic about people. They may see the hope of the world in a religious or philosophic ideal, and devote themselves to communicating that as a means to freedom.

MERCURY IN AQUARIUS

Here is a clever and original thinker. Mercury in Aquarius individuals are the observers of the world. What they see they put together into a complete whole, so they are usually able to give very illuminating views and see solutions that other people have not even touched.

These people often are topnotch scientists and inventors. They have an unconscious urge to discover, so they are endowed with a penetrating vision. They are not so-called thinkers; they don't sit down and ponder through their perceptions and memories. They "see" things swiftly. They are able to connect seemingly isolated events and phenomena in a flash. This is true inspiration.

But, of course, there is a negative side. If Mercury is unsupported by some solid planetary influence, these people can be very superficial. They may not chatter on or make spectacles of themselves, for they are rather reserved. But they can make gossip and the trivial comings and goings of companions the center of their interests. They still observe the scene, but it lacks the penetration and depth of perception of which they are capable.

Mercury in Aquarius individuals can be vague, inquisitive, erratic, and unpredictable.

The developed Mercury in Aquarius person is an excellent judge of human nature. These individuals are able to observe a person clinically, without allowing their emotions to get in the way. So they often hit upon the truth.

They can have a special interest in trying to improve the lot of their fellow man. They are more interested in people and humanity as a whole than in individual problems. They make friends easily, liking to make contact at all levels of society, so they can absorb the total picture.

Anyone who is looking for a close personal relationship with Mercury in Aquarius people is likely to be disappointed. Even in romantic and marital situations, they seem to keep their distance. They have a detached way about them, which can appear to be cold uninterest to the more emotional types of the Zodiac.

It is this quality of detachment that allows them to be such good scientists and helpers, especially in the social field. They can focus totally, ignoring day-to-day needs, even the people around them. They can become so absorbed in a subject that they may be labeled "absent-minded."

Mercury in Aquarius folk are agreeable as a rule. If their Sun is in Capricorn, they may be more reserved and studious, with a tendency to look more on the practical side than the idealistic one. They are likely to be aware of their own position, which can make them more self-centered and self-seeking than otherwise would be the case.

With both Mercury and the Sun in Aquarius, individuals can be a little too brilliant and erratic for their own good. There is such an emphasis on intellectual pursuits and values that the person is inclined to lose touch with the more feeling and emotional side of life.

People having Mercury in Aquarius and the Sun in Pisces will be inclined to turn their attentions to artistic pursuits rather than scientific and strictly mental endeavors. These people may be entertainers or performers, who reach a wide public through television or radio. However, they tend to lack a solid opinion of themselves, and so can be inclined toward moodiness and depression. They may spend their time fighting for a sense of independence they do not really want.

Mercury in Aquarius individuals are often far ahead of their times. If they have the patience to wait, they eventually find the public embracing their ideas, which were once ignored.

MERCURY IN PISCES

Here Mercury is in danger of drowning in the emotional sea of Pisces. These people can be lacking in logical thought. But they should never be underestimated. They depend mainly on their feelings to perceive what is going on in the world. And they can be uncannily accurate and intuitive. People with Mercury in Pisces are not easy to pin down. To argue or even debate with them can be a frustrating experience. Their mentality tends to skate over contradictions. Gaps and double-talk are normal parts of communicating. They can be infuriatingly vague, unreasonable, and indecisive.

They have wonderful memories, though. Their recollections are vivid, colored with all the emotional nuances of the moment, even if the moment was years ago. But their memory is selective.

Mercury in Pisces individuals are not anxious to remember events and things that did not appeal to them—unless there was someone or something to blame! This often is the case. Then they are unusually vindictive and unforgiving in their condemnations. They can have strong prejudices, which may last for ages, long after experiencing that they have been mistaken.

These people are subtle and ultrasensitive. They can be offended by remarks that other people accept as normal. Language has a special meaning for them. In a positive way, they can express their appreciation for things mortal and beautiful in poetry, song, and story.

They can be great talkers, spilling out their experiences and reliving them with a light that comes into their eyes. Every time they retell them, which is often, they wax more poetic. They are humorous people, easy to take to once their peculiar logic and way of seeing things are understood.

With Mercury in Pisces, a person often suffers from self-doubt. They may worry that their mind is empty and slow. In fact, their mind is crowded with keen perceptions. These people are very bright, and can demonstrate it if they will overcome their tendency to see everything through an emotional screen.

These people have a great capacity for understanding the problems of others. They are sympathetic and genuinely caring. They can pick up bad vibrations in an instant, and become distressed and disturbed. They can dwell too long and intensely on their problems, which affects their health. These people need to keep their thinking optimistic and practical.

Mercury in Pisces individuals are very good listeners. They hear people's problems with a third ear. They are capable of giving sympathy combined with good advice. They are diplomatic and subtle in tricky situations. They know how to get their way by working behind the scenes.

These people have very changeable emotions. They can be wholeheartedly in favor of one thing one moment, then opposed to it the next. They often do not know their own mind. They have to be careful making important decisions affecting their future. They need sufficient time to think through all the consequences. They can be impulsive as well as ambivalent.

Mercury in Pisces people love to fantasize and daydream. They can drift off into another world in the middle of a conversation. They often use their imagination as a means of escape when the pressures of life become too much for them, which is likely to happen fairly frequently.

With both the Sun and Mercury in Pisces, there is a tendency for a person to be lazy or listless. This combination requires practical support from the placements of other planets. Ideas, however, can be brilliant, and give rise to shrewd moneymaking schemes. But more energetic folk are likely to be required to do the physical work.

If Mercury in Pisces individuals have their Sun in Aries, their mental gymnastics keep them leaping from task to task. Action, though sometimes ineffective, replaces listlessness. If their Sun is in Aquarius, they can make rigorous intellectual productions over each and every mood. Emotion replaces reason.

Venus in the Signs

Venus stands for love and beauty. Its quality is attraction, union. Venus has a major influence on romance and love life.

At its best, Venus confers gracious, artistic, and refined sensibilities. At its worst, this planet represents sensuality. In adverse combination with other planets, such as Saturn, it can create unhappiness through lack of feeling, possessiveness, and selfishness.

Venus is considered to be the second most fortunate planet, after Jupiter. As Venus stands for beauty, love, charm, artistry, and all that is pleasing, it follows that people with a strong Venus influence are going to be popular. They will attract favorable attention and aid, giving them an easier ride in life.

But a strong Venus influence also can make individuals so desirous of comfort, ease, and freedom from the ordinary stresses and strains of life that they become dependent, lazy, demanding, indecisive, and ineffectual. In this case, too much of a good thing goes sour, for both men and women. Idealistic Venus needs to get her feet dirty in the solid, fruitful Earth. Then she has much to give in partnership, relatedness, agreeableness, serenity, charm, generosity, good humor, appreciation, and encouragement.

Venus is considered feminine, Mars masculine. All men and women have a bit of each in them, which is what gives added stimulation to love and sexual attraction. We want the opposite, we need the same. Venus takes, Mars gives. Venus represents cooperation, Mars singleness of purpose.

If a person has both Venus and Mars in the same sign, he or she will be amorous, erotic, and passionate, with a strong tendency toward impulsiveness and indiscretion. If two lovers have the same Venus or Mars placement, they are likely to achieve sexual harmony easily and naturally, spontaneously enjoying the physical side of lovemaking.

Venus is the origin of the word "veins," which according to medical lore return the "tired" blood gently to the heart, the center of the living body. The Venus principle, analogously, circulates the affections to the heart, there to be rejuvenated and to spring forth once more fresh and pure. Venus is favorably situated in Taurus and Libra, the signs it rules.

VENUS IN ARIES

Here is a person who loves to embark on romantic ventures. Venus in Aries individuals are passionate, physical, and impulsive. They often take the initiative in love affairs. What they like they tend to go after with great gusto.

These people have the charm that comes through directness and love of action. They are too impatient to play the love game for long. They are spontaneous with their gifts, often too generous. But they want the fruits of wooing as soon as possible. Sometimes they scale up the apple tree before the fruit is ripe, and are disappointed. But they also have much enviable success.

Venus in Aries people are honest and open. Although they may seem intent on the physical side of love at times, they also need to pursue the beautiful. This is why their affections and attractions can be short-lived. They are looking for love and the exquisite. Until they find both, they do tend to have a dazzling array of lovers.

These people are often extremely good at sports and physical activity. They can become true artists of the gymnasts and ballet bar, the football and baseball fields, and the basketball court. They have a keen competitive spirit that aims just as much at excelling as at winning.

Their emotions are not so deep as to get in the way of their need for new experiences. In spite of all their activity, they do not lose sight of their objective. Many of them have a devotion to an impossible ideal. It might be finding the perfect male or female, or reaching the heights of style and artistry in creative expression.

Venus in Aries individuals are enthusiastic lovers and performers. They seek harmony through mental activity when they cannot find it in the physical. They are demonstrative people.

For a woman this combination can be a bit aggressive. Aries is the most purely masculine of all the signs. There is not much leeway here for using the feminine charms that entice by suggestion and subtlety.

In Aries, Venus is consumed before she has time to work her gentle magic.

Venus in Aries people often throw caution to the winds. They are prepared to gamble with their emotions as well as with other people's. They love the pursuit of love. The adventure often means more to them than the realization of their desires.

With the Sun in Taurus and Venus in Aries, the person is likely to become engaged at some time in his or her life in a serious secret love affair. There can be more desire for security where the emotions are concerned. The person will be more inclined to settle down and conform to domestic expectations.

With the Sun in Pisces and Venus in Aries, the person will be even more of a romantic. They are likely to put their loved ones on a pedestal and expect the impossible from them. As a result, they will frequently be disappointed, lamenting their lack of luck in love. However, there people will have quick powers of recovery from romantic disenchantment—and are likely to repeat enthusiastically the same mistakes.

Individuals with both Venus and the Sun in Aries may take many years or experiences to learn that the chase is never-ending. Eventually they discover there is no substitute for abiding love.

VENUS IN TAURUS

Taurus is the natural home of Venus. Here the planet of love and beauty can have full expression. A person with this combination can be extremely attractive, a passionate lover, charming, and gracious. But somewhere in their makeup is a touch of selfishness, of self-indulgence. They can be too attracted to the good things in life, and so make the acquisition of them their reason for living.

People with Venus in Taurus are practical. They may dream about castles in Spain, dashing princes, and alluring maidens. But they know the realities of life. If they want these things, they have to go out and get them.

They are in many ways hardheaded people. An abiding stubborn streak usually ensures that they get what they want. But it is the manner of getting that varies so much.

With Venus in Taurus, a person usually is drawn to some kind of artistic pursuit. But it will not be a flighty one. It will have a quality of earthiness about it. It will be something practical that will lead to a good living.

A woman or a man with Venus in Taurus can use their physical attractiveness to make another person work for them. They may look around to marry into money. Or they may persevere in the fields of design, handicrafts, or fashion. In such jobs they can express their artistic or creative urges, and so get to the top or a position of comfort that way.

These people have great powers of perseverance. They do not give up. Once they have fixed their target, they plod on and on. They may not be very adventurous. They do not take risks that have not been calculated. They have a great need for comfort and security. And they are prepared to work as long as it is necessary to get it.

But Venus in Taurus creates irritations if rewards are too slow in coming. Although there is loyalty in the combination, the desire for comfort can induce this person eventually to look around for an easier and more comfortable existence.

These people like to surround themselves with attractive things, which may include men or women who appeal to their senses. They have strong feelings, sensual ones. They like the feel of expensive cloth. Luxury can be more important to them than they realize.

Individuals with Venus in Taurus have a way with their lovers. They understand them and can anticipate their desires. Knowing how to please gets them the lovely things they want. There is a hint of opportunism in this placement.

Venus in Taurus people love to surround themselves with their possessions. It is impossible for them ever to imagine that they could get tired of living in the lap of luxury. Even if the placement of other planets makes their tastes less exotic, they will still exhibit a liking for what is stylish or beautiful.

These people make good nest builders. They are not inclined to move around except to better themselves. Once they have a home of their liking, they will pour all their energies and most of their money into it to make it more attractive and comfortable.

With the Sun also in Taurus, security through good investments, especially in homes and real estate, will be particularly important. With the Sun in Aries, and Venus in Taurus, there is likely to be more house moving. The love of comfort and beautiful things will be reflected in pioneering and perhaps even reckless endeavors to obtain more of them.

Venus in Taurus usually confers a love of nature. These people manage to have a lovely garden, even if it consists only of a few attractive flower boxes or potted plants in a city apartment.

These people are not known for their austere type of living. They believe in giving themselves the best even though it means living up to their income. They like to give the impression that they are doing well.

VENUS IN GEMINI

This person likes the idea of love more than the actual physical contact. Venus in Gemini individuals are flirtatious. Or they content themselves with sexual fantasies. They have extremely active imaginations, which are not dependent on actual experiences.

In Gemini, Venus is up in the air. She cannot get down to earth, where she is at her best. So the person seldom is able to make the most of her physical propensities.

There is a lack of devotion in these people. They love with their heads; they frequently experience changes of affection. They are unable to maintain a passionate relationship. Theirs is more an enthusiastic approach, which touches as it goes past on its way to the next adventure. Emotion is something these people can feel but seldom can express.

People with Venus in Gemini like to talk about art. They can be clever and popular writers of fact and fiction, seeming to have a deep insight into human emotions. But their perceptions are mostly superficial, the kind found in people who like to imagine experiences without having them. The deep reality can be missing.

But Venus in Gemini individuals are amusing and impressive conversationalists and speakers. They make fine critics. They have an appreciation of beauty that might be expressed through love of flowers, colors, music, or sketching. They can make good actors or mimics. There is a refinement about them.

These people often possess a quality of youthfulness that continues right through into old age. They are sympathetic and spontaneous. They make friends very easily and are usually found at the center of events at parties.

Venus in Gemini people need to be liked. They flee from unpleasantness or discord. They will often say what they think the other person wants to hear instead of giving a straightforward reply that might not be appreciated. They are inclined to be a bit opportunistic. It is easy for them, especially if their Sun also is in Gemini, to take life rather unseriously. These people often marry more than once. They can have several romantic attachments going at one time. They love to travel and meet new people. They search for harmony through relationships, but can fail to give satisfaction once the initial excitement is over. They may take more out of an association than they put into it.

Venus in Gemini individuals love to travel. Their partners or close associates often have to get used to being left alone without warning—or having to pack their bags and be off on a visit or journey at a moment's notice. These fleet-footed Venus in Gemini characters find it difficult to turn down any opportunity to experience a change of scene.

It has to be remembered that Gemini is the sign of the Twins. Venus is the sign of comfort and beauty. One Twin, one side of the personality, may like to luxuriate in a well-appointed apartment. The other Twin may love to get out in the country. Often there is a fierce tug-of-war between the two, which can result in irritability, indecision, and instability.

These are people who love the fun of living but often shy away from its obligations. They do not like to be pinned down to one kind of work. Although they enjoy the trappings of wealth and success, they are not prepared to join in the often grubby rough-and-tumble climb up. They prefer to skim along the surface. Their ready wit and amusing personality often provide them with the means of making a good living and a good life.

VENUS IN CANCER

This is a person who is capable of great love and affection. And he or she expects the same in return. Family men or women will devote themselves untiringly to their loved ones. Venus in Cancer folk are the mother type.

Venus in Cancer can make a person ideally domestic. They are good homemakers and cooks. They like to bring a touch of artistry to the home. They often show admirable taste in furnishings, decor, and color schemes. Their table usually features special dishes, not just the routine home-cooked fare. They take great pleasure in being hospitable to visitors and guests.

As lovers, Venus in Cancer people can be delightful. They have a cuddly and responsive temperament. They are strongly intuitive and seem to know how to please their beloved. They work very hard at this. They like to please.

But they also can be very demanding. They need a great deal of attention and mothering themselves. They are incurably romantic. They can never be satisfied by any mortal show of love or affection. It seems they always want a little more. This can become wearying for mate or beloved.

Venus in Cancer individuals are also inclined to sink into moodiness, especially if they feel they are not being sufficiently appreciated. Whether it is a lover, their children, or their spouse, they are inclined to be clinging.

Love life does not usually run smoothly for these people. They are often too soft and romantic. They can be imposed on and exploited. They will often do anything for love. If they can't find it, they may turn mystical. Or they can wither away in fretful unhappiness.

Nevertheless, Venus in Cancer folk are kind, understanding, and comforting. They love beauty, especially nature. They can be attracted to literature, music, poetry, and art. They have a great attachment to the past. Past loves—even unhappy ones—grow gloriously in their imagination.

These people often have a mother complex. They may find it hard to break away from the home or an aging parent. They can be fortunate through real estate or land and its products. They should always try to express their emotions positively and not allow them to get bottled up.

Venus in Cancer individuals can moon around unhappily. They should try to avoid putting all their love into one person or thing.

These people can cut themselves off from the rest of society at times in order to escape pressures. They would rather ruminate in an imaginary world of their own making than try to cope with all the demands they feel are being made upon them.

Men with Venus in Cancer are often attracted to older women. These men have a definite charm and a maturity, which appeals to sophisticated women. Their manners and way of speaking have an Old World character about them. They are protective and considerate.

It is not unusual for Venus in Cancer people to be acquisitive. They may like to fill their homes with beautiful things. Sometimes money and property come to them from the maternal side of the family. They may not, however, be prepared to put a great deal of personal effort into fulfilling their materialistic appetites. They may depend on others to do the hard work, relying on their own ingratiating charm to bring them benefits.

People born with Venus in Cancer have a great need to be liked and looked up to. This often propels them into doing some kind of charity work. They are the types who will be found cheerfully working at the tables at the local church or street fair. They have many good qualities—and they want to be admired for them.

VENUS IN LEO

Here the planet of love and luxury is in the sign of romance and pleasure! The result is a person who can very easily overstep the mark in these things and make problems for himself or herself.

Venus in Leo people have a great deal of creative talent. They are dramatic, masters of the flourish and the trumpet. They love displays in which they can take a central part. They can put their ideas across to the public. They do this in love and romance.

These are people who have no problem attracting the attention of the opposite sex. They usually dress splendidly, with a touch of the flamboyant. Even though they might not have a penny to spare, they somehow manage to give the impression of being somebody or going somewhere.

They have a great talent for self-expression. They love social affairs where they can take the center of the floor, discoursing easily on this or that. Their object at all times is to be the cynosure of all eyes. They love applause and are suckers for flattery. They can become a bit tiresome with their posturing and need for compliments.

Venus in Leo people are faithful and kind. Whether it is love of a person or work, they put their whole heart into it. They may make fools of themselves sometimes in their rather childish scrambling for plaudits. But no one could ever doubt their sincerity when it comes to their affections.

They are impossibly romantic. They are inclined to believe any story about how much they are loved. Their heart rules their head. They are frequently disillusioned, heartbroken through love affairs. But they keep coming back for more, with the same ingenuous faith and trust. And probably make the same mistakes again!

As lovers, they are generous, responsive, and proud. One thing Venus in Leo lovers cannot stand is being made a fool of.

The love of pleasure and entertainment, along with the many opportunities that seem to arise to enjoy them, can make these people a bit shallow and tinselly unless there are strengthening influences in the chart.

The Sun also in Leo, for example, will impart an even greater love of pleasure but will carry with it a responsible element. The positive and creative side will be emphasized. There will then be accomplishments in which pride can be justified.

With the Sun in Virgo and Venus in Leo, there will be more emphasis on efficiency and less on imagination. The person will be more critical and inclined to look for a perfection that may never be realized. These people may dream about love affairs, but have difficulty expressing their feelings in actual romances. This combination encourages a tendency to become involved in secret emotional alliances.

The Sun in Cancer and Venus in Leo confer a softer and gentler influence, with strong sensual feelings. The emotions can get out of control more easily. Discrimination in choice of companions is necessary. These people make good lovers, but can be very possessive and jealous.

All Venus in Leo people have to beware that they do not put too much store in appearances. They can easily be distracted by glamor. In seeking romantic companions, they may fail to look for the more enduringly admirable qualities beneath the surface.

Also, Venus in Leo individuals can frequently become preoccupied with fashion and style in dress. Clothes can become so important to them that they tend to dismiss or overlook deeper values. Concern about what people are thinking can make them unpredictable, erratic, and superficial.

VENUS IN VIRGO

Venus in Virgo is a rather cool placement for love and romance. A person with this combination is exceedingly cautious about whom they give their heart to. They are nervous, almost suspicious, of anything that suggests physical contact and that may develop into intimacy. They like to put a lot of distance between themselves and the alluring suggestions of the planet of love and beauty.

These people are searching for moral beauty. In a physical and emotional world, where sex is natural, they do not feel at ease. They prefer to avoid intimate relationships. But being human, they can be tempted. Sometimes, when real love exists, they discover a reflection of the purity that means so much to them.

People with Venus in Virgo have a firm hold on their feelings and affections. They prefer to serve an idea rather than a person. They find it difficult to surrender themselves. They can change their mind at the very last moment, because they never intended to go ahead at all.

Venus in Virgo individuals are very discriminating when it comes to settling down. They are attractive people with a touch of aloofness that intrigues, increasing the suggestion of mystery. They are inclined to select their partners by rationalizing their conventional qualities. Seldom indeed do they throw themselves with abandon into the arms of love.

These people have a strong desire to be liked and accepted. But they never put themselves forward. They prefer to be a face in the crowd, to weigh the situation, before making any moves. They need to feel they are on familiar ground, among people they know before they can take the initiative.

This planetary position is very helpful for a person who wants to enter the medical profession as a doctor or nurse. The urge to be of useful service to mankind is strong in Virgo, and the presence of Venus confers an added touch of tenderness and devotion. Through self-denial these people often develop a self-fulfilling capacity for serving others.

Venus in Virgo induces a critical temperament. The person cannot help analyzing the actions and attitudes of others, especially in relation to their emotions and affections. Even though they may not say what they think, the judging still goes on in their heads.

Sometimes these people are worried by their own criticalness. Then they try to compensate by showing exaggerated concern, especially about other people's health. Venus in Virgo individuals often have a flair for improving health through natural food and diets.

Venus in Virgo men tend to be more sexually oriented than women having this placement. But the men like to think the woman they eventually marry "saved herself" for them. They have an old-fashioned respect for virginity, and a double standard for the sexes. Nevertheless, the men are controlled in their passions, atthough this may not be quite so evident if the Sun is in Leo.

With both the Sun and Venus in Virgo, the person can very easily become celibate. They either genuinely want to save themselves for the love of their life, or they have developed a strong moral conscience about sexual behavior. However, once the ice has been broken, all people with Venus in Virgo are more likely to forget their inhibitions. But if the first sexual experience is unhappy, they may never risk another.

VENUS IN LIBRA

Venus in Libra makes for harmony. Here is a person with an outstanding ability to get along with others. Such individuals are charming, sociable, and dignified. They go out of their way to please without having to try at all. Being nice, reasonable, and agreeable comes naturally to them. Venus, the planet of love and beauty, is in its own sign. This emphasizes the artistic and refining qualities of Venus. These people have a distaste for anything that is sordid or jarring. They are always seeking to soothe and smoothe their sensibilities in compatible company, for they can find this world a constantly prickling experience.

Venus in Libra people are kind and fortunately very adaptable. They have a wonderful way of accepting people exactly as they are, and of communicating this by an interested and pleasing manner. Although they prefer and usually manage to mix in the more elegant levels of their society, they are quite at home with everyone. But they cannot tolerate arguments and aggressive behavior. They make very nice excuses—and flee.

People with Venus in Libra have a love of color, proportion, and etiquette. Their good taste shows in everything they do, from the way they furnish and decorate their homes to the stylish and smart way they dress. They love the formalities of entertaining.

These people make the finest mates and partners in the Zodiac, especially if their Sun also is in Libra. Of course, this ideality is often marred by other planetary influences. But generally, Venus in Libra individuals flower in partnership. They manage to give the other person a great deal that is pleasing, even though the association may not work out or last long.

The love life of these people is not always happy. They are susceptible. In their hunger for harmony, they tend to believe every nice thing said. They are terribly romantic. They are easily misled by a show of affection. They are not fools by any means, but they are vulnerable to love and the idle flatteries of romance.

They often have beauty that is deeper than surface looks. A quality of refinement shows in their actions and manner. They are magnetic. But they can be flighty, flirtatious, selfish, self-indulgent, dependent, and sentimental. They can be too refined and delicate to cope with this hard world.

Venus in Libra individuals unconsciously impose heavy demands on their romantic partners. They are always looking for them to live up to their ideals of beauty and conduct. A constant analysis is going on behind the scenes, which often exhausts them physically and forces them to lie down, sometimes for days. This is especially so if the Sun is in Libra as well as in Venus.

The Venus in Libra combination warns against hasty and impulsive marriages. There is a great deal of variability in the temperament. The tendency is to try to compensate for this by formalizing relationships through contracts and ceremonies. It is not unlike whistling in the dark, because in the course of time the Libra changeableness may assert itself if the affections do not have a deep foundation.

Venus in Libra people are inclined to put on a show to cover up what might be lacking in a relationship or a situation. They like everything in the garden to be lovely, so much so that self-deception is a strong possibility. They live in a world of mental ideals. Of course, they can pretend that a situation lives up to their expectations. But in reality the opposite may be true, and they are dissatisfied and lonely.

VENUS IN SCORPIO

Venus in Scorpio is a highly sexual placement. Eroticism and sexual urge can be expressed in any number of ways. There can be a straightforward hunger for sexual experience, which seeks gratification in the actual act of lovemaking. Or sexual impulse can go too far to extremes. There will be a tendency not only to overindulge but also to wallow—and perhaps to sink into degrading experiences. Or the sexual urge can be associated with perversity, cruelty, and pain.

It must be understood that this is an isolated placement. Because of the modifying influence of the other planets, no one with Venus in Scorpio will be exactly as described here. But such individuals will exhibit evidence of these traits, if not to others, then to themselves.

These people have a love of sensation. They enjoy luxury, flattery, and secrecy. Their emotions are extremely strong and are almost in a constant state of arousal. They can really hate, with a venom that people without a Scorpio connection can't even imagine.

Venus in Scorpio people can be vindictive. They have tremendous powers of self-control when they have a clear objective in mind. Their aim often is to get even with someone who may have rejected them or slighted them. They can wait years for the right opportunity for revenge.

They are proud people, much more sensitive than they ever seem. They repress their seething emotions. They can appear cool, calm, and collected when just the opposite is the case.

People with Venus in Scorpio often are tactless. They say what they feel. They have an urge to discover the truth, and they don't mind dropping it on other people's toes. They often make the same mistakes twice, especially where love is concerned.

These are possessive and passionate people. Whatever is theirs they hold onto fiercely. They do not allow the person they love much freedom. They can be cruelly jealous, wildly suspicious. They are not beyond sacrificing the interests of others in order to save their own skins.

They are deeply perceptive, though not particularly artistic. They have great insights into the mysteries of life, and they accept their insights as matters of fact. Where others are amazed, Venus in Scorpio individuals can be indifferent.

Venus in Scorpio individuals are proud without being egotistical. There is a hidden side to their nature, which they do not allow others to see or suspect. They are constantly under pressure from sexual forces that might drive others to disastrous extremes. But the strength of these people in restraining their impulses is often amazing.

However, such control has its price. Venus in Scorpio people need to sublimate their desires if they do not express them. Otherwise, severe inner conflicts are possible, which can make life a misery for them as well as for the people they live with. Energies need to be redirected into productive channels.

Often these people can release themselves through activities requiring personal sacrifice. They may decide to serve a higher purpose such as the good of mankind. They are capable of great privation and dedication once the decision to serve has been made.

Venus, the planet of love and beauty, is not very comfortable in Scorpio, a sign ruled by Mars, the planet of war and destruction. The emotions and affections are too often wrenched and tortured by fate and circumstances as well as by insatiable appetites.

VENUS IN SAGITTARIUS

Venus in Sagittarius is an enthusiastic placement for romance. In love, these people hold out a great deal of promise. They are idealistic. They beckon with suggestions of heady delights just over the horizon. But if anyone can catch them, there is a strong possibility of disappointment. The moment of coming together may be splendid, or it may not. But there is little chance of a continuing and satisfying attachment.

People with Venus in Sagittarius are impulsive in their affections. One minute they want to make love, the next they have moved on to another interest or another place. Not that they are insincere. It's just that they lack the depth of persistent passion that most people expect.

Individuals with this combination want what they want when they want it. They are not too subtle in the ways of love. They don't have much time, literally, for the preambles of wooing. They are physical lovers, but only when they feel like it. They are tentative and easily rebuffed.

Venus in Sagittarius confers on a person a love of the great outdoors. They are high-spirited and fun-loving. They enjoy uncomplicated relationships that leave them free to come and go as they please. They are generous and frank and usually very popular. They make friends easily. They are better "buddies" than lovers.

These people are inclined to make promises without considering the consequences or all that is involved. This can make them unreliable when it comes to important decisions about getting married. They may think it's a great idea, but when the time comes, they split. They are hard to commit.

Venus in Sagittarius individuals love their freedom. They will not be pinned down. The urge to travel is strong. They are always seeking new horizons. They are great explorers and don't like to stay in the same place for long.

These people are often very indulgent of their loved ones in an effort to get closer to them. They can wed two or three times. If conditions become too demanding, or people emotionally binding, they are likely to solve the situation neatly and simply—by walking out.

Venus in Sagittarius suggests many passing love affairs. It is not a placement ideal for settling down, sinking roots, or nest building.

Yet people born with Venus in Sagittarius can be very sincere. Unless there are adverse planetary placements, these folk will not deliberately mislead another person. They have the best of intentions, even though their freewheeling disposition suggests otherwise at times.

Once people with Venus in Sagittarius have given their word in romantic matters, they will do their best to stick to it. They have a strong social conscience, which recognizes the need for fair play. But in a partnership they need shared interests to make a go of it. Too often people who fall in love with Venus in Sagittarius individuals mistakingly feel that once the knot is tied their spouse will alter his or her ways.

As parents, people with this combination love and indulge their children. But if they have the opportunity, they may be inclined to send the kids to boarding schools. This move can have two aims. The first is to give their youngsters the best start in life possible, with a good grounding in all the social graces and the possibility of making influential friends and acquaintances. The other is to give themselves more freedom to go their independent ways.

VENUS IN CAPRICORN

Venus in Capricorn suggests a bit of timidity in love and romance. It makes a person interestingly shy about expressing affection. They are likely to arouse the passions of the more daring types of the Zodiac. They present a challenge that is hard to resist. On the surface they may seem a bit serious. But underneath are passions waiting to be released by the right person.

Venus in Capricorn people can be very sensual. They may not be easy conquests. They generally keep their affections well locked up. No one gets a preview without some effort. They love pleasure, but don't like to admit it. They have a fear of being made to look foolish. They can be scornful of people who show too much emotion. They are easily embarrassed.

People with Venus in Capricorn are sincere. Once they fall in love, they remain true. They are usually more successful marrying later in life, when their repressed fears and emotions have had time to surface. In the early stages of life they can make mistakes by choosing partners who do not intrude on their inner world. They later discover that without deep interaction between two people, there is little chance of happiness.

These people are always aiming at self-reliance. They can feel it is a weakness to depend on someone else, even for emotional reasons. They often hold back, when they would love to reach out. The right partner can give them the means of self-expression they need so much.

Physical compatibility is very important to Venus in Capricorn individuals. Often it is only through the act of lovemaking that they are able to show their deepest feelings.

They love domestic life. They can sink into it and luxuriate. They enjoy being in familiar surroundings where there are not likely to be unexpected problems to deal with. They are creatures of habit. Too much of the family life can make them dull and uninteresting.

Venus in Capricorn people often marry someone much older or younger. They are very protective of their loved ones, especially their children. But they have to work at not becoming rigid with the younger generation. The fear of being rebuffed can prevent them from taking the initiative other people are longing for.

There is a developed and undeveloped type in this combination of Venus and Capricorn. The less developed type is more worldly and self-seeking. Such individuals want to surround themselves with possessions and material symbols of security. They like others to know how well they are doing. They are inclined to measure everything by the value of money. They frequently marry for money, prestige, or power. The developed aspect of this combination is reflected in an ability to love through all sorts of trials. This person is not afraid to switch traditional roles in partnership. A woman will go to work to support her man. A man will do the domestic chores and raise the kids.

There is much that is appealingly old-fashioned in Venus in Capricorn people. They possess a strong sense of right and wrong. Although physically passionate, they are not as a rule the promiscuous type. They prefer to let themselves go only with a person they love. If they do have casual affairs, it is not without a sense of seriousness. They are prepared to accept their responsibilities.

These people do not look for love at first sight. They like a relationship to develop slowly, so they can be sure there will be no mistake. Often, however, they allow practical considerations to get in the way, which can unnecessarily delay their day of fulfillment and happiness.

VENUS IN AQUARIUS

People with Venus in Aquarius can be a bit erratic in their love life. Mostly they prefer a lot of distance in relationships, as far as emotion is concerned. They can't stand clinging vines, for instance. And they like their companions to be intellectual, at least able to indulge in interesting conversations. While a love mate wants to get on with the more physical side, these people may prefer a chat.

Yet they can be suddenly aroused. Without warning, they can throw their books and blueprints out the window, then plunge into splendid love-making. They can be interesting and exciting lovers with a fondness for experimentation.

With Venus in Aquarius, a person has a love of social life. They enjoy getting around, meeting as many interesting people as possible. They like to develop their intellect. They are friendly and good listeners. They encourage people to talk about themselves, so they can study human nature. They often make very inspired observations about living and personal relationships.

These people are idealistic. They have a very good idea of the type of person they *might* want to fall in love with, but events seldom turn out that way. They often do the unexpected, which surprises them as much as their families and associates. They can make odd and improbable marriages and alliances. The less promising, the more likely they are to succeed.

People with Venus in Aquarius usually do things in moderation. As much as they enjoy social affairs, they are unlikely to eat or drink too much. They are self-controlled. Even under stressful and unusual circumstances, they show stability.

They are tolerant people. Nothing much shocks them. They have their own fixed ideas, but don't allow these to interfere with their relationships. They accept other people's beliefs without argument. They are not prejudiced.

Venus in Aquarius people have a compulsion to be independent and free of restriction. Some of them, especially if under strong parental or family strictures, may sleep around just to make the point. Venus in Aquarius individuals are attracted to people who are different. They do not like the run-of-the-mill type. Even if they are not particularly outstanding themselves, they will still look for extraordinariness in their closest associates, lovers, and mates. Erratic and unpredictable behavior often turns them on. Although they may appear to be ordinary themselves, not very deep underneath lurks a most unconventional disposition. They can be attracted to far-out philosophies and to occult subjects.

These people do not have a great deal of time for personal attachments and responsibilities. They would rather be active in political groups, influencing others to work toward a life of greater independence. They cannot stand to see people bowing down to any form of authority. And for this reason they refuse to allow themselves to become the slave of their emotions.

Music, poetry, and painting can be among their interests. There is a love of beauty here, but it is the kind that does not need to possess it. These people are just as happy seeing a work of art in a museum as in having it in their own home. They have a keen sense for sharing.

Venus in Aquarius individuals often become very good parents, confounding the predictions of their friends who may be used to their preference for unfettered relationships. They can treat their kids like friends, and so enjoy sharing family life.

VENUS IN PISCES

This is a person who has an unmistakable love of beauty in some form or other. It may be music, poetry, flowers. Or it could be romantic dreams, which may reach heights of earthly unobtainability. These individuals, regardless of any modifying influences from the other planets, are tender-souled to the core.

Venus in Pisces people can be terribly vague and unworldly. They are likely to spend much of their time daydreaming, picturing themselves and their lovers in impossibly romantic situations. Venus, the planet of love and beauty, is strongest in dreamy, watery Pisces. Without a good deal of strengthening from, say, the Sun in Aries, these people can become slaves of their emotions and feelings. This is especially so if the Sun or Moon also is in Pisces.

People with Venus in Pisces are extremely sensitive, generous, and kind. Their compassion for others is easily aroused. They have a strong self-sacrificing nature, which can be used as a means of escape from pressure and reality.

In love, it is possible for these individuals to become so devoted to a lover that they are almost slavish. These people can really get a kick out of surrendering their "all." It makes them feel strangely pure, something like the sacrificial lamb. This is the way their minds work; they are either victim or villain. And as villain, they then seek punishment for their wrongs and guilt.

One guilty secret is their longing for sexual experience. Venus in Pisces individuals can be promiscuous. This is not so much out of sensuality, but out of a need to share emotional experiences with others. Unless there are strengthening factors, these people may prefer not to work. They will take any easy way out, which will give them a peaceful and comfortable life. They can be very, very lazy.

Venus in Pisces people are trusting. They are too yielding and forgiving to make enemies, except for their rivals in love and romance. Women with this placement are ultrafeminine, often possessing a remarkably soft texture of body.

These people are sociable. But they do like periods of peace and quiet. They may at times retreat into themselves. Their withdrawal is aggravating to their mates and partners, who also are frequently disconcerted by their inexplicable changes of mood.

Venus in Pisces confers a great deal of compassion. These people often get involved in some sort of caretaking or charity work. They are secretive and very sensitive to what other people may be thinking about them. They love to be loved. Without love, they sink into depression.

Venus in Pisces individuals are easily influenced. But their enthusiasms are often short-lived. They can be mad about something or someone today, and totally disinterested tomorrow. They are difficult people to follow, even harder to pin down. But they are very forgivable.

People born with Venus in Pisces have a habit of putting their loved ones on pedestals. If someone comes along who even vaguely resembles one of their idealistic images, they are inclined to regard him or her as the real thing. They can blind themselves with their own emotional projections. Needless to say, they are frequently taken for a ride and shocked into eventual disillusionment.

But they do have the long-suffering, martyr mentality. It can allow them to cling to the vine of their dreams long after autumn and winter have come and gone.

With Venus in Pisces, a person may be slow to stand up for his or her own rights. Depending on the position of the Sun and Mars, they may allow others to walk over them, feeling a greater need for peace and serenity than for justice. This can lead to involuntary frustration, which may have its release in feelings of failure and self-doubt.

Mars in the Signs

Mars is the planet of enterprise, ambition, self-assertion, combativeness, and energetic expression. Its quality is forcefulness. At its best, it is pioneering, vigorous, courageous, strong. At its worst, it is cruel, aggressive, violent, quick-tempered. Mars is the force in us that gets things done. It is the principle of the ancient war god. It is associated with heat, blood, pain, and action.

A person with a strong Mars placement is a doer. He and she tend to be impatient and impulsive, always champing at the bit to be on the move, to get things under way.

Mars gives great organizing and executive ability. It is the dynamic business and professional man or woman.

It also is the impulse that makes heroes—not necessarily on a grand scale, when individuals think and plan, but on an everyday level. Those who just step into a gap where action or help is needed, without considering social consequences or personal safety, are demonstrating the proud Mars principle.

It is Mars that provides sexual strength in romantic desire. It drives us to go after what we want, whether we are being indiscreet or foolish. Mars sees what it wants and grabs it.

Venus loves the games, the preamble, the promise, the tantalizing fragrance of passion without contact, the exquisite contemplation of final unity. Mars can't wait. Mars thrusts through Venus's dreams, bruising the flesh, scalding the emotions, searing the sensibilities. And sometimes seems to consume the very soul, oblivious to all but the conquest of passion over restraint, ideals, and intentions.

When Saturn, the planet of depression and restriction, settles its forces on man or woman, it is Mars that can break through into the clear again, snapping bonds, shattering illusions, and pummeling obstacles into the dust with blind anger or sheer combative glee.

Mars is fierce determination once an idea or objective is targeted. But it is an energy that thrives on results. If these are slow in coming, or are not impressive enough, the dynamic attention may turn to newer and more challenging ventures. Mars represents the body's resistance to disease, its fighting and survival capabilities. It is the iron that makes the blood red and the nerves steely. Mars also stands for accidents and injuries through haste and impatience. It is loss of temper, burns, scalds, fevers—all that is hot, fiery, and eruptive. Mars is especially strong in association with Aries and Scorpio, the signs it rules.

MARS IN ARIES

Mars in Aries individuals have strong desires. They are always busy doing something. Their capacity for energetic activity is enormous. They are intensely ambitious, not so much for the power and position as for the delight they get out of the rough and tumble of getting there.

They are enterprising and enthusiastic. They are always ready to fight for the things they believe in. Mars, the planet of energy and strength, is in its own sign in Aries, and so is especially powerful. These people are good organizers and executives. They can round up resources and spur others into action. Given a task to accomplish, they will seldom admit defeat. What they can't solve with their considerable mental gifts, they get around or eliminate with audacious actions.

People with Mars in Aries have to learn self-control. They continually make life difficult for themselves by being impulsive. Their often brilliant ideas never stay in their head for reflection; they are translated into action immediately, without any regard for timing. They often fall flat on their face; but they are up again instantly, hammering away at the opposition with indefatigable energy.

Mars in Aries individuals are spontaneous. They are as quick with the open hand to someone needing help as they are with a push to someone getting in their way. They love freedom and plenty of room to act in. They make superior fighting men and women, surgeons, engineers, and police officers.

Venus in Pisces gives the Mars in Aries placement a softening, artistic touch. This can make such individuals fine writers, journalists, and artists.

With Mars in Aries, a person can be accident-prone. Haste and impatience are their worst enemies. But they have an outstanding resistance to illness. If they do get sick, recovery usually is quicker than expected.

Dauntless, they often take on impossible tasks that have to be left half finished. They also are inclined to lose interest in a project once they see the end in sight. Then it is no longer a challenge.

In love, Mars in Aries people are ardent and impulsive. They need a mate who is physically compatible and understands their uncomplicated nature. They are good at sports. They need plenty of exercise to work off their great abundance of energy if their fires are not consumed in lovemaking.

In love, they also know what they want. Both the men and the women are aggressive lovers. An Aries woman is not the type to take the traditional female role of coyness and uncertainty when it comes to wooing. With more reserved men, she is the one who is likely to make the first move and set the pace.

Mars in Aries individuals are idealistic. When they decide for themselves that something has to be done to improve their community or society, there are no half measures. They have a strong sense of commitment.

A fondness for any adventure or dare is outstanding in these people. They are great vacation mates when long distances have to be traveled and numerous difficulties overcome. They will take charge right from the word go. The problem for less hardy people is not only putting up with them but also keeping up with them.

There is often a lack of sympathy and tolerance in people born with Mars in Aries. Most situations seem black and white to them. They find difficulty coping with people of finer sensibilities. They are likely to dismiss such people's feelings as weak, or just ride roughshod over them.

MARS IN TAURUS

Mars in Taurus individuals are determined to get their share of worldly goods. There is a tendency to be a bit too materialistic. Money and possessions become the main interests in life. This, of course will be offset or emphasized by the position of the other planets.

A person with Mars in Taurus is very persistent. Early in life, they form an idea of what they want. Their desires usually relate to the good things in life. And they go after them in a calm and practical manner, seldom discouraged by setbacks and hard work.

Although these people have a strong hankering for comfort and luxury, they are not dreamers. They usually know their limitations. They have made a shrewd assessment of the problems that lie ahead. Often they have to plod on for a long time before achieving worthwhile results. They can sometimes waste time by battling anticipated difficulties that may not even arise.

Mars in Taurus eventually brings financial success. These people crave security. They want money in the bank and their names on the deeds of property. They have a strong fear of being left penniless in their old age. They are often physically attractive people with good common sense. They have noted the toll that the years can take. They are not as a rule the religious or mystical type. They put their faith in tangible things. And any reward that might be coming they want in their lifetime, the sooner the better.

These people are extremely stubborn. They will never give up. Once they have an idea in their head, it's there for good, or at least until it is proved· to their satisfaction that it does not work. They are doubting Thomases, not out of cynicism but out of pure hardheadedness. They don't take chances. They rely on their own judgment. They are self-contained individuals.

Sex is vital to them. They love the physical, sensual side. They are especially stimulated by touch and touching. They are possessive but good to their lovers. Jealousy can often make marriages more of a trial than should be. These people are faithful and good providers. They love children and can teach them to cope with the world.

Mars in Taurus people have great control of their emotions, but loss of temper can mean violence. Jealousy and possessiveness are their weak spots. Threatened by a mate's flirtatiousness or infidelity, they act out their rage with little restraint. They also are made anxious when their love partner seeks even innocent forms of independence.

Mars in Taurus individuals are often skilled in craftsmaking. They have a knack for designing fine and pretty things in fabric, wood, or metal. They have a good eye for practical decoration. They may do well in the building, real estate, or design industries. There is nothing flighty about their artistic and creative productions.

These people often seem to act out of character. One day they may be conservative and contented, the next impatient and discontented. They are inclined to spend extravagantly on luxuries and entertainment. Their generosity can go to extremes. They also can be wildly self-indulgent.

People with Mars in Taurus usually are prepared to work hard to get their own homes. They feel a basic need for economic security, which their impulsive actions may seem to contradict. They are often pulled between the urge to get up and go and to stay where they are. They are the types who can get in a rut and then suddenly break out.

Taurus usually confers a love of nature. But the presence of Mars there induces an urge to transform nature. These people can often be successful as developers and engineers, building highways, dams, tunnels, turnpikes, and thoroughfares.

MARS IN GEMINI

Mars in Gemini creates a forceful speaker. Such individuals have a way with words. Their ideas are often inspirational and capture the public imagination. They make good politicians, lecturers, lawyers, and teachers. As writers, they can keep the ideas coming quick and fast. They have a knack for whipping up flagging enthusiasm, which makes them admirable for addressing action groups and getting people to work together.

Mars and Gemini people can be sarcastic, satirical, and witty. They also can be blunt and bruising when it suits them. They have to be careful in company. When they mix, they tend to get hold of a pet idea and belabor everyone with it as though it were the most important invention since the wheel.

But as convincing as they are in communicating good ideas, they are not so adept at putting the ideas into action. These people have a fitful physical energy, which is not suited for prolonged activity. They tire easily. They are deft with their hands and minds. And they might have a talent for tap dancing, judo, or boxing. They are swift movers. They avoid heavy work.

People with Mars in Gemini seldom ever have one job or career. They like to do different things, either at the same time or in succession. They are sometimes ambidextrous. They love variety and change.

A person with Mars in Gemini is usually talkative. They are inclined to provoke arguments with their friends and associates for the sheer pleasure of matching wits against others. They are usually well-informed, being natural gatherers of information.

They have a way with mechanical appliances. They can repair tools and machines without special technical knowledge. Their homes usually display a host of ingenious gadgets, some of them handmade.

People with Mars in Gemini often become irritable. They build up mental energy, which is hard for them to release adequately. They become restless, discontented. Then they take out their frustrations on those around them.

Mars in Gemini, without balance from other placements, can make a person disagreeable and nasty. He or she is always having trouble with relatives or neighbors. Concentration can be difficult. Instability may develop.

Mars in Gemini people need to circulate freely. This tendency makes them poor candidates for long and committed love affairs. They see family ties as threats to their freedom. Although they love kids, they prefer to enjoy other people's.

In love, no one can take a Mars in Gemini individual for granted without being left promptly on their own and lonesome. These people do not as a rule become closely attached. They like to keep their relationships fluid, so they can move swiftly in and out as the mood takes them.

Often they do not know themselves what they are going to do the next moment. They live on a live wire, which makes them mentally and physically restless. They need to get their teeth into a project, to give it everything they have, to feel really fulfilled. But the trouble is, they are too easily distracted and dart off in new directions.

Mars in Gemini individuals work from inspirational flashes. Some of their ideas can be brilliant. These people usually gather around them an active and intelligent group of friends. They have a fondness for chat, new experiences, and late nights. There is seldom a dull moment—one way or another—when these rascals are around.

The early education of Mars in Gemini people is often erratic. They may have attended a lot of schools. Or they devoted more time to sports, hobbies, and leisure activities than to study. Concentration and continuity of thought can be more difficult to attain than their alert and observant manner suggests.

MARS IN CANCER

Mars in Cancer has produced some of the world's best writers, artists, and thinkers. The fiery energies of Mars stimulate the emotional waters of Cancer, allowing the person to dive deeper than usual into his or her own instinctive feelings. These people can discover truly original thoughts and ideas lodged in the subconscious.

Mars in Cancer gives a person strong desires. These can be sensuous, heightening the need for emotional and physical pleasure. These people can be romantic and stimulating lovers. But they can be very changeable in their moods. One minute they are all over a lover, the next peevish and resentful. They imagine slights where none was meant. They exaggerate their hard luck and the minor problems as well. They can be very demanding and very hard to please. Irritability can create frequent arguments.

There is a strong streak of rebellion in Mars in Cancer people. They are always looking for independence, when their nature is to hold onto what they've got. They can become confused by their contradictions. They may make progress in worldly affairs by giving up one job or career after another. The stimulus of change creates even more vivid imagination, so that the natural urge for some kind of artistic expression gets released.

If Mars in Cancer individuals do not find a release, their health can be affected. There is a tendency for the emotions to disturb the digestion. If such individuals indulge food or drink to excess, or alternatively inhibit their tastes, gastritis and ulcers can develop.

With Mars in Cancer there is little chance of compatibility with maternal figures, including the real mother in this person's life. Or the women with whom they associate may cause trouble and friction.

There is, though, a powerful love of the home and a need to find peace and quiet there. But this may never be achieved to the person's satisfaction. They will be protective of their children and loved ones, but have to avoid trying to take over their lives.

There also can be a lack of direction, which increases their feelings of discontent and frustration. They may be too timid to insist on loved ones cooperating with important plans for the family or home. Or they are unsure of what they want. So progress goes by the board.

A person with Mars in Cancer is inclined to put great value on the past. They may do their utmost to bring back some of the good old days. They can muse nostalgically, but often wind up moody and brooding when the remembrances of childhood fail to materialize here and now.

Mars in Cancer folk like to fill their homes with knickknacks and bric-a-brac, especially relics in which they take considerable pride. They are often collectors of books, photographs, and souvenirs, particularly those with a martial, or warlike, flavor.

These individuals are inclined to be rigidly patriotic and prejudiced. They have a strong sense of self-preservation, which makes them suspicious of diverse groups, strangers, and unfamiliar people. Anything unknown can threaten the peace of mind and security of the Mars in Cancer individual. They fantasize striking swiftly at their imagined enemies, then brood when the moment of confrontation passes silently.

Mars in Cancer people worry too much. They are inclined to fuss around their families. They imagine the worst has happened if anyone is late arriving home. The childhood of these people is often disturbed by association with uncongenial people. Their memory constantly reflects these emotional difficulties in adult life. It is not easy for them to decide what they want to do with their lives.

Homemaking and raising families are not enough to satisfy the deeper needs of Mars in Cancer individuals. Their innate fondness for family life is too often undermined by their own forceful and aggressive attitudes. These people are likely to make a success of an occupation connected with catering—running an institution, a hotel, or a restaurant. Housing and real-estate projects also attract their interest, and provide a constructive outlet for their energies.

MARS IN LEO

Mars in Leo gives a strong sense of purpose and creative ability. The drive to outdistance and outshine any rivals is compulsive. This person is determined to get to the top of the tree, and is not too fussy about who gets pushed and shoved around in the process.

Once Mars in Leo people get an idea in their head, no one is going to change their minds for them. They tend to fix a target for their considerable ambitions, then pour enormous physical and mental energy into that objective until it is attained.

They are born showmen and showwomen. But they lack subtlety in their attempts to attract the attention and admiration of the crowd, which mean so much to them. They can be ham-fisted as well as hams. They are likely to be looking over their shoulder constantly to see what impression they are having. It is not money or social position that these people strive for. It is recognition and image.

Individuals born with Mars in Leo are extremely passionate and strongly sexed. They are born romantics. They not only imagine themselves in heroic situations, but also they like to act these out. They are often foolhardy in their desire to make an impression on members of the opposite sex. They may throw money around and show a penchant for fast and showy cars.

These people also are flamboyant dressers. Often they favor bright colors, like red and yellow, even though these shades may not suit their complexions. They are people of strong desires, who frequently go for what they like rather than for what is good for them. They are fast talkers with a great sense of the dramatic.

People with Mars in Leo seldom are happy until they reach a position of leadership. Even then, they soon become impatient to extend their authority. They love to bask in glory. And it has to be said that they are brave and courageous, depending, of course, on the influences of the other planets. These people, when they do make promises, do their utmost to deliver the goods.

They are not lazy. And they will accept responsibility. They love nothing more than to meet a challenge, especially one that exploits their vivid imagination, their undoubted initiative, and their creative turn of mind. They usually have a flair for writing and verbal expression.

Mars in Leo people are often hot-tempered and independent. They love to order other people around. They are bossy and dictatorial. They have a good idea what has to be done most times, especially in emergencies. Their conviction induces others to give them power and authority.

Their enthusiasm for projects that take their fancy is unbounded. They can inspire others into supporting their schemes through the sheer power of their personalities and their disregard for danger and discomfort.

There are seldom any back doors about people born with Mars in Leo. In fact, they are often so frank and direct as to be rude and insensitive. Tact and diplomacy are not among their virtues, unless these qualities are conferred by other planetary placements.

People with Mars in Leo tend to lack humility. They are so sure of their own infallibility that they find it difficult to listen to advice, now matter how well intended. So they are prone to make mistakes, especially of the emotional kind. They can be undisciplined in their expenditure of energy.

MARS IN VIRGO

Individuals born with Mars in Virgo have a keenness for detail. Their analytical powers fit them for a career in science. They are especially suited for working in laboratories where medical, chemical, and metallurgical problems have to be solved. These people can be dedicated researchers. In their determination to find a cure or a remedy, they put all other considerations aside.

There is usually a strong urge to serve in Mars in Virgo people. They make the most energetic employees. However, they do need a special objective to work toward. Otherwise, their considerable energies start to back up, and they can become troublemakers.

If not totally absorbed, these people can stir up teammates. They can do this by fussing about unimportant details and nonessentials. Or they may draw attention to unhygienic or unhealthy working conditions, and so create discontent among the work force.

Mars in Virgo individuals have considerable technical and executive ability. They are very good with figures. They have a special gift for analytical thought. They are able to reduce a vast amount of detail to a logical essence. They are usually exceptionally clear and fast makers of reports. They are good people to head inquiries, especially when there are attempts to conceal the facts.

One problem with Mars in Virgo is that it makes an individual extremely critical. This is an advantage if the trait is employed in constructive ways. But without direction, criticalness can degenerate into picking and nagging. Such a person also can be officious and coldly calculating.

Mars in Virgo people often have sharp tongues and are argumentative. And unless the individual is mature, he or she may lack physical courage. If their jibes or criticisms are challenged, such individuals wilt into the background, there to make intrigue and trouble.

The developed individual with Mars in Virgo is extremely capable of dealing with emergencies. They are not the types to lose their head. While others may panic or run around ineffectively, they will quietly stand their ground looking for practical solutions. They are not beyond indulging in a bit of scheming either, if it suits them.

Lack of spontaneous emotional response often makes these people seem cold and aloof. They have difficulty expressing their feelings. They will hide behind a mask of indifference rather than risk making a fool of themselves. There is often a great deal more going on deep inside than their bland appearance may suggest.

Sometimes Mars in Virgo people become health and diet faddists. They are the types to be found jogging around the park first thing in the morning. They are not exercise buffs, but their logical minds tell them it is good for them. They also can damage their health by taking diets to extreme.

These individuals are terrible worriers. They do their best not to show it and to appear cool as a cucumber. They can suffer from stomach pains and indigestion due to nerves and repressed anxieties.

People born with Mars in Virgo often like talking as a pastime more than anything else. They do not seek the public eye. They prefer to remain on the sidelines until they see a safe opportunity to put their oar in. Then they delight all and sundry with their magical ability to transform the most everyday experiences into fascinating tales of mystery and intrigue.

Mars in Virgo individuals are not great innovators or experimentalists. But they do possess a talent for solving work and production problems. They have a knack for improvising that would make them extremely handy people to have along in any environment.

MARS IN LIBRA

Mars in Libra fosters extremes in action or decision-making. This placement produces a person who is likely to swing violently to one side or another. It marks an individual who probably will be impatient and intolerant of any injustice or exploitation of others. Such people might put a great deal of energy into righting such wrongs. Or they may run around in circles, making a lot of noise but accomplishing very little.

Mars in Libra people do not like to argue or get involved in stand-up fights if they can be avoided. But in a tight spot, they will stand their ground and give as much as they receive. They prefer to solve disputes by compromise. They are adroit at maneuvering others into positions where cooperation seems to be the only sensible alternative.

These people make persuasive and firm diplomats. They are exceptionally suited for the courtroom. Here they can argue a case with telling effect. They also make excellent negotiators and go-betweens, especially if there is distinct hostility between the parties involved. In times of war, they can put on just the right show of force to make an enemy hesitate, while they increase their defenses during the pause.

As much as they love peace, truce, and moderation, individuals born with Mars in Libra usually manage to get involved in conflicts. They may seem always to strive for a state of equilibrium, especially on the domestic front. But here they often make problems for themselves by selecting a mate who is the exact opposite of themselves. So home life can be a trial or an uneasy truce.

It has to be remembered that Libra is ruled by Venus, the planet of love and beauty. When Mars, the planet of war and raw energy, is placed in this position, the result obviously involves conflict and contradiction.

These people yearn for true love, but often try too hard to obtain it. They can be attractive, passionate, skilled lovers. Mars the warrior and Venus the artist come together in an ecstasy of union. Often these people are involved in love-at-first-sight affairs. They are impulsive and ardent. But when it comes to living with a partner, the differences start to show and the arguments begin. These individuals know instinctively what is good for them. So they often choose to move on, renouncing deeply committed relationships.

Mars in Libra people do not have a lot of physical staying power. They put tremendous energy into their projects, then burn out quickly. They can lose interest in the face of prolonged delays, aggravations, and petty conflicts.

These are rash people. It does not take much to upset their equilibrium, especially in their personal life. They can overreact. They can fall in love one day and be indifferent the next. Due to their impulsiveness, they often marry early in life—and learn to regret it. They may marry more than once. Lovers and mates seem to create the main problems in their life.

Usually, Mars in Libra confers artistic talent or a penetrating appreciation of art, as may be found in a gallery owner, dealer, or critic. Their own artistic productions may be motivated by a sense of urgency, and so come across as lacking in detail. Strong colors and broad strokes are their forte.

Mars in Libra individuals are animated talkers. They love discussions about politics and international affairs. Such topics allow them to express their particular views about the unjust treatment of others. They have to avoid a tendency to advocate extreme measures.

MARS IN SCORPIO

Mars in Scorpio is a powerful and dangerous placement. It is a bundle of dynamite that can explode at any moment. The question for the individual with this placement is whether to use the explosive energies positively or negatively.

Mars in Scorpio people give out intense vibes. They have only to be in a room to stir up reactions of dislike or attraction. They are the kind of people who cannot be ignored.

Mars, the planet of driving force and aggression, is the coruler of Scorpio, together with the mysterious, seething planet Pluto. Scorpio stands for penetration at any cost, the urge to find the secret of life even at the expense of death. There are no half measures here.

This man or woman is a hard-driving individual who knows exactly what he or she wants—and how to go about it. They are relentlessly determined. Once they start on a certain course, they never give up. They are absolutely fearless and contemptuous of any opposition. They have unlimited faith in their own self-sufficiency and their ability to overcome all obstacles.

Mars in Scorpio individuals have an unusual approach to time. Although they are impatient in their desires to keep forever moving toward the one objective they fix for themselves, they are prepared to wait years for the final result. Anything that gets in their way they are inclined to stomp on. They possess a near indestructibility. They are sustained in whatever they undertake by an unshakable sense of purpose. These can be dangerous rivals and deadly enemies. If they are undeveloped and immature, they can be cruel, heartless, vindictive. They have a natural ability to discern the weaknesses in people. And they never fail to exploit these weaknesses in the pursuit of their own aims.

People with Mars in Scorpio can do a great deal to benefit humanity or the community in which they live. They have nerves of steel. They are just the kind of people who can dedicate themselves to eliminating criminal or corrupt practices. They make excellent spies, investigators, and undercover agents. They also make good surgeons, military leaders, and corporation heads.

These are hard-working and practical people. They have the power to command. Their physical strength and endurance are exceptional. They make fearless executives, especially the troubleshooting kind. Hardship means nothing to them. They bore unremittingly toward their goal.

It is a good idea for individuals born with Mars in Scorpio periodically to take stock of the direction their life is taking. It is not difficult for them to get on the downgrade toward an unlawful or undesirable existence. The power and resource available to them can lead them into excesses. Also, since they have very fixed ideas, they are inclined to put their head down and seldom look up to see if anything has changed since the original commitment was made.

Mars in Scorpio individuals usually like to work alone. They are not the kind to look for advice or to accept it. Their faith in their own opinions and beliefs can be so strong that they become dogmatic and even fanatical.

They often have to cultivate a more humane outlook. They can take people around them for granted, or even use them ruthlessly. They have strong sexual urges, which can be expressed or repressed. When repressed, Mars in Scorpio people must find an outlet for their energies. A constructive and self-fulfilling endeavor is an added compensation.

MARS IN SAGITTARIUS

Mars in Sagittarius people are among the most impulsive in the Zodiac. Their associates cannot predict what they will be doing next, or where they will be. Mars in Sagittarius individuals are restless, and forever on the move physically and mentally. They also can be reckless.

They are great lovers of outdoor activities. All sports and games, especially of the vigorously competitive type, appeal to them. As they grow older and their waistlines grow broader, they are likely to become good-natured coaches, the generous patrons of clubs, or jovial and active committee members.

Sagittarius normally is a sign that gives a love of the good life without much regard for tomorrow. Money is something to be used, not held onto, once the basics are provided. With Mars in Sagittarius, there is a tendency to go farther, even to extremes. These people can be extravagant to the point of foolishness. They are likely to put on weight through dietary indulgences and to drive their bodies to the limit.

Mars in Sagittarius individuals have extraordinary resources of energy, especially when it is needed to pursue a new adventure. Otherwise, their staying power is not great. They are inclined to work in fits and starts. They become easily bored with routine and cannot stand to be tied down in one place for long.

There is another side to the nature, which, if dominant, produces a more philosophically minded person. These individuals, although not particularly self-searching—unless the Sun or another planet is in Scorpio—use their experiences to look for a greater meaning to life. They are, however, inclined to stick to conventional beliefs. They may become zealous advocates of an established religion.

Mars in Sagittarius people are often distinguished by an extraordinary optimism. They have great faith in the future, especially in good luck, on which they rely. They are inclined to gamble, taking high risks with money, their careers, and positions, as well as with their own physical safety.

These are extremely independent individuals. Their love of freedom can be so pronounced that they find it difficult to work in an ordinary nine-to-five job. They are likely to switch jobs regularly. If they do not end up working for themselves, they may settle for work that gives them a minimum of responsibility and the opportunity to travel around and meet new people.

Their enthusiasm is boundless. They are usually looking for pie in the sky, one big transaction, or that surefire adventure that will solve all their financial problems forever. They do not necessarily believe this, but they live as though they do. They are people with high ambitions and a great amount of energy to use in trying to get to the top. They usually take the unconventional way up and often attain fame and fortune, confounding the dire predictions of their critics.

Mars in Sagittarius people can be pompous. They get on their associates' nerves at times with their moralizing. They may argue for the sake of hearing their own views expressed. They can be extremely tactless and blunt. They not only call a spade a spade, but also hit their audience over the head with it.

Exaggeration is often one of their main faults. They are inclined to make promises they cannot keep. They also can be boastful and slapdash. But they do have deep insights into human nature, and can often deliver jewels of wisdom in a few words.

Mars in Sagittarius individuals need to find an aim in life and keep to it.

MARS IN CAPRICORN

People with Mars in Capricorn are particularly well suited for getting ahead and eventually to the top in this world. Mars, the planet of energy, drive, and ambition, is exalted in Capricorn. That means Mars is most powerful here. Also, Capricorn is the sign of material achievement and organizing ability. Together, they represent a person to be reckoned with.

These people have great driving force. But it is controlled, contained, like the air in a tire. The pressure, although released slowly, drives inexorably forward. As hard as rocks both in determination and outlook, these individuals are prepared to plod a long, hard course that would weary any but the most dauntless competitor.

In fact, it is possible for their associates to dismiss these people for a while as being too serious and methodical ever to make it to the top. But eventually, these same people are likely to find themselves working for a Mars in Capricorn boss.

Mars in Capricorn confers a tremendous desire to obtain prestige and authority. These individuals enjoy the feeling of power, but probably more than anything they yearn to be respected. And they usually deserve whatever notch they rise to.

They are extremely conscientious. They are not the type of worker who watches the clock. While there is work to be done, they are available. Their bosses soon learn that they are most reliable employees who can be trusted to carry out instructions to the letter. No one takes their responsibilities more seriously than people born with Mars in Capricorn.

Although they are inclined to work on their own, minding their own business, they have a keen appreciation of the need for all the parts of an organization to work efficiently for the common good. When they become elevated to positions of authority, they display a rare ability to understand the workings of all departments. They know exactly what is going on in each of them and when. A company or organization can seldom become too large for a chief born with Mars in Capricorn.

These people are often strict disciplinarians. They believe in sticking to rules. Yet they would never ask another person to perform a job they would not do themselves. Usually these people on the way up have made a point of familiarizing themselves with the operations of every branch of their company. No external discipline could ever be more than what they are inclined to impose on themselves.

They are prudent, resourceful, and cautious. They are rehearsed in everything they attempt. They never risk failure by leaving anything to chance. They are not particularly imaginative or creative. But they are consummate planners, with an eye for detail and a shrewd ability to assess character.

These are not the type of people to waste time struggling against resistance. They leave that to more stubborn types who have something to prove apart from the attainment of the objective. Mars in Capricorn individuals overcome difficulties by making the best possible use of all the forces and resources at their disposal. They do not run up blind alleys or hammer on doors unless they already have planned the next move.

However, in the face of prolonged delays, these people can show evidence of frustration. They may become increasingly irritable. If their ambitions are obviously thwarted, they may be subject to violent explosions of temper.

MARS IN AQUARIUS

People born with Mars in Aquarius are usually at the hub in their community or friendship group. They seem to attract numerous acquaintances and would-be associates. Often they are members of societies and associations with humanitarian objectives. These people usually are concerned with making the world a better place to live in.

Although they are friendly and take a great interest in what others are doing and what is happening to them, they manage to keep their relationships fairly detached. They are the first to help anyone in trouble. Frequently they take home individuals who are down in their luck and give them a bed for the night. But at the first sign of any emotional demands, they lose interest.

Mars in Aquarius people are radical thinkers. They can hold strong antiauthoritarian views. They attack through writings and speeches whatever established order exists in their time or in their community. They often become involved in political agitations. They are more inclined to incite others to take action than actually to get in there themselves.

In spite of their dislike of authority, they are motivated by a strong desire for personal power. This is not obvious, because they are not interested in giving orders. Their power complex is satisfied by being in the position to change other people's views and beliefs. In this way they can be quite destructive, especially if they have a bee in their bonnet and are not objective.

Mars in Aquarius people are persuasive and plausible. They believe in freedom. They do not necessarily object to law and order, except when these are used as excuses for muzzling an individual's freedom of speech or association.

They are original thinkers and are often found in the forefront of scientific research. They are never happier than when they are experimenting either with the slide rule, the test tube, a current political idea, or an unusual hobby.

If they are not moving at great speed in their minds, they like to move around people. They take interesting journeys and make unconventional associations. They often are creditable writers. Some Mars in Aquarius individuals have well-developed musical talents.

The energy these people can put into causes is immense. But they are rather selective about the kind of work they will do. It has to offer them a good deal of freedom. They are not particularly concerned with amassing a fortune. But they do like to have a secure and comfortable home.

Because of their fiercely independent nature, Mars in Aquarius individuals are not often blessed with a great deal of domestic harmony. Much will depend on the positions of the other planets, as well as those of their mates or family members.

They can be blunt to the point of rudeness. They have strong enthusiasms. But they need a good deal of variety and intellectual stimulation to keep them interested.

They are difficult people in a close relationship, especially marriage. Disappointment awaits the partner who is looking for warmth and affection. Mars in Aquarius individuals are not particularly physical or demonstrative. They are more attracted by a marriage of minds.

These people often prefer to mix with types who have different ideas and habits from the rest of society. In this company, they can air their unusual views without risking rejection. Once they get an idea in their head, no matter how bizarre, it is usually there to stay until experience proves it to be false. They are themselves not easily swayed.

In many respects Mars in Aquarius individuals live a moderate and regular life. Yet there is something unpredictable about them. They may go along conventional lines for a time, then suddenly do something that appears completely out of character. They are sometimes the catalyst of radical change for the people they associate with.

MARS IN PISCES

Mars in Pisces is not an easy position, but it is a promising one. People born with this placement often are obliged to sort out confusing situations—both in themselves and in their environment. They have strong feelings and compulsive drives. But when it comes to expressing them or putting them into action, the result usually falls short of their expectations.

These are people who are no strangers to frustration. They have to learn to bridge the gap between feelings and mind. They must coordinate sensation with sense. What they want to do sometimes does not make sense to others, and they feel restricted and inhibited. It is not always easy for them to see basic issues.

Mars is a fiery, self-assertive planet. Pisces is a watery, self-repressive sign. And when Mars plunges into this psychological pool, there is created seething currents below, dense and steamy clouds above.

Mars in Pisces is intense, dramatic. It gives the person a determined attitude to exploit his or her artistic potential, especially talents utilized in theater and performing. These individuals also will be inclined to take more than a passing interest in the sufferings of others. They may even be attracted to working as caretakers for the sick, hurt, and needy. But there could be more sympathetic talk than action in such a role.

Mars in Pisces people have extremely fertile imaginations. They are likely to spend a good deal of their time daydreaming and living in their feelings, stimulated by thoughts of the past. They can be intuitive and kindly, prepared to involve themselves in other people's troubles.

One of the most admirable traits about these individuals is an honest secretiveness. They are likely to work assiduously for others behind the scenes. Although they may not be particularly energetic in physical ways, they can focus their heart and mind on other people's problems.

Their understanding and genuine desire to be of help can make them valuable social and charity workers. Even if other influences induce them to seek personal recognition for their efforts, it is often difficult for them to bask in glory without guilt.

It is important for Mars in Pisces people to recognize that they probably are more effective in trying to reach their goals by indirect means. They have a knack for infiltration and surreptitious maneuver. They can wheedle people, and often achieve more spectacular results than the direct methods of their associates.

Mars in Pisces does imbue a person with an interest in the occult, mysticism, or parapsychology. They often use their own sensitivity to analyze their emotions, which makes them susceptible to prophetic visions and dreams.

Mars in Pisces also heightens sensual desires. If there is a lack of control due to other planetary positions, the search for excitement and stimulation can be taken to extremes. An immature Mars in Pisces individual can become preoccupied with trying to experience every sensation the body has to offer.

They can be impressionable, easily influenced, and permissive. The strong compulsion to fantasize in the face of frustrations makes the excessive use of alcohol and drugs a danger.

Mars in Pisces people usually have a good sense of humor. They have a strong desire to please and be liked. They are diplomatic, sometimes even to the point of dishonesty. They can lack push and self-reliance. They need an aim in life or they are likely to misdirect their energies.

Jupiter in the Signs

Jupiter is the planet of good fortune. It stands for expansion through foresight. It makes a person optimistic, cheerful, generous, frank, a good friend, and a wise adviser.

Jupiter, being the planet of expansion, naturally has the reputation for bringing material gains through business, personal endeavors, and good luck. When strongly placed, it makes us the kind of people others like to be with. Like Venus, which is fortunate because it attracts, Jupiter is fortunate because it expands—friendship, good will, and joy.

Jupiter is the planet of wisdom, the kind of wisdom that comes from being able to accept trials philosophically, knowing in the end that things usually turn out for the best. For this reason, the Jupiter person often gives the impression of being too confident and easygoing.

Jupiter also gives a desire for travel and adventure. If these journeys cannot be physical or geographical, they must be mental and intellectual. The imagination must be stimulated and broadened. Jupiter likes to wander. In its wanderings, wisdom is culled.

When adverse influences are at work, the Jupiter influence can endow individuals with too much faith in the future and their own good luck. So they may take silly risks with their money or with their reputations. But being philosophical, they are able to adopt the wider view and accept things as they are. The result is they are seldom downhearted for long, and so tend to attract helpful people.

The negative side of Jupiter takes all the good influences to extremes, so like the extremes of Venus they become problems. Jupiter's expansive tendencies can make a person extravagant and too fond of the good things in life. It can mean indulgence in food or drink, with excesses causing problems of fitness and health.

Promises can be made as a matter of convenience to expand the conviviality of social occasions, with no intention ever to honor them. Gambling—again the willingness to depend on luck—can become an irresistible lure; debts are left strewn in the wake of the buoyant, good-humored, fun-loving, irresponsible Jupiter. Jupiter's travel urge, when divorced from any particular aim in life, can produce a rolling stone.

But favorably placed, Jupiter contributes dignity, justice, honesty, broad-mindedness, and fine judgment. It confers a respect for law and order and a high tone of morality expressed through a philosophic or religious ideal.

Jupiter is favorably associated with Sagittarius and Pisces, the signs it rules.

JUPITER IN ARIES

People with Jupiter in Aries have big ideas, big ambitions, and loads of energy to see them through. They are extremely independent and self-confident. Their enthusiasm for their numerous projects is boundless. They are pushers, go-getters, men and women who seldom fail to get results. But often their disdain for detail and their refusal to draw up thorough plans plunge them into disaster. Their failures are frequently as large as their successes.

These are people who love to travel and get around. They seldom spend much time in one place. They are often great car enthusiasts, speedboat fanatics, or fliers. Any activity that gives them the sensation of speed or sets the adrenalin pumping attracts them. They are the types who love sports and games. They are hikers, mountain climbers, skiers, adventurers.

These are self-made men and women. Although other planetary placements will have an effect, people with Jupiter in Aries usually end up working for themselves in their own business. Or they rise to positions of authority where they enjoy all the freedom that their individualistic natures demand.

Jupiter in Aries individuals are usually pioneers and leaders. They like to set the pace. They refuse to follow others. If they do, they manage to branch off in a spectacular way, endeavoring to improve on the original idea. They believe in whatever they do. They embrace their projects body and soul, often being captivated more by the idea of the thing than any practical considerations.

These are among the natural gamblers of the Zodiac. Their faith in themselves and the future is unlimited. They are brave and courageous. They have an almost absurd disregard for physical danger. They often succeed in their ambitions through sheer audacity. They will take chances with money, reputations, and relationships that would make their more conservative colleagues shudder.

These people are impulsive and tremendously optimistic. Wishful thinking is one of their main faults. Although they have all the zest and zeal to go with their confident expectations, they frequently fail to live up to what they have promised. Being fun-loving and seeking pleasurable social pursuits, they easily get carried away by the euphoria of an occasion.

Jupiter in Aries can produce a person with strong religious beliefs. They are inclined to preach their own unorthodox doctrines to support whom they gather around them. They are not the club-joining types, but they do like to be at the center of a group or set of which they are the acknowledged leader. These people often are seized with a personal sense of mission. They slip easily into the role of crusader.

There is a certain rebelliousness in the nature of people born with Jupiter in Aries. Although usually supporters of the need for law and order, they are inclined to be against most forms of authority without necessarily having a clear idea of why.

They are great freedom lovers. Although rash and impetuous, they have a steady side that reveals itself when they are engaged in active occupations. They are at their best having to deal with moving situations. They can adapt and change direction without disturbance, and are able to make the best of whatever is happening.

JUPITER IN TAURUS

Jupiter in Taurus produces a person who usually ends up in a fairly comfortable financial position. Jupiter is the planet symbolizing expansion through material growth. Taurus is the sign of worldly accumulation and material pleasures. Together they sound a rich note.

These people may either continuously fight against or yield to extravagant urges. They have a great love of luxury and beautiful things. They are inclined to measure a person's success by his or her material possessions. They love to relax in comfort surrounded by as many symbols of the good life as possible.

Even in the tough times, these people find it very difficult to live in economical ways. They believe firmly that the highest price usually indicates the best quality, and that nothing less than the best is a good buy. They are quite capable of going without if they have to. But their last dollar is likely to be spent on a trifle. They live in style, these Jupiter in Taurus characters, or they go without.

Jupiter in Taurus individuals have fixed opinions. They believe in supporting the establishment in all its forms. They usually become businesspeople and business owners, with some of their cash always invested in real estate or other blue-chip holdings. The establishment stands for the protection of property, so why wouldn't they be all for it?

These people are not particularly imaginative. Although solidly practical and adept at making and holding onto money, they are inclined to cling to ideas and methods that have proved to be reliable. However, what they lack in originality, they make up for in their capacity for hard work.

They are patient people with strong qualities of perseverance. They can devote themselves to a project for years, as long as they are convinced that it is going to give them a good return. They do not trust much to luck, although invariably they seem to have more than their fair share of it. This probably is because they are single-minded in their aim to make money.

They are extremely good managers and are the kind who can become millionaires. They have a flair for banking, ranching, mining, construction, and merchandising operations.

Jupiter in Taurus makes a person want value for money. Although they can be charitable, they are not the types to give handouts unless the recipient is prepared to do his or her share to help themselves. They are very conscious of position and prestige. They like to be seen in the company of successful people. They are good mixers and love the social life. They always have an eye out for an influential person who may be helpful to them in the future. They are inclined to join prestigious professional and business clubs.

Undeveloped individuals born with Jupiter in Taurus can be so self-indulgent and lazy that they never amount to anything. They are inclined to live off others, to be greedy and possessive. They are not afraid of lying or deceiving those who befriend them.

There is a stubborn streak in all people with Jupiter in Taurus. They generally know what they want. They do not give up without a fight. They are particularly fond of having a fine residence, where they can entertain their prominent and socially acceptable friends, and show off their many lovely possessions.

In love, they are sincere, devoted, and possessive. They insist on giving their partners expensive gifts, especially clothes, as they want them to look as attractive as possible. They have expansive and sometimes ostentatious tastes. They have to watch their waistlines.

JUPITER IN GEMINI

Here the planet of expansion is in the sign of logical thought. Jupiter in Gemini people are big thinkers. Even the smallest, interesting idea they can swiftly escalate into a full-blown scheme. They have a good eye for detail and are amazingly adaptive, so any snags in their mental creations can be quickly changed without affecting the main plan.

The main trouble is that these people are often not practical, but they are bright. These are excellent individuals to bounce ideas off. But they need solid placements of the other planets to keep their feet on the ground.

A person born with Jupiter in Gemini believes in self-education. They are avid readers, conversationalists, and travelers. They are forever on the move mentally or physically. They love change and novelty.

These people often have a natural gift for writing. They should endeavor to develop any signs of this talent. It is possible for them to make their living from writing, or to add to their income through it. They can produce great volumes of thought, but the writing may suffer from lack of economy and control over their material.

The pressure of ideas keeps people born with Jupiter in Gemini continuously restless, so much so that it is sometimes difficult for them to stick to one activity for very long. Although they possess considerable power of expression, they lack perseverance. They need to see immediate results for what they do, or they get bored.

These people are extremely versatile. They have a continuous flow of new and wonderful ideas passing through their heads. As quickly as they start to develop one idea, another appears. They can make intellectual mountains out of molehills.

Jupiter in Gemini individuals often manage to get into the news. If they are not writing or lecturing to the public, the public often gets to talking or hearing about them.

These are usually clever and witty people. They make excellent company at social functions. They love to be the center of attention. They usually manage to keep a roomful of people amused and entertained with their stories and anecdotes.

They often have strong philosophic or religious beliefs. They tend to air these views to anyone who is prepared to listen. They usually have a remarkable knack for being able to talk about any subject at length without saying anything specific and yet keep it interesting and convincing.

Jupiter in Gemini individuals are especially suited for careers in politics and professions that require diplomacy and an air of knowledge. These people do have a way of being able to convey the most abstract ideas in simple-to-understand terms. They can make good teachers, but usually will require a greater sense of movement than instructing a class of children. The role of university professors, with its opportunities to make an impression on the highest circles, is more suitable to their style.

At their worst, Jupiter in Gemini people can become con artists or demagogues. They are not above using false claims to gain personal advantage.

Sometimes these people make lots of promises they cannot keep. Or they may get carried away with a situation and make commitments they mean wholeheartedly at the time but forget about.

Jupiter in Gemini individuals frequently waste their considerable energies and mental talents by scattering them over too many operations. They are inclined to get involved in numerous different activities, giving too little to each really to make a go of any. They always seem busy. But under the froth and bubble there may be very little of lasting value accomplished.

JUPITER IN CANCER

People born with Jupiter in Cancer usually dote on their families. They are intent on providing their loved ones with a secure and comfortable home. They are prepared to work very hard for those whom they regard as their own. They will accept all the responsibilities that go with being the head of a household. But they can be demanding in their need to be appreciated for what they do.

These are charitable people. They love to help anyone who stirs their sympathies. It would be very rare for anyone to ask for their assistance and not to receive it. They have a strong protective instinct. Once they take anyone or anything under their wing, they will see them through.

These Jupiter in Cancer people love to entertain at home. Their homes are often filled with their families, relatives, and friends. Jupiter in Cancer people may complain sometimes about all they have to do for others on the domestic front—but actually they love it. When someone leaves home, perhaps a teenager who is going out into the world, the Jupiter in Cancer person can be desolate.

Jupiter in Cancer individuals are often lucky. They have sharp financial judgment and business acumen. Often they have a talent for dealing in real estate or land and its products. Often they can guide a family into a business enterprise, in which every member has a particular job and responsibility. Acquisitiveness is frequently one of their faults. They may start by accumulating household possessions, then people, then business interests. They never seem to be able to discard things that ever have meant anything to them. In the home they can become surrounded with old and worn-out possessions.

Jupiter in Cancer people are also the type to keep on faithful employees who have served them for many years. They are loyal and grateful, even though such a demonstration of gratitude may not be in their financial interests.

These are people with heart. But they are not without their faults. Sometimes they are their own worst enemies. They love food, and can be guilty of indulgence. It is very easy for them to become overweight, even at an early age. They may have strong sexual appetites and be unable to resist fantasizing, which can cause emotional problems.

The emotions of these people are more active than their minds. They are motivated by their feelings, which are strongly conditioned by the environment of their childhood. They have a binding attachment to the past, and they love to talk and reminisce about the past. Their parents mean a great deal to them, even though they may not get along with them.

People born with Jupiter in Cancer often have a deep respect for the best traditions of society. They tend to follow the religious indoctrination of their childhood. Although often interested in philosophic questions, they are inclined to be more orthodox than exploratory, even though their personal insights can be exceptionally profound and mystically revealing.

These people have a way of influencing the public if they ever enter the business scene. Even in their immediate community environment they are likely to be among the most socially active people. They tend to support worthy causes and local charities. They will generously cook and serve for social functions. They will organize an event so that everyone has a share in the work and the praise.

Cancer is the best sign for Jupiter to be placed in at a person's birth. Jupiter, the planet of expansion and benevolence, is exalted in Cancer. This means it is at its strongest and in its most compatible sign. Cancer is the sign of home and family, so Jupiter helps one to expand and the other to multiply.

JUPITER IN LEO

Jupiter in Leo produces a person of immense optimism and self-assurance. The planet of expansion in the sign of leadership makes such individuals feel they can accomplish anything. They often appear to have tremendous egos, but usually this is accompanied by an ability to carry out much of what they claim. However, depending much on the placements of the other planets, they can also be vain, boastful, and ineffectual.

These are people with high ambitions. But they are not seeking worldly wealth or possessions. They want admiration and praise. For these they will bring all their considerable talents to bear, without a great deal of thought for the material rewards.

Jupiter in Leo people love to be in the public eye. But they have a high regard for their own importance and the need of dignity to go with it. They like to dress for the occasion; they aim to attract the maximum amount of attention, without appearing to be foolish. As they are often impulsive and childish or immature in their tastes, they can select clothes and colors that are ostentatious. It is easy for these people to be show-offs.

Leo is the sign of drama. Jupiter here expands the person's sense of theater and display. These people love to mix in the higher echelons of society. Often they manage to be among the social leaders in their communities. They like to "hold court" in these situations, gathering around them their circle of admirers and handing out any favors with royal dispensation. Leo is said to be the sign of kingship. These people can be among the last to realize the age of kings is dead.

Jupiter in Leo people are fitted for running large, established businesses, and for holding top posts in government. They are not too proud to be figureheads, if necessary. Usually they manage to bring some of their own original ideas to whatever they attempt. They are not afraid of responsibility. They can be snobbish and autocratic, inclined to lord it over the people they depend on for performing the menial tasks.

However, there is much that is noble in their natures. They are generous and compassionate. They cannot help looking on the bright side, although they often risk being too confident. They are inclined to be jovial types who enjoy parties and all kinds of pleasurable activities. They can indulge drink or food to excess.

Jupiter in Leo is a propitious placement for people engaged in artistic work. Leo is the sign of imagination and self-expression. The presence of Jupiter enlarges these capacities, and adds a quality of luck that halts the disasters these fiery and impulsive characters can bring down upon themselves.

In love, these individuals are passionate, larger than life. There is nothing they will not do for the idol of their affections. They spoil, pamper, and indulge their lovers. They like their romantic companions to be attractive and desirable to other people. Then their own feelings of pride and position are enhanced.

Jupiter in Leo people are conscientious in their efforts to help others. They are quite prepared to be served; in fact, they demand homage. But they cannot stand to see a person acting in a servile way even if he or she occupies a menial position. They have a great respect for the dignity of the human race. Sometimes they consider themselves responsible for improving or saving it. They can easily become fanatical about reforms, which they feel are necessary for their fellow man.

These people often make talented writers, musicians, painters, sculptors, and entrepreneurs—always tending to be a little more dramatic and flamboyant than the next artist. Their self-confidence makes them successful actors and actresses, with a flair for obtaining publicity that is seldom rivaled.

JUPITER IN VIRGO

People born with Jupiter in Virgo accumulate knowledge as though it were a virtue. And often, in their hands and if put to worthwhile use, it can be. But frequently these people just go on and on picking over detail after detail until everyone has lost interest except themselves.

Jupiter in Virgo produces people who can be relied upon to carry out important research, especially areas that will be helpful to mankind as a whole. There is an ability to handle an amazing amount of detail, to see patterns of significance where others may discern only stunning tedium and monotony.

These individuals possess special technical skill. Problems that have gummed up the works through overload of detail and trivia can be quickly spotted and sorted out by these highly discriminating people. They make excellent laboratory workers, time-and-motion engineers, and systems analysts.

Jupiter in Virgo people can be prolific writers and talkers. Although fairly conservative and cautious, once they feel they are on secure or familiar ground, the expansive side of their nature starts to assert itself. Their imaginings can take on fantastic proportions, with every appearance of originality. But when it comes down to the world of ordinary living, they often are unable to go beyond an almost commonplace approach.

These individuals would rather talk imaginatively than live imaginatively. They can be too materialistic, inclined to hold onto their possessions as representing the highest value in life. They are practical people as a rule, and have a great respect for order and neatness.

People with Jupiter in Virgo have to cultivate a greater sense of feeling and compassion. Of course, other planetary placements may provide the warmth of emotions. But on their own, Jupiter and Virgo can be too down-to-earth and intellectual.

It is easy for Jupiter in Virgo people to be cynics. They can put too much emphasis on the importance of formalities, and overlook the human need for spontaneity, even error. In their minds, they think they have the solution to all of life's problems if only people would listen to them.

When they do endeavor to put their thoughts into action, they are extremely good at overcoming practical difficulties. But again, the need for something more human than statistics and common sense can escape them.

These people are often drawn to the manufacturing industries. They can work with computers, machines, production lines, microcircuits—all the electronic gadgetry of modern industry. They are specialists in supplying small goods and services.

In religious outlook, people born with Jupiter in Virgo can be so skeptical that they analyze the finest teaching down to being simply words on a page. It is often beyond them even to want to see anything more than what their senses tell them.

These people often make distinguished writers. Their intellects can soar to heights that their feelings can never reach. They can lock themselves away for long stretches at a time and become lost in their own literary productions. They have a way of turning a single idea into a wonderful structure. They are the type of people who can always make the most of the materials at hand.

The minds of Jupiter in Virgo individuals are exceptionally alert and clear. They are always on the lookout to learn new things, and for opportunities to teach others. They can be painstaking in their attempts to explain the most intricate scientific theory, which, even as laypeople, they are likely to understand.

JUPITER IN LIBRA

Jupiter in Libra individuals fall over themselves to please. They are among the most socially conscious types in the Zodiac. They want to win the acceptance of others at any price. They crave for approval. They feel that they need solid external support. For this, they pin their hopes and expectations on others. They are afraid to be themselves.

But Jupiter in Libra people also are most genial and likable. They shine in the role of host or hostess. Their hospitality leaves nothing to be desired. They can be a bit lavish and certainly extravagant. But everything is always done in such good taste and with such grace that they are more often forgiven than condemned.

Libra is the sign of relationships and diplomacy. With Jupiter, the planet of expansion and excess in this sign, it is easy to understand how these people can go too far in trying to make social contacts as pleasant and harmonious as possible. They believe—and rightly so, for they are so good at it—that their effusiveness is doing a job for mankind by bringing people together.

Nevertheless, conflict does come to Jupiter in Libra individuals. Despite their best intentions, these people often find themselves in the middle of argument or strife. And they detest conflict!

But conflict is inevitable. Libra is also a sign of war as well as of peace. Alliance is Libra's strategy. It can break down, exposing the parties to battle anew. And with Jupiter in Libra, expansionist aims are freed. Trouble can come through too much of a good thing.

But again, with Jupiter's fortunate help, Jupiter in Libra individuals may slip away from relationships or situations in the nick of time. Just before conflict escalates into chaos, they escape, leaving the mess for others to clean up.

Jupiter in Libra produces a person who usually has finely balanced judgment. These people as a rule are born conciliators and judges. They are frequently found in the legal profession or in top areas of government and big business where a breadth of vision combined with an extreme delicacy of judgment are required. They can be superlatively objective. They sincerely wish to do the right thing. They are humane.

These people often carry generosity to a fault. They are inclined to give very expensive gifts. Their unconscious urge is to win approval, which means so much to them.

Jupiter in Libra individuals are humanitarians. They believe in the spirit of the law, not only the letter of it. They can be fairly orthodox in their views, but usually they strain toward the broad humanitarian outlook. They can be great fighters for the underdog. As much as they yearn for peace and harmony, they will battle against injustice with a determination that can seem quite out of character. Nothing gets their blood up more than seeing a human being treated unfairly or exploited.

Jupiter in Libra people often have to fight against an indulgent streak in themselves. They can develop such a liking for comfort and the good life that it becomes their natural expectation. They can become lazy and effete without knowing it. They can make lovely speeches and sympathetic utterances about reforms, but fail to exert themselves in any practical way to achieve these goals.

These people usually have strong artistic impulses. Their homes reflect their expensive and refined tastes. They are fond of the best in everything. They like exotic furnishings and decor, stylish clothes and cars. They are often involved in the beautifying professions.

JUPITER IN SCORPIO

Jupiter in Scorpio is a good placement. Jupiter balances some of the less likable characteristics of Scorpio, which under worse influences can turn to bitterness and poison. Jupiter in Scorpio produces a person who usually is determined to make something worthwhile of his or her life.

These individuals have a natural feeling for business and finance. They can anticipate trends. They can predict with fair accuracy the commercial conditions that will be operating in the near future. They have a breadth of vision, but it can become stuck in one frame if they do not keep updating what they have seen.

Jupiter in Scorpio people think big and build big. Money is often their most powerful tool. These people are not intent on the pleasures that money can provide. They want the power money can give them. More power to dominate their immediate surroundings and relationships is what drives them on. They know the value of money as a means to achieve this end.

These people are often attracted to occupations connected with research and investigation. They have a way of being able to get to the bottom of things. They are relentless and untiring when they are on the trail.

They make first-rate detectives, undercover agents, and psychoanalysts. As psychologists, they dig deep to root out blocks, and so help people reconstruct their lives from within. These individuals also like to be involved in converting natural resources into useful products. They make good engineers and chemists.

Jupiter in Scorpio endows a person with considerable personal magnetism. They have tremendous willpower, which makes it necessary for them to direct their energies into worthwhile projects instead of antisocial activities. They can become devoted to whatever they pursue. They have to guard against a tendency to become fanatical about their enterprises. Their self-confidence can seem almost unlimited; this may degenerate into the pride that comes before a fall.

Jupiter in Scorpio individuals are passionate. They have strong sexual and sensual urges. There is a tendency to experiment to find new ways of heightening sensations. They can be reckless in this regard, and may be tempted to use drugs and alcohol to excess.

Yet people with Jupiter in Scorpio have an extraordinary capacity for self-control. They can hide their feelings. In fact, they can repress their emotions so much that they are in danger sometimes of exploding into rages. It is a good thing if they find an associate in whom they can confide, and let off steam before it builds up into dangerous proportions.

Jupiter in Scorpio provides artistic ability. These people find art to be an outlet for their unused energies. It is through art that they can sublimate their deeper and darker emotions, and so give the world the benefit of their extraordinary insights.

Scorpio is the sign of sex and regeneration and death. Jupiter here gives a far-seeing quality. It can enable the individual to delve beyond material and physical limitations, to envision connections of soul and sense, to "see" into psychic phenomena.

There is often an avid interest in occult matters. With their talent for getting at the essence behind the appearance, these people may make a major contribution to human knowledge of the psychic world. In this way, they calm the fears of those who dread the thought of an end to mortal existence.

People with Jupiter in Scorpio are good to be with in times of crisis. They can keep their cool and risk their necks to ensure another person's safety.

JUPITER IN SAGITTARIUS

Sagittarius is a most comfortable and fortunate place for Jupiter. Here Jupiter is in its own sign. Jupiter bestows on a person the bonuses of life, the good things that come without necessarily having to be earned. In its own sign, Sagittarius, it can make the person plain lucky!

Jupiter cannot be counted on, however. It would be silly to rush into risky and daring ventures hoping that Jupiter will provide protection and success. Strangely enough, this is just what Jupiter in Sagittarius people are inclined to do. They take chances naturally, without thought.

Jupiter in Sagittarius individuals never challenge the force of their luck. They just can't help believing in it. As a result, they often land themselves in trouble. Financial and business schemes threaten. Yet they scrape through. More often than not, they get away with it.

These people usually are genial, jovial, and generous. It could be said that they have a fair amount to smile about. But they also have their fair share of strife and trouble. They just refuse to take the setbacks and difficulties too seriously. Unlike many other people, they have great faith in the future. They are prepared to cut their losses at any time, and walk away without a backward glance.

Jupiter in Sagittarius produces an interest in religion and philosophy, and an ability to see the truth. But unfortunately these people do not like to go too deep into themselves, even though they have the faculty to do so. What they see down deep in themselves they often do not like. So they do not look too often. They prefer to remain on the surface and to express surface emotions.

Such individuals are inclined to stick to orthodox religious and philosophic beliefs. They are not nearly as daring or experimental here as they are in other areas of their life. There is a type of Jupiter in Sagittarius person who is acutely self-analyzing. But such a one is rare, and probably has other planets in Scorpio.

Jupiter in Sagittarius people usually love an active outdoor life. They have an enthusiastic interest in sports and games. If not athletes themselves, they often become promoters and coaches in spectator sports.

Travel is especially stimulating to these people. They have loads of energy. They keep on the go, mentally and physically. Visiting other countries is particularly appealing. They like to live with the people and absorb their culture. Not for them the guided tour, if they can help it. These are adventurers at heart, born trailblazers.

A person with Jupiter in Sagittarius loves freedom. They do not find it easy to settle down to a nine-to-five existence or humdrum domesticity. Even though there may be planets in the fixed and cautious signs, such a person would still feel the conflict of a settled life if his or her imagination was ever excited by a picture of distant and exotic places. The freewheeling gypsy life is for such a person.

These people often end up in positions of prestige and authority despite their nonconformity. On the way up they may have envisioned and espoused all sorts of reforms that could be made if they had the chance. But on arrival at the top, they may be too busy doing other things to get around to what they once thought so necessary. They can be guilty of hypocrisy.

With Jupiter in Sagittarius, a person has a great desire to be recognized for doing the right thing. They will placate and satisfy the demands of a group rather than risk unpopularity by going the other way. However, this man or woman has a genuine desire to do good. On a personal level, he or she can always be depended on to help anyone seeking to get out of trouble.

JUPITER IN CAPRICORN

Jupiter in Capricorn produces a fairly straitlaced, prudent, and conscientious person. He or she will have a strong sense of duty. They will conduct their affairs along conventional lines with due regard for tradition. They are quietly but determinedly ambitious, and are prepared to get to the top slowly and surely.

These are people who very often end up in charge of large business corporations. They think on an expansive scale but never overlook the immediate details. They can generate the most imaginative visions and extract the fine practical nucleus, which they then set about patiently and industriously implementing.

These are not the types of people who take chances. They work strictly to the rules, so much so that they can lose any spontaneity. They can become fixed and impersonal in their dealings with other people. There is always a danger that they will overlook the human side of a situation, and insist on the letter of the law being enforced rather than the spirit of it.

Jupiter in Capricorn individuals often become wealthy. They are the kind of people who can become married to their jobs and work, spending longer hours than are really necessary with their noses to the grindstone— and enjoying every moment of it. Their diligence and perseverance seldom escape the attention of grateful superiors. So they gradually, if not spectacularly, move up to the top of the ladder.

These people do best at managing and expanding established enterprises and businesses. They can be too cautious and lacking in self-confidence to launch a venture of their own. They have the willpower and hard-working ability, but not the flexibility. They are reluctant to take chances, an attitude that so often contributes to the success of a new operation.

Jupiter in Capricorn people want to be financially secure. They are usually thrifty and self-denying. With adverse influences from other planetary placements, they can be stingy and ever-complaining. But for the most part they are prepared to spend much of their early life scrimping and scraping as necessary to reach a position of independence through wealth or authority.

Sometimes they are subject to bouts of extravagance, but not often until they achieve their goals. When and if they do amass wealth, they are the kind of people who will spend fortunes on their homes for entertaining business associates. Yet they will argue about the milk bill! They want value for their money.

Jupiter in Capricorn individuals do have genuine unselfish urges. They can be generous patrons and sponsors. But usually they support causes that have practical value. They are not too likely to sponsor purely artistic endeavors, unless this act gains for them a high degree of prestige.

It is the desire for authority and respect that can take over the lives of these people and provide them with very little joy and simple pleasure. Everything they do is likely to be measured against what people will think of them.

They cannot stand being laughed at or ridiculed. Their sense of dignity can be so inflated that it is impossible for them eventually to act naturally. Sometimes the final reward for a life given to the pursuit of their ambitions is loneliness in a room at the top.

Jupiter in Capricorn individuals can do much good in the world, as long as they do not lose sight of themselves and their needs. Their desire for love and affection is strong, but they have to learn to give both in order to receive.

JUPITER IN AQUARIUS

Soon or later, a person born with Jupiter in Aquarius is likely to give the world, or their community, an original idea that will help to bring changes for the good. Often the ideas of these people are so far ahead of the times that the ideas are not fully appreciated until the people have gone. Jupiter in Aquarius is a very good placement for people who are engaged in mental pursuits. It is ideal for politicians, social workers, idealists, and crusaders. Humanitarian considerations usually are very strong in these people. They are not frightened to criticize authority or to call for reforms on which the establishment may frown. They are often freedom fighters.

People with Jupiter in Aquarius have inventive minds. They are intuitive, imaginative, and fiercely dedicated when dealing with the rights of their fellow man. They like to live an active intellectual life that does not stop at airing their usually strong reformist views. They are prepared to practice what they preach. They will get in there when the going is tough with the followers they usually draw to them.

They are especially good at handling groups of people. They have a friendly, sociable way about them that makes other people feel at ease. They will accept people for what they are. But they will try to make people aware of any exploiting authority that is standing in the way of their full development.

Jupiter in Aquarius individuals are tolerant and just. They can devise important new theories that may be laughed at now but that will be hailed as great discoveries in the future. Their minds are always filled with new ideas clamoring for expression.

These people make better friends than marriage partners, as a rule. They are too inclined to circulate in groups, hanging around with their many acquaintances, exchanging views and ideas, and mounting the next offensive against ignorance or suppression.

These people make excellent scientists employed in such frontier fields as space technology, microelectronics, and atomic and nuclear research. They like to contribute to the welfare of society and humanity. They seldom will give their time to anything that is not associated with progress.

Jupiter in Aquarius produces people who are interested in philosophical questions. They have a deep desire to realize the higher potentialities of man. They are not materialists, although the placements of the other planets will have a considerable bearing on this. Even so, people with Jupiter in Aquarius will always be inclined to use their money to try to make the world in some way or other a better place in which to live.

With help from the other planets, these individuals may devote their entire lives to the welfare of other people. They are often to be found at the forefront of charitable and political movements. They are not the kind usually to preach revolution, as they believe in enlightened law and order. They would prefer to bring about improvements through more peaceful and conservative means than violence.

On the adverse side, they have to beware of a tendency to be erratic and unpredictable. Their theoretical schemes can be impractical. They have to be sure to set an example by action and not just become doctrinaire spokespeople.

People with Jupiter in Aquarius often collect odd characters among their friends. They are not the type to disown anyone just because he or she is unconventional.

JUPITER IN PISCES

Jupiter in Pisces individuals have a delicious sense of humor. Not the rollicking, life-of-the-party kind, but a quiet and subtle kind that ripples out and delights the soul. They are great observers of life, almost painfully aware of its cruel reality and yet ecstatic at times with the beauty they feel around them. These are optimistic, understanding, and charitable people.

They also have periods of gloom and deep introspection. They oscillate for much of the time between highs and lows. They are always trying to fit their individual observation and experience of life into a broad and comprehensive pattern, one that possibly would explain the mystery once and for all. They are always looking for answers that they never manage to find.

These people are often religious or have a deep interest in philosophic questions. But they are not theorists in their ideas of good. They have a strong feeling to serve others who are less fortunate, or at least to reduce their pain and misery.

They are generous to others, both in their time and with their money. They have a great amount of patience and understanding. They will listen to another person pour out their heart with a genuine sympathy that seldom fails to provide a measure of relief. These individuals born with Jupiter in Pisces can easily become devoted to a life of charitable works.

However, they enjoy the good life, too. Although there is always a touch of the saint or the martyr in them, if they are blessed with worldly wealth and possessions, they know how to enjoy them. They may at times retreat into themselves or into some sabbatical isolation, but they manage to come out smiling and eager for the next round.

Jupiter in Pisces people are fairly easygoing. They can take life as it comes. But they do not like pressure and uncongenial people or situations. These they will flee from. They use money, but they are not hungry for it. They will not work for long hours for peanuts, saving for their old age. They want to live, either delving into humanity's feelings and suffering, or getting about mixing and experiencing.

They love to get back to nature at times. They have a need to surrender themselves to simplicity. Periods spent among beautiful scenery, especially near the water, can act as a tonic to their health. These people love change. They frequently will spend as much time as possible between two homes or bases if they can afford it.

Usually, people born with Jupiter in Pisces are fairly lucky. Because of their fluctuating emotions, they often are impulsive and do things spontaneously they are likely to regret the next day. Sometimes they can even wonder how they possibly could make such a move. Naturally, some of these decisions involve money, and they often lose it. But their fortunes are frequently restored.

They can be extravagant. Their imagination knows no bounds. They are easily influenced and can be drawn into speculative ventures that would best be left alone. They have great faith in the future, so much so that they often are inclined to sit back and do nothing.

Jupiter in Pisces individuals are given to daydreaming. They live more in their emotions than in their minds. They can be very difficult to pin down. Their schemes are often unrealistic or impractical. Yet they frequently get brilliant ideas that can make them and their associates a lot of money.

Saturn in the Signs

Saturn is the planet of responsibility. Its quality is restraint. Saturn represents the power of limitation and discipline.

Saturn is the taskmaster of the Zodiac. It is cold, depressing, limiting, anxious, fearful, and conservative. At its worst it is repressive, possessive, selfish, envious, grasping, miserly, and grudging.

Saturn is the seventh and the last of the personal planets. The last three planets out from Saturn—Uranus, Neptune, and Pluto—are known as the spiritual planets. Because they take so long to traverse the Solar System, their influence mainly is expressed through eras, ages, generations. There is a tremendous gap in solar space between Saturn, which represents the outer skin of man, and the orbit of Uranus, the first spiritual planet.

Saturn, too, is very far away from the sun. So it represents all that is suppressive and least desirable to warmth-loving man. It symbolizes the bony skeleton, which keeps him upright yet is the most enduring and rigid part of the body.

Being the last personal planet from the Sun, Saturn stands at the gate to the heavens, the barrier that man has to cross to reach his final reward. Through the trials and tribulations its energy inflicts on man, Saturn provides the necessary discipline.

Saturn is the sober balance in man. It keeps in check the exuberance of the Sun, the optimism of Jupiter, the luxuriousness of Venus, the fertility of the Moon, the fire of Mars, the frivolity of Mercury. If any expectation can be spoiled, Saturn will do it. Saturn teaches us to control our passions, excitement, and enthusiasm. What the other planets give, Saturn tests.

Whereas Jupiter teaches man to be philosophical and hopeful in the bad times, Saturn teaches that there is no such thing as hope. The individual must patiently accept his lot without thought of escape. Saturn instructs the hard way, through despair and surrender. Jupiter instructs through hope and faith in the future.

Saturn is the main cause of delays and obstructions, all that drags on and complicates. Saturn turns shortcuts into long hauls, mistakes into misery. Saturn weakens the constitution, causes nervous depression, colds, arthritis, and skin diseases. It is the planetary force that blemishes beauty, reduces self-indulgent wealth to poverty or wretchedness, destroys the selfish family clique, turns self-satisfaction into self-disgust.

But when Saturn's lessons have been learned—and not one day before—the surly old planet known as Father Time and the Grim Reaper will give individuals their just rewards. These can exceed anything ever hoped for!

Saturn makes a person conscientious and industrious. There is a thoroughness, which often makes any job a little harder. But the responsibility and care shown often will attract the favorable attention of people in authority, so that position and standing are consistently advanced.

Saturn helps people to work well under pressure, but creates a dislike of change. It provides a strict public sense of right and wrong, which sometimes can be a bit puritanical. Saturn helps people to keep secrets and to give practical advice.

A weak Saturn makes a person pessimistic, fearful, slow-witted. Such individuals are inclined to miss opportunities through dithering or fear of change and progress. They can be self-pitying, backbiting, critical killjoys.

Saturn is favorably situated in Capricorn and Aquarius, the signs it rules.

SATURN IN ARIES

Saturn in Aries is not an easy placement. This person will often be at war with himself or herself. The planet of restraint in the sign of initiative and adventure gives an underlying feeling of frustration. The nature cannot be satisfactorily expressed. People may want to act, yet suppress themselves, or realize that the time is wrong for making a certain move, but find themselves doing it all the same.

Saturn in Aries does produce a person who is extremely self-reliant. They will press on indomitably in the face of all hardships and obstacles. They are likely to be too proud or afraid of being ridiculed or laughed at to ask for help. These are people who appear to have an iron will.

There is a strong sense of duty here. Saturn in Aries individuals are hard on themselves and also expect a lot of others. It is easy for these people to become disciplinarians if they have any authority. It is the sort of stressful placement that may be found in the chart of a straw boss, a drill sergeant, or a relentless servant.

These people have to avoid strain. Although they generally have great reserves of energy, they are likely to spend their lives trying too hard. Much of their exertions are likely to be due to correcting moves made at the wrong time. Their sense of timing is not strategic.

Saturn in Aries individuals are not easy to please. Often life for them consists of one obstacle after another. They surmount them, though. But doing so gets them into the habit of expecting the worst and being protectively aggressive. They can resort to authoritarian ways to compensate for their own inner frustrations.

In spite of these problems, people born with Saturn in Aries often succeed in the end. They are so persistent and persevering that they tend to wear down and exhaust the opposing forces. They are strong characters. These people have to avoid being jealous. They may be inclined to be too guarded toward their loved ones, especially to their children when they are teenagers. Their domestic rule may need to be tempered with a bit more understanding of other people's need for freedom. Often these individuals have had to contend with a harsh or demanding parent, possibly a father, in their childhood. If so, in dealing with their children they should endeavor to remember their own unhappy experiences.

Saturn in Aries is not an influence that adds to a person's sociability. In fact, it induces a tendency to be retiring and watchfully aloof. There is a great need to be respected by others. And it can be felt that any softening of behavior or attitudes may be interpreted as a sign of weakness. These people are not the type to forgive any insult or slight, particularly if it is made in public.

Saturn in Aries can produce a certain puritanical outlook. There is a strong desire to be known for doing the accepted thing. Laws and rules may be the guiding principle. Mainly such order is used as a defense or protection against the person's own spontaneity, of which they are mistrustful. They would like to be spontaneous, but cannot bear the thought of the uncertainty it produces.

These people like to know exactly where they are going. But frequently they misjudge a situation, acting when they should not and not acting when they should. Within themselves they are likely to be a playground of emotional contradictions. These may be revealed through irritability and sudden explosions of temper.

Saturn in Aries individuals need to cultivate the habit of self-sacrifice.

SATURN IN TAURUS

Here are the makings of a very solid citizen. Saturn in Taurus people will want a good hold on the earth. Money and material possessions will mean a great deal to them. They will love saving up, putting the pennies side by side where they can watch the little mounds grow every week. This is not to say they are miserly. They are just careful, frugal, and almost fanatical about security.

Saturn, a psychologically weighty planet, is not uncomfortable in Taurus. Taurus is the sign of material wealth. And Saturn gives an even greater determination to the character to amass whatever wealth is possible, without taking any risks.

These people are not afraid of hard work. They realize that there is only one sure way of keeping the wolf from the door. They are not interested in taking shortcuts to riches. They know that there is no such thing as a free lunch. They are not interested in speculative and risky ventures. A bird in the hand is all they want. And they will gradually build their own aviary of security with patience and good, honest sweat.

Not surprisingly, Saturn in Taurus individuals often have a long haul on the way up, and frequently a difficult one. But in the end they usually win out. Their achievements do not have to be great to satisfy their desires. They possess a fondness for beautiful things, the more practical the better, but not the usual Taurus love of luxury. This, of course, will depend on whether the individual has any other planets in Taurus.

Saturn in Taurus is conducive to a purposeful personality. The tendency is to fix an overriding aim—probably to be economically independent—then butt for it. These individuals lower the head like a working bull, butt and plod resolutely toward the aim, come what may. These are not people to be deflected easily once they have made up their minds. In fact, they can become so fixed in their ideas and their way of life that they fall into a rut and seldom get out of it.

Stubbornness is one of their main faults. They can be very difficult people to live with if they do not learn the art of compromise. They also can lack spontaneity, being always inclined to follow the same old routine. These are people who can easily endure a nine-to-five existence and a fairly uneventful domestic life as long as they do not have to worry about tomorrow.

Saturn in Taurus individuals are often too cautious. Although they have a flair for handling finance and other business affairs, they often wait too long weighing the pros and cons and so miss opportunities. They would rather be slow and sure. So they will shrug off lost chances as being all for the best in the long run.

They have to avoid being possessive and avaricious. They can be inclined to live by material values, judging other people by their apparent wealth or possessions. They enjoy their homes and endeavor to make them as comfortable as possible without overdoing it.

Saturn in Taurus individuals like to entertain intimate friends, but are not too enthusiastic about public appearances. There their self-image may be challenged.

These people have due respect for law and order. They believe in tradition. They stick to tried and trusted ways. They believe in a good day's work for a good day's pay. They are conservative in their views and not particularly adventurous.

In love, they know what they want and they are prepared to wait for the right person to come along. They will have their affairs, but very seldom get carried away.

As parents, Saturn in Taurus individuals have to be careful not to become too exacting. They may confuse prudence with prudishness.

SATURN IN GEMINI

Saturn in Gemini? Unimaginably good! Saturn is the taskmaster planet of the Zodiac and usually means some hard lines for the individual in whatever sign it is placed. But Gemini is one of the best positions for this weighty influence to get tucked away in. Gemini normally is a flighty, scatterbrained sign, giving agility and restlessness of mind. Saturns tones all this down. People born with Saturn in Gemini are serious, orderly thinkers. They can at time become a bit gloomy and depressed, being inclined to concentrate on minor probtems, which they can magnify into alarming proportions. They should not take their problems or themselves so seriously.

These people often make good scholars. Their disciplined way of thinking fits them for occupations in science and research. They are able to make precise comparisons and measurements. They are extremely good critics. They often find an outlet for their need to communicate at a serious level in teaching, where challenge and controversy are not frowned on.

They have a rather stern air about them that does not encourage banter or tomfoolery. Their minds are cautious and calculating, usually one jump ahead in anticipating what would be advantageous personally in any developing situation.

Saturn in Gemini individuals love to gather facts. They usually are avid readers. They enjoy serious conversations, but spend a lot of their time summing up the other person. One might, at times, get the feeling of being alone and talking alone in the presence of these studiously silent creatures.

Usually they have a talent for writing. They choose their words with great care. They are inclined to write about important and controversial current issues in politics, the law, and perhaps even religion. Specific interests will depend on the placements of the Sun and Jupiter.

Saturn in Gemini people do suffer from lack of confidence. They may at times not say what they mean for fear of being ridiculed or made to look a fool. They can be very thin-skinned about their intellectual abilities. They may take offense when none was intended.

At times, they are impulsive. Words jump out of their mouth, for which they are immediately sorry. They are inclined to be critical of their own mental efforts, and yet resent anyone else's criticism.

These people prefer to use their minds rather than move around a great deal physically. They like to get where they are going fast, though, then start concentrating on the job in hand. They travel more in the line of duty than for pleasure.

Saturn in Gemini often brings problems concerning relatives or neighbors. There can be tedious responsibilities connected with brothers or sisters. The health of other people can interfere with the daily routine of these individuals.

It often is difficult for Saturn in Gemini people to make decisions. Their minds are more peaceful when they are following a set line of inquiry. They make good secretaries, clerks, and office managers where routine is firmly established. They are very good at writing reports; they put great emphasis on reaching correct conclusions. They like to take their time, so they can be as thorough as possible.

But Saturn in Gmini individuals may lack application. Under the slightest strain or threat, they may lose their ability to concentrate. They can be quickly irritated in such situations, and so become quarrelsome or sink into sullen silence.

People born with Saturn in Gemini often grow into polished and accomplished speakers. The years seldom fail to add an attractive maturity to the speaking and writing ability. They have a remarkable power of observation, which they can convert into successful books and articles for publication. Quite often they possess a good sense of humor, which belies their serious outlook.

SATURN IN CANCER

Saturn in Cancer can bring the moody blues. Cancer for mood, Saturn for gloom. Yet the essential dignity of both Cancer and Saturn can help the individual rise above all manner of problems and deceits, which all too often are produced when Saturn is in Cancer.

People born with Saturn in Cancer often have to contend with troublesome domestic conditions. Their childhood may have been disrupted by a broken marriage or the death or illness of one of their parents. Or a dominant parent may have instilled such a sense of self-discipline that they never really recover their buoyancy.

However, these are people who do their very best to make their homes run smoothly and orderly. They may not receive all the respect and appreciation from their families that they feel are due to them for their efforts. But they are individuals who will conscientiously work on, aware that the world is not a very thankful place.

Saturn in Cancer folk take all their responsibilities very seriously. And they worry about the slightest thing affecting the home or any member of the family. They feel it is their task to look after everyone. They are inclined to be a bit authoritarian. They will complain if others do not give a hand— and also if they do.

Sometimes these people feel inadequate in coping with home and family affairs. They can become sorry for themselves and feel like giving up. They never get enough recognition at the fact they are doing a good job and would be sadly missed.

It is not easy for Saturn in Cancer individuals to express their emotions. They care tremendously for their loved ones, but may never feel they can express this adequately. They can become depressed. It is especially important for these people in partnership to have a harmonious sexual relationship. It is through physical contact that they are best able to release their feelings and communicate the love they feel.

Despite love and tenderness from others, Saturn in Cancer people are not particularly tolerant. They have to cultivate a more sympathetic attitude if they hope to attract the kind of affection they feel they need so much. They can be too acquisitive and protective of their worldly possessions.

The homes of these people are often cluttered with old things. They find it difficult to discard anything that has an important connection with the past. They are likely to keep childhood souvenirs and toys well into their old age. They love to reminisce about the good old days, which probably were not so good at all.

These people do not like physical change. They seldom move home if they have any say about it. But frequently they are forced to move, and it takes them lots of time to settle in again.

A person born with Saturn in Cancer has to find a good reason for living to be happy. They have much to give. Often they find it difficult to discover something worthwhile and satisfying to absorb their energies. They are too self-absorbed for their own good. They have to learn to take a greater interest in the world around them.

These people have a natural ability for controlling affairs connected with the public welfare. This gift offers scope for their executive abilities. It particularly addresses their need to feel they are doing some good for others.

When occupied in a task that appeals to them, Saturn in Cancer individuals are tremendous workers. They have great powers of perseverance. They are tenacious in the pursuits of their goals. They have to be careful how they handle others, as they can be bossy and too opinionated.

These people need constant reassurance that they are needed. If they feel their efforts are unappreciated, they are likely to lose interest very quickly. They can fall back into a state of inactivity and self-pity, the moody blues being their only memory of the good life.

SATURN IN LEO

Saturn in Leo banks the fires, but keeps the coals glowing embers. Neither heat nor light nor matter is extinguished, just kept on a slow burner, a low flame. Every now and then is a sputter and burst, evidence that something is cooking.

The Saturn in Leo individual has strong qualities of leadership and an equally strong sense of moral responsibility. They tend to take themselves very seriously. They consider that they have the answer to many of the world's problems. And they are prepared to wait patiently until the public discovers how much their leadership is needed.

In other words, they have big ideas about themselves. It's justified! If given the opportunity, they frequently are capable of exercising authority on a large scale and in constructive ways. People born with Saturn in Leo can become powerful figures in government and politics. They have an inspired way of getting to the kernel of a problem, of cutting through personal considerations and inhibitions to reveal what *has* to be done.

If what *has* to be done is unpalatable to others but necessary to the welfare of an organization or a community, they are just the people to put efficiency first. They make first-rate administrators, businessmen, and businesswomen.

However, Saturn in Leo individuals do have a touch of the dictator in them. Discipline is something they understand, and they regard it as essential to any successful operation requiring people to work together. They are not individuals who believe in loose-knit, easygoing working arrangements. Although the position of the other planets will have a strong modifying influence, these people by nature tend to be aloof. Staying apart from the gang allows them to nurture the big ideas.

They have a keen sense of dignity. They feel that to let their hair down and join in beyond a certain point is to jeopardize the respect and prestige they demand and crave. Usually they are respected, but not for the reasons they may assume. Their coworkers and subordinates cannot help but admire their conscientiousness and hard-working ability.

At a party, the Saturn in Leo person is likely to be found in serious conversation on the sidelines, but always at the center of what's important. Having a good time is not likely to be the main object as far as they are concerned. Business can always be mixed with pleasure to make pleasure more pleasurable!

Close associations are not their forte, and intimate associates are few. They have trouble expressing their emotions freely. They prefer to bottle them up. This serves a dual purpose: protection and control. They will, though, adopt a compensatory façade of seemingly tolerant authority. This pose can become a dominant facet of their personality.

People born with Saturn in Leo can be badly misunderstood in love. Inside they have much affection to give. And they need love, perhaps even more than some other types. But their unbending attitude can give a potential lover the wrong impression that they are cool and calculating.

It is especially important for these individuals as parents to remember their own inner feelings and frustrations. In this way, they can be loving and tender to their children. If they are too demanding of children "for their own good," they can pass on the capacity for inhibition and frustration. Insisting on disciplined behavior can undermine a youngster's spontaneity.

Also, parents who have children with Saturn in Leo should make a point of emphasizing the togetherness and warmth of the family circle. These children should not be loaded too heavily or too early with responsibilities, which they may appear precociously willing and able to undertake. Parents must remember that these children take obligations gravely. Other children can throw them off when they feel like it, but not these children.

SATURN IN VIRGO

Saturn, the planet of restriction, makes life just a bit harder wherever it appears in a sign. But here in Virgo, its solid earthiness blends with the natural characteristics of the sign. A person with Saturn in Virgo will be practical and have a good deal of common sense.

This placement bestows mental stability. There is seldom any flightiness in these people. In fact, they can be overly concerned most of the time with the impression they are making on others, having an innate fear of appearing foolish. They can be very self-conscious, even bashful. But Saturn in Virgo individuals are not prudish, merely prudent.

Saturn in Virgo people often are very good with words. Although they may not like to become involved in public debates, once they are sure of their ground, they can express themselves with great clarity and penetration. They are often drawn to literary pursuits and are capable of working for long hours in isolation. They are the types who can produce books that are regarded as making a major contribution to solving society's problems.

Saturn in Virgo individuals are not particularly humanitarian folk, though. Personally they can lack feeling and the ability to communicate affection and love. But their minds are discriminating. They can analyze situations with tremendous precision, being especially attentive to detail. In this way, they often describe the ills of society, and come up with practical solutions or systems for dealing with them. These people often are involved in occupations connected with diet, health, and sanitation. Virgo is the sign of work, and develops the "perfect" employee who is conscientious and receives his or her satisfaction from being able to do a good job. Saturn, the planet of perseverance, improves on the scheme. Here is an even more dogged and industrious individual. However, there are some drawbacks. Although these people generally have a high regard for the prevailing moral code, they can carry their esteem too far and become narrow-minded and puritanical. Admirable uprightness can be turned into rigidity. They have to be careful to keep in touch with their fellow creatures. They must not lock themselves away, either in their minds through the rigidity of their opinions, or in their lifestyle, following a hermit's existence.

Saturn in Virgo individuals must beware of becoming so involved in their work that the lighter side of life and its pleasures become a bore. They can suffer down moods, depression. They have to keep active to prevent themselves from brooding on their anxieties. They are individuals who can worry over anything or nothing.

But the thing that upsets these people most is uncertainty or the unknown. Saturn in Virgo individuals need to know where they are going. They like to have the constant reassurance of material security.

However, people with Saturn in Virgo often are motivated to produce great accomplishments through their fears of insecurity. They are inclined to be more successful in later life, probably because they spend their earlier years in hard and concentrated effort, ignoring the opportunities to gamble or take a chance.

It is not unusual for Saturn in Virgo to generate hypochondria in its subjects. These people are inclined to be fastidious about their diet. If any complaint is going around, they imagine they will catch the ailment. Often they can worry so much that they suffer from digestive problems, and so bring on the chronic discomfort they dread so much.

Saturn in Virgo people can be critical. They can get on their associates' nerves by always carping about the faults they see in others. They also can be suspicious, constantly looking for the catch or the con. They need to cultivate self-confidence and a belief in other people.

A bit of faith and a lot of love for themselves and for humanity can go a long way toward making Saturn in Virgo individuals the true protectors of earthy values and rewards.

SATURN IN LIBRA

Saturn in Libra is a sobering and regularizing influence. It helps individuals strive to maintain balance in their life and their relationships. They are very much aware of the need to do the right thing. They are not going to risk upsetting the applecart in any way by their own foolish actions, if they can help it. They know how easy it is to bring trouble down on themselves. Yet they often manage to do just that.

How well Saturn works in Libra, the sign of partners and partnership, will depend on how well developed is the individual's sense of sharing. If individuals tend to be selfish and inconsiderate because of other planetary placements, they are in for some depressing circumstances in their relationships.

But if they have managed to learn the lessons of sharing and the values of harmony and togetherness, they can make this a constructive placement. They will practice a bit of self-denial.

As a rule, Saturn in Libra people are honorable. They manage their affairs with neatness and orderliness. They believe in the golden rule, honesty in marriage, integrity in business and social relationships. They can be sticklers for good form. They are inclined to frown strongly on anyone who is too demonstrative or showy.

In this lies a danger of their being intolerant. They are so intent on keeping their affairs on a solid equilibrium, they may begin to resent anything that is discordant with their own judgments and feelings. They have to learn to live and let live, especially in the little things.

Saturn in Libra people do have a tendency to become opinionated. They are particular about their style of dress; they have good taste. They have a liking for objects of art, which they may feel makes them an expert, at least a connoisseur.

They also have to guard against insincerity. Saturn in Libra individuals have an almost painful need to be accepted by others, especially at the social level. To gain this kind of treatment they may use guile and flattery. These people often encounter their own faults in their associates, especially in marriage partners. Until they have mastered these shortcomings in themselves, they have to put up with some disturbing relationships.

People born with Saturn in Libra often flourish in the legal profession. They possess extraordinarily good judgment and an ability to maintain impartiality. They make fair-minded administrators and executives. A scientific career also suits them.

Libra is the sign of art, color, and harmony. Saturn provides a realistic approach to these largely Venusian activities, which ordinarily can attract dabblers and arty types who are more interested in the show than the showing. People with Saturn in Libra have a no-nonsense approach to their creative enterprises. They take firm control of their projects, and work methodically toward worthwhile objectives.

People with less weighty planets in Libra are often flirtatious and flighty. They are inclined to have numerous affairs, not because they are so sensual but out of their sense of romance and search for the ideal of love. Saturn in Libra individuals are more realistic. They are inclined to settle for the best partner they can find without looking for the impossible.

These people like to regularize their relationships. Although they may have their share of love affairs, they like to make them lawful by marrying or avoiding involvements with people who are already attached. They are firm believers in equal rights, provided their other planetary placements are favorable.

SATURN IN SCORPIO

Saturn in Scorpio can be a scalding combination—for the individual as well as for their close associates. But it can be a teaching influence. With Saturn in Scorpio comes the test of endurance. The individual can learn to control angry emotions and the destructive side of his or her nature. Much will depend also on the placements of the other planets; no one placement can ever be taken to represent the whole person.

Saturn in Scorpio individuals have a tremendous ability to stick to their aim. They can be relentless in the pursuit of their ambitions. Once they decide they want something, or to achieve something, they are prepared to undergo unbelievable hardships to get there.

They are exacting, cold, and calculating. They can use people to attain their own ends. They possess a talent for being able to sum people up in an instant, and especially to identify their weak points, which they then concentrate on. They can be very dangerous enemies.

These people, unless they have some strongly modifying planets elsewhere, never forget an insult. They tend to hold grudges for as long as it takes them to get even. One of the unfortunate things is that they often imagine slights and insults where none was intended. They find it very difficult to accept criticism. They can be excruciatingly thin-skinned and touchy.

It is not easy for people with Saturn in Scorpio to change their opinions. Inflexibility is one of their main faults. It often prevents them from making the success of their lives that their skills and determination would otherwise have made possible. They can be one of the most stubborn people in the Zodiac.

These individuals are intensely secretive. Their reserved exterior always conceals great emotional activity. One of their problems is that they will not allow their inner feelings any latitude or release. They are constantly in the grip of their own cool reserve. If and when they ever do release their emotions, it is usually in the form of an explosion. They have violent tempers because of this.

Saturn in Scorpio individuals can be strongly sexual. They emit a magnetism that either repels or attracts. Their pride and aloofness can act like a lure to curious members of the opposite sex. They are not the kind of people to flirt with. They mean business. And they will not play around for long.

These are highly sensitive people. In love, their passions are fixed and enduring. But they are difficult types to get away from. They tend to play for keeps. Their jealousy can amount almost to mania, and may engender cruelty.

Although intensely proud, these are not as a rule vain people. They are too hardheaded to allow themselves such an indulgence, which they regard as a weakness. They have a great talent for being able to get to the bottom of things, to see through façades and pretensions, and to solve mysteries.

People born with Saturn in Scorpio are deep and devious. They often prefer the cat-and-mouse game to the straightforward deal. They are masters at intrigue. They make good detectives, secret agents, and psychologists. They can be counted on to track down the problem or the person.

These people have considerable executive ability. They can stay cool in a crisis, and marshal the forces at their disposal. They do not lose their nerve, even when faced with imminent disaster.

SATURN IN SAGITTARIUS

Sagittarius is a bounding, forward-looking, enthusiastic sign, which can easily go to extremes. The weighty and restricting planet Saturn in this position tones all that down. Saturn in Sagittarius produces a person who is well balanced and has a lot to give to the world in the way of natural wisdom.

These people often go a long way in business. They are extremely ambitious and farsighted. They tend to work toward distant goals, which they have firmly visualized so that slipups are reduced as much as possible. Although idealistic, they keep their feet on the ground. Their plans are imaginative but practical.

Saturn in Sagittarius individuals are genial types. They enjoy getting around and meeting people, especially when it involves the possibility of making a few bucks. They prefer to mix business with pleasure and pleasure with profit.

Saturn in Sagittarius is conducive to meditation and a serious inner search for the meaning of life. They are not the kind of people who display their religious or philosophic efforts, but they often are renowned among their friends and associates as being fairly wise. If the placements of the other planets are not helpful, however, these people can spend a lot of time boring their friends by moralizing, believing they are helping others to finding a better way of life.

These are persistent people. They appreciate that their objectives may take a long time to reach. But they compensate for this by the scope of their plans, which often lead them to considerable success and possibly wealth in their later years. It is important for people with this placement to know what they want early in life and to work toward it.

Saturn in Sagittarius gives people a fear of personal restriction. They must always feel that they are going ahead. To be in a bottleneck creates tremendous inner frustrations. Such a buildup of energy can explode into a violent loss of temper.

There are times in which these people show a lack of restraint. The serious side of their nature seems to be put aside, and they can break out into seemingly uncharacteristic behavior. They can be impulsive one moment, deliberate the next. They have to avoid getting into a stop-and-go routine.

The typical Saturn in Sagittarius individual tries to be open and frank. But frequently their dread of being criticized or publicly ridiculed can prevent them from saying all that they think. They are individuals who are very much aware of other people's pain and problems. They try to be kind and compassionate.

It is usually in the later years, after these people have made a success of their lives, that they tend to take up some philanthropic activity. They may be financial patrons to struggling but practical artists and innovators. They admire people with new and workable ideas. They also may become leading members of community and charity groups, especially those sponsored by a religious organization. These are independent people. They cannot stand relationships in which emotional demands are made on them. They are quite prepared to accept their responsibilities, but only those that they themselves select and recognize. They have to avoid a tendency to be cynical. Unless the other planets are favorably placed, they can be destructively critical of other people's ideas. They also can cling to outdated concepts and try to force these on their work and business associates.

In love, Saturn in Sagittarius individuals are inclined to look for a reliable partner rather than be carried away by romantic dreams.

SATURN IN CAPRICORN

This is a very strong placement, for Saturn is the ruler of Capricorn. Saturn in Capricorn provides a person with great ability to persevere to the bitter, or sweet, end in whatever life objectives they set themselves.

But the trouble is that Saturn in Capricorn can make the person very materialistic, even grasping. Much depends on the placement of the Sun and the other planets. However, if the ambitions are directed and channeled along constructive and satisfying lines, this is one of the most helpful influences for an individual.

Saturn in Capricorn people may take some time in their early years to work out exactly what they want to do. It is important for them always to keep their options open while they are in this period. They should try to avoid getting settled into a dull, nine-to-five routine that offers nothing in the end or in between.

The tendency is for Saturn in Capricorn people to get into ruts. They can be inclined to take the easy way out when there is nothing special on the scene, and to sink farther and farther into a drudge routine. This may not seem so bad to them, for they are quite capable of putting up with the most difficult as well as the most boring conditions once they get used to them. But their lives can slip away from them.

Saturn in Capricorn individuals have great organizing ability. They need to be in an occupation that stretches their capabilities. Then they can discover for themselves just what they can do. They can be something like a precious stone that remains hidden in the land because no one recognizes it.

These people can be successful in business, especially in controlling large corporations, including international conglomerates. Their minds are able to retain a great amount of detail connected with various simultaneous operations. They do not waste their time or effort. They plan and aim at taking as few chances as possible. They are cautious, economical, and practical. They believe in hard work. They never fail to set an example to their associates and subordinates that is difficult to emulate.

Saturn in Capricorn individuals have great respect for the law of cause and effect. They realize that as a man sows so he reaps. There is a depth of practical wisdom in these people that often induces others to seek their advice in worldly matters. But it must be remembered Saturn in Capricorn usually matures the individual in the latter half of life. Earlier the person may not seem to be very sure of where he or she is going. It also is inclined to bring some difficult times, which have to be patiently worked through.

One of the dangers of Saturn in Capricorn is that the person may tend to live for work. They can become so immersed in earning a living, or fulfilling their ambitions, that they have no time for other activities, especially relaxation. The loved ones of Saturn in Capricorn people have to make sure that they take their vacations and get regular exercise on the golf course or the tennis court.

These people often have a flair for writing. They can become the authors of serious and respected works, which may be regarded almost as a final authority on a subject. They can put complex ideas into simple words. This placement is also conducive to a career in science or mathematics as well as teaching.

People born with Saturn in Capricorn are often said to be success-prone, due, not in the least, to their relentless dedication to the job at hand.

SATURN IN AQUARIUS

Saturn in Aquarius individuals can do a lot of good in the world. They are not selfish types. They have high humanitarian ideals. Sooner or later they are bound to be involved in some kind of activity that makes the world, or their community, a better place to live in.

Saturn in Aquarius individuals have a knack for being objective. They can stand back from a problem and discern solutions. They do not allow personal considerations to interfere with their judgments. They look for the broader effects that their decisions will have. They can be regarded as being a bit cool and detached as far as the individual is concerned.

These people have a compulsive desire to do away with exploitive or pretentious authority. They do not like the idea of people having to kowtow to bureaucracy and officialdom, which really get their power from the masses. Although they are cautious and deliberate in their considerations, deep within the psyche of these people is a revolutionary trying to get out.

The typical Saturn in Aquarius individual has a scientific mind. Although original and inventive, they are not the types to try to rush ahead without proper preparations. They have a pronounced ability for understanding basic principles. And even in everyday life their discernment is often valuable enough for their friends and associates to seek their counsel.

These are people who generally have an admirable indifference to personal fame and success. Like the scientist who is dedicated to the task of finding the solution to a problem without worrying about who is going to get the kudos, these people can be oblivious to their own entitlement to reward. They usually gravitate to an occupation that they feel in some way or other serves the greater interests of humanity.

This indifference to success can often be infuriating for their loved ones. Saturn in Aquarius individuals are not the easiest people to live with. Although friendly and easygoing, they are inclined to put more importance on their group and altruistic activities than on family relationships. They cannot as a rule stand emotional demands being made on them.

One of their faults is they can be mentally obstinate. Once they get an idea fixed in their head, it is usually there to stay until they see it through or until experience teaches them otherwise. They also can impose their opinions on others. They have an intensity of presence, which can be a bit overpowering for people who enjoy the lighter side of life. Saturn in Aquarius folk usually have serious projects on their mind.

These are subtle people. Their intellects are finely developed. They are quick to observe the lay of the land, whether they are dealing with a person or with a situation. They also are highly intuitive.

Sometimes these people seem to lack initiative. Depending on the placements of the other planets, they may be inclined to espouse their reformative schemes loudly, but when the time comes for action, they are missing. There is a tendency to be perverse, to go in the opposite direction from everyone else, especially from established authority.

It is not unusual for Saturn in Aquarius people to court trouble. If they become involved in public agitations, they might run up against the law or get drawn into legal actions. These can be the kind that drag on interminably or are fought from court to court.

These individuals have to be careful that their zeal does not become fanaticism and ruin all their good work.

As a rule, Saturn in Aquarius people manage to keep a good balance in their lives, especially once they have found a worthwhile vocation into which to pour their talents.

SATURN IN PISCES

Saturn in Pisces is a sensitive placement and not such an easy one. It represents the coming together of the material and the immaterial. One side of the nature wants to give all, and the other side wants to hold back. Sometimes people with Saturn in Pisces despair that they will ever be able to reach their goals. Yet if they can persevere, it is almost certain that they will.

However, Saturn in Pisces is not a placement that allows for many shortcuts. Achievement has to be earned.

Saturn in Pisces individuals usually possess artistic and creative abilities, which they should strive to formulate. Too often they feel the urge to create, but do not get around to making a practical effort. They can bewail their inability to find some suitable outlet for their sensibilities when all they need to do is sit down and try.

These people are sympathetic and compassionate. They usually are drawn to an occupation that brings them in contact with people who are underprivileged or in need of help or care. They can make other people's lives happier by their sheer ability to listen and understand their problems. People with Saturn in Pisces often lack courage and self-reliance. They are inclined to be self-pitying and evasive. They may wallow in their emotions. They can be moody and forever blaming others for their own shortcomings. Or they project their fears onto others, and so have an excuse for not trying.

Although extremely sensitive and understanding, they can be cruelly inconsiderate of their loved ones when they are under the pressure of their own emotions. They can make unbelievable demands and fly into tantrums if they are not filled to their self-indulgent satisfaction. Although perceptive of the truth most of the time, they can in their moodiness seem deliberately to avoid seeing it.

Saturn in Pisces individuals can become recluses. These are people who in their worst moments can dislike and even hate humanity. Yet in their more heightened perceptions, they can make great self-sacrifices on humanity's behalf. They are often found working in hospitals and institutions. The more psychologically evolved type is prepared to do the most menial tasks in the service of those for whom they feel compassion.

Sometimes these people can be drawn to renounce material existence. This is an extreme action, and it will be indicated also in the placements of the other planets. But Saturn in Pisces is a combination that is always in danger of running to extremes.

The need to be alone is usually very strong at times. And yet at the same time there can be a morbid fear of isolation.

These people's sufferings are also often due to others. Although they bring much upon themselves with their fluctuating moods, they are often the rather innocent bystander who gets caught up in a chaotic stream of events started by someone else.

Saturn in Pisces individuals can have a good head for business. Their ideas for making money are often brilliant. Although they find it difficult to cope with the ordinary pressures of life, in business they can play a very cool game. They can push a transaction to the limit without batting an eye or revealing the personal uncertainty they may be feeling.

Saturn in Pisces individuals may lack self-confidence. If so, they can become very dependent on the people who love them. But in their more positive moments they have much to give.

Uranus in the Signs

U ranus is the surprise packet, the anything-can-happen planet, the unexpected and eccentric force of the Zodiac. It brings drastic change and is related to science, revolution, and independence. All this is not surprising when the events that followed the planet's discovery in 1781 are considered.

The American Revolution ended to launch what was to become the most technologically advanced nation on Earth in less than two hundred years. The first hot-air balloon flights were made (1783). The power loom was invented, heralding the Industrial Revolution. The French Revolution and the Napoleonic Wars changed the face of Europe. Britain abolished the slave trade (1807). The United States abolished slavery (1863). The first railway operated. Steamships crossed the Atlantic. Electricity, the telephone, and telegraph illuminated and shrunk the world. Antiseptic surgery eased humanity's pain. Then the airplane, radio, television, nuclear power, and space travel defied even more unimaginable limits of the natural world. And all during the nineteenth and twentieth centuries, wars of liberation spread like wildfire from one part of the globe to another.

So the discovery of Uranus marked the beginning of the scientific age and the ages of independence and liberation, fostering a brilliant succession of ideas, discoveries, and inventions, and the brilliant, often eccentric individuals who produced them.

Even the physical characteristics of Uranus are eccentric. It has peculiar markings visible through telescopes. Its axis of rotation is so tipped that it lies almost in the plane of its orbit around the Sun. So it seems to rotate on its side as it revolves around the Sun.

Also, its revolutionary path is eccentric. It was noticed by observers that Uranus didn't follow the path predicted for it. Uranus wobbles along on an irregular orbit around the Sun, slowing down and speeding up. What could cause Uranus to move in such a strange way?

Characteristic of its association with genius, invention, and discovery, the peculiar motion of Uranus itself was used to make a brilliant discovery. Two astronomers, working independently on the peculiar motion of Uranus, and using only mathematics—not observing the planet—found the answer. They suggested the presence of another planet, unknown at the time (1843–46), causing Uranus to wobble.

In 1846 astronomers sighted this new planet just where the mathematicians said it might be, and it was named Neptune. (Neptune's "hidden" presence certainly earns it the designation of planet of mystery!) But back to Uranus

Uranus takes eighty-four years to complete an orbit around the Sun, which the Earth manages in one year. This means that Uranus spends an average of seven years in each sign. But here again, Uranus refuses to conform! Due to the eccentricity of its orbit—it wobbles off path—it may spend as many as thirteen years in a sign!

The quality Uranus imparts to a person or a generation is its originality. It stands for all that is inventive, transforming, and disruptive. The planet is treated by traditional astrologers as being "malefic"—that is, it does not contribute to the peace of mind of a person. Uranus does bring unforeseeable and unalterable changes in life, but these may turn out for the better.

Just as the Uranus force in recent history has disrupted the established patterns of nations and societies, its effect is to upset the attitudes and opinions of the individual so he or she can start afresh.

Uranus is the spark of genius that often makes the brilliant person seem odd. It is unconventional, a breakaway force, which refuses to behave in established ways. Whatever sign Uranus is in at the time of birth, the lifestyle of the person will be somewhat different, a bit erratic in relation to those matters.

Uranus is more than just imaginative. It is eccentric, even nuclear, and seems to bring the blinding flash of inspiration that makes the inventor, the scientist, or the ordinary person exclaim, "Eureka!"

Uranus is an emotionally detached energy that circulates. The individual will tend to move among a wide circle of friends and acquaintances, without allowing any relationship to become too close. While the Moon and Venus tend to form cloying associations based on sentiment and erotic notions, Uranus always keeps its distance. It is concerned with the wider and broader issues that will advance the welfare of humanity as a whole, rather than personal attachments or preferences.

Uranus can provide a ripping urge for freedom, even a rip-roaring one such as opened up the American West. It is an energy that can make a person or a nation suddenly discard heartfelt traditions in favor of independence and individual expression.

Uranus is the force behind radical political movements, reforms, crusades, and worthy causes. Sometimes, though, the energy becomes too free and independent. Fanatical zeal may set the scene for dictatorships and anarchy.

Uranus can express its energy negatively in antisocial actions and in sexual perversions. Being an emotional force of nervous and mental origin, it focuses on idea and action rather than on value or consequence. Uranus is said to rule the sex glands. The sexual side of this planet's influence is more pronounced when the planet transits Scorpio (1975–81).

Uranus is especially strong in the sign of Aquarius, which it rules together with Saturn.

URANUS IN ARIES

Uranus in Aries introduces into the character an erratic and impulsive influence. These people need to learn to think twice. They should try not to act on their first impulse. The spontaneousness of Aries, the first sign of the Zodiac, can become nerve-racking unpredictability under the added stimulation of Uranus.

These are fiercely independent people. They are proud that they make a point of never bowing to anyone. They have indeflatable self-confidence. They are not the kind of person who ever asks for help if this can possibly be avoided. And then the request is likely to be made in such a way that it appears they are doing the other person the favor!

Uranus in Aries individuals are leaders. Whether asked to or not, they will usually jump into the front rank. They either will be trailblazing or haranguing a mob. They combine physical with intellectual courage.

Often these people are drawn to a political career. They are far from diplomatic, but they are experts at rough-and-tumble. They can think quickly when under attack. Instinctively they anticipate their opponent's next move. But due to their impetuous nature, they can often make the most silly blunders. It is usually only in maturity that they learn to curb this side of their nature.

Uranus in Aries people love to get involved in crusades and reforms. They are the types who may be found at the head of protest marches and demonstrations. They often champion radical changes that bring them into conflict with the ruling establishment. They are the revolutionary pioneers.

These are physically daring and adventurous people. They love meeting challenges. Once their mind is made up, they are indomitable. At least they think and act as though they are. The best of them are troubleshooters.

The less evolved type of person with Uranus in Aries tends to be intolerant and unscrupulous. They may be rabble-rousers and troublemakers. They get the thrill of power from leading gangs of inferior-minded individuals.

Uranus in Aries individuals are often responsible for new ideas and changes that mark the beginning of new epochs. Sometimes their schemes are so original that they spend their lives fighting to get them accepted. Sometimes the acceptance comes long after the individuals have gone.

Ordinarily, Uranus in Aries people do not dwell on their failures. They are not the types to cry over spilled milk. In their lives, they spill quite a few gallons with their harebrained schemes and impulsive actions. But they seldom fail to add something to the progress of the world.

These people sometimes have explosive tempers. They have little time for those who do not agree with their views and plans. They tend to gather around them groups of supporters, many of whom have ideas just as odd or unusual as their own.

Uranus in Aries individuals like to destroy sacred cows. They seem to make it a mission of their life to pull down any vulnerable authority. They believe wholeheartedly in personal freedom, especially the kind that they espouse.

Uranus in Aries confers a great deal of enthusiasm. Any project that catches the individual's fancy is embraced with great gusto. There is an impatience for results, the quicker the better. Details are often overlooked, preparations neglected. Sudden changes in direction may be made. For their own good, Uranus in Aries people have to cultivate a sense of caution. The fires of their zeal, fanned by the currents of change, can all too easily consume their good works.

URANUS IN TAURUS

Uranus in Taurus is a solid but at times sensitive placement from the material point of view. It provides a person with a flair for discovering new ways of making money or adding to their assets. Their ideas may be far-out, perhaps ahead of their times, but they get results. So Uranus in Taurus people should not get into the habit of dismissing their ideas, which is a possibility for the more retiring types with this placement.

Taurus is a fixed and conservative sign. It does not provide any fondness for taking chances; it is unadventurous. But Uranus is the planet of flashing inspiration. All that is new and inventive it embraces. The contradictions that this placement can induce in a person are obvious. But if individuals know the ingredients in their nature, they will have a better chance of turning them into positive value.

Uranus in Taurus people have to be prepared for sudden eventualities. They are likely to undergo some radical changes in their lives. They may win a fortune or lose a fortune. Even if their life follows a fairly orderly pattern, they will have distinct periods of ups and downs in their finances.

They will often have a yearning for more comfort. They may move house more frequently than other people do, always in an effort to improve their accommodations and surroundings. They do not really like packing up and leaving familiar places and people. But it is an urge they may find hard to resist. These people may horrify themselves at times at the things they do on the spur of the moment.

Uranus in Taurus individuals often get drawn into big business. They have a way with finance, which tends to attract the attention of people who have money to invest. As long as the other planetary placements of the individual do not exaggerate the unconventionality of Uranus, they can do well as builders, farmers, bankers, industrialists, civil servants, auctioneers, economists, and architects.

Uranus in Taurus people also have a sense of art, beauty, and harmony. And they tend to bring new ideas into any projects connected with traditional forms and functions. All they have to be careful of is that their ideas are practical. Fortunately, Taurus is a down-to-earth sign, which will help to keep the fancy but sometimes erratic feet of Uranus firmly on the ground.

Individuals with Uranus in Taurus can be terribly stubborn. Once they get an idea in their head, it is usually there to stay. They can even be fanatical about their schemes. And such may range from reforming the banking system to revolutionizing the holding and protection of property. They can do a lot more talking and advocating than getting down to action.

It is not unusual for some people with Uranus in Taurus to be singers or sculptors. They endeavor to bring art into the world in practical ways. They may also have a gift for writing. These people work well with others. Although they are independent, they enjoy being a member of a team working toward an objective that is of benefit to mankind as a whole. As well as looking after their own interests and security, they like to feel their efforts also are helping others. Scientific research may attract them.

Uranus in Taurus individuals often gather around them some odd companions. These associates are not always good for them. More often than not, their kooky pals land them in difficult situations. They are very loyal to their friends, though, and will believe nothing bad about them. They will support a mate in trouble through thick and thin.

Uranus in Taurus folk have a love of nature. They have a frequent urge to throw off their impediments and get back to the simple life. But usually this is far easier felt than done. They really like to be involved in the here and now of the world. When the time for retiring arrives, their mood has probably changed.

URANUS IN GEMINI

Uranus in Gemini can produce a person with a touch of genius about them. But like all those with a highly developed mental potential, they can be eccentric. Sometimes these people are so far ahead of the times in their thinking that they appear to be dotty. Yet an ungrateful world or community may end up employing the very ideas that were scorned—after the person has left the scene.

These people are especially well suited to a career in science, particularly those branches associated with electronics, computers, and space technology. Their minds are seldom still. They are always working out something.

These individuals like to concern themselves with the problems of humanity. They are at their happiest pitting their mental faculties against the ignorance and pretensions of fad, fashion, and controversy—especially the foolishness of authority, which they will attack with a vengeance.

Uranus in Gemini individuals love to be always on the move. They are very inquisitive people. They spend a great deal of time on the telephone. They are likely to pop in on their friends and associates at any time of the day or night. They do not believe in conventional restraints. People have to take them or leave them. They make friends very easily, and can get away with unorthodox conduct that would not be tolerated in others.

These individuals are great freedom lovers. It is not so easy for them to hold down a steady job as a result. They are impulsive and tend to say exactly what they think. Their love of independence makes it difficult for them to conform. However, if these people are employed in work that gives them ample opportunity to express their creative and inspirational talents, they can be very happy—and irreplaceable.

Anyone with Uranus in Gemini will have within them a fondness for the unusual. They may satisfy this by reading or through writing. Their imaginations are extremely inventive. They can make topnotch science-fiction authors. They are ingenious and devious and fantastic. These people are also very persuasive. They are the types who can make inspired speeches that rally public support. But usually their ideas appeal to a minority. They are more concerned with reforms in the community than bulwarking it. They seek changes that have not been discerned by the majority. Often they have to contend with fierce opposition to their beliefs.

Uranus in Gemini is an agitated placement. Of course, the placements of the other planets and especially the Sun will have a considerable modifying effect. Nevertheless, Uranus in Gemini is a mental placement, and its agitation and restlessness may be hidden under more obvious physical and emotional influences. But those tendencies will be there.

Uranus in Gemini is inclined to make a person irritable and nervy. The flow of ideas keeps them in their head most of the time. They can be very restless. They find it difficult to relax unless they have something totally absorbing to attend to.

These people also are easily discontented unless they find occupations that are to their liking. They may change their jobs frequently. Or they may endavor to become self-employed so they can be their own boss.

They do not take easily to authority, but they do take to novel ideas. Trends are the patterns Uranus in Gemini individuals have discovered long before they are accepted as such. Frontiers of intellectual change are their battlefields.

Sudden changes in their personal lives are something that people born with Uranus in Gemini often have to contend with. Sometimes their education is interrupted in their youth. They may leave school early or be forced by domestic moves to change from one school to another. Relatives may be prominent in their early upbringing.

These people have to choose their friends with more discretion. They certainly can become involved in dubious company. The less mature Uranus in Gemini individuals may find it impossible to stick to any kind of routine. Concentration can be very difficult. Distractions take them away from the pursuit of frontier thinking that can so benefit their generation.

URANUS IN CANCER

People born with Uranus in Cancer usually make a point of equipping their home with the very latest appliances. They believe in making life as easy as possible by the use of modern gadgetry. They usually have inventive minds. Although possessing a deep respect for the achievements of the past, they are always on the lookout for something new.

Uranus in Cancer individuals have very active imaginations. They have to guard against allowing their imaginings to assume fantastic proportions. They can easily get carried away into a world of unreality. In the young or immature type, daydreaming can be a substitute for work and action.

These are people with strong instincts. They can live on their nerves and emotions. They have to guard against a tendency to get upset about every little thing. Worry and uncertainty tend to affect their digestion. They are extrmely sensitive people. They like to be surrounded by their loved ones, whom they cherish very dearly. Yet they often yearn to be alone and to be free of their responsibilities and obligations. They can have an almost love-hate relationship with some family members, appreciating their attentive concern one moment and resisting it the next.

People with Uranus in Cancer take a great interest in their domestic affairs. They would like to work at home. Sometimes they are drawn to a literary occupation, which enables them eventually to do this. But usually they spend a good bit of their lives trying to find out what they really want to do.

They are often found in advertising and business. They are unobtrusive types as a rule. They have a way of influencing the public through their writings and unusual ideas. They work very well with groups of people. They are artistic.

One of the most impressive things about people born with Uranus in Cancer is their intuitive insights. They are very impressionable to psychic influences. Their emotions often color their thoughts.

In love, they are romantics although they do not like to be tied down. They can express themselves with a good deal of Old World charm, which makes them attractive to older people. They tend to be protective of their loved ones and to expect them to do as they say.

Uranus in Cancer folk are patriotic people. But they will not support any national policy that tends to exploit others. They believe in equality and the freedom of the individual to choose what political system he or she wants to live under. They can be inconsistent, tending to lay down the law themselves and to oppose others who do the same thing.

They are the types of people who are attracted to fighting lost causes. They are deeply affected by injustice. They have many progressive political ideas, but can be too attached to their local community scene to get out and give the wider world the benefit of their views.

Also, these people can be a bit lazy. They need to be strongly motivated to get beyond the talking and haranguing stage. They are inclined to leave the hard physical work to others. They are often restless and inclined to chase rainbows.

Uranus in Cancer individuals can be touchy and thin-skinned. The less developed type may be moody and bad-tempered. If the other planets are unfavorably placed, it is easy for these people to be untidy around the house. They may not take much care with their personal appearance. They can be domineering.

Women are often important influences in the lives of Uranus in Cancer people—for good and otherwise.

URANUS IN LEO

Uranus in Leo is conducive to a personality who loves the drama and theater of life. There is something of the showperson about them. They aim to create an effect in whatever they do. They are especially interested in putting their ideas across to large groups of people.

These people can be true revolutionaries. They may aim to bring down any kind of establishment or authority they consider to be a threat to freedom. The trouble is, however, they are likely to be guided by their own judgments alone and to ignore the opinions of others.

Uranus in Leo peqple can be dictatorial. If given the chance, they may be inclined to replace one tyranny with another of their own making. They are often extremists.

Uranus in Leo individuals do not do things by halves. When they become involved in a project, it is usually a total commitment. They generally reserve their enthusiasm for enterprises that they imagine will be helpful to their fellow man. The fact that they regard themselves as the natural leader of any group they affiliate with often causes resentment and ill feeling, and involves them in power struggles.

Even so, these people do have the will to command. They are not as selfish and egocentric as they may appear. As a rule, they genuinely want to improve the lot of people by making them more aware of the dangers of authority. It is one of their inconsistencies that they are prepared to overlook or ignore their own vulnerability to being similarly accused.

Uranus in Leo individuals have pride and passion. They are not afraid to give orders and to stand by them. They are prepared to mete out any punishment that may be necessary in their position as leader. They have the courage of their convictions.

But much of the time of these people is given to making speeches and airing their views. They depend a lot on their ability to sway others into supporting their schemes. They do this by the written as well as the spoken word. They are often first-rate writers and powerful speakers.

Uranus in Leo people like to get down to the grass roots. In positions of command, they are the types who will sleep with their troops. They believe strongly that all power stems from the masses. They are usually popular and magnetic.

Uranus in Leo individuals have a love of pleasure. They enjoy being at the center of a night's entertainment. They like to be admired and praised. They can easily go to excess. They are impulsive and inclined to be erratic. Much will depend on the placements of the other planets, especially the Sun.

These are people with considerable organizing ability. They have a sense of style and ceremony that can appeal to the crowd. They also make good teachers and instructors. They have a way with young people, who tend to trust and admire them. They are proud of their accomplishments.

Uranus in Leo people also are among the most stubborn in the Zodiac. They hate to admit that they are wrong. They will usually find a good excuse for any failures.

The lives of Uranus in Leo individuals often undergo radical changes. It is difficult for them to keep on a straight course for long. They tend to court disaster, or at least the unfavorable attention of those in power.

Often, their revolutionary activities are directed toward scientific achievements. These are the kind of people who inspired the conquest of space. They also were responsible for much of the new technology without which space exploration would have been impossible.

URANUS IN VIRGO

People with Uranus in Virgo usually have a deeper than normal interest in health and hygiene. Although this interest is expressed in keeping themselves fit and clean, they also desire to make the world a less toxic place in which to live. They are inclined to frown on noxious pesticides, industrial pollutants, and the addition of unnecessary artificial ingredients to processed foods.

Much depends on the favorable placements of the other planets, for if these are adverse, these same people can go the other way. They may be the very ones who create or are responsible for similar problems, which they may be endeavoring to eliminate in another area. Uranus in Virgo is not consistent.

These people can be analytical scientists, the types who introduce chemical and other devices to clean up the place, and actually make it worse. In their zeal—either in their private lives or in their professional capacities—they can upset the natural balance.

Uranus in Virgo individuals are extremely discriminating. They can mentally dissect a problem down to the finest of details. They are unconsciously motivated by a desire for purification and perfection. They have to be careful not to go to extremes. Their concern, once they get a bee in their bonnet, can be more of a nuisance than the problem they are trying to solve.

These people do have some brilliant ideas from time to time, particularly connected with solving work and production problems. This is not so surprising, as Virgo is the sign of work and service, and Uranus is the planet of invention and progress. Uranus in Virgo folk like to get their teeth into a knotty project, especially one that tests their ingenuity.

Although mentally active and discerning, these are as a rule cautious people. They like to remain on the outskirts of the crowd, observing everything that is happening but not drawing attention to themselves.

Uranus in Virgo individuals can be truly detached. They can be counted on not to take sides on an issue or in a dispute. They are inclined always to want to do the best job possible, without worrying too much about personal reward or fame.

These people are genuinely interested in helping mankind to live a fuller existence, with less dependence on external authority. They are not the revolutionary type. But they tend to feel that man has within him the potential for perfection. If he can find this, it is all the authority he really needs. As was said, Uranus in Virgo people are perfectionists.

They can also be dogmatic. With the support of other planets, they can believe that their ideas are the only correct ones. To ignore them means disaster, or at least lack of progress, for everyone. They are inclined to analyze every little thing and to erect intellectual structures that may not stand up well in the light of experience.

They also can be contrary. They may take an opposite stand to anyone they do not like, even if they secretly support their opinions. They can be very sharp-tongued and critical. It is not easy for these people to resist telling others what they should or should not be doing. And the infuriating thing about this habit is that they are very often correct.

Uranus in Virgo people mean well, but often are misunderstood. Unless the placements of the other planets give warmth and affection, they can be a bit lacking in human feeling and compassion. They may be too intellectual, and not emotional enough to enjoy truly the fruits of their works.

URANUS IN LIBRA

Uranus in Libra strives for grace under pressure. These are people with delicately balanced temperaments and minds. It does not take much to upset their equilibrium. They are easily distracted, and quick to take up new interests before older ones have been fully pursued or absorbed. They can be fickle.

This is not an unfavorable placement for Uranus, the planet of invention and inspiration. But it needs some solid practical support from the other planetary placements, particularly the Sun.

Libra is a mentally active sign. The presence here of the planet of brilliant insights, and sudden changes can upset the scales. The person can lose poise through agitation, and become eccentric in his or her ideas.

Libra gives artistic inclinations, and Uranus adds the innovative touch, which can produce progressive changes in style and form of art. These people can establish trends in art. Although they may be vogues and not long-lasting, these new forms will make a contribution to the general evolution of creative expression.

With support from the other planets, especially the Sun, Uranus in Libra individuals are the types who can easily influence groups of people, especially artists. They can be teachers or lecturers. They can begin new movements in the arts, which others may build into schools of thought that will radically change attitudes and perspectives.

However, these people often can create chaos around them. Although compulsively committed to trying to harmonize their relationships and surroundings, often they have the opposite effect. People are inclined to polarize under their influence. Libras' efforts often force people to split into camps of differing opinions.

Libra is the sign of peace—and also war. It endeavors to maintain harmony by cooperativeness. But as the whole world knows, you cannot please everyone. An unenlightened attempt will generate antagonism and friction. Uranus in Libra heightens the desire to bring peace though the written and spoken word regardless of whom the message addresses.

These are people who believe in freedom. They cannot stand any authority that exploits or oppresses mankind. They have very strong humanitarian instincts. As much as they love harmony, when their indignation at injustice is aroused they will fight to the bitter end for their principles.

Uranus in Libra individuals have to avoid stop-and-start activity. They should endeavor to follow through whatever they begin. Unless their deeper feelings are involved, which may not be very often, they are inclined to be fitful in their efforts. The need of novelty and change can lead to restlessness. Without strong support from the other planets, they can become easily discontented.

Uranus in Libra individuals can have a high turnover of friends. They can be a bit disloyal, shedding yesterday's friends for more interesting ones found today. They do not have deep attachments to people. They love to move from group to group. They are inclined to cultivate friends who are high on the social register, or who have money. Immature individuals with Uranus in Libra do not have an easy love life. Their romantic affairs are characterized by many changes, some of which can have drastic results. They can be involved in divorces and other lawsuits. The erratic and unpredictable actions of partners can force radical changes in their lives. There is likely to be an attraction to fashion. It is easy for these people to give the lead to a new dress style. But they also can go to extremes and experiment with way-out costumes and gear. They are the lost leaders of a current era.

Uranus in Libra is conducive to unusual unions and partnerships, both of the emotional and business kind. These people are highly tolerant of the most unconventional views and ideas. They often are stimulated by being in the company of eccentrics, and can take such far-out views a stage farther to displays or limited productions.

URANUS IN SCORPIO

Uranus in Scorpio embraces the spectrum of idea and emotion, intellectuality, and spirituality. Or this placement can seek the extreme, cutting off one way of sensing and knowing in favor of another. Uranus in Scorpio is a most decisive placement.

Scorpio is a masterful sign with great power. When Uranus, the planet of inspiration and deviation, drops into this slot at a person's birth, the results can be very good for the world at large—or very bad. This person can easily go to extremes. They can use their penetrating minds to help their fellow man, or to make his life a misery.

They are especially suited for scientific occupations. They are inventive and mechanical-minded. They have great powers of concentration. They have a sixth sense, which informs them when there is a coverup or a puzzle at the bottom of a problem. They love difficult investigations in which an important discovery might be made.

These individuals can pour over problems night and day, making infinitesimal progress but never giving up. In the laboratories of the world, such people have been responsible for some of man's most progressive and curative discoveries.

The undeveloped individual with Uranus in Scorpio can turn to crime. Much will depend on the placements of the other planets. These people can be ruthless. Once they put their minds to anything, they never give up. They are especially sensitive to criticism, and are inclined to look for insults. They do not show their feelings. And they do not forgive or forget an affront.

These people also have a heightened sensitivity and search for ways to explore sensuality. They may be drawn to experimentation, always endeavoring to reach higher intensities of feeling. They should be careful not to use drugs and alcohol to excess.

Uranus in Scorpio individuals are tenacious to a fault. They can be very obstinate. Once they make up their minds, they are not easily shifted. They can easily be unreasonable, feeling that they alone have the right answers. People with Uranus in Scorpio are often attracted to working in groups. Although rather secretive and aloof, they appreciate that many minds are needed to make the greatest progress in any endeavor. Even so, they always tend to regard their own views as the essential ones. These are very self-sufficient people. They have great mental stamina. They are not easily swayed. They are quite prepared to undergo any kind of trial for the sake of the principles in which they believe. They cannot be brainwashed. But they are the types who can brainwash others, and not worry about any niceties in the process. In extreme cases, they can be guilty of mental cruelty.

Uranus in Scorpio people often are very interested in metaphysics and the occult. They have an ability to discover psychic realities, or to expose pretenders. Their minds are sharply penetrative and can see through delusion.

Yet they can be self-delusive. This arises from their tendency to be compartment thinkers, refusing to see that one compartment often is the antithesis of another.

These are realists, however, when it comes to dealing with the world. They appreciate strength and are disdainful of weakness. They try to influence their associates with pressure if more subtle methods are not successful.

Although straightforward in giving their views on worldly matters, they are wily people with a great sensitivity for intrigue. It is difficult ever to be sure whether they have an ulterior motive. However, when they are straight, they are straight. And they make undeviating supporters once they have committed themselves.

Uranus in Scorpio individuals have to beware of losing their temper. They impose considerable mental pressures on themselves by not sharing their thoughts with others. Continuous suppression of this kind leads to a buildup of energy, which eventually has to break out, often quite violently.

URANUS IN SAGITTARIUS

Uranus in Sagittarius individuals as a rule have a highly developed social consciousness. They would truly like to see Utopia come to earth. They have a sense of vision that is often prophetic. But frequently their wonderful ideas and insights are too far ahead of the times to be taken seriously. Sometimes they may even have to grin and bear it while latecomers receive the credit for ideas they had earlier expressed.

These people are often excitable. They find it very difficult to remain in one place for long, either physically or mentally. They usually pursue a course that leads them from place to place, from idea to idea, or from person to person. They are not very stable types.

There is, however, a strong desire to see the world become a more moral and orderly place. Although these people may espouse what seem to be revolutionary doctrines, they are at heart conventionalists. They want to demolish in order to restore—not the old structures but the old ideas of goodness and justice. These people tend to believe wholeheartedly in the golden rule of how one person should treat another. They have a great deal of energy. They love to get caught up in reform movements and causes in which they believe. As younger people they often can be found out front in protest marches and demonstrations. They are not afraid of a fight or a challenge.

Uranus in Sagittarius endows a person with a great love and respect for freedom. They cannot tolerate any authority that tries to brainwash its populace with foolish or bigoted propaganda. It is this that makes these basically law-supporting people often appear to be anarchists. Their high-founded motives can be easily misunderstood.

The Uranus in Sagittarius individual is often too independent-minded to accept the tenets of orthodox religion. They often tend to develop a philosophy of life for themselves that they then try to pass on to their associates. They have to be careful not to become too fanatical in their views, or they may be accused of trying to set up some kind of authority of their own.

The less developed Uranus in Sagittarius individuals can be reckless in their social experiments. They may fail to give sufficient thought to the schemes in which they involve others. They can be irresponsible and immature.

These people enjoy travel, especially to other countries. If they do not get the chance to travel, they are inclined to read about foreign places. They are inclined to write about their experiences and can become successful authors and journalists.

Uranus in Sagittarius makes a person keenly aware of the benefits of education. But they prefer an educational system that does not put too much emphasis on books. They believe people learn more quickly by doing and example. They do their best to live up to what they preach.

In love, Uranus in Sagittarius does not endow a person with a great amount of feeling or emotion. Such people are inclined to take love as it comes, but not to get too deeply involved. In fact, these individuals can be marriage-shy. They are too aware of their need for intellectual and physical freedom to roam where they please. They won't compromise without a fight.

These are generous people. They will seldom turn down a request for help from a friend. They have a wide circle of acquaintances, who usually number a good proportion of people with eccentric ideas.

URANUS IN CAPRICORN

Uranus in Capricorn is valuable for people intent on fulfilling their ambitions. It is especially helpful to business and political aspirations. It gives shrewdness and a sense of mission.

The minds of these people work very swiftly where finances are concerned. They have a way of spotting opportunities for making money in even the most commonplace situations. They are especially aware of the necessity for teamwork. They try to give everyone with whom they are involved in an enterprise a fair shake.

However, the urge to succeed in life can be very strong. Uranus in Capricorn people can be grinds. They also imagine themselves to be indispensable. They may refuse to take a break or a vacation in their desire to get a job finished. The trouble is that their lives can become completely dedicated to work. Everything else, including their closest relationships, can fail to get developed.

It is extremely important for Uranus in Capricorn individuals to keep a balance in their lives. They must try to relax and not allow their responsibilities to take them over. Without the modifying support of other planets, especially the Sun, they can become too far removed from the pleasures of life.

These people have great powers of perseverance. Anything they put their minds to they will see through to the end. Uranus, the planet of sudden change and inspiration, helps to break down the earthiness of Capricorn and introduces a greater flexibility of mind. Practicality is assisted by showers of often brilliant ideas. And a tendency to plod along in a rut is interrupted by sudden changes of direction, either self-initiated or enforced.

There is not such a fear of change and experimentation as Capricorn usually imposes. Uranus in Capricorn people are more inclined to move with the times. They can insist that organizations and subordinates do the same.

This is the kind of person who can head a very large company or corporation. They have the kind of mind that can keep up with experts in any of the many departments under their control. They encourage progressive thinking. They like to be surrounded by the latest business machines and electronic gadgetry as long as these make a contribution to efficiency.

When they do gain positions of authority, Uranus in Capricorn people treat their staff fairly. Uranus in Capricorn are not the type to encourage close personal relationships. But they do believe in a friendly and congenial atmosphere.

They can lay down the law when they want to. But usually their authority is understood without their having to make any drastic demonstrations. They have the knack of remaining aloof without being distant. Employees respect them, especially for their willingness and ability to perform the work they expect of others.

As employers, they are fair and just. They have a strong regard for the independence of others. They insist on being kept informed, but are prepared to allow a worker to use his or her initiative. They are willing to listen to advice, although they may not take it.

Uranus in Capricorn individuals often have to put up with a succession of major changes in childhood. They may move house or school many times. There can be disruptions in domestic affairs that they may never quite get over.

It is easy for them to become acquisitive if they do not marry or avoid close relationships. They have to cultivate the ability to express their feelings and emotions. They must avoid putting off making close personal contacts, as this tendency can become habitual.

URANUS IN AQUARIUS

Uranus, the planet of originality, inspiration, and independence, posited in its own sign of Aquarius at birth produces a person who is bound to be a progressive thinker. Although the placements of the other planets, especially the Sun, will have a determining influence on the overall character, this person will have a lively intelligence. How he or she uses it is the big question.

People with Uranus in Aquarius sometimes appear to be odd to more conservative types of thinkers. Uranus in Aquarius individuals do not follow accepted norms. They are for progress and reform. They believe change is best accomplished by changing people's ideas.

Their thinking can go to extremes. Once they get an idea in their head that they believe will benefit the community or the world as a whole, they will not abandon it lightly. They are often humanitarians and reformers. They tend to discern social and political problems long before others do. They advocate changes that even the people who would benefit do not fully comprehend. Their ideas can often be so far ahead of the times that they can be dismissed as eccentrics.

Uranus in Aquarius individuals have strong wills. They are likely to pit their ideas against even the strongest established conventions without worrying about the consequences to themselves if they feel that what they are doing is right. The trouble is, if other planetary placements are not favorable, they can become fanatical or their judgment may be faulty. They can propose unrealistic and even damaging reforms that would create more strife and hardship than they were trying to eradicate.

Uranus in Aquarius people can be perverse. They are the types who may oppose any proposal at all just for the sake of taking an opposite stand and hearing their own ideas being expressed. They can alienate their friends and supporters by taking too hard a line on issues. As would-be leaders of public opinion, they are often their own worst enemies.

There is a touch of the revolutionary deep down in all people born with Uranus in Aquarius. The important thing is for them to recognize this and to be selective as to which causes they champion. They can do a lot of good, as they have a powerful ability for influencing others, either through the spoken or the written word. They make topnotch politicians, writers, broadcasters, psychologists, and publishers.

These people often can appear to be a bit cool. They are detached emotionally from the people with whom they deal. They are more concerned with the welfare and goings-on of groups than of individual people. They are not the types who will put up with any emotional demands being made on them. They can be quite sharp and even rude to people who try to get too close to them.

However, when the other planetary lineups are favorable, Uranus in Aquarius individuals are friendly and easy to get along with. They have artistic tendencies, which should be developed as much as possible to compensate for their strong mental inclinations. They need to be in touch with their emotions and finer feelings.

These people are often attracted to work in the sciences. They like to feel that in whatever way they earn their living they are contributing to the overall progress of mankind. They are often in the forefront of important medical discoveries. Space research, physics, and electronics often provide suitable mediums for their inventive minds. They are not sentimental types, as a rule. They prefer to deal in facts more than feelings. They believe in freedom for everyone, even though sometimes they have not managed to think through the ramifications of what they are proposing.

URANUS IN PISCES

People with Uranus in Pisces have to find something to do with their active minds. They need to be productive and to feel they are doing some good, for humanity as a whole or for some one in particular. They can too easily drift into an uncertain existence in which their minds may turn in on themselves, producing self-pity and vague fears.

Uranus is the planet of scientific discovery, invention, and progress. Pisces is the sign of compassion, tears, emotions, and mystical and religious impulses. They are almost opposites. The two influences can work very well together in any occupation that endeavors to serve others who are less fortunate through scientific or compassionate means.

These people have extremely vivid imaginations. Their spiritual insights are sometimes remarkable. From the scientific point of view they may receive flashes of inspiration that can solve problems that have long troubled mankind. Even in business, they have a knack for coming up with unusual ideas for making money.

The problem is they can be dilatory. They may do nothing about their good ideas. They can be too dependent on others to do the work. They may sit back and think that it is enough for them just to come up with the schemes. Also, these people can be very impractical. For every worthwhile suggestion there may be a dozen that are unworkable.

Uranus in Pisces individuals have a tendency to daydream. If they feel they are under pressure, they are inclined to slip into an imaginative world of their own making. They are so easily disillusioned with life that they can become terribly sorry for themselves.

These people have an ability for self-sacrifice. They are especially good at working in hospitals and other institutions where their understanding natures can give much solace to the sick or underprivileged.

They make very good teachers of children, especially at the infant and kindergarten stage. They can comfort as well as instruct. They are often drawn to work in orphanages. Their inventive minds can make life easier for the handicapped; they are very good at dreaming up new ways of doing things.

Uranus in Pisces people often have psychic powers. Their intuition is often remarkable. They also are likely to be interested in occult subjects. They may make first-rate astrologers. This is a placement that destroys materialism. These individuals are inclined to put humane considerations before others.

They love to be with other people. They are sociable and often are to be found taking part in group activities. They have artistic leanings, which can make them affiliate with painting, sculpting, and handicraft groups. But they do tend to sink into reflective moods and to need to get away on their own. They are the types of people who can take up yoga and meditation seriously. They are able to combine mind and body, which makes them sometimes gifted dancers. However, their will can be uncoordinated. They may take up a pastime and quickly tire of it.

These are not as a rule ambitious people, unless the placements of the other planets give that kind of support. They would rather give than take. They are the types who genuinely would like to serve mankind if only they could find a way. Often that way is not clearly defined to their satisfaction, although the people around them who are on the receiving end of their kindly and sympathetic natures would say they have already found what they are looking for.

In love and romance, Uranus in Pisces people can be highly sensuous with a tendency to experiment for heightened sensations.

Neptune in the Signs

Neptune is the planet of mystery. It governs hidden events, peculiar forces behind the scenes. Its influences are the hardest of all to understand and get a grip on. It is regarded as the most spiritual of all the planetary forces.

Neptune brings the quality of inner vision into our lives. Its visionary quality is in direct contrast to the materialism of our own planet and our natural inclinations.

Neptune stands for idealism. It is the principle that allows a person so inclined to transcend the world. It is the mystical planet. At its worst, it represents escapism through self-delusion, drugs, alcohol, and sexual fantasy.

Neptune takes 168 years to journey around the Sun. This means it spends twelve to fifteen years in each sign. There it brings its subtle and pervasive energies to bear on the generations born in those years, causing each to follow a new course according to the sign in which it is placed.

For instance, when Neptune was first sighted in 1846, it was transiting the scientific sign Aquarius. The sighting coincided with a wave of interest around the world, scientific as well as spiritualistic, whether there was life after death. This was reflected in a great deal of research into spiritualism and psychic rappings, as well as an outbreak of the popular nineteenth-century pastime of ghost hunting.

Neptune in its own way added support to the scientific era started by Uranus half a century before. Neptune's strong deceptive and hallucinatory powers were represented by the introduction of anesthetics, and gradually the popular rise of drug taking.

Neptune gives us dreams of better things through the characteristics of the sign in which it appears. It is then up to the individual. The choice is to bring these ideas into the world through resolution and effort. Another is to go on indulgently dreaming and accomplishing little.

It has to be remembered that Neptune takes 168 years to circle the

Sun, spending an average of twelve to fifteen years in each sign. Neptune's influence in a sign applies more to the generation to which the person belongs, and to successive generations, than to the particular individual. Psychologically, the influences work at the subconscious level. In this way they affect the attitudes, beliefs, and preferences of the generation as expressed through individual character and behavior.

Neptune is strongest in association with Pisces, the sign that it rules together with Jupiter.

The following descriptions of Neptune in the signs start with Neptune in Cancer, as this era began in 1902. The Neptune eras before Cancer are not considered in this book because the Planetary Tables begin at the year 1910.

NEPTUNE IN CANCER

People with Neptune in Cancer were born between 1902 and 1916.

Neptune in Cancer individuals all like to feel they belong to something. They take pride in being members of successful movements and establishments. They were born at a time when patriotism was to be tested. They were not found to be lacking, especially in World War II, when so many of them gave so much.

This was a generation of people who had to make very difficult adjustments, passing out of the horse-and-buggy age, into the automobile age, then into the electronics age, and finally into the nuclear and space age.

Cancer is the sign of the home and the family. These people had the task of keeping both together through probably one of the most unpredictable periods in history—a period that is still challenging concepts of home and family.

There is a good deal of emotionality in the Neptune in Cancer generation. Individuals will remember the past as the good old days, forgetting the bitter times or dismissing them as a learning experience or mistake. They love to keep relics of the old days. Old photographs, books, and souvenirs are treasured possessions. Nostalgia has become an industry.

Neptune in Cancer individuals are instinctive people. They are inclined to do good turns without being asked. They like to gather their families around them as often as possible, and with as many generations as possible. They like to be at the center of warmth and affection.

Sometimes these people find it difficult to stay in one place for long. As much as they love their homes and families, they like to travel. They are especially fond of natural and rural surroundings. They would like to have a second home in the country as well if they live in the city.

Neptune in Cancer people cherish their loved ones. But they can be too demanding of attention and respect. They are not particularly materialistic, putting more value on personal attachments, belongings, and relationships than anything else.

They can be self-indulgent. They may also lack the will to engage in any heavy physical exertion. They are frequently psychic, being able to predict events as well as diagnosing illnesses from which people may be suffering.

NEPTUNE IN LEO

People with Neptune in Leo were born between 1917 and 1928.
Neptune in Leo people are great dreamers. They envision a wonderful future in which they themselves play a leading part. Many of this generation are now in the seats of power. From this position they can ensure that some of their dreams come true.

Neptune in Leo can also produce illusions of glory. These people can be distracted from practical endeavors by the enticements of glamorous people or situations. They have to guard against being drawn into speculative ventures. The urge to gamble and to take other unnecessary risks may be strong.

Neptune in Leo individuals tend to be romantics. They are usually drawn to creative work. Or they may enter politics or government and strive to make the world a better place for all to live in. They have the power to lead and inspire. They usually are able to write or speak with persuasion. They have good organizing ability and a great deal of faith in themselves.

The Neptune in Leo generation developed the motorcar and the movie industry. It also made an important contribution to psychoanalytical techniques.

Neptune in Leo individuals have a love of pleasure. They know how to play hard, and how to work for big stakes. They are often misled by people who indulge their weakness for flattery. They can put too much value on appearances.

Neptune in Leo has given rise to many revolutionaries, from the French Revolution to the American Revolution. Leo is the sign of leadership and showmanship. The addition of Neptune, the planet of illusion, can distort the vision and lead to foolhardy escapades.

These are passionate people who put their heart and soul into whatever they attempt. Sometimes they are driven by a lust for power, which can destroy the things they love most. They have to avoid being egotistical and overestimating their own worth.

Neptune in Leo people have a special gift for dealing with children. But the love life of these individuals seldom runs smoothly. They tend to put their loved ones on a pedestal and so invite disillusionment.

Neptune in Leo individuals need to find a constructive outlet for their vast energies.

NEPTUNE IN VIRGO

People with Neptune in Virgo were born between the latter part of 1928 and 1942.

These are people in whom the sense of service is usually well developed. They respond to any opportunity to implement their ideals of how social conditions can be improved. They have a way of being able to make abstract ideas more concrete and readily understandable. They usually are interested in making the community healthier, both mentally and physically. They enjoy preparing and disseminating information on nutrition and hygiene.

Neptune in Virgo individuals can be a bit scheming and cunning, but usually not out of self-interest. They are quick to discern the problems facing their immediate group. They will resort to sly behind-the-scenes maneuvering to help to right them. There is something of the perfectionist in these individuals. They have to be sure of where they are going, or they can create more trouble and confusion than they are trying to eradicate. There is a desire in these people to have everything in its correct place. They can be too precise and exacting. They have to avoid insisting on only the letter of the law having meaning, while ignoring the spirit of it. They can be of considerable practical help, but be a bit short on spiritual vision.

Neptune in Virgo people are usually moved to improve labor and working conditions. They believe in adult education as a means of improving the lot of everyone. They have the power to absorb and teach techniques. They are able to utilize the materials at their disposal. They are not dependent on special tools or conditions to prove their worth. It is through their talent for devising new methods that they overcome old problems.

Neptune in Virgo individuals sometimes have the healing gift. They can be in tune with inner psychic powers, which are channeled into their practical train of mind to do good work in the physical realm. The spirituality of these people, however, may not be so evident.

Neptune in Virgo people are not publicity seekers for any good work they do. Often they fail to receive the recognition of the public, even when it is due them. They are capable of making sacrifices without hullabaloo.

NEPTUNE IN LIBRA

People with Neptune in Libra were born between the latter part of 1942 and 1955.

Libra is the sign of beauty and balance. Neptune is the planet of imagination, idealism, and illusion. Neptune in Libra can inflate any desire to escape into sweetness and light.

The Neptune in Libra years produced the "flower generation," which endeavored to disarm the world with the feeling of love. Although they seem to have failed in a sense, the corrosive materialism and skepticism of the world have been challenged by that idealism.

Neptune in Libra individuals have the power to create harmony. They have high ideals about the way life should be for mankind. Sometimes their thinking is hopelessly impractical. They can get carried away with their own visions. Yet they are prepared to make the effort. They have the courage of their convictions.

Libra also is the sign of war, as well as of peace. Often these people, in spite of their altruism, create disharmony and conflict. Where they hope to spread love, they sow dissension by the sheer vagueness of their message. Neptune in Libra is not an easy placement for dealing with the determined material forces that seem to run the world.

Neptune in Libra individuals find it difficult to hide their feelings. They are compassionate. They cannot stand to see people or other creatures badly treated. They are deeply moved by the suffering of others.

In spite of their good intentions, these people do have a tendency to compromise. They may lack the will to pursue their aim to the bitter end. They feel that even a shaky peace is better than no peace at all.

Neptune in Libra people prefer to work in partnership. They are a bit lost when they are alone for long. They have refined, artistic tastes. They should not allow these to develop into extravagant appetites for the most luxurious and the most expensive.

Neptune in Libra individuals are more intellectual than physical. They may blow hot and cold in their relationships. Often they are attracted to people or situations that turn their lives upside down or inside out. Peculiar things tend to happen to them.

NEPTUNE IN SCORPIO

People with Neptune in Scorpio were born between the latter part of 1955 and early 1970.

Neptune in Scorpio stimulates a craving for any sensation. At some time in their lives, these people are likely to be drawn into a search for heightened sensations. They may learn their lessons, possibly by having their fingers burned. But they can then go beyond their limiting appetites or desires and emerge far wiser and mature human beings.

This was the generation born at a time when the world gave up a little of its hypocrisy about sex. The rigid pretensions and moral codes were challenged. Censorship was relaxed dramatically to give more reality to the movies, theater, and the daily dialogue between people.

Yet it also was a time of excess, one of the dangers of Neptune in Scorpio. Alcoholism, drug addiction, social diseases, and the crime rate soared. America fought in Vietnam, finally not quite sure itself what it had all been about. Neptune, it should be remembered, is the planet of confusion, delusion, and decay.

It is not surprising that during this period of Neptune's passage through Scorpio, the sign of sex, the Pill came into widespread use. After countless centuries of suffering, it gave women a degree of sexual freedom never before experienced. At the same time, Neptune began to confuse the appearance of and distinctions between male and female; women dressed liked men, and men began to look like women.

Neptune in Scorpio individuals have secretive tendencies. They do not take many people into their confidence. Their emotional natures are intense, but they seldom allow their exterior appearance to reveal their inner feelings. They can play a cool cat-and-mouse game.

These people like to get to the bottom of things. They have an intuition that allows them to often see through concealment. They can be confusing and seem mixed up. Yet they seldom lose control of any situation for which they are responsible.

Neptune in Scorpio people can be too indulgent of themselves. But they have a strong regenerative capability. This allows them to turn their excesses into accesses to higher knowledge.

NEPTUNE IN SAGITTARIUS

People with Neptune in Sagittarius were born or will be born between early 1970 and early 1984.

Neptune is the planet of dissolution. In Sagittarius, the sign of religion and philosophy, it tends to break down the old dogmas and creeds. Views become more liberal. The social conscience turns toward freedom, recognizing that the containments and restrictions of yesterday create explosive pressures that can destroy a society.

Yet the sense of respect for lawfulness remains, for Sagittarius, in spite of its love of liberty, believes firmly in many of the conventional values. Liberty without licence is the Sagittarius message.

This generation of young people born with Neptune in Sagittarius are responsive to any cry for frankness and openness. They are particularly concerned with greater openness in government. Gone are the days of secrecy, which bred corruption, distrust and unaccountable power—as far as they are concerned, anyway.

This generation can be sincere in its spiritual aspirations. But in its search for new dimensions of thinking, it must guard against extremes. It could become too ceremonial. It could put more emphasis on pomp and regalia when the time comes for implementing the social platforms it once believed were so urgent.

People born with Neptune in Sagittarius have the power to visualize the future as it should be. But the big question is: Do they have the strength of will and persistence to make it a reality? These individuals are restless. They tend to need constant change of surroundings and activities to keep them interested.

They are an optimistic generation, even though they will have forebodings about the future they are to control. It may be this that introduces the task of the next generation—to talk less, preach less, and do more in practical terms.

When Neptune leaves Sagittarius, the holiday is over and the new order of discipline and authority arrives. Neptune in Capricorn!

NEPTUNE IN CAPRICORN

People with Neptune in Capricorn will be born between the beginning of 1984 and 1999.

Neptune in Capricorn represents the return of the new order. It stands for more emphasis on practical down-to-earth action, and less on theorizing and abstract discussion. It may be a period in which idealism is inhibited. It will be thought that all the blueprints for a better world have already been prepared. It may be a time when traditional and conventional values are reappraised.

Some astrologers have predicted that Neptune's passage through Capricorn will see the first real moves toward world government. This will not be out of any idealistic impulse, but out of consideration for practical realities.

Capricorn is the sign of ambition and materialism. It does not need much of a negative influence from the other planets to turn this into selfishness. Capricorn also is the sign of business acumen. This may be an extremely constructive period for the economic policies of the nations.

Neptune, however, is the planet of illusion, confusion, and chaos. It also is the spiritual planet. In the face of excessive materialistic aims, Neptune is inclined to produce peculiar and unexpected situations and circumstances.

People born into this generation will have the power to persevere and to make sacrifices to reach their objectives. On the world scene, it may be a time of considerable hard work. There may be less time for leisure, probably due to the hotter pursuits of ambitions and material security.

The Neptune in Capricorn years may be rather wearying for those looking for spiritual regeneration. There can be a slackening of the drive for mystical awakening. Or there may be fewer people or groups interested.

The early years of this generation may contain some uncertainty in relation to family life. Individuals, youngsters mainly, may be neglected if parents have to give most of their time to material considerations. Parental influence, however, will be strong, with a good deal of emphasis on discipline and authority.

Pluto in the Signs

Pluto is the force of upheaval, the volcanic spewing out of emotional matter that has been pent up too long. Pluto represents the fires of hell on the surface of the Earth, the underworld coming up for air. Pluto also represents regeneration and renewal. Its influence works at the subconscious level, and so affects the character and behavior of all people. Out of upheaval and destruction come new forces of progress, widespread throughout the consciousness of the generation.

Pluto was discovered in 1930. Its discovery coincided with gangsterism, organized crime, mobism, fascism, and Nazism, the world's worst financial crash and Great Depression, and World War II. Its discovery also coincided with racial and nationalistic struggles for nationhood and independence, and with popular or people's movements to rise from obscurity to identity, from powerlessness to autonomy.

Pluto controls mass movements, armies, and syndicates for such perverse reasons as victimizing and exterminating people in concentration camps or *pogroms*, and conquering and ruling struggling peoples in underprivileged nations.

Pluto governs large organizations and institutions for progressive purposes too, such as big business and labor, national health, welfare, and educational movements.

Pluto is responsible for mass production; the tedium of the assembly line brings yet more jobs, more goods, more time, more pay. The sweep of modern industrial life creates the need for goods and services in all areas of existence.

Pluto stands for sex and money in an abstract and universal way. Males and females wear their hair alike, dress similarly. Women demand equality and want to function in areas reserved for men. Men learn how to raise children, stay home, and keep house. Or a couple works and shares alike. The poor nations of the world and the poor individuals of a society demand equality and equity, too. Their needs create conflicts and struggles; their struggles create change. In each generation there is the sweeping away of the old and the bringing in of the new.

Pluto is the slowest-moving planet of all. Pluto's orbit is so irregular that it spends from 12 to 37 years in each sign. Its lumbering pace around the Zodiac requires 248 years to complete a full circuit.

Pluto stands for progress through irrevocable change. The change is not necessarily good or bad from the point of view of mere mortals, and most change is difficult to adjust to. But through these changes, people, communities, nations—and finally the individual—are transformed for the better in that they would never choose to return to the old ways of doing things.

So Pluto in a sign is an indicator of the basic attitudes of the generation to which the person belongs, rather than his or her individual characteristics. The influences wrought by Pluto in a sign are also passed on and affect the thinking and preferences of succeeding generations.

The sign where Pluto is at the time of birth will be the area in which the individual finds the greatest inner contradictions.

Pluto is strongest in association with Scorpio, the sign that it rules.

The following descriptions of Pluto in the signs start with Pluto in Gemini, as this era began in 1882. The Pluto eras before Gemini are not considered in this book because the Planetary Tables begin at the year 1910.

PLUTO IN GEMINI

People with Pluto in Gemini were born between 1882 and 1914, before the planet was discovered in 1930.

Pluto in Gemini individuals were a generation of people who had to make the most extraordinary adjustments in the field of communications, which Gemini represents. The telephone allowed ideas to be exchanged instantly and over long distances.

Pluto is the sign of money and wealth. The telephone was one of the most potent instruments in founding and extending the empires of the new plutocrats.

Pluto in Gemini people are inventive. They displayed in their most active days an ability to move with the times. They could adjust and adapt their thinking to the tremendous demands of a daily shrinking world.

Their times gave birth to the automobile and the airplane. And as their generation matured, they brought both to a threshold of performance that could hardly have been imagined.

This was the era that started the scramble for speedier ways to do everything. Even entertainment underwent a metamorphosis. The phonograph became popular and was mass-produced, setting the stage for a booming recording industry.

This was a generation that got used to changes. They went through two world wars, the worst depression the world had known, and entry into the nuclear and space ages.

Pluto in Gemini individuals have the power to understand what consumers need. It was they who drew up the blueprints for the miracle of mass production in many industries.

PLUTO IN CANCER

People with Pluto in Cancer were born between 1914 and 1938.

Cancer is the sign of the home and the family. With Pluto, the planet of fundamental change, in Cancer, it was to be expected that these years would see some transformations in attitudes toward domestic life, as well as physical changes in the environment and the lives of people.

World War I destroyed many homes in Europe through the actual conflict of battle. People were left rootless. Family life was unsettled. The subsequent financial crises and the Great Depression of the 1930s left people in Europe and the United States little alternative but to uproot family ties and homesteads and go in search of work. Women, among those separated from their families and mates, either went to find jobs or became the head of the household.

The Pluto in Cancer era ended just before World War II broke out. Women who never would have thought of working left their homes and family duties and poured into the factories, the military services, and other wartime work. When the war ended, woman's traditional role was over. Emancipation from the kitchen had begun.

The idea of woman's liberation, reinforced in the Pluto in Cancer era, took time to filter through to all levels of society. But the female role was never to be quite the same again. Women would continue to question, challenge, and resist being inferior to the male head of the household.

People born with Pluto traversing the sign of Cancer have this revolutionary instinct for change in them. Although they may not enjoy disruption, they tend to be catalysts for it.

They are of the era when the United States and Britain gave women the vote, when hemlines were raised, when labor-saving devices replaced servants. Improved household appliances and even prepared foods made the home modern and functional, which lightened the work of Pluto in Cancer homemakers, for whom food and comfortable furnishings are so important.

Yet people of this generation have strong attachments to the past. In spite of the changes their times effected, they are often nostalgic about the good old days. They are a deeply emotional type of people whose feelings often had to be repressed only to find release in sudden upheavals.

Pluto in Cancer individuals strive to find security. They are tenacious in their efforts to achieve it. They have strong social awareness and tend to take personal responsibility for the condition of the world. They are the types who can cherish their loved ones and what they own.

PLUTO IN LEO

People with Pluto in Leo were born between 1938 and 1957.

Leo is the sign of kings and power. In these nineteen years of Pluto's occupation, more rulers were tumbled from their thrones than probably at any other time in history. Kingship was definitely out of fashion.

But a new kind of power arose—neither vested in the people nor in the authorities who ruled: the atom bomb. Only the need for survival prevented the power-hungry nations from employing it to achieve their expansive and obsessive aims.

Leo also is the sign of young people. Pluto's compelling energy stimulated teenagers, who began to realize their own power to set up a world of their own. Soon arose the plutocratic industries and businesses catering to their fashions and fads, from music to clothes.

People born during this Pluto transit of Leo tend to have a good deal of self-confidence. They have faith in their own ideas to solve many of the problems they see around them. They like to give orders and generally possess an ability for managing and organizing.

Pluto in Leo individuals have to avoid becoming too sure of themselves, especially where their emotions are concerned. They can be self-expressive in productive ways. These are people who have contributed much to the world of art and entertainment.

Pluto in Leo people are likely to be in the forefront of movements developing in the 1980s and 1990s to establish a central world government.

PLUTO IN VIRGO

People with Pluto in Virgo were born between 1957 and 1972.

Virgo is the sign of specialization. It gives the capacity for fine analysis and the grouping of masses of detail into meaningful forms. Pluto, the planet of opportunistic wealth, applied Virgo's abilities to electronics—and the computer age was launched.

Pluto also exploited Virgo's concern for health and hygiene. The people of this era are more conscious of the industrial pollution that poisons their oceans, rivers, land forms, and atmosphere.

Pluto in Virgo individuals have an instinctive interest in order and efficiency. They appreciate the difficulties facing industry and technology, and they have a conscientious wish to help develop preventive measures.

They are the types who believe that progress does require certain sacrifices, and they are confident of their ability to devise techniques for minimizing the dangers of pollution.

The Pluto in Virgo era may prove that industry and higher standards of health are not incompatible.

Pluto is a planet of extremes and profound upheavals. It was during its transit of Virgo that many of the ills of modern terrorism—skyjacking, assassinations, holding innocents hostage—erupted. Everyone and every movement with a protest to make seemed to want to do it with accompanying violence or threat of violence.

It is not by accident that Virgo is a hypercritical sign, notorious for its fault-finding and nagging. The Pluto in Virgo age demanded some sort of move toward perfection. As a result, it often produced the extremes—for better and for worse.

PLUTO IN LIBRA

People with Pluto in Libra were or will be born between 1972 and 1984.

Libra is the sign of peace and war. With Pluto here, anything—or nothing—can happen. The old seething hatreds and divisions can suddenly rise to the surface and crack the world apart.

But Libra is a sign that endeavors always to smooth over any rents. Often peace at any price is the Libra war cry. It could easily be an age of continued stalemate.

Pluto is the planet of the underworld, not only of gangsters and terrorists, their modern counterparts, but also of mineral resources and buried treasures of oil, gold, and coal. This era saw the first oil crisis of 1973, and the subsequent ones.

Libra is the sign of balance. To redress the balance is one of its compelling aims. However, the presence of Pluto raises the danger of going too far, one way or the other.

The Pluto in Libra era is one in which huge fortunes are being made while many people of the world continue to starve. There was a great cry for social justice, and yet a reluctance to take sides to provide the necessary impetus for change by those in authority. Opportunism stepped in and filled the gap. The plutocrats grew wealthier, while economic depression tightened the belts of the people.

This generation of individuals, when they reach the seats of power, will have a compelling desire to achieve harmony in the world. They have to be careful that their well-intended efforts do not encourage greater polarization. Opposing factions and forces can lead to greater unrest and violence.

PLUTO IN SCORPIO

People with Pluto in Scorpio will be born between 1984 and 1995.

Pluto in Scorpio is in its own sign. This can be very good or very bad, with little likelihood of a happy medium.

Pluto brings sweeping changes. In the warlike, ambitious sign of Scorpio, this could be the time when man's lust for power destroys him. Pluto is the planet of nuclear power; the plutonium bomb is recognized as the ultimate of all horrors.

And yet Pluto also is the planet of gold and plenty. Gold—the age-old symbol of the powerful. The plutocrats' massive wealth could be devoted to turning this into a golden age.

Scorpio is the sign of taxation, which means that the little person may also have to pay heavily for utopian schemes. Scorpio is also the sign of insurance. So all people may want to invest in future peace and safety in order to collect real rewards on the living planet Earth.

This can be an age of awakening. Scorpio and Pluto represent the powers of spiritual regeneration. These twelve years are likely to produce great strides in psychotherapy.

The Pluto in Scorpio generation is likely to foster a shrewd business sense, as well as great determination. It will be very important that individual energies are directed along constructive channels. Individuals have the power for good or for bad.

Tables: Cusp Tables for All Signs, Ascendant Tables, and Planetary Tables

Cusp Tables
for All Signs

You probably know your own Sun sign. At least you have always been under the impression that a certain Sun sign was yours. Sun sign dates for each sign, as shown below, are generalized dates, though we follow slightly different ones in the Planetary Tables.

Generalized Sun Sign Dates

Aries	March 21 to April 20
Taurus	April 21 to May 20
Gemini	May 21 to June 20
Cancer	June 21 to July 20
Leo	July 21 to August 21
Virgo	August 22 to September 21
Libra	September 22 to October 22
Scorpio	October 23 to November 22
Sagittarius	November 23 to December 20
Capricorn	December 21 to January 19
Aquarius	January 20 to February 18
Pisces	February 19 to March 20

These generalized dates are not always the actual dates that the Sun changes sign. The actual day a sign changes differs from month to month and from year to year because the time used to measure planetary motion differs from calendar time.

In the year of your birth a sign may have changed on a day different from the generalized date. For example, if you were born on May 21 in 1942, the actual Sun sign was Taurus for that year, not Gemini.

The Cusp Tables on the next five pages give the days the signs change for the years 1910 through 1990. Check your year of birth, and see if you belong to a cusp.

The cusp period—the time it takes for a sign to give way to another sign—lasts about six days. The cusp period goes from the nineteenth to the twenty-fourth of a month. If you were born on any of these six days, you are influenced by the cusp period.

You will then certainly want to read the cusp description that applies to you in the following chapter, "Cusp Signs: Aries Through Pisces." Or you may want to consult the relevant book of the *Astroscope Profile* series for the other Sun sign. By understanding the other sign, you will learn another set of influences that make you uniquely you.

YEAR	ARIES MAR.–APR.	TAURUS APR.–MAY	GEMINI MAY–JUNE	CANCER JUNE–JULY	LEO JULY–AUG.	VIRGO AUG.–SEPT.	LIBRA SEPT.–OCT.	SCORPIO OCT.–NOV.	SAGITTARIUS NOV.–DEC.	CAPRICORN DEC.–JAN.	AQUARIUS JAN.–FEB.	PISCES FEB.–MAR.
1910	22–20	21–21	22–21	22–23	24–23	24–23	24–23	24–22	23–22	23–20	21–19	20–21
1911	22–20	21–21	22–22	23–23	24–23	24–23	24–24	25–22	23–22	23–20	21–19	20–21
1912	21–19	20–20	21–21	22–22	23–23	24–22	23–23	24–22	23–21	22–20	21–19	20–20
1913	21–20	21–21	22–21	22–23	24–23	24–23	24–23	24–22	23–21	22–20	21–18	19–20
1914	21–20	21–21	22–21	22–23	24–23	24–23	24–23	24–22	23–22	23–20	21–18	19–20
1915	22–20	21–21	22–22	23–23	24–23	24–23	24–24	25–22	23–22	23–20	21–19	20–21
1916	21–19	20–20	21–21	22–22	23–23	24–22	23–23	24–22	23–21	22–20	21–19	20–20
1917	21–20	21–21	22–21	22–22	23–23	24–23	24–23	24–22	23–21	22–20	21–18	19–20
1918	21–20	21–21	22–21	22–23	24–23	24–23	24–23	24–22	23–22	23–20	21–18	19–20
1919	22–20	21–21	22–21	22–23	24–23	24–23	23–23	24–22	23–21	23–20	21–19	20–21
1920	21–19	20–20	21–21	22–22	23–22	23–22	23–23	24–22	23–21	22–20	21–19	20–20
1921	21–20	21–21	22–21	22–22	23–23	24–23	24–23	24–22	23–21	22–20	21–18	19–20
1922	21–20	21–21	22–21	22–23	24–23	24–23	24–23	24–22	23–22	23–20	21–18	19–20

Year	1	2	3	4	5	6	7	8	9	10	11	12
1923	20-21	21-19	23-20	23-22	24-22	24-23	24-23	24-23	22-23	22-21	21-21	22-20
1924	20-20	21-19	22-20	23-21	24-22	23-23	23-22	23-22	22-22	21-21	20-20	21-19
1925	19-20	21-18	22-20	23-21	24-22	24-23	24-23	23-23	22-22	22-21	21-21	21-20
1926	19-20	21-18	23-20	23-22	24-22	24-23	24-23	24-23	22-23	22-21	21-21	21-20
1927	20-21	21-19	23-20	23-22	24-22	24-23	24-23	24-23	22-23	22-21	21-21	22-20
1928	20-20	21-19	22-20	23-21	24-22	23-23	23-22	23-22	22-22	21-21	20-20	21-19
1929	19-20	21-18	22-20	23-21	24-22	24-23	24-23	23-23	22-22	22-21	21-21	21-20
1930	19-20	21-18	23-20	23-22	24-22	24-23	24-23	24-23	22-23	22-21	21-21	21-20
1931	20-21	21-19	23-20	23-22	24-22	24-23	24-23	24-23	22-23	22-21	21-21	22-20
1932	20-20	21-19	22-20	23-21	24-22	23-23	23-22	23-22	22-22	21-21	20-20	21-19
1933	19-20	20-18	22-19	23-21	24-22	24-23	24-23	23-23	22-22	22-21	21-21	21-20
1934	19-20	21-18	23-20	23-22	24-22	24-23	24-23	24-23	22-23	22-21	21-21	21-20
1935	20-21	21-19	23-20	23-22	24-22	24-23	24-23	24-23	22-23	22-21	21-21	22-20
1936	20-20	21-19	22-20	22-21	24-21	23-23	23-22	23-22	22-22	21-21	20-20	21-19
1937	19-20	20-18	22-19	23-21	24-22	23-23	24-22	23-23	22-22	21-21	21-21	21-20
1938	19-20	21-18	23-20	23-22	24-22	24-23	24-23	24-23	22-23	22-21	21-21	21-20
1939	20-21	21-19	23-20	23-22	24-22	24-23	24-23	24-23	22-23	22-21	21-21	22-20

Year												
1940	20–20	21–19	22–20	22–21	24–21	23–23	23–22	23–22	22–22	21–21	20–20	21–19
1941	19–20	20–18	22–19	23–21	24–22	23–23	24–22	23–23	22–22	21–21	20–20	21–19
1942	19–20	21–18	22–20	23–21	24–22	24–23	24–23	24–23	22–23	22–21	21–21	21–20
1943	20–21	21–19	23–20	23–22	24–22	24–23	24–23	24–23	22–23	22–21	21–21	22–20
1944	20–20	21–19	22–20	22–21	24–21	23–23	23–22	23–22	22–22	21–21	20–20	21–19
1945	19–20	20–18	22–19	23–21	24–22	23–23	24–22	23–23	22–22	21–21	20–20	21–19
1946	19–20	21–18	22–20	23–21	24–22	24–23	24–23	23–23	22–23	22–21	21–21	21–20
1947	19–20	21–18	23–20	23–22	24–22	24–23	24–23	24–23	22–22	22–21	21–21	21–20
1948	20–20	21–19	22–20	22–21	24–21	23–23	23–22	23–22	22–22	21–21	20–20	21–19
1949	19–20	20–18	22–19	23–21	24–22	23–23	23–22	23–22	22–22	21–21	20–20	21–19
1950	19–20	21–18	22–20	23–21	24–22	24–23	24–23	23–23	22–22	22–21	21–21	21–20
1951	20–21	21–19	23–20	24–22	25–23	24–24	24–23	24–23	23–23	22–22	21–21	22–20
1952	20–20	22–19	22–21	23–21	24–22	24–23	24–23	23–23	22–22	22–21	21–21	21–20
1953	19–20	21–18	23–20	23–22	24–22	24–23	24–23	24–23	22–23	22–21	21–21	21–20
1954	20–21	21–19	23–20	23–22	24–22	24–23	24–23	24–23	22–23	22–21	21–21	22–20
1955	20–21	21–19	23–20	24–22	25–23	24–24	24–23	24–23	23–23	22–22	21–21	22–20
1956	20–20	22–19	22–21	23–21	24–22	24–23	24–23	23–23	22–22	22–21	21–21	21–20

Year												
1957	19-20	21-18	23-20	23-22	24-22	24-23	24-23	24-23	22-23	22-21	21-21	21-20
1958	20-21	21-19	23-20	23-22	24-22	24-23	24-23	24-23	22-23	22-21	21-21	22-20
1959	20-21	21-19	23-20	24-22	25-23	24-24	24-23	24-23	23-23	22-22	21-21	22-20
1960	20-20	22-19	22-21	23-21	24-22	24-23	24-23	23-23	22-22	22-21	21-21	21-20
1961	19-20	21-18	23-20	23-22	24-22	24-23	24-23	24-23	22-23	22-21	21-21	21-20
1962	20-21	21-19	23-20	23-22	24-22	24-23	24-23	24-23	22-23	22-21	21-21	22-20
1963	20-21	21-19	23-20	24-22	25-23	24-24	24-23	24-23	23-23	22-22	21-21	22-20
1964	20-20	22-19	22-21	23-21	24-22	24-23	24-23	23-23	22-22	22-21	21-21	21-20
1965	19-20	21-18	23-20	23-22	24-22	24-23	24-23	24-23	22-23	22-21	21-21	21-20
1966	20-21	21-19	23-20	23-22	24-22	24-23	24-23	24-23	22-23	22-21	21-21	22-20
1967	20-21	21-19	23-20	23-22	25-22	24-24	24-23	24-23	23-23	22-22	21-21	22-20
1968	20-20	21-19	22-20	23-21	24-22	23-23	24-22	23-23	22-22	21-21	21-20	21-20
1969	19-20	21-18	23-20	23-22	24-22	24-23	24-23	24-23	22-23	22-21	21-21	21-20
1970	20-21	21-19	23-20	23-22	24-22	24-23	24-23	24-23	22-23	22-21	21-21	22-20
1971	20-21	21-19	23-20	23-22	25-22	24-24	24-23	24-23	23-23	22-22	21-21	22-20
1972	20-20	21-19	22-20	23-21	24-22	23-23	24-22	23-23	22-22	21-21	20-20	21-19
1973	19-20	21-18	23-20	23-22	24-22	24-23	24-23	23-23	22-22	22-21	21-21	21-20

Year												
1974	20-21	21-19	23-20	23-22	24-22	24-23	24-23	24-23	22-23	22-21	21-21	22-20
1975	20-21	21-19	23-20	23-22	25-22	24-24	24-23	24-23	23-23	22-22	21-21	22-20
1976	20-20	21-19	22-20	23-21	24-22	23-23	24-22	23-23	22-22	21-21	20-20	21-19
1977	19-20	21-18	22-20	23-21	24-22	24-23	24-23	23-23	22-22	22-21	21-21	21-20
1978	20-20	21-19	23-20	23-22	24-22	24-23	24-23	24-23	22-23	22-21	21-21	21-20
1979	20-20	21-19	23-20	23-22	25-22	24-24	24-23	24-23	22-23	22-21	21-21	22-20
1980	20-21	21-19	22-20	23-21	24-22	23-23	23-22	23-22	22-22	21-21	20-20	21-19
1981	20-20	21-18	22-20	23-21	24-22	24-23	24-23	23-23	22-22	22-21	21-21	21-20
1982	19-20	21-18	23-20	23-22	24-22	24-23	24-23	24-23	22-23	22-21	21-21	21-20
1983	19-20	21-19	23-20	23-22	24-22	24-23	24-23	24-23	22-23	22-21	21-21	22-20
1984	20-21	21-19	22-20	23-21	24-22	23-23	23-22	23-22	22-22	21-21	20-20	21-19
1985	20-20	21-18	22-20	23-21	24-22	24-23	24-23	23-23	22-22	22-21	21-21	21-20
1986	19-20	21-18	23-20	23-22	24-22	24-23	24-23	24-23	22-23	22-21	21-21	21-20
1987	19-20	21-19	23-20	23-22	24-22	24-23	24-23	24-23	22-23	22-21	21-21	22-20
1988	20-21	21-19	22-20	23-21	24-22	23-23	23-22	23-22	22-22	21-21	20-20	21-19
1989	20-20	21-18	22-20	23-21	24-22	24-23	24-23	23-23	22-22	22-21	21-21	21-20
1990	19-20	21-18	23-20	23-22	24-22	24-23	24-23	24-23	22-23	22-21	21-21	21-20

Ascendant Tables

These Ascendant Tables give the Rising sign for each hour of the day for every day that corresponds to your Sun sign.

If your Rising sign is the same as your Sun sign, you've got a double whammy going. For example, you are a "double" Aries or a "double" Capricorn or a "double" of another sign. And you probably show the tendencies of the particular sign more strongly than would be expected.

If your Sun sign and Rising sign are different, of course the approach to life is a variation. When you find your Rising sign from the tables that follow, go to the particular chapter "Your Rising Sign" that applies to you.

As you read, you will be amazed at how many facets of your own personality reveal themselves to you. You will be astounded as *Astroscope Profile* helps you on your voyage of self-discovery. And, as the mystery unfolds, you'll be startled to see just how *Astroscope Profile* is zeroing in on your character.

How can you guess your Rising sign if you do not know the time of your birth? Since each sign rises once a day, the odds are twelve to one against. Of course, you can narrow the odds if you know you were born "in the morning," or "around midnight," or "sometime in the afternoon." But the Rising sign lasts only about two hours, so you could make a big mistake. You might guess Libra, but it could be Virgo or Scorpio, depending on how far off your estimate was.

A better way to figure out your Rising sign if you do not know the hour of your birth is to read the chapters "Your Rising Sign," which start on pages 151–245. Skim through each chapter to see which Rising sign description best fits you.

DAYLIGHT SAVING TIME

The hour of birth given in the following Ascendant Tables is for Standard Time anywhere around the world. The US and the UK and many other nations use Daylight Saving Time during the summer, which is one hour later than Standard Time. British Summer Time runs from late March to late October, with the precise dates varying from year to year, and if your birth was recorded during British Summer Time you should *subtract one hour* from that time. Then look up the revised hour in the Ascendant Tables.

LEO ASCENDANT TABLES: YOUR RISING SIGN

	July 23	July 24	July 25	July 26	July 27
Midnight	Taurus	Taurus	Taurus	Taurus	Taurus
1:00 A.M.	Gemini	Gemini	Gemini	Gemini	Gemini
2:00 A.M.	Gemini	Gemini	Gemini	Gemini	Gemini
3:00 A.M.	Cancer	Cancer	Cancer	Cancer	Cancer
4:00 A.M.	Cancer	Cancer	Cancer	Cancer	Cancer
5:00 A.M.	Leo	Leo	Leo	Leo	Leo
6:00 A.M.	Leo	Leo	Leo	Leo	Leo
7:00 A.M.	Leo	Leo	Leo	Leo	Leo
8:00 A.M.	Virgo	Virgo	Virgo	Virgo	Virgo
9:00 A.M.	Virgo	Virgo	Virgo	Virgo	Virgo
10:00 A.M.	Libra	Libra	Libra	Libra	Libra
11:00 A.M.	Libra	Libra	Libra	Libra	Libra
Noon	Libra	Libra	Libra	Libra	Libra
1:00 P.M.	Scorpio	Scorpio	Scorpio	Scorpio	Scorpio
2:00 P.M.	Scorpio	Scorpio	Scorpio	Scorpio	Scorpio
3:00 P.M.	Sagittarius	Sagittarius	Sagittarius	Sagittarius	Sagittarius
4:00 P.M.	Sagittarius	Sagittarius	Sagittarius	Sagittarius	Sagittarius
5:00 P.M.	Sagittarius	Sagittarius	Sagittarius	Sagittarius	Sagittarius
6:00 P.M.	Capricorn	Capricorn	Capricorn	Capricorn	Capricorn
7:00 P.M.	Capricorn	Capricorn	Capricorn	Aquarius	Aquarius
8:00 P.M.	Aquarius	Aquarius	Aquarius	Aquarius	Aquarius
9:00 P.M.	Pisces	Pisces	Pisces	Pisces	Pisces
10:00 P.M.	Aries	Aries	Aries	Aries	Aries
11:00 P.M.	Aries	Aries	Aries	Taurus	Taurus

LEO ASCENDANT TABLES: YOUR RISING SIGN

	July 28	July 29	July 30	July 31	August 1
Midnight	Taurus	Taurus	Taurus	Taurus	Taurus
1:00 A.M.	Gemini	Gemini	Gemini	Gemini	Gemini
2:00 A.M.	Gemini	Gemini	Gemini	Gemini	Gemini
3:00 A.M.	Cancer	Cancer	Cancer	Cancer	Cancer
4:00 A.M.	Cancer	Cancer	Cancer	Cancer	Cancer
5:00 A.M.	Leo	Leo	Leo	Leo	Leo
6:00 A.M.	Leo	Leo	Leo	Leo	Leo
7:00 A.M.	Leo	Leo	Leo	Leo	Virgo
8:00 A.M.	Virgo	Virgo	Virgo	Virgo	Virgo
9:00 A.M.	Virgo	Virgo	Virgo	Virgo	Virgo
10:00 A.M.	Libra	Libra	Libra	Libra	Libra
11:00 A.M.	Libra	Libra	Libra	Libra	Libra
Noon	Libra	Libra	Scorpio	Scorpio	Scorpio
1:00 P.M.	Scorpio	Scorpio	Scorpio	Scorpio	Scorpio
2:00 P.M.	Scorpio	Scorpio	Scorpio	Scorpio	Scorpio
3:00 P.M.	Sagittarius	Sagittarius	Sagittarius	Sagittarius	Sagittarius
4:00 P.M.	Sagittarius	Sagittarius	Sagittarius	Sagittarius	Sagittarius
5:00 P.M.	Capricorn	Capricorn	Capricorn	Capricorn	Capricorn
6:00 P.M.	Capricorn	Capricorn	Capricorn	Capricorn	Capricorn
7:00 P.M.	Aquarius	Aquarius	Aquarius	Aquarius	Aquarius
8:00 P.M.	Aquarius	Aquarius	Aquarius	Aquarius	Aquarius
9:00 P.M.	Pisces	Pisces	Pisces	Pisces	Pisces
10:00 P.M.	Aries	Aries	Aries	Aries	Aries
11:00 P.M.	Taurus	Taurus	Taurus	Taurus	Taurus

	August 2	August 3	August 4	August 5	August 6
Midnight	Gemini	Gemini	Gemini	Gemini	Gemini
1:00 A.M.	Gemini	Gemini	Gemini	Gemini	Gemini
2:00 A.M.	Cancer	Cancer	Cancer	Cancer	Cancer
3:00 A.M.	Cancer	Cancer	Cancer	Cancer	Cancer
4:00 A.M.	Cancer	Cancer	Cancer	Cancer	Cancer
5:00 A.M.	Leo	Leo	Leo	Leo	Leo
6:00 A.M.	Leo	Leo	Leo	Leo	Leo
7:00 A.M.	Virgo	Virgo	Virgo	Virgo	Virgo
8:00 A.M.	Virgo	Virgo	Virgo	Virgo	Virgo
9:00 A.M.	Virgo	Virgo	Virgo	Virgo	Virgo
10:00 A.M.	Libra	Libra	Libra	Libra	Libra
11:00 A.M.	Libra	Libra	Libra	Libra	Libra
Noon	Scorpio	Scorpio	Scorpio	Scorpio	Scorpio
1:00 P.M.	Scorpio	Scorpio	Scorpio	Scorpio	Scorpio
2:00 P.M.	Scorpio	Scorpio	Scorpio	Scorpio	Scorpio
3:00 P.M.	Sagittarius	Sagittarius	Sagittarius	Sagittarius	Sagittarius
4:00 P.M.	Sagittarius	Sagittarius	Sagittarius	Sagittarius	Sagittarius
5:00 P.M.	Capricorn	Capricorn	Capricorn	Capricorn	Capricorn
6:00 P.M.	Capricorn	Capricorn	Capricorn	Capricorn	Capricorn
7:00 P.M.	Aquarius	Aquarius	Aquarius	Aquarius	Aquarius
8:00 P.M.	Aquarius	Pisces	Pisces	Pisces	Pisces
9:00 P.M.	Pisces	Pisces	Pisces	Pisces	Pisces
10:00 P.M.	Aries	Aries	Aries	Aries	Aries
11:00 P.M.	Taurus	Taurus	Taurus	Taurus	Taurus

LEO ASCENDANT TABLES: YOUR RISING SIGN

	August 7	August 8	August 9	August 10	August 11
Midnight	Gemini	Gemini	Gemini	Gemini	Gemini
1:00 A.M.	Gemini	Gemini	Gemini	Gemini	Gemini
2:00 A.M.	Cancer	Cancer	Cancer	Cancer	Cancer
3:00 A.M.	Cancer	Cancer	Cancer	Cancer	Cancer
4:00 A.M.	Leo	Leo	Leo	Leo	Leo
5:00 A.M.	Leo	Leo	Leo	Leo	Leo
6:00 A.M.	Leo	Leo	Leo	Leo	Leo
7:00 A.M.	Virgo	Virgo	Virgo	Virgo	Virgo
8:00 A.M.	Virgo	Virgo	Virgo	Virgo	Virgo
9:00 A.M.	Libra	Libra	Libra	Libra	Libra
10:00 A.M.	Libra	Libra	Libra	Libra	Libra
11:00 A.M.	Libra	Libra	Libra	Libra	Libra
Noon	Scorpio	Scorpio	Scorpio	Scorpio	Scorpio
1:00 P.M.	Scorpio	Scorpio	Scorpio	Scorpio	Scorpio
2:00 P.M.	Sagittarius	Sagittarius	Sagittarius	Sagittarius	Sagittarius
3:00 P.M.	Sagittarius	Sagittarius	Sagittarius	Sagittarius	Sagittarius
4:00 P.M.	Sagittarius	Sagittarius	Sagittarius	Sagittarius	Sagittarius
5:00 P.M.	Capricorn	Capricorn	Capricorn	Capricorn	Capricorn
6:00 P.M.	Capricorn	Capricorn	Capricorn	Capricorn	Aquarius
7:00 P.M.	Aquarius	Aquarius	Aquarius	Aquarius	Aquarius
8:00 P.M.	Pisces	Pisces	Pisces	Pisces	Pisces
9:00 P.M.	Pisces	Aries	Aries	Aries	Aries
10:00 P.M.	• Aries	Aries	Aries	Aries	Taurus
11:00 P.M.	Taurus	Taurus	Taurus	Taurus	Taurus

	August 12	August 13	August 14	August 15	August 16	August 17
Midnight	Gemini	Gemini	Gemini	Gemini	Gemini	Gemini
1:00 A.M.	Gemini	Gemini	Gemini	Gemini	Gemini	Gemini
2:00 A.M.	Cancer	Cancer	Cancer	Cancer	Cancer	Cancer
3:00 A.M.	Cancer	Cancer	Cancer	Cancer	Cancer	Cancer
4:00 A.M.	Leo	Leo	Leo	Leo	Leo	Leo
5:00 A.M.	Leo	Leo	Leo	Leo	Leo	Leo
6:00 A.M.	Leo	Leo	Leo	Leo	Virgo	Virgo
7:00 A.M.	Virgo	Virgo	Virgo	Virgo	Virgo	Virgo
8:00 A.M.	Virgo	Virgo	Virgo	Virgo	Virgo	Virgo
9:00 A.M.	Libra	Libra	Libra	Libra	Libra	Libra
10:00 A.M.	Libra	Libra	Libra	Libra	Libra	Libra
11:00 A.M.	Libra	Libra	Scorpio	Scorpio	Scorpio	Scorpio
Noon	Scorpio	Scorpio	Scorpio	Scorpio	Scorpio	Scorpio
1:00 P.M.	Scorpio	Scorpio	Scorpio	Scorpio	Scorpio	Scorpio
2:00 P.M.	Sagittarius	Sagittarius	Sagittarius	Sagittarius	Sagittarius	Sagittarius
3:00 P.M.	Sagittarius	Sagittarius	Sagittarius	Sagittarius	Sagittarius	Sagittarius
4:00 P.M.	Capricorn	Capricorn	Capricorn	Capricorn	Capricorn	Capricorn
5:00 P.M.	Capricorn	Capricorn	Capricorn	Capricorn	Capricorn	Capricorn
6:00 P.M.	Aquarius	Aquarius	Aquarius	Aquarius	Aquarius	Aquarius
7:00 P.M.	Aquarius	Aquarius	Aquarius	Aquarius	Aquarius	Aquarius
8:00 P.M.	Pisces	Pisces	Pisces	Pisces	Pisces	Pisces
9:00 P.M.	Aries	Aries	Aries	Aries	Aries	Aries
10:00 P.M.	Taurus	Taurus	Taurus	Taurus	Taurus	Taurus
11:00 P.M.	Taurus	Taurus	Taurus	Taurus	Taurus	Taurus

LEO ASCENDANT TABLES: YOUR RISING SIGN

	August 18	August 19	August 20	August 21	August 22	August 23
Midnight	Gemini	Gemini	Gemini	Gemini	Gemini	Gemini
1:00 A.M.	Cancer	Cancer	Cancer	Cancer	Cancer	Cancer
2:00 A.M.	Cancer	Cancer	Cancer	Cancer	Cancer	Cancer
3:00 A.M.	Cancer	Cancer	Cancer	Cancer	Leo	Leo
4:00 A.M.	Leo	Leo	Leo	Leo	Leo	Leo
5:00 A.M.	Leo	Leo	Leo	Leo	Leo	Leo
6:00 A.M.	Virgo	Virgo	Virgo	Virgo	Virgo	Virgo
7:00 A.M.	Virgo	Virgo	Virgo	Virgo	Virgo	Virgo
8:00 A.M.	Virgo	Virgo	Virgo	Libra	Libra	Libra
9:00 A.M.	Libra	Libra	Libra	Libra	Libra	Libra
10:00 A.M.	Libra	Libra	Libra	Libra	Libra	Libra
11:00 A.M.	Scorpio	Scorpio	Scorpio	Scorpio	Scorpio	Scorpio
Noon	Scorpio	Scorpio	Scorpio	Scorpio	Scorpio	Scorpio
1:00 P.M.	Scorpio	Scorpio	Scorpio	Scorpio	Sagittarius	Sagittarius
2:00 P.M.	Sagittarius	Sagittarius	Sagittarius	Sagittarius	Sagittarius	Sagittarius
3:00 P.M.	Sagittarius	Sagittarius	Sagittarius	Sagittarius	Sagittarius	Sagittarius
4:00 P.M.	Capricorn	Capricorn	Capricorn	Capricorn	Capricorn	Capricorn
5:00 P.M.	Capricorn	Capricorn	Capricorn	Capricorn	Capricorn	Capricorn
6:00 P.M.	Aquarius	Aquarius	Aquarius	Aquarius	Aquarius	Aquarius
7:00 P.M.	Pisces	Pisces	Pisces	Pisces	Pisces	Pisces
8:00 P.M.	Pisces	Pisces	Pisces	Aries	Aries	Aries
9:00 P.M.	Aries	Aries	Aries	Aries	Aries	Aries
10:00 P.M.	Taurus	Taurus	Taurus	Taurus	Taurus	Taurus
11:00 P.M.	Gemini	Gemini	Gemini	Gemini	Gemini	Gemini

Planetary Tables

Our *Astroscope Profile* system of constructing a personal astroscope is really simple. Just turn to your birthday tables. These tables, on colored/banded pages, give the planetary positions for your Sun sign every day for the eighty-one years 1910–90. Once you have located your birth year and day, you can see at a glance the astrological makeup contributed by the planets of the Solar System.

HOW TO USE THE TABLES

Select the page on which your year of birth appears. Note the column headings at the top of the page. They denote each planet of the solar system: Moon (actually a satellite of Earth), Mercury, Venus, Mars, Jupiter, Saturn, Uranus, Neptune, and Pluto. Going down the column, you see the zodiacal signs in which each of the planets is located for a specific day.

Now run down the month to find your day of birth. From your birth date read across the page, stopping at each column to learn your true placement of planets in signs.

Is it a true placement? It is, except for two possible cautions. One concerns time zones around the world; the other concerns Daylight Saving Time. These cautions could apply to you, so read the sections below.

TIME ZONES AROUND THE WORLD

The times given in the tables for the Moon entering a new sign are given in New York time, which is Eastern Standard Time. If you were born in a different time zone, you may need to adjust your recorded birth time to Eastern Standard Time.

Look at the map "Time Zones Around the World" on the next page.

Time Zones Around The World

Figure 8

For explanation of Time Zone Map, see page 396.

The time zone marked "0" is the New York, or Eastern Standard, Time Zone. If you were born in that area, you don't have to adjust your birth hour. It corresponds to Moon times given in the tables (except during Daylight Saving Time hours).

But if you were born in any other time zone, here is how you can convert your birth time.

Find on the map where you were born. Then look at the number above that place. That number tells you how many hours you must add or subtract to your birth time for the conversion.

The numbers to the left of New York (going west) are minus numbers: −1, −2, and so on. If you were born in zone −3, say, you must subtract three hours from your recorded birth time to get the correct New York time.

The numbers to the right of New York (going east) are plus numbers: +1, +2, and so on. If, for example, you were born in zone +5, you must add five hours to your recorded birth time to get the corresponding New York time.

DAYLIGHT SAVING TIME

As has been mentioned, the Moon times in the tables are given in Eastern Standard Time, but if your birth was recorded during British Summer Time (or Daylight Saving Time) you may need to *subtract one hour,* as well as converting your birth hour for Eastern Standard Time, if you need to do so.

LEO PLANETARY TABLES

1910

	MOON FROM	IN	MERCURY	VENUS	MARS	JUPITER	SATURN	URANUS	NEPTUNE	PLUTO
July										
24	11:56 A.M.	Pisces	Leo	Gemini	Leo	Libra	Taurus	Capricorn	Cancer	Gemini
25			Leo	Cancer	Leo	Libra	Taurus	Capricorn	Cancer	Gemini
26	4:07 P.M.	Aries	Leo	Cancer	Leo	Libra	Taurus	Capricorn	Cancer	Gemini
27			Leo	Cancer	Leo	Libra	Taurus	Capricorn	Cancer	Gemini
28	7:26 P.M.	Taurus	Leo	Cancer	Leo	Libra	Taurus	Capricorn	Cancer	Gemini
29			Leo	Cancer	Leo	Libra	Taurus	Capricorn	Cancer	Gemini
30	10:19 P.M.	Gemini	Leo	Cancer	Leo	Libra	Taurus	Capricorn	Cancer	Gemini
31			Leo	Cancer	Leo	Libra	Taurus	Capricorn	Cancer	Gemini
August										
1	0:53 A.M.	Cancer	Leo	Cancer	Leo	Libra	Taurus	Capricorn	Cancer	Gemini
2			Leo	Cancer	Leo	Libra	Taurus	Capricorn	Cancer	Gemini
3			Leo	Cancer	Leo	Libra	Taurus	Capricorn	Cancer	Gemini
4	4:39 A.M.	Leo	Leo	Cancer	Leo	Libra	Taurus	Capricorn	Cancer	Gemini
5			Leo	Cancer	Leo	Libra	Taurus	Capricorn	Cancer	Gemini
6	9:57 A.M.	Virgo	Virgo	Cancer	Virgo	Libra	Taurus	Capricorn	Cancer	Gemini
7			Virgo	Cancer	Virgo	Libra	Taurus	Capricorn	Cancer	Gemini
8	6:12 P.M.	Libra	Virgo	Cancer	Virgo	Libra	Taurus	Capricorn	Cancer	Gemini
9			Virgo	Cancer	Virgo	Libra	Taurus	Capricorn	Cancer	Gemini
10			Virgo	Cancer	Virgo	Libra	Taurus	Capricorn	Cancer	Gemini
11	5:33 A.M.	Scorpio	Virgo	Cancer	Virgo	Libra	Taurus	Capricorn	Cancer	Gemini
12			Virgo	Cancer	Virgo	Libra	Taurus	Capricorn	Cancer	Gemini
13	6:26 P.M.	Sagittarius	Virgo	Cancer	Virgo	Libra	Taurus	Capricorn	Cancer	Gemini
14			Virgo	Cancer	Virgo	Libra	Taurus	Capricorn	Cancer	Gemini
15			Virgo	Cancer	Virgo	Libra	Taurus	Capricorn	Cancer	Gemini
16	6:04 A.M.	Capricorn	Virgo	Cancer	Virgo	Libra	Taurus	Capricorn	Cancer	Gemini
17			Virgo	Cancer	Virgo	Libra	Taurus	Capricorn	Cancer	Gemini
18	2:29 P.M.	Aquarius	Virgo	Cancer	Virgo	Libra	Taurus	Capricorn	Cancer	Gemini
19			Virgo	Leo	Virgo	Libra	Taurus	Capricorn	Cancer	Gemini
20	7:39 P.M.	Pisces	Virgo	Leo	Virgo	Libra	Taurus	Capricorn	Cancer	Gemini
21			Virgo	Leo	Virgo	Libra	Taurus	Capricorn	Cancer	Gemini
22	10:41 P.M.	Aries	Virgo	Leo	Virgo	Libra	Taurus	Capricorn	Cancer	Gemini
23			Virgo	Leo	Virgo	Libra	Taurus	Capricorn	Cancer	Gemini

LEO PLANETARY TABLES

1911

	MOON FROM	IN	MERCURY	VENUS	MARS	JUPITER	SATURN	URANUS	NEPTUNE	PLUTO
July										
24	Cancer		Leo	Virgo	Taurus	Scorpio	Taurus	Capricorn	Cancer	Gemini
25	12:24 P.M.	Leo	Leo	Virgo	Taurus	Scorpio	Taurus	Capricorn	Cancer	Gemini
26	1:26 P.M.	Virgo	Leo	Virgo	Taurus	Scorpio	Taurus	Capricorn	Cancer	Gemini
27			Leo	Virgo	Taurus	Scorpio	Taurus	Capricorn	Cancer	Gemini
28			Leo	Virgo	Taurus	Scorpio	Taurus	Capricorn	Cancer	Gemini
29	5:32 P.M.	Libra	Leo	Virgo	Taurus	Scorpio	Taurus	Capricorn	Cancer	Gemini
30			Leo	Virgo	Taurus	Scorpio	Taurus	Capricorn	Cancer	Gemini
31			Virgo	Virgo	Taurus	Scorpio	Taurus	Capricorn	Cancer	Gemini
August										
1	1:45 A.M.	Scorpio	Virgo	Virgo	Taurus	Scorpio	Taurus	Capricorn	Cancer	Gemini
2			Virgo	Virgo	Taurus	Scorpio	Taurus	Capricorn	Cancer	Gemini
3	1:23 P.M.	Sagittarius	Virgo	Virgo	Taurus	Scorpio	Taurus	Capricorn	Cancer	Gemini
4			Virgo	Virgo	Taurus	Scorpio	Taurus	Capricorn	Cancer	Gemini
5			Virgo	Virgo	Taurus	Scorpio	Taurus	Capricorn	Cancer	Gemini
6	2:08 A.M.	Capricorn	Virgo	Virgo	Taurus	Scorpio	Taurus	Capricorn	Cancer	Gemini
7			Virgo	Virgo	Taurus	Scorpio	Taurus	Capricorn	Cancer	Gemini
8	2:01 P.M.	Aquarius	Virgo	Virgo	Taurus	Scorpio	Taurus	Capricorn	Cancer	Gemini
9			Virgo	Virgo	Taurus	Scorpio	Taurus	Capricorn	Cancer	Gemini
10	11:59 P.M.	Pisces	Virgo	Virgo	Taurus	Scorpio	Taurus	Capricorn	Cancer	Gemini
11			Virgo	Virgo	Taurus	Scorpio	Taurus	Capricorn	Cancer	Gemini
12			Virgo	Virgo	Taurus	Scorpio	Taurus	Capricorn	Cancer	Gemini
13	8:01 A.M.	Aries	Virgo	Virgo	Taurus	Scorpio	Taurus	Capricorn	Cancer	Gemini
14			Virgo	Virgo	Taurus	Scorpio	Taurus	Capricorn	Cancer	Gemini
15	2:10 P.M.	Taurus	Virgo	Virgo	Taurus	Scorpio	Taurus	Capricorn	Cancer	Gemini
16			Virgo	Virgo	Taurus	Scorpio	Taurus	Capricorn	Cancer	Gemini
17	6:22 P.M.	Gemini	Virgo	Virgo	Taurus	Scorpio	Taurus	Capricorn	Cancer	Gemini
18			Virgo	Virgo	Taurus	Scorpio	Taurus	Capricorn	Cancer	Gemini
19	8:41 P.M.	Cancer	Virgo	Virgo	Taurus	Scorpio	Taurus	Capricorn	Cancer	Gemini
20			Virgo	Virgo	Taurus	Scorpio	Taurus	Capricorn	Cancer	Gemini
21	9:53 P.M.	Leo	Virgo	Virgo	Taurus	Scorpio	Taurus	Capricorn	Cancer	Gemini
22			Virgo	Virgo	Taurus	Scorpio	Taurus	Capricorn	Cancer	Gemini
23	11:26 P.M.	Virgo	Virgo	Virgo	Taurus	Scorpio	Taurus	Capricorn	Cancer	Gemini

1912

	MOON FROM	IN	MERCURY	VENUS	MARS	JUPITER	SATURN	URANUS	NEPTUNE	PLUTO
July										
23	10:21 A.M.	Sagittarius	Leo	Leo	Virgo	Sagittarius	Gemini	Aquarius	Cancer	Gemini
24			Leo	Leo	Virgo	Sagittarius	Gemini	Aquarius	Cancer	Gemini
25	11:41 P.M.	Capricorn	Leo	Leo	Virgo	Sagittarius	Gemini	Aquarius	Cancer	Gemini
26			Virgo	Leo	Virgo	Sagittarius	Gemini	Aquarius	Cancer	Gemini
27			Virgo	Leo	Virgo	Sagittarius	Gemini	Aquarius	Cancer	Gemini
28	11:59 A.M.	Aquarius	Virgo	Leo	Virgo	Sagittarius	Gemini	Aquarius	Cancer	Gemini
29			Virgo	Leo	Virgo	Sagittarius	Gemini	Aquarius	Cancer	Gemini
30			Virgo	Leo	Virgo	Sagittarius	Gemini	Aquarius	Cancer	Gemini
31	0:39 A.M.	Pisces	Virgo	Leo	Virgo	Sagittarius	Gemini	Aquarius	Cancer	Gemini
August										
1			Virgo	Leo	Virgo	Sagittarius	Gemini	Aquarius	Cancer	Gemini
2	12:38 P.M.	Aries	Virgo	Leo	Virgo	Sagittarius	Gemini	Aquarius	Cancer	Gemini
3			Virgo	Leo	Virgo	Sagittarius	Gemini	Aquarius	Cancer	Gemini
4	10:35 P.M.	Taurus	Virgo	Leo	Virgo	Sagittarius	Gemini	Aquarius	Cancer	Gemini
5			Virgo	Leo	Virgo	Sagittarius	Gemini	Aquarius	Cancer	Gemini
6			Virgo	Leo	Virgo	Sagittarius	Gemini	Aquarius	Cancer	Gemini
7	5:08 A.M.	Gemini	Virgo	Leo	Virgo	Sagittarius	Gemini	Aquarius	Cancer	Gemini
8			Virgo	Leo	Virgo	Sagittarius	Gemini	Aquarius	Cancer	Gemini
9	7:56 A.M.	Cancer	Virgo	Leo	Virgo	Sagittarius	Gemini	Aquarius	Cancer	Gemini
10			Virgo	Leo	Virgo	Sagittarius	Gemini	Aquarius	Cancer	Gemini
11	7:59 A.M.	Leo	Virgo	Leo	Virgo	Sagittarius	Gemini	Aquarius	Cancer	Gemini
12			Virgo	Leo	Virgo	Sagittarius	Gemini	Aquarius	Cancer	Gemini
13	7:13 A.M.	Virgo	Virgo	Virgo	Virgo	Sagittarius	Gemini	Aquarius	Cancer	Gemini
14			Virgo	Virgo	Virgo	Sagittarius	Gemini	Aquarius	Cancer	Gemini
15	7:48 A.M.	Libra	Virgo	Virgo	Virgo	Sagittarius	Gemini	Aquarius	Cancer	Gemini
16			Virgo	Virgo	Virgo	Sagittarius	Gemini	Aquarius	Cancer	Gemini
17	11:28 A.M.	Scorpio	Virgo	Virgo	Virgo	Sagittarius	Gemini	Aquarius	Cancer	Gemini
18			Virgo	Virgo	Virgo	Sagittarius	Gemini	Aquarius	Cancer	Gemini
19	6:58 P.M.	Sagittarius	Virgo	Virgo	Virgo	Sagittarius	Gemini	Aquarius	Cancer	Gemini
20			Virgo	Virgo	Virgo	Sagittarius	Gemini	Aquarius	Cancer	Gemini
21			Leo	Virgo	Virgo	Sagittarius	Gemini	Aquarius	Cancer	Gemini
22	5:42 A.M.	Capricorn	Leo	Virgo	Virgo	Sagittarius	Gemini	Aquarius	Cancer	Gemini
23			Leo	Virgo	Virgo	Sagittarius	Gemini	Aquarius	Cancer	Gemini

LEO PLANETARY TABLES

1913

	MOON FROM	IN	MERCURY	VENUS	MARS	JUPITER	SATURN	URANUS	NEPTUNE	PLUTO
July										
24		Aries	Leo	Gemini	Taurus	Capricorn	Gemini	Aquarius	Cancer	Cancer
25	11:28 P.M.	Taurus	Leo	Gemini	Taurus	Capricorn	Gemini	Aquarius	Cancer	Cancer
26			Leo	Gemini	Taurus	Capricorn	Gemini	Aquarius	Cancer	Cancer
27			Leo	Gemini	Taurus	Capricorn	Gemini	Aquarius	Cancer	Cancer
28	8:56 A.M.	Gemini	Leo	Gemini	Taurus	Capricorn	Gemini	Aquarius	Cancer	Cancer
29			Leo	Gemini	Gemini	Capricorn	Gemini	Aquarius	Cancer	Cancer
30	2:21 P.M.	Cancer	Leo	Gemini	Gemini	Capricorn	Gemini	Aquarius	Cancer	Cancer
31			Leo	Gemini	Gemini	Capricorn	Gemini	Aquarius	Cancer	Cancer
August										
1	4:23 P.M.	Leo	Leo	Gemini	Gemini	Capricorn	Gemini	Aquarius	Cancer	Cancer
2			Leo	Gemini	Gemini	Capricorn	Gemini	Aquarius	Cancer	Cancer
3	4:43 P.M.	Virgo	Leo	Gemini	Gemini	Capricorn	Gemini	Aquarius	Cancer	Cancer
4			Leo	Gemini	Gemini	Capricorn	Gemini	Aquarius	Cancer	Cancer
5	5:12 P.M.	Libra	Leo	Gemini	Gemini	Capricorn	Gemini	Aquarius	Cancer	Cancer
6			Leo	Cancer	Gemini	Capricorn	Gemini	Aquarius	Cancer	Cancer
7	7:21 P.M.	Scorpio	Leo	Cancer	Gemini	Capricorn	Gemini	Aquarius	Cancer	Cancer
8			Leo	Cancer	Gemini	Capricorn	Gemini	Aquarius	Cancer	Cancer
9			Leo	Cancer	Gemini	Capricorn	Gemini	Aquarius	Cancer	Cancer
10	0:03 A.M.	Sagittarius	Leo	Cancer	Gemini	Capricorn	Gemini	Aquarius	Cancer	Cancer
11			Leo	Cancer	Gemini	Capricorn	Gemini	Aquarius	Cancer	Cancer
12	7:24 A.M.	Capricorn	Leo	Cancer	Gemini	Capricorn	Gemini	Aquarius	Cancer	Cancer
13			Leo	Cancer	Gemini	Capricorn	Gemini	Aquarius	Cancer	Cancer
14	5:09 P.M.	Aquarius	Leo	Cancer	Gemini	Capricorn	Gemini	Aquarius	Cancer	Cancer
15			Leo	Cancer	Gemini	Capricorn	Gemini	Aquarius	Cancer	Cancer
16			Leo	Cancer	Gemini	Capricorn	Gemini	Aquarius	Cancer	Cancer
17	4:51 A.M.	Pisces	Leo	Cancer	Gemini	Capricorn	Gemini	Aquarius	Cancer	Cancer
18			Leo	Cancer	Gemini	Capricorn	Gemini	Aquarius	Cancer	Cancer
19	5:47 P.M.	Aries	Leo	Cancer	Gemini	Capricorn	Gemini	Aquarius	Cancer	Cancer
20			Leo	Cancer	Gemini	Capricorn	Gemini	Aquarius	Cancer	Cancer
21			Leo	Cancer	Gemini	Capricorn	Gemini	Aquarius	Cancer	Cancer
22	6:29 A.M.	Taurus	Leo	Cancer	Gemini	Capricorn	Gemini	Aquarius	Cancer	Cancer
23			Leo	Cancer	Gemini	Capricorn	Gemini	Aquarius	Cancer	Cancer

1914

July	MOON FROM / IN	MERCURY	VENUS	MARS	JUPITER	SATURN	URANUS	NEPTUNE	PLUTO
24	Leo	Cancer	Virgo	Virgo	Aquarius	Gemini	Aquarius	Cancer	Cancer
25	2:59 A.M. Virgo	Cancer	Virgo	Virgo	Aquarius	Gemini	Aquarius	Cancer	Cancer
26		Cancer	Virgo	Virgo	Aquarius	Gemini	Aquarius	Cancer	Cancer
27	6:04 A.M. Libra	Cancer	Virgo	Virgo	Aquarius	Gemini	Aquarius	Cancer	Cancer
28		Cancer	Virgo	Virgo	Aquarius	Gemini	Aquarius	Cancer	Cancer
29	8:44 A.M. Scorpio	Cancer	Virgo	Virgo	Aquarius	Gemini	Aquarius	Cancer	Cancer
30		Cancer	Virgo	Virgo	Aquarius	Gemini	Aquarius	Cancer	Cancer
31	11:35 A.M. Sagittarius	Cancer	Virgo	Virgo	Aquarius	Gemini	Aquarius	Cancer	Cancer
August									
1		Cancer	Virgo	Virgo	Aquarius	Gemini	Aquarius	Cancer	Cancer
2	3:14 P.M. Capricorn	Cancer	Virgo	Virgo	Aquarius	Gemini	Aquarius	Cancer	Cancer
3		Cancer	Virgo	Virgo	Aquarius	Gemini	Aquarius	Cancer	Cancer
4	8:26 P.M. Aquarius	Cancer	Virgo	Virgo	Aquarius	Gemini	Aquarius	Cancer	Cancer
5		Cancer	Virgo	Virgo	Aquarius	Gemini	Aquarius	Cancer	Cancer
6		Cancer	Virgo	Virgo	Aquarius	Gemini	Aquarius	Cancer	Cancer
7	4:03 A.M. Pisces	Cancer	Virgo	Virgo	Aquarius	Gemini	Aquarius	Cancer	Cancer
8		Cancer	Virgo	Virgo	Aquarius	Gemini	Aquarius	Cancer	Cancer
9	2:25 P.M. Aries	Cancer	Virgo	Virgo	Aquarius	Gemini	Aquarius	Cancer	Cancer
10		Cancer	Virgo	Virgo	Aquarius	Gemini	Aquarius	Cancer	Cancer
11		Leo	Libra	Virgo	Aquarius	Gemini	Aquarius	Cancer	Cancer
12	2:45 A.M. Taurus	Leo	Libra	Virgo	Aquarius	Gemini	Aquarius	Cancer	Cancer
13		Leo	Libra	Virgo	Aquarius	Gemini	Aquarius	Cancer	Cancer
14	3:05 P.M. Gemini	Leo	Libra	Virgo	Aquarius	Gemini	Aquarius	Cancer	Cancer
15		Leo	Libra	Virgo	Aquarius	Gemini	Aquarius	Cancer	Cancer
16	1:09 A.M. Cancer	Leo	Libra	Libra	Aquarius	Gemini	Aquarius	Cancer	Cancer
17		Leo	Libra	Libra	Aquarius	Gemini	Aquarius	Cancer	Cancer
18	7:51 A.M. Leo	Leo	Libra	Libra	Aquarius	Gemini	Aquarius	Cancer	Cancer
19		Leo	Libra	Libra	Aquarius	Gemini	Aquarius	Cancer	Cancer
20	11:29 A.M. Virgo	Leo	Libra	Libra	Aquarius	Gemini	Aquarius	Cancer	Cancer
21		Leo	Libra	Libra	Aquarius	Gemini	Aquarius	Cancer	Cancer
22	1:17 P.M. Libra	Leo	Libra	Libra	Aquarius	Gemini	Aquarius	Cancer	Cancer
23		Leo	Libra	Libra	Aquarius	Gemini	Aquarius	Cancer	Cancer

LEO PLANETARY TABLES

1915

		MOON FROM	IN	MERCURY	VENUS	MARS	JUPITER	SATURN	URANUS	NEPTUNE	PLUTO
July	24	2:04 A.M.	Capricorn	Cancer	Cancer	Gemini	Pisces	Cancer	Aquarius	Leo	Cancer
	25	3:11 A.M.	Aquarius	Cancer	Cancer	Gemini	Pisces	Cancer	Aquarius	Leo	Cancer
	26			Cancer	Cancer	Gemini	Pisces	Cancer	Aquarius	Leo	Cancer
	27	6:05 A.M.	Pisces	Cancer	Cancer	Gemini	Pisces	Cancer	Aquarius	Leo	Cancer
	28			Cancer	Cancer	Gemini	Pisces	Cancer	Aquarius	Leo	Cancer
	29	12:08 P.M.	Aries	Cancer	Cancer	Gemini	Pisces	Cancer	Aquarius	Leo	Cancer
	30			Cancer	Cancer	Gemini	Pisces	Cancer	Aquarius	Leo	Cancer
	31	9:40 P.M.	Taurus	Cancer	Cancer	Gemini	Pisces	Cancer	Aquarius	Leo	Cancer
August	1			Cancer	Cancer	Gemini	Pisces	Cancer	Aquarius	Leo	Cancer
	2			Cancer	Cancer	Gemini	Pisces	Cancer	Aquarius	Leo	Cancer
	3	9:43 A.M.	Gemini	Cancer	Cancer	Gemini	Pisces	Cancer	Aquarius	Leo	Cancer
	4			Leo	Leo	Gemini	Pisces	Cancer	Aquarius	Leo	Cancer
	5			Leo	Leo	Gemini	Pisces	Cancer	Aquarius	Leo	Cancer
	6	10:11 P.M.	Cancer	Leo	Leo	Gemini	Pisces	Cancer	Aquarius	Leo	Cancer
	7			Leo	Leo	Gemini	Pisces	Cancer	Aquarius	Leo	Cancer
	8			Leo	Leo	Gemini	Pisces	Cancer	Aquarius	Leo	Cancer
	9	9:08 A.M.	Leo	Leo	Leo	Gemini	Pisces	Cancer	Aquarius	Leo	Cancer
	10			Leo	Leo	Gemini	Pisces	Cancer	Aquarius	Leo	Cancer
	11	5:42 P.M.	Virgo	Leo	Leo	Gemini	Pisces	Cancer	Aquarius	Leo	Cancer
	12			Leo	Leo	Gemini	Pisces	Cancer	Aquarius	Leo	Cancer
	13	11:55 P.M.	Libra	Leo	Leo	Gemini	Pisces	Cancer	Aquarius	Leo	Cancer
	14			Leo	Leo	Gemini	Pisces	Cancer	Aquarius	Leo	Cancer
	15			Leo	Leo	Gemini	Pisces	Cancer	Aquarius	Leo	Cancer
	16	4:16 A.M.	Scorpio	Leo	Leo	Gemini	Pisces	Cancer	Aquarius	Leo	Cancer
	17			Leo	Leo	Gemini	Pisces	Cancer	Aquarius	Leo	Cancer
	18	7:19 A.M.	Sagittarius	Leo	Leo	Gemini	Pisces	Cancer	Aquarius	Leo	Cancer
	19			Virgo	Leo	Cancer	Pisces	Cancer	Aquarius	Leo	Cancer
	20	9:38 A.M.	Capricorn	Virgo	Leo	Cancer	Pisces	Cancer	Aquarius	Leo	Cancer
	21			Virgo	Leo	Cancer	Pisces	Cancer	Aquarius	Leo	Cancer
	22	12:04 P.M.	Aquarius	Virgo	Leo	Cancer	Pisces	Cancer	Aquarius	Leo	Cancer
	23			Virgo	Leo	Cancer	Pisces	Cancer	Aquarius	Leo	Cancer

1916

	MOON		MERCURY	VENUS	MARS	JUPITER	SATURN	URANUS	NEPTUNE	PLUTO
July	FROM	IN								
23	Taurus		Cancer	Cancer	Libra	Taurus	Cancer	Aquarius	Leo	Cancer
24	5:36 A.M.	Gemini	Cancer	Cancer	Libra	Taurus	Cancer	Aquarius	Leo	Cancer
25			Cancer	Cancer	Libra	Taurus	Cancer	Aquarius	Leo	Cancer
26	6:53 P.M.	Cancer	Leo	Cancer	Libra	Taurus	Cancer	Aquarius	Leo	Cancer
27			Leo	Cancer	Libra	Taurus	Cancer	Aquarius	Leo	Cancer
28			Leo	Cancer	Libra	Taurus	Cancer	Aquarius	Leo	Cancer
29	7:56 A.M.	Leo	Leo	Cancer	Libra	Taurus	Cancer	Aquarius	Leo	Cancer
30			Leo	Cancer	Libra	Taurus	Cancer	Aquarius	Leo	Cancer
31	8:18 P.M.	Virgo	Leo	Cancer	Libra	Taurus	Cancer	Aquarius	Leo	Cancer
August										
1			Leo	Cancer	Libra	Taurus	Cancer	Aquarius	Leo	Cancer
2			Leo	Cancer	Libra	Taurus	Cancer	Aquarius	Leo	Cancer
3	6:54 A.M.	Libra	Leo	Cancer	Libra	Taurus	Cancer	Aquarius	Leo	Cancer
4			Leo	Cancer	Libra	Taurus	Cancer	Aquarius	Leo	Cancer
5	2:55 P.M.	Scorpio	Leo	Cancer	Libra	Taurus	Cancer	Aquarius	Leo	Cancer
6			Leo	Cancer	Libra	Taurus	Cancer	Aquarius	Leo	Cancer
7	7:57 P.M.	Sagittarius	Leo	Cancer	Libra	Taurus	Cancer	Aquarius	Leo	Cancer
8			Leo	Cancer	Libra	Taurus	Cancer	Aquarius	Leo	Cancer
9	10:08 P.M.	Capricorn	Leo	Cancer	Libra	Taurus	Cancer	Aquarius	Leo	Cancer
10			Virgo	Cancer	Libra	Taurus	Cancer	Aquarius	Leo	Cancer
11	10:28 P.M.	Aquarius	Virgo	Cancer	Libra	Taurus	Cancer	Aquarius	Leo	Cancer
12			Virgo	Cancer	Libra	Taurus	Cancer	Aquarius	Leo	Cancer
13	10:30 P.M.	Pisces	Virgo	Cancer	Libra	Taurus	Cancer	Aquarius	Leo	Cancer
14			Virgo	Cancer	Libra	Taurus	Cancer	Aquarius	Leo	Cancer
15			Virgo	Cancer	Libra	Taurus	Cancer	Aquarius	Leo	Cancer
16	0:03 A.M.	Aries	Virgo	Cancer	Libra	Taurus	Cancer	Aquarius	Leo	Cancer
17			Virgo	Cancer	Libra	Taurus	Cancer	Aquarius	Leo	Cancer
18	4:46 A.M.	Taurus	Virgo	Cancer	Libra	Taurus	Cancer	Aquarius	Leo	Cancer
19			Virgo	Cancer	Libra	Taurus	Cancer	Aquarius	Leo	Cancer
20	1:28 P.M.	Gemini	Virgo	Cancer	Libra	Taurus	Cancer	Aquarius	Leo	Cancer
21			Virgo	Cancer	Libra	Taurus	Cancer	Aquarius	Leo	Cancer
22			Virgo	Cancer	Libra	Taurus	Cancer	Aquarius	Leo	Cancer
23	1:22 A.M.	Cancer	Virgo	Cancer	Libra	Taurus	Cancer	Aquarius	Leo	Cancer

LEO PLANETARY TABLES

1917

Date	MOON FROM / IN	MERCURY	VENUS	MARS	JUPITER	SATURN	URANUS	NEPTUNE	PLUTO
July									
23	Virgo	Leo	Leo	Gemini	Gemini	Leo	Aquarius	Leo	Cancer
24	7:33 A.M. Libra	Leo	Leo	Gemini	Gemini	Leo	Aquarius	Leo	Cancer
25		Leo	Leo	Gemini	Gemini	Leo	Aquarius	Leo	Cancer
26	6:41 P.M. Scorpio	Leo	Leo	Gemini	Gemini	Leo	Aquarius	Leo	Cancer
27		Leo	Leo	Cancer	Gemini	Leo	Aquarius	Leo	Cancer
28		Leo	Leo	Cancer	Gemini	Leo	Aquarius	Leo	Cancer
29	2:37 A.M. Sagittarius	Leo	Virgo	Cancer	Gemini	Leo	Aquarius	Leo	Cancer
30		Leo	Virgo	Cancer	Gemini	Leo	Aquarius	Leo	Cancer
31	6:48 A.M. Capricorn	Leo	Virgo	Cancer	Gemini	Leo	Aquarius	Leo	Cancer
August									
1	7:50 A.M. Aquarius	Leo	Virgo	Cancer	Gemini	Leo	Aquarius	Leo	Cancer
2		Leo	Virgo	Cancer	Gemini	Leo	Aquarius	Leo	Cancer
3		Virgo	Virgo	Cancer	Gemini	Leo	Aquarius	Leo	Cancer
4	7:20 A.M. Pisces	Virgo	Virgo	Cancer	Gemini	Leo	Aquarius	Leo	Cancer
5		Virgo	Virgo	Cancer	Gemini	Leo	Aquarius	Leo	Cancer
6	7:19 A.M. Aries	Virgo	Virgo	Cancer	Gemini	Leo	Aquarius	Leo	Cancer
7		Virgo	Virgo	Cancer	Gemini	Leo	Aquarius	Leo	Cancer
8	9:38 A.M. Taurus	Virgo	Virgo	Cancer	Gemini	Leo	Aquarius	Leo	Cancer
9		Virgo	Virgo	Cancer	Gemini	Leo	Aquarius	Leo	Cancer
10	3:25 P.M. Gemini	Virgo	Virgo	Cancer	Gemini	Leo	Aquarius	Leo	Cancer
11		Virgo	Virgo	Cancer	Gemini	Leo	Aquarius	Leo	Cancer
12		Virgo	Virgo	Cancer	Gemini	Leo	Aquarius	Leo	Cancer
13	0:40 A.M. Cancer	Virgo	Virgo	Cancer	Gemini	Leo	Aquarius	Leo	Cancer
14		Virgo	Virgo	Cancer	Gemini	Leo	Aquarius	Leo	Cancer
15	12:20 P.M. Leo	Virgo	Virgo	Cancer	Gemini	Leo	Aquarius	Leo	Cancer
16		Virgo	Virgo	Cancer	Gemini	Leo	Aquarius	Leo	Cancer
17		Virgo	Virgo	Cancer	Gemini	Leo	Aquarius	Leo	Cancer
18	1:02 A.M. Virgo	Virgo	Virgo	Cancer	Gemini	Leo	Aquarius	Leo	Cancer
19		Virgo	Virgo	Cancer	Gemini	Leo	Aquarius	Leo	Cancer
20	1:42 P.M. Libra	Virgo	Virgo	Cancer	Gemini	Leo	Aquarius	Leo	Cancer
21		Virgo	Libra	Cancer	Gemini	Leo	Aquarius	Leo	Cancer
22		Virgo	Libra	Cancer	Gemini	Leo	Aquarius	Leo	Cancer
23	1:15 A.M. Scorpio	Virgo	Libra	Cancer	Gemini	Leo	Aquarius	Leo	Cancer

1918

July	MOON FROM	IN	MERCURY	VENUS	MARS	JUPITER	SATURN	URANUS	NEPTUNE	PLUTO
24	Aquarius		Leo	Gemini	Libra	Cancer	Leo	Aquarius	Leo	Cancer
25	5:32 P.M.	Pisces	Leo	Cancer	Libra	Cancer	Leo	Aquarius	Leo	Cancer
26			Leo	Cancer	Libra	Cancer	Leo	Aquarius	Leo	Cancer
27	6:59 P.M.	Aries	Leo	Cancer	Libra	Cancer	Leo	Aquarius	Leo	Cancer
28			Virgo	Cancer	Libra	Cancer	Leo	Aquarius	Leo	Cancer
29	9:07 P.M.	Taurus	Virgo	Cancer	Libra	Cancer	Leo	Aquarius	Leo	Cancer
30			Virgo	Cancer	Libra	Cancer	Leo	Aquarius	Leo	Cancer
31			Virgo	Cancer	Libra	Cancer	Leo	Aquarius	Leo	Cancer
August										
1	0:49 A.M.	Gemini	Virgo	Cancer	Libra	Cancer	Leo	Aquarius	Leo	Cancer
2			Virgo	Cancer	Libra	Cancer	Leo	Aquarius	Leo	Cancer
3	6:22 A.M.	Cancer	Virgo	Cancer	Libra	Cancer	Leo	Aquarius	Leo	Cancer
4			Virgo	Cancer	Libra	Cancer	Leo	Aquarius	Leo	Cancer
5	1:50 P.M.	Leo	Virgo	Cancer	Libra	Cancer	Leo	Aquarius	Leo	Cancer
6			Virgo	Cancer	Libra	Cancer	Leo	Aquarius	Leo	Cancer
7	11:18 P.M.	Virgo	Virgo	Cancer	Libra	Cancer	Leo	Aquarius	Leo	Cancer
8			Virgo	Cancer	Libra	Cancer	Leo	Aquarius	Leo	Cancer
9			Virgo	Cancer	Libra	Cancer	Leo	Aquarius	Leo	Cancer
10	10:46 A.M.	Libra	Virgo	Cancer	Libra	Cancer	Leo	Aquarius	Leo	Cancer
11			Virgo	Cancer	Libra	Cancer	Leo	Aquarius	Leo	Cancer
12	11:27 P.M.	Scorpio	Virgo	Cancer	Libra	Cancer	Leo	Aquarius	Leo	Cancer
13			Virgo	Cancer	Libra	Cancer	Leo	Aquarius	Leo	Cancer
14			Virgo	Cancer	Libra	Cancer	Leo	Aquarius	Leo	Cancer
15	11:22 A.M.	Sagittarius	Virgo	Cancer	Libra	Cancer	Leo	Aquarius	Leo	Cancer
16			Virgo	Cancer	Libra	Cancer	Leo	Aquarius	Leo	Cancer
17	8:17 P.M.	Capricorn	Virgo	Cancer	Scorpio	Cancer	Leo	Aquarius	Leo	Cancer
18			Virgo	Cancer	Scorpio	Cancer	Leo	Aquarius	Leo	Cancer
19			Virgo	Leo	Scorpio	Cancer	Leo	Aquarius	Leo	Cancer
20	1:10 A.M.	Aquarius	Virgo	Leo	Scorpio	Cancer	Leo	Aquarius	Leo	Cancer
21			Virgo	Leo	Scorpio	Cancer	Leo	Aquarius	Leo	Cancer
22	2:48 A.M.	Pisces	Virgo	Leo	Scorpio	Cancer	Leo	Aquarius	Leo	Cancer
23			Virgo	Leo	Scorpio	Cancer	Leo	Aquarius	Leo	Cancer

LEO PLANETARY TABLES

1919

Date	MOON FROM	IN	MERCURY	VENUS	MARS	JUPITER	SATURN	URANUS	NEPTUNE	PLUTO
July 24	4:25 P.M.	Cancer	Leo	Virgo	Cancer	Cancer	Leo	Pisces	Leo	Cancer
25	7:04 P.M.	Leo	Leo	Virgo	Cancer	Cancer	Leo	Pisces	Leo	Cancer
26			Leo	Virgo	Cancer	Cancer	Leo	Pisces	Leo	Cancer
27			Leo	Virgo	Cancer	Cancer	Leo	Pisces	Leo	Cancer
28	11:29 P.M.	Virgo	Leo	Virgo	Cancer	Cancer	Leo	Pisces	Leo	Cancer
29			Leo	Virgo	Cancer	Cancer	Leo	Pisces	Leo	Cancer
30			Leo	Virgo	Cancer	Cancer	Leo	Pisces	Leo	Cancer
31	7:07 A.M.	Libra	Leo	Virgo	Cancer	Cancer	Leo	Pisces	Leo	Cancer
August 1			Leo	Virgo	Cancer	Cancer	Leo	Pisces	Leo	Cancer
2	6:08 P.M.	Scorpio	Leo	Virgo	Cancer	Leo	Leo	Pisces	Leo	Cancer
3			Leo	Virgo	Cancer	Leo	Leo	Pisces	Leo	Cancer
4			Leo	Virgo	Cancer	Leo	Leo	Pisces	Leo	Cancer
5	6:58 A.M.	Sagittarius	Leo	Virgo	Cancer	Leo	Leo	Pisces	Leo	Cancer
6			Leo	Virgo	Cancer	Leo	Leo	Pisces	Leo	Cancer
7	6:52 P.M.	Capricorn	Leo	Virgo	Cancer	Leo	Leo	Pisces	Leo	Cancer
8			Leo	Virgo	Cancer	Leo	Leo	Pisces	Leo	Cancer
9			Leo	Virgo	Cancer	Leo	Leo	Pisces	Leo	Cancer
10	3:56 P.M.	Aquarius	Leo	Virgo	Cancer	Leo	Leo	Pisces	Leo	Cancer
11			Leo	Virgo	Cancer	Leo	Leo	Pisces	Leo	Cancer
12	9:59 P.M.	Pisces	Leo	Virgo	Cancer	Leo	Virgo	Pisces	Leo	Cancer
13			Leo	Virgo	Cancer	Leo	Virgo	Pisces	Leo	Cancer
14	1:59 P.M.	Aries	Leo	Virgo	Cancer	Leo	Virgo	Pisces	Leo	Cancer
15			Leo	Virgo	Cancer	Leo	Virgo	Pisces	Leo	Cancer
16	5:05 P.M.	Taurus	Leo	Virgo	Cancer	Leo	Virgo	Pisces	Leo	Cancer
17			Leo	Virgo	Cancer	Leo	Virgo	Pisces	Leo	Cancer
18	8:03 P.M.	Gemini	Leo	Virgo	Cancer	Leo	Virgo	Aquarius	Leo	Cancer
19			Leo	Virgo	Cancer	Leo	Virgo	Aquarius	Leo	Cancer
20	11:14 P.M.	Cancer	Leo	Virgo	Cancer	Leo	Virgo	Aquarius	Leo	Cancer
21			Leo	Virgo	Cancer	Leo	Virgo	Aquarius	Leo	Cancer
22			Leo	Virgo	Cancer	Leo	Virgo	Aquarius	Leo	Cancer
23	3:00 A.M.	Leo	Leo	Virgo	Leo	Leo	Virgo	Aquarius	Leo	Cancer

1920

	MOON									
July	FROM	IN	MERCURY	VENUS	MARS	JUPITER	SATURN	URANUS	NEPTUNE	PLUTO
23	Scorpio		Leo	Leo	Scorpio	Leo	Virgo	Pisces	Leo	Cancer
24			Leo	Leo	Scorpio	Leo	Virgo	Pisces	Leo	Cancer
25	2:32 A.M.	Sagittarius	Leo	Leo	Scorpio	Leo	Virgo	Pisces	Leo	Cancer
26			Leo	Leo	Scorpio	Leo	Virgo	Pisces	Leo	Cancer
27	3:22 P.M.	Capricorn	Leo	Leo	Scorpio	Leo	Virgo	Pisces	Leo	Cancer
28			Leo	Leo	Scorpio	Leo	Virgo	Pisces	Leo	Cancer
29			Leo	Leo	Scorpio	Leo	Virgo	Pisces	Leo	Cancer
30	3:36 A.M.	Aquarius	Leo	Leo	Scorpio	Leo	Virgo	Pisces	Leo	Cancer
31			Leo	Leo	Scorpio	Leo	Virgo	Pisces	Leo	Cancer
August										
1	2:18 P.M.	Pisces	Leo	Leo	Scorpio	Leo	Virgo	Pisces	Leo	Cancer
2			Leo	Leo	Scorpio	Leo	Virgo	Pisces	Leo	Cancer
3	11:09 P.M.	Aries	Cancer	Leo	Scorpio	Leo	Virgo	Pisces	Leo	Cancer
4			Cancer	Leo	Scorpio	Leo	Virgo	Pisces	Leo	Cancer
5			Cancer	Leo	Scorpio	Leo	Virgo	Pisces	Leo	Cancer
6	5:56 A.M.	Taurus	Cancer	Leo	Scorpio	Leo	Virgo	Pisces	Leo	Cancer
7			Cancer	Leo	Scorpio	Leo	Virgo	Pisces	Leo	Cancer
8	10:14 A.M.	Gemini	Cancer	Leo	Scorpio	Leo	Virgo	Pisces	Leo	Cancer
9			Cancer	Leo	Scorpio	Leo	Virgo	Pisces	Leo	Cancer
10	12:11 P.M.	Cancer	Leo	Leo	Scorpio	Leo	Virgo	Pisces	Leo	Cancer
11			Leo	Leo	Scorpio	Leo	Virgo	Pisces	Leo	Cancer
12	12:42 P.M.	Leo	Leo	Virgo	Scorpio	Leo	Virgo	Pisces	Leo	Cancer
13			Leo	Virgo	Scorpio	Leo	Virgo	Pisces	Leo	Cancer
14	1:28 P.M.	Virgo	Leo	Virgo	Scorpio	Leo	Virgo	Pisces	Leo	Cancer
15			Leo	Virgo	Scorpio	Leo	Virgo	Pisces	Leo	Cancer
16	4:29 P.M.	Libra	Leo	Virgo	Scorpio	Leo	Virgo	Pisces	Leo	Cancer
17			Leo	Virgo	Scorpio	Leo	Virgo	Pisces	Leo	Cancer
18	11:14 P.M.	Scorpio	Leo	Virgo	Scorpio	Leo	Virgo	Pisces	Leo	Cancer
19			Leo	Virgo	Scorpio	Leo	Virgo	Pisces	Leo	Cancer
20			Leo	Virgo	Scorpio	Leo	Virgo	Pisces	Leo	Cancer
21	9:46 A.M.	Sagittarius	Leo	Virgo	Scorpio	Leo	Virgo	Pisces	Leo	Cancer
22			Leo	Virgo	Scorpio	Leo	Virgo	Pisces	Leo	Cancer

LEO PLANETARY TABLES

1921

MOON FROM	IN	MERCURY	VENUS	MARS	JUPITER	SATURN	URANUS	NEPTUNE	PLUTO
July									
23	Pisces	Cancer	Gemini	Cancer	Virgo	Virgo	Pisces	Leo	Cancer
24		Cancer	Gemini	Cancer	Virgo	Virgo	Pisces	Leo	Cancer
25	2:41 A.M. Aries	Cancer	Gemini	Cancer	Virgo	Virgo	Pisces	Leo	Cancer
26		Cancer	Gemini	Cancer	Virgo	Virgo	Pisces	Leo	Cancer
27	12:57 P.M. Taurus	Cancer	Gemini	Cancer	Virgo	Virgo	Pisces	Leo	Cancer
28		Cancer	Gemini	Cancer	Virgo	Virgo	Pisces	Leo	Cancer
29	7:37 P.M. Gemini	Cancer	Gemini	Cancer	Virgo	Virgo	Pisces	Leo	Cancer
30		Cancer	Gemini	Cancer	Virgo	Virgo	Pisces	Leo	Cancer
31	10:17 P.M. Cancer	Cancer	Gemini	Cancer	Virgo	Virgo	Pisces	Leo	Cancer
August									
1		Cancer	Gemini	Cancer	Virgo	Virgo	Pisces	Leo	Cancer
2	10:11 P.M. Leo	Cancer	Gemini	Cancer	Virgo	Virgo	Pisces	Leo	Cancer
3		Cancer	Gemini	Leo	Virgo	Virgo	Pisces	Leo	Cancer
4	9:19 P.M. Virgo	Cancer	Gemini	Leo	Virgo	Virgo	Pisces	Leo	Cancer
5		Cancer	Gemini	Leo	Virgo	Virgo	Pisces	Leo	Cancer
6	9:53 P.M. Libra	Cancer	Cancer	Leo	Virgo	Virgo	Pisces	Leo	Cancer
7		Leo	Cancer	Leo	Virgo	Virgo	Pisces	Leo	Cancer
8		Leo	Cancer	Leo	Virgo	Virgo	Pisces	Leo	Cancer
9	1:35 A.M. Scorpio	Leo	Cancer	Leo	Virgo	Virgo	Pisces	Leo	Cancer
10		Leo	Cancer	Leo	Virgo	Virgo	Pisces	Leo	Cancer
11	9:00 A.M. Sagittarius	Leo	Cancer	Leo	Virgo	Virgo	Pisces	Leo	Cancer
12		Leo	Cancer	Leo	Virgo	Virgo	Pisces	Leo	Cancer
13	7:30 P.M. Capricorn	Leo	Cancer	Leo	Virgo	Virgo	Pisces	Leo	Cancer
14		Leo	Cancer	Leo	Virgo	Virgo	Pisces	Leo	Cancer
15		Leo	Cancer	Leo	Virgo	Virgo	Pisces	Leo	Cancer
16	7:42 A.M. Aquarius	Leo	Cancer	Leo	Virgo	Virgo	Pisces	Leo	Cancer
17		Leo	Cancer	Leo	Virgo	Virgo	Pisces	Leo	Cancer
18	8:20 P.M. Pisces	Leo	Cancer	Leo	Virgo	Virgo	Pisces	Leo	Cancer
19		Leo	Cancer	Leo	Virgo	Virgo	Pisces	Leo	Cancer
20		Leo	Cancer	Leo	Virgo	Virgo	Pisces	Leo	Cancer
21	8:30 A.M. Aries	Leo	Cancer	Leo	Virgo	Virgo	Pisces	Leo	Cancer
22		Leo	Cancer	Leo	Virgo	Virgo	Pisces	Leo	Cancer
23	7:07 P.M. Taurus	Leo	Cancer	Leo	Virgo	Virgo	Pisces	Leo	Cancer

1922

	MOON FROM	IN	MERCURY	VENUS	MARS	JUPITER	SATURN	URANUS	NEPTUNE	PLUTO
July										
24	6:27 A.M.	Leo	Cancer	Virgo	Sagittarius	Libra	Libra	Pisces	Leo	Cancer
25			Cancer	Virgo	Sagittarius	Libra	Libra	Pisces	Leo	Cancer
26	7:22 A.M.	Virgo	Cancer	Virgo	Sagittarius	Libra	Libra	Pisces	Leo	Cancer
27			Cancer	Virgo	Sagittarius	Libra	Libra	Pisces	Leo	Cancer
28	7:09 A.M.	Libra	Cancer	Virgo	Sagittarius	Libra	Libra	Pisces	Leo	Cancer
29			Cancer	Virgo	Sagittarius	Libra	Libra	Pisces	Leo	Cancer
30	11:00 A.M.	Scorpio	Cancer	Virgo	Sagittarius	Libra	Libra	Pisces	Leo	Cancer
31			Cancer	Virgo	Sagittarius	Libra	Libra	Pisces	Leo	Cancer
August										
1	3:36 P.M.	Sagittarius	Leo	Virgo	Sagittarius	Libra	Libra	Pisces	Leo	Cancer
2			Leo	Virgo	Sagittarius	Libra	Libra	Pisces	Leo	Cancer
3	10:23 P.M.	Capricorn	Leo	Virgo	Sagittarius	Libra	Libra	Pisces	Leo	Cancer
4			Leo	Virgo	Sagittarius	Libra	Libra	Pisces	Leo	Cancer
5			Leo	Virgo	Sagittarius	Libra	Libra	Pisces	Leo	Cancer
6	7:19 A.M.	Aquarius	Leo	Virgo	Sagittarius	Libra	Libra	Pisces	Leo	Cancer
7			Leo	Virgo	Sagittarius	Libra	Libra	Pisces	Leo	Cancer
8	6:23 P.M.	Pisces	Leo	Virgo	Sagittarius	Libra	Libra	Pisces	Leo	Cancer
9			Leo	Libra	Sagittarius	Libra	Libra	Pisces	Leo	Cancer
10	7:06 A.M.	Aries	Leo	Libra	Sagittarius	Libra	Libra	Pisces	Leo	Cancer
11			Leo	Libra	Sagittarius	Libra	Libra	Pisces	Leo	Cancer
12			Leo	Libra	Sagittarius	Libra	Libra	Pisces	Leo	Cancer
13	7:57 P.M.	Taurus	Leo	Libra	Sagittarius	Libra	Libra	Pisces	Leo	Cancer
14			Leo	Libra	Sagittarius	Libra	Libra	Pisces	Leo	Cancer
15			Virgo	Libra	Sagittarius	Libra	Libra	Pisces	Leo	Cancer
16	6:43 A.M.	Gemini	Virgo	Libra	Sagittarius	Libra	Libra	Pisces	Leo	Cancer
17			Virgo	Libra	Sagittarius	Libra	Libra	Pisces	Leo	Cancer
18	1:39 P.M.	Cancer	Virgo	Libra	Sagittarius	Libra	Libra	Pisces	Leo	Cancer
19			Virgo	Libra	Sagittarius	Libra	Libra	Pisces	Leo	Cancer
20	4:45 P.M.	Leo	Virgo	Libra	Sagittarius	Libra	Libra	Pisces	Leo	Cancer
21			Virgo	Libra	Sagittarius	Libra	Libra	Pisces	Leo	Cancer
22	5:16 P.M.	Virgo	Virgo	Libra	Sagittarius	Libra	Libra	Pisces	Leo	Cancer
23			Virgo	Libra	Sagittarius	Libra	Libra	Pisces	Leo	Cancer

LEO PLANETARY TABLES

1923

Date	Moon FROM	Moon IN	MERCURY	VENUS	MARS	JUPITER	SATURN	URANUS	NEPTUNE	PLUTO
July 24		Sagittarius	Leo	Cancer	Leo	Scorpio	Libra	Pisces	Leo	Cancer
25	6:33 A.M.	Capricorn	Leo	Cancer	Leo	Scorpio	Libra	Pisces	Leo	Cancer
26			Leo	Cancer	Leo	Scorpio	Libra	Pisces	Leo	Cancer
27	10:43 A.M.	Aquarius	Leo	Cancer	Leo	Scorpio	Libra	Pisces	Leo	Cancer
28			Leo	Cancer	Leo	Scorpio	Libra	Pisces	Leo	Cancer
29	5:24 P.M.	Pisces	Leo	Cancer	Leo	Scorpio	Libra	Pisces	Leo	Cancer
30			Leo	Cancer	Leo	Scorpio	Libra	Pisces	Leo	Cancer
31			Leo	Cancer	Leo	Scorpio	Libra	Pisces	Leo	Cancer
August 1	3:12 A.M.	Aries	Leo	Cancer	Leo	Scorpio	Libra	Pisces	Leo	Cancer
2			Leo	Cancer	Leo	Scorpio	Libra	Pisces	Leo	Cancer
3	3:22 P.M.	Taurus	Leo	Cancer	Leo	Scorpio	Libra	Pisces	Leo	Cancer
4			Leo	Leo	Leo	Scorpio	Libra	Pisces	Leo	Cancer
5			Leo	Leo	Leo	Scorpio	Libra	Pisces	Leo	Cancer
6	3:47 A.M.	Gemini	Leo	Leo	Leo	Scorpio	Libra	Pisces	Leo	Cancer
7			Leo	Leo	Leo	Scorpio	Libra	Pisces	Leo	Cancer
8	2:07 P.M.	Cancer	Virgo	Leo	Leo	Scorpio	Libra	Pisces	Leo	Cancer
9			Virgo	Leo	Leo	Scorpio	Libra	Pisces	Leo	Cancer
10	9:19 P.M.	Leo	Virgo	Leo	Leo	Scorpio	Libra	Pisces	Leo	Cancer
11			Virgo	Leo	Leo	Scorpio	Libra	Pisces	Leo	Cancer
12			Virgo	Leo	Leo	Scorpio	Libra	Pisces	Leo	Cancer
13	1:43 A.M.	Virgo	Virgo	Leo	Leo	Scorpio	Libra	Pisces	Leo	Cancer
14			Virgo	Leo	Leo	Scorpio	Libra	Pisces	Leo	Cancer
15	4:27 A.M.	Libra	Virgo	Leo	Leo	Scorpio	Libra	Pisces	Leo	Cancer
16			Virgo	Leo	Leo	Scorpio	Libra	Pisces	Leo	Cancer
17	6:38 A.M.	Scorpio	Virgo	Leo	Leo	Scorpio	Libra	Pisces	Leo	Cancer
18			Virgo	Leo	Leo	Scorpio	Libra	Pisces	Leo	Cancer
19	9:12 A.M.	Sagittarius	Virgo	Leo	Leo	Scorpio	Libra	Pisces	Leo	Cancer
20			Virgo	Leo	Leo	Scorpio	Libra	Pisces	Leo	Cancer
21	12:50 P.M.	Capricorn	Virgo	Leo	Leo	Scorpio	Libra	Pisces	Leo	Cancer
22			Virgo	Leo	Leo	Scorpio	Libra	Pisces	Leo	Cancer
23	6:03 P.M.	Aquarius	Virgo	Leo	Leo	Scorpio	Libra	Pisces	Leo	Cancer

1924

July	MOON FROM	IN	MERCURY	VENUS	MARS	JUPITER	SATURN	URANUS	NEPTUNE	PLUTO
23	10:37 A.M.	Taurus	Leo	Cancer	Pisces	Sagittarius	Libra	Pisces	Leo	Cancer
24			Leo	Cancer	Pisces	Sagittarius	Libra	Pisces	Leo	Cancer
25	10:37 P.M.	Gemini	Leo	Cancer	Pisces	Sagittarius	Libra	Pisces	Leo	Cancer
26			Leo	Cancer	Pisces	Sagittarius	Libra	Pisces	Leo	Cancer
27			Leo	Cancer	Pisces	Sagittarius	Libra	Pisces	Leo	Cancer
28	11:11 A.M.	Cancer	Leo	Cancer	Pisces	Sagittarius	Libra	Pisces	Leo	Cancer
29			Leo	Cancer	Pisces	Sagittarius	Libra	Pisces	Leo	Cancer
30	10:38 P.M.	Leo	Leo	Cancer	Pisces	Sagittarius	Libra	Pisces	Leo	Cancer
31			Virgo	Cancer	Pisces	Sagittarius	Libra	Pisces	Leo	Cancer
August										
1	8:05 A.M.	Virgo	Virgo	Cancer	Pisces	Sagittarius	Libra	Pisces	Leo	Cancer
2			Virgo	Cancer	Pisces	Sagittarius	Libra	Pisces	Leo	Cancer
3	3:19 P.M.	Libra	Virgo	Cancer	Pisces	Sagittarius	Libra	Pisces	Leo	Cancer
4			Virgo	Cancer	Pisces	Sagittarius	Libra	Pisces	Leo	Cancer
5			Virgo	Cancer	Pisces	Sagittarius	Libra	Pisces	Leo	Cancer
6	8:24 P.M.	Scorpio	Virgo	Cancer	Pisces	Sagittarius	Libra	Pisces	Leo	Cancer
7			Virgo	Cancer	Pisces	Sagittarius	Libra	Pisces	Leo	Cancer
8	11:31 P.M.	Sagittarius	Virgo	Cancer	Pisces	Sagittarius	Libra	Pisces	Leo	Cancer
9			Virgo	Cancer	Pisces	Sagittarius	Libra	Pisces	Leo	Cancer
10			Virgo	Cancer	Pisces	Sagittarius	Libra	Pisces	Leo	Cancer
11	1:20 A.M.	Capricorn	Virgo	Cancer	Pisces	Sagittarius	Libra	Pisces	Leo	Cancer
12			Virgo	Cancer	Pisces	Sagittarius	Libra	Pisces	Leo	Cancer
13	2:52 A.M.	Aquarius	Virgo	Cancer	Pisces	Sagittarius	Libra	Pisces	Leo	Cancer
14			Virgo	Cancer	Pisces	Sagittarius	Libra	Pisces	Leo	Cancer
15	5:29 A.M.	Pisces	Virgo	Cancer	Pisces	Sagittarius	Libra	Pisces	Leo	Cancer
16			Virgo	Cancer	Pisces	Sagittarius	Libra	Pisces	Leo	Cancer
17	10:33 A.M.	Aries	Virgo	Cancer	Pisces	Sagittarius	Libra	Pisces	Leo	Cancer
18			Virgo	Cancer	Pisces	Sagittarius	Libra	Pisces	Leo	Cancer
19	6:54 P.M.	Taurus	Virgo	Cancer	Pisces	Sagittarius	Libra	Pisces	Leo	Cancer
20			Virgo	Cancer	Pisces	Sagittarius	Libra	Pisces	Leo	Cancer
21			Virgo	Cancer	Pisces	Sagittarius	Libra	Pisces	Leo	Cancer
22	6:15 A.M.	Gemini	Virgo	Cancer	Pisces	Sagittarius	Libra	Pisces	Leo	Cancer

LEO PLANETARY TABLES

1925

	MOON FROM	IN	MERCURY	VENUS	MARS	JUPITER	SATURN	URANUS	NEPTUNE	PLUTO
July										
23	10:17 A.M.	Virgo	Leo	Leo	Leo	Capricorn	Scorpio	Pisces	Leo	Cancer
24			Leo	Leo	Leo	Capricorn	Scorpio	Pisces	Leo	Cancer
25	9:29 P.M.	Libra	Leo	Leo	Leo	Capricorn	Scorpio	Pisces	Leo	Cancer
26			Virgo	Leo	Leo	Capricorn	Scorpio	Pisces	Leo	Cancer
27			Virgo	Leo	Leo	Capricorn	Scorpio	Pisces	Leo	Cancer
28	5:56 A.M.	Scorpio	Virgo	Virgo	Leo	Capricorn	Scorpio	Pisces	Leo	Cancer
29			Virgo	Virgo	Leo	Capricorn	Scorpio	Pisces	Leo	Cancer
30	10:55 A.M.	Sagittarius	Virgo	Virgo	Leo	Capricorn	Scorpio	Pisces	Leo	Cancer
31			Virgo	Virgo	Leo	Capricorn	Scorpio	Pisces	Leo	Cancer
August										
1	12:46 P.M.	Capricorn	Virgo	Virgo	Leo	Capricorn	Scorpio	Pisces	Leo	Cancer
2			Virgo	Virgo	Leo	Capricorn	Scorpio	Pisces	Leo	Cancer
3	12:41 P.M.	Aquarius	Virgo	Virgo	Leo	Capricorn	Scorpio	Pisces	Leo	Cancer
4			Virgo	Virgo	Leo	Capricorn	Scorpio	Pisces	Leo	Cancer
5	12:24 P.M.	Pisces	Virgo	Virgo	Leo	Capricorn	Scorpio	Pisces	Leo	Cancer
6			Virgo	Virgo	Leo	Capricorn	Scorpio	Pisces	Leo	Cancer
7	1:48 P.M.	Aries	Virgo	Virgo	Leo	Capricorn	Scorpio	Pisces	Leo	Cancer
8			Virgo	Virgo	Leo	Capricorn	Scorpio	Pisces	Leo	Cancer
9	6:25 P.M.	Taurus	Virgo	Virgo	Leo	Capricorn	Scorpio	Pisces	Leo	Cancer
10			Virgo	Virgo	Leo	Capricorn	Scorpio	Pisces	Leo	Cancer
11			Virgo	Virgo	Leo	Capricorn	Scorpio	Pisces	Leo	Cancer
12	2:58 A.M.	Gemini	Virgo	Virgo	Leo	Capricorn	Scorpio	Pisces	Leo	Cancer
13			Virgo	Virgo	Virgo	Capricorn	Scorpio	Pisces	Leo	Cancer
14	2:39 P.M.	Cancer	Virgo	Virgo	Virgo	Capricorn	Scorpio	Pisces	Leo	Cancer
15			Virgo	Virgo	Virgo	Capricorn	Scorpio	Pisces	Leo	Cancer
16			Virgo	Virgo	Virgo	Capricorn	Scorpio	Pisces	Leo	Cancer
17	3:41 A.M.	Leo	Virgo	Virgo	Virgo	Capricorn	Scorpio	Pisces	Leo	Cancer
18			Virgo	Virgo	Virgo	Capricorn	Scorpio	Pisces	Leo	Cancer
19	4:12 P.M.	Virgo	Virgo	Virgo	Virgo	Capricorn	Scorpio	Pisces	Leo	Cancer
20			Virgo	Virgo	Virgo	Capricorn	Scorpio	Pisces	Leo	Cancer
21			Virgo	Virgo	Virgo	Capricorn	Scorpio	Pisces	Leo	Cancer
22	3:05 A.M.	Libra	Virgo	Libra	Virgo	Capricorn	Scorpio	Pisces	Leo	Cancer
23			Virgo	Libra	Virgo	Capricorn	Scorpio	Pisces	Leo	Cancer

1926

	MOON FROM	IN	MERCURY	VENUS	MARS	JUPITER	SATURN	URANUS	NEPTUNE	PLUTO
July										
24	9:48 P.M.	Aquarius	Leo	Cancer	Aries	Aquarius	Scorpio	Pisces	Leo	Cancer
25			Leo	Cancer	Aries	Aquarius	Scorpio	Pisces	Leo	Cancer
26	9:46 P.M.	Pisces	Leo	Cancer	Aries	Aquarius	Scorpio	Pisces	Leo	Cancer
27			Leo	Cancer	Aries	Aquarius	Scorpio	Pisces	Leo	Cancer
28	10:14 P.M.	Aries	Leo	Cancer	Aries	Aquarius	Scorpio	Pisces	Leo	Cancer
29			Leo	Cancer	Aries	Aquarius	Scorpio	Pisces	Leo	Cancer
30			Leo	Cancer	Aries	Aquarius	Scorpio	Pisces	Leo	Cancer
31	0:48 A.M.	Taurus	Leo	Cancer	Aries	Aquarius	Scorpio	Pisces	Leo	Cancer
August										
1			Leo	Cancer	Taurus	Aquarius	Scorpio	Pisces	Leo	Cancer
2	6:25 A.M.	Gemini	Leo	Cancer	Taurus	Aquarius	Scorpio	Pisces	Leo	Cancer
3			Leo	Cancer	Taurus	Aquarius	Scorpio	Pisces	Leo	Cancer
4	3:09 P.M.	Cancer	Leo	Cancer	Taurus	Aquarius	Scorpio	Pisces	Leo	Cancer
5			Leo	Cancer	Taurus	Aquarius	Scorpio	Pisces	Leo	Cancer
6			Leo	Cancer	Taurus	Aquarius	Scorpio	Pisces	Leo	Cancer
7	2:13 A.M.	Leo	Leo	Cancer	Taurus	Aquarius	Scorpio	Pisces	Leo	Cancer
8			Leo	Cancer	Taurus	Aquarius	Scorpio	Pisces	Leo	Cancer
9	2:39 P.M.	Virgo	Leo	Cancer	Taurus	Aquarius	Scorpio	Pisces	Leo	Cancer
10			Leo	Cancer	Taurus	Aquarius	Scorpio	Pisces	Leo	Cancer
11			Leo	Cancer	Taurus	Aquarius	Scorpio	Pisces	Leo	Cancer
12	3:26 A.M.	Libra	Leo	Cancer	Taurus	Aquarius	Scorpio	Pisces	Leo	Cancer
13			Leo	Cancer	Taurus	Aquarius	Scorpio	Pisces	Leo	Cancer
14	3:17 P.M.	Scorpio	Leo	Cancer	Taurus	Aquarius	Scorpio	Pisces	Leo	Cancer
15			Leo	Cancer	Taurus	Aquarius	Scorpio	Pisces	Leo	Cancer
16			Leo	Cancer	Taurus	Aquarius	Scorpio	Pisces	Leo	Cancer
17	0:38 A.M.	Sagittarius	Leo	Cancer	Taurus	Aquarius	Scorpio	Pisces	Leo	Cancer
18			Leo	Leo	Taurus	Aquarius	Scorpio	Pisces	Leo	Cancer
19	6:23 A.M.	Capricorn	Leo	Leo	Taurus	Aquarius	Scorpio	Pisces	Leo	Cancer
20			Leo	Leo	Taurus	Aquarius	Scorpio	Pisces	Leo	Cancer
21	8:30 A.M.	Aquarius	Leo	Leo	Taurus	Aquarius	Scorpio	Pisces	Leo	Cancer
22			Leo	Leo	Taurus	Aquarius	Scorpio	Pisces	Leo	Cancer
23	8:14 A.M.	Pisces	Leo	Leo	Taurus	Aquarius	Scorpio	Pisces	Leo	Cancer

1927

LEO PLANETARY TABLES

Date	MOON FROM / IN	MERCURY	VENUS	MARS	JUPITER	SATURN	URANUS	NEPTUNE	PLUTO
July 24	Gemini	Cancer	Virgo	Leo	Aries	Sagittarius	Aries	Leo	Cancer
25	9:31 P.M. Cancer	Cancer	Virgo	Virgo	Aries	Sagittarius	Aries	Leo	Cancer
26		Cancer	Virgo	Virgo	Aries	Sagittarius	Aries	Leo	Cancer
27		Cancer	Virgo	Virgo	Aries	Sagittarius	Aries	Leo	Cancer
28	4:01 A.M. Leo	Cancer	Virgo	Virgo	Aries	Sagittarius	Aries	Leo	Cancer
29		Cancer	Virgo	Virgo	Aries	Sagittarius	Aries	Leo	Cancer
30	12:43 P.M. Virgo	Cancer	Virgo	Virgo	Aries	Sagittarius	Aries	Leo	Cancer
31		Cancer	Virgo	Virgo	Aries	Sagittarius	Aries	Leo	Cancer
August 1	11:44 P.M. Libra	Cancer	Virgo	Virgo	Aries	Sagittarius	Aries	Leo	Cancer
2		Cancer	Virgo	Virgo	Aries	Sagittarius	Aries	Leo	Cancer
3		Cancer	Virgo	Virgo	Aries	Sagittarius	Aries	Leo	Cancer
4	12:16 P.M. Scorpio	Cancer	Virgo	Virgo	Aries	Sagittarius	Aries	Leo	Cancer
5		Cancer	Virgo	Virgo	Aries	Sagittarius	Aries	Leo	Cancer
6		Cancer	Virgo	Virgo	Aries	Sagittarius	Aries	Leo	Cancer
7	0:13 A.M. Sagittarius	Cancer	Virgo	Virgo	Aries	Sagittarius	Aries	Leo	Cancer
8		Cancer	Virgo	Virgo	Aries	Sagittarius	Aries	Leo	Cancer
9	9:22 A.M. Capricorn	Cancer	Virgo	Virgo	Aries	Sagittarius	Aries	Leo	Cancer
10		Cancer	Virgo	Virgo	Aries	Sagittarius	Aries	Leo	Cancer
11	2:45 P.M. Aquarius	Cancer	Virgo	Virgo	Aries	Sagittarius	Aries	Leo	Cancer
12		Leo	Virgo	Virgo	Aries	Sagittarius	Aries	Leo	Cancer
13	5:05 P.M. Pisces	Leo	Virgo	Virgo	Aries	Sagittarius	Aries	Leo	Cancer
14		Leo	Virgo	Virgo	Aries	Sagittarius	Aries	Leo	Cancer
15	5:57 P.M. Aries	Leo	Virgo	Virgo	Aries	Sagittarius	Aries	Leo	Cancer
16		Leo	Virgo	Virgo	Aries	Sagittarius	Aries	Leo	Cancer
17	7:12 P.M. Taurus	Leo	Virgo	Virgo	Aries	Sagittarius	Aries	Leo	Cancer
18		Leo	Virgo	Virgo	Aries	Sagittarius	Aries	Leo	Cancer
19	10:09 P.M. Gemini	Leo	Virgo	Virgo	Aries	Sagittarius	Aries	Leo	Cancer
20		Leo	Virgo	Virgo	Aries	Sagittarius	Aries	Leo	Cancer
21		Leo	Virgo	Virgo	Aries	Sagittarius	Aries	Leo	Cancer
22	3:20 A.M. Cancer	Leo	Virgo	Virgo	Aries	Sagittarius	Aries	Leo	Cancer
23		Leo	Virgo	Virgo	Aries	Sagittarius	Aries	Leo	Cancer

1928

	MOON FROM	IN	MERCURY	VENUS	MARS	JUPITER	SATURN	URANUS	NEPTUNE	PLUTO
July										
23	Libra		Cancer	Leo	Taurus	Taurus	Sagittarius	Aries	Leo	Cancer
24	6:48 A.M.	Scorpio	Cancer	Leo	Taurus	Taurus	Sagittarius	Aries	Leo	Cancer
25			Cancer	Leo	Taurus	Taurus	Sagittarius	Aries	Leo	Cancer
26	7:34 P.M.	Sagittarius	Cancer	Leo	Taurus	Taurus	Sagittarius	Aries	Leo	Cancer
27			Cancer	Leo	Taurus	Taurus	Sagittarius	Aries	Leo	Cancer
28			Cancer	Leo	Taurus	Taurus	Sagittarius	Aries	Leo	Cancer
29	7:47 A.M.	Capricorn	Cancer	Leo	Taurus	Taurus	Sagittarius	Aries	Leo	Cancer
30			Cancer	Leo	Taurus	Taurus	Sagittarius	Aries	Leo	Cancer
31	5:33 P.M.	Aquarius	Cancer	Leo	Taurus	Taurus	Sagittarius	Aries	Leo	Cancer
August										
1			Cancer	Leo	Taurus	Taurus	Sagittarius	Aries	Leo	Cancer
2			Cancer	Leo	Taurus	Taurus	Sagittarius	Aries	Leo	Cancer
3	0:34 A.M.	Pisces	Cancer	Leo	Taurus	Taurus	Sagittarius	Aries	Leo	Cancer
4			Cancer	Leo	Taurus	Taurus	Sagittarius	Aries	Leo	Cancer
5	5:33 A.M.	Aries	Leo	Leo	Taurus	Taurus	Sagittarius	Aries	Leo	Cancer
6			Leo	Leo	Taurus	Taurus	Sagittarius	Aries	Leo	Cancer
7	9:18 A.M.	Taurus	Leo	Leo	Taurus	Taurus	Sagittarius	Aries	Leo	Cancer
8			Leo	Leo	Taurus	Taurus	Sagittarius	Aries	Leo	Cancer
9	12:22 P.M.	Gemini	Leo	Leo	Gemini	Taurus	Sagittarius	Aries	Leo	Cancer
10			Leo	Leo	Gemini	Taurus	Sagittarius	Aries	Leo	Cancer
11	3:03 P.M.	Cancer	Leo	Leo	Gemini	Taurus	Sagittarius	Aries	Leo	Cancer
12			Leo	Virgo	Gemini	Taurus	Sagittarius	Aries	Leo	Cancer
13	5:57 P.M.	Leo	Leo	Virgo	Gemini	Taurus	Sagittarius	Aries	Leo	Cancer
14			Leo	Virgo	Gemini	Taurus	Sagittarius	Aries	Leo	Cancer
15	10:08 P.M.	Virgo	Leo	Virgo	Gemini	Taurus	Sagittarius	Aries	Leo	Cancer
16			Leo	Virgo	Gemini	Taurus	Sagittarius	Aries	Leo	Cancer
17			Leo	Virgo	Gemini	Taurus	Sagittarius	Aries	Leo	Cancer
18	4:54 A.M.	Libra	Leo	Virgo	Gemini	Taurus	Sagittarius	Aries	Leo	Cancer
19			Leo	Virgo	Gemini	Taurus	Sagittarius	Aries	Leo	Cancer
20	2:58 P.M.	Scorpio	Virgo	Virgo	Gemini	Taurus	Sagittarius	Aries	Leo	Cancer
21			Virgo	Virgo	Gemini	Taurus	Sagittarius	Aries	Leo	Cancer
22			Virgo	Virgo	Gemini	Taurus	Sagittarius	Aries	Leo	Cancer

LEO PLANETARY TABLES

1929

	MOON FROM / IN	MERCURY	VENUS	MARS	JUPITER	SATURN	URANUS	NEPTUNE	PLUTO
July									
23	Aquarius	Cancer	Gemini	Virgo	Gemini	Sagittarius	Aries	Leo	Cancer
24	4:39 A.M. Pisces	Cancer	Gemini	Virgo	Gemini	Sagittarius	Aries	Virgo	Cancer
25		Cancer	Gemini	Virgo	Gemini	Sagittarius	Aries	Virgo	Cancer
26	2:13 P.M. Aries	Cancer	Gemini	Virgo	Gemini	Sagittarius	Aries	Virgo	Cancer
27		Cancer	Gemini	Virgo	Gemini	Sagittarius	Aries	Virgo	Cancer
28	9:25 P.M. Taurus	Leo	Gemini	Virgo	Gemini	Sagittarius	Aries	Virgo	Cancer
29		Leo	Gemini	Virgo	Gemini	Sagittarius	Aries	Virgo	Cancer
30		Leo	Gemini	Virgo	Gemini	Sagittarius	Aries	Virgo	Cancer
31	1:43 A.M. Gemini	Leo	Gemini	Virgo	Gemini	Sagittarius	Aries	Virgo	Cancer
August									
1		Leo	Gemini	Virgo	Gemini	Sagittarius	Aries	Virgo	Cancer
2	3:15 A.M. Cancer	Leo	Gemini	Virgo	Gemini	Sagittarius	Aries	Virgo	Cancer
3		Leo	Gemini	Virgo	Gemini	Sagittarius	Aries	Virgo	Cancer
4	3:11 A.M. Leo	Leo	Gemini	Virgo	Gemini	Sagittarius	Aries	Virgo	Cancer
5		Leo	Cancer	Virgo	Gemini	Sagittarius	Aries	Virgo	Cancer
6	3:23 A.M. Virgo	Leo	Cancer	Virgo	Gemini	Sagittarius	Aries	Virgo	Cancer
7		Leo	Cancer	Virgo	Gemini	Sagittarius	Aries	Virgo	Cancer
8	5:56 A.M. Libra	Leo	Cancer	Virgo	Gemini	Sagittarius	Aries	Virgo	Cancer
9		Leo	Cancer	Virgo	Gemini	Sagittarius	Aries	Virgo	Cancer
10	12:22 P.M. Scorpio	Leo	Cancer	Virgo	Gemini	Sagittarius	Aries	Virgo	Cancer
11		Leo	Cancer	Virgo	Gemini	Sagittarius	Aries	Virgo	Cancer
12	10:45 P.M. Sagittarius	Virgo	Cancer	Virgo	Gemini	Sagittarius	Aries	Virgo	Cancer
13		Virgo	Cancer	Virgo	Gemini	Sagittarius	Aries	Virgo	Cancer
14		Virgo	Cancer	Virgo	Gemini	Sagittarius	Aries	Virgo	Cancer
15	11:21 A.M. Capricorn	Virgo	Cancer	Virgo	Gemini	Sagittarius	Aries	Virgo	Cancer
16		Virgo	Cancer	Virgo	Gemini	Sagittarius	Aries	Virgo	Cancer
17	11:50 P.M. Aquarius	Virgo	Cancer	Virgo	Gemini	Sagittarius	Aries	Virgo	Cancer
18		Virgo	Cancer	Virgo	Gemini	Sagittarius	Aries	Virgo	Cancer
19		Virgo	Cancer	Virgo	Gemini	Sagittarius	Aries	Virgo	Cancer
20	10:46 A.M. Pisces	Virgo	Cancer	Virgo	Gemini	Sagittarius	Aries	Virgo	Cancer
21		Virgo	Cancer	Virgo	Gemini	Sagittarius	Aries	Virgo	Cancer
22	7:47 P.M. Aries	Virgo	Cancer	Libra	Gemini	Sagittarius	Aries	Virgo	Cancer

1930

July	MOON FROM IN	MERCURY	VENUS	MARS	JUPITER	SATURN	URANUS	NEPTUNE	PLUTO
24	Cancer	Leo	Virgo	Gemini	Cancer	Capricorn	Aries	Virgo	Cancer
25	12:19 P.M. Leo	Leo	Virgo	Gemini	Cancer	Capricorn	Aries	Virgo	Cancer
26		Leo	Virgo	Gemini	Cancer	Capricorn	Aries	Virgo	Cancer
27	11:35 A.M. Virgo	Leo	Virgo	Gemini	Cancer	Capricorn	Aries	Virgo	Cancer
28		Leo	Virgo	Gemini	Cancer	Capricorn	Aries	Virgo	Cancer
29	12:19 P.M. Libra	Leo	Virgo	Gemini	Cancer	Capricorn	Aries	Virgo	Cancer
30		Leo	Virgo	Gemini	Cancer	Capricorn	Aries	Virgo	Cancer
31	4:08 P.M. Scorpio	Leo	Virgo	Gemini	Cancer	Capricorn	Aries	Virgo	Cancer
August									
1		Leo	Virgo	Gemini	Cancer	Capricorn	Aries	Virgo	Cancer
2	11:25 P.M. Sagittarius	Leo	Virgo	Gemini	Cancer	Capricorn	Aries	Virgo	Cancer
3		Leo	Virgo	Gemini	Cancer	Capricorn	Aries	Virgo	Cancer
4		Virgo	Virgo	Gemini	Cancer	Capricorn	Aries	Virgo	Cancer
5	9:35 A.M. Capricorn	Virgo	Virgo	Gemini	Cancer	Capricorn	Aries	Virgo	Cancer
6		Virgo	Virgo	Gemini	Cancer	Capricorn	Aries	Virgo	Cancer
7	9:27 P.M. Aquarius	Virgo	Virgo	Gemini	Cancer	Capricorn	Aries	Virgo	Cancer
8		Virgo	Virgo	Gemini	Cancer	Capricorn	Aries	Virgo	Cancer
9		Virgo	Virgo	Gemini	Cancer	Capricorn	Aries	Virgo	Cancer
10	10:03 A.M. Pisces	Virgo	Libra	Gemini	Cancer	Capricorn	Aries	Virgo	Cancer
11		Virgo	Libra	Gemini	Cancer	Capricorn	Aries	Virgo	Cancer
12	10:32 P.M. Aries	Virgo	Libra	Gemini	Cancer	Capricorn	Aries	Virgo	Cancer
13		Virgo	Libra	Gemini	Cancer	Capricorn	Aries	Virgo	Cancer
14		Virgo	Libra	Gemini	Cancer	Capricorn	Aries	Virgo	Cancer
15	9:37 A.M. Taurus	Virgo	Libra	Gemini	Cancer	Capricorn	Aries	Virgo	Cancer
16		Virgo	Libra	Gemini	Cancer	Capricorn	Aries	Virgo	Cancer
17	5:46 P.M. Gemini	Virgo	Libra	Gemini	Cancer	Capricorn	Aries	Virgo	Cancer
18		Virgo	Libra	Gemini	Cancer	Capricorn	Aries	Virgo	Cancer
19	10:01 P.M. Cancer	Virgo	Libra	Gemini	Cancer	Capricorn	Aries	Virgo	Cancer
20		Virgo	Libra	Gemini	Cancer	Capricorn	Aries	Virgo	Cancer
21	10:57 P.M. Leo	Virgo	Libra	Gemini	Cancer	Capricorn	Aries	Virgo	Cancer
22		Virgo	Libra	Gemini	Cancer	Capricorn	Aries	Virgo	Cancer
23	10:14 P.M. Virgo	Virgo	Libra	Gemini	Cancer	Capricorn	Aries	Virgo	Cancer

LEO PLANETARY TABLES

1931

	MOON FROM	IN	MERCURY	VENUS	MARS	JUPITER	SATURN	URANUS	NEPTUNE	PLUTO
July 24	7:19 A.M.	Sagittarius	Leo	Cancer	Virgo	Leo	Capricorn	Aries	Virgo	Cancer
25			Leo	Cancer	Virgo	Leo	Capricorn	Aries	Virgo	Cancer
26	1:23 P.M.	Capricorn	Leo	Cancer	Virgo	Leo	Capricorn	Aries	Virgo	Cancer
27			Leo	Cancer	Virgo	Leo	Capricorn	Aries	Virgo	Cancer
28	9:25 P.M.	Aquarius	Leo	Cancer	Virgo	Leo	Capricorn	Aries	Virgo	Cancer
29			Virgo	Cancer	Virgo	Leo	Capricorn	Aries	Virgo	Cancer
30			Virgo	Cancer	Virgo	Leo	Capricorn	Aries	Virgo	Cancer
31	7:46 A.M.	Pisces	Virgo	Cancer	Virgo	Leo	Capricorn	Aries	Virgo	Cancer
August 1			Virgo	Cancer	Virgo	Leo	Capricorn	Aries	Virgo	Cancer
2	8:10 P.M.	Aries	Virgo	Cancer	Libra	Leo	Capricorn	Aries	Virgo	Cancer
3			Virgo	Leo	Libra	Leo	Capricorn	Aries	Virgo	Cancer
4			Virgo	Leo	Libra	Leo	Capricorn	Aries	Virgo	Cancer
5	9:05 A.M.	Taurus	Virgo	Leo	Libra	Leo	Capricorn	Aries	Virgo	Cancer
6			Virgo	Leo	Libra	Leo	Capricorn	Aries	Virgo	Cancer
7	8:01 P.M.	Gemini	Virgo	Leo	Libra	Leo	Capricorn	Aries	Virgo	Cancer
8			Virgo	Leo	Libra	Leo	Capricorn	Aries	Virgo	Cancer
9			Virgo	Leo	Libra	Leo	Capricorn	Aries	Virgo	Cancer
10	3:09 A.M.	Cancer	Virgo	Leo	Libra	Leo	Capricorn	Aries	Virgo	Cancer
11			Virgo	Leo	Libra	Leo	Capricorn	Aries	Virgo	Cancer
12	6:31 A.M.	Leo	Virgo	Leo	Libra	Leo	Capricorn	Aries	Virgo	Cancer
13			Virgo	Leo	Libra	Leo	Capricorn	Aries	Virgo	Cancer
14	7:25 A.M.	Virgo	Virgo	Leo	Libra	Leo	Capricorn	Aries	Virgo	Cancer
15			Virgo	Leo	Libra	Leo	Capricorn	Aries	Virgo	Cancer
16	7:45 A.M.	Libra	Virgo	Leo	Libra	Leo	Capricorn	Aries	Virgo	Cancer
17			Virgo	Leo	Libra	Leo	Capricorn	Aries	Virgo	Cancer
18	9:11 A.M.	Scorpio	Virgo	Leo	Libra	Leo	Capricorn	Aries	Virgo	Cancer
19			Virgo	Leo	Libra	Leo	Capricorn	Aries	Virgo	Cancer
20	12:48 P.M.	Sagittarius	Virgo	Leo	Libra	Leo	Capricorn	Aries	Virgo	Cancer
21			Virgo	Leo	Libra	Leo	Capricorn	Aries	Virgo	Cancer
22	6:58 P.M.	Capricorn	Virgo	Leo	Libra	Leo	Capricorn	Aries	Virgo	Cancer
23			Virgo	Leo	Libra	Leo	Capricorn	Aries	Virgo	Cancer

1932

July	MOON FROM	IN	MERCURY	VENUS	MARS	JUPITER	SATURN	URANUS	NEPTUNE	PLUTO
23	Aries		Leo	Gemini	Gemini	Leo	Aquarius	Aries	Virgo	Cancer
24			Leo	Gemini	Gemini	Leo	Aquarius	Aries	Virgo	Cancer
25	3:54 A.M.	Taurus	Leo	Gemini	Gemini	Leo	Aquarius	Aries	Virgo	Cancer
26			Leo	Gemini	Gemini	Leo	Aquarius	Aries	Virgo	Cancer
27	4:26 P.M.	Gemini	Leo	Gemini	Gemini	Leo	Aquarius	Aries	Virgo	Cancer
28			Virgo	Cancer	Gemini	Leo	Aquarius	Aries	Virgo	Cancer
29			Virgo	Cancer	Gemini	Leo	Aquarius	Aries	Virgo	Cancer
30	3:07 A.M.	Cancer	Virgo	Cancer	Gemini	Leo	Aquarius	Aries	Virgo	Cancer
31			Virgo	Cancer	Gemini	Leo	Aquarius	Aries	Virgo	Cancer
August										
1	10:57 A.M.	Leo	Virgo	Cancer	Gemini	Leo	Aquarius	Aries	Virgo	Cancer
2			Virgo	Cancer	Gemini	Leo	Aquarius	Aries	Virgo	Cancer
3	4:15 P.M.	Virgo	Virgo	Cancer	Gemini	Leo	Aquarius	Aries	Virgo	Cancer
4			Virgo	Cancer	Cancer	Leo	Aquarius	Aries	Virgo	Cancer
5	7:56 P.M.	Libra	Virgo	Cancer	Cancer	Leo	Aquarius	Aries	Virgo	Cancer
6			Virgo	Cancer	Cancer	Leo	Aquarius	Aries	Virgo	Cancer
7	10:49 P.M.	Scorpio	Virgo	Cancer	Cancer	Leo	Aquarius	Aries	Virgo	Cancer
8			Virgo	Cancer	Cancer	Leo	Aquarius	Aries	Virgo	Cancer
9			Virgo	Cancer	Cancer	Leo	Aquarius	Aries	Virgo	Cancer
10	1:32 A.M.	Sagittarius	Leo	Cancer	Cancer	Leo	Aquarius	Aries	Virgo	Cancer
11			Leo	Cancer	Cancer	Virgo	Aquarius	Aries	Virgo	Cancer
12	4:38 A.M.	Capricorn	Leo	Cancer	Cancer	Virgo	Aquarius	Aries	Virgo	Cancer
13			Leo	Cancer	Cancer	Virgo	Aquarius	Aries	Virgo	Cancer
14	8:54 A.M.	Aquarius	Leo	Cancer	Cancer	Virgo	Capricorn	Aries	Virgo	Cancer
15			Leo	Cancer	Cancer	Virgo	Capricorn	Aries	Virgo	Cancer
16	3:14 P.M.	Pisces	Leo	Cancer	Cancer	Virgo	Capricorn	Aries	Virgo	Cancer
17			Leo	Cancer	Cancer	Virgo	Capricorn	Aries	Virgo	Cancer
18			Leo	Cancer	Cancer	Virgo	Capricorn	Aries	Virgo	Cancer
19	0:18 A.M.	Aries	Leo	Cancer	Cancer	Virgo	Capricorn	Aries	Virgo	Cancer
20			Leo	Cancer	Cancer	Virgo	Capricorn	Aries	Virgo	Cancer
21	11:56 A.M.	Taurus	Leo	Cancer	Cancer	Virgo	Capricorn	Aries	Virgo	Cancer
22			Leo	Cancer	Cancer	Virgo	Capricorn	Aries	Virgo	Cancer

LEO PLANETARY TABLES

1933

MOON FROM	IN	MERCURY	VENUS	MARS	JUPITER	SATURN	URANUS	NEPTUNE	PLUTO
July									
23 Leo		Leo	Leo	Libra	Virgo	Aquarius	Aries	Virgo	Cancer
24 10:35 P.M.	Virgo	Leo	Leo	Libra	Virgo	Aquarius	Aries	Virgo	Cancer
25		Leo	Leo	Libra	Virgo	Aquarius	Aries	Virgo	Cancer
26		Leo	Leo	Libra	Virgo	Aquarius	Aries	Virgo	Cancer
27 6:44 A.M.	Libra	Leo	Leo	Libra	Virgo	Aquarius	Aries	Virgo	Cancer
28		Leo	Virgo	Libra	Virgo	Aquarius	Aries	Virgo	Cancer
29 12:20 P.M.	Scorpio	Leo	Virgo	Libra	Virgo	Aquarius	Aries	Virgo	Cancer
30		Leo	Virgo	Libra	Virgo	Aquarius	Aries	Virgo	Cancer
31 3:26 P.M.	Sagittarius	Leo	Virgo	Libra	Virgo	Aquarius	Aries	Virgo	Cancer
August									
1		Leo	Virgo	Libra	Virgo	Aquarius	Aries	Virgo	Cancer
2 4:40 P.M.	Capricorn	Leo	Virgo	Libra	Virgo	Aquarius	Aries	Virgo	Cancer
3		Leo	Virgo	Libra	Virgo	Aquarius	Aries	Virgo	Cancer
4 5:22 P.M.	Aquarius	Leo	Virgo	Libra	Virgo	Aquarius	Aries	Virgo	Cancer
5		Leo	Virgo	Libra	Virgo	Aquarius	Aries	Virgo	Cancer
6 7:11 P.M.	Pisces	Leo	Virgo	Libra	Virgo	Aquarius	Aries	Virgo	Cancer
7		Leo	Virgo	Libra	Virgo	Aquarius	Aries	Virgo	Cancer
8 11:42 P.M.	Aries	Leo	Virgo	Libra	Virgo	Aquarius	Aries	Virgo	Cancer
9		Leo	Virgo	Libra	Virgo	Aquarius	Aries	Virgo	Cancer
10		Leo	Virgo	Libra	Virgo	Aquarius	Aries	Virgo	Cancer
11 7:45 A.M.	Taurus	Leo	Virgo	Libra	Virgo	Aquarius	Aries	Virgo	Cancer
12		Leo	Virgo	Libra	Virgo	Aquarius	Aries	Virgo	Cancer
13 6:57 P.M.	Gemini	Leo	Virgo	Libra	Virgo	Aquarius	Aries	Virgo	Cancer
14		Leo	Virgo	Libra	Virgo	Aquarius	Aries	Virgo	Cancer
15		Leo	Virgo	Libra	Virgo	Aquarius	Aries	Virgo	Cancer
16 7:32 A.M.	Cancer	Leo	Virgo	Libra	Virgo	Aquarius	Aries	Virgo	Cancer
17		Leo	Virgo	Libra	Virgo	Aquarius	Aries	Virgo	Cancer
18 7:23 P.M.	Leo	Leo	Virgo	Libra	Virgo	Aquarius	Aries	Virgo	Cancer
19		Leo	Virgo	Libra	Virgo	Aquarius	Aries	Virgo	Cancer
20		Leo	Virgo	Libra	Virgo	Aquarius	Aries	Virgo	Cancer
21 5:07 A.M.	Virgo	Leo	Virgo	Libra	Virgo	Aquarius	Aries	Virgo	Cancer
22		Leo	Libra	Libra	Virgo	Aquarius	Aries	Virgo	Cancer
23 12:29 P.M.	Libra	Leo	Libra	Libra	Virgo	Aquarius	Aries	Virgo	Cancer

1934

	MOON		MERCURY	VENUS	MARS	JUPITER	SATURN	URANUS	NEPTUNE	PLUTO
July	FROM	IN								
24	3:04 A.M.	Capricorn	Cancer	Cancer	Cancer	Libra	Aquarius	Taurus	Virgo	Cancer
25	2:43 A.M.	Aquarius	Cancer	Cancer	Cancer	Libra	Aquarius	Taurus	Virgo	Cancer
26			Cancer	Cancer	Cancer	Libra	Aquarius	Taurus	Virgo	Cancer
27			Cancer	Cancer	Cancer	Libra	Aquarius	Taurus	Virgo	Cancer
28	2:20 A.M.	Pisces	Cancer	Cancer	Cancer	Libra	Aquarius	Taurus	Virgo	Cancer
29			Cancer	Cancer	Cancer	Libra	Aquarius	Taurus	Virgo	Cancer
30	3:46 A.M.	Aries	Cancer	Cancer	Cancer	Libra	Aquarius	Taurus	Virgo	Cancer
31			Cancer	Cancer	Cancer	Libra	Aquarius	Taurus	Virgo	Cancer
August										
1	8:25 A.M.	Taurus	Cancer	Cancer	Cancer	Libra	Aquarius	Taurus	Virgo	Cancer
2	4:49 P.M.	Gemini	Cancer	Cancer	Cancer	Libra	Aquarius	Taurus	Virgo	Cancer
3			Cancer	Cancer	Cancer	Libra	Aquarius	Taurus	Virgo	Cancer
4			Cancer	Cancer	Cancer	Libra	Aquarius	Taurus	Virgo	Cancer
5			Cancer	Cancer	Cancer	Libra	Aquarius	Taurus	Virgo	Cancer
6	4:13 A.M.	Cancer	Cancer	Cancer	Cancer	Libra	Aquarius	Taurus	Virgo	Cancer
7			Cancer	Cancer	Cancer	Libra	Aquarius	Taurus	Virgo	Cancer
8	5:08 P.M.	Leo	Cancer	Cancer	Cancer	Libra	Aquarius	Taurus	Virgo	Cancer
9			Cancer	Cancer	Cancer	Libra	Aquarius	Taurus	Virgo	Cancer
10			Leo	Cancer	Cancer	Libra	Aquarius	Taurus	Virgo	Cancer
11	5:59 A.M.	Virgo	Leo	Cancer	Cancer	Libra	Aquarius	Taurus	Virgo	Cancer
12			Leo	Cancer	Cancer	Libra	Aquarius	Taurus	Virgo	Cancer
13	5:32 P.M.	Libra	Leo	Cancer	Cancer	Libra	Aquarius	Taurus	Virgo	Cancer
14			Leo	Cancer	Cancer	Libra	Aquarius	Taurus	Virgo	Cancer
15			Leo	Cancer	Cancer	Libra	Aquarius	Taurus	Virgo	Cancer
16	2:51 A.M.	Scorpio	Leo	Cancer	Cancer	Libra	Aquarius	Taurus	Virgo	Cancer
17			Leo	Cancer	Cancer	Libra	Aquarius	Taurus	Virgo	Cancer
18	9:11 A.M.	Sagittarius	Leo	Leo	Cancer	Libra	Aquarius	Taurus	Virgo	Cancer
19			Leo	Leo	Cancer	Libra	Aquarius	Taurus	Virgo	Cancer
20	12:27 P.M.	Capricorn	Leo	Leo	Cancer	Libra	Aquarius	Taurus	Virgo	Cancer
21			Leo	Leo	Cancer	Libra	Aquarius	Taurus	Virgo	Cancer
22	1:18 P.M.	Aquarius	Leo	Leo	Cancer	Libra	Aquarius	Taurus	Virgo	Cancer
23			Leo	Leo	Cancer	Libra	Aquarius	Taurus	Virgo	Cancer

LEO PLANETARY TABLES

1935

Date	MOON FROM	MOON IN	MERCURY	VENUS	MARS	JUPITER	SATURN	URANUS	NEPTUNE	PLUTO
July 24	9:42 P.M.	Gemini	Cancer	Virgo	Libra	Scorpio	Pisces	Taurus	Virgo	Cancer
25			Cancer	Virgo	Libra	Scorpio	Pisces	Taurus	Virgo	Cancer
26	5:43 A.M.	Cancer	Cancer	Virgo	Libra	Scorpio	Pisces	Taurus	Virgo	Cancer
27			Cancer	Virgo	Libra	Scorpio	Pisces	Taurus	Virgo	Cancer
28			Cancer	Virgo	Libra	Scorpio	Pisces	Taurus	Virgo	Cancer
29	4:04 P.M.	Leo	Cancer	Virgo	Libra	Scorpio	Pisces	Taurus	Virgo	Cancer
30			Cancer	Virgo	Scorpio	Scorpio	Pisces	Taurus	Virgo	Cancer
31			Cancer	Virgo	Scorpio	Scorpio	Pisces	Taurus	Virgo	Cancer
August 1	4:06 A.M.	Virgo	Cancer	Virgo	Scorpio	Scorpio	Pisces	Taurus	Virgo	Cancer
2	4:54 P.M.	Libra	Leo	Virgo	Scorpio	Scorpio	Pisces	Taurus	Virgo	Cancer
3			Leo	Virgo	Scorpio	Scorpio	Pisces	Taurus	Virgo	Cancer
4			Leo	Virgo	Scorpio	Scorpio	Pisces	Taurus	Virgo	Cancer
5	4:57 A.M.	Scorpio	Leo	Virgo	Scorpio	Scorpio	Pisces	Taurus	Virgo	Cancer
6			Leo	Virgo	Scorpio	Scorpio	Pisces	Taurus	Virgo	Cancer
7	2:24 P.M.	Sagittarius	Leo	Virgo	Scorpio	Scorpio	Pisces	Taurus	Virgo	Cancer
8			Leo	Virgo	Scorpio	Scorpio	Pisces	Taurus	Virgo	Cancer
9	8:10 P.M.	Capricorn	Leo	Virgo	Scorpio	Scorpio	Pisces	Taurus	Virgo	Cancer
10			Leo	Virgo	Scorpio	Scorpio	Pisces	Taurus	Virgo	Cancer
11	10:21 P.M.	Aquarius	Leo	Virgo	Scorpio	Scorpio	Pisces	Taurus	Virgo	Cancer
12			Leo	Virgo	Scorpio	Scorpio	Pisces	Taurus	Virgo	Cancer
13	10:18 P.M.	Pisces	Leo	Virgo	Scorpio	Scorpio	Pisces	Taurus	Virgo	Cancer
14			Leo	Virgo	Scorpio	Scorpio	Pisces	Taurus	Virgo	Cancer
15	9:55 P.M.	Aries	Leo	Virgo	Scorpio	Scorpio	Pisces	Taurus	Virgo	Cancer
16			Leo	Virgo	Scorpio	Scorpio	Pisces	Taurus	Virgo	Cancer
17	11:08 P.M.	Taurus	Virgo	Virgo	Scorpio	Scorpio	Pisces	Taurus	Virgo	Cancer
18			Virgo	Virgo	Scorpio	Scorpio	Pisces	Taurus	Virgo	Cancer
19			Virgo	Virgo	Scorpio	Scorpio	Pisces	Taurus	Virgo	Cancer
20	3:25 A.M.	Gemini	Virgo	Virgo	Scorpio	Scorpio	Pisces	Taurus	Virgo	Cancer
21			Virgo	Virgo	Scorpio	Scorpio	Pisces	Taurus	Virgo	Cancer
22	11:17 A.M.	Cancer	Virgo	Virgo	Scorpio	Scorpio	Pisces	Taurus	Virgo	Cancer
23			Virgo	Virgo	Scorpio	Scorpio	Pisces	Taurus	Virgo	Cancer

1936

July	MOON FROM	IN	MERCURY	VENUS	MARS	JUPITER	SATURN	URANUS	NEPTUNE	PLUTO
23	12:31 P.M.	Libra	Cancer	Leo	Cancer	Sagittarius	Pisces	Taurus	Virgo	Cancer
24			Leo	Leo	Cancer	Sagittarius	Pisces	Taurus	Virgo	Cancer
25	0:54 A.M.	Scorpio	Leo	Leo	Cancer	Sagittarius	Pisces	Taurus	Virgo	Cancer
26			Leo	Leo	Cancer	Sagittarius	Pisces	Taurus	Virgo	Cancer
27			Leo	Leo	Cancer	Sagittarius	Pisces	Taurus	Virgo	Cancer
28	12:36 P.M.	Sagittarius	Leo	Leo	Cancer	Sagittarius	Pisces	Taurus	Virgo	Cancer
29			Leo	Leo	Cancer	Sagittarius	Pisces	Taurus	Virgo	Cancer
30	10:23 P.M.	Capricorn	Leo	Leo	Cancer	Sagittarius	Pisces	Taurus	Virgo	Cancer
31			Leo	Leo	Cancer	Sagittarius	Pisces	Taurus	Virgo	Cancer

August	MOON FROM	IN	MERCURY	VENUS	MARS	JUPITER	SATURN	URANUS	NEPTUNE	PLUTO
1			Leo	Leo	Cancer	Sagittarius	Pisces	Taurus	Virgo	Cancer
2	4:25 A.M.	Aquarius	Leo	Leo	Cancer	Sagittarius	Pisces	Taurus	Virgo	Cancer
3			Leo	Leo	Cancer	Sagittarius	Pisces	Taurus	Virgo	Cancer
4	7:36 A.M.	Pisces	Leo	Leo	Cancer	Sagittarius	Pisces	Taurus	Virgo	Cancer
5			Leo	Leo	Cancer	Sagittarius	Pisces	Taurus	Virgo	Cancer
6	9:21 A.M.	Aries	Leo	Leo	Cancer	Sagittarius	Pisces	Taurus	Virgo	Cancer
7			Leo	Leo	Cancer	Sagittarius	Pisces	Taurus	Virgo	Cancer
8	11:12 A.M.	Taurus	Virgo	Leo	Cancer	Sagittarius	Pisces	Taurus	Virgo	Cancer
9			Virgo	Leo	Cancer	Sagittarius	Pisces	Taurus	Virgo	Cancer
10	2:12 P.M.	Gemini	Virgo	Leo	Leo	Sagittarius	Pisces	Taurus	Virgo	Cancer
11			Virgo	Virgo	Leo	Sagittarius	Pisces	Taurus	Virgo	Cancer
12	6:52 P.M.	Cancer	Virgo	Virgo	Leo	Sagittarius	Pisces	Taurus	Virgo	Cancer
13			Virgo	Virgo	Leo	Sagittarius	Pisces	Taurus	Virgo	Cancer
14			Virgo	Virgo	Leo	Sagittarius	Pisces	Taurus	Virgo	Cancer
15	1:20 A.M.	Leo	Virgo	Virgo	Leo	Sagittarius	Pisces	Taurus	Virgo	Cancer
16			Virgo	Virgo	Leo	Sagittarius	Pisces	Taurus	Virgo	Cancer
17	9:45 A.M.	Virgo	Virgo	Virgo	Leo	Sagittarius	Pisces	Taurus	Virgo	Cancer
18			Virgo	Virgo	Leo	Sagittarius	Pisces	Taurus	Virgo	Cancer
19	8:17 P.M.	Libra	Virgo	Virgo	Leo	Sagittarius	Pisces	Taurus	Virgo	Cancer
20			Virgo	Virgo	Leo	Sagittarius	Pisces	Taurus	Virgo	Cancer
21			Virgo	Virgo	Leo	Sagittarius	Pisces	Taurus	Virgo	Cancer
22	8:36 A.M.	Scorpio	Virgo	Virgo	Leo	Sagittarius	Pisces	Taurus	Virgo	Cancer

LEO PLANETARY TABLES

1937

	MOON FROM	IN	MERCURY	VENUS	MARS	JUPITER	SATURN	URANUS	NEPTUNE	PLUTO
July										
23	7:19 A.M.	Aquarius	Leo	Gemini	Scorpio	Capricorn	Aries	Taurus	Virgo	Cancer
24			Leo	Gemini	Scorpio	Capricorn	Aries	Taurus	Virgo	Cancer
25	3:18 P.M.	Pisces	Leo	Gemini	Scorpio	Capricorn	Aries	Taurus	Virgo	Cancer
26			Leo	Gemini	Scorpio	Capricorn	Aries	Taurus	Virgo	Cancer
27	9:13 P.M.	Aries	Leo	Gemini	Scorpio	Capricorn	Aries	Taurus	Virgo	Cancer
28			Leo	Gemini	Scorpio	Capricorn	Aries	Taurus	Virgo	Cancer
29			Leo	Gemini	Scorpio	Capricorn	Aries	Taurus	Virgo	Cancer
30	1:29 A.M.	Taurus	Leo	Gemini	Scorpio	Capricorn	Aries	Taurus	Virgo	Cancer
31			Leo	Gemini	Scorpio	Capricorn	Aries	Taurus	Virgo	Cancer
August										
1	4:28 A.M.	Gemini	Virgo	Gemini	Scorpio	Capricorn	Aries	Taurus	Virgo	Cancer
2			Virgo	Gemini	Scorpio	Capricorn	Aries	Taurus	Virgo	Cancer
3	6:33 A.M.	Cancer	Virgo	Gemini	Scorpio	Capricorn	Aries	Taurus	Virgo	Cancer
4			Virgo	Gemini	Scorpio	Capricorn	Aries	Taurus	Virgo	Cancer
5	8:36 A.M.	Leo	Virgo	Cancer	Scorpio	Capricorn	Aries	Taurus	Virgo	Cancer
6			Virgo	Cancer	Scorpio	Capricorn	Aries	Taurus	Virgo	Cancer
7	11:56 A.M.	Virgo	Virgo	Cancer	Scorpio	Capricorn	Aries	Taurus	Virgo	Cancer
8			Virgo	Cancer	Scorpio	Capricorn	Aries	Taurus	Virgo	Cancer
9	6:03 P.M.	Libra	Virgo	Cancer	Sagittarius	Capricorn	Aries	Taurus	Virgo	Cancer
10			Virgo	Cancer	Sagittarius	Capricorn	Aries	Taurus	Virgo	Cancer
11			Virgo	Cancer	Sagittarius	Capricorn	Aries	Taurus	Virgo	Cancer
12	3:38 A.M.	Scorpio	Virgo	Cancer	Sagittarius	Capricorn	Aries	Taurus	Virgo	Cancer
13			Virgo	Cancer	Sagittarius	Capricorn	Aries	Taurus	Virgo	Cancer
14	3:59 P.M.	Sagittarius	Virgo	Cancer	Sagittarius	Capricorn	Aries	Taurus	Virgo	Cancer
15			Virgo	Cancer	Sagittarius	Capricorn	Aries	Taurus	Virgo	Cancer
16			Virgo	Cancer	Sagittarius	Capricorn	Aries	Taurus	Virgo	Cancer
17	4:36 A.M.	Capricorn	Virgo	Cancer	Sagittarius	Capricorn	Aries	Taurus	Virgo	Cancer
18			Virgo	Cancer	Sagittarius	Capricorn	Aries	Taurus	Virgo	Cancer
19	3:02 P.M.	Aquarius	Virgo	Cancer	Sagittarius	Capricorn	Aries	Taurus	Virgo	Cancer
20			Virgo	Cancer	Sagittarius	Capricorn	Aries	Taurus	Virgo	Cancer
21	10:25 P.M.	Pisces	Virgo	Cancer	Sagittarius	Capricorn	Aries	Taurus	Virgo	Cancer
22			Virgo	Cancer	Sagittarius	Capricorn	Aries	Taurus	Virgo	Cancer
23			Virgo	Cancer	Sagittarius	Capricorn	Aries	Taurus	Virgo	Cancer

1938

	MOON		MERCURY	VENUS	MARS	JUPITER	SATURN	URANUS	NEPTUNE	PLUTO
July	FROM	IN								
24	5:54 A.M.	Cancer	Leo	Virgo	Leo	Pisces	Aries	Taurus	Virgo	Cancer
25	5:25 P.M.	Leo	Leo	Virgo	Leo	Pisces	Aries	Taurus	Virgo	Cancer
26			Leo	Virgo	Leo	Pisces	Aries	Taurus	Virgo	Cancer
27	5:18 P.M.	Virgo	Virgo	Virgo	Leo	Pisces	Aries	Taurus	Virgo	Cancer
28			Virgo	Virgo	Leo	Pisces	Aries	Taurus	Virgo	Cancer
29			Virgo	Virgo	Leo	Pisces	Aries	Taurus	Virgo	Cancer
30	7:42 P.M.	Libra	Virgo	Virgo	Leo	Aquarius	Aries	Taurus	Virgo	Cancer
31			Virgo	Virgo	Leo	Aquarius	Aries	Taurus	Virgo	Cancer
August										
1	1:53 A.M.	Scorpio	Virgo	Virgo	Leo	Aquarius	Aries	Taurus	Virgo	Cancer
2			Virgo	Virgo	Leo	Aquarius	Aries	Taurus	Virgo	Leo
3	12:04 P.M.	Sagittarius	Virgo	Virgo	Leo	Aquarius	Aries	Taurus	Virgo	Leo
4			Virgo	Virgo	Leo	Aquarius	Aries	Taurus	Virgo	Leo
5			Virgo	Virgo	Leo	Aquarius	Aries	Taurus	Virgo	Leo
6			Virgo	Virgo	Leo	Aquarius	Aries	Taurus	Virgo	Leo
7	0:34 A.M.	Capricorn	Virgo	Virgo	Leo	Aquarius	Aries	Taurus	Virgo	Leo
8			Virgo	Virgo	Leo	Aquarius	Aries	Taurus	Virgo	Leo
9	1:15 P.M.	Aquarius	Virgo	Libra	Leo	Aquarius	Aries	Taurus	Virgo	Leo
10			Virgo	Libra	Leo	Aquarius	Aries	Taurus	Virgo	Leo
11			Virgo	Libra	Leo	Aquarius	Aries	Taurus	Virgo	Leo
12	0:43 A.M.	Pisces	Virgo	Libra	Leo	Aquarius	Aries	Taurus	Virgo	Leo
13			Virgo	Libra	Leo	Aquarius	Aries	Taurus	Virgo	Leo
14	10:33 A.M.	Aries	Virgo	Libra	Leo	Aquarius	Aries	Taurus	Virgo	Leo
15			Virgo	Libra	Leo	Aquarius	Aries	Taurus	Virgo	Leo
16	6:22 P.M.	Taurus	Virgo	Libra	Leo	Aquarius	Aries	Taurus	Virgo	Leo
17			Virgo	Libra	Leo	Aquarius	Aries	Taurus	Virgo	Leo
18	11:47 P.M.	Gem:ni	Virgo	Libra	Leo	Aquarius	Aries	Taurus	Virgo	Leo
19			Virgo	Libra	Leo	Aquarius	Aries	Taurus	Virgo	Leo
20			Virgo	Libra	Leo	Aquarius	Aries	Taurus	Virgo	Leo
21	2:37 A.M.	Cancer	Virgo	Libra	Leo	Aquarius	Aries	Taurus	Virgo	Leo
22	3:26 A.M.	Leo	Virgo	Libra	Leo	Aquarius	Aries	Taurus	Virgo	Leo
23			Virgo	Libra	Leo	Aquarius	Aries	Taurus	Virgo	Leo

LEO PLANETARY TABLES

1939

Date	MOON FROM	IN	MERCURY	VENUS	MARS	JUPITER	SATURN	URANUS	NEPTUNE	PLUTO
July										
24		Scorpio	Leo	Cancer	Capricorn	Aries	Taurus	Taurus	Virgo	Leo
25	2:13 P.M.	Sagittarius	Leo	Cancer	Capricorn	Aries	Taurus	Taurus	Virgo	Leo
26			Leo	Cancer	Capricorn	Aries	Taurus	Taurus	Virgo	Leo
27	11:53 P.M.	Capricorn	Leo	Cancer	Capricorn	Aries	Taurus	Taurus	Virgo	Leo
28			Leo	Cancer	Capricorn	Aries	Taurus	Taurus	Virgo	Leo
29			Leo	Cancer	Capricorn	Aries	Taurus	Taurus	Virgo	Leo
30	11:15 A.M.	Aquarius	Leo	Cancer	Capricorn	Aries	Taurus	Taurus	Virgo	Leo
31			Leo	Cancer	Capricorn	Aries	Taurus	Taurus	Virgo	Leo
August										
1	11:41 P.M.	Pisces	Leo	Cancer	Capricorn	Aries	Taurus	Taurus	Virgo	Leo
2			Leo	Cancer	Capricorn	Aries	Taurus	Taurus	Virgo	Leo
3			Leo	Leo	Capricorn	Aries	Taurus	Taurus	Virgo	Leo
4	12:21 P.M.	Aries	Leo	Leo	Capricorn	Aries	Taurus	Taurus	Virgo	Leo
5			Leo	Leo	Capricorn	Aries	Taurus	Taurus	Virgo	Leo
6			Leo	Leo	Capricorn	Aries	Taurus	Taurus	Virgo	Leo
7	4:04 A.M.	Taurus	Leo	Leo	Capricorn	Aries	Taurus	Taurus	Virgo	Leo
8			Leo	Leo	Capricorn	Aries	Taurus	Taurus	Virgo	Leo
9	8:04 A.M.	Gemini	Leo	Leo	Capricorn	Aries	Taurus	Taurus	Virgo	Leo
10			Leo	Leo	Capricorn	Aries	Taurus	Taurus	Virgo	Leo
11	12:18 P.M.	Cancer	Leo	Leo	Capricorn	Aries	Taurus	Taurus	Virgo	Leo
12			Leo	Leo	Capricorn	Aries	Taurus	Taurus	Virgo	Leo
13	1:07 P.M.	Leo	Leo	Leo	Capricorn	Aries	Taurus	Taurus	Virgo	Leo
14			Leo	Leo	Capricorn	Aries	Taurus	Taurus	Virgo	Leo
15	12:20 P.M.	Virgo	Leo	Leo	Capricorn	Aries	Taurus	Taurus	Virgo	Leo
16			Leo	Leo	Capricorn	Aries	Taurus	Taurus	Virgo	Leo
17	12:05 P.M.	Libra	Leo	Leo	Capricorn	Aries	Taurus	Taurus	Virgo	Leo
18			Leo	Leo	Capricorn	Aries	Taurus	Taurus	Virgo	Leo
19	2:25 P.M.	Scorpio	Leo	Leo	Capricorn	Aries	Taurus	Taurus	Virgo	Leo
20			Leo	Leo	Capricorn	Aries	Taurus	Taurus	Virgo	Leo
21	8:18 P.M.	Sagittarius	Leo	Leo	Capricorn	Aries	Taurus	Taurus	Virgo	Leo
22			Leo	Leo	Capricorn	Aries	Taurus	Taurus	Virgo	Leo
23			Leo	Leo	Capricorn	Aries	Taurus	Taurus	Virgo	Leo

1940

July	MOON FROM IN	MERCURY	VENUS	MARS	JUPITER	SATURN	URANUS	NEPTUNE	PLUTO
23	Pisces	Cancer	Gemini	Leo	Taurus	Taurus	Taurus	Virgo	Leo
24	9:02 A.M. Aries	Cancer	Gemini	Leo	Taurus	Taurus	Taurus	Virgo	Leo
25		Cancer	Gemini	Leo	Taurus	Taurus	Taurus	Virgo	Leo
26	9:53 P.M. Taurus	Cancer	Gemini	Leo	Taurus	Taurus	Taurus	Virgo	Leo
27		Cancer	Gemini	Leo	Taurus	Taurus	Taurus	Virgo	Leo
28		Cancer	Gemini	Leo	Taurus	Taurus	Taurus	Virgo	Leo
29	9:03 A.M. Gemini	Cancer	Gemini	Leo	Taurus	Taurus	Taurus	Virgo	Leo
30		Cancer	Gemini	Leo	Taurus	Taurus	Taurus	Virgo	Leo
31	4:27 P.M. Cancer	Cancer	Gemini	Leo	Taurus	Taurus	Taurus	Virgo	Leo
August									
1		Cancer	Cancer	Leo	Taurus	Taurus	Taurus	Virgo	Leo
2	8:16 P.M. Leo	Cancer	Cancer	Leo	Taurus	Taurus	Taurus	Virgo	Leo
3		Cancer	Cancer	Leo	Taurus	Taurus	Taurus	Virgo	Leo
4	9:49 P.M. Virgo	Cancer	Cancer	Leo	Taurus	Taurus	Taurus	Virgo	Leo
5		Cancer	Cancer	Leo	Taurus	Taurus	Taurus	Virgo	Leo
6	10:51 P.M. Libra	Cancer	Cancer	Leo	Taurus	Taurus	Taurus	Virgo	Leo
7		Cancer	Cancer	Leo	Taurus	Taurus	Taurus	Virgo	Leo
8		Cancer	Cancer	Leo	Taurus	Taurus	Taurus	Virgo	Leo
9	0:48 A.M. Scorpio	Cancer	Cancer	Leo	Taurus	Taurus	Taurus	Virgo	Leo
10		Cancer	Cancer	Leo	Taurus	Taurus	Taurus	Virgo	Leo
11	4:30 A.M. Sagittarius	Cancer	Cancer	Leo	Taurus	Taurus	Taurus	Virgo	Leo
12		Leo	Cancer	Leo	Taurus	Taurus	Taurus	Virgo	Leo
13	10:17 A.M. Capricorn	Leo	Cancer	Leo	Taurus	Taurus	Taurus	Virgo	Leo
14		Leo	Cancer	Leo	Taurus	Taurus	Taurus	Virgo	Leo
15	6:11 P.M. Aquarius	Leo	Cancer	Leo	Taurus	Taurus	Taurus	Virgo	Leo
16		Leo	Cancer	Leo	Taurus	Taurus	Taurus	Virgo	Leo
17		Leo	Cancer	Leo	Taurus	Taurus	Taurus	Virgo	Leo
18	4:11 A.M. Pisces	Leo	Cancer	Leo	Taurus	Taurus	Taurus	Virgo	Leo
19		Leo	Cancer	Leo	Taurus	Taurus	Taurus	Virgo	Leo
20	4:16 P.M. Aries	Leo	Cancer	Virgo	Taurus	Taurus	Taurus	Virgo	Leo
21		Leo	Cancer	Virgo	Taurus	Taurus	Taurus	Virgo	Leo
22		Leo	Cancer	Virgo	Taurus	Taurus	Taurus	Virgo	Leo

LEO PLANETARY TABLES

1941

Date	MOON FROM	IN	MERCURY	VENUS	MARS	JUPITER	SATURN	URANUS	NEPTUNE	PLUTO
July 23	Cancer		Cancer	Leo	Aries	Gemini	Taurus	Taurus	Virgo	Leo
24	0:46 A.M.	Leo	Cancer	Leo	Aries	Gemini	Taurus	Taurus	Virgo	Leo
25			Cancer	Leo	Aries	Gemini	Taurus	Taurus	Virgo	Leo
26	7:04 A.M.	Virgo	Cancer	Leo	Aries	Gemini	Taurus	Taurus	Virgo	Leo
27			Cancer	Virgo	Aries	Gemini	Taurus	Taurus	Virgo	Leo
28	11:40 A.M.	Libra	Cancer	Virgo	Aries	Gemini	Taurus	Taurus	Virgo	Leo
29			Cancer	Virgo	Aries	Gemini	Taurus	Taurus	Virgo	Leo
30	3:07 P.M.	Scorpio	Cancer	Virgo	Aries	Gemini	Taurus	Taurus	Virgo	Leo
31			Cancer	Virgo	Aries	Gemini	Taurus	Taurus	Virgo	Leo
August										
1	5:49 P.M.	Sagittarius	Cancer	Virgo	Aries	Gemini	Taurus	Taurus	Virgo	Leo
2			Cancer	Virgo	Aries	Gemini	Taurus	Taurus	Virgo	Leo
3	9:27 P.M.	Capricorn	Cancer	Virgo	Aries	Gemini	Taurus	Taurus	Virgo	Leo
4			Cancer	Virgo	Aries	Gemini	Taurus	Taurus	Virgo	Leo
5	11:35 P.M.	Aquarius	Cancer	Virgo	Aries	Gemini	Taurus	Taurus	Virgo	Leo
6			Leo	Virgo	Aries	Gemini	Taurus	Taurus	Virgo	Leo
7			Leo	Virgo	Aries	Gemini	Taurus	Gemini	Virgo	Leo
8	4:52 A.M.	Pisces	Leo	Virgo	Aries	Gemini	Taurus	Gemini	Virgo	Leo
9			Leo	Virgo	Aries	Gemini	Taurus	Gemini	Virgo	Leo
10	1:15 P.M.	Aries	Leo	Virgo	Aries	Gemini	Taurus	Gemini	Virgo	Leo
11			Leo	Virgo	Aries	Gemini	Taurus	Gemini	Virgo	Leo
12			Leo	Virgo	Aries	Gemini	Taurus	Gemini	Virgo	Leo
13	0:33 A.M.	Taurus	Leo	Virgo	Aries	Gemini	Taurus	Gemini	Virgo	Leo
14			Leo	Virgo	Aries	Gemini	Taurus	Gemini	Virgo	Leo
15	1:08 P.M.	Gemini	Leo	Virgo	Aries	Gemini	Taurus	Gemini	Virgo	Leo
16			Leo	Virgo	Aries	Gemini	Taurus	Gemini	Virgo	Leo
17			Leo	Virgo	Aries	Gemini	Taurus	Gemini	Virgo	Leo
18	0:34 A.M.	Cancer	Leo	Virgo	Aries	Gemini	Taurus	Gemini	Virgo	Leo
19			Leo	Virgo	Aries	Gemini	Taurus	Gemini	Virgo	Leo
20	9:14 A.M.	Leo	Leo	Virgo	Aries	Gemini	Taurus	Gemini	Virgo	Leo
21			Virgo	Libra	Aries	Gemini	Taurus	Gemini	Virgo	Leo
22	2:50 P.M.	Virgo	Virgo	Libra	Aries	Gemini	Taurus	Gemini	Virgo	Leo
23			Virgo	Libra	Aries	Gemini	Taurus	Gemini	Virgo	Leo

1942

July	MOON FROM IN	MERCURY	VENUS	MARS	JUPITER	SATURN	URANUS	NEPTUNE	PLUTO
24	Sagittarius	Cancer	Cancer	Leo	Cancer	Gemini	Gemini	Virgo	Leo
25	7:38 A.M. Capricorn	Cancer	Cancer	Leo	Cancer	Gemini	Gemini	Virgo	Leo
26		Cancer	Cancer	Leo	Cancer	Gemini	Gemini	Virgo	Leo
27	7:37 A.M. Aquarius	Cancer	Cancer	Leo	Cancer	Gemini	Gemini	Virgo	Leo
28		Cancer	Cancer	Leo	Cancer	Gemini	Gemini	Virgo	Leo
29	8:51 A.M. Pisces	Leo	Cancer	Leo	Cancer	Gemini	Gemini	Virgo	Leo
30		Leo	Cancer	Leo	Cancer	Gemini	Gemini	Virgo	Leo
31	12:59 P.M. Aries	Leo	Cancer	Leo	Cancer	Gemini	Gemini	Virgo	Leo
August									
1		Leo	Cancer	Virgo	Cancer	Gemini	Gemini	Virgo	Leo
2		Leo	Cancer	Virgo	Cancer	Gemini	Gemini	Virgo	Leo
3	0:26 A.M. Taurus	Leo	Cancer	Virgo	Cancer	Gemini	Gemini	Virgo	Leo
4		Leo	Cancer	Virgo	Cancer	Gemini	Gemini	Virgo	Leo
5	7:55 A.M. Gemini	Leo	Cancer	Virgo	Cancer	Gemini	Gemini	Virgo	Leo
6		Leo	Cancer	Virgo	Cancer	Gemini	Gemini	Virgo	Leo
7	8:29 P.M. Cancer	Leo	Cancer	Virgo	Cancer	Gemini	Gemini	Virgo	Leo
8		Leo	Cancer	Virgo	Cancer	Gemini	Gemini	Virgo	Leo
9		Leo	Cancer	Virgo	Cancer	Gemini	Gemini	Virgo	Leo
10	8:39 A.M. Leo	Leo	Cancer	Virgo	Cancer	Gemini	Gemini	Virgo	Leo
11		Leo	Cancer	Virgo	Cancer	Gemini	Gemini	Virgo	Leo
12	7:06 P.M. Virgo	Leo	Cancer	Virgo	Cancer	Gemini	Gemini	Virgo	Leo
13		Virgo	Cancer	Virgo	Cancer	Gemini	Gemini	Virgo	Leo
14		Virgo	Cancer	Virgo	Cancer	Gemini	Gemini	Virgo	Leo
15	3:29 A.M. Libra	Virgo	Cancer	Virgo	Cancer	Gemini	Gemini	Virgo	Leo
16	9:36 A.M. Scorpio	Virgo	Cancer	Virgo	Cancer	Gemini	Gemini	Virgo	Leo
17		Virgo	Leo	Virgo	Cancer	Gemini	Gemini	Virgo	Leo
18	1:33 P.M. Sagittarius	Virgo	Leo	Virgo	Cancer	Gemini	Gemini	Virgo	Leo
19		Virgo	Leo	Virgo	Cancer	Gemini	Gemini	Virgo	Leo
20	3:45 P.M. Capricorn	Virgo	Leo	Virgo	Cancer	Gemini	Gemini	Virgo	Leo
21		Virgo	Leo	Virgo	Cancer	Gemini	Gemini	Virgo	Leo
22	5:07 P.M. Aquarius	Virgo	Leo	Virgo	Cancer	Gemini	Gemini	Virgo	Leo
23		Virgo	Leo	Virgo	Cancer	Gemini	Gemini	Virgo	Leo

LEO PLANETARY TABLES

1943

Date	MOON FROM	IN	MERCURY	VENUS	MARS	JUPITER	SATURN	URANUS	NEPTUNE	PLUTO
July 24	Taurus		Leo	Virgo	Taurus	Leo	Gemini	Gemini	Virgo	Leo
25			Leo	Virgo	Taurus	Leo	Gemini	Gemini	Virgo	Leo
26	7:04 A.M.	Gemini	Leo	Virgo	Taurus	Leo	Gemini	Gemini	Virgo	Leo
27			Leo	Virgo	Taurus	Leo	Gemini	Gemini	Virgo	Leo
28	6:05 P.M.	Cancer	Leo	Virgo	Taurus	Leo	Gemini	Gemini	Virgo	Leo
29			Leo	Virgo	Taurus	Leo	Gemini	Gemini	Virgo	Leo
30			Leo	Virgo	Taurus	Leo	Gemini	Gemini	Virgo	Leo
31	6:43 A.M.	Leo	Leo	Virgo	Taurus	Leo	Gemini	Gemini	Virgo	Leo
August 1	7:44 P.M.	Virgo	Leo	Virgo	Taurus	Leo	Gemini	Gemini	Virgo	Leo
2			Leo	Virgo	Taurus	Leo	Gemini	Gemini	Libra	Leo
3	7:51 A.M.	Libra	Leo	Virgo	Taurus	Leo	Gemini	Gemini	Libra	Leo
4			Leo	Virgo	Taurus	Leo	Gemini	Gemini	Libra	Leo
5	5:35 P.M.	Scorpio	Virgo	Virgo	Taurus	Leo	Gemini	Gemini	Libra	Leo
6			Virgo	Virgo	Taurus	Leo	Gemini	Gemini	Libra	Leo
7			Virgo	Virgo	Taurus	Leo	Gemini	Gemini	Libra	Leo
8			Virgo	Virgo	Taurus	Leo	Gemini	Gemini	Libra	Leo
9			Virgo	Virgo	Taurus	Leo	Gemini	Gemini	Libra	Leo
10	0:03 A.M.	Sagittarius	Virgo	Virgo	Taurus	Leo	Gemini	Gemini	Libra	Leo
11			Virgo	Virgo	Taurus	Leo	Gemini	Gemini	Libra	Leo
12	3:06 A.M.	Capricorn	Virgo	Virgo	Taurus	Leo	Gemini	Gemini	Libra	Leo
13			Virgo	Virgo	Taurus	Leo	Gemini	Gemini	Libra	Leo
14	3:36 A.M.	Aquarius	Virgo	Virgo	Taurus	Leo	Gemini	Gemini	Libra	Leo
15			Virgo	Virgo	Taurus	Leo	Gemini	Gemini	Libra	Leo
16	3:07 A.M.	Pisces	Virgo	Virgo	Taurus	Leo	Gemini	Gemini	Libra	Leo
17			Virgo	Virgo	Taurus	Leo	Gemini	Gemini	Libra	Leo
18	3:34 A.M.	Aries	Virgo	Virgo	Taurus	Leo	Gemini	Gemini	Libra	Leo
19			Virgo	Virgo	Taurus	Leo	Gemini	Gemini	Libra	Leo
20	6:39 A.M.	Taurus	Virgo	Virgo	Taurus	Leo	Gemini	Gemini	Libra	Leo
21			Virgo	Virgo	Taurus	Leo	Gemini	Gemini	Libra	Leo
22	1:39 P.M.	Gemini	Virgo	Virgo	Taurus	Leo	Gemini	Gemini	Libra	Leo
23			Virgo	Virgo	Taurus	Leo	Gemini	Gemini	Libra	Leo

1944

July	MOON FROM / IN	MERCURY	VENUS	MARS	JUPITER	SATURN	URANUS	NEPTUNE	PLUTO
23	Virgo	Leo	Leo	Virgo	Leo	Cancer	Gemini	Libra	Leo
24		Leo	Leo	Virgo	Leo	Cancer	Gemini	Libra	Leo
25	6:07 A.M. Libra	Leo	Leo	Virgo	Leo	Cancer	Gemini	Libra	Leo
26		Leo	Leo	Virgo	Virgo	Cancer	Gemini	Libra	Leo
27	6:14 P.M. Scorpio	Leo	Leo	Virgo	Virgo	Cancer	Gemini	Libra	Leo
28		Leo	Leo	Virgo	Virgo	Cancer	Gemini	Libra	Leo
29		Virgo	Leo	Virgo	Virgo	Cancer	Gemini	Libra	Leo
30	3:48 A.M. Sagittarius	Virgo	Leo	Virgo	Virgo	Cancer	Gemini	Libra	Leo
31		Virgo	Leo	Virgo	Virgo	Cancer	Gemini	Libra	Leo
August									
1	9:39 A.M. Capricorn	Virgo	Leo	Virgo	Virgo	Cancer	Gemini	Libra	Leo
2		Virgo	Leo	Virgo	Virgo	Cancer	Gemini	Libra	Leo
3	12:09 P.M. Aquarius	Virgo	Leo	Virgo	Virgo	Cancer	Gemini	Libra	Leo
4		Virgo	Leo	Virgo	Virgo	Cancer	Gemini	Libra	Leo
5	10:02 A.M. Pisces	Virgo	Leo	Virgo	Virgo	Cancer	Gemini	Libra	Leo
6		Virgo	Leo	Virgo	Virgo	Cancer	Gemini	Libra	Leo
7	12:45 P.M. Aries	Virgo	Leo	Virgo	Virgo	Cancer	Gemini	Libra	Leo
8		Virgo	Leo	Virgo	Virgo	Cancer	Gemini	Libra	Leo
9	2:23 P.M. Taurus	Virgo	Leo	Virgo	Virgo	Cancer	Gemini	Libra	Leo
10		Virgo	Virgo	Virgo	Virgo	Cancer	Gemini	Libra	Leo
11	6:43 P.M. Gemini	Virgo	Virgo	Virgo	Virgo	Cancer	Gemini	Libra	Leo
12		Virgo	Virgo	Virgo	Virgo	Cancer	Gemini	Libra	Leo
13		Virgo	Virgo	Virgo	Vargo	Cancer	Gemini	Libra	Leo
14	2:06 A.M. Cancer	Virgo	Virgo	Virgo	Virgo	Cancer	Gemini	Libra	Leo
15		Virgo	Virgo	Virgo	Virgo	Cancer	Gemini	Libra	Leo
16	12:09 P.M. Lec	Virgo	Virgo	Virgo	Virgo	Cancer	Gemini	Libra	Leo
17		Virgo	Virgo	Virgo	Virgo	Cancer	Gemini	Libra	Leo
18		Virgo	Virgo	Virgo	Virgo	Cancer	Gemini	Libra	Leo
19	0:01 A.M. Virgo	Virgo	Virgo	Virgo	Virgo	Cancer	Gemini	Libra	Leo
20		Virgo	Virgo	Virgo	Virgo	Cancer	Gemini	Libra	Leo
21	12:44 P.M. Libra	Virgo	Virgo	Virgo	Virgo	Cancer	Gemini	Libra	Leo
22		Virgo	Virgo	Virgo	Virgo	Cancer	Gemini	Libra	Leo

LEO PLANETARY TABLES

1945

July	MOON FROM IN	MERCURY	VENUS	MARS	JUPITER	SATURN	URANUS	NEPTUNE	PLUTO
23	Capricorn	Leo	Gemini	Gemini	Virgo	Cancer	Gemini	Libra	Leo
24	6:12 P.M. Aquarius	Leo	Gemini	Gemini	Virgo	Cancer	Gemini	Libra	Leo
25	10:25 P.M. Pisces	Leo	Gemini	Gemini	Virgo	Cancer	Gemini	Libra	Leo
26		Leo	Gemini	Gemini	Virgo	Cancer	Gemini	Libra	Leo
27		Virgo	Gemini	Gemini	Virgo	Cancer	Gemini	Libra	Leo
28		Virgo	Gemini	Gemini	Virgo	Cancer	Gemini	Libra	Leo
29	1:07 A.M. Aries	Virgo	Gemini	Gemini	Virgo	Cancer	Gemini	Libra	Leo
30		Virgo	Gemini	Gemini	Virgo	Cancer	Gemini	Libra	Leo
31	3:30 A.M. Taurus	Virgo	Gemini	Gemini	Virgo	Cancer	Gemini	Libra	Leo
August									
1		Virgo	Gemini	Gemini	Virgo	Cancer	Gemini	Libra	Leo
2	6:22 A.M. Gemini	Virgo	Gemini	Gemini	Virgo	Cancer	Gemini	Libra	Leo
3		Virgo	Gemini	Gemini	Virgo	Cancer	Gemini	Libra	Leo
4	10:23 A.M. Cancer	Virgo	Cancer	Gemini	Virgo	Cancer	Gemini	Libra	Leo
5		Virgo	Cancer	Gemini	Virgo	Cancer	Gemini	Libra	Leo
6	3:54 P.M. Leo	Virgo	Cancer	Gemini	Virgo	Cancer	Gemini	Libra	Leo
7		Virgo	Cancer	Gemini	Virgo	Cancer	Gemini	Libra	Leo
8	11:26 P.M. Virgo	Virgo	Cancer	Gemini	Virgo	Cancer	Gemini	Libra	Leo
9		Virgo	Cancer	Gemini	Virgo	Cancer	Gemini	Libra	Leo
10		Virgo	Cancer	Gemini	Virgo	Cancer	Gemini	Libra	Leo
11	9:23 A.M. Libra	Virgo	Cancer	Gemini	Virgo	Cancer	Gemini	Libra	Leo
12		Virgo	Cancer	Gemini	Virgo	Cancer	Gemini	Libra	Leo
13	9:26 P.M. Scorpio	Virgo	Cancer	Gemini	Virgo	Cancer	Gemini	Libra	Leo
14		Virgo	Cancer	Gemini	Virgo	Cancer	Gemini	Libra	Leo
15		Virgo	Cancer	Gemini	Virgo	Cancer	Gemini	Libra	Leo
16	9:55 A.M. Sagittarius	Virgo	Cancer	Gemini	Virgo	Cancer	Gemini	Libra	Leo
17		Leo	Cancer	Gemini	Virgo	Cancer	Gemini	Libra	Leo
18	8:25 P.M. Capricorn	Leo	Cancer	Gemini	Virgo	Cancer	Gemini	Libra	Leo
19		Leo	Cancer	Gemini	Virgo	Cancer	Gemini	Libra	Leo
20		Leo	Cancer	Gemini	Virgo	Cancer	Gemini	Libra	Leo
21	3:29 A.M. Aquarius	Leo	Cancer	Gemini	Virgo	Cancer	Gemini	Libra	Leo
22		Leo	Cancer	Gemini	Virgo	Cancer	Gemini	Libra	Leo
23	7:05 A.M. Pisces	Leo	Cancer	Gemini	Virgo	Cancer	Gemini	Libra	Leo

1946

July	MOON FROM	IN	MERCURY	VENUS	MARS	JUPITER	SATURN	URANUS	NEPTUNE	PLUTO
23	8:15 P.M.	Gemini	Leo	Virgo	Virgo	Libra	Cancer	Gemini	Libra	Leo
24			Leo	Virgo	Virgo	Libra	Cancer	Gemini	Libra	Leo
25	9:43 P.M.	Cancer	Leo	Virgo	Virgo	Libra	Cancer	Gemini	Libra	Leo
26			Leo	Virgo	Virgo	Libra	Cancer	Gemini	Libra	Leo
27	11:01 P.M.	Leo	Leo	Virgo	Virgo	Libra	Cancer	Gemini	Libra	Leo
28			Leo	Virgo	Virgo	Libra	Cancer	Gemini	Libra	Leo
29			Leo	Virgo	Virgo	Libra	Cancer	Gemini	Libra	Leo
30	1:41 A.M.	Virgo	Leo	Virgo	Virgo	Libra	Cancer	Gemini	Libra	Leo
31			Leo	Virgo	Virgo	Libra	Cancer	Gemini	Libra	Leo
August										
1	7:09 A.M.	Libra	Leo	Virgo	Virgo	Libra	Cancer	Gemini	Libra	Leo
2			Leo	Virgo	Virgo	Libra	Leo	Gemini	Libra	Leo
3	4:30 P.M.	Scorpio	Leo	Virgo	Virgo	Libra	Leo	Gemini	Libra	Leo
4			Leo	Virgo	Virgo	Libra	Leo	Gemini	Libra	Leo
5			Leo	Virgo	Virgo	Libra	Leo	Gemini	Libra	Leo
6	4:38 A.M.	Sagittarius	Leo	Virgo	Virgo	Libra	Leo	Gemini	Libra	Leo
7			Leo	Virgo	Virgo	Libra	Leo	Gemini	Libra	Leo
8	5:19 P.M.	Capricorn	Leo	Libra	Virgo	Libra	Leo	Gemini	Libra	Leo
9			Leo	Libra	Virgo	Libra	Leo	Gemini	Libra	Leo
10			Leo	Libra	Libra	Libra	Leo	Gemini	Libra	Leo
11	4:19 A.M.	Aquarius	Leo	Libra	Libra	Libra	Leo	Gemini	Libra	Leo
12			Leo	Libra	Libra	Libra	Leo	Gemini	Libra	Leo
13	12:36 P.M.	Pisces	Leo	Libra	Libra	Libra	Leo	Gemini	Libra	Leo
14			Leo	Libra	Libra	Libra	Leo	Gemini	Libra	Leo
15	6:33 P.M.	Aries	Leo	Libra	Libra	Libra	Leo	Gemini	Libra	Leo
16			Leo	Libra	Libra	Libra	Leo	Gemini	Libra	Leo
17	10:56 P.M.	Taurus	Leo	Libra	Libra	Libra	Leo	Gemini	Libra	Leo
18			Leo	Libra	Libra	Libra	Leo	Gemini	Libra	Leo
19			Leo	Libra	Libra	Libra	Leo	Gemini	Libra	Leo
20	2:20 A.M.	Gemini	Leo	Libra	Libra	Libra	Leo	Gemini	Libra	Leo
21			Leo	Libra	Libra	Libra	Leo	Gemini	Libra	Leo
22	5:07 A.M.	Cancer	Leo	Libra	Libra	Libra	Leo	Gemini	Libra	Leo
23			Leo	Libra	Libra	Libra	Leo	Gemini	Libra	Leo

LEO PLANETARY TABLES

1947

	MOON FROM	IN	MERCURY	VENUS	MARS	JUPITER	SATURN	URANUS	NEPTUNE	PLUTO
July										
24	3:46 P.M.	Scorpio	Cancer	Cancer	Gemini	Scorpio	Leo	Gemini	Libra	Leo
25			Cancer	Cancer	Gemini	Scorpio	Leo	Gemini	Libra	Leo
26	1:44 A.M.	Sagittarius	Cancer	Cancer	Gemini	Scorpio	Leo	Gemini	Libra	Leo
27			Cancer	Cancer	Gemini	Scorpio	Leo	Gemini	Libra	Leo
28	2:02 P.M.	Capricorn	Cancer	Cancer	Gemini	Scorpio	Leo	Gemini	Libra	Leo
29			Cancer	Cancer	Gemini	Scorpio	Leo	Gemini	Libra	Leo
30			Cancer	Cancer	Gemini	Scorpio	Leo	Gemini	Libra	Leo
31			Cancer	Cancer	Gemini	Scorpio	Leo	Gemini	Libra	Leo
August										
1	2:50 A.M.	Aquarius	Cancer	Cancer	Gemini	Scorpio	Leo	Gemini	Libra	Leo
2			Cancer	Leo	Gemini	Scorpio	Leo	Gemini	Libra	Leo
3	2:48 P.M.	Pisces	Cancer	Leo	Gemini	Scorpio	Leo	Gemini	Libra	Leo
4			Cancer	Leo	Gemini	Scorpio	Leo	Gemini	Libra	Leo
5			Cancer	Leo	Gemini	Scorpio	Leo	Gemini	Libra	Leo
6	1:19 A.M.	Aries	Cancer	Leo	Gemini	Scorpio	Leo	Gemini	Libra	Leo
7			Cancer	Leo	Gemini	Scorpio	Leo	Gemini	Libra	Leo
8	10:37 A.M.	Taurus	Cancer	Leo	Gemini	Scorpio	Leo	Gemini	Libra	Leo
9			Cancer	Leo	Gemini	Scorpio	Leo	Gemini	Libra	Leo
10	3:14 P.M.	Gemini	Cancer	Leo	Gemini	Scorpio	Leo	Gemini	Libra	Leo
11			Leo	Leo	Gemini	Scorpio	Leo	Gemini	Libra	Leo
12	5:45 P.M.	Cancer	Leo	Leo	Gemini	Scorpio	Leo	Gemini	Libra	Leo
13			Leo	Leo	Gemini	Scorpio	Leo	Gemini	Libra	Leo
14	6:06 P.M.	Leo	Leo	Leo	Cancer	Scorpio	Leo	Gemini	Libra	Leo
15			Leo	Leo	Cancer	Scorpio	Leo	Gemini	Libra	Leo
16	5:53 P.M.	Virgo	Leo	Leo	Cancer	Scorpio	Leo	Gemini	Libra	Leo
17			Leo	Leo	Cancer	Scorpio	Leo	Gemini	Libra	Leo
18	7:10 P.M.	Libra	Leo	Leo	Cancer	Scorpio	Leo	Gemini	Libra	Leo
19			Leo	Leo	Cancer	Scorpio	Leo	Gemini	Libra	Leo
20	11:40 P.M.	Scorpio	Leo	Leo	Cancer	Scorpio	Leo	Gemini	Libra	Leo
21			Leo	Leo	Cancer	Scorpio	Leo	Gemini	Libra	Leo
22			Leo	Leo	Cancer	Scorpio	Leo	Gemini	Libra	Leo
23	8:36 A.M.	Sagittarius	Leo	Leo	Cancer	Scorpio	Leo	Gemini	Libra	Leo

1948

	MOON		MERCURY	VENUS	MARS	JUPITER	SATURN	URANUS	NEPTUNE	PLUTO
July	FROM	IN								
23	1:14 P.M.	Pisces	Cancer	Gemini	Libra	Sagittarius	Leo	Gemini	Libra	Leo
24			Cancer	Gemini	Libra	Sagittarius	Leo	Gemini	Libra	Leo
25	1:57 A.M.	Aries	Cancer	Gemini	Libra	Sagittarius	Leo	Gemini	Libra	Leo
26			Cancer	Gemini	Libra	Sagittarius	Leo	Gemini	Libra	Leo
27	1:30 P.M.	Taurus	Cancer	Gemini	Libra	Sagittarius	Leo	Gemini	Libra	Leo
28			Cancer	Gemini	Libra	Sagittarius	Leo	Gemini	Libra	Leo
29			Cancer	Gemini	Libra	Sagittarius	Leo	Gemini	Libra	Leo
30	9:56 P.M.	Gemini	Cancer	Gemini	Libra	Sagittarius	Leo	Gemini	Libra	Leo
31			Cancer	Gemini	Libra	Sagittarius	Leo	Gemini	Libra	Leo
August										
1	2:17 A.M.	Cancer	Cancer	Gemini	Libra	Sagittarius	Leo	Gemini	Libra	Leo
2			Cancer	Gemini	Libra	Sagittarius	Leo	Gemini	Libra	Leo
3	3:11 A.M.	Leo	Leo	Cancer	Libra	Sagittarius	Leo	Gemini	Libra	Leo
4			Leo	Cancer	Libra	Sagittarius	Leo	Gemini	Libra	Leo
5			Leo	Cancer	Libra	Sagittarius	Leo	Gemini	Libra	Leo
6	2:26 A.M.	Virgo	Leo	Cancer	Libra	Sagittarius	Leo	Gemini	Libra	Leo
7			Leo	Cancer	Libra	Sagittarius	Leo	Gemini	Libra	Leo
8	2:33 A.M.	Libra	Leo	Cancer	Libra	Sagittarius	Leo	Gemini	Libra	Leo
9			Leo	Cancer	Libra	Sagittarius	Leo	Gemini	Libra	Leo
10	4:58 A.M.	Scorpio	Leo	Cancer	Libra	Sagittarius	Leo	Gemini	Libra	Leo
11			Leo	Cancer	Libra	Sagittarius	Leo	Gemini	Libra	Leo
12	10:52 A.M.	Sagittarius	Leo	Cancer	Libra	Sagittarius	Leo	Gemini	Libra	Leo
13			Leo	Cancer	Libra	Sagittarius	Leo	Gemini	Libra	Leo
14	7:54 P.M.	Capricorn	Leo	Cancer	Libra	Sagittarius	Leo	Gemini	Libra	Leo
15			Leo	Cancer	Libra	Sagittarius	Leo	Gemini	Libra	Leo
16			Leo	Cancer	Libra	Sagittarius	Leo	Gemini	Libra	Leo
17	7:02 A.M.	Aquarius	Virgo	Cancer	Libra	Sagittarius	Leo	Gemini	Libra	Leo
18			Virgo	Cancer	Libra	Sagittarius	Leo	Gemini	Libra	Leo
19	7:23 P.M.	Pisces	Virgo	Cancer	Libra	Sagittarius	Leo	Gemini	Libra	Leo
20			Virgo	Cancer	Libra	Sagittarius	Leo	Gemini	Libra	Leo
21			Virgo	Cancer	Libra	Sagittarius	Leo	Gemini	Libra	Leo
22	8:04 A.M.	Aries	Virgo	Cancer	Libra	Sagittarius	Leo	Gemini	Libra	Leo

LEO PLANETARY TABLES

1949

Date	MOON FROM	IN	MERCURY	VENUS	MARS	JUPITER	SATURN	URANUS	NEPTUNE	PLUTO
July 23	5:51 A.M.	Cancer	Cancer	Leo	Cancer	Capricorn	Virgo	Cancer	Libra	Leo
24	10:18 A.M.	Leo	Cancer	Leo	Cancer	Capricorn	Virgo	Cancer	Libra	Leo
25			Leo	Leo	Cancer	Capricorn	Virgo	Cancer	Libra	Leo
26	12:35 P.M.	Virgo	Leo	Leo	Cancer	Capricorn	Virgo	Cancer	Libra	Leo
27			Leo	Virgo	Cancer	Capricorn	Virgo	Cancer	Libra	Leo
28			Leo	Virgo	Cancer	Capricorn	Virgo	Cancer	Libra	Leo
29	2:21 P.M.	Libra	Leo	Virgo	Cancer	Capricorn	Virgo	Cancer	Libra	Leo
30			Leo	Virgo	Cancer	Capricorn	Virgo	Cancer	Libra	Leo
31	4:46 P.M.	Scorpio	Leo	Virgo	Cancer	Capricorn	Virgo	Cancer	Libra	Leo
August 1			Leo	Virgo	Cancer	Capricorn	Virgo	Cancer	Libra	Leo
2	8:26 P.M.	Sagittarius	Leo	Virgo	Cancer	Capricorn	Virgo	Cancer	Libra	Leo
3			Leo	Virgo	Cancer	Capricorn	Virgo	Cancer	Libra	Leo
4			Leo	Virgo	Cancer	Capricorn	Virgo	Cancer	Libra	Leo
5	1:37 A.M.	Capricorn	Leo	Virgo	Cancer	Capricorn	Virgo	Cancer	Libra	Leo
6			Leo	Virgo	Cancer	Capricorn	Virgo	Cancer	Libra	Leo
7			Leo	Virgo	Cancer	Capricorn	Virgo	Cancer	Libra	Leo
8	8:34 A.M.	Aquarius	Leo	Virgo	Cancer	Capricorn	Virgo	Cancer	Libra	Leo
9			Virgo	Virgo	Cancer	Capricorn	Virgo	Cancer	Libra	Leo
10	5:49 P.M.	Pisces	Virgo	Virgo	Cancer	Capricorn	Virgo	Cancer	Libra	Leo
11			Virgo	Virgo	Cancer	Capricorn	Virgo	Cancer	Libra	Leo
12			Virgo	Virgo	Cancer	Capricorn	Virgo	Cancer	Libra	Leo
13	5:20 A.M.	Aries	Virgo	Virgo	Cancer	Capricorn	Virgo	Cancer	Libra	Leo
14			Virgo	Virgo	Cancer	Capricorn	Virgo	Cancer	Libra	Leo
15	6:18 P.M.	Taurus	Virgo	Virgo	Cancer	Capricorn	Virgo	Cancer	Libra	Leo
16			Virgo	Virgo	Cancer	Capricorn	Virgo	Cancer	Libra	Leo
17			Virgo	Virgo	Cancer	Capricorn	Virgo	Cancer	Libra	Leo
18	6:22 A.M.	Gemini	Virgo	Virgo	Cancer	Capricorn	Virgo	Cancer	Libra	Leo
19			Virgo	Virgo	Cancer	Capricorn	Virgo	Cancer	Libra	Leo
20	3:09 P.M.	Cancer	Virgo	Virgo	Cancer	Capricorn	Virgo	Cancer	Libra	Leo
21			Virgo	Libra	Cancer	Capricorn	Virgo	Cancer	Libra	Leo
22	8:02 P.M.	Leo	Virgo	Libra	Cancer	Capricorn	Virgo	Cancer	Libra	Leo

1950

	MOON FROM IN	MERCURY	VENUS	MARS	JUPITER	SATURN	URANUS	NEPTUNE	PLUTO
July									
23	Scorpio	Leo	Cancer	Libra	Pisces	Virgo	Cancer	Libra	Leo
24	9:54 A.M. Sagittarius	Leo	Cancer	Libra	Pisces	Virgo	Cancer	Libra	Leo
25		Leo	Cancer	Libra	Pisces	Virgo	Cancer	Libra	Leo
26	11:39 A.M. Capricorn	Leo	Cancer	Libra	Pisces	Virgo	Cancer	Ljbra	Leo
27		Leo	Cancer	Libra	Pisces	Virgo	Cancer	Libra	Leo
28	1:58 P.M. Aquarius	Leo	Cancer	Libra	Pisces	Virgo	Cancer	Libra	Leo
29		Leo	Cancer	Libra	Pisces	Virgo	Cancer	Libra	Leo
30	6:24 P.M. Pisces	Leo	Cancer	Libra	Pisces	Virgo	Cancer	Libra	Leo
31		Leo	Cancer	Libra	Pisces	Virgo	Cancer	Libra	Leo
August									
1		Leo	Cancer	Libra	Pisces	Virgo	Cancer	Libra	Leo
2	2:05 A.M. Aries	Virgo	Cancer	Libra	Pisces	Virgo	Cancer	Libra	Leo
3		Virgo	Cancer	Libra	Pisces	Virgo	Cancer	Libra	Leo
4	1:07 P.M. Taurus	Virgo	Cancer	Libra	Pisces	Virgo	Cancer	Libra	Leo
5		Virgo	Cancer	Libra	Pisces	Virgo	Cancer	Libra	Leo
6		Virgo	Cancer	Libra	Pisces	Virgo	Cancer	Libra	Leo
7	1:43 A.M. Gemini	Virgo	Cancer	Libra	Pisces	Virgo	Cancer	Libra	Leo
8		Virgo	Cancer	Libra	Pisces	Virgo	Cancer	Libra	Leo
9	11:28 A.M. Cancer	Virgo	Cancer	Libra	Pisces	Virgo	Cancer	Libra	Leo
10		Virgo	Cancer	Libra	Pisces	Virgo	Cancer	Libra	Leo
11	10:33 P.M. Leo	Virgo	Cancer	Scorpio	Pisces	Virgo	Cancer	Libra	Leo
12		Virgo	Cancer	Scorpio	Pisces	Virgo	Cancer	Libra	Leo
13		Virgo	Cancer	Scorpio	Pisces	Virgo	Cancer	Libra	Leo
14	5:02 A.M. Virgo	Virgo	Cancer	Scorpio	Pisces	Virgo	Cancer	Libra	Leo
15		Virgo	Cancer	Scorpio	Pisces	Virgo	Cancer	Libra	Leo
16	9:30 A.M. Libra	Virgo	Cancer	Scorpio	Pisces	Virgo	Cancer	Libra	Leo
17		Virgo	Leo	Scorpio	Pisces	Virgo	Cancer	Libra	Leo
18	12:48 P.M. Scorpio	Virgo	Leo	Scorpio	Pisces	Virgo	Cancer	Libra	Leo
19		Virgo	Leo	Scorpio	Pisces	Virgo	Cancer	Libra	Leo
20	3:35 P.M. Sagittarius	Virgo	Leo	Scorpio	Pisces	Virgo	Cancer	Libra	Leo
21		Virgo	Leo	Scorpio	Pisces	Virgo	Cancer	Libra	Leo
22	6:23 P.M. Capricorn	Virgo	Leo	Scorpio	Pisces	Virgo	Cancer	Libra	Leo
23		Virgo	Leo	Scorpio	Pisces	Virgo	Cancer	Libra	Leo

LEO PLANETARY TABLES

1951

	MOON FROM	IN	MERCURY	VENUS	MARS	JUPITER	SATURN	URANUS	NEPTUNE	PLUTO
July										
24	Aries		Leo	Virgo	Cancer	Aries	Virgo	Cancer	Libra	Leo
25	10:08 A.M.	Taurus	Leo	Virgo	Cancer	Aries	Virgo	Cancer	Libra	Leo
26			Leo	Virgo	Cancer	Aries	Virgo	Cancer	Libra	Leo
27	9:09 P.M.	Gemini	Leo	Virgo	Cancer	Aries	Virgo	Cancer	Libra	Leo
28			Virgo	Virgo	Cancer	Aries	Virgo	Cancer	Libra	Leo
29			Virgo	Virgo	Cancer	Aries	Virgo	Cancer	Libra	Leo
30	9:42 A.M.	Cancer	Virgo	Virgo	Cancer	Aries	Virgo	Cancer	Libra	Leo
31			Virgo	Virgo	Cancer	Aries	Virgo	Cancer	Libra	Leo
August										
1	10:06 P.M.	Leo	Virgo	Virgo	Cancer	Aries	Virgo	Cancer	Libra	Leo
2			Virgo	Virgo	Cancer	Aries	Virgo	Cancer	Libra	Leo
3			Virgo	Virgo	Cancer	Aries	Virgo	Cancer	Libra	Leo
4	9:17 A.M.	Virgo	Virgo	Virgo	Cancer	Aries	Virgo	Cancer	Libra	Leo
5			Virgo	Virgo	Cancer	Aries	Virgo	Cancer	Libra	Leo
6	6:30 P.M.	Libra	Virgo	Virgo	Cancer	Aries	Virgo	Cancer	Libra	Leo
7			Virgo	Virgo	Cancer	Aries	Virgo	Cancer	Libra	Leo
8			Virgo	Virgo	Cancer	Aries	Virgo	Cancer	Libra	Leo
9	1:21 A.M.	Scorpio	Virgo	Virgo	Cancer	Aries	Virgo	Cancer	Libra	Leo
10	5:29 A.M.	Sagittarius	Virgo	Virgo	Cancer	Aries	Virgo	Cancer	Libra	Leo
11			Virgo	Virgo	Cancer	Aries	Virgo	Cancer	Libra	Leo
12	7:18 A.M.	Capricorn	Virgo	Virgo	Cancer	Aries	Virgo	Cancer	Libra	Leo
13			Virgo	Virgo	Cancer	Aries	Libra	Cancer	Libra	Leo
14	7:18 A.M.	Aquarius	Virgo	Virgo	Cancer	Aries	Libra	Cancer	Libra	Leo
15			Virgo	Virgo	Cancer	Aries	Libra	Cancer	Libra	Leo
16			Virgo	Virgo	Cancer	Aries	Libra	Cancer	Libra	Leo
17	9:20 P.M.	Pisces	Virgo	Virgo	Cancer	Aries	Libra	Cancer	Libra	Leo
18			Virgo	Virgo	Cancer	Aries	Libra	Cancer	Libra	Leo
19	12:01 P.M.	Aries	Virgo	Virgo	Leo	Aries	Libra	Cancer	Libra	Leo
20			Virgo	Virgo	Leo	Aries	Libra	Cancer	Libra	Leo
21	6:31 P.M.	Taurus	Virgo	Virgo	Leo	Aries	Libra	Cancer	Libra	Leo
22			Virgo	Virgo	Leo	Aries	Libra	Cancer	Libra	Leo
23			Virgo	Virgo	Leo	Aries	Libra	Cancer	Libra	Leo

1952

July	MOON FROM	IN	MERCURY	VENUS	MARS	JUPITER	SATURN	URANUS	NEPTUNE	PLUTO
23	Leo		Leo	Leo	Scorpio	Taurus	Libra	Cancer	Libra	Leo
24	9:26 A.M.	Virgo	Leo	Leo	Scorpio	Taurus	Libra	Cancer	Libra	Leo
25			Leo	Leo	Scorpio	Taurus	Libra	Cancer	Libra	Leo
26	9:36 P.M.	Libra	Leo	Leo	Scorpio	Taurus	Libra	Cancer	Libra	Leo
27			Leo	Leo	Scorpio	Taurus	Libra	Cancer	Libra	Leo
28			Leo	Leo	Scorpio	Taurus	Libra	Cancer	Libra	Leo
29	8:08 A.M.	Scorpio	Leo	Leo	Scorpio	Taurus	Libra	Cancer	Libra	Leo
30			Leo	Leo	Scorpio	Taurus	Libra	Cancer	Libra	Leo
31	2:57 P.M.	Sagittarius	Leo	Leo	Scorpio	Taurus	Libra	Cancer	Libra	Leo
August										
1			Leo	Leo	Scorpio	Taurus	Libra	Cancer	Libra	Leo
2	5:52 P.M.	Capricorn	Leo	Leo	Scorpio	Taurus	Libra	Cancer	Libra	Leo
3			Leo	Leo	Scorpio	Taurus	Libra	Cancer	Libra	Leo
4	6:26 P.M.	Aquarius	Leo	Leo	Scorpio	Taurus	Libra	Cancer	Libra	Leo
5			Leo	Leo	Scorpio	Taurus	Libra	Cancer	Libra	Leo
6	5:42 P.M.	Pisces	Leo	Leo	Scorpio	Taurus	Libra	Cancer	Libra	Leo
7			Leo	Leo	Scorpio	Taurus	Libra	Cancer	Libra	Leo
8	6:08 P.M.	Aries	Leo	Leo	Scorpio	Taurus	Libra	Cancer	Libra	Leo
9			Leo	Leo	Scorpio	Taurus	Libra	Cancer	Libra	Leo
10	9:01 P.M.	Taurus	Leo	Virgo	Scorpio	Taurus	Libra	Cancer	Libra	Leo
11			Leo	Virgo	Scorpio	Taurus	Libra	Cancer	Libra	Leo
12			Leo	Virgo	Scorpio	Taurus	Libra	Cancer	Libra	Leo
13	3:36 A.M.	Gemini	Leo	Virgo	Scorpio	Taurus	Libra	Cancer	Libra	Leo
14			Leo	Virgo	Scorpio	Taurus	Libra	Cancer	Libra	Leo
15	2:24 P.M.	Cancer	Leo	Virgo	Scorpio	Taurus	Libra	Cancer	Libra	Leo
16			Leo	Virgo	Scorpio	Taurus	Libra	Cancer	Libra	Leo
17			Leo	Virgo	Scorpio	Taurus	Libra	Cancer	Libra	Leo
18	2:23 A.M.	Leo	Leo	Virgo	Scorpio	Taurus	Libra	Cancer	Libra	Leo
19			Leo	Virgo	Scorpio	Taurus	Libra	Cancer	Libra	Leo
20	3:04 P.M.	Virgo	Leo	Virgo	Scorpio	Taurus	Libra	Cancer	Libra	Leo
21			Leo	Virgo	Scorpio	Taurus	Libra	Cancer	Libra	Leo
22			Leo	Virgo	Scorpio	Taurus	Libra	Cancer	Libra	Leo
23	3:01 A.M.	Libra	Leo	Virgo	Scorpio	Taurus	Libra	Cancer	Libra	Leo

LEO PLANETARY TABLES

1953

July	MOON FROM	IN	MERCURY	VENUS	MARS	JUPITER	SATURN	URANUS	NEPTUNE	PLUTO
24		Capricorn	Leo	Gemini	Cancer	Gemini	Libra	Cancer	Libra	Leo
25			Leo	Gemini	Cancer	Gemini	Libra	Cancer	Libra	Leo
26	2:13 A.M.	Aquarius	Leo	Gemini	Cancer	Gemini	Libra	Cancer	Libra	Leo
27			Leo	Gemini	Cancer	Gemini	Libra	Cancer	Libra	Leo
28	3:15 A.M.	Pisces	Leo	Gemini	Cancer	Gemini	Libra	Cancer	Libra	Leo
29			Cancer	Gemini	Cancer	Gemini	Libra	Cancer	Libra	Leo
30	4:07 A.M.	Aries	Cancer	Gemini	Leo	Gemini	Libra	Cancer	Libra	Leo
31			Cancer	Gemini	Leo	Gemini	Libra	Cancer	Libra	Leo

August	MOON FROM	IN	MERCURY	VENUS	MARS	JUPITER	SATURN	URANUS	NEPTUNE	PLUTO
1	5:50 A.M.	Taurus	Cancer	Gemini	Leo	Gemini	Libra	Cancer	Libra	Leo
2			Cancer	Gemini	Leo	Gemini	Libra	Cancer	Libra	Leo
3	10:26 A.M.	Gemini	Cancer	Gemini	Leo	Gemini	Libra	Cancer	Libra	Leo
4			Cancer	Gemini	Leo	Gemini	Libra	Cancer	Libra	Leo
5	5:14 P.M.	Cancer	Cancer	Cancer	Leo	Gemini	Libra	Cancer	Libra	Leo
6			Cancer	Cancer	Leo	Gemini	Libra	Cancer	Libra	Leo
7			Cancer	Cancer	Leo	Gemini	Libra	Cancer	Libra	Leo
8	2:23 A.M.	Leo	Cancer	Cancer	Leo	Gemini	Libra	Cancer	Libra	Leo
9			Cancer	Cancer	Leo	Gemini	Libra	Cancer	Libra	Leo
10	1:19 P.M.	Virgo	Cancer	Cancer	Leo	Gemini	Libra	Cancer	Libra	Leo
11			Cancer	Cancer	Leo	Gemini	Libra	Cancer	Libra	Leo
12			Leo	Cancer	Leo	Gemini	Libra	Cancer	Libra	Leo
13	1:45 A.M.	Libra	Leo	Cancer	Leo	Gemini	Libra	Cancer	Libra	Leo
14			Leo	Cancer	Leo	Gemini	Libra	Cancer	Libra	Leo
15	2:33 P.M.	Scorpio	Leo	Cancer	Leo	Gemini	Libra	Cancer	Libra	Leo
16			Leo	Cancer	Leo	Gemini	Libra	Cancer	Libra	Leo
17			Leo	Cancer	Leo	Gemini	Libra	Cancer	Libra	Leo
18	1:38 A.M.	Sagittarius	Leo	Cancer	Leo	Gemini	Libra	Cancer	Libra	Leo
19			Leo	Cancer	Leo	Gemini	Libra	Cancer	Libra	Leo
20	9:16 A.M.	Capricorn	Leo	Cancer	Leo	Gemini	Libra	Cancer	Libra	Leo
21			Leo	Cancer	Leo	Gemini	Libra	Cancer	Libra	Leo
22	12:21 P.M.	Aquarius	Leo	Cancer	Leo	Gemini	Libra	Cancer	Libra	Leo
23			Leo	Cancer	Leo	Gemini	Libra	Cancer	Libra	Leo

1954

	MOON FROM	IN	MERCURY	VENUS	MARS	JUPITER	SATURN	URANUS	NEPTUNE	PLUTO
July										
24	Taurus		Cancer	Virgo	Sagittarius	Cancer	Scorpio	Cancer	Libra	Leo
25	2:36 A.M.	Gemini	Cancer	Virgo	Sagittarius	Cancer	Scorpio	Cancer	Libra	Leo
26			Cancer	Virgo	Sagittarius	Cancer	Scorpio	Cancer	Libra	Leo
27	5:48 A.M.	Cancer	Cancer	Virgo	Sagittarius	Cancer	Scorpio	Cancer	Libra	Leo
28			Cancer	Virgo	Sagittarius	Cancer	Scorpio	Cancer	Libra	Leo
29	10:10 A.M.	Leo	Cancer	Virgo	Sagittarius	Cancer	Scorpio	Cancer	Libra	Leo
30			Cancer	Virgo	Sagittarius	Cancer	Scorpio	Cancer	Libra	Leo
31	3:09 P.M.	Virgo	Cancer	Virgo	Sagittarius	Cancer	Scorpio	Cancer	Libra	Leo
August										
1			Cancer	Virgo	Sagittarius	Cancer	Scorpio	Cancer	Libra	Leo
2	9:57 P.M.	Libra	Cancer	Virgo	Sagittarius	Cancer	Scorpio	Cancer	Libra	Leo
3			Cancer	Virgo	Sagittarius	Cancer	Scorpio	Cancer	Libra	Leo
4			Cancer	Virgo	Sagittarius	Cancer	Scorpio	Cancer	Libra	Leo
5	10:01 A.M.	Scorpio	Cancer	Virgo	Sagittarius	Cancer	Scorpio	Cancer	Libra	Leo
6			Cancer	Virgo	Sagittarius	Cancer	Scorpio	Cancer	Libra	Leo
7	10:52 P.M.	Sagittarius	Cancer	Virgo	Sagittarius	Cancer	Scorpio	Cancer	Libra	Leo
8			Leo	Virgo	Sagittarius	Cancer	Scorpio	Cancer	Libra	Leo
9			Leo	Virgo	Sagittarius	Cancer	Scorpio	Cancer	Libra	Leo
10	9:27 A.M.	Capricorn	Leo	Libra	Sagittarius	Cancer	Scorpio	Cancer	Libra	Leo
11			Leo	Libra	Sagittarius	Cancer	Scorpio	Cancer	Libra	Leo
12	4:44 P.M.	Aquarius	Leo	Libra	Sagittarius	Cancer	Scorpio	Cancer	Libra	Leo
13			Leo	Libra	Sagittarius	Cancer	Scorpio	Cancer	Libra	Leo
14	9:10 P.M.	Pisces	Leo	Libra	Sagittarius	Cancer	Scorpio	Cancer	Libra	Leo
15			Leo	Libra	Sagittarius	Cancer	Scorpio	Cancer	Libra	Leo
16	11:34 P.M.	Aries	Leo	Libra	Sagittarius	Cancer	Scorpio	Cancer	Libra	Leo
17			Leo	Libra	Sagittarius	Cancer	Scorpio	Cancer	Libra	Leo
18			Leo	Libra	Sagittarius	Cancer	Scorpio	Cancer	Libra	Leo
19	1:33 A.M.	Taurus	Leo	Libra	Sagittarius	Cancer	Scorpio	Cancer	Libra	Leo
20			Leo	Libra	Sagittarius	Cancer	Scorpio	Cancer	Libra	Leo
21	4:13 A.M.	Gemini	Leo	Libra	Sagittarius	Cancer	Scorpio	Cancer	Libra	Leo
22			Leo	Libra	Sagittarius	Cancer	Scorpio	Cancer	Libra	Leo
23	8:04 A.M.	Cancer	Virgo	Libra	Sagittarius	Cancer	Scorpio	Cancer	Libra	Leo

LEO PLANETARY TABLES

1955

	MOON FROM / IN	MERCURY	VENUS	MARS	JUPITER	SATURN	URANUS	NEPTUNE	PLUTO
July 24	Libra	Cancer	Cancer	Leo	Leo	Scorpio	Cancer	Libra	Leo
25		Cancer	Cancer	Leo	Leo	Scorpio	Cancer	Libra	Leo
26	5:28 A.M. Scorpio	Cancer	Cancer	Leo	Leo	Scorpio	Cancer	Libra	Leo
27		Cancer	Cancer	Leo	Leo	Scorpio	Cancer	Libra	Leo
28	5:41 P.M. Sagittarius	Cancer	Cancer	Leo	Leo	Scorpio	Cancer	Libra	Leo
29		Cancer	Cancer	Leo	Leo	Scorpio	Cancer	Libra	Leo
30		Cancer	Cancer	Leo	Leo	Scorpio	Cancer	Libra	Leo
31	6:36 A.M. Capricorn	Leo	Cancer	Leo	Leo	Scorpio	Cancer	Libra	Leo
August 1		Leo	Cancer	Leo	Leo	Scorpio	Cancer	Libra	Leo
2	5:19 P.M. Aquarius	Leo	Leo	Leo	Leo	Scorpio	Cancer	Libra	Leo
3		Leo	Leo	Leo	Leo	Scorpio	Cancer	Libra	Leo
4		Leo	Leo	Leo	Leo	Scorpio	Cancer	Libra	Leo
5	2:33 A.M. Pisces	Leo	Leo	Leo	Leo	Scorpio	Cancer	Libra	Leo
6		Leo	Leo	Leo	Leo	Scorpio	Cancer	Libra	Leo
7	10:03 A.M. Aries	Leo	Leo	Leo	Leo	Scorpio	Cancer	Libra	Leo
8		Leo	Leo	Leo	Leo	Scorpio	Cancer	Libra	Leo
9	3:04 P.M. Taurus	Leo	Leo	Leo	Leo	Scorpio	Cancer	Libra	Leo
10		Leo	Leo	Leo	Leo	Scorpio	Cancer	Libra	Leo
11	6:51 P.M. Gemini	Leo	Leo	Leo	Leo	Scorpio	Cancer	Libra	Leo
12		Leo	Leo	Leo	Leo	Scorpio	Cancer	Libra	Leo
13	8:50 P.M. Cancer	Leo	Leo	Leo	Leo	Scorpio	Cancer	Libra	Leo
14		Leo	Leo	Leo	Leo	Scorpio	Cancer	Libra	Leo
15	10:44 P.M. Leo	Virgo	Leo	Leo	Leo	Scorpio	Cancer	Libra	Leo
16		Virgo	Leo	Leo	Leo	Scorpio	Cancer	Libra	Leo
17		Virgo	Leo	Leo	Leo	Scorpio	Cancer	Libra	Leo
18	1:11 A.M. Virgo	Virgo	Leo	Leo	Leo	Scorpio	Cancer	Libra	Leo
19		Virgo	Leo	Leo	Leo	Scorpio	Cancer	Libra	Leo
20	5:32 A.M. Libra	Virgo	Leo	Leo	Leo	Scorpio	Cancer	Libra	Leo
21		Virgo	Leo	Leo	Leo	Scorpio	Cancer	Libra	Leo
22	1:38 P.M. Scorpio	Virgo	Leo	Leo	Leo	Scorpio	Cancer	Libra	Leo
23		Virgo	Leo	Leo	Leo	Scorpio	Cancer	Libra	Leo

1956

Date	MOON FROM	IN	MERCURY	VENUS	MARS	JUPITER	SATURN	URANUS	NEPTUNE	PLUTO
July										
23	Aquarius		Leo	Gemini	Pisces	Virgo	Scorpio	Leo	Libra	Leo
24			Leo	Gemini	Pisces	Virgo	Scorpio	Leo	Libra	Leo
25	4:49 A.M.	Pisces	Leo	Gemini	Pisces	Virgo	Scorpio	Leo	Libra	Leo
26			Leo	Gemini	Pisces	Virgo	Scorpio	Leo	Libra	Leo
27	4:12 P.M.	Aries	Leo	Gemini	Pisces	Virgo	Scorpio	Leo	Libra	Leo
28			Leo	Gemini	Pisces	Virgo	Scorpio	Leo	Libra	Leo
29			Leo	Gemini	Pisces	Virgo	Scorpio	Leo	Libra	Leo
30	1:09 A.M.	Taurus	Leo	Gemini	Pisces	Virgo	Scorpio	Leo	Libra	Leo
31			Leo	Gemini	Pisces	Virgo	Scorpio	Leo	Libra	Leo
August										
1	6:29 A.M.	Gemini	Leo	Gemini	Pisces	Virgo	Scorpio	Leo	Libra	Leo
2			Leo	Gemini	Pisces	Virgo	Scorpio	Leo	Libra	Leo
3	8:27 A.M.	Cancer	Leo	Gemini	Pisces	Virgo	Scorpio	Leo	Libra	Leo
4			Leo	Gemini	Pisces	Virgo	Scorpio	Leo	Libra	Leo
5	8:25 A.M.	Leo	Leo	Cancer	Pisces	Virgo	Scorpio	Leo	Libra	Leo
6			Virgo	Cancer	Pisces	Virgo	Scorpio	Leo	Libra	Leo
7	8:08 A.M.	Virgo	Virgo	Cancer	Pisces	Virgo	Scorpio	Leo	Libra	Leo
8			Virgo	Cancer	Pisces	Virgo	Scorpio	Leo	Libra	Leo
9	9:13 A.M.	Libra	Virgo	Cancer	Pisces	Virgo	Scorpio	Leo	Libra	Leo
10			Virgo	Cancer	Pisces	Virgo	Scorpio	Leo	Libra	Leo
11	1:45 P.M.	Scorpio	Virgo	Cancer	Pisces	Virgo	Scorpio	Leo	Libra	Leo
12			Virgo	Cancer	Pisces	Virgo	Scorpio	Leo	Libra	Leo
13	9:54 P.M.	Sagittarius	Virgo	Cancer	Pisces	Virgo	Scorpio	Leo	Libra	Leo
14			Virgo	Cancer	Pisces	Virgo	Scorpio	Leo	Libra	Leo
15			Virgo	Cancer	Pisces	Virgo	Scorpio	Leo	Libra	Leo
16	9:51 A.M.	Capricorn	Virgo	Cancer	Pisces	Virgo	Scorpio	Leo	Libra	Leo
17			Virgo	Cancer	Pisces	Virgo	Scorpio	Leo	Libra	Leo
18	10:44 P.M.	Aquarius	Virgo	Cancer	Pisces	Virgo	Scorpio	Leo	Libra	Leo
19			Virgo	Cancer	Pisces	Virgo	Scorpio	Leo	Libra	Leo
20			Virgo	Cancer	Pisces	Virgo	Scorpio	Leo	Libra	Leo
21	10:55 A.M.	Pisces	Virgo	Cancer	Pisces	Virgo	Scorpio	Leo	Libra	Leo
22			Virgo	Cancer	Pisces	Virgo	Scorpio	Leo	Libra	Leo
23	9:38 P.M.	Aries	Virgo	Cancer	Pisces	Virgo	Scorpio	Leo	Libra	Leo

LEO PLANETARY TABLES

1957

Date	MOON FROM	MOON IN	MERCURY	VENUS	MARS	JUPITER	SATURN	URANUS	NEPTUNE	PLUTO
July 24	3:58 P.M.	Cancer	Leo	Leo	Leo	Virgo	Sagittarius	Leo	Libra	Leo
25	5:24 P.M.	Leo	Leo	Leo	Leo	Virgo	Sagittarius	Leo	Libra	Leo
26			Leo	Leo	Leo	Virgo	Sagittarius	Leo	Libra	Leo
27	5:24 P.M.	Virgo	Leo	Virgo	Leo	Virgo	Sagittarius	Leo	Libra	Leo
28			Leo	Virgo	Leo	Virgo	Sagittarius	Leo	Libra	Leo
29			Leo	Virgo	Leo	Virgo	Sagittarius	Leo	Libra	Leo
30	5:54 P.M.	Libra	Leo	Virgo	Leo	Virgo	Sagittarius	Leo	Libra	Leo
31			Virgo	Virgo	Leo	Virgo	Sagittarius	Leo	Libra	Leo
August 1	8:02 P.M.	Scorpio	Virgo	Virgo	Leo	Virgo	Sagittarius	Leo	Libra	Leo
2			Virgo	Virgo	Leo	Virgo	gsagittarius	Leo	Libra	Leo
3			Virgo	Virgo	Leo	Virgo	Sagittarius	Leo	Libra	Leo
4	1:44 A.M.	Sagittarius	Virgo	Virgo	Leo	Virgo	Sagittarius	Leo	Libra	Leo
5			Virgo	Virgo	Leo	Virgo	Sagittarius	Leo	Libra	Leo
6	10:08 A.M.	Capricorn	Virgo	Virgo	Leo	Virgo	Sagittarius	Leo	Libra	Leo
7			Virgo	Virgo	Leo	Virgo	Sagittarius	Leo	Libra	Leo
8	9:10 P.M.	Aquarius	Virgo	Virgo	Leo	Libra	Sagittarius	Leo	Scorpio	Leo
9			Virgo	Virgo	Virgo	Libra	Sagittarius	Leo	Scorpio	Leo
10			Virgo	Virgo	Virgo	Libra	Sagittarius	Leo	Scorpio	Leo
11	9:02 A.M.	Pisces	Virgo	Virgo	Virgo	Libra	Sagittarius	Leo	Scorpio	Leo
12			Virgo	Virgo	Virgo	Libra	Sagittarius	Leo	Scorpio	Leo
13	9:46 P.M.	Aries	Virgo	Virgo	Virgo	Libra	Sagittarius	Leo	Scorpio	Leo
14			Virgo	Virgo	Virgo	Libra	Sagittarius	Leo	Scorpio	Leo
15			Virgo	Virgo	Virgo	Libra	Sagittarius	Leo	Scorpio	Leo
16	10:08 A.M.	Taurus	Virgo	Virgo	Virgo	Libra	Sagittarius	Leo	Scorpio	Leo
17			Virgo	Virgo	Virgo	Libra	Sagittarius	Leo	Scorpio	Leo
18	7:50 P.M.	Gemini	Virgo	Virgo	Virgo	Libra	Sagittarius	Leo	Scorpio	Leo
19			Virgo	Virgo	Virgo	Libra	Sagittarius	Leo	Scorpio	Leo
20			Virgo	Virgo	Virgo	Libra	Sagittarius	Leo	Scorpio	Virgo
21	1:45 A.M.	Cancer	Virgo	Libra	Virgo	Libra	Sagittarius	Leo	Scorpio	Virgo
22			Virgo	Libra	Virgo	Libra	Sagittarius	Leo	Scorpio	Virgo
23	3:52 A.M.	Leo	Virgo	Libra	Virgo	Libra	Sagittarius	Leo	Scorpio	Virgo

1958

July	MOON FROM	IN	MERCURY	VENUS	MARS	JUPITER	SATURN	URANUS	NEPTUNE	PLUTO
24	Scorpio		Leo	Cancer	Taurus	Libra	Sagittarius	Leo	Scorpio	Virgo
25	12:22 P.M.	Sagittarius	Leo	Cancer	Taurus	Libra	Sagittarius	Leo	Scorpio	Virgo
26			Leo	Cancer	Taurus	Libra	Sagittarius	Leo	Scorpio	Virgo
27	5:02 P.M.	Capricorn	Virgo	Cancer	Taurus	Libra	Sagittarius	Leo	Scorpio	Virgo
28			Virgo	Cancer	Taurus	Libra	Sagittarius	Leo	Scorpio	Virgo
29	11:15 P.M.	Aquarius	Virgo	Cancer	Taurus	Libra	Sagittarius	Leo	Scorpio	Virgo
30			Virgo	Cancer	Taurus	Libra	Sagittarius	Leo	Scorpio	Virgo
31			Virgo	Cancer	Taurus	Libra	Sagittarius	Leo	Scorpio	Virgo
August										
1	7:24 A.M.	Pisces	Virgo	Cancer	Taurus	Libra	Sagittarius	Leo	Scorpio	Virgo
2			Virgo	Cancer	Taurus	Libra	Sagittarius	Leo	Scorpio	Virgo
3	6:24 P.M.	Aries	Virgo	Cancer	Taurus	Libra	Sagittarius	Leo	Scorpio	Virgo
4			Virgo	Cancer	Taurus	Libra	Sagittarius	Leo	Scorpio	Virgo
5			Virgo	Cancer	Taurus	Libra	Sagittarius	Leo	Scorpio	Virgo
6	6:48 A.M.	Taurus	Virgo	Cancer	Taurus	Libra	Sagittarius	Leo	Scorpio	Virgo
7			Virgo	Cancer	Taurus	Libra	Sagittarius	Leo	Scorpio	Virgo
8	7:47 P.M.	Gemini	Virgo	Cancer	Taurus	Libra	Sagittarius	Leo	Scorpio	Virgo
9			Virgo	Cancer	Taurus	Libra	Sagittarius	Leo	Scorpio	Virgo
10			Virgo	Cancer	Taurus	Libra	Sagittarius	Leo	Scorpio	Virgo
11	4:45 A.M.	Cancer	Virgo	Cancer	Taurus	Libra	Sagittarius	Leo	Scorpio	Virgo
12			Virgo	Cancer	Taurus	Libra	Sagittarius	Leo	Scorpio	Virgo
13	9:45 A.M.	Leo	Virgo	Cancer	Taurus	Libra	Sagittarius	Leo	Scorpio	Virgo
14			Virgo	Cancer	Taurus	Libra	Sagittarius	Leo	Scorpio	Virgo
15	12:27 P.M.	Virgo	Virgo	Cancer	Taurus	Libra	Sagittarius	Leo	Scorpio	Virgo
16			Virgo	Cancer	Taurus	Libra	Sagittarius	Leo	Scorpio	Virgo
17	1:41 P.M.	Libra	Virgo	Leo	Taurus	Libra	Sagittarius	Leo	Scorpio	Virgo
18			Virgo	Leo	Taurus	Libra	Sagittarius	Leo	Scorpio	Virgo
19	2:44 P.M.	Scorpio	Virgo	Leo	Taurus	Libra	Sagittarius	Leo	Scorpio	Virgo
20			Virgo	Leo	Taurus	Libra	Sagittarius	Leo	Scorpio	Virgo
21	5:34 P.M.	Sagittarius	Virgo	Leo	Taurus	Libra	Sagittarius	Leo	Scorpio	Virgo
22	10:30 P.M.	Capricorn	Virgo	Leo	Taurus	Libra	Sagittarius	Leo	Scorpio	Virgo
23			Virgo	Leo	Taurus	Libra	Sagittarius	Leo	Scorpio	Virgo

LEO PLANETARY TABLES

1959

	MOON FROM IN	MERCURY	VENUS	MARS	JUPITER	SATURN	URANUS	NEPTUNE	PLUTO
July									
24	3:12 P.M. Aries	Leo	Virgo	Virgo	Scorpio	Capricorn	Leo	Scorpio	Virgo
25		Leo	Virgo	Virgo	Scorpio	Capricorn	Leo	Scorpio	Virgo
26	1:51 P.M. Taurus	Leo	Virgo	Virgo	Scorpio	Capricorn	Leo	Scorpio	Virgo
27		Leo	Virgo	Virgo	Scorpio	Capricorn	Leo	Scorpio	Virgo
28		Leo	Virgo	Virgo	Scorpio	Capricorn	Leo	Scorpio	Virgo
29	2:37 P.M. Gemini	Leo	Virgo	Virgo	Scorpio	Capricorn	Leo	Scorpio	Virgo
30		Leo	Virgo	Virgo	Scorpio	Capricorn	Leo	Scorpio	Virgo
31		Leo	Virgo	Virgo	Scorpio	Capricorn	Leo	Scorpio	Virgo
August									
1	2:31 A.M. Cancer	Leo	Virgo	Virgo	Scorpio	Capricorn	Leo	Scorpio	Virgo
2		Leo	Virgo	Virgo	Scorpio	Capricorn	Leo	Scorpio	Virgo
3	12:21 P.M. Leo	Leo	Virgo	Virgo	Scorpio	Capricorn	Leo	Scorpio	Virgo
4		Leo	Virgo	Virgo	Scorpio	Capricorn	Leo	Scorpio	Virgo
5	7:26 P.M. Virgo	Leo	Virgo	Virgo	Scorpio	Capricorn	Leo	Scorpio	Virgo
6		Leo	Virgo	Virgo	Scorpio	Capricorn	Leo	Scorpio	Virgo
7		Leo	Virgo	Virgo	Scorpio	Capricorn	Leo	Scorpio	Virgo
8	0:53 A.M. Libra	Leo	Virgo	Virgo	Scorpio	Capricorn	Leo	Scorpio	Virgo
9		Leo	Virgo	Virgo	Scorpio	Capricorn	Leo	Scorpio	Virgo
10	4:35 A.M. Scorpio	Leo	Virgo	Virgo	Scorpio	Capricorn	Leo	Scorpio	Virgo
11		Leo	Virgo	Virgo	Scorpio	Capricorn	Leo	Scorpio	Virgo
12	7:41 A.M. Sagittarius	Leo	Virgo	Virgo	Scorpio	Capricorn	Leo	Scorpio	Virgo
13		Leo	Virgo	Virgo	Scorpio	Capricorn	Leo	Scorpio	Virgo
14	10:14 A.M. Capricorn	Leo	Virgo	Virgo	Scorpio	Capricorn	Leo	Scorpio	Virgo
15		Leo	Virgo	Virgo	Scorpio	Capricorn	Leo	Scorpio	Virgo
16	1:13 P.M. Aquarius	Leo	Virgo	Virgo	Scorpio	Capricorn	Leo	Scorpio	Virgo
17		Leo	Virgo	Virgo	Scorpio	Capricorn	Leo	Scorpio	Virgo
18	5:19 P.M. Pisces	Leo	Virgo	Virgo	Scorpio	Capricorn	Leo	Scorpio	Virgo
19		Leo	Virgo	Virgo	Scorpio	Capricorn	Leo	Scorpio	Virgo
20		Leo	Virgo	Virgo	Scorpio	Capricorn	Leo	Scorpio	Virgo
21	0:09 A.M. Aries	Leo	Virgo	Virgo	Scorpio	Capricorn	Leo	Scorpio	Virgo
22	9:38 A.M. Taurus	Leo	Virgo	Virgo	Scorpio	Capricorn	Leo	Scorpio	Virgo
23		Leo	Virgo	Virgo	Scorpio	Capricorn	Leo	Scorpio	Virgo

1960

July	MOON FROM	IN	MERCURY	VENUS	MARS	JUPITER	SATURN	URANUS	NEPTUNE	PLUTO
23	12:03 P.M.	Leo	Cancer	Leo	Taurus	Sagittarius	Capricorn	Leo	Scorpio	Virgo
24			Cancer	Leo	Taurus	Sagittarius	Capricorn	Leo	Scorpio	Virgo
25	11:44 P.M.	Virgo	Cancer	Leo	Taurus	Sagittarius	Capricorn	Leo	Scorpio	Virgo
26			Cancer	Leo	Taurus	Sagittarius	Capricorn	Leo	Scorpio	Virgo
27			Cancer	Leo	Taurus	Sagittarius	Capricorn	Leo	Scorpio	Virgo
28	9:38 A.M.	Libra	Cancer	Leo	Taurus	Sagittarius	Capricorn	Leo	Scorpio	Virgo
29			Cancer	Leo	Taurus	Sagittarius	Capricorn	Leo	Scorpio	Virgo
30	5:02 P.M.	Scorpio	Cancer	Leo	Taurus	Sagittarius	Capricorn	Leo	Scorpio	Virgo
31			Cancer	Leo	Taurus	Sagittarius	Capricorn	Leo	Scorpio	Virgo
August										
1	8:52 P.M.	Sagittarius	Cancer	Leo	Taurus	Sagittarius	Capricorn	Leo	Scorpio	Virgo
2			Cancer	Leo	Taurus	Sagittarius	Capricorn	Leo	Scorpio	Virgo
3	10:51 P.M.	Capricorn	Cancer	Leo	Gemini	Sagittarius	Capricorn	Leo	Scorpio	Virgo
4			Cancer	Leo	Gemini	Sagittarius	Capricorn	Leo	Scorpio	Virgo
5	10:42 P.M.	Aquarus	Cancer	Leo	Gemini	Sagittarius	Capricorn	Leo	Scorpio	Virgo
6			Cancer	Leo	Gemini	Sagittarius	Capricorn	Leo	Scorpio	Virgo
7	11:20 P.M.	Pisces	Cancer	Leo	Gemini	Sagittarius	Capricorn	Leo	Scorpio	Virgo
8			Cancer	Leo	Gemini	Sagittarius	Capricorn	Leo	Scorpio	Virgo
9			Cancer	Leo	Gemini	Sagittarius	Capricorn	Leo	Scorpio	Virgo
10	1:30 A.M.	Aries	Cancer	Virgo	Gemini	Sagittarius	Capricorn	Leo	Scorpio	Virgo
11			Leo	Virgo	Gemini	Sagittarius	Capricorn	Leo	Scorpio	Virgo
12	7:45 A.M.	Taurus	Leo	Virgo	Gemini	Sagittarius	Capricorn	Leo	Scorpio	Virgo
13			Leo	Virgo	Gemini	Sagittarius	Capricorn	Leo	Scorpio	Virgo
14	5:41 P.M.	Gemini	Leo	Virgo	Gemini	Sagittarius	Capricorn	Leo	Scorpio	Virgo
15			Leo	Virgo	Gemini	Sagittarius	Capricorn	Leo	Scorpio	Virgo
16			Leo	Virgo	Gemini	Sagittarius	Capricorn	Leo	Scorpio	Virgo
17	6:23 A.M.	Cancer	Leo	Virgo	Gemini	Sagittarius	Capricorn	Leo	Scorpio	Virgo
18			Leo	Virgo	Gemini	Sagittarius	Capricorn	Leo	Scorpio	Virgo
19	6:42 P.M.	Leo	Leo	Virgo	Gemini	Sagittarius	Capricorn	Leo	Scorpio	Virgo
20			Leo	Virgo	Gemini	Sagittarius	Capricorn	Leo	Scorpio	Virgo
21			Leo	Virgo	Gemini	Sagittarius	Capricorn	Leo	Scorpio	Virgo
22	5:50 A.M.	Virgo	Leo	Virgo	Gemini	Sagittarius	Capricorn	Leo	Scorpio	Virgo
23			Leo	Virgo	Gemini	Sagittarius	Capricorn	Leo	Scorpio	Virgo

LEO PLANETARY TABLES

1961

	MOON FROM	IN	MERCURY	VENUS	MARS	JUPITER	SATURN	URANUS	NEPTUNE	PLUTO
July										
24		Sagittarius	Cancer	Gemini	Virgo	Aquarius	Capricorn	Leo	Scorpio	Virgo
25	7:49 A.M.	Capricorn	Cancer	Gemini	Virgo	Aquarius	Capricorn	Leo	Scorpio	Virgo
26			Cancer	Gemini	Virgo	Aquarius	Capricorn	Leo	Scorpio	Virgo
27	8:17 A.M.	Aquarius	Cancer	Gemini	Virgo	Aquarius	Capricorn	Leo	Scorpio	Virgo
28			Cancer	Gemini	Virgo	Aquarius	Capricorn	Leo	Scorpio	Virgo
29	7:38 A.M.	Pisces	Cancer	Gemini	Virgo	Aquarius	Capricorn	Leo	Scorpio	Virgo
30			Cancer	Gemini	Virgo	Aquarius	Capricorn	Leo	Scorpio	Virgo
31	8:10 A.M.	Aries	Cancer	Gemini	Virgo	Aquarius	Capricorn	Leo	Scorpio	Virgo
August										
1			Cancer	Gemini	Virgo	Aquarius	Capricorn	Leo	Scorpio	Virgo
2	11:08 A.M.	Taurus	Cancer	Gemini	Virgo	Aquarius	Capricorn	Leo	Scorpio	Virgo
3			Cancer	Gemini	Virgo	Aquarius	Capricorn	Leo	Scorpio	Virgo
4	5:53 P.M.	Gemini	Cancer	Gemini	Virgo	Aquarius	Capricorn	Leo	Scorpio	Virgo
5			Leo	Cancer	Virgo	Aquarius	Capricorn	Leo	Scorpio	Virgo
6			Leo	Cancer	Virgo	Aquarius	Capricorn	Leo	Scorpio	Virgo
7	4:02 A.M.	Cancer	Leo	Cancer	Virgo	Aquarius	Capricorn	Leo	Scorpio	Virgo
8			Leo	Cancer	Virgo	Aquarius	Capricorn	Leo	Scorpio	Virgo
9	4:17 P.M.	Leo	Leo	Cancer	Virgo	Aquarius	Capricorn	Leo	Scorpio	Virgo
10			Leo	Cancer	Virgo	Aquarius	Capricorn	Leo	Scorpio	Virgo
11			Leo	Cancer	Virgo	Aquarius	Capricorn	Leo	Scorpio	Virgo
12	4:48 A.M.	Virgo	Leo	Cancer	Virgo	Aquarius	Capricorn	Leo	Scorpio	Virgo
13			Leo	Cancer	Virgo	Aquarius	Capricorn	Leo	Scorpio	Virgo
14	5:05 P.M.	Libra	Leo	Cancer	Virgo	Capricorn	Capricorn	Leo	Scorpio	Virgo
15			Leo	Cancer	Virgo	Capricorn	Capricorn	Leo	Scorpio	Virgo
16			Leo	Cancer	Virgo	Capricorn	Capricorn	Leo	Scorpio	Virgo
17	4:30 A.M.	Scorpio	Leo	Cancer	Virgo	Capricorn	Capricorn	Leo	Scorpio	Virgo
18			Leo	Cancer	Virgo	Capricorn	Capricorn	Leo	Scorpio	Virgo
19	12:47 P.M.	Sagittarius	Virgo	Cancer	Libra	Capricorn	Capricorn	Leo	Scorpio	Virgo
20			Virgo	Cancer	Libra	Capricorn	Capricorn	Leo	Scorpio	Virgo
21	5:28 P.M.	Capricorn	Virgo	Cancer	Libra	Capricorn	Capricorn	Leo	Scorpio	Virgo
22			Virgo	Cancer	Libra	Capricorn	Capricorn	Leo	Scorpio	Virgo
23	6:37 P.M.	Aquarius	Virgo	Cancer	Libra	Capricorn	Capricorn	Leo	Scorpio	Virgo

1962

July	MOON FROM	IN	MERCURY	VENUS	MARS	JUPITER	SATURN	URANUS	NEPTUNE	PLUTO
24	Taurus		Cancer	Virgo	Gemini	Pisces	Aquarius	Leo	Scorpio	Virgo
25			Cancer	Virgo	Gemini	Pisces	Aquarius	Leo	Scorpio	Virgo
26		2:24 A.M. Gemini	Cancer	Virgo	Gemini	Pisces	Aquarius	Leo	Scorpio	Virgo
27			Leo	Virgo	Gemini	Pisces	Aquarius	Leo	Scorpio	Virgo
28		8:40 A.M. Cancer	Leo	Virgo	Gemini	Pisces	Aquarius	Leo	Scorpio	Virgo
29			Leo	Virgo	Gemini	Pisces	Aquarius	Leo	Scorpio	Virgo
30		4:43 P.M. Leo	Leo	Virgo	Gemini	Pisces	Aquarius	Leo	Scorpio	Virgo
31			Leo	Virgo	Gemini	Pisces	Aquarius	Leo	Scorpio	Virgo
August										
1			Leo	Virgo	Gemini	Pisces	Aquarius	Leo	Scorpio	Virgo
2		2:43 A.M. Virgo	Leo	Virgo	Gemini	Pisces	Aquarius	Leo	Scorpio	Virgo
3			Leo	Virgo	Gemini	Pisces	Aquarius	Leo	Scorpio	Virgo
4		2:52 P.M. Libra	Leo	Virgo	Gemini	Pisces	Aquarius	Leo	Scorpio	Virgo
5			Leo	Virgo	Gemini	Pisces	Aquarius	Leo	Scorpio	Virgo
6			Leo	Virgo	Gemini	Pisces	Aquarius	Leo	Scorpio	Virgo
7		3:33 A.M. Scorpio	Leo	Virgo	Gemini	Pisces	Aquarius	Leo	Scorpio	Virgo
8			Leo	Virgo	Gemini	Pisces	Aquarius	Leo	Scorpio	Virgo
9		2:50 P.M. Sagittarius	Leo	Virgo	Gemini	Pisces	Aquarius	Leo	Scorpio	Virgo
10			Leo	Libra	Gemini	Pisces	Aquarius	Virgo	Scorpio	Virgo
11		10:24 P.M. Capricorn	Virgo	Libra	Gemini	Pisces	Aquarius	Virgo	Scorpio	Virgo
12			Virgo	Libra	Gemini	Pisces	Aquarius	Virgo	Scorpio	Virgo
13			Virgo	Libra	Gemini	Pisces	Aquarius	Virgo	Scorpio	Virgo
14		1:59 A.M. Aquarius	Virgo	Libra	Gemini	Pisces	Aquarius	Virgo	Scorpio	Virgo
15			Virgo	Libra	Gemini	Pisces	Aquarius	Virgo	Scorpio	Virgo
16		3:16 A.M. Pisces	Virgo	Libra	Gemini	Pisces	Aquarius	Virgo	Scorpio	Virgo
17			Virgo	Libra	Gemini	Pisces	Aquarius	Virgo	Scorpio	Virgo
18		3:16 A.M. Aries	Virgo	Libra	Gemini	Pisces	Aquarius	Virgo	Scorpio	Virgo
19			Virgo	Libra	Gemini	Pisces	Aquarius	Virgo	Scorpio	Virgo
20		4:43 A.M. Taurus	Virgo	Libra	Gemini	Pisces	Aquarius	Virgo	Scorpio	Virgo
21			Virgo	Libra	Gemini	Pisces	Aquarius	Virgo	Scorpio	Virgo
22		7:43 A.M. Gemini	Virgo	Libra	Gemini	Pisces	Aquarius	Virgo	Scorpio	Virgo
23			Virgo	Libra	Cancer	Pisces	Aquarius	Virgo	Scorpio	Virgo

LEO PLANETARY TABLES

1963

Date	MOON FROM	MOON IN	MERCURY	VENUS	MARS	JUPITER	SATURN	URANUS	NEPTUNE	PLUTO
July 24		Virgo	Leo	Cancer	Virgo	Aries	Aquarius	Virgo	Scorpio	Virgo
25	10:56 A.M.	Libra	Leo	Cancer	Virgo	Aries	Aquarius	Virgo	Scorpio	Virgo
26			Leo	Cancer	Virgo	Aries	Aquarius	Virgo	Scorpio	Virgo
27	10:44 P.M.	Scorpio	Leo	Cancer	Virgo	Aries	Aquarius	Virgo	Scorpio	Virgo
28			Leo	Cancer	Libra	Aries	Aquarius	Virgo	Scorpio	Virgo
29			Leo	Cancer	Libra	Aries	Aquarius	Virgo	Scorpio	Virgo
30	11:39 A.M.	Sagittarius	Leo	Cancer	Libra	Aries	Aquarius	Virgo	Scorpio	Virgo
31			Leo	Cancer	Libra	Aries	Aquarius	Virgo	Scorpio	Virgo
August 1	10:25 P.M.	Capricorn	Leo	Leo	Libra	Aries	Aquarius	Virgo	Scorpio	Virgo
2			Leo	Leo	Libra	Aries	Aquarius	Virgo	Scorpio	Virgo
3			Leo	Leo	Libra	Aries	Aquarius	Virgo	Scorpio	Virgo
4	6:18 A.M.	Aquarius	Virgo	Leo	Libra	Aries	Aquarius	Virgo	Scorpio	Virgo
5			Virgo	Leo	Libra	Aries	Aquarius	Virgo	Scorpio	Virgo
6	11:23 A.M.	Pisces	Virgo	Leo	Libra	Aries	Aquarius	Virgo	Scorpio	Virgo
7			Virgo	Leo	Libra	Aries	Aquarius	Virgo	Scorpio	Virgo
8	3:04 P.M.	Aries	Virgo	Leo	Libra	Aries	Aquarius	Virgo	Scorpio	Virgo
9			Virgo	Leo	Libra	Aries	Aquarius	Virgo	Scorpio	Virgo
10	5:41 P.M.	Taurus	Virgo	Leo	Libra	Aries	Aquarius	Virgo	Scorpio	Virgo
11			Virgo	Leo	Libra	Aries	Aquarius	Virgo	Scorpio	Virgo
12	8:31 P.M.	Gemini	Virgo	Leo	Libra	Aries	Aquarius	Virgo	Scorpio	Virgo
13			Virgo	Leo	Libra	Aries	Aquarius	Virgo	Scorpio	Virgo
14	11:56 P.M.	Cancer	Virgo	Leo	Libra	Aries	Aquarius	Virgo	Scorpio	Virgo
15			Virgo	Leo	Libra	Aries	Aquarius	Virgo	Scorpio	Virgo
16			Virgo	Leo	Libra	Aries	Aquarius	Virgo	Scorpio	Virgo
17	4:21 A.M.	Leo	Virgo	Leo	Libra	Aries	Aquarius	Virgo	Scorpio	Virgo
18			Virgo	Leo	Libra	Aries	Aquarius	Virgo	Scorpio	Virgo
19	10:44 A.M.	Virgo	Virgo	Leo	Libra	Aries	Aquarius	Virgo	Scorpio	Virgo
20			Virgo	Leo	Libra	Aries	Aquarius	Virgo	Scorpio	Virgo
21	7:18 P.M.	Libra	Virgo	Leo	Libra	Aries	Aquarius	Virgo	Scorpio	Virgo
22			Virgo	Leo	Libra	Aries	Aquarius	Virgo	Scorpio	Virgo
23			Virgo	Leo	Libra	Aries	Aquarius	Virgo	Scorpio	Virgo

1964

MOON FROM	IN	MERCURY	VENUS	MARS	JUPITER	SATURN	URANUS	NEPTUNE	PLUTO
July									
23	Capricorn	Leo	Gemini	Gemini	Taurus	Pisces	Virgo	Scorpio	Virgo
24	7:24 A.M. Aquarius	Leo	Gemini	Gemini	Taurus	Pisces	Virgo	Scorpio	Virgo
25		Leo	Gemini	Gemini	Taurus	Pisces	Virgo	Scorpio	Virgo
26	5:18 P.M. Pisces	Leo	Gemini	Gemini	Taurus	Pisces	Virgo	Scorpio	Virgo
27		Leo	Gemini	Gemini	Taurus	Pisces	Virgo	Scorpio	Virgo
28		Virgo	Gemini	Gemini	Taurus	Pisces	Virgo	Scorpio	Virgo
29	1:31 A.M. Aries	Virgo	Gemini	Gemini	Taurus	Pisces	Virgo	Scorpio	Virgo
30		Virgo	Gemini	Gemini	Taurus	Pisces	Virgo	Scorpio	Virgo
31	7:31 A.M. Taurus	Virgo	Gemini	Cancer	Taurus	Pisces	Virgo	Scorpio	Virgo
August									
1	10:42 A.M. Gemini	Virgo	Gemini	Cancer	Taurus	Pisces	Virgo	Scorpio	Virgo
2		Virgo	Gemini	Cancer	Taurus	Pisces	Virgo	Scorpio	Virgo
3		Virgo	Gemini	Cancer	Taurus	Pisces	Virgo	Scorpio	Virgo
4	12:14 P.M. Cancer	Virgo	Gemini	Cancer	Taurus	Pisces	Virgo	Scorpio	Virgo
5		Virgo	Gemini	Cancer	Taurus	Pisces	Virgo	Scorpio	Virgo
6	1:06 P.M. Leo	Virgo	Cancer	Cancer	Taurus	Pisces	Virgo	Scorpio	Virgo
7		Virgo	Cancer	Cancer	Taurus	Pisces	Virgo	Scorpio	Virgo
8	2:51 P.M. Virgo	Virgo	Cancer	Cancer	Taurus	Pisces	Virgo	Scorpio	Virgo
9		Virgo	Cancer	Cancer	Taurus	Pisces	Virgo	Scorpio	Virgo
10	6:50 P.M. Libra	Virgo	Cancer	Cancer	Taurus	Pisces	Virgo	Scorpio	Virgo
11		Virgo	Cancer	Cancer	Taurus	Pisces	Virgo	Scorpio	Virgo
12		Virgo	Cancer	Cancer	Taurus	Pisces	Virgo	Scorpio	Virgo
13	2:24 A.M. Scorpio	Virgo	Cancer	Cancer	Taurus	Pisces	Virgo	Scorpio	Virgo
14		Virgo	Cancer	Cancer	Taurus	Pisces	Virgo	Scorpio	Virgo
15	1:52 P.M. Sagittarius	Virgo	Cancer	Cancer	Taurus	Pisces	Virgo	Scorpio	Virgo
16		Virgo	Cancer	Cancer	Taurus	Pisces	Virgo	Scorpio	Virgo
17		Virgo	Cancer	Cancer	Taurus	Pisces	Virgo	Scorpio	Virgo
18	2:46 A.M. Capricorn	Virgo	Cancer	Cancer	Taurus	Pisces	Virgo	Scorpio	Virgo
19		Virgo	Cancer	Cancer	Taurus	Pisces	Virgo	Scorpio	Virgo
20	2:32 P.M. Aquarius	Virgo	Cancer	Cancer	Taurus	Pisces	Virgo	Scorpio	Virgo
21		Virgo	Cancer	Cancer	Taurus	Pisces	Virgo	Scorpio	Virgo
22	11:53 P.M. Pisces	Virgo	Cancer	Cancer	Taurus	Pisces	Virgo	Scorpio	Virgo
23		Virgo	Cancer	Cancer	Taurus	Pisces	Virgo	Scorpio	Virgo

LEO PLANETARY TABLES

1965

July	MOON FROM	IN	MERCURY	VENUS	MARS	JUPITER	SATURN	URANUS	NEPTUNE	PLUTO
24	Gemini		Leo	Leo	Libra	Gemini	Pisces	Virgo	Scorpio	Virgo
25	10:58 P.M.	Cancer	Leo	Leo	Libra	Gemini	Pisces	Virgo	Scorpio	Virgo
26	10:55 P.M.	Leo	Leo	Virgo	Libra	Gemini	Pisces	Virgo	Scorpio	Virgo
27			Leo	Virgo	Libra	Gemini	Pisces	Virgo	Scorpio	Virgo
28			Leo	Virgo	Libra	Gemini	Pisces	Virgo	Scorpio	Virgo
29	10:16 P.M.	Virgo	Leo	Virgo	Libra	Gemini	Pisces	Virgo	Scorpio	Virgo
30			Leo	Virgo	Libra	Gemini	Pisces	Virgo	Scorpio	Virgo
31	11:14 P.M.	Libra	Leo	Virgo	Libra	Gemini	Pisces	Virgo	Scorpio	Virgo
August										
1			Virgo	Virgo	Libra	Gemini	Pisces	Virgo	Scorpio	Virgo
2			Virgo	Virgo	Libra	Gemini	Pisces	Virgo	Scorpio	Virgo
3	3:35 A.M.	Scorpio	Virgo	Virgo	Libra	Gemini	Pisces	Virgo	Scorpio	Virgo
4			Leo	Virgo	Libra	Gemini	Pisces	Virgo	Scorpio	Virgo
5	11:44 A.M.	Sagittarius	Leo	Virgo	Libra	Gemini	Pisces	Virgo	Scorpio	Virgo
6			Leo	Virgo	Libra	Gemini	Pisces	Virgo	Scorpio	Virgo
7	11:24 P.M.	Capricorn	Leo	Virgo	Libra	Gemini	Pisces	Virgo	Scorpio	Virgo
8			Leo	Virgo	Libra	Gemini	Pisces	Virgo	Scorpio	Virgo
9			Leo	Virgo	Libra	Gemini	Pisces	Virgo	Scorpio	Virgo
10	12:06 P.M.	Aquarius	Leo	Virgo	Libra	Gemini	Pisces	Virgo	Scorpio	Virgo
11			Leo	Virgo	Libra	Gemini	Pisces	Virgo	Scorpio	Virgo
12			Leo	Virgo	Libra	Gemini	Pisces	Virgo	Scorpio	Virgo
13	0:33 A.M.	Pisces	Leo	Virgo	Libra	Gemini	Pisces	Virgo	Scorpio	Virgo
14			Leo	Virgo	Libra	Gemini	Pisces	Virgo	Scorpio	Virgo
15	12:04 P.M.	Aries	Leo	Virgo	Libra	Gemini	Pisces	Virgo	Scorpio	Virgo
16			Leo	Virgo	Libra	Gemini	Pisces	Virgo	Scorpio	Virgo
17	9:44 P.M.	Taurus	Leo	Virgo	Libra	Gemini	Pisces	Virgo	Scorpio	Virgo
18			Leo	Virgo	Libra	Gemini	Pisces	Virgo	Scorpio	Virgo
19			Leo	Virgo	Libra	Gemini	Pisces	Virgo	Scorpio	Virgo
20	4:39 A.M.	Gemini	Leo	Libra	Libra	Gemini	Pisces	Virgo	Scorpio	Virgo
21			Leo	Libra	Scorpio	Gemini	Pisces	Virgo	Scorpio	Virgo
22	8:10 A.M.	Cancer	Leo	Libra	Scorpio	Gemini	Pisces	Virgo	Scorpio	Virgo
23			Leo	Libra	Scorpio	Gemini	Pisces	Virgo	Scorpio	Virgo

1966

July	MOON FROM	IN		MERCURY	VENUS	MARS	JUPITER	SATURN	URANUS	NEPTUNE	PLUTO
24	11:44 A.M.	Scorpio		Leo	Cancer	Cancer	Cancer	Pisces	Virgo	Scorpio	Virgo
25				Leo	Cancer	Cancer	Cancer	Pisces	Virgo	Scorpio	Virgo
26	5:18 P.M.	Sagittarius		Leo	Cancer	Cancer	Cancer	Pisces	Virgo	Scorpio	Virgo
27				Leo	Cancer	Cancer	Cancer	Pisces	Virgo	Scorpio	Virgo
28				Leo	Cancer	Cancer	Cancer	Pisces	Virgo	Scorpio	Virgo
29	1:08 A.M.	Capricorn		Leo	Cancer	Cancer	Cancer	Pisces	Virgo	Scorpio	Virgo
30				Leo	Cancer	Cancer	Cancer	Pisces	Virgo	Scorpio	Virgo
31	11:05 A.M.	Aquarius		Leo	Cancer	Cancer	Cancer	Pisces	Virgo	Scorpio	Virgo
August											
1				Leo	Cancer	Cancer	Cancer	Pisces	Virgo	Scorpio	Virgo
2	10:40 P.M.	Pisces		Leo	Cancer	Cancer	Cancer	Pisces	Virgo	Scorpio	Virgo
3				Leo	Cancer	Cancer	Cancer	Pisces	Virgo	Scorpio	Virgo
4				Leo	Cancer	Cancer	Cancer	Pisces	Virgo	Scorpio	Virgo
5	11:17 A.M.	Aries		Leo	Cancer	Cancer	Cancer	Pisces	Virgo	Scorpio	Virgo
6				Leo	Cancer	Cancer	Cancer	Pisces	Virgo	Scorpio	Virgo
7	11:50 P.M.	Taurus		Leo	Cancer	Cancer	Cancer	Pisces	Virgo	Scorpio	Virgo
8				Leo	Cancer	Cancer	Cancer	Pisces	Virgo	Scorpio	Virgo
9				Leo	Cancer	Cancer	Cancer	Pisces	Virgo	Scorpio	Virgo
10	9:37 A.M.	Gemini		Leo	Cancer	Cancer	Cancer	Pisces	Virgo	Scorpio	Virgo
11				Leo	Cancer	Cancer	Cancer	Pisces	Virgo	Scorpio	Virgo
12	3:38 P.M.	Cancer		Leo	Cancer	Cancer	Cancer	Pisces	Virgo	Scorpio	Virgo
13				Leo	Cancer	Cancer	Cancer	Pisces	Virgo	Scorpio	Virgo
14	5:51 P.M.	Leo		Leo	Cancer	Cancer	Cancer	Pisces	Virgo	Scorpio	Virgo
15				Leo	Cancer	Cancer	Cancer	Pisces	Virgo	Scorpio	Virgo
16	6:02 P.M.	Virgo		Leo	Leo	Cancer	Cancer	Pisces	Virgo	Scorpio	Virgo
17				Leo	Leo	Cancer	Cancer	Pisces	Virgo	Scorpio	Virgo
18	5:36 P.M.	Libra		Leo	Leo	Cancer	Cancer	Pisces	Virgo	Scorpio	Virgo
19				Leo	Leo	Cancer	Cancer	Pisces	Virgo	Scorpio	Virgo
20	6:51 P.M.	Scorpio		Leo	Leo	Cancer	Cancer	Pisces	Virgo	Scorpio	Virgo
21				Leo	Leo	Cancer	Cancer	Pisces	Virgo	Scorpio	Virgo
22	10:54 P.M.	Sagittarius		Leo	Leo	Cancer	Cancer	Pisces	Virgo	Scorpio	Virgo
23				Leo	Leo	Cancer	Cancer	Pisces	Virgo	Scorpio	Virgo

LEO PLANETARY TABLES

1967

	MOON		MERCURY	VENUS	MARS	JUPITER	SATURN	URANUS	NEPTUNE	PLUTO
July	FROM	IN								
24	Pisces		Cancer	Virgo	Scorpio	Leo	Aries	Virgo	Scorpio	Virgo
25			Cancer	Virgo	Scorpio	Leo	Aries	Virgo	Scorpio	Virgo
26	7:12 A.M.	Aries	Cancer	Virgo	Scorpio	Leo	Aries	Virgo	Scorpio	Virgo
27			Cancer	Virgo	Scorpio	Leo	Aries	Virgo	Scorpio	Virgo
28	7:55 P.M.	Taurus	Cancer	Virgo	Scorpio	Leo	Aries	Virgo	Scorpio	Virgo
29			Cancer	Virgo	Scorpio	Leo	Aries	Virgo	Scorpio	Virgo
30			Cancer	Virgo	Scorpio	Leo	Aries	Virgo	Scorpio	Virgo
31	8:11 A.M.	Gemini	Cancer	Virgo	Scorpio	Leo	Aries	Virgo	Scorpio	Virgo
August										
1			Cancer	Virgo	Scorpio	Leo	Aries	Virgo	Scorpio	Virgo
2	5:24 P.M.	Cancer	Cancer	Virgo	Scorpio	Leo	Aries	Virgo	Scorpio	Virgo
3			Cancer	Virgo	Scorpio	Leo	Aries	Virgo	Scorpio	Virgo
4	11:21 P.M.	Leo	Cancer	Virgo	Scorpio	Leo	Aries	Virgo	Scorpio	Virgo
5			Cancer	Virgo	Scorpio	Leo	Aries	Virgo	Scorpio	Virgo
6			Cancer	Virgo	Scorpio	Leo	Aries	Virgo	Scorpio	Virgo
7			Cancer	Virgo	Scorpio	Leo	Aries	Virgo	Scorpio	Virgo
8			Cancer	Virgo	Scorpio	Leo	Aries	Virgo	Scorpio	Virgo
9	2:52 A.M.	Virgo	Leo	Virgo	Scorpio	Leo	Aries	Virgo	Scorpio	Virgo
10	4:43 A.M.	Libra	Leo	Virgo	Scorpio	Leo	Aries	Virgo	Scorpio	Virgo
11	6:41 A.M.	Scorpio	Leo	Virgo	Scorpio	Leo	Aries	Virgo	Scorpio	Virgo
12			Leo	Virgo	Scorpio	Leo	Aries	Virgo	Scorpio	Virgo
13	9:45 A.M.	Sagittarius	Leo	Virgo	Scorpio	Leo	Aries	Virgo	Scorpio	Virgo
14			Leo	Virgo	Scorpio	Leo	Aries	Virgo	Scorpio	Virgo
15	2:17 P.M.	Capricorn	Leo	Virgo	Scorpio	Leo	Aries	Virgo	Scorpio	Virgo
16			Leo	Virgo	Scorpio	Leo	Aries	Virgo	Scorpio	Virgo
17	8:29 P.M.	Aquarius	Leo	Virgo	Scorpio	Leo	Aries	Virgo	Scorpio	Virgo
18			Leo	Virgo	Scorpio	Leo	Aries	Virgo	Scorpio	Virgo
19			Leo	Virgo	Scorpio	Leo	Aries	Virgo	Scorpio	Virgo
20	4:33 A.M.	Pisces	Leo	Virgo	Scorpio	Leo	Aries	Virgo	Scorpio	Virgo
21			Leo	Virgo	Scorpio	Leo	Aries	Virgo	Scorpio	Virgo
22	2:56 P.M.	Aries	Leo	Virgo	Scorpio	Leo	Aries	Virgo	Scorpio	Virgo
23			Leo	Virgo	Scorpio	Leo	Aries	Virgo	Scorpio	Virgo

1968

MOON FROM	IN	MERCURY	VENUS	MARS	JUPITER	SATURN	URANUS	NEPTUNE	PLUTO
July									
23 Cancer		Cancer	Leo	Cancer	Virgo	Aries	Virgo	Scorpio	Virgo
24		Cancer	Leo	Cancer	Virgo	Aries	Virgo	Scorpio	Virgo
25 2:11 A.M.	Leo	Cancer	Leo	Cancer	Virgo	Aries	Virgo	Scorpio	Virgo
26		Cancer	Leo	Cancer	Virgo	Aries	Virgo	Scorpio	Virgo
27 10:20 A.M.	Virgo	Cancer	Leo	Cancer	Virgo	Aries	Virgo	Scorpio	Virgo
28		Cancer	Leo	Cancer	Virgo	Aries	Virgo	Scorpio	Virgo
29 4:34 P.M.	Libra	Cancer	Leo	Cancer	Virgo	Aries	Virgo	Scorpio	Virgo
30		Cancer	Leo	Cancer	Virgo	Aries	Virgo	Scorpio	Virgo
31 8:53 P.M.	Scorpio	Cancer	Leo	Cancer	Virgo	Aries	Virgo	Scorpio	Virgo
August									
1		Leo	Leo	Cancer	Virgo	Aries	Virgo	Scorpio	Virgo
2 11:52 P.M.	Sagittarius	Leo	Leo	Cancer	Virgo	Aries	Virgo	Scorpio	Virgo
3		Leo	Leo	Cancer	Virgo	Aries	Virgo	Scorpio	Virgo
4		Leo	Leo	Cancer	Virgo	Aries	Virgo	Scorpio	Virgo
5 2:02 A.M.	Capricorn	Leo	Leo	Cancer	Virgo	Aries	Virgo	Scorpio	Virgo
6		Leo	Leo	Leo	Virgo	Aries	Virgo	Scorpio	Virgo
7 3:53 A.M.	Aquarius	Leo	Leo	Leo	Virgo	Aries	Virgo	Scorpio	Virgo
8		Leo	Leo	Leo	Virgo	Aries	Virgo	Scorpio	Virgo
9 7:21 A.M.	Pisces	Leo	Virgo	Leo	Virgo	Aries	Virgo	Scorpio	Virgo
10		Leo	Virgo	Leo	Virgo	Aries	Virgo	Scorpio	Virgo
11 10:07 P.M.	Aries	Leo	Virgo	Leo	Virgo	Aries	Virgo	Scorpio	Virgo
12		Leo	Virgo	Leo	Virgo	Aries	Virgo	Scorpio	Virgo
13 10:25 P.M.	Taurus	Leo	Virgo	Leo	Virgo	Aries	Virgo	Scorpio	Virgo
14		Leo	Virgo	Leo	Virgo	Aries	Virgo	Scorpio	Virgo
15		Leo	Virgo	Leo	Virgo	Aries	Virgo	Scorpio	Virgo
16 10:52 A.M.	Gemini	Virgo	Virgo	Leo	Virgo	Aries	Virgo	Scorpio	Virgo
17		Virgo	Virgo	Leo	Virgo	Aries	Virgo	Scorpio	Virgo
18 11:24 P.M.	Cancer	Virgo	Virgo	Leo	Virgo	Aries	Virgo	Scorpio	Virgo
19		Virgo	Virgo	Leo	Virgo	Aries	Virgo	Scorpio	Virgo
20		Virgo	Virgo	Leo	Virgo	Aries	Virgo	Scorpio	Virgo
21 10:02 A.M.	Leo	Virgo	Virgo	Leo	Virgo	Aries	Virgo	Scorpio	Virgo
22		Virgo	Virgo	Leo	Virgo	Aries	Virgo	Scorpio	Virgo
23 7:19 A.M.	Virgo	Virgo	Virgo	Leo	Virgo	Aries	Virgo	Scorpio	Virgo

LEO PLANETARY TABLES

1969

Date	MOON FROM / IN	MERCURY	VENUS	MARS	JUPITER	SATURN	URANUS	NEPTUNE	PLUTO
July									
24	12:12 P.M. Sagittarius	Leo	Gemini	Sagittarius	Libra	Taurus	Libra	Scorpio	Virgo
25	1:22 P.M. Capricorn	Leo	Gemini	Sagittarius	Libra	Taurus	Libra	Scorpio	Virgo
26		Leo	Gemini	Sagittarius	Libra	Taurus	Libra	Scorpio	Virgo
27	1:05 P.M. Aquarius	Leo	Gemini	Sagittarius	Libra	Taurus	Libra	Scorpio	Virgo
28		Leo	Gemini	Sagittarius	Libra	Taurus	Libra	Scorpio	Virgo
29	1:03 P.M. Pisces	Leo	Gemini	Sagittarius	Libra	Taurus	Libra	Scorpio	Virgo
30		Leo	Gemini	Sagittarius	Libra	Taurus	Libra	Scorpio	Virgo
31		Leo	Gemini	Sagittarius	Libra	Taurus	Libra	Scorpio	Virgo
August									
1	3:01 P.M. Aries	Leo	Gemini	Sagittarius	Libra	Taurus	Libra	Scorpio	Virgo
2		Leo	Gemini	Sagittarius	Libra	Taurus	Libra	Scorpio	Virgo
3	8:57 P.M. Taurus	Leo	Gemini	Sagittarius	Libra	Taurus	Libra	Scorpio	Virgo
4		Leo	Cancer	Sagittarius	Libra	Taurus	Libra	Scorpio	Virgo
5		Leo	Cancer	Sagittarius	Libra	Taurus	Libra	Scorpio	Virgo
6	6:37 A.M. Gemini	Leo	Cancer	Sagittarius	Libra	Taurus	Libra	Scorpio	Virgo
7	7:19 P.M. Cancer	Leo	Cancer	Sagittarius	Libra	Taurus	Libra	Scorpio	Virgo
8		Virgo	Cancer	Sagittarius	Libra	Taurus	Libra	Scorpio	Virgo
9		Virgo	Cancer	Sagittarius	Libra	Taurus	Libra	Scorpio	Virgo
10	8:00 A.M. Leo	Virgo	Cancer	Sagittarius	Libra	Taurus	Libra	Scorpio	Virgo
11		Virgo	Cancer	Sagittarius	Libra	Taurus	Libra	Scorpio	Virgo
12	7:24 P.M. Virgo	Virgo	Cancer	Sagittarius	Libra	Taurus	Libra	Scorpio	Virgo
13		Virgo	Cancer	Sagittarius	Libra	Taurus	Libra	Scorpio	Virgo
14		Virgo	Cancer	Sagittarius	Libra	Taurus	Libra	Scorpio	Virgo
15	5:39 A.M. Libra	Virgo	Cancer	Sagittarius	Libra	Taurus	Libra	Scorpio	Virgo
16		Virgo	Cancer	Sagittarius	Libra	Taurus	Libra	Scorpio	Virgo
17		Virgo	Cancer	Sagittarius	Libra	Taurus	Libra	Scorpio	Virgo
18	1:14 P.M. Scorpio	Virgo	Cancer	Sagittarius	Libra	Taurus	Libra	Scorpio	Virgo
19		Virgo	Cancer	Sagittarius	Libra	Taurus	Libra	Scorpio	Virgo
20	6:59 P.M. Sagittarius	Virgo	Cancer	Sagittarius	Libra	Taurus	Libra	Scorpio	Virgo
21		Virgo	Cancer	Sagittarius	Libra	Taurus	Libra	Scorpio	Virgo
22	7:54 P.M. Capricorn	Virgo	Cancer	Sagittarius	Libra	Taurus	Libra	Scorpio	Virgo
23		Virgo	Cancer	Sagittarius	Libra	Taurus	Libra	Scorpio	Virgo

1970

Date	MOON FROM IN	MERCURY	VENUS	MARS	JUPITER	SATURN	URANUS	NEPTUNE	PLUTO
July 24	Aries	Leo	Virgo	Leo	Libra	Taurus	Libra	Scorpio	Virgo
25	2:36 A.M. Taurus	Leo	Virgo	Leo	Libra	Taurus	Libra	Scorpio	Virgo
26		Leo	Virgo	Leo	Libra	Taurus	Libra	Scorpio	Virgo
27	9:17 A.M. Gemini	Leo	Virgo	Leo	Libra	Taurus	Libra	Scorpio	Virgo
28		Leo	Virgo	Leo	Libra	Taurus	Libra	Scorpio	Virgo
29	6:53 P.M. Cancer	Leo	Virgo	Leo	Libra	Taurus	Libra	Scorpio	Virgo
30		Leo	Virgo	Leo	Libra	Taurus	Libra	Scorpio	Virgo
31		Leo	Virgo	Leo	Libra	Taurus	Libra	Scorpio	Virgo
August 1	6:02 A.M. Leo	Virgo	Virgo	Leo	Libra	Taurus	Libra	Scorpio	Virgo
2		Virgo	Virgo	Leo	Libra	Taurus	Libra	Scorpio	Virgo
3	6:30 P.M. Virgo	Virgo	Virgo	Leo	Libra	Taurus	Libra	Scorpio	Virgo
4		Virgo	Virgo	Leo	Libra	Taurus	Libra	Scorpio	Virgo
5		Virgo	Virgo	Leo	Libra	Taurus	Libra	Scorpio	Virgo
6	7:12 A.M. Libra	Virgo	Virgo	Leo	Libra	Taurus	Libra	Scorpio	Virgo
7		Virgo	Virgo	Leo	Libra	Taurus	Libra	Scorpio	Virgo
8	6:43 P.M. Scorpio	Virgo	Virgo	Leo	Libra	Taurus	Libra	Scorpio	Virgo
9		Virgo	Libra	Leo	Libra	Taurus	Libra	Scorpio	Virgo
10		Virgo	Libra	Leo	Libra	Taurus	Libra	Scorpio	Virgo
11	3:28 A.M. Sagittarius	Virgo	Libra	Leo	Libra	Taurus	Libra	Scorpio	Virgo
12		Virgo	Libra	Leo	Libra	Taurus	Libra	Scorpio	Virgo
13	7:41 A.M. Capricorn	Virgo	Libra	Leo	Libra	Taurus	Libra	Scorpio	Virgo
14		Virgo	Libra	Leo	Libra	Taurus	Libra	Scorpio	Virgo
15	8:55 A.M. Aquarius	Virgo	Libra	Leo	Libra	Taurus	Libra	Scorpio	Virgo
16		Virgo	Libra	Leo	Scorpio	Taurus	Libra	Scorpio	Virgo
17	8:25 A.M. Pisces	Virgo	Libra	Leo	Scorpio	Taurus	Libra	Scorpio	Virgo
18		Virgo	Libra	Leo	Scorpio	Taurus	Libra	Scorpio	Virgo
19	8:09 A.M. Aries	Virgo	Libra	Leo	Scorpio	Taurus	Libra	Scorpio	Virgo
20		Virgo	Libra	Leo	Scorpio	Taurus	Libra	Scorpio	Virgo
21	10:04 A.M. Taurus	Virgo	Libra	Leo	Scorpio	Taurus	Libra	Scorpio	Virgo
22		Virgo	Libra	Leo	Scorpio	Taurus	Libra	Scorpio	Virgo
23	3:08 P.M. Gemini	Virgo	Libra	Leo	Scorpio	Taurus	Libra	Scorpio	Virgo

LEO PLANETARY TABLES

1971

	MOON FROM	IN	MERCURY	VENUS	MARS	JUPITER	SATURN	URANUS	NEPTUNE	PLUTO
July										
24	4:15 P.M.	Virgo	Leo	Cancer	Aquarius	Scorpio	Gemini	Libra	Sagittarius	Virgo
25			Leo	Cancer	Aquarius	Scorpio	Gemini	Libra	Sagittarius	Virgo
26			Leo	Cancer	Aquarius	Scorpio	Gemini	Libra	Sagittarius	Virgo
27	4:00 A.M.	Libra	Virgo	Cancer	Aquarius	Scorpio	Gemini	Libra	Sagittarius	Virgo
28			Virgo	Cancer	Aquarius	Scorpio	Gemini	Libra	Sagittarius	Virgo
29	4:53 P.M.	Scorpio	Virgo	Cancer	Aquarius	Scorpio	Gemini	Libra	Sagittarius	Virgo
30			Virgo	Cancer	Aquarius	Scorpio	Gemini	Libra	Sagittarius	Virgo
31			Virgo	Cancer	Aquarius	Scorpio	Gemini	Libra	Sagittarius	Virgo
August										
1	4:06 A.M.	Sagittarius	Virgo	Leo	Aquarius	Scorpio	Gemini	Libra	Sagittarius	Virgo
2			Virgo	Leo	Aquarius	Scorpio	Gemini	Libra	Sagittarius	Virgo
3	11:50 A.M.	Capricorn	Virgo	Leo	Aquarius	Scorpio	Gemini	Libra	Sagittarius	Virgo
4			Virgo	Leo	Aquarius	Scorpio	Gemini	Libra	Sagittarius	Virgo
5	3:53 P.M.	Aquarius	Virgo	Leo	Aquarius	Scorpio	Gemini	Libra	Sagittarius	Virgo
6			Virgo	Leo	Aquarius	Scorpio	Gemini	Libra	Sagittarius	Virgo
7	5:40 P.M.	Pisces	Virgo	Leo	Aquarius	Scorpio	Gemini	Libra	Sagittarius	Virgo
8			Virgo	Leo	Aquarius	Scorpio	Gemini	Libra	Sagittarius	Virgo
9	6:26 P.M.	Aries	Virgo	Leo	Aquarius	Scorpio	Gemini	Libra	Sagittarius	Virgo
10			Virgo	Leo	Aquarius	Scorpio	Gemini	Libra	Sagittarius	Virgo
11	8:00 P.M.	Taurus	Virgo	Leo	Aquarius	Scorpio	Gemini	Libra	Sagittarius	Virgo
12			Virgo	Leo	Aquarius	Scorpio	Gemini	Libra	Sagittarius	Virgo
13	11:14 P.M.	Gemini	Virgo	Leo	Aquarius	Scorpio	Gemini	Libra	Sagittarius	Virgo
14			Virgo	Leo	Aquarius	Scorpio	Gemini	Libra	Sagittarius	Virgo
15			Virgo	Leo	Aquarius	Scorpio	Gemini	Libra	Sagittarius	Virgo
16	5:13 A.M.	Cancer	Virgo	Leo	Aquarius	Scorpio	Gemini	Libra	Sagittarius	Virgo
17			Virgo	Leo	Aquarius	Scorpio	Gemini	Libra	Sagittarius	Virgo
18	1:25 P.M.	Leo	Virgo	Leo	Aquarius	Scorpio	Gemini	Libra	Sagittarius	Virgo
19			Virgo	Leo	Aquarius	Scorpio	Gemini	Libra	Sagittarius	Virgo
20			Virgo	Leo	Aquarius	Scorpio	Gemini	Libra	Sagittarius	Virgo
21	11:31 P.M.	Virgo	Virgo	Leo	Aquarius	Scorpio	Gemini	Libra	Sagittarius	Virgo
22			Virgo	Leo	Aquarius	Scorpio	Gemini	Libra	Sagittarius	Virgo
23	11:04 A.M.	Libra	Virgo	Leo	Aquarius	Scorpio	Gemini	Libra	Sagittarius	Virgo

1972

July	MOON FROM IN	MERCURY	VENUS	MARS	JUPITER	SATURN	URANUS	NEPTUNE	PLUTO
23	11:26 A.M. Capricorn	Leo	Gemini	Leo	Capricorn	Gemini	Libra	Sagittarius	Virgo
24	8:12 P.M. Aquarius	Leo	Gemini	Leo	Capricorn	Gemini	Libra	Sagittarius	Virgo
25		Leo	Gemini	Leo	Sagittarius	Gemini	Libra	Sagittarius	Virgo
26		Leo	Gemini	Leo	Sagittarius	Gemini	Libra	Sagittarius	Virgo
27		Leo	Gemini	Leo	Sagittarius	Gemini	Libra	Sagittarius	Virgo
28	2:30 A.M. Pisces	Leo	Gemini	Leo	Sagittarius	Gemini	Libra	Sagittarius	Virgo
29		Leo	Gemini	Leo	Sagittarius	Gemini	Libra	Sagittarius	Virgo
30	7:00 A.M. Aries	Leo	Gemini	Leo	Sagittarius	Gemini	Libra	Sagittarius	Virgo
31		Leo	Gemini	Leo	Sagittarius	Gemini	Libra	Sagittarius	Libra
August									
1	10:02 A.M. Taurus	Leo	Gemini	Leo	Sagittarius	Gemini	Libra	Sagittarius	Libra
2		Leo	Gemini	Leo	Sagittarius	Gemini	Libra	Sagittarius	Libra
3	12:45 P.M. Gemini	Leo	Gemini	Leo	Sagittarius	Gemini	Libra	Sagittarius	Libra
4		Leo	Gemini	Leo	Sagittarius	Gemini	Libra	Sagittarius	Libra
5	3:31 P.M. Cancer	Leo	Gemini	Leo	Sagittarius	Gemini	Libra	Sagittarius	Libra
6		Leo	Gemini	Leo	Sagittarius	Gemini	Libra	Sagittarius	Libra
7	7:08 P.M. Leo	Leo	Cancer	Leo	Sagittarius	Gemini	Libra	Sagittarius	Libra
8		Leo	Cancer	Leo	Sagittarius	Gemini	Libra	Sagittarius	Libra
9		Leo	Cancer	Leo	Sagittarius	Gemini	Libra	Sagittarius	Libra
10	0:19 A.M. Virgo	Leo	Cancer	Leo	Sagittarius	Gemini	Libra	Sagittarius	Libra
11		Leo	Cancer	Leo	Sagittarius	Gemini	Libra	Sagittarius	Libra
12	8:10 A.M. Libra	Leo	Cancer	Leo	Sagittarius	Gemini	Libra	Sagittarius	Libra
13		Leo	Cancer	Leo	Sagittarius	Gemini	Libra	Sagittarius	Libra
14	7:06 P.M. Scorpio	Leo	Cancer	Leo	Sagittarius	Gemini	Libra	Sagittarius	Libra
15		Leo	Cancer	Virgo	Sagittarius	Gemini	Libra	Sagittarius	Libra
16		Leo	Cancer	Virgo	Sagittarius	Gemini	Libra	Sagittarius	Libra
17	7:49 A.M. Sagittarius	Leo	Cancer	Virgo	Sagittarius	Gemini	Libra	Sagittarius	Libra
18		Leo	Cancer	Virgo	Sagittarius	Gemini	Libra	Sagittarius	Libra
19	7:53 P.M. Capricorn	Leo	Cancer	Virgo	Sagittarius	Gemini	Libra	Sagittarius	Libra
20		Leo	Cancer	Virgo	Sagittarius	Gemini	Libra	Sagittarius	Libra
21		Leo	Cancer	Virgo	Sagittarius	Gemini	Libra	Sagittarius	Libra
22	4:49 A.M. Aquarius	Leo	Cancer	Virgo	Sagittarius	Gemini	Libra	Sagittarius	Libra
23		Leo	Cancer	Virgo	Sagittarius	Gemini	Libra	Sagittarius	Libra

LEO PLANETARY TABLES

1973

Date	MOON FROM	IN	MERCURY	VENUS	MARS	JUPITER	SATURN	URANUS	NEPTUNE	PLUTO
July 23	Taurus		Cancer	Leo	Aries	Aquarius	Gemini	Libra	Sagittarius	Libra
24			Cancer	Leo	Aries	Aquarius	Gemini	Libra	Sagittarius	Libra
25		2:27 A.M. Gemini	Cancer	Leo	Aries	Aquarius	Gemini	Libra	Sagittarius	Libra
26			Cancer	Virgo	Aries	Aquarius	Gemini	Libra	Sagittarius	Libra
27		3:24 A.M. Cancer	Cancer	Virgo	Aries	Aquarius	Gemini	Libra	Sagittarius	Libra
28			Cancer	Virgo	Aries	Aquarius	Gemini	Libra	Sagittarius	Libra
29		3:51 A.M. Leo	Cancer	Virgo	Aries	Aquarius	Gemini	Libra	Sagittarius	Libra
30			Cancer	Virgo	Aries	Aquarius	Gemini	Libra	Sagittarius	Libra
31		4:52 A.M. Virgo	Cancer	Virgo	Aries	Aquarius	Gemini	Libra	Sagittarius	Libra
August 1			Cancer	Virgo	Aries	Aquarius	Gemini	Libra	Sagittarius	Libra
2		7:55 A.M. Libra	Cancer	Virgo	Aries	Aquarius	Cancer	Libra	Sagittarius	Libra
3			Cancer	Virgo	Aries	Aquarius	Cancer	Libra	Sagittarius	Libra
4		3:33 P.M. Scorpio	Cancer	Virgo	Aries	Aquarius	Cancer	Libra	Sagittarius	Libra
5			Cancer	Virgo	Aries	Aquarius	Cancer	Libra	Sagittarius	Libra
6			Cancer	Virgo	Aries	Aquarius	Cancer	Libra	Sagittarius	Libra
7		2:39 A.M. Sagittarius	Cancer	Virgo	Aries	Aquarius	Cancer	Libra	Sagittarius	Libra
8			Cancer	Virgo	Aries	Aquarius	Cancer	Libra	Sagittarius	Libra
9		3:39 P.M. Capricorn	Cancer	Virgo	Aries	Aquarius	Cancer	Libra	Sagittarius	Libra
10			Cancer	Virgo	Aries	Aquarius	Cancer	Libra	Sagittarius	Libra
11			Cancer	Virgo	Aries	Aquarius	Cancer	Libra	Sagittarius	Libra
12		3:40 A.M. Aquarius	Leo	Virgo	Aries	Aquarius	Cancer	Libra	Sagittarius	Libra
13			Leo	Virgo	Aries	Aquarius	Cancer	Libra	Sagittarius	Libra
14		1:53 P.M. Pisces	Leo	Virgo	Taurus	Aquarius	Cancer	Libra	Sagittarius	Libra
15			Leo	Virgo	Taurus	Aquarius	Cancer	Libra	Sagittarius	Libra
16		10:16 P.M. Aries	Leo	Virgo	Taurus	Aquarius	Cancer	Libra	Sagittarius	Libra
17			Leo	Virgo	Taurus	Aquarius	Cancer	Libra	Sagittarius	Libra
18			Leo	Virgo	Taurus	Aquarius	Cancer	Libra	Sagittarius	Libra
19		4:10 A.M. Taurus	Leo	Virgo	Taurus	Aquarius	Cancer	Libra	Sagittarius	Libra
20			Leo	Libra	Taurus	Aquarius	Cancer	Libra	Sagittarius	Libra
21		8:41 A.M. Gemini	Leo	Libra	Taurus	Aquarius	Cancer	Libra	Sagittarius	Libra
22			Leo	Libra	Taurus	Aquarius	Cancer	Libra	Sagittarius	Libra
23		11:20 A.M. Cancer	Leo	Libra	Taurus	Aquarius	Cancer	Libra	Sagittarius	Libra

1974

July	MOON FROM	IN	MERCURY	VENUS	MARS	JUPITER	SATURN	URANUS	NEPTUNE	PLUTO
24	Libra		Cancer	Cancer	Leo	Pisces	Cancer	Libra	Sagittarius	Libra
25	6:01 P.M.	Scorpio	Cancer	Cancer	Leo	Pisces	Cancer	Libra	Sagittarius	Libra
26			Cancer	Cancer	Leo	Pisces	Cancer	Libra	Sagittarius	Libra
27			Cancer	Cancer	Leo	Pisces	Cancer	Libra	Sagittarius	Libra
28	2:02 A.M.	Sagittarius	Cancer	Cancer	Virgo	Pisces	Cancer	Libra	Sagittarius	Libra
29			Cancer	Cancer	Virgo	Pisces	Cancer	Libra	Sagittarius	Libra
30	1:25 P.M.	Capricorn	Cancer	Cancer	Virgo	Pisces	Cancer	Libra	Sagittarius	Libra
31			Cancer	Cancer	Virgo	Pisces	Cancer	Libra	Sagittarius	Libra
August										
1	1:33 A.M.	Aquarius	Cancer	Cancer	Virgo	Pisces	Cancer	Libra	Sagittarius	Libra
2			Cancer	Cancer	Virgo	Pisces	Cancer	Libra	Sagittarius	Libra
3	2:04 P.M.	Pisces	Cancer	Cancer	Virgo	Pisces	Cancer	Libra	Sagittarius	Libra
4			Cancer	Cancer	Virgo	Pisces	Cancer	Libra	Sagittarius	Libra
5			Cancer	Cancer	Virgo	Pisces	Cancer	Libra	Sagittarius	Libra
6	2:11 A.M.	Aries	Leo	Cancer	Virgo	Pisces	Cancer	Libra	Sagittarius	Libra
7			Leo	Cancer	Virgo	Pisces	Cancer	Libra	Sagittarius	Libra
8	12:27 P.M.	Taurus	Leo	Cancer	Virgo	Pisces	Cancer	Libra	Sagittarius	Libra
9			Leo	Cancer	Virgo	Pisces	Cancer	Libra	Sagittarius	Libra
10	7:14 P.M.	Gemini	Leo	Cancer	Virgo	Pisces	Cancer	Libra	Sagittarius	Libra
11			Leo	Cancer	Virgo	Pisces	Cancer	Libra	Sagittarius	Libra
12			Leo	Cancer	Virgo	Pisces	Cancer	Libra	Sagittarius	Libra
13	10:37 P.M.	Cancer	Leo	Cancer	Virgo	Pisces	Cancer	Libra	Sagittarius	Libra
14			Leo	Cancer	Virgo	Pisces	Cancer	Libra	Sagittarius	Libra
15	11:20 P.M.	Leo	Leo	Leo	Virgo	Pisces	Cancer	Libra	Sagittarius	Libra
16			Leo	Leo	Virgo	Pisces	Cancer	Libra	Sagittarius	Libra
17	10:46 P.M.	Virgo	Leo	Leo	Virgo	Pisces	Cancer	Libra	Sagittarius	Libra
18			Leo	Leo	Virgo	Pisces	Cancer	Libra	Sagittarius	Libra
19	11:07 P.M.	Libra	Leo	Leo	Virgo	Pisces	Cancer	Libra	Sagittarius	Libra
20			Leo	Leo	Virgo	Pisces	Cancer	Libra	Sagittarius	Libra
21			Virgo	Leo	Virgo	Pisces	Cancer	Libra	Sagittarius	Libra
22	1:51 A.M.	Scorpio	Virgo	Leo	Virgo	Pisces	Cancer	Libra	Sagittarius	Libra
23			Virgo	Leo	Virgo	Pisces	Cancer	Libra	Sagittarius	Libra

LEO PLANETARY TABLES

1975

Date	MOON FROM / IN	MERCURY	VENUS	MARS	JUPITER	SATURN	URANUS	NEPTUNE	PLUTO
July 24	Aquarius	Cancer	Virgo	Taurus	Aries	Cancer	Libra	Sagittarius	Libra
25	12:12 P.M. Pisces	Cancer	Virgo	Taurus	Aries	Cancer	Libra	Sagittarius	Libra
26		Cancer	Virgo	Taurus	Aries	Cancer	Libra	Sagittarius	Libra
27		Cancer	Virgo	Taurus	Aries	Cancer	Libra	Sagittarius	Libra
28	0:51 A.M. Aries	Cancer	Virgo	Taurus	Aries	Cancer	Libra	Sagittarius	Libra
29		Leo	Virgo	Taurus	Aries	Cancer	Libra	Sagittarius	Libra
30	1:19 P.M. Taurus	Leo	Virgo	Taurus	Aries	Cancer	Libra	Sagittarius	Libra
31		Leo	Virgo	Taurus	Aries	Cancer	Libra	Sagittarius	Libra
August 1	11:00 P.M. Gemini	Leo	Virgo	Taurus	Aries	Cancer	Libra	Sagittarius	Libra
2		Leo	Virgo	Taurus	Aries	Cancer	Libra	Sagittarius	Libra
3		Leo	Virgo	Taurus	Aries	Cancer	Libra	Sagittarius	Libra
4	5:15 A.M. Cancer	Leo	Virgo	Taurus	Aries	Cancer	Libra	Sagittarius	Libra
5		Leo	Virgo	Taurus	Aries	Cancer	Libra	Sagittarius	Libra
6	7:40 A.M. Leo	Leo	Virgo	Taurus	Aries	Cancer	Libra	Sagittarius	Libra
7		Leo	Virgo	Taurus	Aries	Cancer	Libra	Sagittarius	Libra
8	8:07 A.M. Virgo	Leo	Virgo	Taurus	Aries	Cancer	Libra	Sagittarius	Libra
9		Leo	Virgo	Taurus	Aries	Cancer	Libra	Sagittarius	Libra
10	8:10 A.M. Libra	Leo	Virgo	Taurus	Aries	Cancer	Libra	Sagittarius	Libra
11		Leo	Virgo	Taurus	Aries	Cancer	Libra	Sagittarius	Libra
12	8:17 A.M. Scorpio	Leo	Virgo	Taurus	Aries	Cancer	Libra	Sagittarius	Libra
13		Virgo	Virgo	Taurus	Aries	Cancer	Libra	Sagittarius	Libra
14	2:04 P.M. Sagittarius	Virgo	Virgo	Taurus	Aries	Cancer	Libra	Sagittarius	Libra
15		Virgo	Virgo	Gemini	Aries	Cancer	Libra	Sagittarius	Libra
16	9:29 P.M. Capricorn	Virgo	Virgo	Gemini	Aries	Cancer	Libra	Sagittarius	Libra
17		Virgo	Virgo	Gemini	Aries	Cancer	Libra	Sagittarius	Libra
18		Virgo	Virgo	Gemini	Aries	Cancer	Libra	Sagittarius	Libra
19	7:12 A.M. Aquarius	Virgo	Virgo	Gemini	Aries	Cancer	Libra	Sagittarius	Libra
20		Virgo	Virgo	Gemini	Aries	Cancer	Libra	Sagittarius	Libra
21	6:30 P.M. Pisces	Virgo	Virgo	Gemini	Aries	Cancer	Libra	Sagittarius	Libra
22		Virgo	Virgo	Gemini	Aries	Cancer	Libra	Sagittarius	Libra
23		Virgo	Virgo	Gemini	Aries	Cancer	Libra	Sagittarius	Libra

1976

	MOON		MERCURY	VENUS	MARS	JUPITER	SATURN	URANUS	NEPTUNE	PLUTO
July	FROM	IN								
23	Gemini		Leo	Leo	Virgo	Taurus	Leo	Scorpio	Sagittarius	Libra
24	6:49 A.M.	Cancer	Leo	Leo	Virgo	Taurus	Leo	Scorpio	Sagittarius	Libra
25			Leo	Leo	Virgo	Taurus	Leo	Scorpio	Sagittarius	Libra
26	1:23 P.M.	Leo	Leo	Leo	Virgo	Taurus	Leo	Scorpio	Sagittarius	Libra
27			Leo	Leo	Virgo	Taurus	Leo	Scorpio	Sagittarius	Libra
28	5:38 P.M.	Virgo	Leo	Leo	Virgo	Taurus	Leo	Scorpio	Sagittarius	Libra
29			Leo	Leo	Virgo	Taurus	Leo	Scorpio	Sagittarius	Libra
30	8:36 P.M.	Libra	Leo	Leo	Virgo	Taurus	Leo	Scorpio	Sagittarius	Libra
31			Leo	Leo	Virgo	Taurus	Leo	Scorpio	Sagittarius	Libra
August										
1	10:57 P.M.	Scorpio	Leo	Leo	Virgo	Taurus	Leo	Scorpio	Sagittarius	Libra
2			Leo	Leo	Virgo	Taurus	Leo	Scorpio	Sagittarius	Libra
3			Leo	Leo	Virgo	Taurus	Leo	Scorpio	Sagittarius	Libra
4	1:54 A.M.	Sagittarius	Virgo	Leo	Virgo	Taurus	Leo	Scorpio	Sagittarius	Libra
5			Virgo	Leo	Virgo	Taurus	Leo	Scorpio	Sagittarius	Libra
6	5:38 A.M.	Capricorn	Virgo	Leo	Virgo	Taurus	Leo	Scorpio	Sagittarius	Libra
7			Virgo	Leo	Virgo	Taurus	Leo	Scorpio	Sagittarius	Libra
8	11:00 A.M.	Aquarius	Virgo	Leo	Virgo	Taurus	Leo	Scorpio	Sagittarius	Libra
9			Virgo	Virgo	Virgo	Taurus	Leo	Scorpio	Sagittarius	Libra
10	6:19 P.M.	Pisces	Virgo	Virgo	Virgo	Taurus	Leo	Scorpio	Sagittarius	Libra
11			Virgo	Virgo	Virgo	Taurus	Leo	Scorpio	Sagittarius	Libra
12			Virgo	Virgo	Virgo	Taurus	Leo	Scorpio	Sagittarius	Libra
13	4:02 A.M.	Aries	Virgo	Virgo	Virgo	Taurus	Leo	Scorpio	Sagittarius	Libra
14			Virgo	Virgo	Virgo	Taurus	Leo	Scorpio	Sagittarius	Libra
15	4:10 P.M.	Taurus	Virgo	Virgo	Virgo	Taurus	Leo	Scorpio	Sagittarius	Libra
16			Virgo	Virgo	Virgo	Taurus	Leo	Scorpio	Sagittarius	Libra
17			Virgo	Virgo	Virgo	Taurus	Leo	Scorpio	Sagittarius	Libra
18	4:49 A.M.	Gemini	Virgo	Virgo	Virgo	Taurus	Leo	Scorpio	Sagittarius	Libra
19			Virgo	Virgo	Virgo	Taurus	Leo	Scorpio	Sagittarius	Libra
20	3:46 P.M.	Cancer	Virgo	Virgo	Virgo	Taurus	Leo	Scorpio	Sagittarius	Libra
21			Virgo	Virgo	Virgo	Taurus	Leo	Scorpio	Sagittarius	Libra
22	10:39 P.M.	Leo	Virgo	Virgo	Virgo	Taurus	Leo	Scorpio	Sagittarius	Libra
23			Virgo	Virgo	Virgo	Taurus	Leo	Scorpio	Sagittarius	Libra

LEO PLANETARY TABLES

1977

Date	MOON FROM / IN	MERCURY	VENUS	MARS	JUPITER	SATURN	URANUS	NEPTUNE	PLUTO
July									
23	1:18 P.M. Scorpio	Leo	Gemini	Gemini	Gemini	Leo	Scorpio	Sagittarius	Libra
24		Leo	Gemini	Gemini	Gemini	Leo	Scorpio	Sagittarius	Libra
25	4:07 P.M. Sagittarius	Leo	Gemini	Gemini	Gemini	Leo	Scorpio	Sagittarius	Libra
26		Leo	Gemini	Gemini	Gemini	Leo	Scorpio	Sagittarius	Libra
27	5:17 P.M. Capricorn	Leo	Gemini	Gemini	Gemini	Leo	Scorpio	Sagittarius	Libra
28		Leo	Gemini	Gemini	Gemini	Leo	Scorpio	Sagittarius	Libra
29	6:36 P.M. Aquarius	Virgo	Gemini	Gemini	Gemini	Leo	Scorpio	Sagittarius	Libra
30		Virgo	Gemini	Gemini	Gemini	Leo	Scorpio	osagittarius	Libra
31	8:53 P.M. Pisces	Virgo	Gemini	Gemini	Gemini	Leo	Scorpio	Sagittarius	Libra
August									
1		Virgo	Gemini	Gemini	Gemini	Leo	Scorpio	Sagittarius	Libra
2		Virgo	Gemini	Gemini	Gemini	Leo	Scorpio	Sagittarius	Libra
3	2:04 A.M. Aries	Virgo	Cancer	Gemini	Gemini	Leo	Scorpio	Sagittarius	Libra
4		Virgo	Cancer	Gemini	Gemini	Leo	Scorpio	Sagittarius	Libra
5	11:21 A.M. Taurus	Virgo	Cancer	Gemini	Gemini	Leo	Scorpio	Sagittarius	Libra
6		Virgo	Cancer	Gemini	Gemini	Leo	Scorpio	Sagittarius	Libra
7	11:32 P.M. Gemini	Virgo	Cancer	Gemini	Gemini	Leo	Scorpio	Sagittarius	Libra
8		Virgo	Cancer	Gemini	Gemini	Leo	Scorpio	Sagittarius	Libra
9		Virgo	Cancer	Gemini	Gemini	Leo	Scorpio	Sagittarius	Libra
10	12:15 P.M. Cancer	Virgo	Cancer	Gemini	Gemini	Leo	Scorpio	Sagittarius	Libra
11		Virgo	Cancer	Gemini	Gemini	Leo	Scorpio	Sagittarius	Libra
12	11:15 P.M. Leo	Virgo	Cancer	Gemini	Gemini	Leo	Scorpio	Sagittarius	Libra
13		Virgo	Cancer	Gemini	Gemini	Leo	Scorpio	Sagittarius	Libra
14		Virgo	Cancer	Gemini	Gemini	Leo	Scorpio	Sagittarius	Libra
15	7:44 A.M. Virgo	Virgo	Cancer	Gemini	Gemini	Leo	Scorpio	Sagittarius	Libra
16		Virgo	Cancer	Gemini	Gemini	Leo	Scorpio	Sagittarius	Libra
17	1:38 P.M. Libra	Virgo	Cancer	Gemini	Gemini	Leo	Scorpio	Sagittarius	Libra
18		Virgo	Cancer	Gemini	Gemini	Leo	Scorpio	Sagittarius	Libra
19	6:25 P.M. Scorpio	Virgo	Cancer	Gemini	Gemini	Leo	Scorpio	Sagittarius	Libra
20		Virgo	Cancer	Gemini	Gemini	Leo	Scorpio	Sagittarius	Libra
21		Virgo	Cancer	Gemini	Cancer	Leo	Scorpio	Sagittarius	Libra
22	9:46 P.M. Sagittarius	Virgo	Cancer	Gemini	Cancer	Leo	Scorpio	Sagittarius	Libra
23		Virgo	Cancer	Gemini	Cancer	Leo	Scorpio	Sagittarius	Libra

1978

	MOON		MERCURY	VENUS	MARS	JUPITER	SATURN	URANUS	NEPTUNE	PLUTO
July	FROM	IN								
24	5:14 A.M.	Aries	Leo	Virgo	Virgo	Cancer	Leo	Scorpio	Sagittarius	Libra
25			Leo	Virgo	Virgo	Cancer	Leo	Scorpio	Sagittarius	Libra
26	10:48 A.M.	Taurus	Leo	Virgo	Virgo	Cancer	Leo	Scorpio	Sagittarius	Libra
27			Leo	Virgo	Virgo	Cancer	Virgo	Scorpio	Sagittarius	Libra
28	8:42 P.M.	Gemini	Virgo	Virgo	Virgo	Cancer	Virgo	Scorpio	Sagittarius	Libra
29			Virgo	Virgo	Virgo	Cancer	Virgo	Scorpio	Sagittarius	Libra
30			Virgo	Virgo	Virgo	Cancer	Virgo	Scorpio	Sagittarius	Libra
31	8:49 A.M.	Cancer	Virgo	Virgo	Virgo	Cancer	Virgo	Scorpio	Sagittarius	Libra
August										
1			Virgo	Virgo	Virgo	Cancer	Virgo	Scorpio	Sagittarius	Libra
2	9:21 P.M.	Leo	Virgo	Virgo	Virgo	Cancer	Virgo	Scorpio	Sagittarius	Libra
3			Virgo	Virgo	Virgo	Cancer	Virgo	Scorpio	Sagittarius	Libra
4			Virgo	Virgo	Virgo	Cancer	Virgo	Scorpio	Sagittarius	Libra
5	9:13 A.M.	Virgo	Virgo	Virgo	Libra	Cancer	Virgo	Scorpio	Sagittarius	Libra
6			Virgo	Virgo	Libra	Cancer	Virgo	Scorpio	Sagittarius	Libra
7	8:15 P.M.	Libra	Virgo	Virgo	Libra	Cancer	Virgo	Scorpio	Sagittarius	Libra
8			Virgo	Virgo	Libra	Cancer	Virgo	Scorpio	Sagittarius	Libra
9			Virgo	Libra	Libra	Cancer	Virgo	Scorpio	Sagittarius	Libra
10	4:57 A.M.	Scorpio	Virgo	Libra	Libra	Cancer	Virgo	Scorpio	Sagittarius	Libra
11			Virgo	Libra	Libra	Cancer	Virgo	Scorpio	Sagittarius	Libra
12	10:37 A.M.	Sagittarius	Virgo	Libra	Libra	Cancer	Virgo	Scorpio	Sagittarius	Libra
13			Virgo	Libra	Libra	Cancer	Virgo	Scorpio	Sagittarius	Libra
14	1:08 P.M.	Capricorn	Leo	Libra	Libra	Cancer	Virgo	Scorpio	Sagittarius	Libra
15			Leo	Libra	Libra	Cancer	Virgo	Scorpio	Sagittarius	Libra
16	1:32 P.M.	Aquarius	Leo	Libra	Libra	Cancer	Virgo	Scorpio	Sagittarius	Libra
17			Leo	Libra	Libra	Cancer	Virgo	Scorpio	Sagittarius	Libra
18	1:37 P.M.	Pisces	Leo	Libra	Libra	Cancer	Virgo	Scorpio	Sagittarius	Libra
19			Leo	Libra	Libra	Cancer	Virgo	Scorpio	Sagittarius	Libra
20	2:54 P.M.	Aries	Leo	Libra	Libra	Cancer	Virgo	Scorpio	Sagittarius	Libra
21			Leo	Libra	Libra	Cancer	Virgo	Scorpio	Sagittarius	Libra
22	7:11 P.M.	Taurus	Leo	Libra	Libra	Cancer	Virgo	Scorpio	Sagittarius	Libra
23			Leo	Libra	Libra	Cancer	Virgo	Scorpio	Sagittarius	Libra

LEO PLANETARY TABLES

1979

		MOON		MERCURY	VENUS	MARS	JUPITER	SATURN	URANUS	NEPTUNE	PLUTO
		FROM	IN								
July	24	Leo		Leo	Cancer	Gemini	Leo	Virgo	Scorpio	Sagittarius	Libra
	25	8:01 A.M.	Virgo	Leo	Cancer	Gemini	Leo	Virgo	Scorpio	Sagittarius	Libra
	26			Leo	Cancer	Gemini	Leo	Virgo	Scorpio	Sagittarius	Libra
	27	8:56 P.M.	Libra	Leo	Cancer	Gemini	Leo	Virgo	Scorpio	Sagittarius	Libra
	28			Leo	Cancer	Gemini	Leo	Virgo	Scorpio	Sagittarius	Libra
	29			Leo	Cancer	Gemini	Leo	Virgo	Scorpio	Sagittarius	Libra
	30			Leo	Cancer	Gemini	Leo	Virgo	Scorpio	Sagittarius	Libra
	31	8:44 A.M.	Scorpio	Leo	Leo	Gemini	Leo	Virgo	Scorpio	Sagittarius	Libra
August	1	5:01 P.M.	Sagittarius	Leo	Leo	Gemini	Leo	Virgo	Scorpio	Sagittarius	Libra
	2			Leo	Leo	Gemini	Leo	Virgo	Scorpio	Sagittarius	Libra
	3	9:16 P.M.	Capricorn	Leo	Leo	Gemini	Leo	Virgo	Scorpio	Sagittarius	Libra
	4			Leo	Leo	Gemini	Leo	Virgo	Scorpio	Sagittarius	Libra
	5	10:38 P.M.	Aquarius	Leo	Leo	Gemini	Leo	Virgo	Scorpio	Sagittarius	Libra
	6			Leo	Leo	Gemini	Leo	Virgo	Scorpio	Sagittarius	Libra
	7			Leo	Leo	Gemini	Leo	Virgo	Scorpio	Sagittarius	Libra
	8	10:17 P.M.	Pisces	Leo	Leo	Gemini	Leo	Virgo	Scorpio	Sagittarius	Libra
	9			Leo	Leo	Cancer	Leo	Virgo	Scorpio	Sagittarius	Libra
	10	10:21 P.M.	Aries	Leo	Leo	Cancer	Leo	Virgo	Scorpio	Sagittarius	Libra
	11			Leo	Leo	Cancer	Leo	Virgo	Scorpio	Sagittarius	Libra
	12			Leo	Leo	Cancer	Leo	Virgo	Scorpio	Sagittarius	Libra
	13	0:16 A.M.	Taurus	Leo	Leo	Cancer	Leo	Virgo	Scorpio	Sagittarius	Libra
	14	5:33 A.M.	Gemini	Leo	Leo	Cancer	Leo	Virgo	Scorpio	Sagittarius	Libra
	15			Leo	Leo	Cancer	Leo	Virgo	Scorpio	Sagittarius	Libra
	16			Leo	Leo	Cancer	Leo	Virgo	Scorpio	Sagittarius	Libra
	17	2:28 P.M.	Cancer	Leo	Leo	Cancer	Leo	Virgo	Scorpio	Sagittarius	Libra
	18			Leo	Leo	Cancer	Leo	Virgo	Scorpio	Sagittarius	Libra
	19			Leo	Leo	Cancer	Leo	Virgo	Scorpio	Sagittarius	Libra
	20	1:51 A.M.	Leo	Leo	Leo	Cancer	Leo	Virgo	Scorpio	Sagittarius	Libra
	21	2:13 P.M.	Virgo	Leo	Leo	Cancer	Leo	Virgo	Scorpio	Sagittarius	Libra
	22			Leo	Leo	Cancer	Leo	Virgo	Scorpio	Sagittarius	Libra
	23			Leo	Leo	Cancer	Leo	Virgo	Scorpio	Sagittarius	Libra

1980

July	MOON FROM	IN	MERCURY	VENUS	MARS	JUPITER	SATURN	URANUS	NEPTUNE	PLUTO
23	Sagittarius		Cancer	Gemini	Libra	Virgo	Virgo	Scorpio	Sagittarius	Libra
24			Cancer	Gemini	Libra	Virgo	Virgo	Scorpio	Sagittarius	Libra
25	1:12 A.M.	Capricorn	Cancer	Gemini	Libra	Virgo	Virgo	Scorpio	Sagittarius	Libra
26			Cancer	Gemini	Libra	Virgo	Virgo	Scorpio	Sagittarius	Libra
27	5:38 A.M.	Aquarius	Cancer	Gemini	Libra	Virgo	Virgo	Scorpio	Sagittarius	Libra
28			Cancer	Gemini	Libra	Virgo	Virgo	Scorpio	Sagittarius	Libra
29	8:29 A.M.	Pisces	Cancer	Gemini	Libra	Virgo	Virgo	Scorpio	Sagittarius	Libra
0			Cancer	Gemini	Libra	Virgo	Virgo	Scorpio	Sagittarius	Libra
31	9:49 A.M.	Aries	Cancer	Gemini	Libra	Virgo	Virgo	Scorpio	Sagittarius	Libra

August	MOON FROM	IN	MERCURY	VENUS	MARS	JUPITER	SATURN	URANUS	NEPTUNE	PLUTO
1			Cancer	Gemini	Libra	Virgo	Virgo	Scorpio	Sagittarius	Libra
2	11:53 A.M.	Taurus	Cancer	Gemini	Libra	Virgo	Virgo	Scorpio	Sagittarius	Libra
3			Cancer	Gemini	Libra	Virgo	Virgo	Scorpio	Sagittarius	Libra
4	3:21 P.M.	Gemini	Cancer	Gemini	Libra	Virgo	Virgo	Scorpio	Sagittarius	Libra
5			Cancer	Gemini	Libra	Virgo	Virgo	Scorpio	Sagittarius	Libra
6	8:32 P.M.	Cancer	Cancer	Gemini	Libra	Virgo	Virgo	Scorpio	Sagittarius	Libra
7			Cancer	Cancer	Libra	Virgo	Virgo	Scorpio	Sagittarius	Libra
8			Cancer	Cancer	Libra	Virgo	Virgo	Scorpio	Sagittarius	Libra
9	3:51 A.M.	Leo	Cancer	Cancer	Libra	Virgo	Virgo	Scorpio	Sagittarius	Libra
10			Leo	Cancer	Libra	Virgo	Virgo	Scorpio	Sagittarius	Libra
11	1:07 P.M.	Virgo	Leo	Cancer	Libra	Virgo	Virgo	Scorpio	Sagittarius	Libra
12			Leo	Cancer	Libra	Virgo	Virgo	Scorpio	Sagittarius	Libra
13			Leo	Cancer	Libra	Virgo	Virgo	Scorpio	Sagittarius	Libra
14	9:12 A.M.	Libra	Leo	Cancer	Libra	Virgo	Virgo	Scorpio	Sagittarius	Libra
15			Leo	Cancer	Libra	Virgo	Virgo	Scorpio	Sagittarius	Libra
16	1:04 P.M.	Scorpio	Leo	Cancer	Libra	Virgo	Virgo	Snorpio	Sagittarius	Libra
17			Leo	Cancer	Libra	Virgo	Virgo	Scorpio	Sagittarius	Libra
18			Leo	Cancer	Libra	Virgo	Virgo	Scorpio	Sagittarius	Libra
19	1:26 A.M.	Sagittarius	Leo	Cancer	Libra	Virgo	Virgo	Scorpio	Sagittarius	Libra
20			Leo	Cancer	Libra	Virgo	Virgo	Scorpio	Sagittarius	Libra
21	10:40 A.M.	Capricorn	Leo	Cancer	Libra	Virgo	Virgo	Scorpio	Sagittarius	Libra
22			Leo	Cancer	Libra	Virgo	Virgo	Scorpio	Sagittarius	Libra
23	3:38 P.M.	Aquarius	Leo	Cancer	Libra	Virgo	Virgo	Scorpio	Sagittarius	Libra

1981

LEO PLANETARY TABLES

	MOON FROM	IN	MERCURY	VENUS	MARS	JUPITER	SATURN	URANUS	NEPTUNE	PLUTO
July										
23		Aries	Cancer	Leo	Cancer	Libra	Libra	Scorpio	Sagittarius	Libra
24	2:41 A.M.	Taurus	Cancer	Leo	Cancer	Libra	Libra	Scorpio	Sagittarius	Libra
25	5:19 A.M.	Gemini	Cancer	Virgo	Cancer	Libra	Libra	Scorpio	Sagittarius	Libra
26			Cancer	Virgo	Cancer	Libra	Libra	Scorpio	Sagittarius	Libra
27	7:30 A.M.	Cancer	Cancer	Virgo	Cancer	Libra	Libra	Scorpio	Sagittarius	Libra
28			Cancer	Virgo	Cancer	Libra	Libra	Scorpio	Sagittarius	Libra
29	9:54 A.M.	Leo	Cancer	Virgo	Cancer	Libra	Libra	Scorpio	Sagittarius	Libra
30			Cancer	Virgo	Cancer	Libra	Libra	Scorpio	Sagittarius	Libra
31			Cancer	Virgo	Cancer	Libra	Libra	Scorpio	Sagittarius	Libra
August										
1	1:55 P.M.	Virgo	Cancer	Virgo	Cancer	Libra	Libra	Scorpio	Sagittarius	Libra
2			Leo	Virgo	Cancer	Libra	Libra	Scorpio	Sagittarius	Libra
3	8:59 P.M.	Libra	Leo	Virgo	Cancer	Libra	Libra	Scorpio	Sagittarius	Libra
4			Leo	Virgo	Cancer	Libra	Libra	Scorpio	Sagittarius	Libra
5			Leo	Virgo	Cancer	Libra	Libra	Scorpio	Sagittarius	Libra
6	7:37 A.M.	Scorpio	Leo	Virgo	Cancer	Libra	Libra	Scorpio	Sagittarius	Libra
7			Leo	Virgo	Cancer	Libra	Libra	Scorpio	Sagittarius	Libra
8	8:38 P.M.	Sagittarius	Leo	Virgo	Cancer	Libra	Libra	Scorpio	Sagittarius	Libra
9			Leo	Virgo	Cancer	Libra	Libra	Scorpio	Sagittarius	Libra
10			Leo	Virgo	Cancer	Libra	Libra	Scorpio	Sagittarius	Libra
11	8:34 A.M.	Capricorn	Leo	Virgo	Cancer	Libra	Libra	Scorpio	Sagittarius	Libra
12			Leo	Virgo	Cancer	Libra	Libra	Scorpio	Sagittarius	Libra
13	5:48 P.M.	Aquarius	Leo	Virgo	Cancer	Libra	Libra	Scorpio	Sagittarius	Libra
14			Leo	Virgo	Cancer	Libra.	Libra	Scorpio	Sagittarius	Libra
15			Leo	Virgo	Cancer	Libra	Libra	Scorpio	Sagittarius	Libra
16	0:28 A.M.	Pisces	Leo	Virgo	Cancer	Libra	Libra	Scorpio	Sagittarius	Libra
17			Virgo	Virgo	Cancer	Libra	Libra	Scorpio	Sagittarius	Libra
18	4:31 A.M.	Aries	Virgo	Virgo	Cancer	Libra	Libra	Scorpio	Sagittarius	Libra
19			Virgo	Libra	Cancer	Libra	Libra	Scorpio	Sagittarius	Libra
20	7:51 A.M.	Taurus	Virgo	Libra	Cancer	Libra	Libra	Scorpio	Sagittarius	Libra
21			Virgo	Libra	Cancer	Libra	Libra	Scorpio	Sagittarius	Libra
22	10:35 P.M.	Gemini	Virgo	Libra	Cancer	Libra	Libra	Scorpio	Sagittarius	Libra
23			Virgo	Libra	Cancer	Libra	Libra	Scorpio	Sagittarius	Libra

1982

MOON FROM	IN	MERCURY	VENUS	MARS	JUPITER	SATURN	URANUS	NEPTUNE	PLUTO
July									
24	9:53 P.M. Libra	Cancer	Cancer	Libra	Scorpio	Libra	Sagittarius	Sagittarius	Libra
25		Leo	Cancer	Libra	Scorpio	Libra	Sagittarius	Sagittarius	Libra
26		Leo	Cancer	Libra	Scorpio	Libra	Sagittarius	Sagittarius	Libra
27	4:57 A.M. Scorpio	Leo	Cancer	Libra	Scorpio	Lbra	Sagittarius	Sagittarius	Libra
28		Leo	Cancer	Libra	Scorpio	Libra	Sagittarius	Sagittarius	Libra
29	4:13 P.M. Sagittarius	Leo	Cancer	Libra	Scorpio	Libra	Sagittarius	Sagittarius	Libra
30		Leo	Cancer	Libra	Scorpio	Libra	Sagittarius	Sagittarius	Libra
31		Leo	Cancer	Libra	Scorpio	Libra	Sagittarius	Sagittarius	Libra
August									
1	4:49 P.M. Capricorn	Leo	Cancer	Libra	Scorpio	Libra	Sagittarius	Sagittarius	Libra
2	5:15 P.M. Aquarius	Leo	Cancer	Libra	Scorpio	Libra	Sagittarius	Sagittarius	Libra
3		Leo	Cancer	Libra	Scorpio	Libra	Sagittarius	Sagittarius	Libra
4		Leo	Cancer	Scorpio	Scorpio	Libra	Sagittarius	Sagittarius	Libra
5		Leo	Cancer	Scorpio	Scorpio	Libra	Sagittarius	Sagittarius	Libra
6	3:53 A.M. Pisces	Leo	Cancer	Scorpio	Scorpio	Libra	Sagittarius	Sagittarius	Libra
7		Leo	Cancer	Scorpio	Scorpio	Libra	Sagittarius	Sagittarius	Libra
8	1:12 A.M. Aries	Leo	Cancer	Scorpio	Scorpio	Libra	Sagittarius	Sagittarius	Libra
9		Virgo	Cancer	Scorpio	Scorpio	Libra	Sagittarius	Sagittarius	Libra
10	8:06 P.M. Taurus	Virgo	Cancer	Scorpio	Scorpio	Libra	Sagittarius	Sagittarius	Libra
11		Virgo	Cancer	Scorpio	Scorpio	Libra	Sagittarius	Sagittarius	Libra
12		Virgo	Cancer	Scorpio	Scorpio	Libra	Sagittarius	Sagittarius	Libra
13	0:39 A.M. Gemini	Virgo	Cancer	Scorpio	Scorpio	Libra	Sagittarius	Sagittarius	Libra
14	3:02 A.M. Cancer	Virgo	Cancer	Scorpio	Scorpio	Libra	Sagittarius	Sagittarius	Libra
15		Virgo	Leo	Scorpio	Scorpio	Libra	Sagittarius	Sagittarius	Libra
16		Virgo	Leo	Scorpio	Scorpio	Libra	Sagittarius	Sagittarius	Libra
17	3:58 A.M. Leo	Virgo	Leo	Scorpio	Scorpio	Libra	Sagittarius	Sagittarius	Libra
18		Virgo	Leo	Scorpio	Scorpio	Libra	Sagittarius	Sagittarius	Libra
19	4:34 A.M. Virgo	Virgo	Leo	Scorpio	Scorpio	Libra	Sagittarius	Sagittarius	Libra
20		Virgo	Leo	Scorpio	Scorpio	Libra	Sagittarius	Sagittarius	Libra
21	7:21 A.M. Libra	Virgo	Leo	Scorpio	Scorpio	Libra	Sagittarius	Sagittarius	Libra
22		Virgo	Leo	Scorpio	Scorpio	Libra	Sagittarius	Sagittarius	Libra
23	1:25 P.M. Scorpio	Virgo	Leo	Scorpio	Scorpio	Libra	Sagittarius	Sagittarius	Libra

LEO PLANETARY TABLES

1983

	MOON		MERCURY	VENUS	MARS	JUPITER	SATURN	URANUS	NEPTUNE	PLUTO
July	FROM	IN								
24	3:37 P.M.	Aquarius	Leo	Virgo	Cancer	Sagittarius	Libra	Sagittarius	Sagittarius	Libra
25			Leo	Virgo	Cancer	Sagittarius	Libra	Sagittarius	Sagittarius	Libra
26			Leo	Virgo	Cancer	Sagittarius	Libra	Sagittarius	Sagittarius	Libra
27	4:34 A.M.	Pisces	Leo	Virgo	Cancer	Sagittarius	Libra	Sagittarius	Sagittarius	Libra
28			Leo	Virgo	Cancer	Sagittarius	Libra	Sagittarius	Sagittarius	Libra
29	4:46 P.M.	Aries	Leo	Virgo	Cancer	Sagittarius	Libra	Sagittarius	Sagittarius	Libra
30			Leo	Virgo	Cancer	Sagittarius	Libra	Sagittarius	Sagittarius	Libra
31			Leo	Virgo	Cancer	Sagittarius	Libra	Sagittarius	Sagittarius	Libra
August										
1	2:41 A.M.	Taurus	Leo	Virgo	Cancer	Sagittarius	Libra	Sagittarius	Sagittarius	Libra
2			Virgo	Virgo	Cancer	Sagittarius	Libra	Sagittarius	Sagittarius	Libra
3	9:56 A.M.	Gemini	Virgo	Virgo	Cancer	Sagittarius	Libra	Sagittarius	Sagittarius	Libra
4			Virgo	Virgo	Cancer	Sagittarius	Libra	Sagittarius	Sagittarius	Libra
5	1:03 P.M.	Cancer	Virgo	Virgo	Cancer	Sagittarius	Libra	Sagittarius	Sagittarius	Libra
6			Virgo	Virgo	Cancer	Sagittarius	Libra	Sagittarius	Sagittarius	Libra
7	1:29 P.M.	Leo	Virgo	Virgo	Cancer	Sagittarius	Libra	Sagittarius	Sagittarius	Libra
8			Virgo	Virgo	Cancer	Sagittarius	Libra	Sagittarius	Sagittarius	Libra
9	12:45 P.M.	Virgo	Virgo	Virgo	Cancer	Sagittarius	Libra	Sagittarius	Sagittarius	Libra
10			Virgo	Virgo	Cancer	Sagittarius	Libra	Sagittarius	Sagittarius	Libra
11	1:08 P.M.	Libra	Virgo	Virgo	Cancer	Sagittarius	Libra	Sagittarius	Sagittarius	Libra
12			Virgo	Virgo	Cancer	Sagittarius	Libra	Sagittarius	Sagittarius	Libra
13	3:56 P.M.	Scorpio	Virgo	Virgo	Leo	Sagittarius	Libra	Sagittarius	Sagittarius	Libra
14			Virgo	Virgo	Leo	Sagittarius	Libra	Sagittarius	Sagittarius	Libra
15	10:49 P.M.	Sagittarius	Virgo	Virgo	Leo	Sagittarius	Libra	Sagittarius	Sagittarius	Libra
16			Virgo	Virgo	Leo	Sagittarius	Libra	Sagittarius	Sagittarius	Libra
17			Virgo	Virgo	Leo	Sagittarius	Libra	Sagittarius	Sagittarius	Libra
18	9:00 A.M.	Capricorn	Virgo	Virgo	Leo	Sagittarius	Libra	Sagittarius	Sagittarius	Libra
19			Virgo	Virgo	Leo	Sagittarius	Libra	Sagittarius	Sagittarius	Libra
20	9:21 P.M.	Aquarius	Virgo	Virgo	Leo	Sagittarius	Libra	Sagittarius	Sagittarius	Libra
21			Virgo	Virgo	Leo	Sagittarius	Libra	Sagittarius	Sagittarius	Libra
22			Virgo	Virgo	Leo	Sagittarius	Libra	Sagittarius	Sagittarius	Libra
23	4:51 A.M.	Pisces	Virgo	Virgo	Leo	Sagittarius	Libra	Sagittarius	Sagittarius	Libra

1984

July	MOON FROM IN	MERCURY	VENUS	MARS	JUPITER	SATURN	URANUS	NEPTUNE	PLUTO
23	12:27 P.M. Gemini	Leo	Leo	Scorpio	Capricorn	Scorpio	Sagittarius	Sagittarius	Libra
24	6:49 P.M. Cancer	Leo	Leo	Scorpio	Capricorn	Scorpio	Sagittarius	Sagittarius	Libra
25		Leo	Leo	Scorpio	Capricorn	Scorpio	Sagittarius	Sagittarius	Libra
26		Leo	Leo	Scorpio	Capricorn	Scorpio	Sagittarius	Sagittarius	Libra
27	9:46 P.M. Leo	Virgo	Leo	Scorpio	Capricorn	Scorpio	Sagittarius	Sagittarius	Libra
28		Virgo	Leo	Scorpio	Capricorn	Scorpio	Sagittarius	Sagittarius	Libra
29	10:44 P.M. Virgo	Virgo	Leo	Scorpio	Capricorn	Scorpio	Sagittarius	Sagittarius	Libra
30		Virgo	Leo	Scorpio	Capricorn	Scorpio	Sagittarius	Sagittarius	Libra
31	11:23 P.M. Libra	Virgo	Leo	Scorpio	Capricorn	Scorpio	Sagittarius	Sagittarius	Libra
August									
1		Virgo	Leo	Scorpio	Capricorn	Scorpio	Sagittarius	Sagittarius	Libra
2		Virgo	Leo	Scorpio	Capricorn	Scorpio	Sagittarius	Sagittarius	Libra
3	1:13 A.M. Scorpio	Virgo	Leo	Scorpio	Capricorn	Scorpio	Sagittarius	Sagittarius	Libra
4		Virgo	Leo	Scorpio	Capricorn	Scorpio	Sagittarius	Sagittarius	Libra
5	5:37 A.M. Sagittarius	Virgo	Leo	Scorpio	Capricorn	Scorpio	Sagittarius	Sagittarius	Libra
6		Virgo	Leo	Scorpio	Capricorn	Scorpio	Sagittarius	Sagittarius	Libra
7	12:27 P.M. Capricorn	Virgo	Leo	Scorpio	Capricorn	Scorpio	Sagittarius	Sagittarius	Libra
8		Virgo	Virgo	Scorpio	Capricorn	Scorpio	Sagittarius	Sagittarius	Libra
9	9:18 P.M. Aquarius	Virgo	Virgo	Scorpio	Capricorn	Scorpio	Sagittarius	Sagittarius	Libra
10		Virgo	Virgo	Scorpio	Capricorn	Scorpio	Sagittarius	Sagittarius	Libra
11		Virgo	Virgo	Scorpio	Capricorn	Scorpio	Sagittarius	Sagittarius	Libra
12	8:12 A.M. Pisces	Virgo	Virgo	Scorpio	Capricorn	Scorpio	Sagittarius	Sagittarius	Libra
13		Virgo	Virgo	Scorpio	Capricorn	Scorpio	Sagittarius	Sagittarius	Libra
14	8:38 P.M. Aries	Virgo	Virgo	Scorpio	Capricorn	Scorpio	Sagittarius	Sagittarius	Libra
15		Virgo	Virgo	Scorpio	Capricorn	Scorpio	Sagittarius	Sagittarius	Libra
16		Virgo	Virgo	Scorpio	Capricorn	Scorpio	Sagittarius	Sagittarius	Libra
17	9:15 A.M. Taurus	Virgo	Virgo	Sagittarius	Capricorn	Scorpio	Sagittarius	Sagittarius	Libra
18		Virgo	Virgo	Sagittarius	Capricorn	Scorpio	Sagittarius	Sagittarius	Libra
19	8:37 P.M. Gemini	Virgo	Virgo	Sagittarius	Capricorn	Scorpio	Sagittarius	Sagittarius	Libra
20		Virgo	Virgo	Sagittarius	Capricorn	Scorpio	Sagittarius	Sagittarius	Libra
21		Virgo	Virgo	Sagittarius	Capricorn	Scorpio	Sagittarius	Sagittarius	Libra
22	4:30 A.M. Cancer	Virgo	Virgo	Sagittarius	Capricorn	Scorpio	Sagittarius	Sagittarius	Libra

LEO PLANETARY TABLES

1985

Date	Moon From	Moon In	Mercury	Venus	Mars	Jupiter	Saturn	Uranus	Neptune	Pluto
July 23	Libra		Leo	Gemini	Cancer	Aquarius	Scorpio	Sagittrius	Capricorn	Scorpio
24	3:41 P.M.	Scorpio	Leo	Gemini	Cancer	Aquarius	Scorpio	Sagittarius	Capricorn	Scorpio
25	6:10 P.M.	Sagittarius	Leo	Gemini	Cancer	Aquarius	Scorpio	Sagittarius	Capricorn	Scorpio
26			Leo	Gemini	Leo	Aquarius	Scorpio	Sagittarius	Capricorn	Scorpio
27			Leo	Gemini	Leo	Aquarius	Scorpio	Sagittarius	Capricorn	Scorpio
28	9:37 P.M.	Capricorn	Leo	Gemini	Leo	Aquarius	Scorpio	Sagittarius	Capricorn	Scorpio
29			Leo	Gemini	Leo	Aquarius	Scorpio	Sagittarius	Capricorn	Scorpio
30			Leo	Gemini	Leo	Aquarius	Scorpio	Sagittarius	Capricorn	Scorpio
31	1:38 A.M.	Aquarius	Leo	Gemini	Leo	Aquarius	Scorpio	Sagittarius	Capricorn	Scorpio
August 1	7:33 A.M.	Pisces	Leo	Gemini	Leo	Aquarius	Scorpio	Sagittrius	Capricorn	Scorpio
2			Leo	Gemini	Leo	Aquarius	Scorpio	Sagittarius	Capricorn	Scorpio
3	4:57 P.M.	Aries	Leo	Cancer	Leo	Aquarius	Scorpio	Sagittarius	Capricorn	Scorpio
4			Leo	Cancer	Leo	Aquarius	Scorpio	Sagittarius	Capricorn	Scorpio
5			Leo	Cancer	Leo	Aquarius	Scorpio	Sagittarius	Capricorn	Scorpio
6			Leo	Cancer	Leo	Aquarius	Scorpio	Sagittarius	Capricorn	Scorpio
7	4:57 A.M.	Taurus	Leo	Cancer	Leo	Aquarius	Scorpio	Sagittarius	Capricorn	Scorpio
8			Leo	Cancer	Leo	Aquarius	Scorpio	Sagittarius	Capricorn	Scorpio
9	5:30 P.M.	Gemini	Leo	Cancer	Leo	Aquarius	Scorpio	Sagittarius	Capricorn	Scorpio
10			Leo	Cancer	Leo	Aquarius	Scorpio	Sagittarius	Capricorn	Scorpio
11			Leo	Cancer	Leo	Aquarius	Scorpio	Sagittarius	Capricorn	Scorpio
12	4:33 A.M.	Cancer	Leo	Cancer	Leo	Aquarius	Scorpio	Sagittarius	Capricorn	Scorpio
13			Leo	Cancer	Leo	Aquarius	Scorpio	Sagittarius	Capricorn	Scorpio
14	11:59 A.M.	Leo	Leo	Cancer	Leo	Aquarius	Scorpio	Sagittarius	Capricorn	Scorpio
15			Leo	Cancer	Leo	Aquar us	Scorpio	Sagittarius	Capricorn	Scorpio
16	4:28 P.M.	Virgo	Leo	Cancer	Leo	Aquarius	Scorpio	Sagittarius	Capricorn	Scorpio
17			Leo	Cancer	Leo	Aquarius	Scorpio	Sagittarius	Capricorn	Scorpio
18	6:56 P.M.	Libra	Leo	Cancer	Leo	Aquarius	Scorpio	Sagittarius	Capricorn	Scorpio
19			Leo	Cancer	Leo	Aquarius	Scorpio	Sagittarius	Capricorn	Scorpio
20	9:04 P.M.	Scorpio	Leo	Cancer	Leo	Aquarius	Scorpio	Sagittarius	Capricorn	Scorpio
21			Leo	Cancer	Leo	Aquarius	Scorpio	Sagittarius	Capricorn	Scorpio
22	11:24 P.M.	Sagittarius	Leo	Cancer	Leo	Aquarius	Scorpio	Sagittarius	Capricorn	Scorpio
23			Leo	Cancer	Leo	Aquarius	Scorpio	Sagittarius	Capricorn	Scorpio

1986

	MOON		MERCURY	VENUS	MARS	JUPITER	SATURN	URANUS	NEPTUNE	PLUTO
July	FROM	IN								
24	Pisces		Cancer	Virgo	Capricorn	Pisces	Sagittarius	Sagittarius	Capricorn	Scorpio
25	3:26 P.M.	Aries	Cancer	Virgo	Capricorn	Pisces	Sagittarius	Sagittarius	Capricorn	Scorpio
26			Cancer	Virgo	Capricorn	Pisces	Sagittarius	Sagittarius	Capricorn	Scorpio
27			Cancer	Virgo	Capricorn	Pisces	Sagittarius	Sagittarius	Capricorn	Scorpio
28	0:30 A.M.	Taurus	Cancer	Virgo	Capricorn	Pisces	Sagittarius	Sagittarius	Capricorn	Scorpio
29			Cancer	Virgo	Capricorn	Pisces	Sagittarius	Sagittarius	Capricorn	Scorpio
30	12:27 P.M.	Gemini	Cancer	Virgo	Capricorn	Pisces	Sagittarius	Sagittarius	Capricorn	Scorpio
31			Cancer	Virgo	Capricorn	Pisces	Sagittarius	Sagittarius	Capricorn	Scorpio
August										
1	1:09 A.M.	Cancer	Cancer	Virgo	Capricorn	Pisces	Sagittarius	Sagittarius	Capricorn	Scorpio
2			Cancer	Virgo	Capricorn	Pisces	Sagittarius	Sagittarius	Capricorn	Scorpio
3	12:19 P.M.	Leo	Cancer	Virgo	Capricorn	Pisces	Sagittarius	Sagittarius	Capricorn	Scorpio
4			Cancer	Virgo	Capricorn	Pisces	Sagittarius	Sagittarius	Capricorn	Scorpio
5			Cancer	Virgo	Capricorn	Pisces	Sagittarius	Sagittarius	Capricorn	Scorpio
6	9:44 P.M.	Virgo	Cancer	Virgo	Capricorn	Pisces	Sagittarius	Sagittarius	Capricorn	Scorpio
7			Cancer	Virgo	Capricorn	Pisces	Sagittarius	Sagittarius	Capricorn	Scorpio
8			Cancer	Libra	Capricorn	Pisces	Sagittarius	Sagittarius	Capricorn	Scorpio
9	5:12 A.M.	Libra	Cancer	Libra	Capricorn	Pisces	Sagittarius	Sagittarius	Capricorn	Scorpio
10			Cancer	Libra	Capricorn	Pisces	Sagittarius	Sagittarius	Capricorn	Scorpio
11	10:20 A.M.	Scorpio	Cancer	Libra	Capricorn	Pisces	Sagittarius	Sagittarius	Capricorn	Scorpio
12			Leo	Libra	Capricorn	Pisces	Sagittarius	Sagittarius	Capricorn	Scorpio
13	1:53 P.M.	Sagittarius	Leo	Libra	Capricorn	Pisces	Sagittarius	Sagittarius	Capricorn	Scorpio
14			Leo	Libra	Capricorn	Pisces	Sagittarius	Sagittarius	Capricorn	Scorpio
15	4:21 P.M.	Capricorn	Leo	Libra	Capricorn	Pisces	Sagittarius	Sagittarius	Capricorn	Scorpio
16			Leo	Libra	Capricorn	Pisces	Sagittarius	Sagittarius	Capricorn	Scorpio
17	5:50 P.M.	Aquarius	Leo	Libra	Capricorn	Pisces	Sagittarius	Sagittarius	Capricorn	Scorpio
18			Leo	Libra	Capricorn	Pisces	Sagittarius	Sagittarius	Capricorn	Scorpio
19	8:38 P.M.	Pisces	Leo	Libra	Capricorn	Pisces	Sagittarius	Sagittarius	Capricorn	Scorpio
20			Leo	Libra	Capricorn	Pisces	Sagittarius	Sagittarius	Capricorn	Scorpio
21			Leo	Libra	Capricorn	Pisces	Sagittarius	Sagittarius	Capricorn	Scorpio
22	0:47 A.M.	Aries	Leo	Libra	Capricorn	Pisces	Sagittarius	Sagittarius	Capricorn	Scorpio
23			Leo	Libra	Capricorn	Pisces	Sagittarius	Sagittarius	Capricorn	Scorpio

LEO PLANETARY TABLES

1987

July	MOON FROM — IN	MERCURY	VENUS	MARS	JUPITER	SATURN	URANUS	NEPTUNE	PLUTO
24	Cancer	Cancer	Cancer	Leo	Aries	Sagittarius	Sagittarius	Capricorn	Scorpio
25	11:13 A.M. Leo	Cancer	Cancer	Leo	Aries	Sagittarius	Sagittarius	Capricorn	Scorpio
26		Cancer	Cancer	Leo	Aries	Sagittarius	Sagittarius	Capricorn	Scorpio
27	11:32 P.M. Virgo	Cancer	Cancer	Leo	Aries	Sagittarius	Sagittarius	Capricorn	Scorpio
28		Cancer	Cancer	Leo	Aries	Sagittarius	Sagittarius	Capricorn	Scorpio
29		Cancer	Cancer	Leo	Aries	Sagittarius	Sagittarius	Capricorn	Scorpio
30	10:55 A.M. Libra	Cancer	Cancer	Leo	Aries	Sagittarius	Sagittarius	Capricorn	Scorpio
31		Cancer	Leo	Leo	Aries	Sagittarius	Sagittarius	Capricorn	Scorpio
August									
1	7:49 P.M. Scorpio	Cancer	Leo	Leo	Aries	Sagittarius	Sagittarius	Capricorn	Scorpio
2		Cancer	Leo	Leo	Aries	Sagittarius	Sagittarius	Capricorn	Scorpio
3		Cancer	Leo	Leo	Aries	Sagittarius	Sagittarius	Capricorn	Scorpio
4	1:35 A.M. Sagittarius	Cancer	Leo	Leo	Aries	Sagittarius	Sagittarius	Capricorn	Scorpio
5		Cancer	Leo	Leo	Aries	Sagittarius	Sagittarius	Capricorn	Scorpio
6	3:41 A.M. Capricorn	Cancer	Leo	Leo	Aries	Sagittarius	Sagittarius	Capricorn	Scorpio
7		Leo	Leo	Leo	Aries	Sagittarius	Sagittarius	Capricorn	Scorpio
8	3:53 A.M. Aquarius	Leo	Leo	Leo	Aries	Sagittarius	Sagittarius	Capricorn	Scorpio
9		Leo	Leo	Leo	Aries	Sagittarius	Sagittarius	Capricorn	Scorpio
10	3:32 A.M. Pisces	Leo	Leo	Leo	Aries	Sagittarius	Sagittarius	Capricorn	Scorpio
11		Leo	Leo	Leo	Aries	Sagittarius	Sagittarius	Capricorn	Scorpio
12	4:34 A.M. Aries	Leo	Leo	Leo	Aries	Sagittarius	Sagittarius	Capricorn	Scorpio
13		Leo	Leo	Leo	Aries	Sagittarius	Sagittarius	Capricorn	Scorpio
14	8:39 A.M. Taurus	Leo	Leo	Leo	Aries	Sagittarius	Sagittarius	Capricorn	Scorpio
15		Leo	Leo	Leo	Aries	Sagittarius	Sagittarius	Capricorn	Scorpio
16	4:52 P.M. Gemini	Leo	Leo	Leo	Aries	Sagittarius	Sagittarius	Capricorn	Scorpio
17		Leo	Leo	Leo	Aries	Sagittarius	Sagittarius	Capricorn	Scorpio
18		Leo	Leo	Leo	Aries	Sagittarius	Sagittarius	Capricorn	Scorpio
19	4:25 A.M. Cancer	Leo	Leo	Leo	Aries	Sagittarius	Sagittarius	Capricorn	Scorpio
20		Leo	Leo	Leo	Aries	Sagittarius	Sagittarius	Capricorn	Scorpio
21	5:24 P.M. Leo	Leo	Leo	Leo	Aries	Sagittarius	Sagittarius	Capricorn	Scorpio
22		Virgo	Leo	Leo	Aries	Sagittarius	Sagittarius	Capricorn	Scorpio
23		Virgo	Leo	Virgo	Aries	Sagittarius	Sagittarius	Capricorn	Scorpio

1988

July	MOON FROM	IN	MERCURY	VENUS	MARS	JUPITER	SATURN	URANUS	NEPTUNE	PLUTO
23	Scorpio		Cancer	Gemini	Aries	Gemini	Sagittarius	Sagittarius	Capricorn	Scorpio
24	7:00 A.M.	Sagittarius	Cancer	Gemini	Aries	Gemini	Sagittarius	Sagittarius	Capricorn	Scorpio
25			Cancer	Gemini	Aries	Gemini	Sagittarius	Sagittarius	Capricorn	Scorpio
26	11:15 A.M.	Capricorn	Cancer	Gemini	Aries	Gemini	Sagittarius	Sagittarius	Capricorn	Scorpio
27			Cancer	Gemini	Aries	Gemini	Sagittarius	Sagittarius	Capricorn	Scorpio
28	12:58 P.M.	Aquarius	Cancer	Gemini	Aries	Gemini	Sagittarius	Sagittarius	Capricorn	Scorpio
29			Leo	Gemini	Aries	Gemini	Sagittarius	Sagittarius	Capricorn	Scorpio
30	12:45 P.M.	Pisces	Leo	Gemini	Aries	Gemini	Sagittarius	Sagittarius	Capricorn	Scorpio
31			Leo	Gemini	Aries	Gemini	Sagittarius	Sagittarius	Capricorn	Scorpio
August										
1	12:48 P.M.	Aries	Leo	Gemini	Aries	Gemini	Sagittarius	Sagittarius	Capricorn	Scorpio
2			Leo	Gemini	Aries	Gemini	Sagittarius	Sagittarius	Capricorn	Scorpio
3	3:12 P.M.	Taurus	Leo	Gemini	Aries	Gemini	Sagittarius	Sagittarius	Capricorn	Scorpio
4			Leo	Gemini	Aries	Gemini	Sagittarius	Sagittarius	Capricorn	Scorpio
5	8:34 P.M.	Gemini	Leo	Gemini	Aries	Gemini	Sagittarius	Sagittarius	Capricorn	Scorpio
6			Leo	Cancer	Aries	Gemini	Sagittarius	Sagittarius	Capricorn	Scorpio
7			Leo	Cancer	Aries	Gemini	Sagittarius	Sagittarius	Capricorn	Scorpio
8	5:07 A.M.	Cancer	Leo	Cancer	Aries	Gemini	Sagittarius	Sagittarius	Capricorn	Scorpio
9			Leo	Cancer	Aries	Gemini	Sagittarius	Sagittarius	Capricorn	Scorpio
10	3:57 P.M.	Leo	Leo	Cancer	Aries	Gemini	Sagittarius	Sagittarius	Capricorn	Scorpio
11			Leo	Cancer	Aries	Gemini	Sagittarius	Sagittarius	Capricorn	Scorpio
12			Leo	Cancer	Aries	Gemini	Sagittarius	Sagittarius	Capricorn	Scorpio
13	3:37 A.M.	Virgo	Virgo	Cancer	Aries	Gemini	Sagittarius	Sagittarius	Capricorn	Scorpio
14			Virgo	Cancer	Aries	Gemini	Sagittarius	Sagittarius	Capricorn	Scorpio
15	4:26 P.M.	Libra	Virgo	Cancer	Aries	Gemini	Sagittarius	Sagittarius	Capricorn	Scorpio
16			Virgo	Cancer	Aries	Gemini	Sagittarius	Sagittarius	Capricorn	Scorpio
17			Virgo	Cancer	Aries	Gemini	Sagittarius	Sagittarius	Capricorn	Scorpio
18	4:37 A.M.	Scorpio	Virgo	Cancer	Aries	Gemini	Sagittarius	Sagittarius	Capricorn	Scorpio
19			Virgo	Cancer	Aries	Gemini	Sagittarius	Sagittarius	Capricorn	Scorpio
20	2:49 P.M.	Sagittarius	Virgo	Cancer	Aries	Gemini	Sagittarius	Sagittarius	Capricorn	Scorpio
21			Virgo	Cancer	Aries	Gemini	Sagittarius	Sagittarius	Capricorn	Scorpio
22	8:45 P.M.	Capricorn	Virgo	Cancer	Aries	Gemini	Sagittarius	Sagittarius	Capricorn	Scorpio

LEO PLANETARY TABLES

1989

Date	MOON FROM	IN	MERCURY	VENUS	MARS	JUPITER	SATURN	URANUS	NEPTUNE	PLUTO
July										
23	1:30 A.M.	Aries	Leo	Leo	Leo	Gemini	Capricorn	Capricorn	Capricorn	Scorpio
24			Leo	Leo	Leo	Gemini	Capricorn	Capricorn	Capricorn	Scorpio
25	4:07 A.M.	Taurus	Leo	Virgo	Leo	Gemini	Capricorn	Capricorn	Capricorn	Scorpio
26			Leo	Virgo	Leo	Gemini	Capricorn	Capricorn	Capricorn	Scorpio
27	7:21 A.M.	Gemini	Leo	Virgo	Leo	Gemini	Capricorn	Capricorn	Capricorn	Scorpio
28			Leo	Virgo	Leo	Gemini	Capricorn	Capricorn	Capricorn	Scorpio
29	12:08 P.M.	Cancer	Leo	Virgo	Leo	Gemini	Capricorn	Capricorn	Capricorn	Scorpio
30			Leo	Virgo	Leo	Gemini	Capricorn	Capricorn	Capricorn	Scorpio
31	6:04 P.M.	Leo	Leo	Virgo	Leo	Cancer	Capricorn	Capricorn	Capricorn	Scorpio
August										
1			Leo	Virgo	Leo	Cancer	Capricorn	Capricorn	Capricorn	Scorpio
2	2:22 A.M.	Virgo	Leo	Virgo	Leo	Cancer	Capricorn	Capricorn	Capricorn	Scorpio
3			Leo	Virgo	Virgo	Cancer	Capricorn	Capricorn	Capricorn	Scorpio
4	1:00 P.M.	Libra	Leo	Virgo	Virgo	Cancer	Capricorn	Capricorn	Capricorn	Scorpio
5			Leo	Virgo	Virgo	Canner	Capricorn	Capricorn	Capricorn	Scorpio
6			Virgo	Virgo	Virgo	Cancer	Capricorn	Capricorn	Capricorn	Scorpio
7			Virgo	Virgo	Virgo	Cancer	Capricorn	Capricorn	Capricorn	Scorpio
8	1:50 A.M.	Scorpio	Virgo	Virgo	Virgo	Cancer	Capricorn	Capricorn	Capricorn	Scorpio
9			Virgo	Virgo	Virgo	Cancer	Capricorn	Capricorn	Capricorn	Scorpio
10	12:50 P.M.	Sagittarius	Virgo	Virgo	Virgo	Cancer	Capricorn	Capricorn	Capricorn	Scorpio
11			Virgo	Virgo	Virgo	Cancer	Capricorn	Capricorn	Capricorn	Scorpio
12	11:26 P.M.	Capricorn	Virgo	Virgo	Virgo	Cancer	Capricorn	Capricorn	Capricorn	Scorpio
13			Virgo	Virgo	Virgo	Cancer	Capricorn	Capricorn	Capricorn	Scorpio
14			Virgo	Virgo	Virgo	Cancer	Capricorn	Capricorn	Capricorn	Scorpio
15	5:05 A.M.	Aquarius	Virgo	Virgo	Virgo	Cancer	Capricorn	Capricorn	Capricorn	Scorpio
16			Virgo	Virgo	Virgo	Cancer	Capricorn	Capricorn	Capricorn	Scorpio
17	7:40 A.M.	Pisces	Virgo	Virgo	Virgo	Cancer	Capricorn	Capricorn	Capricorn	Scorpio
18			Virgo	Virgo	Virgo	Cancer	Capricorn	Capricorn	Capricorn	Scorpio
19	8:50 A.M.	Aries	Virgo	Libra	Virgo	Cancer	Capricorn	Capricorn	Capricorn	Scorpio
20			Virgo	Libra	Virgo	Cancer	Capricorn	Capricorn	Capricorn	Scorpio
21	10:00 A.M.	Taurus	Virgo	Libra	Virgo	Cancer	Capricorn	Capricorn	Capricorn	Scorpio
22			Virgo	Libra	Virgo	Cancer	Capricorn	Capricorn	Capricorn	Scorpio
23	12:46 P.M.	Gemini	Virgo	Libra	Virgo	Cancer	Capricorn	Capricorn	Capricorn	Scorpio

1990

July	MOON FROM	IN	MERCURY	VENUS	MARS	JUPITER	SATURN	URANUS	NEPTUNE	PLUTO
24	3:22 A.M.	Virgo	Leo	Cancer	Taurus	Cancer	Capricorn	Capricorn	Capricorn	Scorpio
25			Leo	Cancer	Taurus	Cancer	Capricorn	Capricorn	Capricorn	Scorpio
26	9:54 A.M.	Libra	Leo	Cancer	Taurus	Cancer	Capricorn	Capricorn	Capricorn	Scorpio
27			Leo	Cancer	Taurus	Cancer	Capricorn	Capricorn	Capricorn	Scorpio
28	8:42 P.M.	Scorpio	Leo	Cancer	Taurus	Cancer	Capricorn	Capricorn	Capricorn	Scorpio
29			Leo	Cancer	Taurus	Cancer	Capricorn	Capricorn	Capricorn	Scorpio
30			Virgo	Cancer	Taurus	Cancer	Capricorn	Capricorn	Capricorn	Scorpio
31	9:13 A.M.	Sagittarius	Virgo	Cancer	Taurus	Cancer	Capricorn	Capricorn	Capricorn	Scorpio

August	MOON FROM	IN	MERCURY	VENUS	MARS	JUPITER	SATURN	URANUS	NEPTUNE	PLUTO
1			Virgo	Cancer	Taurus	Cancer	Capricorn	Capricorn	Capricorn	Scorpio
2	9:17 P.M.	Capricorn	Virgo	Cancer	Taurus	Cancer	Capricorn	Capricorn	Capricorn	Scorpio
3			Virgo	Cancer	Taurus	Cancer	Capricorn	Capricorn	Capricorn	Scorpio
4			Virgo	Cancer	Taurus	Cancer	Capricorn	Capricorn	Capricorn	Scorpio
5	7:11 A.M.	Aquarius	Virgo	Cancer	Taurus	Cancer	Capricorn	Capricorn	Capricorn	Scorpio
6			Virgo	Cancer	Taurus	Cancer	Capricorn	Capricorn	Capricorn	Scorpio
7	2:35 P.M.	Pisces	Virgo	Cancer	Taurus	Cancer	Capricorn	Capricorn	Capricorn	Scorpio
8			Virgo	Cancer	Taurus	Cancer	Capricorn	Capricorn	Capricorn	Scorpio
9	7:47 P.M.	Aries	Virgo	Cancer	Taurus	Cancer	Capricorn	Capricorn	Capricorn	Scorpio
10			Virgo	Cancer	Taurus	Cancer	Capricorn	Capricorn	Capricorn	Scorpio
11	11:52 P.M.	Taurus	Virgo	Cancer	Taurus	Cancer	Capricorn	Capricorn	Capricorn	Scorpio
12			Virgo	Cancer	Taurus	Cancer	Capricorn	Capricorn	Capricorn	Scorpio
13			Virgo	Cancer	Taurus	Cancer	Capricorn	Capricorn	Capricorn	Scorpio
14	2:50 A.M.	Gemini	Virgo	Leo	Taurus	Cancer	Capricorn	Capricorn	Capricorn	Scorpio
15			Virgo	Leo	Taurus	Cancer	Capricorn	Capricorn	Capricorn	Scorpio
16	5:29 A.M.	Cancer	Virgo	Leo	Taurus	Cancer	Capricorn	Capricorn	Capricorn	Scorpio
17			Virgo	Leo	Taurus	Cancer	Capricorn	Capricorn	Capricorn	Scorpio
18	8:14 A.M.	Leo	Virgo	Leo	Taurus	Cancer	Capricorn	Capricorn	Capricorn	Scorpio
19			Virgo	Leo	Taurus	Cancer	Capricorn	Capricorn	Capricorn	Scorpio
20	12:23 P.M.	Virgo	Virgo	Leo	Taurus	Leo	Capricorn	Capricorn	Capricorn	Scorpio
21			Virgo	Leo	Taurus	Leo	Capricorn	Capricorn	Capricorn	Scorpio
22	7:00 P.M.	Libra	Virgo	Leo	Taurus	Leo	Capricorn	Capricorn	Capricorn	Scorpio
23			Virgo	Leo	Taurus	Leo	Capricorn	Capricorn	Capricorn	Scorpio